According to the Revised Syllabus prescribed by the Shivaji University, Kolhapur with effect from the Academic Year 2013-2014

A TEXT BOOK OF
BASIC ELECTRICAL ENGINEERING

FOR
FIRST YEAR DEGREE COURSES IN ENGINEERING
OF
SHIVAJI UNIVERSITY, KOLHAPUR
SEMESTER-I & II
COMMON FOR ALL BRANCHES
THOROUGHLY REVISED SIXTH EDITION

B. H. DESHMUKH

M. E. (Elect.), B. E. (Mech.)
Retired Assistant Professor of Electrical Engineering,
Government College of Engineering,
Pune-411 005.

N2399

BASIC ELECTRICAL ENGINEERING (Shivaji University, F.E., Sem. I & II)   **ISBN 978-93-83525-58-4**

Seventh Edition : July 2015

© : Author

The text of this publication, or any part thereof, should not be reproduced or transmitted in any form or stored in any computer storage system or device for distribution including photocopy, recording, taping or information retrieval system or reproduced on any disc, tape, perforated media or other information storage device etc., without the written permission of Authors with whom the rights are reserved. Breach of this condition is liable for legal action.

Every effort has been made to avoid errors or omissions in this publication. In spite of this, errors may have crept in. Any mistake, error or discrepancy so noted and shall be brought to our notice shall be taken care of in the next edition. It is notified that neither the publisher nor the authors or seller shall be responsible for any damage or loss of action to any one, of any kind, in any manner, therefrom.

Published By :   **Printed By :**
NIRALI PRAKASHAN   **Repro Knowledgecast Limited**

Abhyudaya Pragati, 1312, Shivaji Nagar,
Off J.M. Road, PUNE – 411005
Tel - (020) 25512336/37/39, Fax - (020) 25511379
Email : niralipune@pragationline.com

☞ DISTRIBUTION CENTRES

PUNE
Nirali Prakashan : 119, Budhwar Peth, Jogeshwari Mandir Lane, Pune 411002, Maharashtra
Tel : (020) 2445 2044, 66022708, Fax : (020) 2445 1538
Email : bookorder@pragationline.com, niralilocal@pragationline.com

Nirali Prakashan : S. No. 28/27, Dhyari, Near Pari Company, Pune 411041
Tel : (020) 24690204 Fax : (020) 24690316
Email : dhyari@pragationline.com, bookorder@pragationline.com

MUMBAI
Nirali Prakashan : 385, S.V.P. Road, Rasdhara Co-op. Hsg. Society Ltd.,
Girgaum, Mumbai 400004, Maharashtra
Tel : (022) 2385 6339 / 2386 9976, Fax : (022) 2386 9976
Email : niralimumbai@pragationline.com

☞ DISTRIBUTION BRANCHES

JALGAON
Nirali Prakashan : 34, V. V. Golani Market, Navi Peth, Jalgaon 425001,
Maharashtra, Tel : (0257) 222 0395, Mob : 94234 91860

KOLHAPUR
Nirali Prakashan : New Mahadvar Road, Kedar Plaza, 1st Floor Opp. IDBI Bank
Kolhapur 416 012, Maharashtra. Mob : 9850046155

NAGPUR
Pratibha Book Distributors :   Above Maratha Mandir, Shop No. 3, First Floor,
Rani Jhanshi Square, Sitabuldi, Nagpur 440012, Maharashtra
Tel : (0712) 254 7129

DELHI
Nirali Prakashan : 4593/21, Basement, Aggarwal Lane 15, Ansari Road, Daryaganj
Near Times of India Building, New Delhi 110002
Mob : 08505972553

BENGALURU
Pragati Book House : House No. 1, Sanjeevappa Lane, Avenue Road Cross,
Opp. Rice Church, Bengaluru – 560002.
Tel : (080) 64513344, 64513355,Mob : 9880582331, 9845021552
Email:bharatsavla@yahoo.com

CHENNAI
Pragati Books : 9/1, Montieth Road, Behind Taas Mahal, Egmore,
Chennai 600008 Tamil Nadu, Tel : (044) 6518 3535,
Mob : 94440 01782 / 98450 21552 / 98805 82331,
Email : bharatsavla@yahoo.com

niralipune@pragationline.com | www.pragationline.com

Also find us on   www.facebook.com/niralibooks

PREFACE

Shivaji University, Kolhapur has revised the curriculum of First Year Degree Courses in Engineering with effect from the academic year 2013-2014. The subject of Basic Electrical Engineering continues to be one of the core technology subjects included in the curriculum of the above courses. It gives me great pleasure in bringing out this thoroughly revised edition of my book "**Basic Electrical Engineering**" exclusively written to serve as a text-book for this subject.

The book contains the subject matter which is thoroughly revised and rearranged as per the new syllabus of Shivaji University, Kolhapur. It includes topics on D.C. Circuits, Magnetic Circuits, A.C. Fundamentals, Single-Phase A.C. Circuits, Earthing and Lamps, and Three-Phase A.C. Circuits. Subsequently, Single-Phase Transformers, Single-Phase Alternators and Single-Phase A.C. Motors are also dealt with in an elementary manner. The international system of units is used throughout the book.

A considerable number of worked examples are included in each chapter to enable the students to understand the electrical principles thoroughly. Each chapter is concluded with 'Points to Remember' and 'Important Formulae at a Glance'. The numerical examples (with solutions) and classified theory questions (for self-study) from large number of university examination papers are also added at the end of each chapter to enhance the utility of the book. The opportunity has also been taken of rectifying errors and omissions as have been brought to the author's notice by the readers of the previous editions. I am sure that the student fraternity as well as faculty members will find the book extremely useful.

I am really thankful to my publishers M/s Nirali Prakashan, Pune for bringing out this book in a very short period. Useful and constructive suggestions from the readers for further improvement of this book will be gratefully accepted by the author.

Pune **AUTHOR**

SYLLABUS

SECTION-I

UNIT 1 : D.C. CIRCUITS (8)

(A) Analysis of D.C. Circuits : Kirchhoff's laws, Mesh and node analysis, Energy conversions between electrical, mechanical, thermal quantities.

(B) Magnetic Circuits : Series magnetic circuits.

UNIT 2 : SINGLE-PHASE A.C. CIRCUITS (8)

Generation of sinusoidal voltage, R.M.S. and Average value, Form factor, Phasor representation of A.C. quantities, Impedance, Admittance, R-L, R-C, R-L-C series and parallel circuits, Power, P.F., Power factor improvement by capacitor method.

UNIT 3 : EARTHING AND LAMPS (5)

Necessity of earthing, Earthing methods, Fuse, MCB, Fluorescent tube, CFL, Mercury vapour lamp, LED lamp, Single-line diagram of electrical system, Study of energy meter.

SECTION-II

UNIT 4 : THREE-PHASE A.C. CIRCUITS (8)

Introduction to three-phase supply and its necessity, Generation of three-phase A.C. voltage, Balanced three-phase system, Relation between line and phase quantities.

UNIT 5 : A.C. MACHINES (8)

(A) Single-Phase Transformers : Construction, Operating principle, Types, E.M.F. equation, Ratios of voltage and current, Operation on no load and with load, Power losses, Efficiency, All-day efficiency, Voltage regulation, Applications, Autotransformer.

(B) Single-Phase Alternators : Construction, Types, Operating principle, E.M.F. equation, Alternator on load, Voltage regulation (Theoretical treatment).

UNIT 6 : SINGLE-PHASE A.C. MOTORS (5)

Construction, Operating principle, T-N characteristics, Applications of induction motors and universal motors.

CONTENTS

SECTION - I

Unit - 1

1.	**D.C. CIRCUITS**	**1.1 – 1.86**
1.1	Work, Power and Energy Relations	1.1
	1.1.1 Mechanical Units	1.1
	1.1.2 Electrical Units	1.3
	1.1.3 Thermal Units	1.4
	1.1.4 Efficiency	1.5
1.2	Analysis of D.C. Circuits	1.16
1.3	Classification of Electrical Networks	1.16
1.4	Energy Sources	1.17
	1.4.1 Independent Voltage Sources	1.17
	1.4.2 Independent Current Sources	1.18
	1.4.3 Source Conversion	1.19
1.5	Concept of Open and Short Circuits	1.26
1.6	Solution of Networks	1.27
1.7	Kirchhoff's Laws	1.27
	1.7.1 Point Law or Current Law	1.27
	1.7.2 Mesh Law or Voltage Law	1.28
	1.7.3 Application of Kirchhoff's Laws for Network Solutions (Branch-Current Method)	1.30
1.8	Loop or Mesh Analysis (Maxwell's Loop Current Method)	1.39
	1.8.1 Loop Current Equations in Generalized Form	1.41
1.9	Nodal Analysis	1.49
	1.9.1 Nodal Equations in Generalized Form	1.54
1.10	Points to Remember	1.64
1.11	Important Formulae at a Glance	1.66
1.12	Solutions of Numerical Examples from University Papers	1.67
1.13	Exercises	1.81
	1.13.1 Review Questions	1.81
	1.13.2 Classified Theory Questions from University Papers	1.81
	1.13.3 Examples for Practice	1.82

2.	**MAGNETIC CIRCUITS**		2.1 – 2.42
	2.1	Introduction	2.1
	2.2	Magnetism and its Effects	2.1
	2.3	Magnetic Field due to a Straight Conductor	2.3
	2.4	Force on a Current Carrying Conductor in a Magnetic Field	2.5
	2.5	Magnetic Field due to a Solenoid	2.6
	2.6	Permeability	2.7
	2.7	Force between Two Parallel Current Carrying Conductors	2.9
	2.8	Magnetic Circuits	2.10
		2.8.1 Quantities Associated with a Magnetic Circuit	2.11
		2.8.2 Comparison of Magnetic and Electrical Circuits	2.12
		2.8.3 Magnetization Curves	2.14
		2.8.4 Series Magnetic Circuits	2.16
		2.8.5 Magnetic Leakage and Fringing	2.18
	2.9	Points to Remember	2.24
	2.10	Important Formulae at a Glance	2.25
	2.11	Solutions of Numerical Examples from University Papers	2.27
	2.12	Exercises	2.40
		2.12.1 Review Questions	2.40
		2.12.2 Classified Theory Questions from University Papers	2.40
		2.12.3 Examples for Practice	2.41

Unit - 2

3.	**A.C. FUNDAMENTALS**		3.1 – 3.56
	3.1	Introduction	3.1
	3.2	Electric Circuit Elements R, L and C	3.1
		3.2.1 Resistance Parameter	3.1
		3.2.2 Inductance Parameter	3.3
		3.2.3 Capacitance Parameter	3.4
	3.3	Alternating Current and Voltage	3.6
	3.4	Generation of Alternating Current and Voltage	3.7
		3.4.1 Simple One Loop A.C. Generator or Elementary Alternator	3.7
	3.5	Some Important Terms	3.9
	3.6	Equations of Alternating Voltages and Currents	3.11
	3.7	Effective or Root Mean Square (R.M.S.) Value of Sinusoidal Current or Voltage	3.14
	3.8	Average Value of Sinusoidal Current or Voltage	3.16
	3.9	Peak Factor and Form Factor	3.17
	3.10	Phasor Representation of Alternating Quantities	3.23

3.11	Phase and Phase Difference	3.24
3.12	Phasor Diagrams	3.26
3.13	Addition and Subtraction of Sinusoidal Alternating Quantities	3.28
3.14	Complex Notation	3.32
3.15	Phasors in Rectangular Form	3.32
	3.15.1 The j Operator	3.33
	3.15.2 Addition and Subtraction of Phasors in Rectangular Form	3.33
	3.15.3 Multiplication and Division of Phasors in Rectangular Form	3.33
3.16	Phasors in Polar Form	3.34
	3.16.1 Multiplication and Division of Phasors in Polar Form	3.35
3.17	Interconversion of Rectangular and Polar Forms	3.35
3.18	Response of Pure R, L and C to Sinusoidal A.C. Supplies	3.41
3.19	Purely Resistive A.C. Circuit	3.41
3.20	Purely Inductive A.C. Circuit	3.43
3.21	Purely Capacitive A.C. Circuit	3.46
3.22	Points to Remember	3.50
3.23	Important Formulae at a Glance	3.51
3.24	Solutions of Numerical Examples from University Papers	3.53
3.25	Exercises	3.55
	3.25.1 Review Questions	3.55
	3.25.2 Classified Theory Questions from University Papers	3.55
	3.25.3 Examples for Practice	3.56

4.	**SINGLE-PHASE A.C. SERIES CIRCUITS**	**4.1 – 4.58**
4.1	Introduction	4.1
4.2	Series A.C. Circuits	4.1
4.3	Circuit with Resistance and Inductance in Series	4.1
	4.3.1 Measurement of Power in an Inductive Circuit using Three-Voltmeter Method	4.8
4.4	Circuit with Resistance and Capacitance in Series	4.11
4.5	Circuit with Resistance, Inductance and Capacitance in Series	4.14
4.6	Active Power and Reactive Power in A.C. Circuit	4.19
4.7	Impedances in Series	4.25
4.8	Resonance in the R-L-C Series Circuit	4.27
	4.8.1 Resonant Frequency	4.29
	4.8.2 Bandwidth of a Resonant Circuit	4.29
	4.8.3 Q-Factor of a Series Circuit	4.29
4.9	Application of Complex Notation Method to A.C. Series Circuits	4.33
4.10	Points to Remember	4.45

4.11	Important Formulae at a Glance	4.46
4.12	Solutions of Numerical Examples from University Papers	4.48
4.13	Exercises	4.54
	4.13.1 Review Questions	4.54
	4.13.2 Classified Theory Questions from University Papers	4.55
	4.13.3 Examples for Practice	4.55

5. SINGLE-PHASE A.C. PARALLEL CIRCUITS 5.1 – 5.38

5.1	Parallel A.C. Circuits	5.1
5.2	Solution of Parallel Circuits	5.1
5.3	Phasor Method and its Application to Parallel Circuits	5.1
5.4	Admittance and Allied Concepts	5.4
5.5	Application of Admittance Method to Parallel Circuits	5.5
5.6	Measurement of Power in an Inductive Circuit using Three-Ammeter Method	5.8
5.7	The Practical Importance of Power Factor	5.10
5.8	Capacitor as a Power Factor Improving Device	5.10
5.9	Resonance in Parallel Circuits	5.11
	5.9.1 Resonant Frequency	5.12
	5.9.2 Dynamic Impedance	5.12
	5.9.3 Q-Factor of a Parallel Circuit	5.13
5.10	Comparison of Series and Parallel Resonant Circuits	5.14
5.11	Application of Complex Notation Method to A.C. Parallel Circuits	5.16
5.12	Points to Remember	5.33
5.13	Important Formulae at a Glance	5.34
5.14	Solutions of Numerical Examples from University Papers	5.35
5.15	Exercises	5.36
	5.15.1 Review Questions	5.36
	5.15.2 Classified Theory Questions from University Papers	5.37
	5.15.3 Examples for Practice	5.37

Unit - 3

6. EARTHING AND LAMPS 6.1 – 6.36

6.1	Necessity of Earthing	6.1
6.2	Methods of Earthing	6.2
	6.2.1 Earthing through a Water Main	6.3
	6.2.2 Plate Earthing	6.3
	6.2.3 Pipe Earthing	6.4
6.3	Maximum Permissible Resistance of Earth Systems	6.4
6.4	Wiring Accessories	6.5

6.5	Fuses	6.5
6.6	Types of Fuses	6.6
	6.6.1 Semi-enclosed or Rewirable Type Fuses	6.6
	6.6.2 High Rupturing Capacity (H.R.C.) Cartridge Fuses	6.7
6.7	Current Rating and Minimum Fusing Current	6.8
6.8	Introduction to Low-Voltage Circuit Breakers	6.9
	6.8.1 Moulded Case Circuit Breaker (MCCB)	6.9
	6.8.2 Miniature Circuit Breaker (MCB)	6.10
	6.8.3 Earth Leakage Circuit Breaker (ELCB)	6.11
6.9	Electric Lamps	6.12
6.10	Incandescent Lamps	6.12
6.11	Electric Discharge Lamps	6.13
	6.11.1 Fluorescent Lamps or Fluorescent Tubes	6.13
	6.11.2 Mercury Vapour Lamps	6.16
	6.11.3 Sodium Vapour Lamps	6.17
	6.11.4 Neon Lamps	6.18
	6.11.5 Compact Fluorescent Lamps (C.F.Ls.)	6.20
	6.11.6 Metal Halide Lamps	6.21
	6.11.7 LED Lamps	6.22
6.12	Electrical Power System	6.23
6.13	Transmission and Distribution of Electrical Power	6.23
6.14	Energy Meters	6.25
6.15	Electromechanical Type Energy Meters	6.26
	6.15.1 Induction Type Single-Phase Energy Meters	6.26
	6.15.2 Induction Type Three-Phase Energy Meters	6.29
6.16	Electronic Type Energy Meters	6.31
	6.16.1 Electronic Type Single-Phase Energy Meters	6.31
	6.16.2 Electronic Type Three-Phase Energy Meters	6.33
	6.16.3 Advantages of Electronic Type Energy Meters	6.34
6.17	Exercises	6.35
	6.17.1 Review Questions	6.35
	6.17.2 Classified Theory Questions from University Papers	6.36

SECTION - II

Unit - 4

7.	**THREE-PHASE A.C. CIRCUITS**	7.1 – 7.28
7.1	Polyphase Systems	7.1
7.2	Generation of Three-Phase Voltages	7.2
7.3	Three-Phase Supply Systems	7.4
	7.3.1 Three-Phase, Three-Wire System	7.4
	7.3.2 Three-Phase, Four-Wire System	7.5
7.4	Balanced Load	7.6
7.5	Balanced System	7.7
7.6	Voltage, Current and Power Relations in a Star Connection	7.7
7.7	Voltage, Current and Power Relations in a Delta Connection	7.10
7.8	Apparent Power and Reactive Power	7.14
7.9	Applications of Star and Delta Connections	7.14
7.10	Points to Remember	7.25
7.11	Important Formulae at a Glance	7.26
7.12	Exercises	7.27
	7.12.1 Review Questions	7.27
	7.12.2 Examples for Practice	7.28

Unit - 5

8.	**SINGLE-PHASE TRANSFORMERS**	8.1 – 8.48
8.1	Introduction	8.1
8.2	Principle of Working	8.1
8.3	Constructional Features	8.2
8.4	Types of Transformers	8.5
8.5	E.M.F. Equation of a Transformer	8.7
8.6	Voltage and Current Ratios of a Transformer	8.10
8.7	Kilovolt-Ampere Rating of a Transformer	8.12
8.8	Ideal Transformer	8.14
	8.8.1 Ideal Transformer on No Load	8.14
	8.8.2 Ideal Transformer on Load	8.15
8.9	Practical Transformers	8.15
	8.9.1 Effect of Core Losses	8.16
	8.9.2 Effect of Resistance and Leakage Reactance of Windings	8.17
	8.9.3 Practical Transformer on Load	8.18
8.10	Regulation of a Transformer	8.18

8.11	Transformer Losses	8.20
8.12	Efficiency of a Transformer	8.21
	8.12.1 Condition for Maximum Efficiency of a Transformer	8.22
8.13	Methods of Finding Efficiency and Regulation of a Transformer	8.28
	8.13.1 Efficiency and Regulation by Direct Loading	8.28
8.14	All-Day Efficiency of a Transformer	8.30
8.15	Applications of Transformers	8.32
8.16	Auto-Transformers	8.33
8.17	Points to Remember	8.34
8.18	Important Formulae at a Glance	8.35
8.19	Solutions of Numerical Examples from University Papers	8.38
8.20	Exercises	8.45
	8.20.1 Review Questions	8.45
	8.20.2 Classified Theory Questions from University Papers	8.46
	8.20.3 Examples for Practice	8.47

9. SINGLE-PHASE ALTERNATORS 9.1 – 9.26

9.1	Introduction	9.1
9.2	Types of Alternators	9.1
9.3	Alternator Construction	9.2
	9.3.1 Excitation for Revolving Field System of an Alternator	9.4
9.4	Frequency of Induced E.M.F.	9.5
9.5	Synchronous Speed	9.5
9.6	Winding Terminology	9.6
9.7	Single-Phase Armature Windings	9.7
9.8	E.M.F. Equation of an Alternator	9.9
	9.8.1 Effect of Distributing the Winding on Induced E.M.F.	9.10
	9.8.2 Effect of using Fractional-Pitch Coils on Induced E.M.F.	9.12
	9.8.3 General Expression for the E.M.F. of an Alternator	9.14
9.9	Parameters of Armature Winding	9.16
9.10	Concept of Synchronous Reactance and Impedance	9.17

9.11	Phasor Diagrams of an Alternator on Load	9.17
9.12	Voltage Regulation of an Alternator	9.22
9.13	Determination of Voltage Regulation	9.24
	9.13.1 Voltage Regulation by Direct Loading	9.24
9.14	Applications of Single-Phase Alternators	9.25
9.15	Exercises	9.25
	9.15.1 Review Questions	9.25
	9.15.2 Examples for Practice	9.26

Unit - 6

10. SINGLE-PHASE A.C. MOTORS   10.1 – 10.12

10.1	Introduction	10.1
10.2	Single-Phase Induction Motors	10.1
10.3	Types of Single-Phase Induction Motors	10.4
	10.3.1 Resistance Split-Phase Motors	10.4
	10.3.2 Capacitor Split-Phase Motors	10.5
	10.3.3 Shaded-Pole Motors	10.7
10.4	Universal Motors	10.9
10.5	Exercises	10.11
	10.5.1 Review Questions	10.11
	10.5.2 Classified Theory Questions from University Papers	10.12

University Question papers (Dec. 2014 & May 2015)   P-1 – P-4

CHAPTER 1

D. C. CIRCUITS

1.1 WORK, POWER AND ENERGY RELATIONS

S.I. system is comprehensive, logical and coherent system designed for use in all branches of science, technology and engineering. The S.I. units for work, power and energy can be derived from the following five basic fundamental units :

(i) Metre (m) for length
(ii) Kilogram (kg) for mass
(iii) Second (s) for time
(iv) Ampere (A) for an electric current and
(v) Kelvin (K)* for temperature

1.1.1 Mechanical Units

Mass : Mass is one of the fundamental quantities. *It is the quantity of the matter possessed by a body.* As already mentioned above, unit for the mass is kilogram (kg).

Velocity : It is defined as *the distance travelled per unit time* and can therefore be expressed in *metres per second* (m/s).

Acceleration : Acceleration is *the rate of change of velocity.* It is expressed in *metres per second square* (m/s^2).

Force : *Force is that which changes or tends to change the state of rest or of uniform motion of a body.* The unit of force is the *newton (N). It is the force required to give a mass of one kilogram an acceleration of one metre per second square.*

Hence, the force 'F' required to give a mass 'm' an acceleration 'a' is :

$$F \text{ (newtons)} = m \text{ (kilograms)} \times a \text{ (metres/second}^2) \qquad \ldots (1.1)$$

Weight : The gravitational force exerted by the earth on a body is termed its weight. The weight can be obtained from the mass of a body and the value of gravitational acceleration 'g' which is 9.81 m/s^2. Thus, the weight of a 1 kg mass is equal to 9.81 N or in general,

$$\text{The weight of a body} = m g = 9.81 \times m \text{ newtons} \qquad \ldots (1.2)$$

where m is the mass of the body in kilograms

Turning Moment or Torque : It is the product of a force and a perpendicular distance from the line of action of the force to the axis of rotation. The unit of torque is *newton-metre* (Nm). *If a force of one newton acts at a perpendicular distance of one metre from its line of action to the axis of rotation, then the torque is one newton-metre.* In general, if a force F (in newtons) is acting at right angles to a radius R (in metres) from the axis of rotation,

$$\text{Turning moment or Torque (T)} = F \times R \text{ newton-metres} \qquad \ldots (1.3)$$

---

* *It should be remembered that a temperature interval of 1 °C = a temperature interval of 1 K.*

Work : Work is said to be done when a force acting on a body causes it to move. The S.I. unit of work is the *joule (J)*. *It is the work done in moving the point of application of a force of one newton through a distance of one metre in the direction of the force.* Hence, if a force 'F' acts through a distance 'd' in its own direction,

Work done, W (joules) = F (newtons) × d (metres) ... (1.4)

It should be noted that :

$$1 \text{ joule (J)} = 1 \text{ newton-metre (Nm)}$$

Power : Power can be defined as *the rate of doing work* i.e.

$$\text{Power} = \frac{\text{Work done}}{\text{Time}} \quad \ldots (1.5)$$

Its unit is the *watt (W)*. *Power developed is said to be one watt when work of one joule is done in one second.* Obviously,

$$1 \text{ watt} = 1 \text{ joule / second.}$$

Torque and Power : Consider the pulley of radius R shown in Fig. 1.1. If T is the torque (in newton-metres) due to a circumferential force F acting about an axis of rotation and if n is the resulting speed of the pulley in revolutions per second, then the power developed (P) can be found as follows :

Work done in 1 revolution = F × 2π R joules

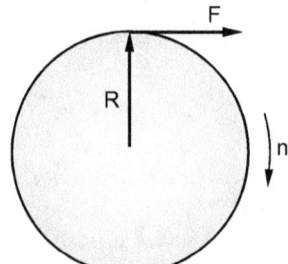

Fig. 1.1 : Torque and Power

Time required for 1 revolution = $\frac{1}{n}$ seconds.

$$\therefore \quad P = \frac{\text{Work done}}{\text{Time}}$$

$$= \frac{F \times 2\pi R}{1/n} = F \times 2\pi R \times n = (F \times R) \times 2\pi n$$

$$= \omega T \text{ joules/second or watts} \quad \ldots (1.6)$$

where ω is the angular velocity in radians / second.

Energy : It is defined as *the capacity to do the work*. Work is done always at the cost of energy. Therefore, work done is taken as measure of the energy used. In other words, energy expended is given by the total work done in a particular period, i.e.

Energy expended = Work done = Power × Time ... (1.7)

Therefore, energy has the same unit as the work, namely the *joule*.

Kinetic Energy : *This is the energy possessed by a body due to its motion.* If a body with mass of m kilograms is moving with velocity of V metres / second, then the amount of energy possessed by it is given by,

$$\text{Kinetic energy} = \frac{1}{2} mV^2 \text{ joules} \qquad \ldots (1.8)$$

Potential Energy : *It is the energy possessed by a body by virtue of its position.* If a body with mass of m kilograms is lifted vertically through height of h metres, and if g metres / second^2 is the gravitational acceleration, then

Potential energy acquired by a body = Work done in lifting the body

$$= mgh = W \times h \text{ joules} \qquad \ldots (1.9)$$

where W is the weight of a body.

1.1.2 Electrical Units

Work : We have seen that quantitatively, an electric current (I) is defined as the rate of transfer of electrical charge (Q) per unit time $\left(\text{i.e. } I = \frac{Q}{t}\right)$. In an electrical circuit, work is said to be done when a charge is moved through a difference of potential (V). Unit is again *the joule* only. *It is the work done electrically in moving a charge of one coulomb through a potential difference of one volt.* Therefore, the work done (W) in moving a charge of Q coulombs through a potential difference of V volts is given by,

$$W = V \cdot Q \text{ joules} \qquad \ldots (1.10)$$
$$= V \cdot I \cdot t \text{ joules} \qquad (\text{since } Q = I \cdot t) \qquad \ldots (1.11)$$

Power : As already seen, *power (P) is the rate of doing work.*

$$\therefore \quad P = \frac{\text{Work done}}{\text{Time}} = \frac{V \cdot I \cdot t}{t} = V \cdot I \qquad \ldots (1.12)$$

Unit for power is *watt (W). The power consumed by the electrical circuit is said to be one watt when the potential difference applied across the circuit is one volt and the current flowing through it is one ampere.* It should be noted that,

1 watt = 1 joule / second

In an electrical circuit with resistance of R ohms and carrying the current of I amperes on application of the voltage of V volts, by Ohm's law, we have

$$V = I \cdot R$$

Or, $$I = \frac{V}{R}$$

Therefore, substituting in the above Equation (1.12), we can have the following alternative forms of the expression for power :

$$P = V \cdot I$$
$$= I^2 \cdot R = \frac{V^2}{R} \text{ watts} \qquad \ldots (1.13)$$

Here, P will be in watts when I is in amperes, V is in volts and R is in ohms.

Energy : Since the work done is always taken as a measure of the energy used,

$$\text{Energy expended} = \text{Work done electrically}$$
$$= V.I.t \text{ joules} \quad \text{(refer to Equation 1.11)}$$
$$= \text{Power} \times \text{Time} \quad \text{(since } P = V.I\text{)}$$

The fundamental unit of energy is *joule*. However, the unit for power being watt and the unit for time being second, the unit for electrical energy is also considered as *watt-second (Ws)*. *Energy consumed by the electrical circuit is said to be one watt-second when it utilizes the power of one watt for one second.* It is obvious that

$$1 \text{ watt-second} = 1 \text{ joule}$$

Since, by Ohm's law, $\quad V = I.R \text{ or } I = \dfrac{V}{R},$

$$\text{Electrical energy} = V.I.t = I^2.R.t$$
$$= \dfrac{V^2 \cdot t}{R} \text{ watt-seconds} \qquad \ldots (1.14)$$

The units for electrical power and energy mentioned above are very small units. Therefore, for commercial purposes, following higher units are frequently employed.

For Power : 1 kilowatt (kW) $\quad = 1000$ watts (W)
For Energy : 1 kilowatt-hour (kWh) $\quad = 1000$ watt-hours (Wh)
$\qquad\qquad\qquad\qquad\qquad\qquad = 3600 \times 1000$ watt-seconds (Ws)

The energy consumed by the electrical circuit is said to be one kilowatt-hour when it utilizes the power of one kilowatt continuously for one hour. Kilowatt-hour is called a Board of Trade Unit (B.O.T.U.) and our bill for electric charges is based on the number of kilowatt-hours consumed.

1.1.3 Thermal Units

The flow of current through a conductor produces heat. By the principle of conservation of energy, the electrical energy expended must equal the heat energy produced, or

$$H = \text{Heat energy (in joules)}$$
$$= I^2.R.t$$
$$= V.I.t \text{ (Joule's Law)} \qquad \ldots (1.15)$$

where, I is the current flowing through the conductor in amperes, R is the resistance of the conductor in ohms and t is the time of current flow in seconds.

Specific Heat Capacity : *The quantity of heat required to raise the temperature of one kilogram of the substance by one kelvin is called the specific heat capacity of that substance.* It is normally expressed in *joules per kilogram kelvin* (J/kg.K). It is important to note that the specific heat capacity of water is 4187 J/kg.K.

Sensible Heat : *It is the quantity of heat gained or lost by a given mass of a substance when a temperature change takes place without change in its state* and is given by the following expression :

$$\text{Sensible heat} = m.s.(t_2 - t_1) \text{ joules} \qquad \ldots (1.16)$$

where,
    m = Mass of a substance in kilograms (kg)
    s = Specific heat capacity of a substance in joules per kilogram kelvin (J/kg.K)
    $t_2 - t_1$ = Final temperature − Initial temperature
    = Temperature change (numerical value) in kelvins (K)

Specific Enthalpy or Specific Latent Heat : *It is the heat required to change the state of one kilogram mass of a substance without change in temperature.*

Latent Heat : *This is the quantity of heat required to change the state of a given mass of a substance without change in temperature* and is given by the expression,

$$\text{Latent heat} = m \times h \text{ joules} \qquad \ldots (1.17)$$

where,

m = Mass of a substance in kilograms

h = Specific enthalpy (or specific latent heat) of a substance in joules per kilogram (J/kg)

Calorific Values : Heat energy can be produced by the combustion of various fuels. The calorific value of a fuel is defined as *the amount of heat produced by completely burning unit mass of that fuel* and it is normally expressed in *kJ/g, MJ/kg or kWh/kg*.

1.1.4 Efficiency

When any device or equipment converts or transforms energy, some of the input energy is always lost due to various reasons during this conversion. The efficiency of this operation is therefore defined as follows :

$$\text{Efficiency} = \frac{\text{Energy output in a given time}}{\text{Energy input in the same time}}$$

$$= \frac{\text{Power output}}{\text{Power input}} \qquad \ldots (1.18)$$

It is invariably less than 1. Higher the value of the power output for the given input, more efficient is the system or the equipment. It should be remembered that efficiency is normally expressed as a percentage, i.e.

$$\% \text{ Efficiency} = \frac{\text{Power output}}{\text{Power input}} \times 100 \qquad \ldots (1.19)$$

With this background, energy conversions between electrical, mechanical and thermal quantities is best illustrated with the help of few examples given below.

Example 1.1 : *Given below are the different electrical appliances used by a family, their ratings and the number of hours they are used daily.*

Description	Rating	No. of hours used (daily)
2 tube lights	40 W, each	4 hours, each
2 bulbs	25 W, each	3 hours, each
An electric iron	450 W	1 hour
A geyser	1500 W	2 hours
2 fans	60 W, each	10 hours, each

Find the electric charges per month (30 days) if the cost per unit is 50 paise.

Solution : Let us first calculate the energy consumed by different appliances daily.

Appliances	Daily energy consumption in watt-hours
Tubes	$2 \times 40 \times 4 = 320$
Bulbs	$2 \times 25 \times 3 = 150$
An electric iron	$450 \times 1 = 450$
A geyser	$1500 \times 2 = 3000$
Fans	$2 \times 60 \times 10 = 1200$
	Total = 5120

Monthly energy consumption

$$= 5120 \times 30$$

$$= 153600 \text{ Wh} = 153.6 \text{ kWh (or Units)}$$

∴ Monthly charge (in Rs.) $= 153.6 \times \dfrac{50}{100} =$ **76.80** ... Ans.

Example 1.2 : *An electric kettle is required to heat 5 litres of water from 15 °C to 96 °C in 30 minutes. Find the rating of the kettle assuming the efficiency of 80 per cent. If the kettle is to operate on 230 V mains, find the resistance of the heating element. Assume the specific heat capacity of water to be 4200 J/kg.K and 1 litre of water to have a mass of 1 kg.*

Solution : Mass of water = 5 kg

Rise of temperature = 96 – 15 = 81°C = 81 K

Hence, from Expression (1.16),

Heat energy required $= 5 \text{ (kg)} \times 4200 \text{ (J/kg.K)} \times 81 \text{ (K)}$

$$= 1701 \times 10^3 \text{ J}$$

∴ Power output required from the kettle

$$= \frac{\text{Energy}}{\text{Time}} = \frac{1701 \times 10^3}{30 \times 60} = 945 \text{ W}$$

∴ Power input to the kettle = Rating

$$= \frac{\text{Power output}}{\text{Efficiency}}$$

$$= \frac{945}{0.8} = 1181.25 \text{ W, say } \mathbf{1200 \text{ W}} \qquad \text{... Ans.}$$

With the supply voltage of 230 V, the resistance of the heating element

$$= \frac{\text{Voltage}^2}{\text{Power rating}} = \frac{230^2}{1200}$$

$$= \mathbf{44 \; \Omega} \qquad \text{... Ans.}$$

Example 1.3 : *An electric furnace is to melt 40 kg of aluminium per hour, the initial temperature of the aluminium being 12 °C. Calculate (a) the power required and (b) the cost of operating the furnace for 20 hours, given that aluminium has the following thermal properties :*

  Specific heat capacity = 950 J/kg.K

  Melting point = 660 °C

Specific latent heat of fusion = 450 kJ/kg.

Assume the efficiency of the furnace to be 85 % and the cost of electrical energy to be 50 paise per unit.

Solution :

Quantity of charge to be melted

$$= 40 \text{ kg.}$$

From the Expression (1.16), heat required to bring the charge to melting point

$$= 40 \text{ (kg)} \times 950 \text{ (J/kg.K)} \times (660 - 12) \text{ (K)}$$
$$= 24.624 \times 10^6 \text{ J}$$

From the Expression (1.17), latent heat i.e. heat required to just melt the charge

$$= 40 \text{ (kg)} \times 450 \text{ (kJ/kg)}$$
$$= 18000 \text{ kJ} = 18 \times 10^6 \text{ J}$$

∴ Total heat required $= 24.624 \times 10^6 + 18 \times 10^6$

$$= 42.624 \times 10^6 \text{ J}$$

∴ Total energy input required for the furnace

$$= \frac{42.624 \times 10^6}{0.85} \text{ J}$$

$$= \frac{42.624 \times 10^6}{0.85 \times 3600 \times 1000} = 13.93 \text{ kWh.}$$

∴ Power input required for the furnace

$$= \frac{\text{Energy input}}{\text{Time}} = \frac{13.93}{1}$$

$$= \mathbf{13.93 \text{ kW}} \qquad \text{… Ans.}$$

If the furnace is operated for 20 hours, then energy consumed

$$= 13.93 \times 20 = 278.6 \text{ kWh}$$

∴ Cost of energy $= 278.6 \times \frac{50}{100}$

$$= \mathbf{139.3 \text{ Rs.}} \qquad \text{… Ans.}$$

Example 1.4 : *An electric boiler has two heating elements each of 230 V, 3.5 kW rating and contains 16 litres of water at 30 °C. Assuming 10 % loss of heat from the boiler, find how long after switching on the heater circuit, will the water boil at the atmospheric pressure if (a) two elements are in parallel, (b) the two elements are in series. The supply voltage is 230 V. Assume, specific heat capacity of water is 4200 J/kg.K and 1 litre of water to have a mass of 1 kg.*

Solution :

Mass of water to be heated = 16 kg.

Rise of temperature = 100 − 30 = 70°C = 70 K

∴ Heat energy required = 16 × 4200 × 70

$$= 4704 \times 10^3 \text{ J}$$

∴ Input energy $= \dfrac{4704 \times 10^3}{0.9} = 5226.67 \times 10^3$ J ... (I)

(a) Elements in Parallel :

When the two elements are connected in parallel, each will draw a power of 3.5 kW from 230 V supply.

∴ Total input power = 2 × 3.5 = 7 kW = 7000 W

Let t seconds be the required time to heat the water.

∴ Input energy = 7000 × t Ws or J ... (II)

Equating expressions (I) and (II), we have

$$7000\, t = 5226.67 \times 10^3$$

∴ $t = \dfrac{5226.67 \times 10^3}{7000}$

$$= 746.67 \text{ s} \qquad \text{... Ans.}$$

(b) Elements in Series :

Rating of each element = 3.5 kW = 3500 W

∴ Resistance of each element,

$$R = \dfrac{230^2}{3500} = 15.11 \ \Omega$$

∴ Total resistance of two elements connected in series

= 2R = 2 × 15.11 = 30.22 Ω

∴ Circuit current, $I = \dfrac{230}{30.22} = 7.61$ A

∴ Total input power = $2 \times 7.61^2 \times 15.11 = 1750.1$ W

If t seconds is the required time in this case to heat the water, then

Input energy = 1750.1 × t Ws or J ... (III)

∴ Equating expressions (I) and (III), we get

$$1750.1 \times t = 5226.67 \times 10^3$$

∴ $$t = \frac{5226.67 \times 10^3}{1750.1} = \mathbf{2986.5\ s} \qquad \text{... Ans.}$$

Example 1.5 : *A belt driven pulley 0.4 m in diameter rotates at a speed of 4 revolutions per second. The tension in the tight side of the belt is 420 N and in the slack side 80 N. Calculate : (a) The torque on the pulley, (b) The power developed.*

Solution :

$$\text{Radius of a pulley} = \frac{0.4}{2} = 0.2\ m$$

Net force acting tangentially on the pulley

$$= 420 - 80 = 340\ N$$

∴ Torque on the pulley $= F \times R = 340 \times 0.2$

$$= \mathbf{68.0\ Nm} \qquad \text{... Ans.}$$

Now, using the Expression (1.6),

Power developed $= T \times 2\pi n$

$$= 68 \times 2\pi \times 4$$

$$= \mathbf{1709.03\ W\ or\ 1.709\ kW} \qquad \text{... Ans.}$$

Example 1.6 : *A pump driven by a d.c. electric motor lifts 1.5 m³ of water per minute to a height of 40 m. The pump has an efficiency of 90 per cent and the motor an efficiency of 85 per cent. Determine (a) the power input to the motor; (b) the current taken from a 480 V supply; (c) the electrical energy consumed when the motor runs at this load for 8 hours. Assume the mass of 1 m³ of water to be 1000 kg.*

Solution :

Mass of water lifted $= 1.5 \times 1000 = 1500\ kg$

∴ Weight of water lifted $= mg = 1500 \times 9.81 = 14715\ N$

Height $= 40\ m$

∴ Work done $= 14715 \times 40 = 588.6 \times 10^3\ J$

∴ Output power $= \dfrac{\text{Work done}}{\text{Time}} = \dfrac{588.6 \times 10^3}{60}$

$$= 9810\ J/s\ \text{or}\ W$$

With pump efficiency $= 90\ \%$

Pump input $=$ Motor output $= \dfrac{9810}{0.9} = 10900\ W$

Now, with motor efficiency = 85 %

(a) Motor power input = $\dfrac{10900}{0.85}$ = **12823.529 W** ... Ans.

(b) Current drawn by motor = $\dfrac{12823.529}{480}$ = **26.72 A** ... Ans.

(c) Electrical energy consumed by the motor = 12.824×8 = **102.592 kWh** ... Ans.

Example 1.7 : *An electric lift makes 12 double journeys per hour. A load of 5×10^3 kg is raised by it through a height of 50 m and it returns empty. The lift takes 65 seconds to go up and 48 seconds to return. The mass of empty cage is 500 kg and that of a counter weight is 2.5×10^3 kg. The efficiency of the equipment is 68 %. Find the energy consumption for one hour in kWh.*

Solution :

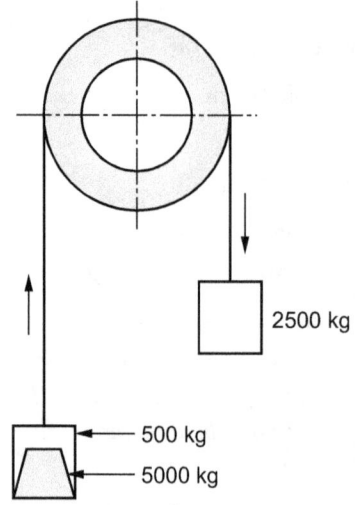

Fig. 1.2 : An electric lift during upward journey

Referring to Fig. 1.2, net mass raised during upward journey
= Mass of a load + Mass of empty cage − Mass of a counter weight
= 5000 + 500 − 2500 = 3000 kg

∴ Net weight lifted in upward journey = m × g
= 3000 × 9.81 = 29430 N

Distance travelled = 50 m

∴ Work done during upward journey
= 29430 × 50 = 1471.5×10^3 J

Now, net mass raised during downward journey
= Mass of a counter weight − Mass of a cage
= 2500 − 500 = 2000 kg

∴ Net weight lifted during downward journey

$$= 2000 \times 9.81 = 19620 \text{ N}$$

Distance travelled $= 50$ m

Hence, work done during downward journey

$$= 19620 \times 50 = 981 \times 10^3 \text{ J}$$

∴ Total work done per double journey

$$= 1471.5 \times 10^3 + 981 \times 10^3 = 2452.5 \times 10^3 \text{ J}$$

Efficiency of the equipment $= 68\%$

∴ Energy consumed per double journey

$$= \frac{2452.5 \times 10^3}{0.68} = 3606.62 \times 10^3 \text{ J}$$

$$= \frac{3606.62 \times 10^3}{3600 \times 1000} \text{ kWh} = 1.002 \text{ kWh}$$

Number of double journeys per hour

$$= 12$$

∴ Energy consumption per hour

$$= 1.002 \times 12$$

$$= \mathbf{12.024 \text{ kWh}} \quad \text{... Ans.}$$

Example 1.8 : *Calculate the current required by a 1500 V d.c. locomotive when driving a total load of 100×10^3 kg at 25 km per hour up an incline of 1 in 100. Assume tractive resistance of 0.069 N/kg and efficiency of the motors and gearing as 70 %.*

Solution : Total load (mass) $= 100 \times 10^3$ kg

∴ Total weight driven by a locomotive (W) $= m \times g = 100 \times 10^3 \times 9.81 = 981 \times 10^3$ N

Fig. 1.3 shows the different forces acting on a locomotive when it moves up the inclined plane.

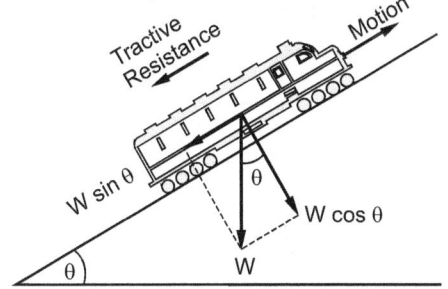

Fig. 1.3 : A locomotive driving load up an incline

Component of the weight acting downwards = W sin θ

$$= 981 \times 10^3 \times \frac{1}{100} = 9.81 \times 10^3 \text{ N}$$

Tractive resistance opposing motion $= 0.069 \times 100 \times 10^3 = 6.9 \times 10^3$ N

Total opposing force $= 9.81 \times 10^3 + 6.9 \times 10^3 = 16.71 \times 10^3$ N

Distance travelled per second $= \dfrac{25 \times 1000}{3600} = 6.94$ m/s

∴ Work done per second $= 16.71 \times 10^3 \times 6.94 = 115.97 \times 10^3$ J

∴ Net power output of the locomotive $= 115.97 \times 10^3$ W

$= 115.97$ kW   (since 1 J/s = 1 W)

Hence, power input $= \dfrac{115.97}{0.7} = 165.67$ kW

∴ Current drawn $= \dfrac{165.67 \times 10^3}{1500} = \mathbf{110.45 \text{ A}}$ ... **Ans.**

Example 1.9 : *A hydro-electric generating plant is supplied from a reservoir of capacity 20×10^6 m³ with a head of 200 m. The hydraulic efficiency of the plant is 0.8 and the electric efficiency is 0.9. What is the total available energy ? If the plant supplies a load of 12 MW for 3 hours, calculate the fall in the level of the reservoir during this period. Area of the reservoir is 3.0 km². Assume 1 m³ of water has a mass of 1000 kg.*

Solution :

Part-1 :

Weight of water $= 20 \times 10^6 \times 1000 \times 9.81 = 196.2 \times 10^9$ N

Water head $= 200$ m

∴ Potential energy stored in this much quantity of water

$= W.h = 196.2 \times 10^9 \times 200$

$= 392.4 \times 10^{11}$ J

Overall efficiency of the station

$= 0.8 \times 0.9 = 0.72$

∴ Energy available $= 392.4 \times 10^{11} \times 0.72$

$= 282.528 \times 10^{11}$ J

$= \dfrac{282.528 \times 10^{11}}{3600 \times 1000}$ kWh $= \mathbf{7.848 \times 10^6}$ **kWh**   ... **Ans.**

Part-2 :

$$\text{Energy supplied} = 12000 \times 3 = 36000 \text{ kWh}$$

∴ Energy drawn from the water stored in the reservoir taking into consideration the overall efficiency of the station

$$= \frac{36000}{0.72} = 5 \times 10^4 \text{ kWh}$$

$$= 5 \times 10^4 \times 10^3 \times 3600$$

$$= 18 \times 10^{10} \text{ Ws or J}$$

If m kg is the mass of water used in 3 hours, then obviously

$$mgh = 18 \times 10^{10}$$

∴ $\quad m \times 9.81 \times 200 = 18 \times 10^{10} \quad$ (since h = 200 m)

∴ $\quad m = 91.74 \times 10^6$ kg

If x metres is the fall in water level, then

$$x \times \text{area} \times \text{density} = \text{Mass of water}$$

∴ $\quad x \times 3 \times 10^6 \times 1000 = 91.74 \times 10^6$

∴ $\quad \mathbf{x = 0.03 \text{ m or } 3 \text{ cm}} \quad$ … Ans.

Example 1.10 : *A steam turbine develops 5 MW. Determine the quantity of oil of calorific value 42 MJ/kg used per minute to heat the boiler if the overall efficiency of the system is 20%.*

Solution :

Power output of steam turbine = 5 MW

Efficiency of the system = 20 %

∴ $\quad$ Power input $= \frac{5}{0.2} = 25$ MW

Energy input needed per minute

$$= 25 \times 10^6 \times 60$$

$$= 15 \times 10^8 \text{ Ws or J}$$

Calorific value of oil = 42 MJ/kg

$$= 42 \times 10^6 \text{ J/kg}$$

∴ $\quad$ Oil used per minute $= \dfrac{15 \times 10^8}{42 \times 10^6}$

$$= \mathbf{35.71 \text{ kg}} \quad \text{… Ans.}$$

Example 1.11 : *An aluminium kettle weighs 3 kg and holds 3000 cm^3 of water. When connected to 200 V supply, its heater element takes current of 12 A. If the efficiency of the kettle is 70 %, find the time required to boil the water from the initial temperature of 30 °C. Assume specific heat capacity of water and aluminium as 4200 J/kg.K and 950 J/kg.K respectively.*

Solution : Mass of 3000 cm³ i.e. 3 litres of water = 3 kg

Total heat energy required to raise the temperature of water and aluminium kettle to 100°C (boiling temperature of water) from 30°C

$$= 3 \times 4200 \times (100 - 30) + 3 \times 950 \times (100 - 30)$$
$$= 1081.5 \times 10^3 \text{ J}$$

$\therefore$ Input energy $= \dfrac{1081.5 \times 10^3}{0.7}$

$$= 1545 \times 10^3 \text{ J}$$

If t seconds is the time required to boil the water, then obviously,

$$V.I.t = 200 \times 12 \times t = 1545 \times 10^3 \text{ J}$$

$\therefore$ t = **643.75 seconds**

= **10.73 minutes** ... Ans.

Example 1.12 : *An electric geyser is used to heat 5 litres of water from 13°C to 83°C. If the heat lost in radiation is 40 kJ and water equivalent of geyser is 100 gm, determine the efficiency of the geyser. Take specific heat of water as 4200 J/kg.K.*

Solution :

Heat output of geyser = $5 \times 4200 \times (83 - 13)$ J
= 1470 kJ

Heat lost in radiation = 40 kJ

Heat absorbed by geyser body = $100 \times 10^{-3} \times 4200 \times (83 - 13)$ J
= 29.4 kJ

$\therefore$ Heat input of geyser = 1470 + 40 + 29.4
= 1539.4 kJ

$\therefore$ Efficiency of geyser = $\dfrac{1470}{1539.4} \times 100$

= **95.49 %** ... Ans.

Example 1.13 : *A crane is designed to lift a mass of 600 kg to a height of 10 m in half minute. The efficiency of crane is 80 %. Select the output rating of motor required. What current will be drawn by the motor when connected to 200 V, d.c. supply ?*

Solution :

Power input to crane = $\dfrac{m.g.h.}{\text{Time} \times \text{Crane efficiency}}$

$= \dfrac{600 \times 9.81 \times 10}{30 \times 0.8}$ W

= 2.4525 kW

∴ Desirable rating of motor = **2.5 kW** ... **Ans.**

Assuming motor efficiency of 80 %,

$$\text{Current drawn by motor} = \frac{2.5 \times 10^3}{0.8 \times 200} = 15.63 \text{ A} \quad \text{... Ans.}$$

Example 1.14 : *In a hydro-electric generating station, the difference in level (head) between the water surface and the turbine driving the generator is 425 m. If 1250 litres of water are required to generate 1 kWh of electrical energy, find the overall efficiency (1 litre of water has a mass of 1 kg).*

Solution : Energy output = 1 kWh

Energy input = Energy drawn from the water stored in the reservoir

= m.g.h

= 1250 × 9.81 × 425 J

= 1.4477 kWh

∴ Efficiency = $\dfrac{\text{Output}}{\text{Input}} \times 100$

= $\dfrac{1}{1.4477} \times 100$

= **0.69 %** ... **Ans.**

Example 1.15 : *A fully charged car battery can give 100 Wh of energy for operating starting mechanism. At each start, the engine has to be cranked at 60 rpm for 10 seconds against a torque of 50 Nm. Assuming an overall efficiency of 30 % of the mechanism, estimate the number of starts before the battery is required to be recharged and the output of the starter motor.*

Solution : Total energy supplied to the engine at each start

$$= \frac{T \times (2\pi N/60) \times \text{Time}}{\text{Efficiency}}$$

$$= \frac{50 \times (2\pi \times 60/60) \times (10/3600)}{0.3}$$

= 2.909 Wh

∴ Number of starts before battery is required to be recharged = $\dfrac{100}{2.909}$

= **34** ... **Ans.**

1.2 ANALYSIS OF D.C. CIRCUITS

In the study of electrical engineering which involves the study of the behaviour of electrical systems and devices, the knowledge of electric circuit theory is very essential. We are therefore beginning our study of electrical circuit theory with the study of some general methods of analysis which have been developed for solving problems on complex electrical networks. Even though the discussion here is restricted to d.c. circuits only, it is equally applicable to a.c. networks. In the case of a.c. networks, the only difference is that the impedances are used instead of just ohmic resistances. Since the impedances as well as currents and voltages in such circuits are expressed by complex numbers, the algebraic manipulations are more extensive.

1.3 CLASSIFICATION OF ELECTRICAL NETWORKS

An electrical circuit or network is a combination of various elements consisting of sources of energy and parameters like resistors, capacitors and inductors, either in lumped or distributed form. The behaviour of entire network depends on the behaviour of its individual elements and accordingly, they can be classified as follows :

(i) Linear Circuits : A circuit whose parameters are always constant irrespective of variations in voltage or current is known as *a linear circuit*. The current flowing in each parameter of such a circuit is directly proportional to the voltage applied across it.

(ii) Non-linear Circuits : A non-linear circuit is one whose parameters change with voltage or current.

(iii) Bilateral Circuits : It is that circuit whose characteristics are the same irrespective of its direction of operation, e.g. a transmission line. It has the same relationship between current and voltage for current flowing in either direction.

(iv) Unilateral Circuits : A circuit whose characteristics are dependent on the direction of its operation is called a *unilateral circuit,* e.g. circuits containing elements like vacuum diodes, silicon diodes, selenium rectifiers, etc., which allow the current to pass only in one direction.

(v) Active Networks : When a network contains a source of energy, it is said to be active. An energy source may be a voltage or current source.

(vi) Passive Networks : A network is said to be passive if it contains no source of energy.

1.4 ENERGY SOURCES

All electric circuits are driven by several kinds of sources of electrical energy. These sources may be independent of other network variables as in the case of d.c. generators, batteries, etc. On the other hand, they may be of a dependent type, such as is frequently encountered in electronic circuits. Discussion here is confined to the independent type energy sources only.

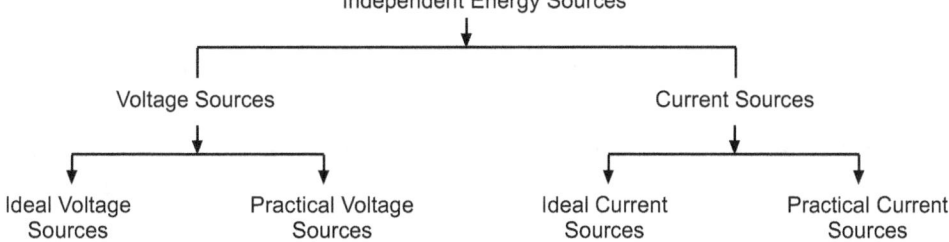

Fig. 1.4 : Classification of independent energy sources

Based on their voltage-current characteristics, independent sources are categorized into voltage sources and current sources (Fig. 1.4).

1.4.1 Independent Voltage Sources

The voltage source is assumed to deliver energy with a specified terminal voltage, which is independent of the amount of current supplied by it. These sources can be further classified as *ideal voltage sources* and *practical voltage sources*.

Ideal Voltage Source : *A voltage source whose terminal voltage remains always constant for all values of output current is known as an ideal voltage source.* Obviously, it has zero internal resistance and is generally represented by a circle with positive (+) and negative (–) polarity marks marked on it as shown in Fig. 1.5 (a). V is its constant terminal voltage.

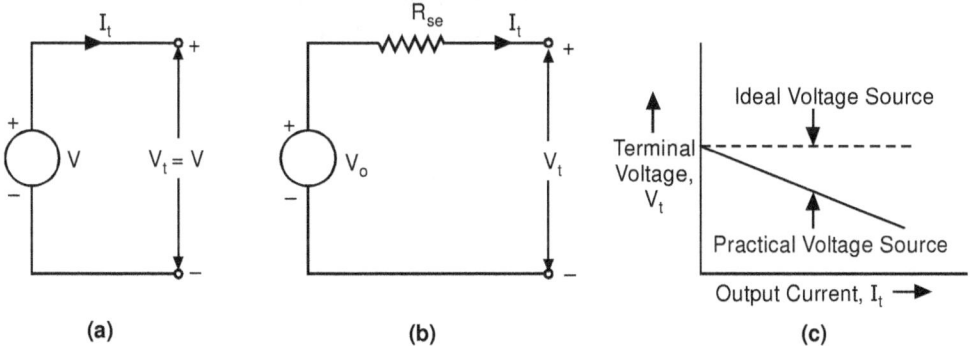

Fig. 1.5 : (a) An ideal voltage source, (b) A practical voltage source,

(c) Voltage-output current characteristics for the ideal and practical voltage sources

In practice, it is impossible to have such a voltage source without any internal resistance.

Practical Voltage Source : In almost all practical voltage sources (e.g. cells, d.c. generators, etc.), a terminal voltage falls with the increase in the output current due to the voltage drop caused by their internal resistance. A practical voltage source can therefore be considered as equivalent to an ideal voltage source having constant voltage equal to open-circuit voltage of the practical voltage source (V_o) in series with the resistance equal to the internal resistance (R_{se}) of the practical voltage source as shown in Fig. 1.5 (b). The series resistor (R_{se}) then accounts for the fall in terminal voltage with the increase in output current. Fig. 1.5 (c) shows the voltage-output current characteristics for the ideal and practical voltage sources.

1.4.2 Independent Current Sources

The current source is assumed to deliver energy with a specified amount of current through its terminals. These sources can also be further classified as *ideal current sources* and *practical current sources*.

Ideal Current Source : *It is that current source which can deliver a constant amount of current irrespective of the value of the load resistance connected across its terminals.* It is generally represented by a circle with an associated arrow indicating the positive direction of the current flow as shown in Fig. 1.6 (a). I is the constant current delivered by the source. In practice, we never come across such a current source.

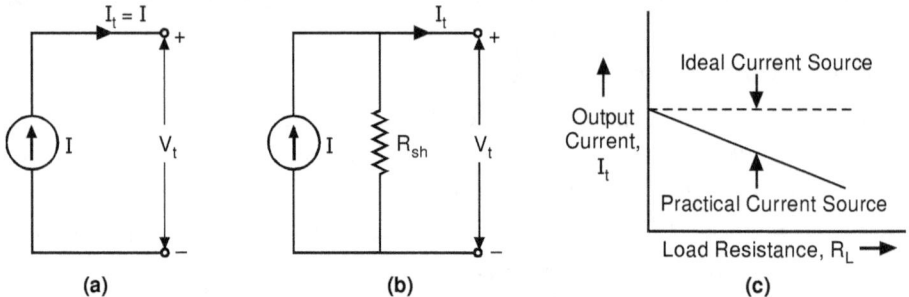

Fig. 1.6 : (a) An ideal current source, (b) A practical current source,
(c) Output current-load resistance characteristics
for the ideal and practical current sources

Practical Current Source : In almost all practical current sources (e.g. photo-electric cells, vacuum tubes, transistors, etc.) output current falls with the increase of load resistance. A practical current source can therefore be considered as equivalent to an ideal current source in parallel with a resistance equal to the internal resistance (R_{sh}) of the practical current source as shown in Fig. 1.6 (b).

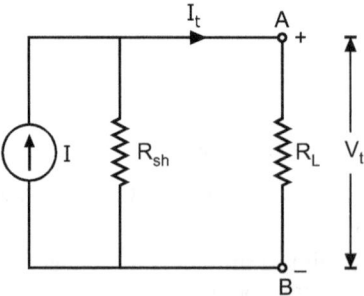

Fig. 1.7 : A current source feeding load

This shunt resistor then accounts for the fall in load current with the increase in the load resistance. Fig. 1.6 (c) shows the output current-load resistance characteristics for the ideal and practical current sources. The ideal conditions of constant current to all loads can be very closely approached if the internal resistance of a practical current source is sufficiently large (it is infinite in the case of an ideal current source). This will be clear from Fig. 1.7 in which a practical current source is shown feeding the load resistance R_L. The load current is obviously given by

$$I_t = \frac{R_{sh}}{R_{sh} + R_L} \times I \qquad \ldots (1.20)$$

Now, if $R_{sh} >> R_L$, $I_t \approx I$. Thus, when the source resistance is very much larger than load resistance, the current delivered to the load nearly equals the source current.

1.4.3 Source Conversion

A practical voltage source can always be replaced by its equivalent practical current source and vice-versa. *Two sources are said to be equivalent if they supply equal load current with the same load resistance connected across their terminals.* Many times, conversion of one source into other becomes essential to facilitate the network analysis. Figs. 1.8 (a) and (b) show respectively the constant voltage source and constant current source with their associated internal resistances, each feeding the load resistance, R_L. Then, with the voltage source, load current is

$$I_t = \frac{V_o}{R_{se} + R_L} \qquad \ldots (1.21)$$

and with the current source, $\quad I_t = \dfrac{R_{sh}}{R_{sh} + R_L} \times I \qquad \ldots (1.22)$

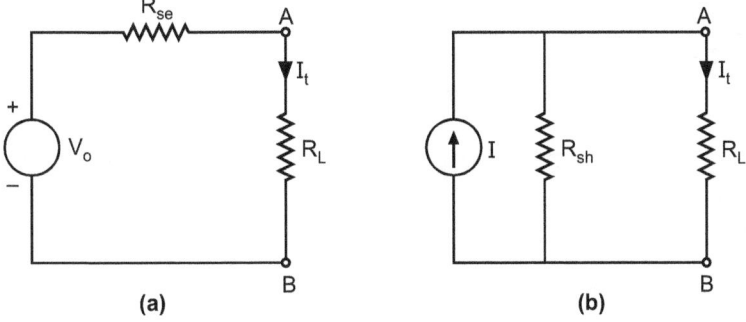

Fig. 1.8 : Source conversion

Now, if two sources are equivalent, then the load current must be the same in each case. Therefore, equating the equations (1.21) and (1.22), we get

$$\frac{V_o}{R_{se} + R_L} = \frac{R_{sh}}{R_{sh} + R_L} \times I \qquad \ldots (1.23)$$

If it is assumed that $R_{se} = R_{sh} = R_s$ (say), then from Equation (1.23), it is obvious that

$$V_o = I \cdot R_s \qquad \ldots (1.24)$$

Thus, from Equation (1.24), it is clear that

(i) A voltage source having voltage V_o and source resistance R_s can be replaced by a current source with current, $I = \dfrac{V_o}{R_s}$ and a source resistance R_s.

(ii) A current source with current I and a source resistance R_s can be replaced by a voltage source with voltage, $V_o = I \cdot R_s$ and source resistance R_s.

Example 1.16 : *Fig. 1.9 (a) shows a voltage source of 40 V with an internal resistance of 4 Ω. Find the equivalent current source.*

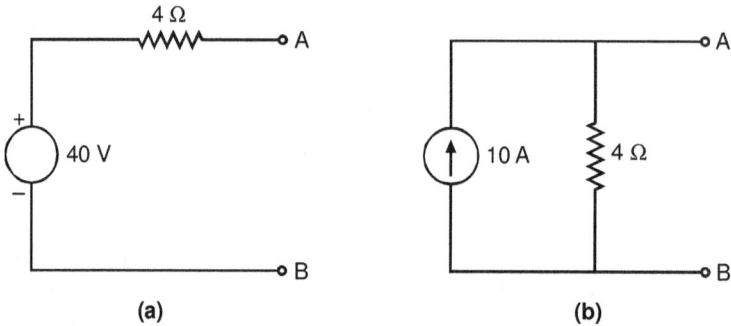

Fig. 1.9 : (a) A practical voltage source, (b) An equivalent practical current source

Solution : Here, it is given that for the voltage source, voltage V_o = 40 V and internal resistance R_s = 4 Ω. Therefore, the equivalent current source will have

$$\text{Current, } I = \frac{V_o}{R_s} = \frac{40}{4} = 10 \text{ A} \qquad \text{... Ans.}$$

Internal resistance, R_s = **4 Ω** ... Ans.

Fig. 1.9 (b) shows the corresponding equivalent circuit.

Example 1.17 : *Fig. 1.10 (a) shows a constant current source of 15 A having an internal resistance of 5 Ω. Find the equivalent voltage source.*

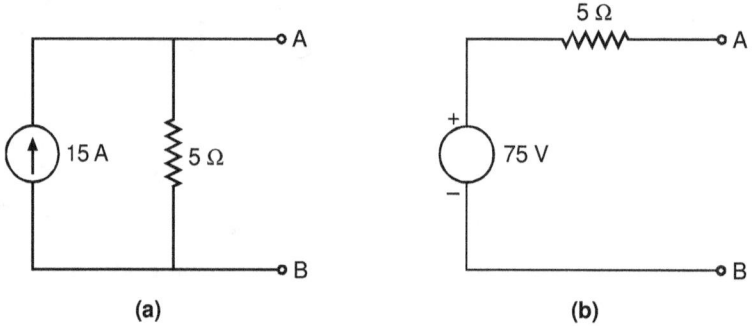

Fig. 1.10 : (a) A practical current source, (b) An equivalent practical voltage source

Solution : Here, it is given that for a practical current source, current I = 15 A and internal resistance R_s = 5 Ω. Therefore, the equivalent voltage source will have

$$\text{Voltage, } V_o = I \cdot R_s$$
$$= 15 \times 5 = \textbf{75 V} \qquad \text{... Ans.}$$

Internal resistance, R_s = **5 Ω** ... Ans.

Fig. 1.10 (b) represents the corresponding equivalent circuit.

Example 1.18 : *Using source conversion, reduce the circuit shown in Fig. 1.11, into a single voltage source in series with single resistance.*

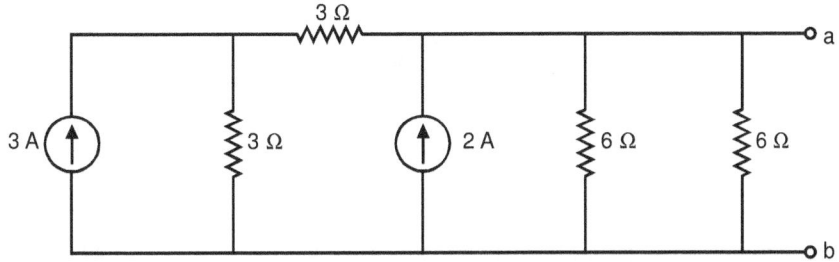

Fig. 1.11 : Network for Example 1.18

Solution :

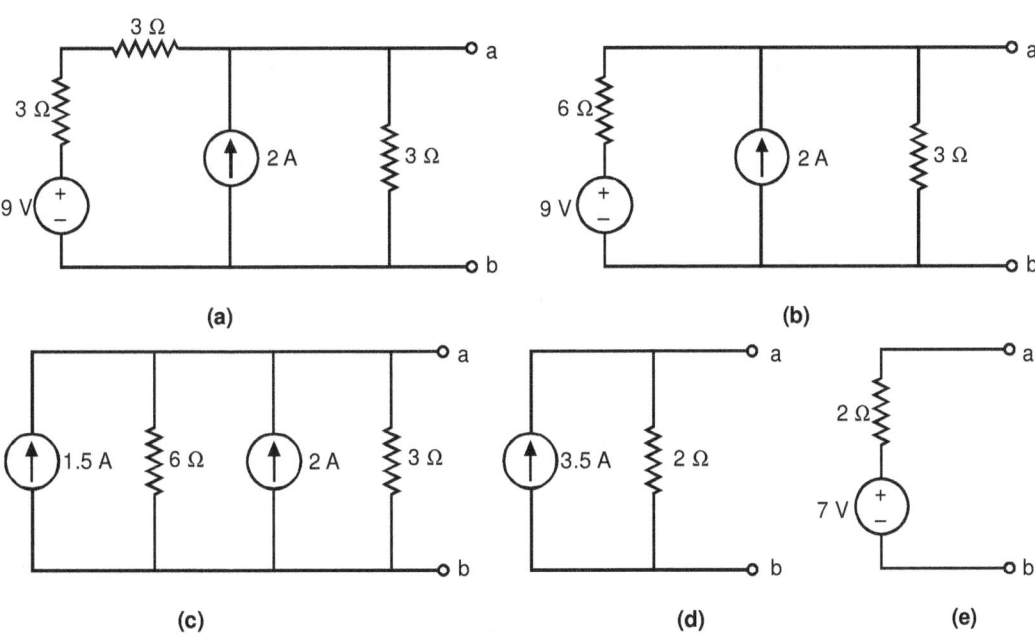

Fig. 1.12 : Different stages of simplification of the network of Fig. 1.11

The current source of 3 A in the circuit of Fig. 1.11 can be replaced by a voltage source and two 6 Ω resistances in parallel can be replaced by their equivalent resistance of 3 Ω as shown in Fig. 1.12 (a). Further, the voltage source in the circuit of Fig. 1.12 (b) can be replaced by a current source as shown in Fig. 1.12 (c). Then, the current sources can be combined into a single source. Similarly, all the resistances in parallel can be combined into a single resistance as shown in Fig. 1.12 (d). Now, a current source of Fig. 1.12 (d) can be replaced by a single voltage source and a series resistance as shown in Fig. 1.12 (e).

Example 1.19 : *Using source conversion, convert the given circuit into an equivalent circuit containing single resistance and voltage source.*

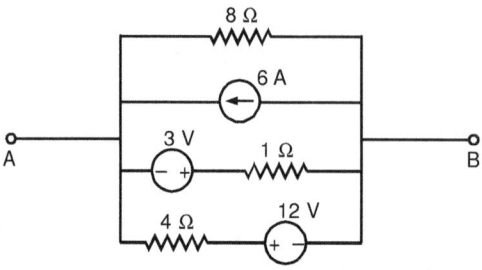

Fig. 1.13 : Network for Example 1.19

Solution : Using source conversion, the given circuit can be converted into an equivalent circuit, containing single resistance and voltage source as illustrated below in Figs. 1.14 (a), (b), (c) and (d).

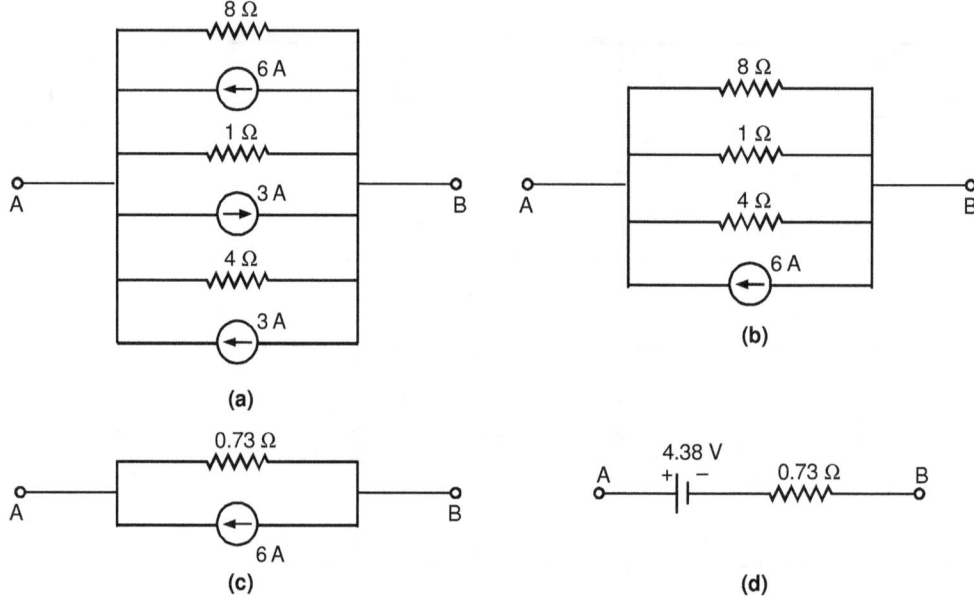

Fig. 1.14 : Different stages of simplification of the network of Fig. 1.13

Example 1.20 : *Using the source conversion technique, find the current through load resistance R_L of the given circuit.*

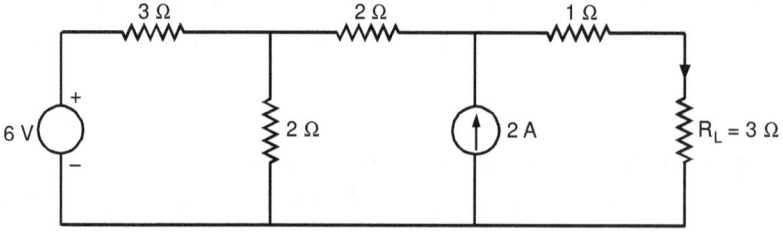

Fig. 1.15 : Network for Example 1.20

Solution : Fig. 1.16 shows the different stages of simplification of the given network using the source conversion technique. Hence,

Current through load resistance $R_L = 2.75 \times \dfrac{3.2}{(3.2 + 1 + 3)} = \mathbf{1.22\ A}$ ... **Ans.**

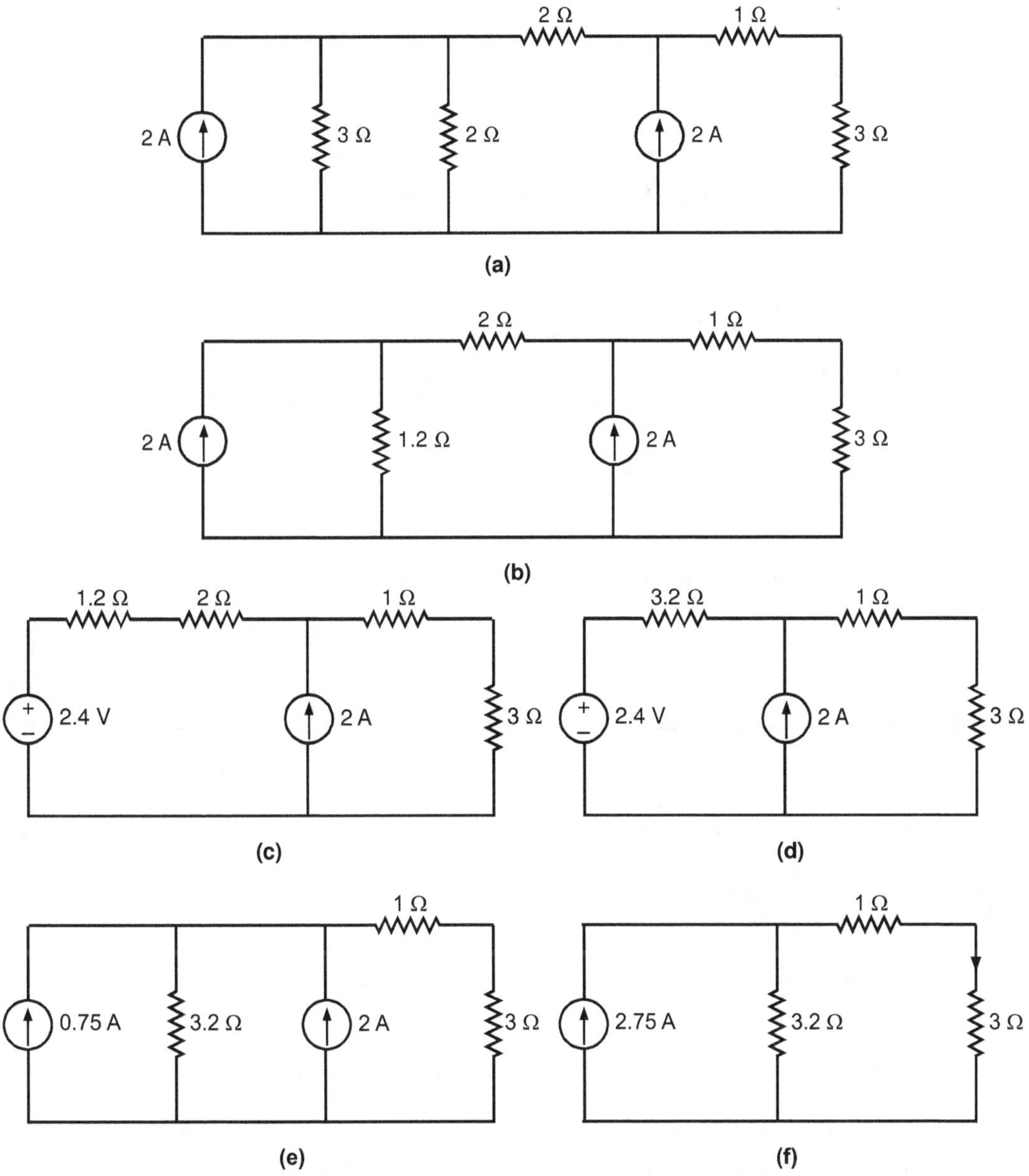

Fig. 1.16 : Different stages of simplification of the network of Fig. 1.15

Example 1.21 : *Using repeated source transformation, find the value of voltage 'v' for the network shown in Fig. 1.17.*

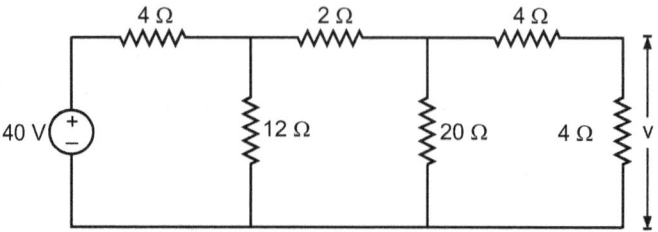

Fig. 1.17 : Network for Example 1.21

Solution :

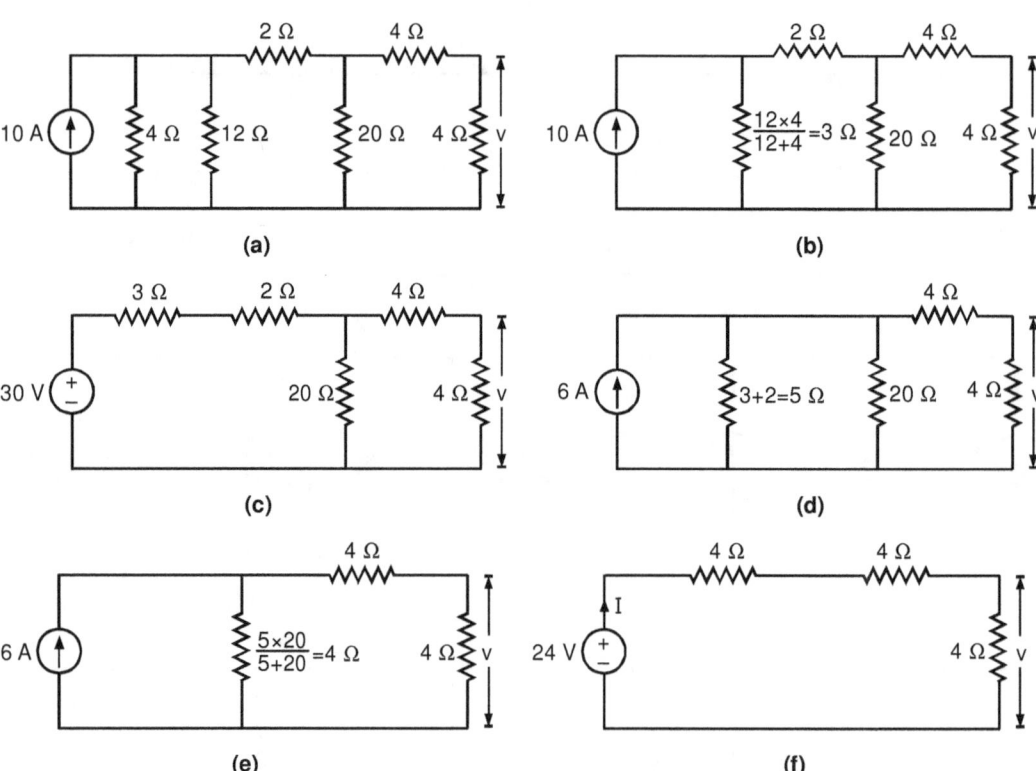

Fig. 1.18 : Different stages of simplification of the network of Fig. 1.17

Figs. 1.18 (a), (b), (c), (d), (e) and (f) show the different stages of simplification of the given network using repeated source transformation. From Fig. 1.18 (f), it is obvious that

$$I = \frac{24}{4+4+4} = 2 \text{ A}$$

∴ Voltage across 4 Ω resistance,

$$v = 4 \times 2 = 8 \text{ V} \qquad \text{... Ans.}$$

Example 1.22 : *Using source transformation, determine the voltage across 5 Ω resistance for the circuit shown in Fig. 1.19.*

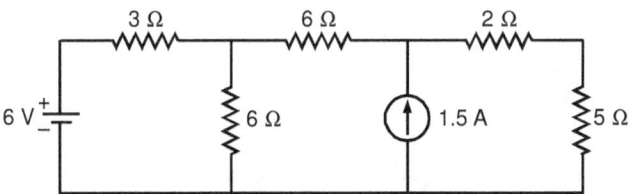

Fig. 1.19 : Network for Example 1.22

Solution : Figs. 1.20 (a), (b), (c), (d), (e) and (f) show the different stages of simplification of the given network using repeated source transformation.

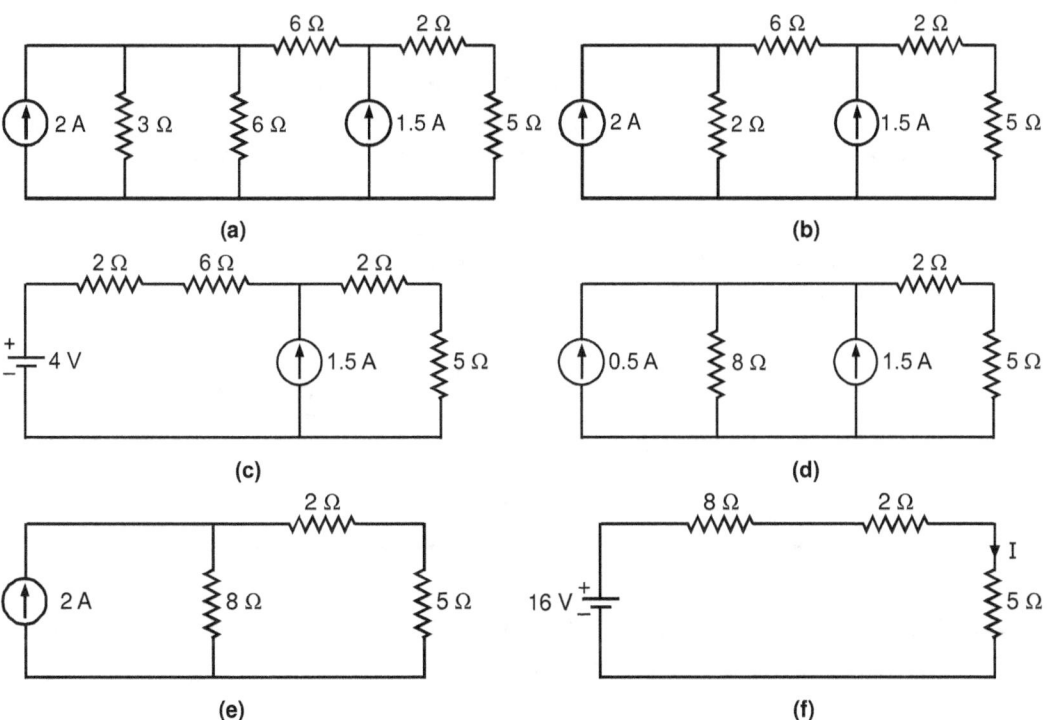

Fig. 1.20 : Different stages of simplification of the network of Fig. 1.19

From Fig. 1.20 (f), it is obvious that

$$I = \frac{16}{(8+2+5)} = 1.067 \text{ A}$$

∴ Voltage across 5 Ω resistance = 1.067×5 = **5.33 V** ... Ans.

1.5 CONCEPT OF OPEN AND SHORT CIRCUITS

The conceptual understanding of open circuits and short circuits is very important in the analysis of electrical networks. Otherwise, they can cause lot of confusion while applying some of the methods or theorems for the solution of electrical networks.

Open Circuits : *An open circuit exists between two isolated terminals of a network which are not connected by an element of any kind.* Under this condition, these terminals can have a potential difference across them but the current flowing through them is always zero amperes. For example, consider the battery of e.m.f. E volts and internal resistance of r ohms shown in Fig. 1.21.

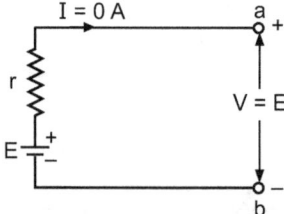

Fig. 1.21 : A battery on open circuit

An open circuit exists between the terminals a and b. There is a voltage of V(=E) volts between these two terminals, but the current flowing between them is zero due to the absence of a closed path for its flow.

Short Circuits : *A direct connection of zero resistance across an element or combination of elements is called a short circuit.* A short circuit can carry a current of very high level but the potential difference across its terminals is always of zero volts.

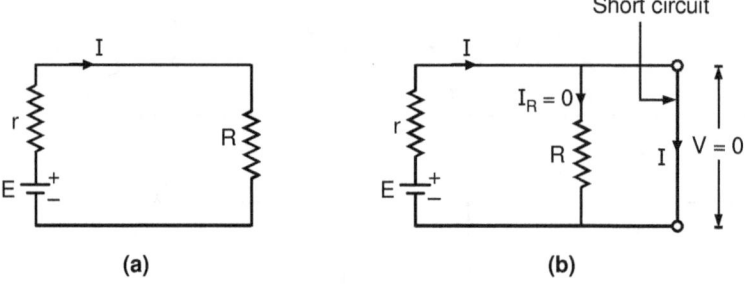

Fig. 1.22 : (a) Battery supplying load of R ohms, (b) A battery with load short circuited

In the circuit of Fig. 1.22 (a), it is obvious that

$$\text{Circuit current, } I = \frac{E}{r+R} \text{ amperes.}$$

Now, if a short circuit is established across the resistor of R ohms as shown in Fig. 1.22 (b), then under this condition,

$$\text{Total resistance of the circuit, } R_T = r + \frac{R \times 0}{R+0} = r \text{ ohms}$$

$$\therefore \qquad \text{Circuit current, } I = \frac{E}{R_T} = \frac{E}{r} \text{ amperes}$$

If the internal resistance (r) of the battery is very small, then this current will be very high. Further, since the current always prefers the path of least resistance, all this current will follow the short circuited path and no current will flow through the resistor R $\left(\because I_R = \dfrac{0}{(0+R)} \times I = 0 \right)$. Also the resistance of a short circuit being zero ohms, the potential difference across its terminals is always zero volts (since, in accordance with Ohm's law, $V = I \times 0 = 0$ volts).

1.6 SOLUTION OF NETWORKS

In the simple series and parallel circuits, it is possible to calculate the equivalent resistance and circuit or branch current by the direct application of Ohm's law. But such a simple solution is not possible if the electric circuit is complex one with more number of branches and energy sources. The methods which are used for the solution of such complex electrical networks can be grouped under two main headings :

(i) Solution by derivation of simultaneous network equations.
(ii) Solution by network reduction.

Kirchhoff's laws are very useful in formulating the network equations. On the other hand, different network theorems and the method like star-delta transformation are often used in the solution by network reduction. We shall study only Kirchhoff's laws and the methods of analysis of d.c. circuits based on these laws in detail in the following sections.

1.7 KIRCHHOFF'S LAWS

In 1847, Gustave Kirchhoff, a German physicist, formulated two fundamental laws which are of immense use in the analysis of electric networks. These laws are discussed below.

1.7.1 Point Law or Current Law

It states that *in any electrical circuit, the algebraic sum of all branch currents that meet at a point (or junction) is always zero*. Mathematically, it can be expressed as

$$\text{At a junction, } \Sigma I = 0$$

where the Greek letter sigma (Σ) represents the algebraic sum of all similar terms. An algebraic sum is one in which the sign of the quantity is taken into account.

Explanation : Consider the simple case of four current carrying conductors meeting at a junction point O as illustrated in Fig. 1.23.

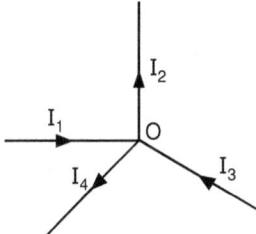

Fig. 1.23 : Circuit to illustrate Kirchhoff's first law

If we assume *a current flowing towards the junction as positive and the other flowing away from it as negative,* then according to the above law, we have

$$\Sigma I = I_1 - I_2 + I_3 - I_4 = 0$$

It means that $\quad I_1 + I_3 = I_2 + I_4$

Thus, *the sum of all currents leaving a junction is always equal to the sum of all the currents entering the junction.* This gives the alternative statement for the law. This is obvious because there cannot be any accumulation of electricity at the junction.

1.7.2 Mesh Law or Voltage Law

This law states that *the algebraic sum of all branch voltages around any closed circuit (or mesh) is always zero* i.e.

$$\text{Around a closed circuit, } \Sigma V = 0$$

In other words, according to this law, *in any closed circuit, the algebraic sum of all the applied electromotive forces (e.m.f.s) and the products of the current and the resistance of each part of the circuit is always zero* i.e.

$$\text{Around any closed circuit, } \Sigma E.M.F. + \Sigma I.R. = 0$$

Explanation : The law is based on the fact that if one starts at a certain point on a closed circuit and goes on noting down the potential changes while travelling in any one particular direction round the circuit until the starting point is reached, then he must be at the same potential with which he started. Therefore, it obviously means that the sum of all the potential rises met on the way must necessarily be equal to the sum of all the potential drops in the various parts of the circuit, thus giving the total change in potential as zero.

Sign Convention : For applying Kirchhoff's voltage law to a closed circuit, we will have to start from one point on it and note down the potential changes while going round the circuit in any one particular direction (clockwise or anticlockwise) till the starting point is reached again. During this process, we will have to follow certain sign convention regarding the potential changes met on the way for making their algebraic addition. Following sign convention can be conveniently adopted :

A rise in potential should be considered as positive. A fall in potential should be considered as negative.

For example, while traversing a source of e.m.f. from its negative terminal to the positive terminal, there is a rise in potential. Hence, in such a condition, this e.m.f. should be considered as positive. On the other hand, while going from the positive terminal of the source to its negative terminal, the potential drops. Naturally, then the e.m.f. will have to be considered as negative. Thus, the direction in which a source of e.m.f. is traversed decides the sign of its e.m.f. and it is independent of direction of current flowing through the branch in which the source is connected.

In the case of a resistor, if we go through it in the direction of the current, then the voltage drops. This is because the current always flows from the point of higher potential to a point of lower potential. Hence, this voltage drop should be taken as negative. However, while going through the resistor in the direction opposite to that of the current, there is a rise in potential. Therefore, this rise in voltage then should be considered as positive. Thus, it should be noted that the direction of the current flowing through the resistor plays important role in deciding the sign of the change in potential across it.

Illustration : Consider the closed circuit ABCDEA shown in Fig. 1.24. Let us apply Kirchhoff's voltage law to this circuit. For that, with the above mentioned sign convention in mind, if we start from point A and travel round the circuit in say, clockwise direction, following voltages will be met on the way :

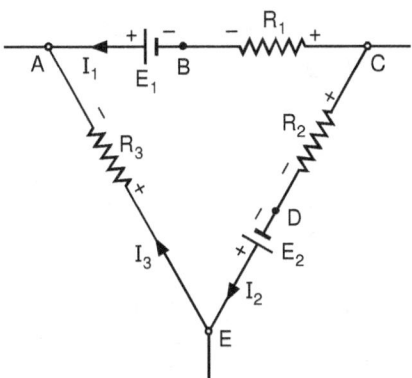

Fig. 1.24 : Circuit to illustrate Kirchhoff's second law

(i) E_1 : It is negative since we are proceeding from the positive plate of a cell to its negative plate.

(ii) I_1R_1 : It is positive since we are traversing the resistance R_1 in the direction opposite to that of the current flowing through it.

(iii) I_2R_2 : It is negative for the reason that we are going through the resistor R_2 in the direction of the current flowing through it.

(iv) E_2 : It is positive since we are proceeding from the negative plate of a cell to the positive plate.

(v) I_3R_3 : It is negative for the reason similar to that mentioned in the earlier case of I_2R_2.

Then, application of Kirchhoff's voltage law will give the following equation :

$$-E_1 + I_1R_1 - I_2R_2 + E_2 - I_3R_3 = 0$$

Definition of Some Important Terms Related to Electric Circuits :

Incidentally, some important terms related with electric circuits are defined below. These terms will be frequently used in our further discussion on Kirchhoff's laws.

Branch : A branch is a part of the network with two terminals across which different circuit elements (like energy sources, resistances, inductances and capacitances) are suitably (in series or in parallel) connected. In Fig. 1.24, AC, CE and EA are the branches of a given network.

Mesh or Loop : A set of branches, forming a closed path in a network is called a mesh or loop. In Fig. 1.24, the closed path ACEA is a mesh or loop.

Junction : It is a common point in a network at which two or more circuit elements are connected. In Fig. 1.24, the points A, B, C, D and E are the junction points.

Node : Every junction point in a network where three or more branches meet is called a node. In Fig. 1.24, A, C and E are the nodes.

1.7.3 Application of Kirchhoff's Laws for Network Solutions (Branch-Current Method)

When properly applied, Kirchhoff's laws are very useful in solving the complex circuits. As already mentioned previously, while applying the second law to a specific problem, it is necessary to adhere to a certain fixed sign convention to avoid errors. In solving the network problems using Kirchhoff's laws, one should follow the following steps :

(i) Draw the circuit diagram from the given description. Letter it and insert the values of all resistances and e.m.f.s.

(ii) Mark on the diagram assumed currents and their directions using Kirchhoff's first law at all junctions. Keep the number of assumed currents to a minimum. The directions for the various currents can be assumed arbitrarily. However, once chosen, these directions must remain unchanged throughout the solution of the problem (after solving the equations, if the value for the particular current is found to be negative, it will indicate that the assumed direction for that current is wrong).

(iii) Noting down the directions of currents through various resistors, mark their terminals of higher and lower potentials by positive and negative signs respectively. This gives quick idea about potential rise or drop across a resistor while applying Kirchhoff's second law.

(iv) Apply Kirchhoff's second law to different closed loops in the network and obtain the corresponding equations. Each equation must contain some element which has not been considered in any previous equation. The law must be applied for sufficient number of loops to include every element in the network atleast once. Total number of independent equations obtained in this manner must be equal to the number of unknowns. It is advisable to go round all the meshes in the same direction (clockwise or anticlockwise) so as to reduce the errors.

(v) Solve the simultaneous equations for the unknowns. The method is illustrated by solving few problems given below.

Example 1.23 : *Determine the current in and the power supplied to 10 Ω resistor in the network shown below in Fig. 1.25.*

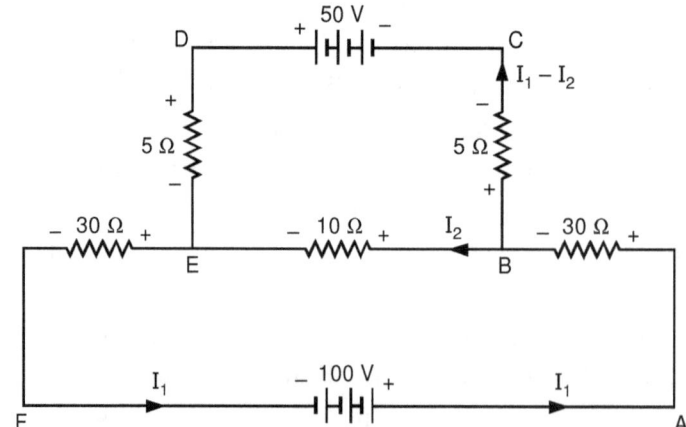

Fig. 1.25 : Network for Example 1.23

Solution : Firstly, the circuit diagram is lettered suitably as shown in Fig. 1.25. Then assumed currents and their directions are marked on the diagram using Kirchhoff's first law at junctions B and E. Noting down the directions of currents through various resistors, their terminals are marked with positive and negative signs as indicated. Since there are two unknowns (I_1 and I_2), we will need two equations. Therefore, let us select following two closed circuits and apply Kirchhoff's voltage law to them.

Circuit ABCDEFA :

$$-30 I_1 - 5 (I_1 - I_2) + 50 - 5(I_1 - I_2) - 30 I_1 + 100 = 0$$

$\therefore \qquad\qquad\qquad\qquad -70 I_1 + 10 I_2 = -150$

Or, $\qquad\qquad\qquad\qquad 70 I_1 - 10 I_2 = 150 \qquad\qquad\qquad \ldots$ (I)

Circuit ABEFA :

$$-30 I_1 - 10 I_2 - 30 I_1 + 100 = 0$$

$\therefore \qquad\qquad\qquad\qquad -60 I_1 - 10 I_2 = -100$

Or, $\qquad\qquad\qquad\qquad 60 I_1 + 10 I_2 = 100 \qquad\qquad\qquad \ldots$ (II)

Multiplying Equation (I) by 6 and Equation (II) by 7, we have

$\qquad\qquad\qquad\qquad 420 I_1 - 60 I_2 = 900 \qquad\qquad\qquad \ldots$ (III)

$\qquad\qquad\qquad\qquad 420 I_1 + 70 I_2 = 700 \qquad\qquad\qquad \ldots$ (IV)

Subtracting Equation (IV) from Equation (III), we get

$\qquad\qquad\qquad\qquad -130 I_2 = 200$

$\therefore \qquad\qquad\qquad\qquad I_2 = -\dfrac{200}{130} = -1.54 \text{ A} \qquad\qquad$ ... Ans.

Thus, the magnitude of the current flowing through the 10 Ω resistor is 1.54 A. However, since its value is found to be negative, it indicates that assumed direction for this current is wrong. Actually, the current will flow from E to B and not from B to E as assumed.

$\qquad$ Power consumed by 10 Ω resistor $= I_2^2 \, R$

$\qquad\qquad\qquad\qquad\qquad\qquad = 1.54^2 \times 10$

$\qquad\qquad\qquad\qquad\qquad\qquad = 23.72 \text{ W} \qquad\qquad\qquad$ ... Ans.

Example 1.24 : *Two storage batteries A and B are connected in parallel for charging from a d.c. source, having an open-circuit voltage of 14 V and internal resistance of 0.15 Ω. The open-circuit voltage of A is 11 V and that of B is 11.5 V. Their internal resistances are 0.06 Ω and 0.05 Ω respectively. Calculate the initial charging currents and the source current.*

Solution : Fig. 1.26 shows the suitably lettered circuit diagram. Assume the initial charging currents for the batteries A and B as I_A and I_B respectively.

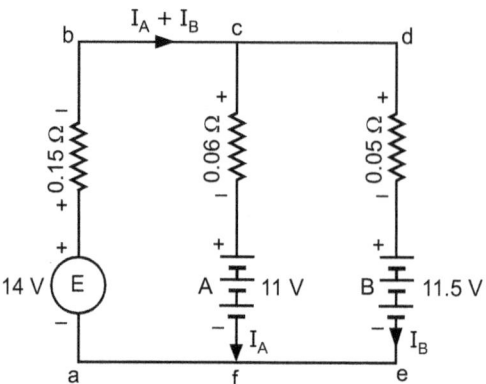

Fig. 1.26 : Circuit diagram for Example 1.24

Applying Kirchhoff's first law at junction c, obviously, the total source current will be $I_A + I_B$.

Now, let us select the following two closed circuits and apply Kirchhoff's voltage law to them.

Circuit abcfa :

$$14 - 0.15 (I_A + I_B) - 0.06 I_A - 11 = 0$$

∴ $-0.21 I_A - 0.15 I_B = -3$

Or, $0.21 I_A + 0.15 I_B = 3$ ... (I)

Circuit abcdefa :

$$14 - 0.15 (I_A + I_B) - 0.05 I_B - 11.5 = 0$$

∴ $-0.15 I_A - 0.2 I_B = -2.5$

Or, $0.15 I_A + 0.2 I_B = 2.5$ ... (II)

Multiplying Equation (I) by 4 and Equation (II) by 3, we get

$$0.84 I_A + 0.60 I_B = 12 \quad \text{... (III)}$$

$$0.45 I_A + 0.60 I_B = 7.5 \quad \text{... (IV)}$$

Subtraction of Equation (IV) from Equation (III) gives

$$0.39 I_A = 4.5$$

∴ $I_A = \mathbf{11.54\ A}$ ... Ans.

Substituting this value of I_A in Equation (I), we have

$$0.21 \times 11.54 + 0.15 I_B = 3$$

∴ $I_B = \mathbf{3.85\ A}$ ... Ans.

Hence,   Total source current, $I_A + I_B = \mathbf{15.39\ A}$ ... Ans.

Example 1.25 : *Find the resistance 'R' in the circuit of Fig. 1.27, if the resistance carries a current of 2 A. Also find the power absorbed by source and each resistance.*

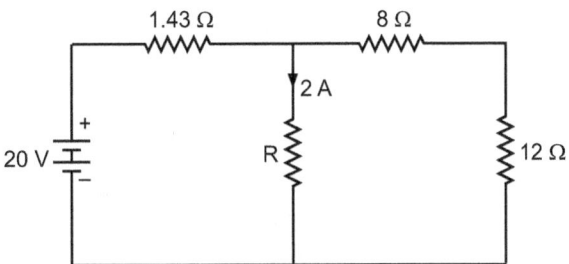

Fig. 1.27 : Circuit diagram for Example 1.25

Solution :

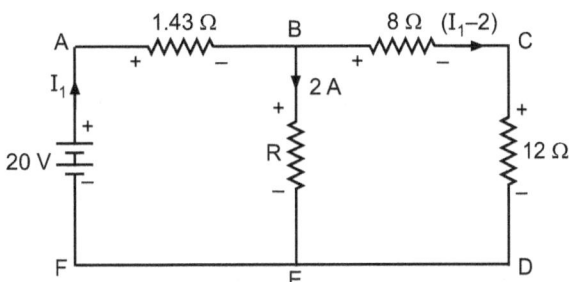

Fig. 1.28 : Circuit of Fig. 1.27 with assumed currents and their directions marked

Fig. 1.28 shows the network with assumed currents and their directions marked.

Loop ABCDEFA : Applying Kirchhoff's voltage law to this loop, we get

$$-1.43\,I_1 - (8+12)(I_1 - 2) + 20 = 0$$

$$\therefore \quad I_1 = 2.8\ \text{A}$$

Hence, the voltage across the resistance R,

$$V = 20 - 2.8 \times 1.43 = 16\ \text{volts}$$

$$\therefore \quad R = \frac{V}{I} = \frac{16}{2} = 8\ \Omega \qquad \text{... Ans.}$$

Further,

$$\text{Power supplied by the source, } P = 20 \times 2.8 = \mathbf{56\ W} \qquad \text{... Ans.}$$

$$P_{1.43} = 2.8^2 \times 1.43 = \mathbf{11.2\ W} \qquad \text{... Ans.}$$

$$P_R = 2^2 \times 8 = \mathbf{32\ W} \qquad \text{... Ans.}$$

$$P_8 = (2.8 - 2)^2 \times 8 = \mathbf{5.12\ W} \qquad \text{... Ans.}$$

$$P_{12} = (2.8 - 2)^2 \times 12 = \mathbf{7.68\ W} \qquad \text{... Ans.}$$

Example 1.26 : *Find the current in the branch A-B in the d.c. circuit shown in Fig. 1.29, using Kirchhoff's laws.*

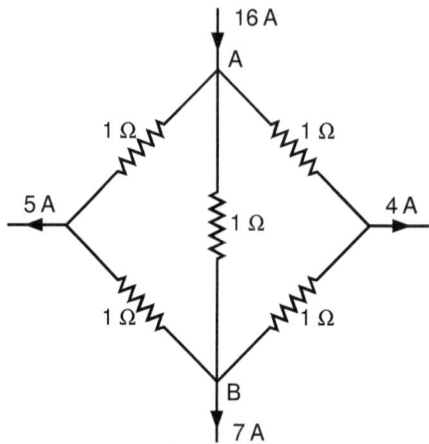

Fig. 1.29 : Circuit diagram for Example 1.26

Solution :

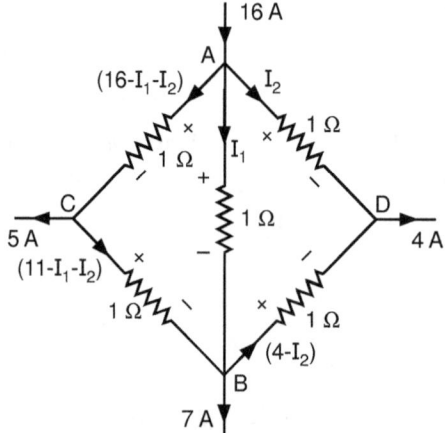

Fig. 1.30 : Circuit of Fig. 1.29 with assumed currents and their directions marked

Fig. 1.30 shows the given network with assumed currents and their directions marked. Choosing the following closed circuits and applying Kirchhoff's voltage law to them, we have

Circuit CABC :

$$(16 - I_1 - I_2) \times 1 - I_1 \times 1 + (11 - I_1 - I_2) \times 1 = 0$$

Or, $\qquad 3 I_1 + 2 I_2 = 27$ ... (I)

Circuit ADBA :

$$- I_2 \times 1 + (4 - I_2) \times 1 + I_1 \times 1 = 0$$

Or, $\qquad I_1 - 2 I_2 = -4$ ... (II)

Solving the equations (I) and (II) simultaneously, we get

Current in branch AB, $I_1 = 5.75$ A ... Ans.

Example 1.27 : *Calculate the currents in the various branches of network shown in Fig. 1.31.*

Solution : Using Kirchhoff's first law at different junction points, currents in the various branches are marked as shown in Fig. 1.31. Following closed circuits are then selected for the purpose of applying Kirchhoff's second law.

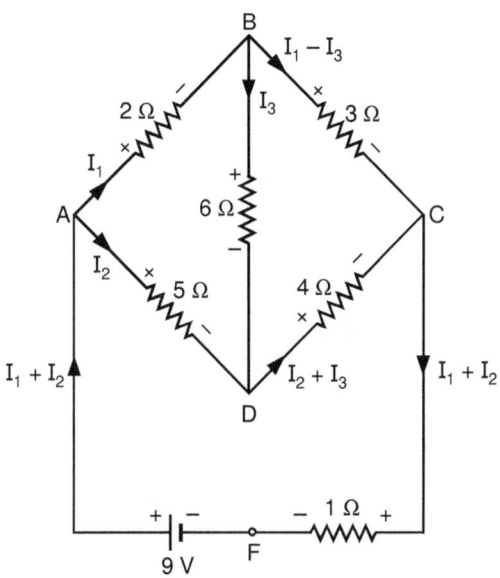

Fig. 1.31 : Network for Example 1.27

Circuit ABCFA :

$$-2I_1 - 3(I_1 - I_3) - (I_1 + I_2) + 9 = 0$$

∴ $\quad -6I_1 - I_2 + 3I_3 = -9$

Or, $\quad 6I_1 + I_2 - 3I_3 = 9 \quad \ldots (I)$

Circuit ADCFA :

$$-5I_2 - 4(I_2 + I_3) - (I_1 + I_2) + 9 = 0$$

∴ $\quad -I_1 - 10I_2 - 4I_3 = -9$

Or, $\quad I_1 + 10I_2 + 4I_3 = 9 \quad \ldots (II)$

Circuit ABDA :

$$-2I_1 - 6I_3 + 5I_2 = 0$$

∴ $\quad 2I_1 - 5I_2 + 6I_3 = 0 \quad \ldots (III)$

Multiplying Equation (I) by 10, we get

$$60 I_1 + 10 I_2 - 30 I_3 = 90 \qquad \ldots \text{(IV)}$$

Subtracting Equation (II) from Equation (IV), we have

$$59 I_1 - 34 I_3 = 81 \qquad \ldots \text{(V)}$$

Similarly, multiplying Equation (I) by 5, we get

$$30 I_1 + 5 I_2 - 15 I_3 = 45 \qquad \ldots \text{(VI)}$$

Adding Equation (III) with Equation (VI), we have

$$32 I_1 - 9 I_3 = 45 \qquad \ldots \text{(VII)}$$

Multiplying Equation (V) by 9 and Equation (VII) by 34, we get the following equations :

$$531 I_1 - 306 I_3 = 729 \qquad \ldots \text{(VIII)}$$

$$1088 I_1 - 306 I_3 = 1530 \qquad \ldots \text{(IX)}$$

Subtracting Equation (VIII) from Equation (IX), we have

$$557 I_1 = 801$$

$$\therefore \qquad I_1 = 1.438 \text{ A}$$

Substituting this value of I_1 in Equation (VII), we get

$$I_3 = 0.113 \text{ A}$$

Hence, substituting the values of I_1 and I_3 in Equation (I), we get

$$I_2 = 0.711 \text{ A}$$

Thus, the currents in the various branches will be as follows :

Current in the branch AB	= I_1	= **1.438 A**	... Ans.
Current in the branch BC	= $I_1 - I_3$	= **1.325 A**	... Ans.
Current in the branch CD	= $I_2 + I_3$	= **0.824 A**	... Ans.
Current in the branch DA	= I_2	= **0.711 A**	... Ans.
Current in the branch BD	= I_3	= **0.113 A**	... Ans.
Current supplied by the battery	= $I_1 + I_2$	= **2.15 A**	... Ans.

Since the values of all branch currents are positive, it means that their assumed directions (marked in Fig. 1.31) are correct.

Solution by Determinants : If the number of unknowns are more, the solution of simultaneous equations by means of determinants gives quick results. According to this method, if we have a set of simultaneous equations of the form :

$$a_{11} x_1 + a_{12} x_2 + \ldots + a_{1n} x_n = k_1$$
$$a_{21} x_1 + a_{22} x_2 + \ldots + a_{2n} x_n = k_2$$
$$\ldots\ldots\ldots\ldots\ldots\ldots\ldots\ldots\ldots\ldots\ldots\ldots\ldots\ldots$$
$$a_{n1} x_1 + a_{n2} x_2 + \ldots + a_{nn} x_n = k_n$$

Then, using Cramer's rule, the solution to such simultaneous equations is given by

$$x_1 = \frac{D_1}{\Delta}, \quad x_2 = \frac{D_2}{\Delta}, \quad \ldots\ldots\ldots, \quad x_n = \frac{D_n}{\Delta}$$

where Δ is the system determinant given by

$$\Delta = \begin{vmatrix} a_{11} & a_{12} & \ldots & a_{1n} \\ a_{21} & a_{22} & \ldots & a_{2n} \\ \ldots & \ldots & \ldots & \ldots \\ a_{n1} & a_{n2} & \ldots & a_{nn} \end{vmatrix}$$

and D_j is the determinant formed by replacing the jth column of the system determinant by the column $k_1, k_2, \ldots k_n$.

As an illustration, let us solve the simultaneous equations in the above problem by this method. The simultaneous equations are :

$$6 I_1 + I_2 - 3 I_3 = 9 \quad \ldots \text{(I)}$$
$$I_1 + 10 I_2 + 4 I_3 = 9 \quad \ldots \text{(II)}$$
$$2 I_1 - 5 I_2 + 6 I_3 = 0 \quad \ldots \text{(III)}$$

Here,
$$\Delta = \begin{vmatrix} 6 & 1 & -3 \\ 1 & 10 & 4 \\ 2 & -5 & 6 \end{vmatrix}$$
$$= 6 (10 \times 6 - 4 \times -5) - (1 \times 6 - 4 \times 2) - 3 (1 \times -5 - 10 \times 2)$$
$$= 557$$

$$D_1 = \begin{vmatrix} 9 & 1 & -3 \\ 9 & 10 & 4 \\ 0 & -5 & 6 \end{vmatrix}$$
$$= 9 (10 \times 6 - 4 \times -5) - 1 (9 \times 6 - 4 \times 0) - 3 (9 \times -5 - 10 \times 0)$$
$$= 801$$

$$D_2 = \begin{vmatrix} 6 & 9 & -3 \\ 1 & 9 & 4 \\ 2 & 0 & 6 \end{vmatrix}$$
$$= 6 (9 \times 6 - 4 \times 0) - 9 (1 \times 6 - 4 \times 2) - 3 (1 \times 0 - 9 \times 2)$$
$$= 396$$

$$D_3 = \begin{vmatrix} 6 & 1 & 9 \\ 1 & 10 & 9 \\ 2 & -5 & 0 \end{vmatrix}$$

$$= 6(10 \times 0 - 9 \times -5) - 1(1 \times 0 - 9 \times 2) + 9(1 \times -5 - 10 \times 2)$$

$$= 63$$

Hence, $I_1 = \dfrac{D_1}{\Delta} = \dfrac{801}{557} = 1.438$ A

$I_2 = \dfrac{D_2}{\Delta} = \dfrac{396}{557} = 0.711$ A

$I_3 = \dfrac{D_3}{\Delta} = \dfrac{63}{557} = 0.113$ A

Thus, the current distribution will be same as before.

Example 1.28 : *For the circuit diagram shown in Fig. 1.32, find V_{CE} and V_{AG}.*

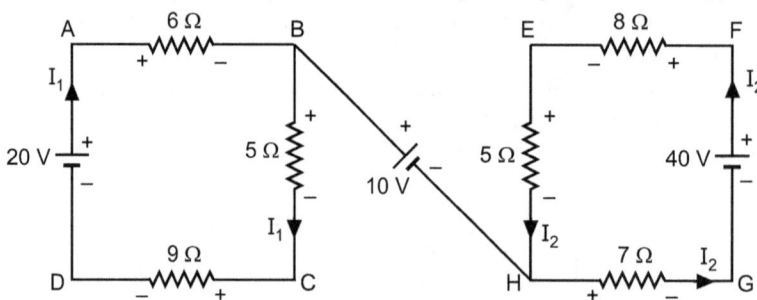

Fig. 1.32 : Network for Example 1.28

Solution : Let I_1 be the current in the closed circuit ABCDA and I_2 be the current in the closed circuit EFGHE. Then, applying Kirchhoff's voltage law to these closed circuits, we have

Circuit ABCDA :

$$-6 I_1 - 5 I_1 - 9 I_1 + 20 = 0$$

∴ $\quad I_1 = 1$ A

Circuit EFGHE :

$$8 I_2 - 40 + 7 I_2 + 5 I_2 = 0$$

∴ $\quad I_2 = 2$ A

$V_{CE} = V_{CB} + V_{BH} + V_{HE}$

$= 5 I_1 - 10 + 5 I_2$

$= 5 \times 1 - 10 + 5 \times 2$

$= \mathbf{5}$ **V, E being at higher potential than C** ... Ans.

$$V_{AG} = V_{AB} + V_{BH} + V_{HG}$$
$$= -6 I_1 - 10 - 7 I_2$$
$$= -6 \times 1 - 10 - 7 \times 2$$
$$= -30 \text{ V, A being at higher potential than G} \quad \text{... Ans.}$$

1.8 LOOP OR MESH ANALYSIS (MAXWELL'S LOOP CURRENT METHOD)

This method of analysis is similar to that seen in the previous article in which Kirchhoff's laws are used for finding directly the branch currents. Only difference is that it employs the system of loop or mesh currents instead of branch currents. The branch currents are then found by taking the algebraic sum of the loop currents which are common to the branch. The required equations in terms of unknown loop currents are obtained by applying Kirchhoff's voltage law in turn to each mesh. Use of loop currents reduces the number of independent equations to be solved and simplifies the calculation work. To illustrate the method, consider the network shown in Fig. 1.33. Since there are three meshes, let I_1, I_2 and I_3 be the corresponding loop currents as shown in Fig. 1.33. Just for convenience, all these currents are assumed to be flowing in the clockwise direction. Then applying Kirchhoff's voltage law to the various loops, we get the following equations (it should be noted that the loops are always referred to by the subscripts of their mesh currents).

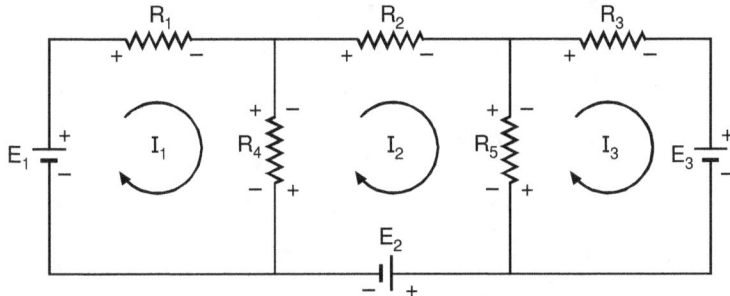

Fig. 1.33: Loop analysis

For Loop-1 :
$$E_1 - I_1 R_1 - (I_1 - I_2) R_4 = 0$$

Here, it is obvious that the net current through R_4 is $(I_1 - I_2)$ in the direction of I_1. Rewriting the above equation, we get

$$I_1 (R_1 + R_4) - I_2 R_4 = E_1 \quad \text{... (1.25)}$$

For Loop-2 :
$$- I_2 R_2 - (I_2 - I_3) R_5 - E_2 - (I_2 - I_1) R_4 = 0$$
Or, $\quad I_1 R_4 - I_2 (R_2 + R_4 + R_5) + I_3 R_5 = E_2 \quad \text{... (1.26)}$

For Loop-3 :
$$- I_3 R_3 - E_3 - (I_3 - I_2) R_5 = 0$$
Or, $\quad I_2 R_5 - I_3 (R_3 + R_5) = E_3 \quad \text{... (1.27)}$

The above equations can then be solved to determine the loop currents and there from the branch currents.

Example 1.29 : *Use loop current analysis to find the currents in the different branches of a d.c. network shown in Fig. 1.34.*

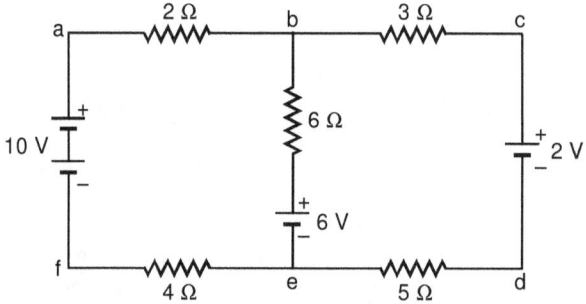

Fig. 1.34 : Network for Example 1.29

Solution : The given network is redrawn in Fig. 1.35 with loop currents marked.

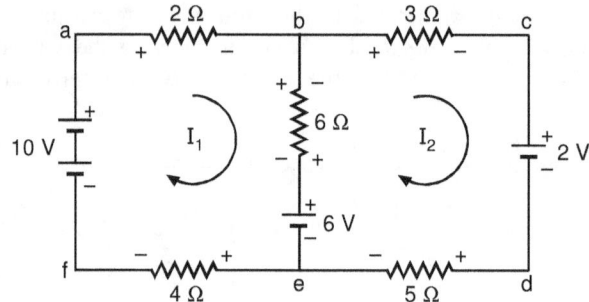

Fig. 1.35 : Network for Example 1.29 with loop currents marked

Applying Kirchhoff's voltage law to the various loops, we get the following equations.

Loop-1 : $\quad 10 - 2 I_1 - 6 (I_1 - I_2) - 6 - 4 I_1 = 0$

Or, $\quad\quad\quad\quad 12 I_1 - 6 I_2 = 4$ ... (I)

Loop-2 : $\quad 6 - 6 (I_2 - I_1) - 3 I_2 - 2 - 5 I_2 = 0$

Or, $\quad\quad\quad\quad 6 I_1 - 14 I_2 = -4$ ... (II)

Solving the above two equations (I) and (II) simultaneously, we get

$$I_1 = 0.606 \text{ A}, \quad I_2 = 0.545 \text{ A}$$

Therefore, the different branch currents are as follows :

$\quad\quad I_{ab} = I_{ef} = I_{fa} = I_1 = \mathbf{0.606 \text{ A}}$ ... **Ans.**

$\quad\quad I_{be} = I_1 - I_2 = \mathbf{0.061 \text{ A}}$ ... **Ans.**

$\quad\quad I_{bc} = I_{cd} = I_{de} = I_2 = \mathbf{0.545 \text{ A}}$ ... **Ans.**

Example 1.30 : *Using mesh current analysis, find the current through 2 Ω resistance shown in Fig. 1.36.*

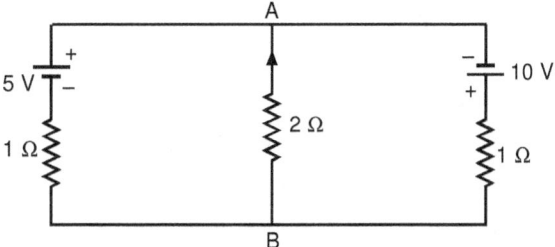

Fig. 1.36 : Network for Example 1.30

Solution :

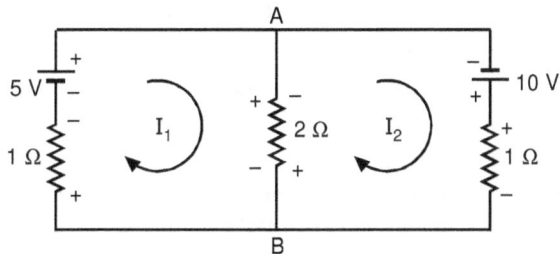

Fig. 1.37 : Network of Fig. 1.36 with loop currents marked

The given network is redrawn in Fig. 1.37 with loop currents marked. Applying Kirchhoff's voltage law to the following loops, we get

Loop-1 : $\quad -1\,I_1 + 5 - 2\,(I_1 - I_2) = 0$

Or, $\quad\quad\quad 3\,I_1 - 2\,I_2 = 5 \quad\quad\quad\quad$ ... (I)

Loop-2 : $\quad -2\,(I_2 - I_1) + 10 - 1\,I_2 = 0$

Or, $\quad\quad\quad 2\,I_1 - 3\,I_2 = -10 \quad\quad\quad\quad$ ... (II)

Solving the above equations simultaneously, we get

$$I_1 = 7\text{ A} \quad \text{and} \quad I_2 = 8\text{ A}$$

∴ Current through 2 Ω resistance

$$= I_2 - I_1 = 8 - 7 = 1\text{ A, from B to A} \quad\quad \text{... Ans.}$$

1.8.1 Loop Current Equations in Generalized Form

In the network of Fig. 1.33 considered earlier, all the circulating loop currents are assumed to be flowing in the same direction i.e. clockwise. This is not necessarily essential as the choice of direction can be made arbitrarily for any loop current. However, if the same direction is chosen for all the loop currents, then the equations for different loops will always be of the generalized form given below :

$$R_{11}\,I_1 + R_{12}\,I_2 + R_{13}\,I_3 + \ldots + R_{1n}\,I_n = V_1$$
$$R_{21}\,I_1 + R_{22}\,I_2 + R_{23}\,I_3 + \ldots + R_{2n}\,I_n = V_2$$
$$R_{31}\,I_1 + R_{32}\,I_2 + R_{33}\,I_3 + \ldots + R_{3n}\,I_n = V_3$$
$$\ldots\ldots\ldots\ldots\ldots\ldots\ldots\ldots\ldots\ldots\ldots\ldots\ldots\ldots\ldots$$
$$R_{n1}\,I_1 + R_{n2}\,I_2 + R_{n3}\,I_3 + \ldots + R_{nn}\,I_n = V_n$$

where,

V_1 = The algebraic sum of the source voltages in Loop-1 in the direction of I_1

V_2 = The algebraic sum of the source voltages in Loop-2 in the direction of I_2, etc.

R_{11} = Sum of all resistances in Loop-1

R_{22} = Sum of all resistances in Loop-2, etc.

$R_{12} = R_{21}$ = Total resistance common to loops 1 and 2

$R_{23} = R_{32}$ = Total resistance common to loops 2 and 3, etc.

Here, it is important to note that the resistance elements (or the co-efficients) R_{11}, R_{22}, R_{33}, etc. which respectively represent the total resistance values on the contours of the loops 1, 2, 3, etc. always carry a positive sign. In other words, it means that in the equation derived for a particular loop, the term which contains loop's own circulating current is always positive e.g. the term $R_{11} I_1$ is always positive in the equation for 1st loop, the term $R_{22} I_2$ is always positive in the equation for 2nd loop and so on. On the other hand, all other resistance elements like R_{12}, R_{21}, R_{23}, R_{32}, etc. representing the total resistance common to two loops carry a positive sign if the two assumed loop currents through them flow in the same direction and a minus sign if these loop currents flow in the opposite directions.

Remembering these rules, it is possible to write the equations necessary for the solution of any network merely by inspecting that network without the necessity for collecting terms with the same co-efficients. Let us verify this by again considering the network shown in Fig. 1.33. The equations for three loops under consideration will be as follows :

For Loop-1 : $R_{11} I_1 + R_{12} I_2 + R_{13} I_3 = V_1$ ... (1.28)

For Loop-2 : $R_{21} I_1 + R_{22} I_2 + R_{23} I_3 = V_2$ ... (1.29)

For Loop-3 : $R_{31} I_1 + R_{32} I_2 + R_{33} I_3 = V_3$ ... (1.30)

where,

$$R_{11} = R_1 + R_4, \quad R_{12} = R_{21} = -R_4, \quad R_{13} = R_{31} = 0$$

$$R_{22} = R_2 + R_4 + R_5, \quad R_{23} = R_{32} = -R_5, \quad R_{33} = R_3 + R_5$$

$$V_1 = E_1, \quad V_2 = -E_2 \text{ and } V_3 = -E_3$$

Substituting these values in the equations (1.28), (1.29) and (1.30), we get

$$(R_1 + R_4) I_1 - R_4 I_2 = E_1 \qquad \ldots (1.31)$$

$$-R_4 I_1 + (R_2 + R_4 + R_5) I_2 - R_5 I_3 = -E_2$$

Or, $R_4 I_1 - (R_2 + R_4 + R_5) I_2 + R_5 I_3 = E_2$ ... (1.32)

and $-R_5 I_2 + (R_3 + R_5) I_3 = -E_3$

Or, $R_5 I_2 - (R_3 + R_5) I_3 = E_3$ ... (1.33)

We find that the equations (1.31), (1.32) and (1.33) are the same as equations (1.25), (1.26) and (1.27). Thus by mere inspection of the network, we can write the required equations very rapidly. In general, the voltage equations for different loops can also be written in the matrix form as given below :

$$\begin{vmatrix} R_{11} & R_{12} & R_{13} & \ldots & R_{1n} \\ R_{21} & R_{22} & R_{23} & \ldots & R_{2n} \\ \ldots & \ldots & \ldots & \ldots & \ldots \\ R_{n1} & R_{n2} & R_{n3} & \ldots & R_{nn} \end{vmatrix} \begin{vmatrix} I_1 \\ I_2 \\ \ldots \\ I_n \end{vmatrix} = \begin{vmatrix} V_1 \\ V_2 \\ \ldots \\ V_n \end{vmatrix}$$

Or, $[R][I] = [V]$

where, [V] and [I] are column matrices, whereas [R] is a square matrix. The elements R_{11}, R_{22}, R_{33}, ... , R_{nn} on the principal diagonal of resistance matrix [R] and its other off diagonal elements like R_{12}, R_{21}, R_{13}, R_{31}, etc., can be written by mere inspection of the network by following the rules already mentioned above.

Before applying this method of loop analysis to any complicated network with several sources, following points should be kept in mind :

(i) In complicated networks with several sources, it is always advantageous to convert constant current sources if present into their equivalent constant voltage sources for the purpose of loop analysis.

(ii) Assume the smallest number of mesh currents so that at least one mesh current links every element. No two loops should be identical.

(iii) In a given circuit, if the current in any one branch is to be calculated, the paths for different loop currents should be so chosen that branch in which the current is to be determined is covered only once i.e. only one loop current should link with this branch. If this precaution is taken, the required branch current can be calculated by applying the Cramer's rule only once.

Example 1.31 : *Write mesh equations for Fig. 1.38.*

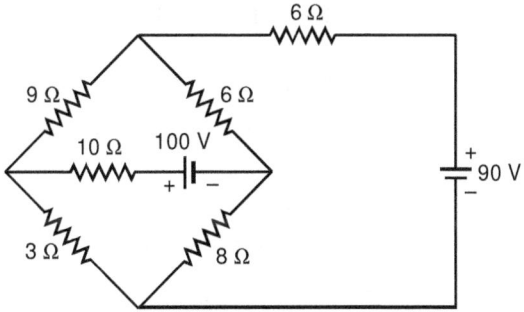

Fig. 1.38 : Network for Example 1.31

Solution : The given network is redrawn in Fig. 1.39 with loop currents marked. Applying Kirchhoff's voltage law to the various loops, we get the following equations :

Loop-1 : $-9I_1 - 6(I_1 - I_3) + 100 - 10(I_1 - I_2) = 0$

Or, $25I_1 - 10I_2 - 6I_3 = 100$ ... (I) ... Ans.

Loop-2 : $-10(I_2 - I_1) - 100 - 8(I_2 - I_3) - 3I_2 = 0$

Or, $\qquad 10I_1 - 21I_2 + 8I_3 = 100 \qquad$ ... (II) ... Ans.

Loop-3 : $-6I_3 - 90 - 8(I_3 - I_2) - 6(I_3 - I_1) = 0$

Or, $\qquad 6I_1 + 8I_2 - 20I_3 = 90 \qquad$ ... (III) ... Ans.

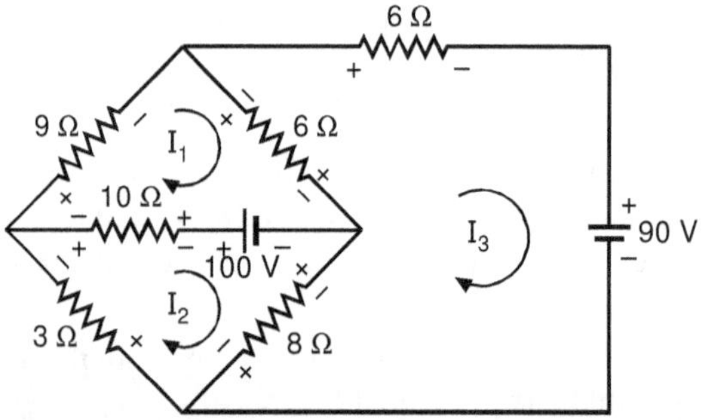

Fig. 1.39 : Network of Fig. 1.38 with loop currents marked

Alternative Method : The above equations in terms of loop currents can also be written by mere inspection of the network as follows :

Loop-1 : $\qquad (9 + 6 + 10)I_1 - 10I_2 - 6I_3 = 100 \qquad (\because R_{11}I_1 + R_{12}I_2 + R_{13}I_3 = V_1)$

Or, $\qquad 25I_1 - 10I_2 - 6I_3 = 100 \qquad$ ... (IV) ... Ans.

Loop-2 : $\qquad -10I_1 + (10 + 8 + 3)I_2 - 8I_3 = -100 \qquad (\because R_{21}I_1 + R_{22}I_2 + R_{23}I_3 = V_2)$

Or, $\qquad 10I_1 - 21I_2 + 8I_3 = 100 \qquad$ ... (V) ... Ans.

Loop-3 : $\qquad -6I_1 - 8I_2 + (6 + 8 + 6)I_3 = -90 \qquad (\because R_{31}I_1 + R_{32}I_2 + R_{33}I_3 = V_3)$

Or, $\qquad 6I_1 + 8I_2 - 20I_3 = 90 \qquad$ ... (VI) ... Ans.

Example 1.32 : *By applying Kirchhoff's laws, write loop equations. Hence, find the current through 6 Ω resistor.*

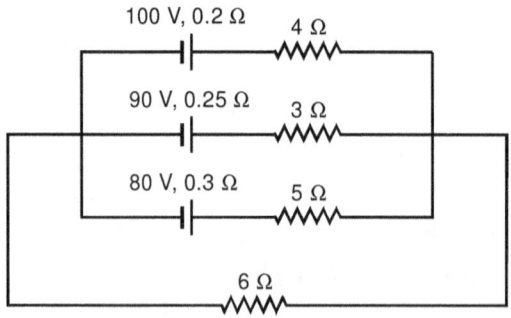

Fig. 1.40 : Network for Example 1.32

Solution : The given network is redrawn in Fig. 1.41 with loop currents marked. Applying Kirchhoff's voltage law to the various loops, we get the following equations :

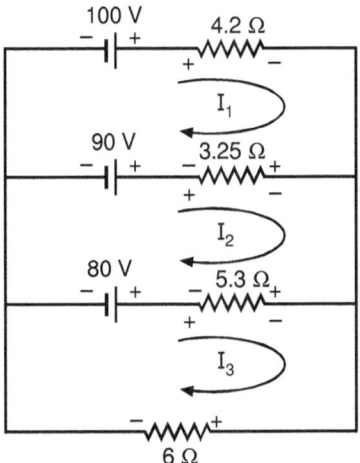

Fig. 1.41 : Network of Fig. 1.40 with loop currents marked

Loop-1 : $100 - 4.2 I_1 - 3.25 (I_1 - I_2) - 90 = 0$

∴ $-7.45 I_1 + 3.25 I_2 = -10$

Or, $7.45 I_1 - 3.25 I_2 = 10$ ... (I)

Loop-2 : $90 - 3.25 (I_2 - I_1) - 5.3 (I_2 - I_3) - 80 = 0$

∴ $3.25 I_1 - 8.55 I_2 + 5.3 I_3 = -10$ ... (II)

Loop-3 : $80 - 5.3 (I_3 - I_2) - 6 I_3 = 0$

∴ $5.3 I_2 - 11.3 I_3 = -80$ ... (III)

The above equations in terms of loop currents can also be written by mere inspection of the network as follows :

Loop-1 : $(4.2 + 3.25) I_1 - 3.25 I_2 = 100 - 90$ $(\because R_{11}I_1 + R_{12}I_2 + R_{13}I_3 = V_1)$

∴ $7.45 I_1 - 3.25 I_2 = 10$ ... (IV)

Loop-2 : $-3.25 I_1 + (3.25 + 5.3) I_2 - 5.3 I_3 = 90 - 80$ $(\because R_{21}I_1 + R_{22}I_2 + R_{23}I_3 = V_2)$

∴ $-3.25 I_1 + 8.55 I_2 - 5.3 I_3 = 10$

Or, $3.25 I_1 - 8.55 I_2 + 5.3 I_3 = -10$ ... (V)

Loop-3 : $-5.3 I_2 + (5.3 + 6) I_3 = 80$ $(\because R_{31}I_1 + R_{32}I_2 + R_{33}I_3 = V_3)$

Or, $5.3 I_2 - 11.3 I_3 = -80$ ... (VI)

Using determinant method for the solution of the above simultaneous equations, we have

$$\Delta = \begin{vmatrix} 7.45 & -3.25 & 0 \\ 3.25 & -8.55 & 5.3 \\ 0 & 5.3 & -11.3 \end{vmatrix}$$

$= 7.45 (96.62 - 28.9) + 3.25 (-36.73 - 0) + 0$

$= 510.55 - 119.37 = 391.18$

$$D_3 = \begin{vmatrix} 7.45 & -3.25 & 10 \\ 3.25 & -8.55 & -10 \\ 0 & 5.3 & -80 \end{vmatrix}$$

$$= 7.45\,(684 + 53) + 3.25\,(-260 - 0) + 10\,(17.23 - 0)$$

$$= 4817.95$$

∴ Current through 6 Ω resistor

$$= I_3 = \frac{D_3}{\Delta} = \frac{4817.95}{391.18} = 12.32 \text{ A} \qquad \text{... Ans.}$$

Example 1.33 : *In Fig. 1.42 shown, determine V_2, which results in zero current in the branch containing V_1, using mesh current analysis.*

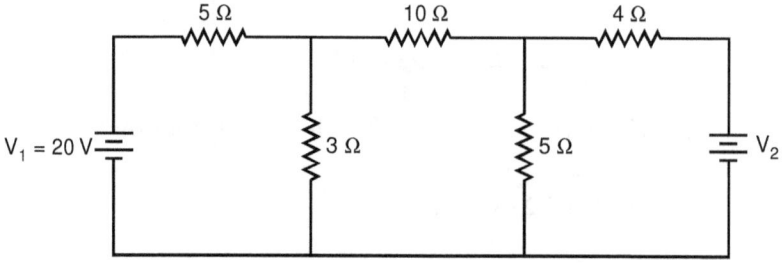

Fig. 1.42 : Network for Example 1.33

Solution : The given network is redrawn in Fig. 1.43 with loop currents marked.

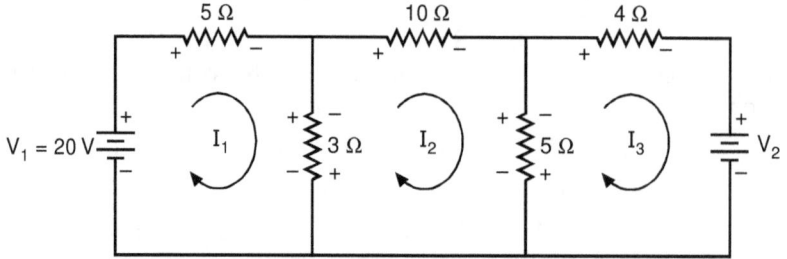

Fig. 1.43 : Network of Fig. 1.42 with loop currents marked

Applying Kirchhoff's voltage law to the various loops, we get the following equations :

Loop-1 : $\qquad 20 - 5 I_1 - 3 (I_1 - I_2) = 0$

Or, $\qquad\qquad\qquad 8 I_1 - 3 I_2 = 20 \qquad\qquad$ ... (I)

Loop-2 : $\qquad -3 (I_2 - I_1) - 10 I_2 - 5 (I_2 - I_3) = 0$

Or, $\qquad\qquad\qquad 3 I_1 - 18 I_2 + 5 I_3 = 0 \qquad\qquad$ ... (II)

Loop-3 : $\qquad -5 (I_3 - I_2) - 4 I_3 - V_2 = 0$

Or, $\qquad\qquad\qquad 5 I_2 - 9 I_3 = V_2 \qquad\qquad$ ... (III)

The above equations in terms of loop currents can also be written by mere inspection of the network as follows :

$$(5 + 3) I_1 - 3 I_2 + 0 \times I_3 = 20 \quad (\because R_{11}I_1 + R_{12}I_2 + R_{13}I_3 = V_1)$$

Or, $\quad 8 I_1 - 3 I_2 = 20 \quad \ldots (I)$

$$-3 I_1 + (3 + 10 + 5) I_2 - 5 I_3 = 0 \quad (\because R_{21}I_1 + R_{22}I_2 + R_{23}I_3 = V_2)$$

Or, $\quad 3 I_1 - 18 I_2 + 5 I_3 = 0 \quad \ldots (II)$

$$0 \times I_1 - 5 I_2 + (5 + 4) I_3 = -V_2 \quad (\because R_{31}I_1 + R_{32}I_2 + R_{33}I_3 = V_3)$$

Or, $\quad 5 I_2 - 9 I_3 = V_2 \quad \ldots (III)$

Further, with $I_1 = 0$ (given), from Equation (I), we get

$$0 - 3 I_2 = 20$$

$\therefore \quad I_2 = -6.67 \text{ A}$

Therefore, from Equation (II), we have

$$0 - 18 \times (-6.67) + 5 I_3 = 0$$

$\therefore \quad I_3 = -24.01 \text{ A}$

Hence, Equation (III) gives

$$5 \times (-6.67) - 9 \times (-24.01) = V_2$$

$\therefore \quad V_2 = \mathbf{182.74 \text{ V}} \quad \ldots \text{ Ans.}$

Example 1.34 : *Find the current through the ammeter using mesh current analysis.*

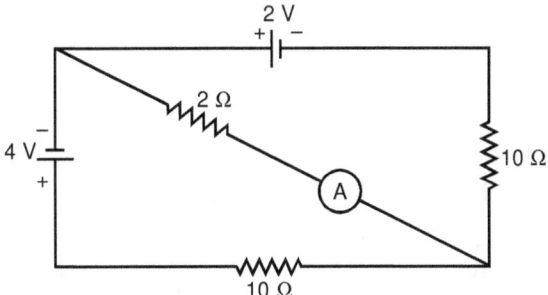

Fig. 1.44 : Network for Example 1.34

Solution :

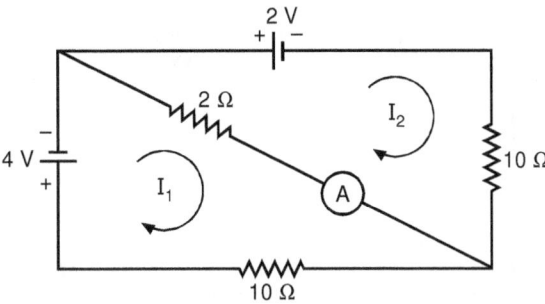

Fig. 1.45 : Network of Fig. 1.44 with loop currents marked

The given network is redrawn in Fig. 1.45 with loop currents marked. The equations in terms of these loop currents can be written by mere inspection of this network as follows :

Loop-1 : $\quad R_{11} I_1 + R_{12} I_2 = V_1$

∴ $\quad (2 + 10) I_1 - 2 I_2 = -4$

Or, $\quad 12 I_1 - 2 I_2 = -4$ ... (I)

Loop-2 : $\quad R_{21} I_1 + R_{22} I_2 = V_2$

∴ $\quad -2 I_1 + (10 + 2) I_2 = -2$

Or, $\quad -2 I_1 + 12 I_2 = -2$ ... (II)

Solving the equations (I) and (II) simultaneously, we get

$$I_1 = -0.37 \text{ A and } I_2 = -0.23 \text{ A}$$

Hence, current through the ammeter

$$= I_2 - I_1 = -0.23 - (-0.37) = \mathbf{0.14 \text{ A}} \quad \text{... Ans.}$$

Example 1.35 : *Find the loop currents for the circuit shown in Fig. 1.46.*

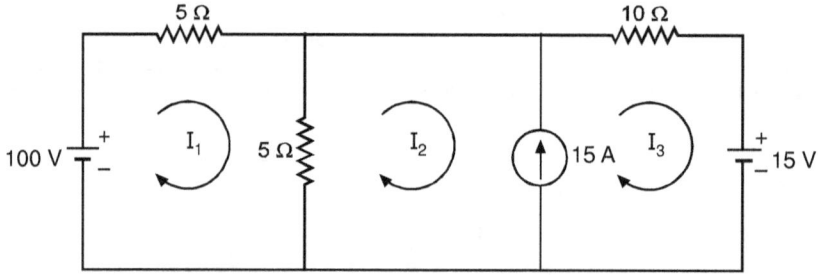

Fig. 1.46 : Network for Example 1.35

Solution : Before applying the method of loop analysis, it is necessary to convert the constant current source of 15 A present in the network into a constant voltage source. Fig. 1.47 shows the network after such conversion. Therefore, the corresponding loop current equations are :

$$(5 + 5) I_1 - 5 I_3 = 100 - 75$$

Or, $\quad 10 I_1 - 5 I_3 = 25$ ... (I)

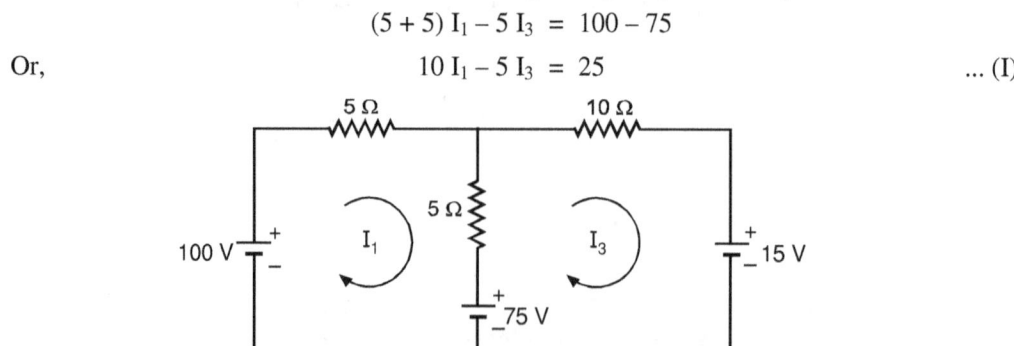

Fig. 1.47 : Network of Fig. 1.46 after source conversion

$$-5I_1 + (5+10)I_3 = 75 - 15$$
Or, $\quad -5I_1 + 15I_3 = 60 \quad \ldots \text{(II)}$

Solving the equations (I) and (II), we have $I_1 = 5.4$ A and $I_3 = 5.8$ A

Now, from the original circuit of Fig. 1.46,

Current through the current source,
$$(I_3 - I_2) = 15 \text{ A}$$
$\therefore \quad I_2 = I_3 - 15 = 5.8 - 15 = -9.2$ A

Thus, **$I_1 = 5.4$ A, $I_2 = -9.2$ A and $I_3 = 5.8$ A** ... Ans.

1.9 NODAL ANALYSIS

The method of nodal analysis is mainly based on Kirchhoff's current law. Every junction point in a network where three or more branches meet is called a *node*. One of the nodes is regarded as the *reference node, datum node or zero potential node*. The potentials of the other nodes are then assumed with respect to this arbitrarily chosen zero potential node. The equations are then written for all the nodes using Kirchhoff's current law. Similar to loop analysis, this method also reduces the number of independent equations to be solved. If n is the number of independent nodes, the number of simultaneous equations to be solved becomes $(n - 1)$. To illustrate the method, consider the network shown in Fig. 1.48 having two current sources and five resistances. There are total four nodes, one of which is considered as a reference or zero potential node and denoted by 0. Other nodes are then numbered as 1, 2 and 3. V_1, V_2 and V_3 represent respectively the potentials of nodes 1, 2 and 3 with respect to zero potential node. Let the currents and their directions which have been chosen arbitrarily be as shown in the figure. Then applying Kirchhoff's current law, we get the following equations for different nodes :

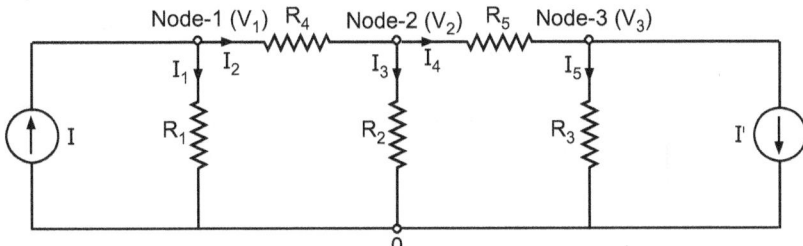

Fig. 1.48 : Nodal analysis

For Node-1 : $\quad I - I_1 - I_2 = 0$

$\therefore \quad I - \dfrac{V_1}{R_1} - \dfrac{(V_1 - V_2)}{R_4} = 0$

Or, $\quad V_1 \left(\dfrac{1}{R_1} + \dfrac{1}{R_4} \right) - \dfrac{V_2}{R_4} = I \quad \ldots (1.34)$

For Node-2 : $\quad I_2 - I_3 - I_4 = 0$

$\therefore \quad \dfrac{(V_1 - V_2)}{R_4} - \dfrac{V_2}{R_2} - \dfrac{(V_2 - V_3)}{R_5} = 0$

Or, $\quad \dfrac{V_1}{R_4} - V_2 \left(\dfrac{1}{R_2} + \dfrac{1}{R_4} + \dfrac{1}{R_5} \right) + \dfrac{V_3}{R_5} = 0 \quad \ldots (1.35)$

For Node-3 :
$$I_4 - I_5 - I' = 0$$

∴
$$\frac{(V_2 - V_3)}{R_5} - \frac{V_3}{R_3} - I' = 0$$

Or,
$$\frac{V_2}{R_5} - V_3\left(\frac{1}{R_3} + \frac{1}{R_5}\right) = I' \qquad \ldots (1.36)$$

The above equations can then be solved to determine the node potentials V_1, V_2 and V_3 and thereafter, the branch currents can be calculated. Here, we have considered the network with current sources only. However, for complicated network with several sources, to facilitate the writing of network equations, all voltage sources in the network should be converted into their equivalent current sources before Kirchhoff's current law is applied at various nodes.

Example 1.36 : *Use nodal analysis to find currents in the different branches of the network shown in Fig. 1.49.*

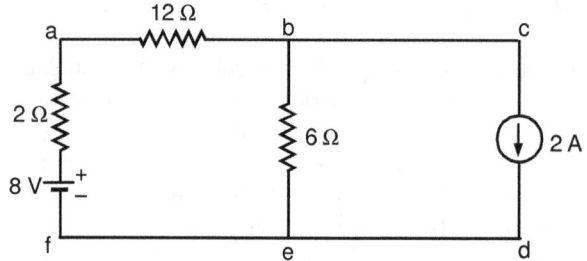

Fig. 1.49 : Network for Example 1.36

Solution : Fig. 1.50 shows the given network after conversion of constant-voltage source of 8 V into its equivalent constant-current source.

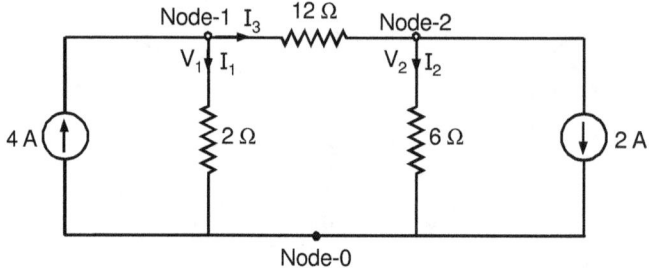

Fig. 1.50: Network of Fig. 1.49 after source conversion

There are total three nodes. These nodes are marked as 0, 1 and 2. The node marked as 0 is considered as zero potential or reference node. V_1 and V_2 represent respectively the potentials of the nodes 1 and 2 with respect to the zero potential node. Let the currents in the various branches of the network be as shown in Fig. 1.50. Then, applying Kirchhoff's current law at Node-1, we have

$$4 - I_1 - I_3 = 0$$

∴
$$I_1 + I_3 = 4$$

Or, $\dfrac{V_1}{2} + \dfrac{(V_1 - V_2)}{12} = 4$

i.e. $7V_1 - V_2 = 48$ ... (I)

Similarly, applying Kirchhoff's current law at Node-2, we get

$$I_3 - I_2 - 2 = 0$$

∴ $I_2 - I_3 = -2$

Or, $\dfrac{V_2}{6} - \dfrac{(V_1 - V_2)}{12} = -2$

i.e. $V_1 - 3V_2 = 24$ ... (II)

Solving the equations (I) and (II) simultaneously, we get

$$V_1 = 6\text{ V} \quad \text{and} \quad V_2 = -6\text{ V}$$

∴ $I_2 = \dfrac{V_2}{6} = \dfrac{-6}{6} = -1\text{ A}$

Here, minus sign indicates that the assumed direction for this current is wrong. Actually, the current I_2 flows in the opposite direction. Further,

$$I_3 = \dfrac{(V_1 - V_2)}{12} = \dfrac{6 - (-6)}{12} = 1\text{ A}$$

Hence, referring back to the original network of Fig. 1.49, we have

Current through 12 Ω resistance = **1 A, from a to b** ... Ans.

Current through 6 Ω resistance = **1 A, from e to b** ... Ans.

Alternative Method : Since the given network is simple, we can directly write the nodal equation of Node-1 (Fig. 1.51) without converting the constant-voltage source of 8 V into its equivalent constant-current source. For that, let the potential at this node be V_1 with respect to zero-potential node 0 and the currents in the various branches of the network be as shown in the figure. Then, applying Kirchhoff's current law at Node-1, we have

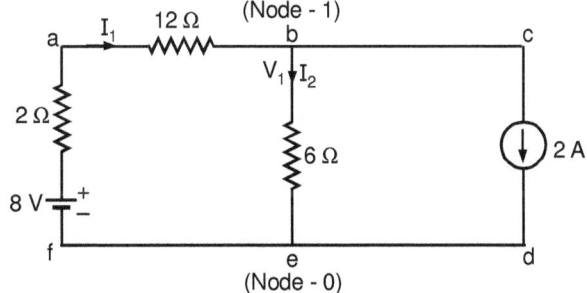

Fig. 1.51 : Network of Fig. 1.49 with nodes marked

$$I_1 - I_2 - 2 = 0$$

Or, $\dfrac{(8 - V_1)}{(12 + 2)} - \dfrac{V_1}{6} - 2 = 0$

∴ $V_1 = -6\text{ V}$

Current through 12 Ω resistance,

$$I_1 = \frac{(8 - V_1)}{(12 + 2)} = \frac{8 - (-6)}{14} = 1 \text{ A, from a to b} \qquad \text{... Ans.}$$

Current through 6 Ω resistance,

$$I_2 = \frac{V_1}{6} = \frac{-6}{6} = -1 \text{ A} \qquad \text{... Ans.}$$

Here, minus sign indicates that current I_2 will not flow from b to e as assumed, but it will actually flow from e to b.

Example 1.37 : *Using nodal voltage method, find current in the 3 Ω resistance for the network shown in Fig. 1.52.*

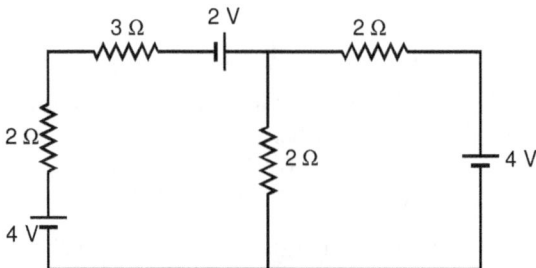

Fig. 1.52 : Network for Example 1.37

Solution : Let the currents in the various branches of the network be as shown in Fig. 1.53. Then, applying Kirchhoff's current law at Node-1, we have

$$I = I_1 + I_2$$

∴ $$\frac{4 + 2 - V_1}{3 + 2} = \frac{V_1}{2} + \frac{V_1 - 4}{2}$$

∴ $$V_1 = 2.67 \text{ V}$$

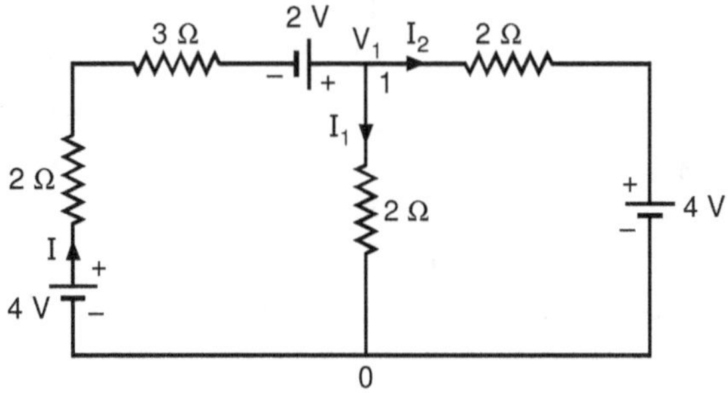

Fig. 1.53 : Network of Fig. 1.52 with nodes marked

∴ Current in 3 Ω resistance, $I = \dfrac{4 + 2 - 2.67}{5} = 0.67 \text{ A} \qquad \text{... Ans.}$

Example 1.38 : *Using the nodal method, determine the currents in the individual resistors of the circuit shown in Fig. 1.54.*

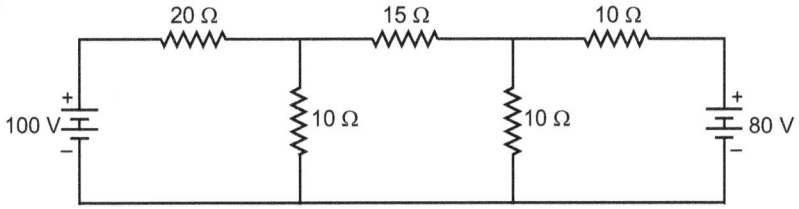

Fig. 1.54 : Network for Example 1.38

Solution :

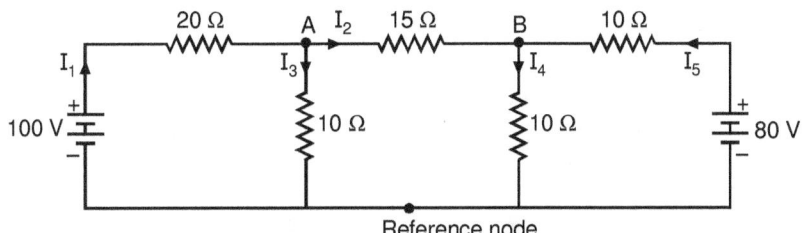

Fig. 1.55 : Network of Fig. 1.54 with nodes marked

Let V_A and V_B be the potentials of the nodes A and B with respect to the reference node (Fig. 1.55). Assume the currents in the different branches of the network as shown in the figure. Applying Kirchhoff's current law at each node point, we get

Node-A : $\qquad I_1 - I_2 - I_3 = 0$

$\therefore \qquad \dfrac{100 - V_A}{20} - \dfrac{V_A - V_B}{15} - \dfrac{V_A}{10} = 0$

$\therefore \qquad -13V_A + 4V_B = -300$

Or, $\qquad 13V_A - 4V_B = 300 \qquad \qquad \text{... (I)}$

Node-B : $\qquad I_2 - I_4 + I_5 = 0$

$\therefore \qquad \dfrac{V_A - V_B}{15} - \dfrac{V_B}{10} + \dfrac{80 - V_B}{10} = 0$

$\therefore \qquad 2V_A - 8V_B = -240 \qquad \qquad \text{... (II)}$

From the equations (I) and (II), we have

$$\Delta = \begin{vmatrix} 13 & -4 \\ 2 & -8 \end{vmatrix} = -104 + 8 = -96$$

$$D_1 = \begin{vmatrix} 300 & -4 \\ -240 & -8 \end{vmatrix} = -2400 - 960 = -3360$$

$$D_2 = \begin{vmatrix} 13 & 300 \\ 2 & -240 \end{vmatrix} = -3120 - 600 = -3720$$

$$\therefore \quad V_A = \frac{D_1}{\Delta} = \frac{-3360}{-96} = 35 \text{ V}$$

$$V_B = \frac{D_2}{\Delta} = \frac{-3720}{-96} = 38.75 \text{ V}$$

From the above values of the node potentials, we can now calculate the various branch currents.

Current through 20 Ω resistor,

$$I_1 = \frac{100 - V_A}{20} = \frac{100 - 35}{20} = 3.25 \text{ A} \qquad \text{... Ans.}$$

Current through 15 Ω resistor,

$$I_2 = \frac{V_A - V_B}{15} = \frac{35 - 38.75}{15} = -0.25 \text{ A} \qquad \text{... Ans.}$$

Current through first 10 Ω resistor,

$$I_3 = \frac{V_A}{10} = \frac{35}{10} = 3.5 \text{ A} \qquad \text{... Ans.}$$

Current through second 10 Ω resistor,

$$I_4 = \frac{V_B}{10} = \frac{38.75}{10} = 3.875 \text{ A} \qquad \text{... Ans.}$$

Current through third 10 Ω resistor,

$$I_5 = \frac{80 - V_B}{10} = \frac{80 - 38.75}{10} = 4.125 \text{ A} \qquad \text{... Ans.}$$

1.9.1 Nodal Equations in Generalized Form

Similar to loop analysis, in nodal analysis also, a method can be developed to write the nodal equations very fast, just by mere inspection of the network. For that, consider again the network of Fig. 1.48. It is redrawn in Fig. 1.56 with all resistances converted into their conductances. Then applying Kirchhoff's current law, we get the following equations for different nodes :

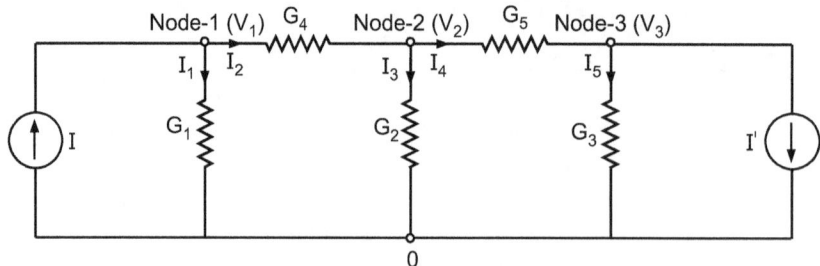

Fig. 1.56 : Nodal analysis

For Node-1 :

$$I - I_1 - I_2 = 0$$

$$\therefore \quad I - V_1 G_1 - (V_1 - V_2) G_4 = 0$$

Or, $\quad V_1 (G_1 + G_4) - V_2 G_4 = I \qquad \text{... (1.37)}$

For Node-2 : $\quad I_2 - I_3 - I_4 = 0$

$\therefore \quad (V_1 - V_2) G_4 - V_2 G_2 - (V_2 - V_3) G_5 = 0$

Or, $\quad V_1 G_4 - V_2 (G_2 + G_4 + G_5) + V_3 G_5 = 0 \qquad \ldots (1.38)$

For Node-3 : $\quad I_4 - I_5 - I' = 0$

$\therefore \quad (V_2 - V_3) G_5 - V_3 G_3 - I' = 0$

Or, $\quad V_2 G_5 - V_3 (G_3 + G_5) = I' \qquad \ldots (1.39)$

The above equations can then be solved to determine the node potentials V_1, V_2 and V_3 and thereafter the branch currents can be calculated.

In any network, such equations for different nodes can always be expressed in the generalized form given below :

$$G_{11} V_1 + G_{12} V_2 + G_{13} V_3 + \ldots + G_{1n} V_n = I_1$$
$$G_{21} V_1 + G_{22} V_2 + G_{23} V_3 + \ldots + G_{2n} V_n = I_2$$
$$G_{31} V_1 + G_{32} V_2 + G_{33} V_3 + \ldots + G_{3n} V_n = I_3$$

$$\ldots\ldots\ldots\ldots\ldots\ldots\ldots\ldots\ldots\ldots\ldots\ldots\ldots\ldots\ldots$$

$$G_{n1} V_1 + G_{n2} V_2 + G_{n3} V_3 + \ldots + G_{nn} V_n = I_n$$

where,

I_1 = The algebraic sum of the source currents meeting at Node-1
(considering the currents towards the node as positive and vice versa)

I_2 = The algebraic sum of the source currents meeting at Node-2, etc.

G_{11} = Sum of all branch conductances meeting at Node-1

G_{22} = Sum of all branch conductances meeting at Node-2, etc.

$G_{12} = G_{21}$ = Sum of all branch conductances connected between Node-1 and Node-2

$G_{23} = G_{32}$ = Sum of all branch conductances connected between Node-2 and Node-3, etc.

Here, it should be remembered that if the same convention regarding positive current is followed for all nodes, then the elements (or co-efficients) G_{11}, G_{22}, G_{33}, etc., in the above equations always carry a positive sign. On the other hand, all other elements like G_{12}, G_{21}, G_{23}, G_{32}, etc. carry a negative sign.

By observing these rules, the node equations necessary for the solution of the network can be written down by mere inspection of that network without the necessity for collecting terms with the same co-efficient. This can be confirmed by again considering the network shown in Fig. 1.56. The generalized equations for three nodes under consideration will be as follows :

For Node-1 :

$$G_{11} V_1 + G_{12} V_2 + G_{13} V_3 = I_1 \qquad \ldots (1.40)$$

For Node-2 :

$$G_{21} V_1 + G_{22} V_2 + G_{23} V_3 = I_2 \qquad \ldots (1.41)$$

For Node-3 :

$$G_{31} V_1 + G_{32} V_2 + G_{33} V_3 = I_3 \qquad \ldots (1.42)$$

where, $G_{11} = G_1 + G_4$, $G_{12} = G_{21} = -G_4$, $G_{13} = G_{31} = 0$,
$G_{22} = G_2 + G_4 + G_5$, $G_{23} = G_{32} = -G_5$, $G_{33} = G_3 + G_5$,
$I_1 = I$, $I_2 = 0$ and $I_3 = -I'$

Substituting these values in the equations (1.40), (1.41) and (1.42), we get

$$(G_1 + G_4) V_1 - G_4 V_2 = I \qquad \ldots (1.43)$$

$$-G_4 V_1 + (G_2 + G_4 + G_5) V_2 - G_5 V_3 = 0$$

Or, $$G_4 V_1 - (G_2 + G_4 + G_5) V_2 + G_5 V_3 = 0 \qquad \ldots (1.44)$$

$$-G_5 V_2 + (G_3 + G_5) V_3 = -I'$$

Or, $$G_5 V_2 - (G_3 + G_5) V_3 = I' \qquad \ldots (1.45)$$

We find that the equations (1.43), (1.44) and (1.45) are the same as equations (1.37), (1.38) and (1.39). Thus by mere inspection of network, we can write required equations. In general, the current equations for different nodes can also be written in the matrix form as given below :

$$\begin{bmatrix} G_{11} & G_{12} & G_{13} & \ldots & G_{1n} \\ G_{21} & G_{22} & G_{23} & \ldots & G_{2n} \\ \ldots & \ldots & \ldots & \ldots & \ldots \\ G_{n1} & G_{n2} & G_{n3} & \ldots & G_{nn} \end{bmatrix} \begin{bmatrix} V_1 \\ V_2 \\ \ldots \\ V_n \end{bmatrix} = \begin{bmatrix} I_1 \\ I_2 \\ \ldots \\ I_n \end{bmatrix}$$

Or, $$[G][V] = [I]$$

where, [V] and [I] are column matrices, whereas [G] is a square matrix. The elements G_{11}, G_{22}, G_{33}, ..., G_{nn} on the principal diagonal of conductance matrix [G] and its other off diagonal elements like G_{12}, G_{21}, G_{23}, G_{32}, etc. can be written by mere inspection of the network by following the rules already mentioned above.

Before applying this method of nodal analysis to any network, following points should be kept in mind :

(i) In complicated networks with several sources, it is always advantageous to convert constant-voltage sources if present into their equivalent constant-current sources for the purpose of nodal analysis.

(ii) All resistances must be expressed in terms of their conductances.

Example 1.39 : *Using node-voltage method, find the magnitude and direction of current I in the network shown in Fig. 1.57.*

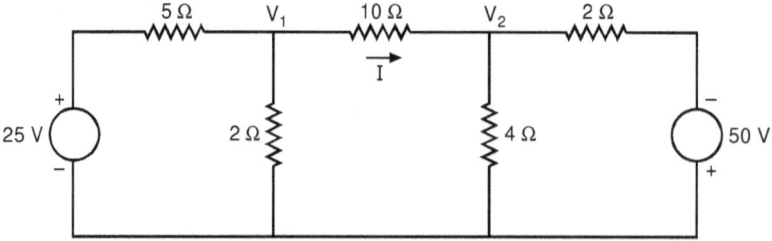

Fig. 1.57 : Network for Example 1.39

Solution : Fig. 1.58 (a) shows the given network after conversion of constant-voltage sources into their equivalent constant-current sources. Fig. 1.58 (b) shows the simplified version of the circuit shown in Fig. 1.58 (a). Let the currents in the various branches of this network be as shown in Fig. 1.58 (b). Then, applying Kirchhoff's current law at various nodes, we get the following equations :

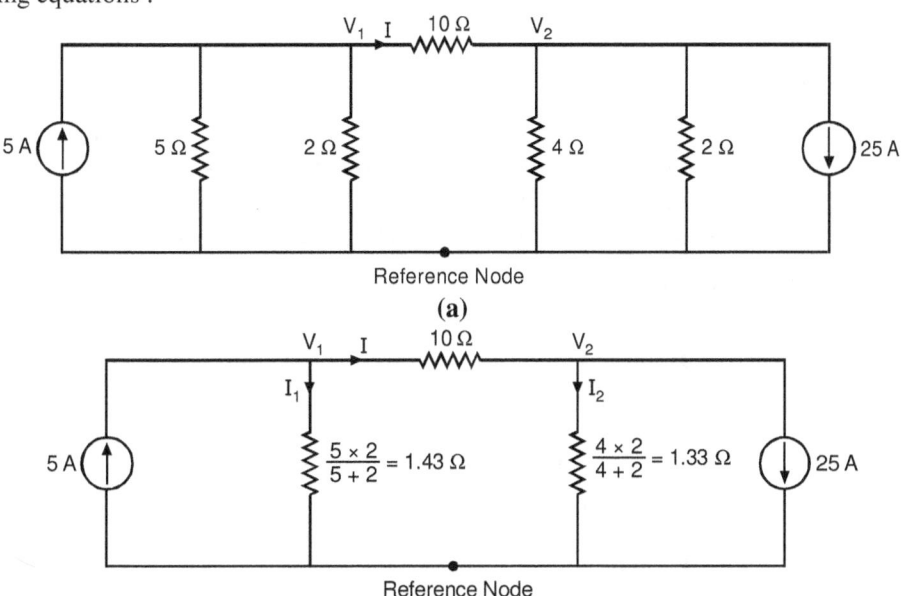

Fig. 1.58 : (a) Network of Fig. 1.57 after source conversion, (b) Simplified circuit

Node-1 : $\quad 5 - I_1 - I = 0$

$\therefore \quad I_1 + I = 5$

Or, $\quad \dfrac{V_1}{1.43} + \dfrac{V_1 - V_2}{10} = 5$

i.e. $\quad 11.43\, V_1 - 1.43\, V_2 = 71.5 \quad \ldots \text{(I)}$

Node-2 : $\quad I - I_2 - 25 = 0$

$\therefore \quad I_2 - I = -25$

Or, $\quad \dfrac{V_2}{1.33} - \dfrac{(V_1 - V_2)}{10} = -25$

i.e. $\quad 1.33\, V_1 - 11.33\, V_2 = 332.5 \quad \ldots \text{(II)}$

Solving the equations (I) and (II) simultaneously, we get

$$V_1 = 2.61 \text{ V} \quad \text{and} \quad V_2 = -29.04 \text{ V}$$

$\therefore \quad I = \dfrac{V_1 - V_2}{10} = \dfrac{2.61 - (-29.04)}{10} = 3.17 \text{ A} \qquad \ldots \textbf{Ans.}$

This current will obviously flow from Node-1 to Node-2 as assumed.

Alternative Method :

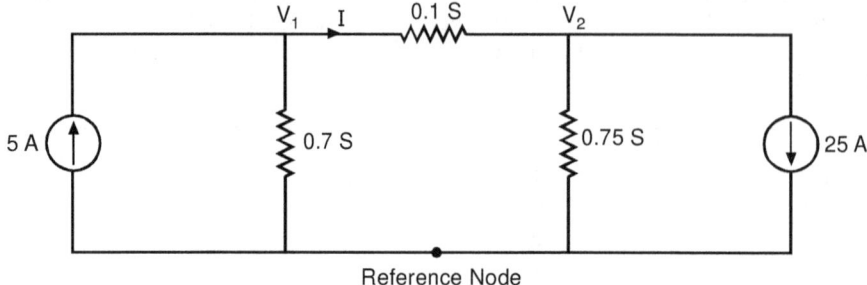

Fig. 1.59 : Network of Fig. 1.58 (b) with conductances marked

Network of Fig. 1.58 (b) is redrawn in Fig. 1.59 with all resistances converted into their conductances. Hence, the different nodal equations can be directly written from the mere inspection of this network as follows :

Node-1 : $\qquad G_{11}V_1 + G_{12}V_2 = I_1$

∴ $\qquad (0.7 + 0.1)V_1 - 0.1 V_2 = 5$

Or, $\qquad 0.8 V_1 - 0.1 V_2 = 5 \qquad$ ... (III)

Node-2 : $\qquad G_{21}V_1 + G_{22}V_2 = I_2$

∴ $\qquad -0.1 V_1 + (0.1 + 0.75) V_2 = -25$

Or, $\qquad 0.1 V_1 - 0.85 V_2 = 25 \qquad$ ... (IV)

Solving the equations (III) and (IV) simultaneously, we get

$$V_1 = 2.61 \text{ V} \quad \text{and} \quad V_2 = -29.1 \text{ V}$$

∴ $\qquad I = (V_1 - V_2) \times 0.1 = [2.61 - (-29.1)] \times 0.1$

$$= 3.17 \text{ A} \qquad \text{... Ans.}$$

Example 1.40 : *Determine V_{AB} by applying Kirchhoff's laws. Verify your answer by using nodal analysis.*

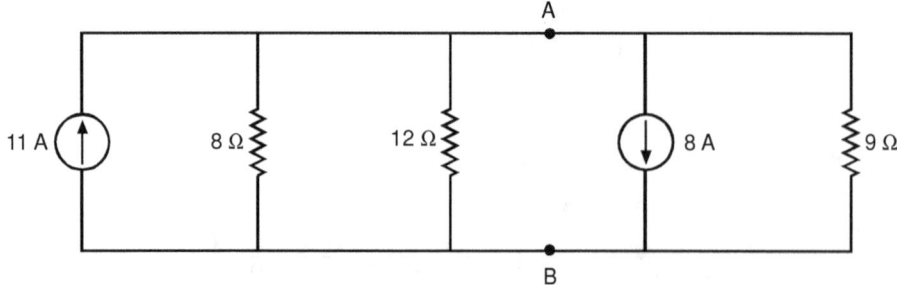

Fig. 1.60 : Network for Example 1.40

Solution : Method-1 : Using Branch Current Method :

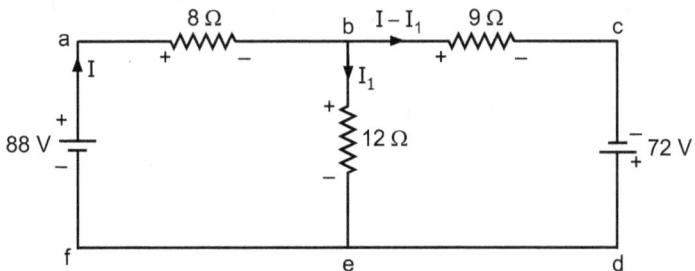

Fig. 1.61 : Network of Fig. 1.60 after source conversion

Fig. 1.61 shows the network of Fig. 1.60 after converting the current sources into their equivalent voltage sources. Assumed branch currents and their directions are marked in this diagram by applying Kirchhoff's current law at Junction b. Now, let us select the following closed circuits and apply Kirchhoff's voltage law to them.

Circuit abefa :

$$-8I - 12I_1 + 88 = 0$$

$$\therefore \quad -8I - 12I_1 = -88$$

Or, $\quad 8I + 12I_1 = 88 \quad \ldots \text{(I)}$

Circuit bcdeb :

$$-9(I - I_1) + 72 + 12I_1 = 0$$

$$\therefore \quad -9I + 21I_1 = -72$$

Or, $\quad 9I - 21I_1 = 72 \quad \ldots \text{(II)}$

Solving the equations (I) and (II) simultaneously, we get

$$I_1 = 0.78 \text{ A}$$

$\therefore \quad V_{AB}$ = Voltage across 12 Ω resistance

$\quad = I_1 \times 12 = 0.78 \times 12 = \mathbf{9.36 \text{ V}} \quad \ldots \text{Ans.}$

Method-2 : Using Nodal Analysis :

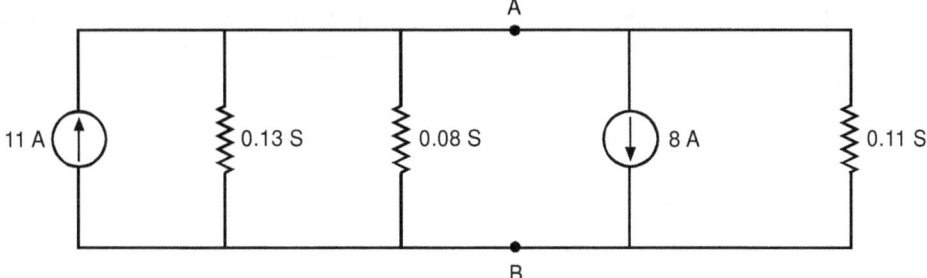

Fig. 1.62 : Network of Fig. 1.60 with conductances marked

Fig. 1.62 shows the given network after converting all the resistances into their conductances. Considering Node-B as a reference or zero-potential node, we can write the equation for Node-A by mere inspection of the network as follows :

$$(0.13 + 0.08 + 0.11) V_A = 11 - 8 \qquad (\because G_{11} V_1 = I_1)$$

∴ Potential of Node-A with respect to Node-B,

$$V_A = 9.38 \text{ V}$$

Hence, $\qquad V_{AB} = V_A = \mathbf{9.38 \text{ V}}$ ... Ans.

Example 1.41 : *Determine the current I_{AB} by nodal analysis.*

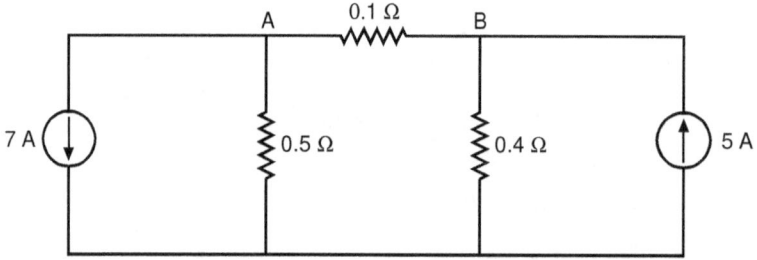

Fig. 1.63 : Network for Example 1.41

Solution :

Method-1 :

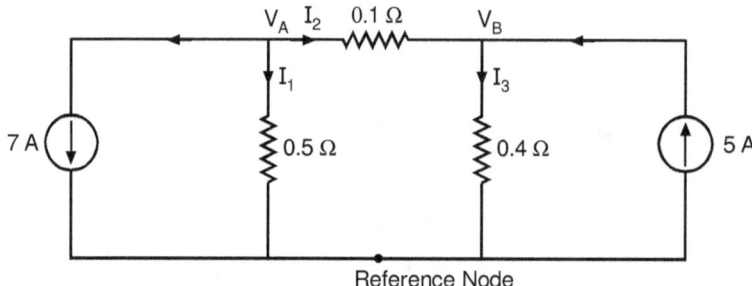

Fig. 1.64 : Network of Fig. 1.63 with node voltages marked

Let V_A and V_B represent respectively the potentials of Node-A and Node-B with respect to the reference node. Let the currents in the various branches of the network be as shown in Fig. 1.64. Then, applying Kirchhoff's current law at Node-A and Node-B, we get the following equations :

Node-A : $\qquad -7 - I_1 - I_2 = 0$

∴ $\qquad I_1 + I_2 = -7$

Or, $\qquad \dfrac{V_A}{0.5} + \dfrac{(V_A - V_B)}{0.1} = -7$

i.e. $\qquad 6V_A - 5V_B = -3.5 \qquad$ ... (I)

Node-B : $\quad I_2 - I_3 + 5 = 0$

$\therefore \quad I_2 - I_3 = -5$

Or, $\quad \dfrac{(V_A - V_B)}{0.1} - \dfrac{V_B}{0.4} = -5$

i.e. $\quad 4V_A - 5V_B = -2 \quad \ldots (II)$

Solving the equations (I) and (II) simultaneously, we get

$$V_A = -0.75 \text{ V} \quad \text{and} \quad V_B = -0.2 \text{ V}$$

$\therefore \quad$ Current, $I_{AB} = I_2 = \dfrac{V_A - V_B}{0.1} = \dfrac{-0.75 - (-0.2)}{0.1} = -5.5 \text{ A} \quad \ldots$ **Ans.**

Method-2 : The given network is redrawn in Fig. 1.65 after converting all the resistances into their conductances. Then, the equations for the nodes A and B can be written by mere inspection of this network as follows :

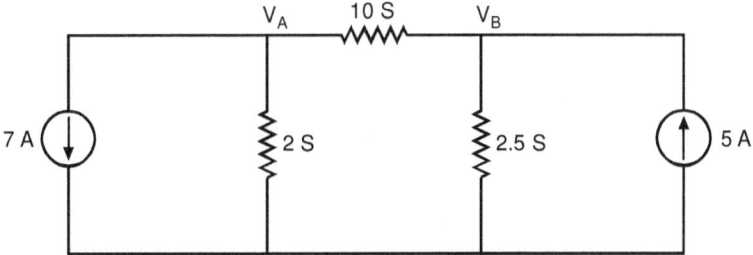

Fig. 1.65 : Network of Fig. 1.64 with conductances marked

Node-A : $\quad (2 + 10) V_A - 10 V_B = -7 \quad\quad (\because G_{11}V_1 + G_{12}V_2 = I_1)$

$\therefore \quad 12 V_A - 10 V_B = -7 \quad \ldots (I)$

Node-B : $\quad -10 V_A + (10 + 2.5) V_B = 5 \quad\quad (\because G_{21}V_1 + G_{22}V_2 = I_2)$

$\therefore \quad 10 V_A - 12.5 V_B = -5 \quad \ldots (II)$

Solving the equations (I) and (II) simultaneously, we get

$$V_A = -0.75 \text{ V} \quad \text{and} \quad V_B = -0.2 \text{ V}$$

$\therefore \quad$ Current, $I_{AB} = (V_A - V_B) \times 10 = (-0.75 + 0.2) \times 10$

$\quad\quad\quad\quad = -5.5 \text{ A} \quad \ldots$ **Ans.**

Here, minus sign for the current indicates that current will actually flow from the terminal B to the terminal A.

Example 1.42 : *Using nodal analysis, find current through 2 Ω resistance of the given circuit in Fig. 1.66.*

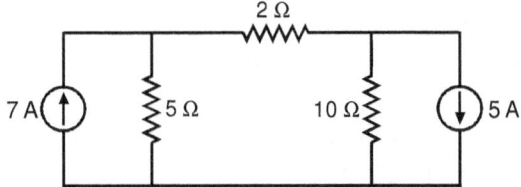

Fig. 1.66 : Circuit for Example 1.42

Solution : Method-1 (From Fundamentals) : Let the current directions which have been chosen arbitrarily be as shown in Fig. 1.67. Then, applying Kirchhoff's current law at Node-1, we get

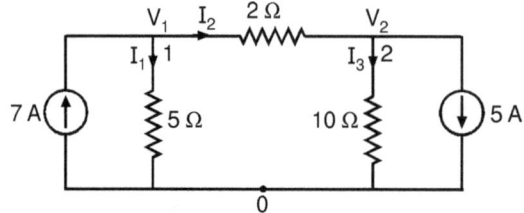

Fig. 1.67 : Circuit of Fig. 1.66 with node voltages marked

$$7 - I_1 - I_2 = 0$$

$$\therefore \quad I_1 + I_2 = 7$$

Or, $\quad \dfrac{V_1}{5} + \dfrac{V_1 - V_2}{2} = 7$

$$\therefore \quad 7V_1 - 5V_2 = 70 \quad \ldots \text{(I)}$$

Similarly, applying Kirchhoff's current law, at Node-2, we have

$$I_2 - I_3 - 5 = 0$$

$$\therefore \quad I_2 - I_3 = 5$$

Or, $\quad \dfrac{V_1 - V_2}{2} - \dfrac{V_2}{10} = 5$

$$\therefore \quad 5V_1 - 6V_2 = 50 \quad \ldots \text{(II)}$$

Solving the equations (I) and (II) simultaneously, we get
$$V_1 = 10 \text{ V and } V_2 = 0$$

∴ Current through 2 Ω resistance,

$$I_2 = \dfrac{V_1 - V_2}{2} = \dfrac{10 - 0}{2} = 5 \text{ A} \quad \ldots \text{Ans.}$$

Method-2 (Using Equations in the Generalized Form) : The given network is redrawn in Fig. 1.68 after converting all the resistances into their conductances.

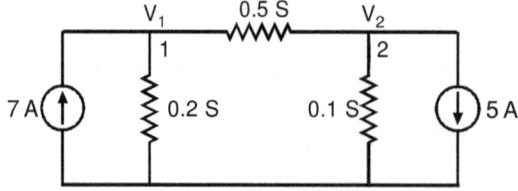

Fig. 1.68 : Circuit of Fig. 1.66 with node voltages and conductances marked

The equations for nodes 1 and 2 in the generalized form will be as follows :

$$G_{11} V_1 + G_{12} V_2 = I_1 \quad \ldots \text{(I)}$$
$$G_{21} V_1 + G_{22} V_2 = I_2 \quad \ldots \text{(II)}$$

where, $G_{11} = 0.2 + 0.5 = 0.7$ S, $G_{12} = G_{21} = -0.5$ S,
$G_{22} = 0.5 + 0.1 = 0.6$ S, $I_1 = 7$ A, $I_2 = -5$ A

Substituting these values in the equations (I) and (II), we get

$$0.7 V_1 - 0.5 V_2 = 7 \quad \ldots \text{(III)}$$
$$-0.5 V_1 + 0.6 V_2 = -5 \quad \ldots \text{(IV)}$$

Solving the above equations simultaneously, we have

$$V_1 = 10 \text{ V and } V_2 = 0$$

∴ Current through 2 Ω resistance (i.e. 0.5 S conductance)

$$= (V_1 - V_2) \times 0.5 = (10 - 0) \times 0.5 = 5 \text{ A} \quad \ldots \text{Ans.}$$

Example 1.43 : *Find the node voltages in the circuit shown in Fig. 1.69.*

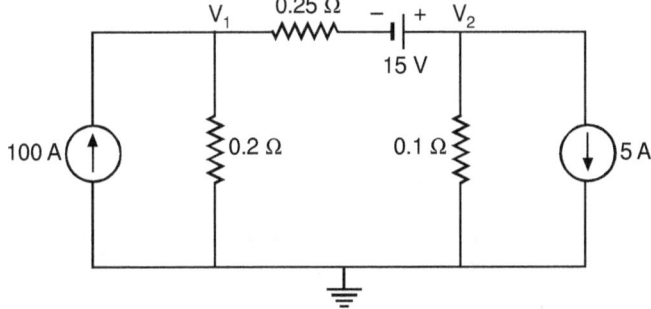

Fig. 1.69 : Network for Example 1.43

Solution : Fig. 1.70 shows the network after conversion of constant-voltage source of 15 V into its equivalent constant-current source and all resistances into their conductances.

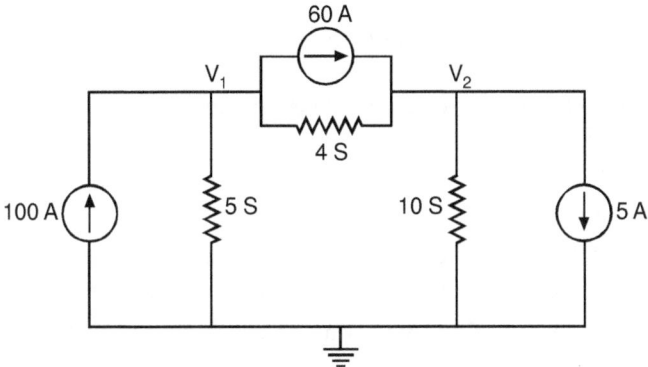

Fig. 1.70 : Network of Fig. 1.69 after source conversion and with resistances replaced by their conductances

Hence, the corresponding nodal equations are

$$(5 + 4) V_1 - 4 V_2 = 100 - 60 \quad (\because G_{11} V_1 + G_{12} V_2 = I_1)$$

Or, $\quad 9 V_1 - 4 V_2 = 40 \quad \ldots \text{(I)}$

$$-4 V_1 + (4 + 10) V_2 = 60 - 5 \quad (\because G_{21} V_1 + G_{22} V_2 = I_2)$$

Or, $\quad -4 V_1 + 14 V_2 = 55 \quad \ldots \text{(II)}$

Solving the equations (I) and (II) simultaneously using determinant method, we have

$$V_1 = \frac{D_1}{\Delta} = \frac{\begin{vmatrix} 40 & -4 \\ 55 & 14 \end{vmatrix}}{\begin{vmatrix} 9 & -4 \\ -4 & 14 \end{vmatrix}}$$

$$= \frac{560 + 220}{126 - 16} = \frac{780}{110} = \mathbf{7.09\ V} \qquad \text{... Ans.}$$

$$V_2 = \frac{D_2}{\Delta} = \frac{\begin{vmatrix} 9 & 40 \\ -4 & 55 \end{vmatrix}}{\begin{vmatrix} 9 & -4 \\ -4 & 14 \end{vmatrix}}$$

$$= \frac{495 + 160}{126 - 16} = \frac{655}{110} = \mathbf{5.95\ V} \qquad \text{... Ans.}$$

1.10 POINTS TO REMEMBER

Work, Power and Energy Relations :
- Mass is the quantity of matter possessed by a body. The unit of mass is kilogram (kg).
- Velocity is defined as the distance travelled per unit time and can therefore be expressed in metres per second (m/s).
- Acceleration is the rate of change of velocity. It is expressed in metres per second per second (m/s^2).
- Force is that which changes or tends to change the state of rest or of uniform motion of a body. The unit of force is newton (N).
- The gravitational force exerted by the earth on a body is termed its weight. The unit of weight is newton (N).
- Turning moment or Torque is the product of a force and a perpendicular distance from the line of action of the force to the axis of rotation. The unit of torque is newton-metre (Nm).
- Work is said to be done when a force acting on a body causes it to move. The S.I. unit of work is the joule (J).
- Power can be defined as the rate of doing work i.e.

$$\text{Power} = \frac{\text{Work done}}{\text{Time}}$$

  The unit of power is watt (W).
- Energy is defined as the capacity to do the work. The unit of energy is joule.
- Kinetic energy is the energy possessed by a body due to its motion. The unit of kinetic energy is joule.

- Potential energy is the energy possessed by a body by virtue of its position. The unit of potential energy is joule.
- In an electrical system, work is the work done electrically in moving a charge of one coulomb through a potential difference of one volt. The unit of work is joule.
- The power consumed by the electrical circuit is said to be one watt when the potential difference applied across the circuit is one volt and the current flowing through it is one ampere. The higher unit of power is kilowatt (kW).
- Energy consumed by the electrical circuit is said to be one watt-second when it utilizes the power of the one watt for one second. The higher units of energy are watt-hour (Wh) and kilowatt-hour (kWh).
- The quantity of heat required to raise the temperature of one kilogram of the substance by one Kelvin is called the specific heat capacity of that substance. It is normally expressed in joules per kilogram kelvin (J/kg.K).
- Sensible heat is the quantity of heat gained or lost by a given mass of a substance when a temperature change takes place without change in its state. The unit of sensible heat is joule.
- Specific enthalpy or specific latent heat is the heat required to change the state of one kilogram mass of a substance without change in temperature. It is normally expressed in joules per kilogram (J/kg).
- Latent heat is the quantity of heat required to change the state of a given mass of a substance without change in temperature. The unit of latent heat is joule.
- The calorific value of a fuel is defined as the amount of heat produced by completely burning unit mass of that fuel and it is normally expressed in kJ/g, MJ/kg or kWh/kg.
- % Efficiency = $\frac{\text{Power output}}{\text{Power input}} \times 100$

Analysis of D.C. Circuits :
- A voltage source whose terminal voltage always remains constant for all values of output current is known as an ideal voltage source.
- An ideal current source is that current source which can deliver a constant amount of current irrespective of the value of the load resistance connected across its terminals.
- An open circuit exists between two isolated terminals of a network which are not connected by an element of any kind.
- A direct connection of zero resistance across an element or combination of elements is called a short circuit.
- **Kirchhoff's Point law or Current law:** It states that in any electrical circuit, the algebraic sum of all branch currents that meet at a point (or junction) is always zero.
- **Kirchhoff's Mesh law or Voltage law:** This law states that the algebraic sum of all branch voltages around any closed circuit (or mesh) is always zero.

1.11 IMPORTANT FORMULAE AT A GLANCE

Work, Power and Energy Relations :

- Power $P = \omega \cdot T$ joules/second or watts

where ω is the angular velocity in radians/second and T is the torque in newton-metres.

- Potential energy acquired by a body

  = Work done in lifting the body = $m \cdot g \cdot h$ joules

where m is the mass of a body in kilograms, g is the gravitational acceleration in metres/second^2 and h is the height in metres through which the body is lifted.

- Electrical power $P = V \cdot I = I^2 \cdot R = \dfrac{V^2}{R}$ watts

  Electrical energy $E = V \cdot I \cdot t = I^2 \cdot R \cdot t = \dfrac{V^2}{R} \cdot t$ watt-seconds

  where,   V = Voltage in volts

  I = Current in amperes

  R = Resistance in ohms

  t = Time in seconds

- Sensible heat = $m \cdot s \cdot (t_2 - t_1)$ joules

  where,   m = Mass of a substance in kilograms (kg)

  s = Specific heat capacity of a substance in joules per kilogram Kelvin (J/kg·K)

  $(t_2 - t_1)$ = Final temperature – Initial temperature

  = Temperature change in Kelvins (K)

- Latent heat = $m \times h$ joules

  where,   m = Mass of a substance in kilograms

  h = Specific enthalpy (i.e. specific latent heat) of a substance in joules per kilogram (J/kg)

Analysis of D.C. Circuits :

Kirchhoff's Point or Current Law :

- At a junction, $\Sigma I = 0$.

  where ΣI = Algebraic sum of all branch currents that meet at a point (or junction)

Kirchhoff's Mesh or Voltage Law :

- Around a closed circuit, $\Sigma V = 0$

  where ΣV = Algebraic sum of all branch voltages around a closed circuit (or mesh)

1.12 SOLUTIONS OF NUMERICAL EXAMPLES FROM UNIVERSITY PAPERS

WORK, POWER AND ENERGY RELATIONS

Example 1.44 : *Find the power in kW taken by a d.c. motor driving a pump to raise 14000 litres of water per minute to a height of 30 m. The motor efficiency is 90% and pump efficiency is 75%. Assume density of water as 1 gm per millilitre.* **(November 2003/8 Marks)**

Solution : Mass of water lifted per minute = 14000 kg

∴ Work done per minute = m.g.h = $14000 \times 9.81 \times 30$ J = 4120.2 kJ

∴ Power output of the pump = $\dfrac{\text{Work done}}{\text{Time}}$ = $\dfrac{4120.2 \times 10^3}{1 \times 60}$ W = 68.67 kW

∴ Power taken by the motor = $\dfrac{\text{Power output of the pump}}{\eta_{\text{pump}} \times \eta_{\text{motor}}}$

= $\dfrac{68.67}{0.75 \times 0.9}$

= **101.73 kW**   ... **Ans.**

Example 1.45 : *An electric iron is marked 250 V, 350 W. What current does it take and what is its hot resistance ? What is the weekly cost of using it 2.5 hours daily at Rs. 2.30 per unit ?*

(November 2003/8 Marks)

Solution : Current drawn by an electric iron when hot,

$$I = \dfrac{P}{V} = \dfrac{350}{250} = \textbf{1.4 A}$$ ... **Ans.**

∴ Hot resistance of an electric iron,

$$R = \dfrac{V}{I} = \dfrac{250}{1.4} = \textbf{178.57 } \Omega$$ ... **Ans.**

Alternatively,

Hot resistance of an electric iron,

$$R = \dfrac{V^2}{P} = \dfrac{250^2}{350} = \textbf{178.57 } \Omega$$ ... **Ans.**

Energy consumption per week = $350 \times 2.5 \times 7$ Wh = 6.125 kWh

∴ Weekly cost = 6.125×2.30 = **Rs. 14.09**   ... **Ans.**

Example 1.46 : *Calculate the time required to heat 15 litres of water from 15°C to the boiling point. The heater is operated at 230 V supply and the resistance of the heating element is 40 Ω. Efficiency of the heater is 84% and specific heat of water is 4180 J/kg.K.*

(November 2004/8 Marks)

Solution : Mass of water to be heated = 15 kg.

Heat energy required to raise the temperature of water to the boiling point

$$= m \cdot s \cdot (t_2 - t_1) = 15 \times 4180 \times (100 - 15) = 5329500 \text{ J}$$

∴ $\quad$ Input energy $= \dfrac{5329500}{0.84} = 6344642.9 \text{ J} \quad \quad \ldots \text{(I)}$

If t seconds is the time required to heat the water, then input energy is also given by

$$\text{Input energy} = \text{Power} \times \text{Time} = \dfrac{V^2}{R} \times \text{Time} = \dfrac{230^2}{40} \times t$$

$$= 1322.5 \times t \quad \quad \ldots \text{(II)}$$

Equating the equations (I) and (II), we get

$$6344642.9 = 1322.5 \times t$$

∴ $\quad$ t = **4797.46 seconds or 1.333 hour** $\quad \quad \ldots$ Ans.

Example 1.47 : *An electric iron is marked 250 V, 350 W. What current does it take and what is its hot resistance ? What is the weekly cost of using it 5 hours daily at Rs. 2.70 per unit ?*

(November 2004/8 Marks)

Solution : Current drawn by an electric iron when hot,

$$I = \dfrac{P}{V} = \dfrac{350}{250} = \mathbf{1.4 \text{ A}} \quad \quad \ldots \text{Ans.}$$

∴ $\quad$ Hot resistance of an electric iron,

$$R = \dfrac{V}{I} = \dfrac{250}{1.4} = \mathbf{178.57 \text{ } \Omega} \quad \quad \ldots \text{Ans.}$$

Alternatively,

Hot resistance of an electric iron,

$$R = \dfrac{V^2}{P} = \dfrac{250^2}{350} = \mathbf{178.57 \text{ } \Omega} \quad \quad \ldots \text{Ans.}$$

Energy consumption per week $= 350 \times 5 \times 7 \text{ Wh} = 12.25 \text{ kWh}$

∴ $\quad$ Weekly cost $= 12.25 \times 2.70 = $ **Rs. 33.08** $\quad \quad \ldots$ Ans.

Example 1.48 : *An electric kettle is required to heat 6 litres of water from 17°C to 98°C in 25 minutes. Find the rating of the kettle assuming the efficiency of 83%. If the kettle is to be operated on 230 V mains, find the resistance of the heating element.*

Assume the specific heat capacity of water to be 4200 J/kg.K and 1 litre of water to have a mass of 1 kg. **(May 2005/8 Marks)**

Solution : Mass of water to be heated = 6 kg.

Heat energy required $= m \cdot s \cdot (t_2 - t_1) = 6 \times 4200 \times (98 - 17)$

$$= 2041.2 \times 10^3 \text{ J}$$

∴ Power output required from the kettle

$$= \frac{\text{Energy}}{\text{Time}} = \frac{2041.2 \times 10^3}{25 \times 60} = 1360.8 \text{ W}$$

∴ Rating of the kettle = Power input to the kettle

$$= \frac{\text{Power output}}{\text{Efficiency}} = \frac{1360.8}{0.83} = \mathbf{1639.52 \text{ W, say 1650 W}} \qquad \text{... Ans.}$$

With the supply voltage of 230 V, the resistance of the heating element

$$= \frac{\text{Voltage}^2}{\text{Power rating}} = \frac{230^2}{1650} = \mathbf{32 \; \Omega} \qquad \text{... Ans.}$$

Example 1.49 : *An electric heater is marked with 250 V and 3 kW. Calculate its resistance and monthly cost of electricity, if heater is used 2 hours per day and cost of electricity is Rs. 4.25 per unit (for 30 days).* **(November 2005/8 Marks)**

Solution : Hot resistance of an electrical heater,

$$R = \frac{V^2}{P} = \frac{250^2}{3 \times 10^3} = \mathbf{20.83 \; \Omega} \qquad \text{... Ans.}$$

Monthly energy consumption = $3 \times 2 \times 30$ = 180 kWh

∴ Monthly cost = 180×4.25 = **Rs. 765** ... Ans.

Example 1.50 : *The cost of boiling 2 kg of water in an electric kettle is 12 paise. The kettle takes 6 minutes to boil the water from an ambient temperature of 20°C. Calculate :*

(i) the efficiency of the kettle, and

(ii) wattage or power rating of the kettle if cost of 1 kWh is 40 paise. **(May 2007/8 Marks)**

Solution : Assuming the specific heat capacity of water to be 4200 J/kg.K, we have

Net heat energy required for boiling the water

$$= m \cdot S \cdot (t_2 - t_1)$$
$$= 2 \times 4200 \times (100 - 20) \qquad (\because \text{Boiling point of the water} = 100°C)$$
$$= 672000 \text{ J}$$

∴ Power output of the kettle

$$= \frac{\text{Energy output}}{\text{Time}} = \frac{672000}{6 \times 60} = 1866.67 \text{ W}$$

Energy consumed by the kettle

$$= \frac{\text{Total cost}}{\text{Cost per kWh}} = \frac{12}{40} = 0.3 \text{ kWh}$$

∴ Power input to the kettle i.e. its power rating

$$= \frac{\text{Energy consumed}}{\text{Time (in hours)}} = \frac{0.3 \times 10^3}{(6/60)} = \mathbf{3000 \text{ W}} \qquad \text{... Ans.}$$

∴ Efficiency of the kettle

$$= \frac{\text{Power output}}{\text{Power input}} \times 100 = \frac{1866.67}{3000} \times 100$$

$$= 62.22 \%$$ ... Ans.

Example 1.51 : *Electricity bill of running of motor pump set is Rs. 6 per hour. Calculate the time required for the motor to fill 1000 kg of water in a tank placed at a height of 10 m. Motor efficiency is 90% and pump efficiency is 78%. Rate of electricity is Rs. 4 per unit.*

(May 2008/8 Marks)

Solution : Energy consumed per hour $= \frac{6}{4} = 1.5$ kWh

∴ Input power $= \frac{\text{Energy}}{\text{Time}} = \frac{1.5 \times 10^3}{1} = 1500$ W ... (I)

Let the time required for the motor to fill 1000 kg of water in a tank be t, in seconds.

Work done during this period

$$= m \cdot g \cdot h = 1000 \times 9.81 \times 10 = 98100 \text{ J or Ws}$$

∴ Output power $= \frac{\text{Work done}}{\text{Time}} = \frac{98100}{t}$ watts

∴ Input power $= \frac{\text{Output power}}{\eta_{pump} \times \eta_{motor}} = \frac{98100}{t \times 0.78 \times 0.90}$

$$= \frac{139743.59}{t} \text{ watts}$$ ... (II)

Equating the input power from Equation (I) with that from Equation (II), we get

$$\frac{139743.59}{t} = 1500$$

∴ Time required for the motor to fill 1000 kg of water in a tank,

$$t = 93.16 \text{ s} \quad \text{or} \quad 1.55 \text{ minute}$$ ... Ans.

Example 1.52 : *A motor lifts 10,000 kg of water to the height of 6.5 m. Pump efficiency is 74%. If the electrical energy consumed by the motor is 0.25 kWh, calculate the motor efficiency.*

(December 2008/8 Marks)

Solution : Given : m = 10000 kg, h = 6.5 m, $\eta_{pump} = 74\%$.

Energy consumed by the motor = 0.25 kWh.

Total energy input required by the motor to lift the water

$$= \frac{m \cdot g \cdot h}{\eta_{pump} \times \eta_{motor}} = \frac{10000 \times 9.81 \times 6.5}{0.74 \times \eta_{motor}} \text{ J or Ws}$$ ... (I)

But Energy consumed by the motor

$$= 0.25 \text{ kWh} = 0.25 \times 1000 \times 3600 \text{ Ws}$$ ... (II)

Hence equating the Equation (I) with Equation (II), we get

Efficiency of the motor, $\eta_{motor} = \mathbf{0.96}$ **or 96%** ... Ans.

Example 1.53 : *A 230 V heater is used to boil 15 kg of water from 15 °C. If heating efficiency is 84% and the resistance of the heating element is 40 Ω, calculate time required to boil the water. Take specific heat of water to be 4180 J/kg.K.* **(December 2008/6 Marks)**

Solution : Given : V = 230 volts, m = 15 kg, t_2 = 100°C, t_1 = 15°C, η = 84%, R = 40 Ω, s = 4180 J/kg.K.

Net heat energy required to boil the water
$$= m.s. (t_2 - t_1) = 15 \times 4180 \times (100 - 15) = 5329500 \text{ J}$$

∴ Total energy input needed $= \dfrac{\text{Net heat energy required}}{\text{Heating efficiency}}$

$$= \dfrac{5329500}{0.84} = 6344642.9 \text{ J or Ws}$$

Power input to the heater $= \dfrac{V^2}{R} = \dfrac{230^2}{40} = 1322.5 \text{ W}$

∴ Time required to boil the water

$$= \dfrac{\text{Energy input}}{\text{Power input}} = \dfrac{6344642.9}{1322.5}$$

$$= \mathbf{4797.46 \text{ seconds or } 1.33 \text{ hour}} \qquad \text{... Ans.}$$

Example 1.54 : *Electricity bill of lifting water in a tank placed at 10 m height is 95 paise. If the motor efficiency is 92% and pump efficiency is 82%, find the tank capacity.*

(May 2009/6 Marks)

Solution : Let the tank capacity be x litres.

∴ Mass of water lifted = x kg

∴ Total energy required to lift the water

$$= \dfrac{mgh}{\eta_{motor} \times \eta_{pump}} = \dfrac{x \times 9.81 \times 10}{0.92 \times 0.82}$$

$$= 130.04 \text{ x joules or watt-seconds}$$

$$= \dfrac{130.04 \text{ x}}{1000 \times 3600} = 3.612 \times 10^{-5} \text{ x kilowatt-hours}$$

Assume the cost of electricity per unit to be Rs. 5.0. Then

Electricity bill $= 3.612 \times 10^{-5} \text{ x} \times 5 = \text{Rs. } 1.806 \times 10^{-4} \text{ x}$ ... (I)

But Electricity bill = Rs. 0.95 (given) ... (II)

Hence, equating the equations (I) and (II), we have

Capacity of the tank, x = **5260 litres** ... Ans.

Example 1.55 : *A d.c. motor is used to lift 2000 kg of water per minute to a height of 21 m. The pump coupled to the motor has an efficiency of 75% and the motor efficiency is 90%. Calculate the power taken in kW by d.c. motor.* **(December 2009/6 Marks)**

Solution : Mass of water lifted, m = 2000 kg.

∴ Total energy input required by the motor to lift the water

$$= \frac{m \cdot g \cdot h}{\eta_{pump} \times \eta_{motor}} = \frac{2000 \times 9.81 \times 21}{0.75 \times 0.9}$$

$$= 610400 \text{ J or Ws}$$

∴ Power taken by the d.c. motor

$$= \frac{\text{Energy input}}{\text{Time}} = \frac{610400}{1 \times 60} \text{ W}$$

$$= \mathbf{10.17 \text{ kW}} \qquad \text{... Ans.}$$

Example 1.56 : *A 230 V water heater is used to heat 10 kg of water from 20°C to 100°C in one hour. If the efficiency of operation is 90%, calculate the resistance of the heating element. Take specific heat of water 4180 J/kg.K.* **(May 2010/6 Marks)**

Solution : Mass of water to be heated = 10 kg.

$$\text{Heat energy required} = m \cdot s \cdot (t_2 - t_1) = 10 \times 4180 \times (100 - 20)$$

$$= 3344 \times 10^3 \text{ J}$$

∴ Power output of the water heater

$$= \frac{\text{Energy}}{\text{Time}} = \frac{3344 \times 10^3}{1 \times 60 \times 60} = 928.89 \text{ W}$$

∴ Rating of the water heater = Power input

$$= \frac{\text{Power output}}{\text{Efficiency}} = \frac{928.89}{0.9} = 1032.1 \text{ W}$$

∴ Resistance of the heating element,

$$R = \frac{\text{Voltage}^2}{\text{Power rating}} = \frac{230^2}{1032.1} = \mathbf{51.25 \ \Omega} \qquad \text{... Ans.}$$

Example 1.57 : *A 40 W, 200 V lamp is to be operated on 230 V, d.c. supply. Calculate the resistance to be added in series with the lamp. Also calculate the power rating of the resistance.*

(December 2010/6 Marks)

Solution : Fig. 1.71 shows the necessary circuit diagram, where R represents lamp and R' the resistance to be added in series with the lamp.

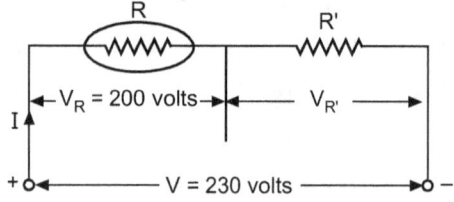

Fig. 1.71

Rated current of the lamp, $\quad I = \dfrac{P}{V} = \dfrac{40}{200} = 0.2 \text{ A}$

Now, $\quad V = V_R + V_{R'}$

∴ $\quad V_{R'} = V - V_R = 230 - 200 = 30 \text{ V}$

∴ Resistance to be added in series with the lamp,

$$R' = \frac{V_{R'}}{I} = \frac{30}{0.2} = 150 \; \Omega \qquad \text{... Ans.}$$

Further, Power rating of the resistance

$$= I^2 \times R' = (0.2)^2 \times 150 = 6 \; W \qquad \text{... Ans.}$$

Alternatively,

$$\text{Power rating of the resistance} = \frac{(V_{R'})^2}{R'} = \frac{30^2}{150} = 6 \; W \qquad \text{... Ans.}$$

Example 1.58 : *Electricity bill of raising the temperature of 5 kg water through 60°C is Rs. 2.10. Rate of electricity is Rs. 5.20 per unit. Calculate the heating efficiency. Consider specific heat of water to be 4200 J/kg.K.* **(December 2010/6 Marks)**

Solution : Energy output of the heater

= Net heat energy required for raising the temperature of the water

= m.s. $(t_2 - t_1)$ = 5 × 4200 × 60 = 1260000 J

Energy input to the heater = Energy actually utilized by the heater

$$= \frac{2.10}{5.20} = 0.4 \; kWh = 0.4 \times 1000 \times 3600 \; J = 1440000 \; J$$

∴ Heating efficiency = $\frac{\text{Energy output}}{\text{Energy input}} \times 100$

$$= \frac{1260000}{1440000} \times 100 = \mathbf{87.5\%} \qquad \text{... Ans.}$$

Example 1.59 : *A resistance R is connected in series with a parallel circuit comprising two resistances of 12 Ω and 8 Ω. The total power dissipated in the circuit is 10 W when the applied voltage across the combination is 12 V. Calculate R.* **(May 2011/6 Marks)**

Solution : Fig. 1.72 (a) shows the necessary circuit diagram and Fig. 1.72 (b) shows its simplified form. Hence,

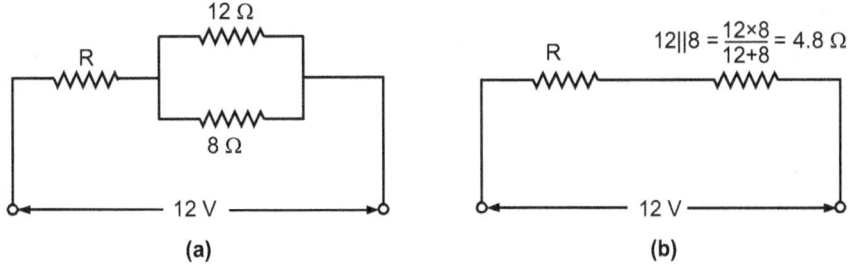

Fig. 1.72

Total resistance of the circuit, R_T = (R + 4.8) Ω

Now, Total power dissipated in the circuit,

$$P_T = \frac{V^2}{R_T}$$

$$\therefore \quad 10 = \frac{12^2}{(R + 4.8)}$$

$$\therefore \quad \text{Resistance, } R = 9.6 \, \Omega \quad \text{... Ans.}$$

Example 1.60 : *A current of 10 A flows through a resistor for 10 minutes and power dissipated by the resistor is 100 W. Find the p.d. across the resistor and energy supplied to the circuit.* **(May 2012/6 Marks)**

Solution : Given : $I = 10$ A, $t = 10$ minutes, $P = 100$ W.

Resistance of the resistor, $\quad R = \dfrac{P}{I^2} = \dfrac{100}{10^2} = 1 \, \Omega$

$\therefore$ P.D. across the resistor, $\quad V = I \cdot R = 10 \times 1 = \mathbf{10\ volts}$ ... Ans.

Energy supplied to the circuit, $\quad E = P \times t = 100 \times \dfrac{10}{60} = \mathbf{16.67\ Wh}$ ... Ans.

KIRCHHOFF'S LAWS

Example 1.61: *A parallel combination of 3 batteries with voltages and internal resistances respectively as (100 V, 0.2 Ω), (105 V, 0.5 Ω), (104 V, 0.1 Ω) is connected to a load resistance of 2 Ω. Determine currents in three batteries and the load current.* **(November 2003/8 Marks)**

Solution :

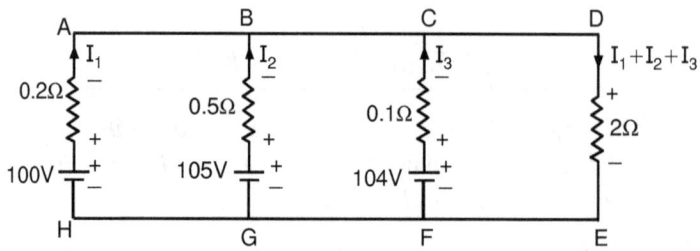

Fig. 1.73

Fig. 1.73 shows the suitably lettered circuit diagram. Assume the currents supplied by the three batteries to be I_1, I_2 and I_3 respectively. Obviously, the total current supplied to the load will be $(I_1 + I_2 + I_3)$. Now, let us select the following closed loops and apply Kirchhoff's voltage law to them.

Loop ABGHA :

$$0.5\, I_2 - 105 + 100 - 0.2\, I_1 = 0$$

$$\therefore \quad -0.2\, I_1 + 0.5\, I_2 = 5$$

Or, $\quad 2I_1 - 5I_2 = -50 \quad$ ... (I)

Loop BCFGB :

$$0.1\,I_3 - 104 + 105 - 0.5\,I_2 = 0$$

$$\therefore \quad -0.5\,I_2 + 0.1\,I_3 = -1$$

Or, $\quad 5\,I_2 - I_3 = 10 \quad \ldots \text{(II)}$

Loop CDEFC :

$$-2\,(I_1 + I_2 + I_3) + 104 - 0.1\,I_3 = 0$$

$$\therefore \quad -2\,I_1 - 2\,I_2 - 2.1\,I_3 = -104$$

Or, $\quad 2\,I_1 + 2\,I_2 + 2.1\,I_3 = 104 \quad \ldots \text{(III)}$

Let us solve the above simultaneous equations by determinant method. Here,

$$\Delta = \begin{vmatrix} 2 & -5 & 0 \\ 0 & 5 & -1 \\ 2 & 2 & 2.1 \end{vmatrix}$$

$$= 2\,(5 \times 2.1 - 2 \times -1) + 5\,(0 \times 0.2 - 2 \times -1) + 0\,(0 \times 2 - 2 \times 5)$$

$$= 35$$

$$D_1 = \begin{vmatrix} -50 & -5 & 0 \\ 10 & 5 & -1 \\ 104 & 2 & 2.1 \end{vmatrix}$$

$$= -50\,(5 \times 2.1 - 2 \times -1) + 5\,(10 \times 2.1 - 104 \times -1) + 0\,(10 \times 2 - 104 \times 5)$$

$$= 0$$

$$D_2 = \begin{vmatrix} 2 & -50 & 0 \\ 0 & 10 & -1 \\ 2 & 104 & 2.1 \end{vmatrix}$$

$$= 2\,(10 \times 2.1 - 104 \times -1) + 50\,(0 \times 2.1 - 2 \times -1) + 0\,(0 \times 104 - 10 \times 2)$$

$$= 350$$

$$D_3 = \begin{vmatrix} 2 & -5 & -50 \\ 0 & 5 & 10 \\ 2 & 2 & 104 \end{vmatrix}$$

$$= 2\,(5 \times 104 - 2 \times 10) + 5\,(0 \times 104 - 10 \times 2) - 50\,(0 \times 2 - 5 \times 2)$$

$$= 1400$$

$$\therefore \quad I_1 = \frac{D_1}{\Delta} = \frac{0}{35} = 0\ \text{A} \quad \ldots \text{Ans.}$$

$$I_2 = \frac{D_2}{\Delta} = \frac{350}{35} = 10 \text{ A} \qquad \text{... Ans.}$$

$$I_3 = \frac{D_3}{\Delta} = \frac{1400}{35} = 40 \text{ A} \qquad \text{... Ans.}$$

$$\text{Load current} = I_1 + I_2 + I_3 = 0 + 10 + 40 = 50 \text{ A} \qquad \text{... Ans.}$$

Example 1.62 : *Two batteries A and B are connected in parallel to supply a load resistance of 5 Ω. Battery A has an e.m.f. of 5 V with an internal resistance of 3 Ω and battery B has an e.m.f. of 3 V with an internal resistance of 6 Ω. Determine the current in each battery and the load resistance.* **(May 2004/8 Marks)**

Solution :

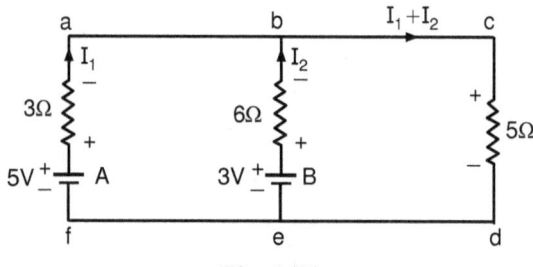

Fig. 1.74

Fig. 1.74 shows the suitably lettered circuit diagram. Assume the currents in the batteries A and B as I_1 and I_2 respectively. Then, applying Kirchhoff's current law at Junction b, the total load current will be $(I_1 + I_2)$. Now, let us select the following two loops and apply Kirchhoff's voltage law to them :

Loop abefa : $\qquad 6 I_2 - 3 + 5 - 3 I_1 = 0$

$\therefore \qquad\qquad\qquad -3 I_1 + 6 I_2 = -2$

Or, $\qquad\qquad\qquad 3 I_1 - 6 I_2 = 2 \qquad$ ... (I)

Loop bcdeb :

$\qquad\qquad\qquad -5 (I_1 + I_2) + 3 - 6 I_2 = 0$

$\therefore \qquad\qquad\qquad -5 I_1 - 11 I_2 = -3$

Or, $\qquad\qquad\qquad 5 I_1 + 11 I_2 = 3 \qquad$ ... (II)

Solving equations (I) and (II) simultaneously, we get

$$I_1 = 0.6349 \text{ A} \quad \text{and} \quad I_2 = -0.0159 \text{ A}$$

Further, $\qquad$ Load current $= I_1 + I_2 = 0.6349 - 0.0159 = 0.619 \text{ A}$

Thus,

$\qquad$ Current supplied by Battery A, $I_1 = \mathbf{0.6349 \text{ A}}$ $\qquad$ ... Ans.

$\qquad$ Current drawn by Battery B, $I_2 = \mathbf{0.0159 \text{ A}}$ $\qquad$ ... Ans.

$\qquad\qquad\qquad$ Load current $= \mathbf{0.619 \text{ A}}$ $\qquad$ ... Ans.

Example 1.63 : *A parallel combination of 3 batteries with voltages and internal resistances respectively as (100 V, 0.2 Ω), (105 V, 0.5 Ω) and (104 V, 0.1 Ω), is connected to a load resistance of 2 Ω. Determine the terminal voltages of the batteries and the load current.*

(November 2004/8 Marks)

Solution : Refer to the solution of Example 1.61 on Page 1.74 for the value of the load current. Further, since the three batteries are in parallel, they will work at the same terminal voltage. This voltage can be found by calculating the terminal voltage for any one battery. Let us select the first battery. Then,

$$\text{Terminal voltage, } V = E_1 - I_1 \cdot r_1 = 100 - 0 \times 0.2 = \mathbf{100 \ V} \quad \ldots \text{Ans.}$$

Example 1.64 : *Two batteries having e.m.fs. 10 V and 12 V with their internal resistances 0.2 Ω and 0.25 Ω are connected in parallel. This combination supplies the load of 5 Ω. Calculate the current flowing through 5 Ω resistance.* **(December 2008/8 Marks)**

Solution : Fig. 1.75 shows the suitably lettered circuit diagram.

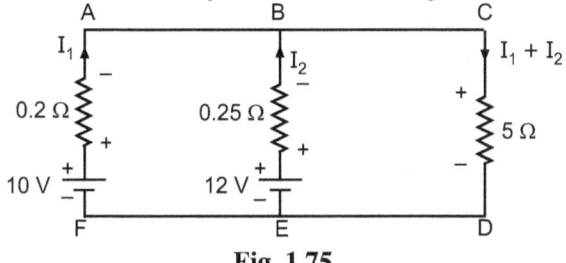

Fig. 1.75

Assume the currents in the two batteries to be I_1 and I_2 as shown in the diagram. Then applying Kirchhoff's current law at the Junction B, the total load current will be $(I_1 + I_2)$. Now, let us select the following two loops and apply Kirchhoff's voltage law to them :

Loop ABEFA : $0.25 \ I_2 - 12 + 10 - 0.2 \ I_1 = 0$

∴ $\quad -0.2 \ I_1 + 0.25 \ I_2 = 2$

Or, $\quad 0.2 \ I_1 - 0.25 \ I_2 = -2 \quad \ldots \text{(I)}$

Loop BCDEB : $-5 \ (I_1 + I_2) + 12 - 0.25 \ I_2 = 0$

∴ $\quad -5 \ I_1 - 5.25 \ I_2 = -12$

Or, $\quad 5 \ I_1 + 5.25 \ I_2 = 12 \quad \ldots \text{(II)}$

Solving the equations (I) and (II) simultaneously, we get

$$I_1 = -3.26 \text{ A and } I_2 = 5.39 \text{ A}$$

∴ Current flowing through 5 Ω resistance

$$= I_1 + I_2 = -3.26 + 5.39 = \mathbf{2.13 \ A} \quad \ldots \text{Ans.}$$

Example 1.65 : *Two batteries A and B connected in parallel supply a load resistance of 15 Ω. Battery A has an e.m.f. of 100 V and internal resistance of 1.5 Ω. Battery B has an internal resistance of 1.2 Ω. If the current flowing through 15 Ω resistance is 8.89 A, calculate the e.m.f. of battery B.* **(May 2009/8 Marks)**

Solution :

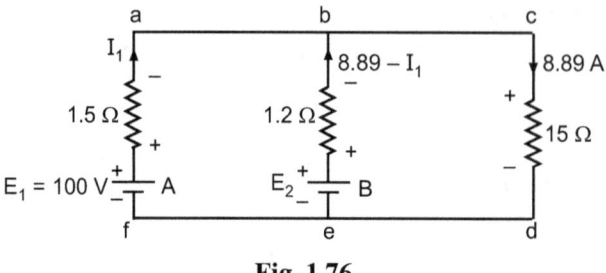

Fig. 1.76

Fig. 1.76 shows the suitably lettered circuit diagram with the assumed currents and their directions marked. Now, let us select the following two loops and apply Kirchhoff's voltage law to them :

Loop abefa :

$$1.2(8.89 - I_1) - E_2 + 100 - 1.5 I_1 = 0$$

$$\therefore \quad -2.7 I_1 - E_2 = -110.67$$

Or, $\quad 2.7 I_1 + E_2 = 110.67 \quad \ldots (I)$

Loop bcdeb :

$$-8.89 \times 15 + E_2 - 1.2(8.89 - I_1) = 0$$

$$\therefore \quad 1.2 I_1 + E_2 = 144.02 \quad \ldots (II)$$

Solving the equations (I) and (II) simultaneously, we get

E.M.F. of battery B, E_2 = **170.7 V** ... **Ans.**

Example 1.66 : *Two batteries A and B are connected in antiparallel. The combination supplies power to 10 Ω resistance when battery A has terminal e.m.f. of 50 V and an internal resistance of 1 Ω, and battery B has terminal voltage of 70 V and an internal resistance of 1 Ω. Calculate the power supplied to 10 Ω resistance.* **(December 2009/8 Marks)**

Solution :

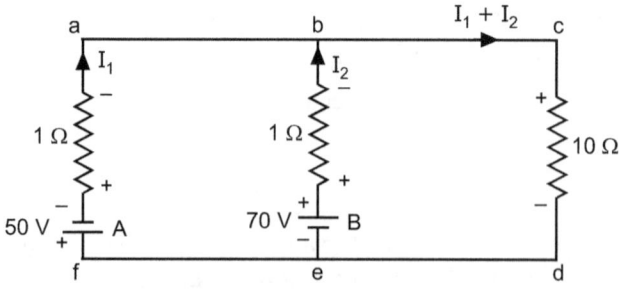

Fig. 1.77

Fig. 1.77 shows the suitably lettered circuit diagram for the given condition with the assumed currents and their directions marked. Now, let us select the following two loops and apply Kirchhoff's voltage law to them :

Loop abefa :

$$I_2 - 70 - 50 - I_1 = 0$$

$$\therefore \quad I_1 - I_2 = -120 \quad \ldots (I)$$

Loop bcdeb :

$$-10(I_1 + I_2) + 70 - I_2 = 0$$

$$\therefore \quad -10 I_1 - 11 I_2 = -70$$

Or, $\quad 10 I_1 + 11 I_2 = 70 \quad \ldots (II)$

Solving the equations (I) and (II) simultaneously, we get

$$I_1 = -59.52 \text{ A} \quad \text{and} \quad I_2 = 60.48 \text{ A}$$

∴ Current supplied to 10 Ω resistance,

$$I = I_1 + I_2 = (-59.52) + 60.48 = 0.96 \text{ A}$$

∴ Power supplied to 10 Ω resistance,

$$P = I^2 R = (0.96)^2 \times 10 = \mathbf{9.22 \text{ W}} \quad \ldots \text{Ans.}$$

Example 1.67 : *Two batteries A and B are connected in antiparallel. The e.m.fs. and internal resistances are 20 V, 1 Ω and 20 V, 1.5 Ω respectively. A resistance of 10 Ω is connected across this combination. Calculate the current flowing through 10 Ω resistance.*

(May 2010/8 Marks)

Solution : Fig. 1.78 shows the suitably lettered circuit diagram for the given condition with the assumed currents and their directions marked.

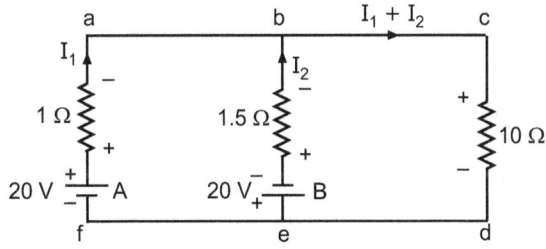

Fig. 1.78

Now, let us select the following two loops and apply Kirchhoff's voltage law to them :

Loop abefa :

$$1.5 I_2 + 20 + 20 - I_1 = 0$$

$$\therefore \quad -I_1 + 1.5 I_2 = -40$$

Or, $\quad I_1 - 1.5 I_2 = 40 \quad \ldots (I)$

Loop bcdeb :

$$-10(I_1 + I_2) - 20 - 1.5 I_2 = 0$$

$$\therefore \quad -10 I_1 - 11.5 I_2 = 20$$

Or, $\quad 10 I_1 + 11.5 I_2 = -20 \quad \ldots \text{(II)}$

Solving the equations (I) and (II) simultaneously, we get

$$I_1 = 16.23 \text{ A} \quad \text{and} \quad I_2 = -15.85 \text{ A}$$

$\therefore$ Current flowing through 10 Ω resistance,

$$I = I_1 + I_2 = 16.23 + (-15.85)$$

$$= 0.38 \text{ A} \quad \ldots \text{Ans.}$$

Example 1.68 : *Applying Kirchhoff's laws, find the potential difference between the points X and Y in the network shown in Fig. 1.79.* **(December 2011/8 Marks)**

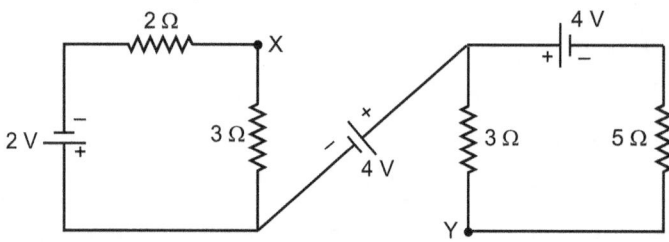

Fig. 1.79

Solution : Fig. 1.80 shows the given network with assumed loop currents marked.

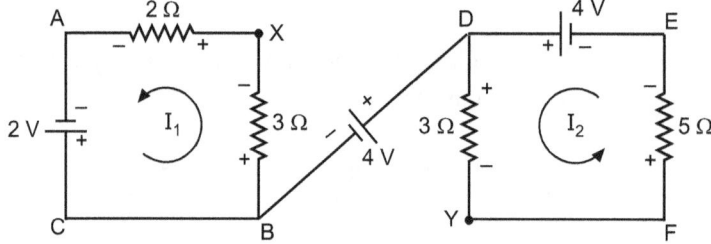

Fig. 1.80

From the above figure, it is obvious that

$$\text{Current in the Loop AXBC, } I_1 = \frac{2}{3+2} = 0.4 \text{ A}$$

$$\text{Current in the Loop DEFY, } I_2 = \frac{4}{3+5} = 0.5 \text{ A}$$

Considering the voltage rise to be positive and voltage drop to be negative, we get

$$V_{XY} = V_{XB} + V_{BD} + V_{DY} = 3 \times 0.4 + 4 - 3 \times 0.5$$

$$= 3.7 \text{ V, Y being at a higher potential than X} \quad \ldots \text{Ans.}$$

1.13 EXERCISES

1.13.1 Review Questions

1. Define work, power and energy. State their S.I. units.
2. Differentiate between the terms :
   (a) Active and passive networks, (b) Unilateral and bilateral networks,
   (c) Linear and non-linear networks.
3. Represent the following by their symbols :
   (a) Ideal and practical voltage sources, (b) Ideal and practical current sources.
4. Derive the equations for converting a constant-voltage source into a constant-current source and vice versa.
5. State and explain Kirchhoff's current and voltage laws.
6. Differentiate between mesh current and branch current. Describe the method of solving a network using mesh analysis.
7. State sequential steps in solving a network by nodal analysis.

1.13.2 Classified Theory Questions from University Papers

1. Explain the following electrical terms :
   (i) Work, (ii) Power, (iii) Energy.
   (Answer : Section 1.1.2)   **(May 2012/6 Marks)**

2. State and explain Kirchhoff's current law.
   (Answer : Section 1.7.1)   **(May 2009/4 Marks)**

3. State and explain : Kirchhoff's voltage law.
   (Answer : Section 1.7.2)   **(December 2010/3 Marks)**

4. State and explain Kirchhoff's current law and voltage law.
   (Answer : Sections 1.7.1, 1.7.2)   **(May 2011, 2012; December 2011, 2012/8 Marks)**

5. State Kirchhoff's current law and voltage law. With the help of a neat circuit diagram, explain how Kirchhoff's equations are written.
   (Answer : Sections 1.7.1, 1.7.2)   **(December 2009/8 Marks)**

6. State Kirchhoff's laws. Explain how these laws are useful to find branch currents of any circuit.
   (Answer : Sections 1.7.1, 1.7.2, 1.7.3)   **(May 2008/8 Marks)**

7. State Kirchhoff's voltage and current laws. Explain how these laws are useful to find the node voltages and branch currents in d.c. circuits.
   (Answer : Sections 1.7.1, 1.7.2, 1.7.3, 1.9)   **(May 2010/8 Marks)**

1.13.3 Examples for Practice

1. An electric iron is marked 250 V, 350 W. What current does it take and what is its hot resistance ? What is the weekly cost of using it for 30 minutes daily at 35 paise per unit ?

    (1.4 A, 178.57 Ω, 43 paise)

2. An electric kettle working on 230 V mains takes 15 minutes to bring 1 kg of water at 15°C to boiling point. Heat efficiency of the kettle is 79 per cent. Determine kW input necessary. (0.502 kW)

3. An electric furnace is used to melt 1000 kg of tin per hour. If the input to the furnace is 50 kW, find the efficiency of the furnace. Assume melting point of tin as 235°C, specific latent heat of fusion for tin as 56 kJ/kg and specific heat of tin as 235 J/kg.K. Initial temperature of the charge is 15°C. (59.83 per cent)

4. A drill is sharpened on a 100 mm diameter grinding wheel rotating at a speed of 7 revolutions per second. The tangential pressure exerted on the drill is 15 N. Calculate the work done on the drill in 30 seconds. What is the input power to the grinder motor if losses amount to 10 % ? (989.6 J, 36.66 W)

5. Find the power in kW taken by a d.c. motor driving a pump to raise 14000 litres of water per minute to a height of 30 m. The motor efficiency is 90 % and pump efficiency is 75 %. Assume 1 litre of water to have a mass of 1 kg. (101.73 kW)

6. An electric lift raises a load of 3000 kg to a height of 50 m. The balance weight has a mass of 2000 kg and the mass of an empty cage is 500 kg. The time taken for either an up or down journey is 1 minute. Calculate the current taken by 250 V d.c. motor fitted to the lift and the daily cost of energy at 50 paise per unit, if the lift makes 100 double journeys a day. Assume efficiency of installation as 60 %. (81.75 A, Rs. 34.06)

7. A car weighing 8 kN reaches the bottom of a 1 in 20 slope at a speed of 60 km/h, at which point it runs out of petrol. How far up the slope will the car ascend, if the frictional resistance to motion is 160 N per kN of its weight ? (67.45 m)

8. The average overall efficiency of a certain car is 50 %. If the car consumes 4 kg of petrol per hour of calorific value 46.89 MJ/kg, determine the power output of the engine.

    (26.05 kW)

9. An electric kettle contains 1.2 kg of water at 20°C. It takes 20 minutes to raise the temperature of the water to 100°C. Assuming the heat lost due to radiation and heating the kettle to be 60 kJ, find the current taken by the kettle from the supply of 230 V. Assume specific heat capacity of water to be 4190 J/kg-K. (1.675 A)

10. Calculate the resistance of the element used to heat 10 litres of the water from 20°C to 100°C in one hour. Efficiency of the operation is 90 % and the supply voltage is 200 V d.c. (38.69 Ω)

11. An electrically driven pump lifts 80 m^3 of water per minute through a height of 12 m. Efficiencies of motor and pump are 70 % and 80 % respectively. Calculate :

    (i) Current drawn by motor if it works on 400 V supply.

(ii) Energy consumption in kWh and cost of the energy at the rate of 75 paise/kWh, if pump operates 2 hours per day for 30 days. Assume 1 m³ of water weighs 1000 kg.

(700.73 A, 16817.4 kWh, Rs. 12613.05)

12. Calculate the time required to heat 15 litres of water from 15°C to the boiling point. The heater is operated at 230 V supply and resistance of heating element is 40 Ω. The efficiency of heater is 84 % and assume specific heat of water 4180 J/kg.K. (80 minutes)

13. Using source transformation, convert the circuit shown in Fig. 1.81 into a single voltage source in series with single resistance.

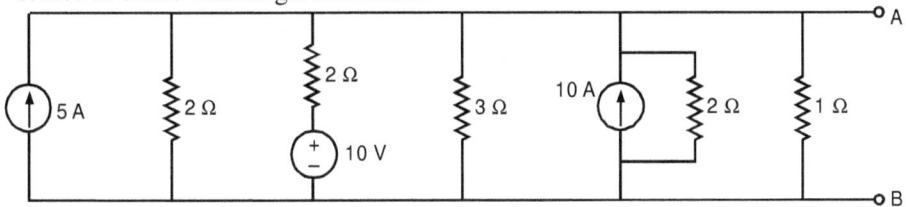

Fig. 1.81

(A source of 7 V in series with a resistance of 0.35 Ω, across the terminals A-B)

14. There are two batteries M and N connected in parallel and they supply to a load of resistance 10 Ω. Battery M has an internal resistance of 2.5 Ω and e.m.f. of 20 V. Battery N has an internal resistance of 2 Ω and an e.m.f. of 23 V. Write down the equations applying Kirchhoff's laws and calculate the current in each of the batteries and in the external load. (I_M = 0.2 A, I_N = 1.75 A, I_L = 1.95 A)

15. A battery consisting of 100 cells in series is connected in parallel to a generator. Each cell of the battery has an e.m.f. of 2 V and an internal resistance of 0.001 Ω. The armature resistance of the generator is 0.5 Ω and its e.m.f. is adjusted to 205 V. A load of resistance 10 Ω is connected across the parallel combination. Find the current supplied by the battery and the generator. (I_G = 11.65 A, I_B = 8.25 A)

16. Two batteries A and B whose e.m.fs. are 109 and 111 V and whose internal resistances are 0.25 and 1.0 Ω respectively are to be charged from a d.c. 125 V source. If for that purpose they were connected in parallel and resistance of 5 Ω was inserted between the supply and the batteries to limit the charging current, determine :

(a) The magnitude and direction of current in each battery.

(b) The current taken from the d.c. source.

(c) The power delivered by the source.

(I_A = 4 A charge, I_B = 1 A discharge, Source current = 3 A, 375 W)

17. The four arms AB, BC, CD and DA of a Wheatstone bridge network ABCD have resistances of 100, 220, 221 and 100 Ω respectively. A 2 V cell is connected between the terminals A and C and galvanometer of 200 Ω resistance between B and D. Estimate the current through the galvanometer. (5.767×10^{-6} A, from D to B)

18. In a Wheatstone bridge network ABCD, resistances AB, BC and DA are 30, 20 and 40 Ω respectively. A milliammeter of resistance 100 Ω is connected between B and D. The unknown resistance R is connected between C and D and a battery of e.m.f. 10 V is connected across A and C. Find the value of R if the ammeter indicates the passage of current of 20 mA. Also find the values of currents in different branches of the network.

$$(7.8\ \Omega,\ I_{AB} = 0.208\ A,\ I_{AD} = 0.206\ A,\ I_{BC} = 0.188\ A,\ I_{CD} = 0.226\ A,$$
Battery current = 0.414 A)

19. For the network shown in Fig. 1.82, calculate the current in the 2 Ω resistor and the currents drawn from each battery.

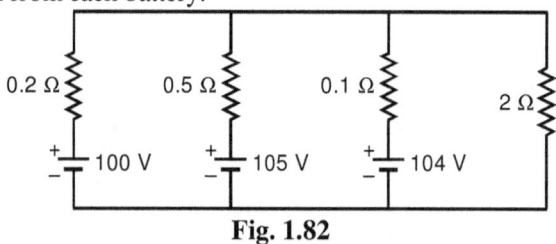

Fig. 1.82

(50 A, 0 A, 40 A, 10 A)

20. Find the currents in the 8 Ω resistors in the network shown in Fig. 1.83. (5 A, each)

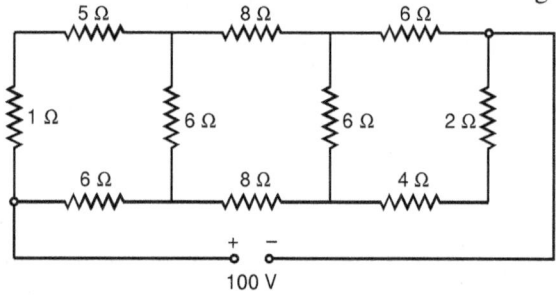

Fig. 1.83

21. Write equations for the loops marked I and II using Kirchhoff's laws for the network shown in Fig. 1.84. Solve the equations and determine the current in each of the voltage source.

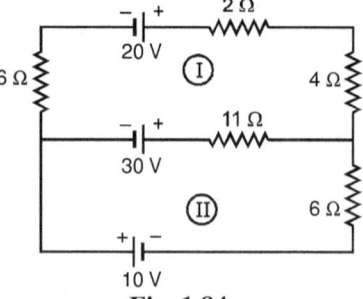

Fig. 1.84

(20 V source : 1A, discharging, 30 V source : 2 A, discharging,
10 V source : 3A, discharging)

22. For the circuit shown in Fig. 1.85, calculate :

    (i) Power output of voltage source, (ii) Voltage across the terminals A and B.

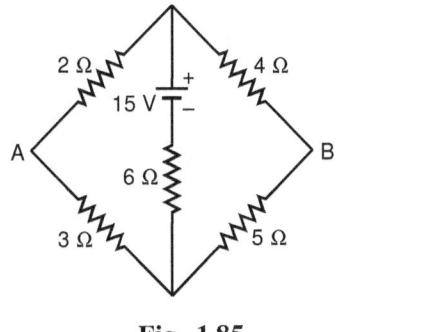

Fig. 1.85   (24.42 W, 0.2325 V)

23. Making use of loop analysis, find currents I_1, I_2 and I_3 for the network shown in Fig. 1.86. From this information, determine the power output of each voltage source.

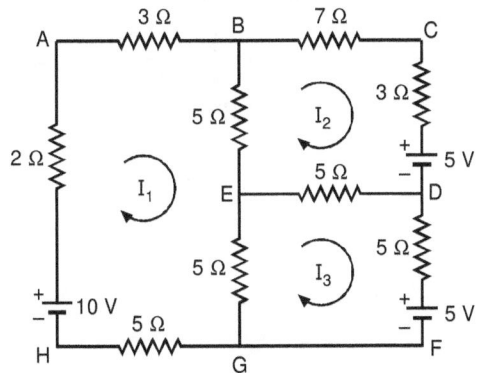

Fig. 1.86

(0.3714 A, − 0.2286 A, − 0.2858 A, 3.714 W, 1.143 W, 1.429 W)

24. Write equations for the loop currents for the network shown in Fig. 1.87. Hence, find the potential difference between the points A and B.

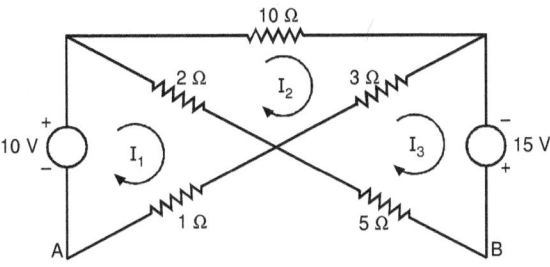

Fig. 1.87   (15.2 V)

25. Find the current in the 5 Ω resistor of network shown in Fig. 1.88 by nodal analysis.

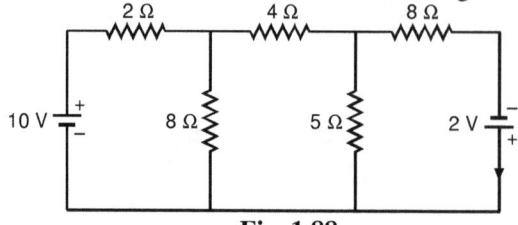

Fig. 1.88 (0.468 A)

26. In the given network shown in Fig. 1.89 below, use nodal analysis to obtain node voltages V_1, V_2 and V_3.

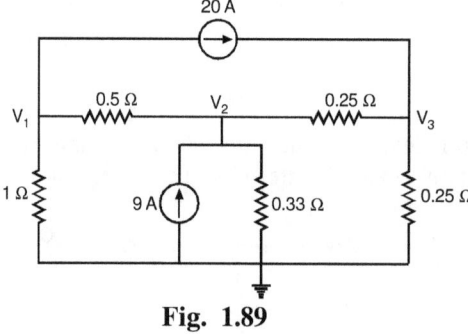

Fig. 1.89 (− 6 V, 1 V, 3 V)

CHAPTER 2

MAGNETIC CIRCUITS

2.1 INTRODUCTION

A conductor carrying a current is always surrounded all along its length by a magnetic field. This important relationship between magnetism and current electricity which was discovered by Oersted in 1820, forms the basis of electromagnetism. *Electromagnetism is the branch of engineering dealing with the magnetic effects of an electric current.* In this chapter, we shall study certain fundamentals of electromagnetism with special emphasis on magnetic circuit principles.

2.2 MAGNETISM AND ITS EFFECTS

Before we begin the study of electromagnetism, some of the common terms used in magnetism are merely summarized below, as it is assumed that students are already familiar with them.

Important Properties of the Magnet :

(i) It attracts small pieces of iron.

(ii) When freely suspended by a piece of silk fibre, it sets itself in a definite direction so that its North pole points towards the North direction and the South pole points towards the South direction.

(iii) Like magnetic poles repel and unlike poles attract each other.

Magnetic Induction : *It is the phenomenon due to which a magnet can induce magnetism in a neighbouring piece of magnetic material (say iron) without actual physical contact.*

Pole Strength : The magnitude of force exerted by one magnet on another magnet gives rise to the idea of pole strength. If under exactly identical conditions, two magnetic poles are exerting equal forces on another pole, then they are said to have equal pole strengths. Unit of pole strength is *weber* (also called *unit pole*) and it is defined *as the strength of that pole which when placed from an identical pole at a distance of 1 metre in free space experiences a force of*

$$\frac{10^7}{16\pi^2} N$$

Laws of Magnetism : The two fundamental laws of magnetism are as follows :

(i) As already mentioned previously, the first law states that like magnetic poles repel and unlike poles attract each other.

(ii) According to the second law which is proved experimentally by Coulomb, the force (F) exerted by one pole on another pole is directly proportional to the product of the pole strengths and inversely proportional to the square of the distance (d) between them. It also depends on the nature of the medium surrounding the poles, i.e.

$$F \propto \frac{m_1 m_2}{d^2} \qquad \ldots (2.1)$$

Or,
$$F = K\frac{m_1 m_2}{d^2} \qquad \ldots (2.2)$$

where m_1 and m_2 are the pole strengths. The value of the constant K depends on the nature of the surrounding medium.

Magnetic Field : *The region in the neighbourhood of a magnet within which the influence of the magnet is felt is termed as magnetic field.* Existence of the magnetic field can be very well tested with the help of a small magnetized compass needle.

Magnetic Lines of Force or Lines of Magnetic Flux : These are the imaginary lines (having no physical existence) introduced by Faraday for the pictorial representation of the distribution of a magnetic field. A line of force may be defined *as a line along which an isolated N-pole would travel if free to move in a magnetic field and it is such that the tangent at any point gives the direction of the resultant force at that point.* The mapping of the magnetic field into a series of magnetic lines of force can be done with the help of a small compass needle (Fig. 2.1).

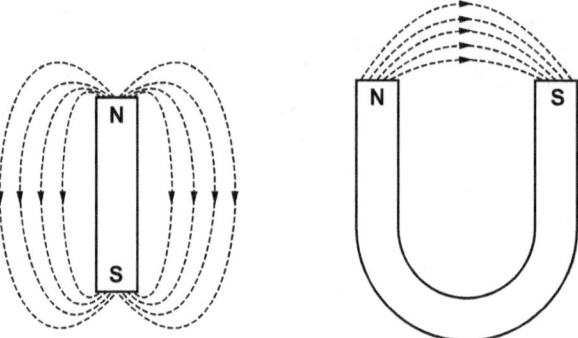

Fig. 2.1 : Magnetic lines of force

Properties of Lines of Force :

(i) Lines of force are always in the form of closed curves originating on a N-pole and terminating on a S-pole.

(ii) Lines of force never cross one another.

(iii) Parallel lines of force acting in the same direction repel one another.

(iv) Lines of force always try to contract in length and thus behave like stretched elastic threads.

(v) Magnetic lines of force always take the path of least reluctance (opposition). Materials which do not readily allow passage of flux lines are said to have a comparatively high reluctance to magnetic fields. Since air, for example, has a greater reluctance to magnetic fields than has iron, the concentration of the magnetic field becomes greater in iron than it does in air.

Magnetic Flux (ϕ) : *The total number of lines of force in any particular magnetic field is called the magnetic flux.* The unit of magnetic flux is also *weber (10^8 lines). The flux which the unit N-pole radiates out is known as one weber.*

Magnetic Flux Density (B) : *The flux per unit area (a) in a plane at right angles to the flux is known as flux density. Its unit is tesla (T).*

$$\therefore \quad B = \frac{\phi}{a} \text{ tesla} \quad \ldots (2.3)$$

Magnetic Field Strength (H) : *The force experienced by a unit North pole (i.e. N-pole with 1 weber pole strength) placed at any point in a magnetic field is known as magnetic field strength at that point.* Higher the value of this force, stronger is the field. Its direction and sense at any point is given by the direction and sense of the line of force passing through the point considered. The unit of magnetic field strength is *newtons per weber (N / Wb) or amperes per metre (A / m).*

2.3 MAGNETIC FIELD DUE TO A STRAIGHT CONDUCTOR

As already mentioned previously, a straight conductor carrying an electric current is always surrounded all along its length by a magnetic field. The lines of force are in the form of concentric circles in planes at right angles to the conductor and their direction is dependent on the direction of the current producing them. This can be very well demonstrated by passing the straight conductor through a cardboard as shown in Fig. 2.2 (a).

When iron filings are sprinkled on the cardboard, they arrange themselves in concentric circles around the current carrying conductor. The direction of the field can be found by replacing the iron filings by compass needles. Fig. 2.2 (b) illustrates the conventional representation of current carrying conductor alongwith the direction of current flowing through it and the direction of the magnetic field around it. Here, the small circle represents the conductor in section. The cross on it represents the rear view of the feathered end of an arrow and indicates a current flowing into the plane of the paper (i.e. away from the observer) in a conventional manner. On the other hand, the dot represents the tip of an arrow and indicates a current flowing out of the plane of the paper (i.e. towards the observer).

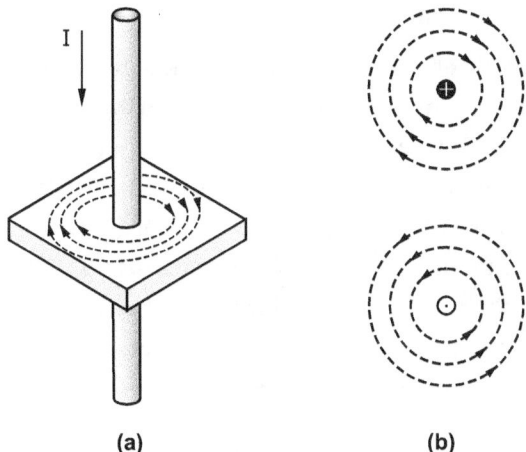

(a)   (b)

Fig. 2.2 : Magnetic field set up around a current carrying conductor

The direction of the field may be quickly determined by means of the following two rules :

(1) The Right Hand Gripping Rule : Grip the current carrying conductor in the right hand with the thumb outstretched parallel to the conductor and pointing in the direction of the current (Fig. 2.3).

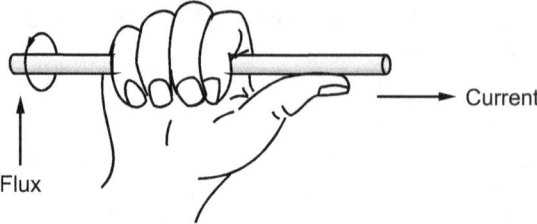

Fig. 2.3 : Right hand gripping rule

The curled fingers then point in the direction of the magnetic field around the conductor.

(2) The Corkscrew Rule : Imagine a right handed corkscrew or wood screw (Fig. 2.4) placed alongside of the current carrying conductor with its axis parallel to the conductor and tip pointing in the direction of the current flow.

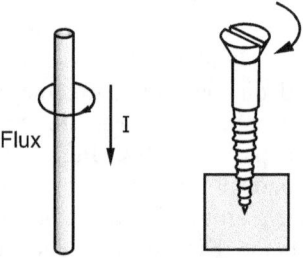

Fig. 2.4 : Corkscrew rule

Then the direction of the magnetic field is given by the direction in which the screw must be turned so as to advance it in the direction of the current.

Magnetic Field Strength of a Long Straight Conductor : Due to magnetic field in the neighbourhood of current carrying conductor, effects are produced very much like those in the vicinity of a permanent magnet i.e. the forces are exerted on magnets, iron or other current carrying conductors which are introduced in this field. It can be experimentally verified that this magnetic effect or in other words, the magnetic field strength (H) at a particular point in the space around the current carrying conductor is proportional to the current in the conductor and decreases as the distance from the conductor increases. It can also be observed that more the number of conductors, more prominent is the magnetic effect.

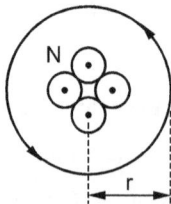

Fig. 2.5 : Magnetic field strength due to long straight conductors

The actual value of magnetic field strength (H) at a point r metres from the centre of the group of N long straight conductors each carrying a current of I amperes in the same direction (Fig. 2.5) is given by the following expression :

$$H = \frac{NI}{2\pi r} \text{ newtons/weber} \qquad \ldots (2.4)$$

The above expression gives another more convenient unit *amperes per metre (A / m)* for the magnetic field strength. It should be noted that the turns (N) is the dimensionless quantity.

2.4 FORCE ON A CURRENT CARRYING CONDUCTOR IN A MAGNETIC FIELD

It is observed that whenever a current carrying straight conductor is placed in a magnetic field, it experiences a mechanical force. This is a very important magnetic effect of an electric current as the operation of the electric motors and other electrical appliances is entirely based on this effect. The magnitude of this force is dependent on the following factors :

(i) Flux density (B) of the magnetic field in which the conductor is placed (in tesla).
(ii) Magnitude of the current (I) in the conductor (in amperes).
(iii) Active length *(l)* of the conductor (in metres). Active length is the part of the total length of the conductor which actually lies in the magnetic field.

If the conductor is at right angles to the magnetic field, then this force (F) is given by the following expression :

$$F = B I l \text{ newtons} \qquad \ldots (2.5)$$

It will be interesting to see how this force is actually produced. Fig. 2.6 shows a straight conductor carrying current in the direction towards the observer and placed in a uniform magnetic field at right angles to it.

The original field and that due to the conductor are shown in Fig. 2.6 (a). These two fields combine to form a single resultant field. It will be seen that in the region below the conductor, both the fields act in the same direction and therefore give a resultant field at any point equal to the sum of the individual fields at that point. In the region above the conductor, one field acts in the direction opposite to that of the other and so the resultant is the difference of the two fields. In general, the original field of the magnet is strengthened at the bottom of the conductor and weakened at the top. The resultant field pattern is shown in Fig. 2.6 (b). In effect, it seems as if some of the lines of force from the top region are transferred to the bottom region.

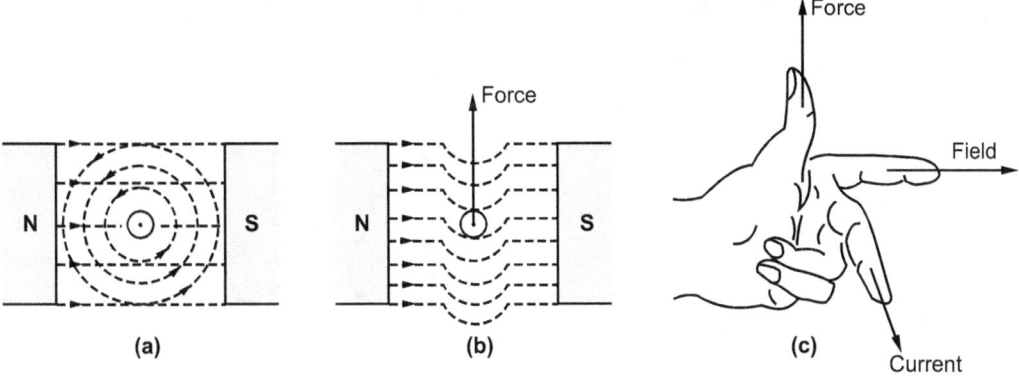

Fig. 2.6 : Force acting on a current carrying conductor placed in a magnetic field

Due to crowding, the lines of force in the lower region get stretched like rubber bands. Therefore, they try to contract and thereby push the conductor upwards. Thus, the conductor experiences a mechanical force in the upward direction.

If the direction of the current in the conductor or the direction of the main field is reversed, the direction of force exerted on the conductor is also reversed. The direction of the force can be easily found by Fleming's left hand rule.

Fleming's Left Hand Rule : Arrange the first finger, the second finger and the thumb of your left hand mutually at right angles to one another (Fig. 2.6 c). Point the first finger in the direction of the field and the second finger in the direction of the current, then the thumb will point in the direction of the force on the conductor.

On applying the above rule to the conductor which we have considered, it will be readily found that it experiences a mechanical force in the upward direction.

Example 2.1 : *A conductor carrying a current of 100 A is placed at right angles to the magnetic field of flux density of 0.5 T. Find the force acting on conductor in newtons per metre run.*

Solution : Equation (2.5) gives $F = B I l$ newtons

Here, $\quad B = 0.5 \text{ T}, \quad I = 100 \text{ A}, \quad l = 1 \text{ m}.$

Substituting these values in the above expression, we get

$$F = 0.5 \times 100 \times 1 = 50 \text{ N} \qquad \text{... Ans.}$$

2.5 MAGNETIC FIELD DUE TO A SOLENOID

When a long conductor is wound with number of turns close together to form a coil whose axial length is several times greater than the diameter of its turns, it is known as a *solenoid*. It may be air cored or wound on long tubular core of magnetic or non-magnetic material (Fig. 2.7 a).

When the current is passed through the solenoid, the magnetic field produced by it acts through the coil along its axis and in the space around the solenoid. Use of iron core intensifies the magnetic field of the solenoid. This is because when the current carrying solenoid is provided with an iron core, the core is acted upon by the original magnetic field and becomes a magnet by the process of magnetic induction. As such, it sets up magnetic lines of force of its own. These induced lines of force in the core being in the same direction as the lines of original magnetic field, in effect, the resultant field of the solenoid becomes more strong. Looking at the field pattern, it will be observed that the magnetic field of a solenoid is similar to that of a bar magnet. The polarity of the solenoid may be obtained by means of the following rules :

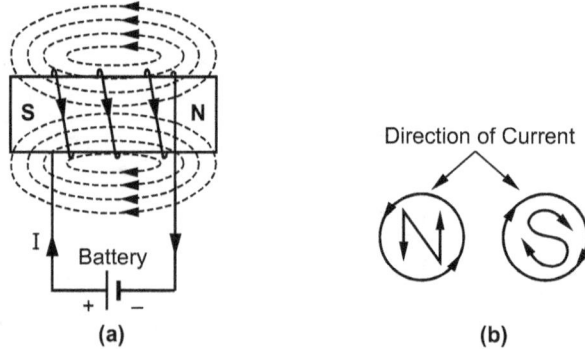

Fig. 2.7 : (a) Solenoid with iron core, (b) End rule for finding polarity

(i) **The Right Hand Gripping Rule :** Grip the solenoid in the right hand with the fingers pointing in the direction of the current. The thumb outstretched parallel to the axis of the solenoid, then points to the North pole of the solenoid.

(ii) **The End Rule :** The polarity may be determined by looking at the solenoid from any one end and noting the direction of the current (Fig. 2.7 b).

(iii) **The Corkscrew Rule :** If the axis of the right handed screw is placed along that of the solenoid and if the screw is turned in the direction of the current, it travels in the direction of the magnetic field inside the solenoid i.e. towards the North pole of the solenoid.

Magnetic Field Strength Inside a Long Solenoid : Similar to a previous case of a long straight conductor, the magnetic field strength along the axis of a solenoid is a function of the number of turns of the coil and the magnitude of the current flowing through it and is given by the following expression :

$$H = \frac{NI}{l} \text{ newtons/weber or amperes/meter} \quad \ldots (2.6)$$

where, N = Number of turns of a solenoid
I = Current in amepres
l = Length of the solenoid in meters

Truly speaking, the above expression is applicable only in the case of a solenoid which is very long in comparison with its diameter, but in actual practice, it is used for all solenoids.

2.6 PERMEABILITY

Conceptually, the current is considered to set up a magnetic field strength (H) at a particular point in the surrounding space. The magnetic field strength at any point in the magnetic field is utilized in maintaining the magnetic flux and producing the particular value of flux density (B) at that point. Thus, H is the cause and B is the effect. The flux density at any point is determined not only by the magnetic field strength at that point but also by the magnetic property of the medium known as its *permeability*. It may be defined as *the ease with which a magnetic flux permeates a medium or in other words, it is the receptiveness of the medium in having flux set up in it.*

Permeability of Free Space or Magnetic Space Constant (μ_o) : *For a magnetic field in vacuum (or free space), the ratio of flux density (in tesla) to magnetic field strength (in amperes/metre) producing that flux density is called the permeability of free space or magnetic space constant.*

It is the measure of the ease with which a magnetic flux permeates (passes through) a vacuum.

It is experimentally verified that for a magnetic field in a vacuum, flux density B_o is everywhere proportional to H and the ratio B_o/H has a constant value of $4\pi \times 10^{-7}$ (this is also true for a magnetic field in air or any other non-magnetic material). Thus, at any point in a magnetic field in a vacuum,

$$\text{Permeability of free space, } \mu_o = \frac{B_o}{H} = 4\pi \times 10^{-7} \text{ H/m} \quad \ldots (2.7)$$

$$\text{Or,} \quad B_o = \mu_o H \text{ tesla} \quad \ldots (2.8)$$

The μ_o in the above Expression (2.7) is often stated without a unit. Strictly speaking, the unit of μ_o is *henry per metre (H/m)* where henry is the unit of inductance.

Absolute Permeability (μ) : *The ratio of magnetic flux density (in tesla) in a particular medium (other than vacuum) to the magnetic field strength (in amperes / metre) at the same location producing that flux density is called the absolute permeability of that medium.* It is also taken as the measure of the ease with which a magnetic flux permeates a medium or in other words, it is a measure of the receptiveness of the medium to having flux set up in it.

Thus,

$$\text{Absolute permeability, } \mu = \frac{B}{H} \text{ henrys per metre} \qquad \ldots (2.9)$$

Or, $\qquad\qquad\qquad B = \mu \cdot H \text{ tesla} \qquad \ldots (2.10)$

The value of the absolute permeability is dependent on the nature of the medium. As already mentioned above, for the magnetic fields in air or non-magnetic materials,

$$\mu = \frac{B}{H} = \mu_o = 4\pi \times 10^{-7} \text{ H/m} \qquad \ldots (2.11)$$

For ferromagnetic materials with non-linear relation between B and H as discussed later, the value of μ is not constant but varies considerably with the degree of magnetization (i.e. with the value of H).

Relative Permeability (μ_r) : In Section (2.5), we have already seen that in the case of a solenoid if the core of iron or any other ferromagnetic material is introduced in the place of air or a former of non-magnetic material, the flux inside the coil is intensified. It means that for the same value of H, the flux density is increased.

The ratio of the flux density produced in a material to the flux density produced in a vacuum (or free space) by the same magnetic field strength under identical conditions is called the relative permeability of that material. If B is the flux density (in tesla) produced in a particular material by a certain value of H and B_o the flux density (in tesla) produced in a vacuum by the same value of H under identical conditions, then by definition,

$$\text{Relative permeability, } \mu_r = \frac{B}{B_o} \qquad \ldots (2.12)$$

But from the expressions (2.8) and (2.10), we know that

$$B_o = \mu_o \cdot H \text{ and } B = \mu \cdot H$$

$\therefore \qquad\qquad \mu_r = \dfrac{B}{B_o} = \dfrac{\mu \cdot H}{\mu_o \cdot H} = \dfrac{\mu}{\mu_o} \qquad \ldots (2.13)$

Or, $\qquad\qquad \mu = \mu_o \cdot \mu_r \text{ henrys per metre} \qquad \ldots (2.14)$

From the Expression (2.13), it is obvious that the relative permeability of the material is nothing but its absolute permeability stated as relative to the permeability of free space. It, being a ratio of absolute permeability to permeability of free space, has no units.

For air and non-magnetic materials,

$$\mu = \mu_o \quad \therefore \quad \mu_r = 1$$

On the other hand, for certain metals like nickel-iron alloys, it may be as high as 100,000.

2.7 FORCE BETWEEN TWO PARALLEL CURRENT CARRYING CONDUCTORS

When two parallel conductors carry electric currents in the same direction (Fig. 2.8 a), the lines of force of each conductor encircle the respective conductor in the same direction (corkscrew rule). The two fields in the space between the conductors being in opposite directions, neutralize each other whereas in the space outside, they assist each other. The resultant field as shown in the figure is an envelope of lines acting like stretched elastic bands tending to pull the conductors together. On the other hand, when two parallel conductors carry currents in the opposite directions, the magnetic fields due to two conductors assist each other in the space between the conductors and the resultant distribution of the flux is as shown in Fig. 2.8 (b). The lateral repulsion between the crowded lines of force between the conductors exerts a force tending to push the conductors apart. Thus, two parallel conductors carrying currents in the same direction attract each other whereas two parallel conductors carrying currents in the opposite directions repel each other.

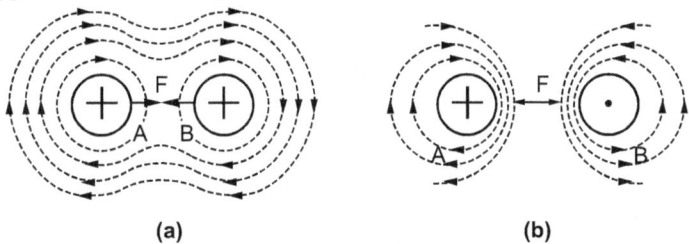

(a)   (b)

Fig. 2.8 : Magnetic fields due to two parallel current carrying conductors

To calculate the magnitude of mutual force between two parallel current carrying conductors, let the currents in the conductors A and B of Fig. 2.8 be I_1 and I_2 amperes respectively and let the distance between their centres be d metres. Then from the Expression (2.4), it follows that magnetic field strength at any point on the conductor B due to current I_1 in the conductor A is

$$H = \frac{I}{2\pi r} = \frac{I_1}{2\pi d} \text{ amperes per metre} \qquad (\because N = 1)$$

and corresponding flux density is

$$B = \mu_o \cdot H = \frac{\mu_o \cdot I_1}{2\pi d} \text{ teslas}$$

If l is the length of conductor B actually lying in this flux density, then from Expression (2.5), the force (either of attraction or repulsion) experienced by it is given by

$$F = B I_2 l = \frac{\mu_o I_1 I_2 l}{2\pi d} = \frac{4\pi \times 10^{-7} I_1 I_2 l}{2\pi d} \qquad (\because \mu_o = 4\pi \times 10^{-7})$$

$$= 2 \times 10^{-7} \frac{I_1 I_2 l}{d} \text{ newtons} \qquad \ldots (2.15)$$

Similarly, being in the magnetic field produced by conductor B, conductor A will also experience an equal force in the opposite direction.

If $I_1 = I_2 = 1$ A, d = 1 m and l = 1 m, then F = 2×10^{-7} N

Hence, we can define *one ampere current as that current which when passing through each of the two parallel straight conductors of infinite length and negligible cross-section and separated by a distance of one metre in vacuum, produces between these conductors a force of 2 x 10⁻⁷ newtons per metre length.*

Example 2.2 : *The parallel conductors A and B placed 150 mm apart in air, carry respectively the currents of 100 A and 75 A in the opposite directions. Calculate :*
  (i) *The force on each conductor per metre length.*
  (ii) *The magnetic field strength at a point C which is 100 mm from conductor A and 50 mm from conductor B.*

Solution : From the Expression (2.15), force between two parallel current carrying conductors is given by

$$F = 2 \times 10^{-7} \frac{I_1 I_2 l}{d} \text{ newtons}$$

Here, $I_1 = 100$ A, $I_2 = 75$ A, $l = 1$ m and $d = 150 \times 10^{-3}$ m

$$\therefore \quad F = 2 \times 10^{-7} \times \frac{100 \times 75 \times 1}{150 \times 10^{-3}}$$

$$= \mathbf{0.01 \text{ N/m}} \quad \ldots \text{ Ans.}$$

Now, from Expression (2.4), the magnetic field strength at any point r metres from the centre of the current carrying conductor is given by

$$H = \frac{I}{2\pi r} \text{ A/m} \quad (\because N = 1)$$

Hence, the magnetic field strength at a point C due to the current of 100 A in conductor A is

$$H_{CA} = \frac{100}{2\pi \times 100 \times 10^{-3}} = 159.16 \text{ A/m}$$

Similarly, the magnetic field strength at point C due to the current of 75 A in conductor B is

$$H_{CB} = \frac{75}{2\pi \times 50 \times 10^{-3}} = 238.73 \text{ A/m}$$

Since the currents in the two conductors flow in the opposite directions, both magnetic field strengths at C act in the same direction. Therefore, the resultant magnetic field strength at C is given by

$$H_C = H_{CA} + H_{CB} = 159.16 + 238.73$$

$$= \mathbf{397.89 \text{ A/m}} \quad \ldots \text{ Ans.}$$

2.8 MAGNETIC CIRCUITS

We have seen that electric circuit is the path provided for electric current. On similar lines, the magnetic circuit can be defined as *the closed path traversed by the magnetic flux.* In the electrical circuit, various electrical quantities like current, e.m.f. and resistance can be easily calculated with the help of simple Ohm's law. In magnetic circuit also, it is possible to determine the values of different magnetic quantities associated with the circuit with the help of simple quantitative relations existing between them. Now, let us study these quantities and quantitative relations existing between them. For that, consider the simple magnetic circuit shown in Fig. 2.9.

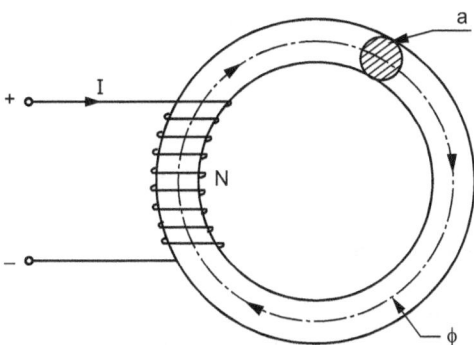

Fig. 2.9 : Simple magnetic circuit

The circuit consists of an iron ring of cross-sectional area 'a' square metres and mean circumference (length of the mean magnetic path) 'l' metres. A coil of 'N' turns is wound on it.

Let,
$\quad$ I = Current flowing through the coil (in amperes)
$\quad \mu, \mu_r$ = Absolute and relative permeabilities of the magnetic material of the ring.

Then, as seen in the Section (2.5), magnetic field strength inside the solenoid will be,
$$H = \frac{NI}{l} \text{ amperes/metre}$$

Now using the Equation (2.10), the flux density in the ring will be given by
$$B = \mu \cdot H = \mu_o \cdot \mu_r H \text{ tesla}$$

Substituting the value of H in the above expression, we get
$$B = \frac{\mu_o \mu_r NI}{l} \text{ tesla}$$

$\therefore$ Total flux in the ring, $\phi = B \cdot a$
$$= \frac{\mu_o \mu_r N I a}{l} \text{ webers}$$

Or,
$$\phi = \frac{NI}{\frac{l}{(\mu_o \mu_r a)}} \text{ webers} \qquad \ldots (2.16)$$

In the above expression, the term 'NI' is known as *magnetomotive force (M.M.F.)* and the term, $\frac{l}{(\mu_o \mu_r a)}$ is called the *reluctance* of the magnetic circuit.

$\therefore \qquad \text{Flux} = \frac{\text{M.M.F.}}{\text{Reluctance}} \qquad \ldots (2.17)$

The above expression which is known as Ohm's law of magnetic circuit, is quite similar to the following expression for electric circuit.
$$\text{Current} = \frac{\text{E.M.F.}}{\text{Resistance}}$$

Obviously, the quantities m.m.f. and reluctance in the magnetic circuit are analogous to the quantities e.m.f. and resistance in an electric circuit. The significance of these and other quantities associated with the magnetic circuit will now be discussed in the following section.

2.8.1 Quantities Associated with a Magnetic Circuit

Magnetomotive Force (M.M.F., also F) : We know that in an electric circuit, electric current is due to the presence of an electromotive force. Similarly, in the magnetic circuit, it can be said that the magnetic flux is due to the presence of magnetomotive force. This magnetomotive force which produces or tends to produce the flux in the magnetic circuit is given by the product of turns on the magnetizing coil (N) and the current flowing in the coil (I) in amperes i.e.

$$\text{M.M.F.} = NI \text{ amperes} \qquad \ldots (2.18)$$

It should be noted that N being a dimensionless number, unit for magnetomotive force is an *ampere (A)*. However, an ampere of m.m.f. is quite different from the current ampere.

The magnetomotive force is usually defined as *the work done in joules on a unit magnetic pole in taking it once round a closed magnetic circuit.*

Reluctance (S) : Reluctance is *the resistance offered by the material to the passage of magnetic flux through it* and corresponds to resistance in the electric circuit. Reluctance is directly proportional to the length of the magnetic circuit (l) and inversely proportional to its cross-sectional area (a) and the relative permeability (μ_r). It is given by the expression :

$$\text{Reluctance, S} = \frac{l}{(\mu_0 \mu_r a)} \text{ amperes/weber} \qquad \ldots (2.19)$$

where 'l' is in metres and 'a' is in square metres. From the Equation (2.16), it is obvious that

$$\text{Reluctance, S} = \frac{\text{M.M.F.}}{\phi}$$

Since m.m.f. is measured in amperes and flux in webers, the unit for reluctance is *ampere per weber (A / Wb)*.

Permeance : The permeance of the magnetic circuit is the reciprocal of its reluctance and may be defined as *that property of the magnetic circuit due to which it permits the passage of magnetic flux through it.* It is analogous to conductance in an electric circuit. Obviously, its unit is *weber per ampere (Wb / A)*. Thus :

$$\text{Permeance} = \frac{1}{\text{Reluctance}} \text{ webers / ampere} \qquad \ldots (2.20)$$

Reluctivity : It is the specific reluctance and corresponds to resistivity or specific resistance in the electric circuit.

2.8.2 Comparison of Magnetic and Electrical Circuits

From the above discussion, it is clear that the magnetic circuit resembles the electric circuit in many ways (Figs. 2.10 a and b).

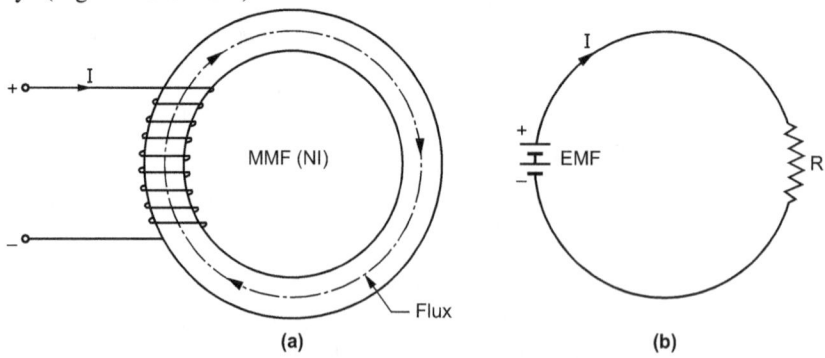

Fig. 2.10 : (a) Magnetic circuit, (b) Electric circuit

A very close comparison as given below can be made between the various electric and magnetic quantities and their relationships. Such a comparison is very useful in developing conceptual understanding about the magnetic circuits.

Magnetic Circuit	Electrical Circuit
Similarities	
(i) Magnetic circuit is the path for magnetic flux.	Electric circuit is the path for electric current.
(ii) M.M.F. (ampere)	E.M.F. (volt)
(iii) Magnetic flux, ϕ (weber)	Electric current, I (ampere)
(iv) Reluctance, S (A/Wb) $$S = \frac{1}{\mu_o \mu_r} \times \frac{l}{a}$$	Resistance, R (ohm) $$R = \rho \frac{l}{a}$$
(v) $\phi = \dfrac{M.M.F.}{S}$	$I = \dfrac{E.M.F.}{R}$
(vi) Flux density, B (T) $$B = \frac{\phi}{a}$$	Current density, δ (A/m^2) $$\delta = \frac{I}{a}$$
(vii) Permeance $= \dfrac{1}{S}$	Conductance $= \dfrac{1}{R}$
(viii) Permeability	Conductivity
Dissimilarities	
(i) With the application of M.M.F., the flux is set up in the magnetic circuit. It does not flow in the sense in which an electric current flows.	With the application of E.M.F., current actually flows in the electric circuit as the electrons drift or physically move.
(ii) Initially, energy is needed only for creating the flux in the magnetic circuit. Once the magnetic flux is set up, no further supply of energy is required for maintaining that flux.	Energy is continuously required to maintain the flow of current in an electric circuit.
(iii) The permeability of magnetic material varies over wide limits depending on the flux density. Reluctance is a function of permeability. Hence, the reluctance of a magnetic circuit may also vary over wide limits with variations in flux density. Over normal working range, it is little affected by changes in temperature.	In an electric circuit, resistance is almost constant under steady temperature conditions and is independent of magnitude of current flowing through it. However, it may be affected appreciably by changes in temperature.
(iv) As there is no known insulator for magnetic flux, it is impossible to confine all the flux to one path.	It is possible to confine the electric current to a definite path using insulation.

2.8.3 Magnetization Curves

Consider the test piece of the magnetic material made up in the form of a ring (C) with a cross-section 'a' square metres and a mean length of magnetic path 'l' metres. Let the ring be wound uniformly with N turns of insulated wire. Connect the terminals of the winding to a battery (E) through a variable resistance (R) as shown in Fig. 2.11.

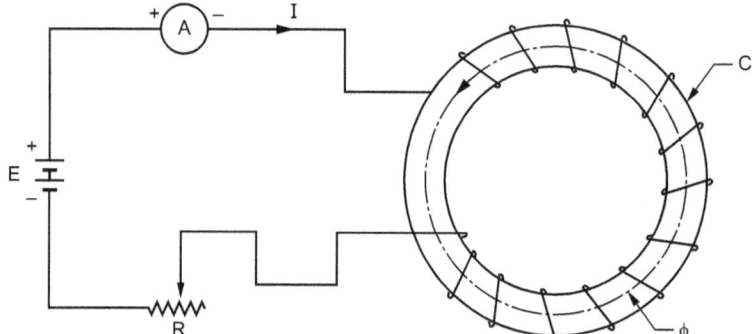

Fig. 2.11 : Determination of the magnetization curve for the magnetic material

Gradually reduce the resistance R so as to increase the current in the winding from zero to some maximum value. Measure the flux (ϕ) for different values of the exciting current (I) by means of some special instruments like flux meter or ballistic galvanometer (not shown). Plot the values of flux density, B $\left(\text{given by } \dfrac{\phi}{a}\right)$ against corresponding values of the magnetic field strength H $\left(\text{given by } \dfrac{NI}{l}\right)$. Then a graph as shown in Fig. 2.12 (b) is obtained.

This graph between flux density (B) and magnetic field strength (H) for the magnetic material is called its magnetization or B-H curve.

It has already been mentioned previously that in air and all other non-magnetic materials, the magnetic flux density is found to be always directly proportional to the magnetic field strength responsible for producing it. Therefore, obviously, the magnetization curve is a straight line passing through the origin (Fig. 2.12 a). That is not the case with magnetic materials. The typical magnetization curve for the magnetic material shown in Fig. 2.12 (b) clearly indicates the non-linear relation between the flux density and the magnetic field strength.

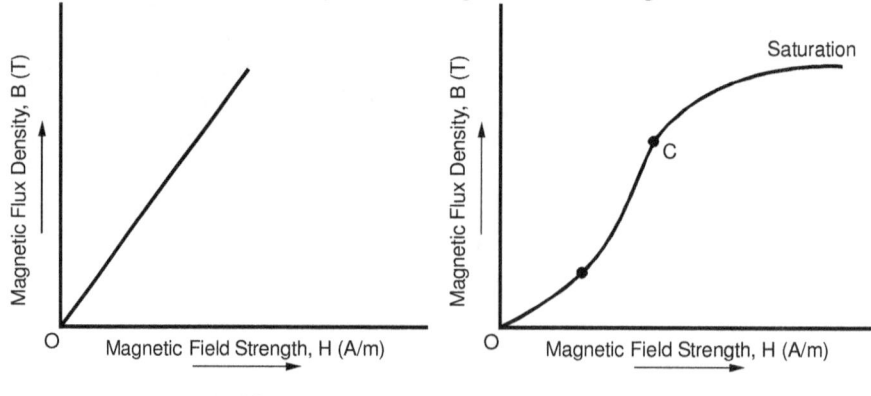

(a)   (b)

**Fig. 2.12 : Typical magnetization curves for
(a) Non-magnetic material, (b) Magnetic material**

At very low values of the magnetic field strength, the flux density at first does not increase rapidly as represented by an initial bend in the curve. Following this initial bend, the flux density increases rapidly as the magnetic field strength is increased until the curve again bends over. The point C where this bend in the curve is pronounced is known as *knee* of the B-H curve.

Beyond this knee, the increase in flux density is less marked. Ultimately, increasing the magnetic field strength makes very little change in the flux density and the magnetic material is said to be *saturated*. The term magnetic saturation is only relative, it means simply that to produce small increase in the flux density, an altogether disproportionately large increase in magnetic field strength is necessary. All magnetic materials exhibit this phenomenon of magnetic saturation. The magnetization curves are, therefore, often called saturation curves.

Magnetization Curve and Relative Permeability :

Since,
$$B = \mu_o \mu_r H$$
$$\mu_r = \frac{B}{\mu_o H} \quad \ldots (2.21)$$

The μ_o in the above expression being a constant having the value of $4\pi \times 10^{-7}$, it is obvious that the slope of B-H curve at a particular point decides the value of the relative permeability of the magnetic material corresponding to the flux density given by the ordinate at that point. Steeper the slope of the magnetization curve, greater is the relative permeability. Using the relationship given by Equation (2.21), relative permeability may be plotted as a function of flux density as shown in Fig. 2.13.

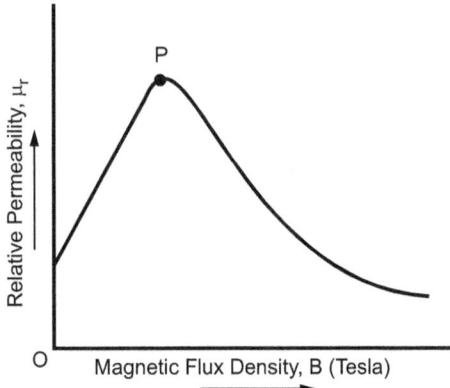

Fig. 2.13 : Permeability characteristic of the magnetic material

The graph shows how the relative permeability actually varies with the flux density. Starting from a comparatively modest value at B = 0, the relative permeability increases to a maximum at point P. Beyond this point, it falls off fairly rapidly as the material saturates, as shown.

In addition to the flux density, relative permeability depends upon the quality of the magnetic material and the mechanical and heat treatments to which it is subjected. In general, lesser the impurities (like sulphur, carbon and phosphorus) in the iron, better is its permeability.

Practical Importance of Magnetization Curves : The magnetic properties of iron, steel and their alloys are generally shown by means of magnetization curves. The permeability curves of the magnetic materials can also be derived from their magnetization curves as already seen above. All these curves are most useful in making magnetic calculations in the design or analysis of the magnetic circuits. For example, the computation of the magnetomotive force necessary to produce some desired value of flux is generally made using magnetization curves. These curves also help in selecting the magnetic material for a particular application.

2.8.4 Series Magnetic Circuits

In practice, a magnetic circuit may consist of several parts of different magnetic materials with different lengths, cross-sectional areas and permeabilities. Such a circuit is known as *composite magnetic circuit*. In a composite magnetic circuit, when the various parts are connected one after the other in such a way that they form a chain, it is called a *series magnetic circuit*. Naturally, upon providing the magnetomotive force, the same flux is established through each part of a series magnetic circuit. Fig. 2.14 (a) shows a series magnetic circuit consisting of three parts A, B and C of different magnetic materials and Fig. 2.14 (b) shows the equivalent electric circuit.

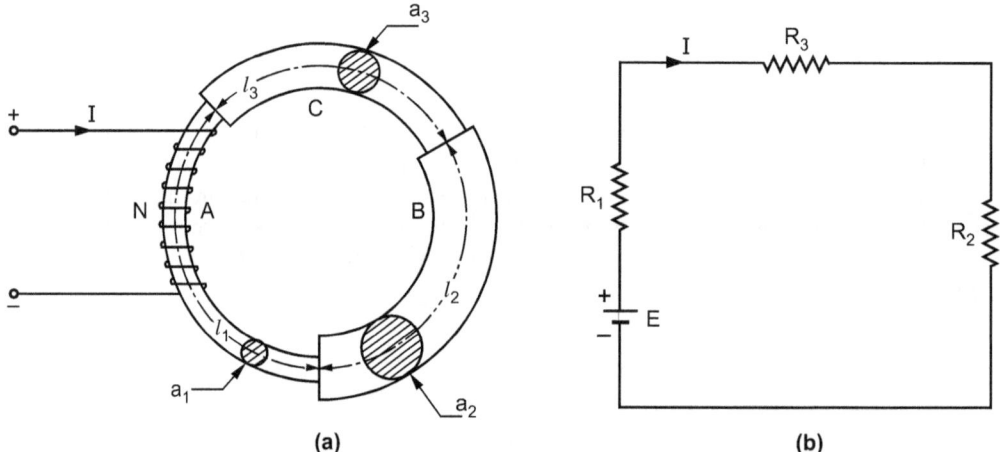

Fig. 2.14 : (a) Series magnetic circuit, (b) Equivalent electric circuit

Let l_1, l_2 and l_3 be the lengths, a_1, a_2 and a_3 be the cross-sectional areas and μ_{r1}, μ_{r2} and μ_{r3} be the relative permeabilities of the parts A, B and C respectively. If S_1, S_2 and S_3 are the reluctances of these three parts, then by Equation (2.19),

$$S_1 = \frac{l_1}{\mu_0 \mu_{r1} a_1}$$

$$S_2 = \frac{l_2}{\mu_0 \mu_{r2} a_2}$$

and

$$S_3 = \frac{l_3}{\mu_0 \mu_{r3} a_3}$$

Let the flux passing in the different components of the magnetic circuit be ϕ webers when the magnetomotive force (F) is supplied by the coil of N turns carrying the current of I amperes as shown.

If F_1, F_2 and F_3 be the m.m.fs. for the three parts, then obviously,

$$\text{Total M.M.F., } F = F_1 + F_2 + F_3 \quad \ldots (2.22)$$

$$= \phi S_1 + \phi S_2 + \phi S_3 \quad \left(\because \text{Flux} = \frac{\text{M.M.F.}}{\text{Reluctance}} \right)$$

But

$$F = \phi S \quad \ldots (2.23)$$

where S is equivalent of the three reluctances in series.

Hence,

$$\phi S = \phi S_1 + \phi S_2 + \phi S_3$$

Dividing each term by ϕ, we get

$$S = S_1 + S_2 + S_3 \qquad \ldots (2.24)$$

Or, substituting values of S_1, S_2 and S_3,

$$S = \frac{l_1}{\mu_o \mu_{r1} a_1} + \frac{l_2}{\mu_o \mu_{r2} a_2} + \frac{l_3}{\mu_o \mu_{r3} a_3} \qquad \ldots (2.25)$$

From the various results obtained above, it will be readily seen that these results are much on the same lines as the corresponding results for the series electric circuit. They can be summarized as below :

(i) The same flux (ϕ) is established through each part.

(ii) The total m.m.f. (F) is equal to the sum of the individual m.m.fs for the various parts i.e.

$$F \text{ (given by N.I)} = F_1 + F_2 + F_3$$

(iii) The equivalent reluctance of number of reluctances joined in series is equal to the sum of the values of the individual reluctances i.e.

$$S = S_1 + S_2 + S_3$$

Computation of Total M.M.F. for Series Magnetic Circuits : We know that in any magnetic circuit, following relation exists between flux, m.m.f. and reluctance.

$$\text{Flux} = \frac{\text{M.M.F.}}{\text{Reluctance}}$$

Therefore, the general expression for total magnetomotive force (given by N.I) necessary to establish a flux ϕ in a series magnetic circuit similar to that considered in Fig. 2.14, can be stated as follows :

$$\begin{aligned}
\text{Total M.M.F.} &= \text{Flux} \times \text{Total reluctance} \\
&= \phi S \\
&= \phi (S_1 + S_2 + S_3) \qquad \ldots (2.26)
\end{aligned}$$

Substituting the values of S_1, S_2 and S_3, this expression can be further modified as

$$\begin{aligned}
\text{Total M.M.F.} &= \phi \left(\frac{l_1}{\mu_o \cdot \mu_{r1} a_1} + \frac{l_2}{\mu_o \cdot \mu_{r2} a_2} + \frac{l_3}{\mu_o \cdot \mu_{r3} a_3} \right) \\
&= \frac{B_1}{\mu_o \cdot \mu_{r1}} \times l_1 + \frac{B_2}{\mu_o \cdot \mu_{r2}} \times l_2 + \frac{B_3}{\mu_o \cdot \mu_{r3}} \times l_3 \qquad \left(\because B = \frac{\phi}{a} \right) \\
&= H_1 l_1 + H_2 l_2 + H_3 l_3 \qquad \left(\because H = \frac{B}{\mu_o \mu_r} \right) \quad \ldots (2.27)
\end{aligned}$$

where B_1, B_2 and B_3 are the flux densities and H_1, H_2 and H_3 are the corresponding magnetic field strengths in the three parts A, B and C respectively.

Thus, if the B-H curves for the different materials are available, then, after reading the values of H corresponding to the various flux densities from these curves, total magnetomotive force can be easily calculated using the Expression (2.27). This method of magnetic calculations is of more practical importance in comparison with that using reluctances (refer to Equation 2.26).

The usual steps followed to find the total m.m.f. for a series magnetic circuit are as follows :

(i) Find the magnetic field strength (H) for each part of the circuit using the relation

$$H = \frac{B}{\mu_o \mu_r}$$ or from the B-H curve for the magnetic material as discussed above.

(ii) Calculate the m.m.f. for each part by using the expression, M.M.F. $= H \times l$.

(iii) Finally, calculate the total m.m.f. for the entire magnetic circuit by adding m.m.f.s for the various parts. Thus,

$$\text{Total M.M.F.} = H_1 l_1 + H_2 l_2 + H_3 l_3 + \ldots$$

2.8.5 Magnetic Leakage and Fringing

In many electromagnetic devices like generators, motors, instruments, etc. their magnetic circuits have an air path or air gap in order that the magnetic flux may be utilized to produce the desired effect. For example, in the instruments like ammeters, voltmeters, etc., the mechanical force required by the operating mechanism may be produced by keeping a piece of iron or a current carrying coil in the magnetic flux passing through the air gap. Therefore, this flux in the air gap which is actually utilized for various purposes depending upon the application is known as *useful flux*.

Even though it is desired that all the flux produced by the magnetizing coil should pass through the air gap where it is to be used, such an ideal condition is never achieved in actual practice. A part of the total flux always leaks out taking short paths partly through air surrounding the iron path and remote from the air gap. This is obviously because the air is not a perfect magnetic insulator. This flux which is not following the intended path for it (i.e. through the air gap) is known as *leakage flux*. Since the leakage flux is not passing through the air gap, it cannot be utilized for the desired purpose. Fig. 2.15 shows useful and leakage fluxes in the case of an iron ring with an air gap.

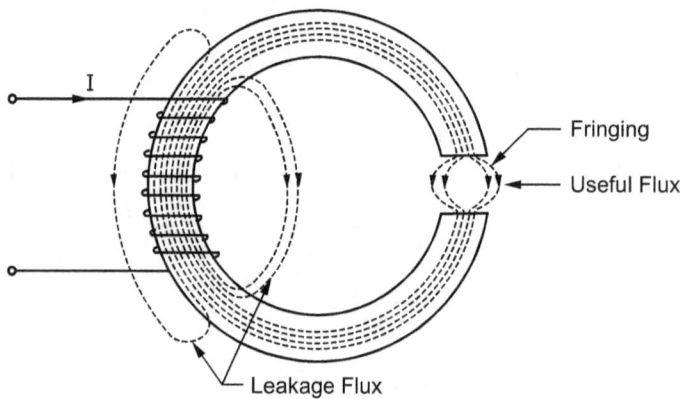

Fig. 2.15 : Magnetic leakage and fringing

The total flux produced by the magnetizing coil is thus the sum of the useful and leakage fluxes.

The ratio of total flux to useful flux is called *Hopkinson's leakage co-efficient* or *leakage factor* and it is denoted by the letter λ. Thus,

$$\text{Leakage co-efficient, } \lambda = \frac{\text{Total flux}}{\text{Useful flux}} \qquad \ldots (2.28)$$

For electrical machines, the value of leakage co-efficient ranges from 1.1 to 1.25. Magnetic leakage is always undesirable for all the electrical appliances because it increases their weight and cost of manufacture.

The parallel lines of force having the same sense experience mutual lateral forces of repulsion while crossing an air gap. Due to this property of lines of force, the useful flux in the air gap always has a tendency to bulge out (spread out) at the edges of the air gap as shown in Fig. 2.15. This effect is known as *fringing*. Fringing increases the effective cross-sectional area of the gap and thereby reduces the flux density in the air gap. Fringing, magnetic leakage and total reluctance of the magnetic circuit can be reduced by making the air gap as narrow as possible.

Example 2.3 : *An iron ring of mean circumference 80 cm is uniformly wound with 500 turns of wire. Calculate the value of flux density that a current of 1 A would produce in the ring. Assume relative permeability of iron to be equal to 1400.*

Solution : Since, magnetic field strength, $H = \dfrac{NI}{l}$ amperes / metre

with $\qquad N = 500, \ I = 1 \text{ A} \ \text{ and } \ l = 80 \times 10^{-2} \text{ m}$

$$H = \dfrac{500 \times 1}{80 \times 10^{-2}} = 625 \text{ A/m}$$

∴ $\qquad B = \mu_o \mu_r H$

$\qquad\qquad = 4\pi \times 10^{-7} \times 1400 \times 625$

$\qquad\qquad = \mathbf{1.1 \text{ T}}$ ... Ans.

Example 2.4 : *A magnetic circuit has uniform cross-sectional area of 5 cm² and a mean length of 80 cms. The data of B-H curve for the material is given below :*

H (A/m)	100	200	300	400	500	600
B (T)	0.76	1.1	1.23	1.3	1.34	1.37

Calculate the total m.m.f. required to produce a flux density of 1.2 T and also the relative permeability of the material at this density.

Solution : Using the data of B-H curve, we get

$\qquad\qquad H = 277 \text{ A/m for } B = 1.2 \text{ T}$

∴ $\qquad$ Total M.M.F. $= H \times l$

$\qquad\qquad\qquad = 277 \times 80 \times 10^{-2}$

$\qquad\qquad\qquad = \mathbf{222 \text{ A}}$ ... Ans.

Also, since $\qquad B = \mu_o \mu_r H$

$$\mu_r = \dfrac{B}{\mu_o \cdot H} = \dfrac{1.2}{4\pi \times 10^{-7} \times 277}$$

$\qquad\qquad = \mathbf{3447}$ ... Ans.

Example 2.5 : *A flux density of 1.2 T is required in 3 mm air gap of an electromagnet wound with 500 turns of wire and having an iron path of 125 cm. Calculate the current required, assuming a relative permeability of 1000 for the iron and neglecting the leakage and fringing.*

Solution :

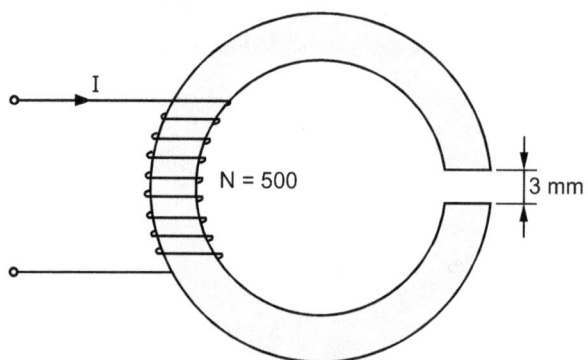

Fig. 2.16 : Magnetic circuit, Example 2.5

For Air Gap :

$$H = \frac{B}{\mu_o \mu_r} = \frac{1.2}{4\pi \times 10^{-7} \times 1} = 95.49 \times 10^4 \text{ A/m}$$

$$l = 3 \text{ mm} = 3 \times 10^{-3} \text{ m}$$

∴ M.M.F. required = $H \times l = 95.49 \times 10^4 \times 3 \times 10^{-3}$

= 2864.70 A

For Iron Path :

$$H = \frac{B}{\mu_o \mu_r} = \frac{1.2}{4\pi \times 10^{-7} \times 1000} = 954.93 \text{ A/m}$$

$$l = 125 \text{ cm} = 1.25 \text{ m}$$

∴ M.M.F. required = $H \times l = 954.93 \times 1.25$

= 1193.66 A

∴ Total M.M.F. required = NI = 2864.70 + 1193.66

= 4058.36 A

∴ $I = \dfrac{4058.36}{500} = \mathbf{8.12 \text{ A}}$ ... **Ans.**

Example 2.6 : *A magnetic circuit has effective iron length of 100 cm and an air gap of 2 mm. It is wound with 800 turns. If the relative permeability of iron is 1200, find the flux density in the air gap when the winding carries a current of 1 A. Neglect leakage and fringing.*

Solution :

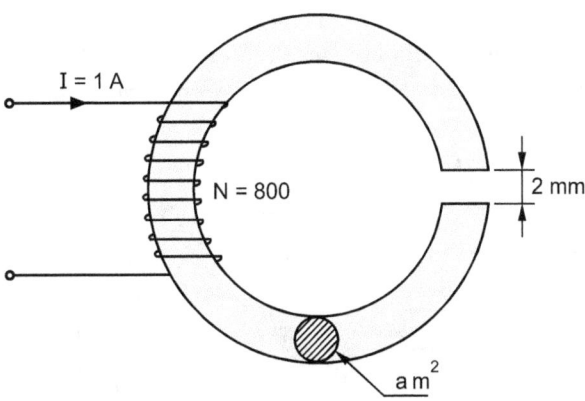

Fig. 2.17 : Magnetic circuit, Example 2.6

Let 'a' be the cross-sectional area of the magnetic circuit in m². We know that

$$\text{Reluctance, } S = \frac{l}{\mu_o \mu_r a}$$

Therefore, substituting the values of various quantities for iron part and an air gap in the above expression, we get

$$\text{Reluctance of iron part, } S_i = \frac{1}{4\pi \times 10^{-7} \times 1200 \times a}$$

$$= \frac{663.15}{a} \text{ A/Wb}$$

$$\text{Reluctance of an air gap, } S_g = \frac{2 \times 10^{-3}}{4\pi \times 10^{-7} \times 1 \times a}$$

$$= \frac{1591.55}{a} \text{ A/Wb}$$

∴ $\quad$ Total reluctance, $S = S_i + S_g$

$$= \frac{663.15}{a} + \frac{1591.55}{a}$$

$$= \frac{2254.7}{a} \text{ A/Wb}$$

Now, $\quad$ M.M.F. provided $= NI = 800 \times 1 = 800$ A

∴ $\quad$ Flux, $\phi = \dfrac{\text{M.M.F.}}{S} = \dfrac{800 \times a}{2254.7}$

$$= 0.3548 \, a \text{ Wb}$$

∴ $\quad$ Flux density, $B = \dfrac{\phi}{a} = \dfrac{0.3548 \, a}{a}$

$$= \mathbf{0.3548 \text{ T}} \quad \text{... Ans.}$$

Example 2.7 : *A soft iron ring of 25 cm mean diameter and circular cross-section of 5 cm diameter is wound with a magnetizing coil. A current of 4 A flowing in the coil produces a flux of 2.5 mWb in the air gap which is 2.5 mm wide. Taking μ_r to be 1000 at this flux density and allowing for a leakage co-efficient of 1.2, find the number of turns on the coil.*

Solution :

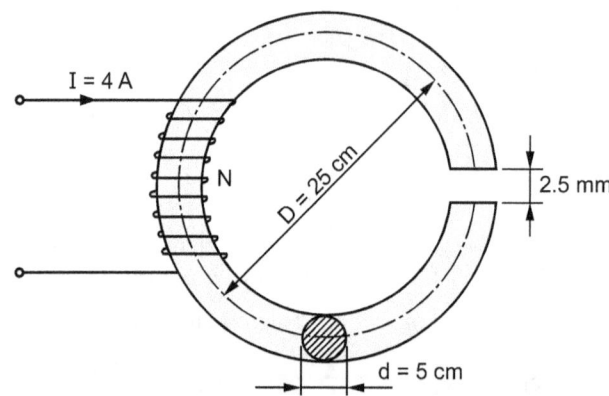

Fig. 2.18 : Magnetic circuit, Example 2.7

For Air Gap :

$$a = \frac{\pi}{4} d^2 = \frac{\pi}{4} \times 5^2 = 19.64 \text{ cm}^2$$

$$\phi = 2.5 \text{ mWb} = 2.5 \times 10^{-3} \text{ Wb}$$

$$\therefore \quad B = \frac{\phi}{a} = \frac{2.5 \times 10^{-3}}{19.64 \times 10^{-4}} = 1.273 \text{ T}$$

$$\therefore \quad H = \frac{B}{\mu_0 \mu_r} = \frac{1.273}{4\pi \times 10^{-7} \times 1} = 101.3 \times 10^4 \text{ A/m}$$

Now, since $l = 2.5 \times 10^{-3}$ m

M.M.F. required $= H \times l = 101.3 \times 10^4 \times 2.5 \times 10^{-3}$
$= 2532.50$ A

For Iron Path :

$$\phi = 1.2 \times 2.5 \times 10^{-3} = 3 \times 10^{-3} \text{ Wb}$$

$$\therefore \quad B = \frac{\phi}{a} = \frac{3 \times 10^{-3}}{19.64 \times 10^{-4}} = 1.528 \text{ T}$$

$$\therefore \quad H = \frac{B}{\mu_0 \mu_r} = \frac{1.528}{4\pi \times 10^{-7} \times 1000} = 1215.94 \text{ A/m}$$

Since, $l = \pi \times D$ – Air gap length
$= \pi \times 25 - 0.25 = 78.29$ cm

$\therefore$ M.M.F. required $= H \times l = 1215.94 \times 78.29 \times 10^{-2}$
$= 952$ A

Thus, Total M.M.F. $= 2532.50 + 952 = 3484.5$ A ... (I)

If the coil has N turns, then with a current of 4 A flowing through it,

Total M.M.F. $= NI = 4N$ ... (II)

Therefore, equating the equations (I) and (II), we have

$$4N = 3484.5$$

∴ $\quad N = \dfrac{3484.5}{4} = 872$ ... Ans.

Example 2.8: *For the magnetic circuit of an iron alloy shown in Fig. 2.19, the mean length of flux path is 100 cm, with an air gap of 0.5 cm, and cross-sectional area of 2 cm × 2 cm. The relative permeability of the iron alloy is 1400. There are three coils A, B and C around the core, with number of turns as 335, 600 and 600 respectively, and they carry currents I_A, I_B and I_C as shown in the figure. Ignoring leakage and fringing, find the flux in the air gap.*

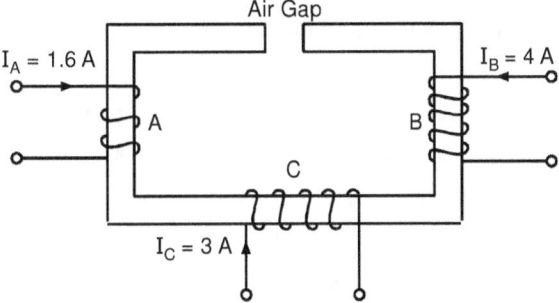

Fig. 2.19 : Magnetic circuit for Example 2.8

Solution: Taking into account the directions of the currents flowing in the three coils, we get

Net m.m.f. acting in the circuit,

$$F = N_A \cdot I_A + N_B \cdot I_B - N_C \cdot I_C$$

$$= (335 \times 1.6) + (600 \times 4) - (600 \times 3)$$

$$= 1136 \text{ A, forcing the flux in the clockwise direction.}$$

Total reluctance of the magnetic circuit,

$$S = S_i + S_g = \dfrac{l_i}{\mu_o \mu_{ri} a} + \dfrac{l_g}{\mu_o a}$$

$$= \dfrac{99.5 \times 10^{-2}}{(4\pi \times 10^{-7}) \times 1400 \times (4 \times 10^{-4})} + \dfrac{0.5 \times 10^{-2}}{(4\pi \times 10^{-7})(4 \times 10^{-4})}$$

$$= 1136 \times 10^4 \text{ A/Wb}$$

∴ Flux produced in the air gap,

$$\phi = \dfrac{F}{S} = \dfrac{1136}{1136 \times 10^4} \text{ Wb} = \mathbf{0.1 \text{ mWb}}$$ ... Ans.

2.9 POINTS TO REMEMBER

DEFINITIONS:

- **Magnetic Induction:** It is the phenomenon due to which a magnet can induce magnetism in a neighbouring piece of magnetic material (say iron) without actual physical contact.

- **Pole Strength:** The unit of pole strength is *weber* and it is defined as the strength of that pole which when placed from an identical pole at a distance of 1 metre in free space experiences a force of $\dfrac{10^7}{16\pi^2}$ newtons.

- **Magnetic Field:** The region in the neighbourhood of a magnet within which the influence of the magnet is felt is termed as magnetic field.

- **Magnetic Lines of Force or Lines of Magnetic Flux:** A line of force may be defined as a line along which an isolated N-pole would travel if free to move in a magnetic field and it is such that the tangent at any point gives the direction of the resultant force at that point.

- **Magnetic Flux (ϕ):** The total number of lines of force in any particular magnetic field is called the magnetic flux. The unit of magnetic flux is also *weber (10^8 lines)*. The flux which the unit N-pole radiates out is known as one weber.

- **Magnetic Flux Density (B):** The flux per unit area (a) in a plane at right angles to the flux is known as flux density. Its unit is *tesla (T)*.

$$\therefore \quad B = \frac{\phi}{a} \text{ tesla}$$

- **Magnetic Field Strength (H):** The force experienced by a unit North pole (i.e. N-pole with 1 weber pole strength) placed at any point in a magnetic field is known as magnetic field strength at that point. The unit of magnetic field strength is *newtons per weber (N / Wb)* or *amperes per metre (A / m)*.

- **Permeability :** It may be defined as the ease with which a magnetic flux permeates a medium or in other words, it is the receptiveness of the medium in having flux set up in it.

- **Permeability of Free Space or Magnetic Space Constant (μ_0):** For a magnetic field in vacuum (or free space), the ratio of flux density (in tesla) to magnetic field strength (in amperes / metre) producing that flux density is called the permeability of free space or magnetic space constant. The unit of μ_0 is *henry per metre (H/m)*.

- **Absolute Permeability (μ):** The ratio of magnetic flux density (in tesla) in a particular medium (other than vacuum) to the magnetic field strength (in amperes / metre) at the same location producing that flux density is called the absolute permeability of that medium. The unit of μ is *henry per metre (H/m)*.

- **Relative Permeability (μ_r):** The ratio of the flux density produced in a material to the flux density produced in a vacuum (or free space) by the same magnetic field strength under identical conditions is called the relative permeability of that material. It being a ratio of absolute permeability to permeability of free space, has no unit.

- **Magnetomotive Force (M.M.F. also F):** The magnetomotive force is usually defined as the work done in joules on a unit magnetic pole in taking it once round a closed magnetic circuit. The unit is *ampere (A)*.

- **Reluctance (S):** It is the resistance offered by the material to the passage of magnetic flux through it and corresponds to resistance in the electric circuit. The unit for reluctance is *ampere per weber (A / Wb)*.

- **Permeance:** The permeance of the magnetic circuit is the reciprocal of its reluctance and may be defined as that property of the magnetic circuit due to which it permits the passage of magnetic flux through it. Its unit is *weber per ampere (Wb/A)*.

- **Hopkinson's Leakage Co-efficient or Leakage Factor:** It is the ratio of total flux to useful flux and denoted by the letter λ. Thus

$$\text{Leakage co-efficient } \lambda = \frac{\text{Total flux}}{\text{Useful flux}}$$

RULES:

- **The Right Hand Gripping Rule for a Straight Conductor Carrying Current:** Grip the current carrying conductor in the right hand with the thumb outstretched parallel to the conductor and pointing in the direction of the current The curled fingers then point in the direction of the magnetic field around the conductor.

- **The Corkscrew Rule for a Straight Conductor Carrying Current:** Imagine a right handed corkscrew or wood screw placed alongside of the current carrying conductor with its axis parallel to the conductor and tip pointing in the direction of the current flow. Then the direction of the magnetic field is given by the direction in which the screw must be turned so as to advance it in the direction of the current.

- **Fleming's Left Hand Rule:** Arrange the first finger, the second finger and the thumb of your left hand mutually at right angles to one another. Point the first finger in the direction of the field and the second finger in the direction of the current, then the thumb will point in the direction of the force on the conductor.

- **Right Hand Gripping Rule for a Solenoid:** Grip the solenoid in the right hand with the fingers pointing in the direction of the current. The thumb outstretched parallel to the axis of the solenoid, then points to the North pole of the solenoid.

2.10 IMPORTANT FORMULAE AT A GLANCE

- Force exerted by one pole on another pole,

$$F = K \frac{m_1 m_2}{d^2}$$

where m_1 and m_2 = Pole strengths of the poles

d = Distance between the two poles

K = Constant. Depends on the nature of the surrounding medium.

- Magnetic field strength at a point due to a group of long straight conductors carrying equal currents in the same direction,

$$H = \frac{NI}{2\pi r} \text{ newtons/weber}$$

where,
N = Number of long straight conductors in a group
I = Current per conductor, in amperes
r = Distance of the point under consideration from the centre of the group of conductors, in metres

- Force experienced by a current carrying conductor placed in a magnetic field at right angles to it,

$$F = B \cdot I \cdot l \text{ newtons}$$

where
B = Flux density of the magnetic field, in teslas
I = Current in the conductor, in amperes
l = Active length of the conductor, in metres

- Magnetic field strength along the axis of a long solenoid,

$$H = \frac{NI}{l} \text{ newtons/weber or amperes/metre}$$

where,
N = Number of turns of a solenoid
I = Current in amperes
l = Length of the solenoid, in metres

- Absolute permeability, $\mu = \frac{B}{H} = \mu_0 \mu_r$ henrys/metre

where
B = Flux density in teslas
H = Magnetic field strength in newtons/weber or amperes/metre
μ_0 = Permeability of free space = $4\pi \times 10^{-7}$ H/m
μ_r = Relative permeability

- Mutual force between two parallel current carrying conductors,

$$F = 2 \times 10^{-7} \frac{I_1 I_2 l}{d} \text{ newtons}$$

where
I_1 and I_2 = Currents in the two conductors, in amperes
l = Active length of either conductor, in metres
d = Distance between the centres of two conductors, in metres

- Magnetomotive force, $F = N \cdot I$ amperes

where
N = Number of turns on the magnetizing coil
I = Current flowing in the magnetizing coil, in amperes

- Reluctance $S = \dfrac{l}{(\mu_0 \mu_r a)}$ amperes/weber

  where
  - l = Length of the magnetic circuit, in metres
  - a = Cross-sectional area of the magnetic circuit, in square metres
  - μ_0 = Permeability of free space = $4\pi \times 10^{-7}$ H/m
  - μ_r = Relative permeability

- Flux = $\dfrac{F}{S}$ webers

  where
  - F = Magnetomotive force, in amperes
  - S = Reluctance of the magnetic circuit, in amperes/weber

- Total reluctance of a series magnetic circuit,

  $$S = S_1 + S_2 + S_3 + \ldots + S_n$$
  $$= \dfrac{l_1}{\mu_0 \mu_{r1} a_1} + \dfrac{l_2}{\mu_0 \mu_{r2} a_2} + \dfrac{l_3}{\mu_0 \mu_{r3} a_3} + \ldots + \dfrac{l_n}{\mu_0 \mu_{rn} a_n} \text{ amperes/weber}$$

  where
  - $S_1, S_2, S_3, \ldots, S_n$ = Individual reluctances of different parts of a series magnetic circuit, in amperes/weber
  - $l_1, l_2, l_3, \ldots, l_n$ = Lengths of different parts of a series magnetic circuit, in metres
  - $a_1, a_2, a_3, \ldots, a_n$ = Cross-sectional areas of different parts of a series magnetic circuit, in square meters
  - $\mu_{r1}, \mu_{r2}, \mu_{r3}, \ldots, \mu_{rn}$ = Relative permeabilities of the materials of different parts of a series magnetic circuit
  - μ_0 = Permeability of free space = $4\pi \times 10^{-7}$ H/m

- Total m.m.f. for a series magnetic circuit,

  $$F = F_1 + F_2 + F_3 + \ldots + F_n \text{ amperes}$$

  where $F_1, F_2, F_3, \ldots, F_n$ = Individual m.m.fs. of different parts of a series magnetic circuit, in amperes

- Total m.m.f. for a series magnetic circuit,

  $$F = H_1 l_1 + H_2 l_2 + H_3 l_3 + \ldots + H_n l_n \text{ amperes}$$

  where $H_1, H_2, H_3, \ldots, H_n$ = Individual field strengths of different parts of a series magnetic circuit, in amperes/metre

  $l_1, l_2, l_3, \ldots, l_n$ = Lengths of different parts of a series magnetic circuit, in metres

2.11 SOLUTIONS OF NUMERICAL EXAMPLES FROM UNIVERSITY PAPERS

Example 2.9 : *A magnetic circuit has effective iron length of 100 cm and an air gap of 2 mm. It is wound with 800 turns. If the relative permeability of iron is 1200, find the flux density in the air gap when the winding carries a current of 1 A. Neglect leakage and assume fringe factor as 1.05.* **(November 2003/12 Marks)**

Solution : Fig. 2.20 shows the necessary magnetic circuit.

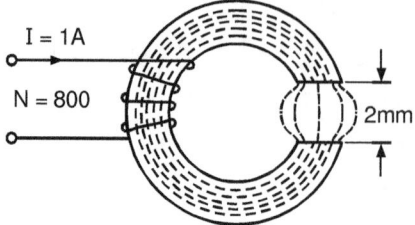

Fig. 2.20

Let 'a' be the cross-sectional area for the iron part of the magnetic circuit, in m². Then,

Reluctance of the iron part,

$$S_i = \frac{l_i}{\mu_0 \mu_{ri} a_i} = \frac{1}{4\pi \times 10^{-7} \times 1200 \times a} = \frac{663.15}{a} \text{ A/Wb}$$

Effective area of an air gap due to fringing effect, in m²

$$a_g = 1.05 \times a$$

∴ Reluctance of an air gap,

$$S_g = \frac{l_g}{\mu_0 \mu_{rg} a_g} = \frac{2 \times 10^{-3}}{4\pi \times 10^{-7} \times 1 \times 1.05 a}$$

$$= \frac{1515.76}{a} \text{ A/Wb}$$

∴ Total reluctance, $S = S_i + S_g = \frac{663.15}{a} + \frac{1515.76}{a}$

$$= \frac{2178.91}{a} \text{ A/Wb}$$

Now, M.M.F. provided $= N \cdot I = 800 \times 1 = 800$ A

∴ Flux, $\phi = \frac{M.M.F}{S} = \frac{800 \times a}{2178.91} = (0.3672 \, a)$ Wb

∴ Flux density in the air gap,

$$B_g = \frac{\phi}{a_g} = \frac{0.3672 \, a}{1.05 \, a}$$

$$= \mathbf{0.3497 \text{ T}} \quad \ldots \text{Ans.}$$

Example 2.10 : *A flux density of 1.3 T is required in 3.5 mm air gap of an electromagnet wound with 550 turns of wire and having an iron path of 130 cm. Calculate the current required assuming that a relative permeability of 1200 for iron and neglecting the leakage and fringing.*

(May 2004/8 Marks)

Solution : Fig. 2.21 shows the magnetic circuit under consideration.

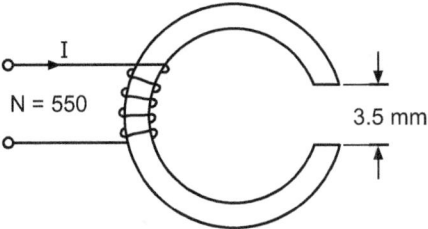

Fig. 2.21

For Air Gap :

$$H = \frac{B}{\mu_o \mu_r} = \frac{1.3}{4\pi \times 10^{-7} \times 1} = 103.451 \times 10^4 \text{ A/m}$$

$$l = 3.5 \text{ mm} = 3.5 \times 10^{-3} \text{ m}$$

∴ M.M.F. required $= H \times l = 103.451 \times 10^4 \times 3.5 \times 10^{-3}$

$= 3620.785$ A

For Iron Path :

$$H = \frac{B}{\mu_o \mu_r} = \frac{1.3}{4\pi \times 10^{-7} \times 1200} = 862.089 \text{ A/m}$$

$$l = 130 \text{ cm} = 1.3 \text{ m}$$

∴ M.M.F. required $= H \times l = 862.089 \times 1.3$

$= 1120.72$ A

∴ Total M.M.F. required $= N \cdot I = 3620.785 + 1120.72$

$= 4741.505$ A

∴ Current required, $I = \dfrac{4741.505}{N} = \dfrac{4741.505}{550}$

$= 8.62$ A ... **Ans.**

Example 2.11 : *A rectangular iron core has mean length of magnetic path of 100 cm. The cross-section is (2 cm × 2 cm). Relative permeability of the iron is 1400 and an air gap of 5 mm is provided in the core. The core has 3 coils wound on it having respective turns and currents as (335, 1.6 A), (600, 4 A), (600, 3 A). If the direction of current in the first and second coils is alike, and is opposite of the direction of current in the third as shown in Fig. 2.22, determine the flux in the air gap.* **(November 2004/12 Marks)**

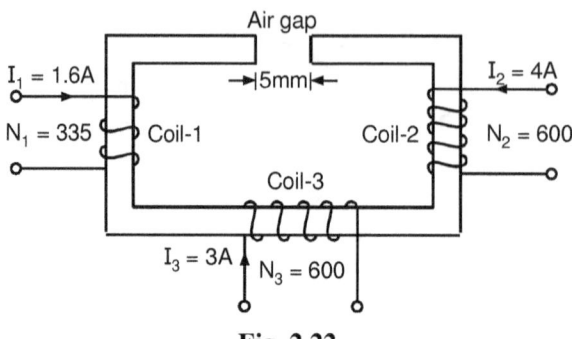

Fig. 2.22

Solution : Refer to the solution of Example 2.8 on page 2.23.

Example 2.12 : A soft iron ring of 27 cm mean diameter and circular cross-section of 7 cm diameter, is wound with a magnetizing coil. A current of 5 A is flowing in the coil producing a flux of 2.5 mWb in the air gap which is 3 mm wide. Taking $\mu_r = 1200$ at this flux density and allowing for a leakage co-efficient of 1.2, find the number of turns on the coil.

(May 2005/6 Marks)

Solution : Fig. 2.23 shows the necessary magnetic circuit.

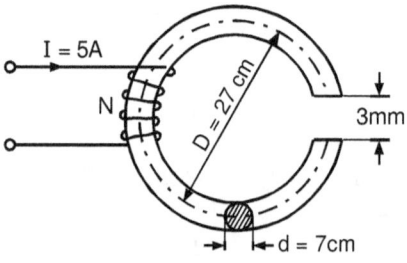

Fig. 2.23

For Air Gap :

$$a = \frac{\pi}{4} d^2 = \frac{\pi}{4} \times 7^2 = 38.48 \text{ cm}^2$$

$$\phi = 2.5 \text{ mWb} = 2.5 \times 10^{-3} \text{ Wb}$$

∴ $$B = \frac{\phi}{a} = \frac{2.5 \times 10^{-3}}{38.48 \times 10^{-4}} = 0.6497 \text{ T}$$

∴ $$H = \frac{B}{\mu_0 \mu_r} = \frac{0.6497}{4\pi \times 10^{-7} \times 1} = 51.7 \times 10^4 \text{ A/m}$$

$$l = 3 \text{ mm} = 3 \times 10^{-3} \text{ m}$$

∴ M.M.F. required $= H \times l = 51.7 \times 10^4 \times 3 \times 10^{-3} = 1551$ A

For Iron Path :

$$\phi = 1.2 \times 2.5 \times 10^{-3} = 3 \times 10^{-3} \text{ Wb}$$

∴ $$B = \frac{\phi}{a} = \frac{3 \times 10^{-3}}{38.48 \times 10^{-4}} = 0.7796 \text{ T}$$

$$\therefore \quad H = \frac{B}{\mu_o \mu_r} = \frac{0.7796}{4\pi \times 10^{-7} \times 1200} = 516.99 \text{ A/m}$$

$$l = \pi D - \text{Air gap length} = \pi \times 27 - 0.3 = 84.523 \text{ cm}$$

$$\therefore \quad \text{M.M.F. required} = H \times l = 516.99 \times 84.523 \times 10^{-2} = 436.98 \text{ A}$$

Thus, Total M.M.F. $= 1551 + 436.98 = 1987.98$ A ... (I)

If the coil has N turns, then with a current of 5 A flowing through it,

$$\text{Total M.M.F.} = NI = 5N \quad \text{... (II)}$$

Therefore, equating equations (I) and (II), we have

$$5N = 1987.98$$

$\therefore$ Number of turns of the coil,

$$N = 398 \quad \text{... Ans.}$$

Example 2.13 : *The magnetic circuit has effective iron length of 105 cm and an air gap of 2.5 mm. It is wound with 825 turns. If the relative permeability of iron is 1175, find the flux density in the air gap when winding carries a current of 1.2 A. Neglect leakage and fringing.*

(May 2006/6 Marks)

Solution : Let 'a' be the cross-sectional area for the iron part of the magnetic circuit, in m². Then,

Reluctance of the iron part,

$$S_i = \frac{l_i}{\mu_o \mu_{ri} a_i} = \frac{1}{4\pi \times 10^{-7} \times 1175 \times a} = \frac{677.26}{a} \text{ A/Wb}$$

Effective cross-sectional area of the air gap,

$$a_g = a \qquad \text{(as fringing is negligible)}$$

$\therefore$ Reluctance of an air gap,

$$S_g = \frac{l_g}{\mu_o \mu_{rg} a_g} = \frac{2.5 \times 10^{-3}}{4\pi \times 10^{-7} \times 1 \times a} = \frac{1989.44}{a} \text{ A/Wb}$$

$\therefore$ Total reluctance, $S = S_i + S_g = \dfrac{677.26}{a} + \dfrac{1989.44}{a}$

$$= \frac{2666.7}{a} \text{ A/Wb}$$

Now, M.M.F. provided $= NI = 825 \times 1.2 = 990$ A

$$\therefore \quad \text{Flux, } \phi = \frac{\text{M.M.F.}}{S} = \frac{990 \times a}{2666.7} = (0.3712\, a) \text{ Wb}$$

$\therefore$ Flux density in the air gap,

$$B_g = \frac{\phi}{a_g} = \frac{0.3712\, a}{a} = 0.3712 \text{ T} \quad \text{... Ans.}$$

Example 2.14 : *A ring has mean diameter of 15 cm, a cross-section of 1.7 cm² and has a radial gap of 0.5 mm cut in it. It is uniformly wound with 1500 turns of insulated wire and current of 1 A produces a flux of 0.1 mWb across the gap. Calculate the relative permeability of iron on the assumption that there is no magnetic leakage.* **(May 2007/8 Marks)**

Solution :

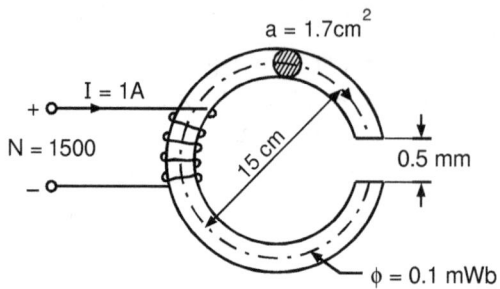

Fig. 2.24

Flux density, $B = \dfrac{\phi}{a} = \dfrac{0.1 \times 10^{-3}}{1.7 \times 10^{-4}} = 0.59$ T

M.M.F. required for air gap,

$$F_g = H_g \times l_g = \dfrac{B}{\mu_o} \times l_g = \dfrac{0.59}{(4\pi \times 10^{-7})} \times 0.5 \times 10^{-3}$$

$$= 234.75 \text{ A}$$

M.M.F. required for iron path,

$$F_i = H_i \times l_i = \dfrac{B}{\mu_o \mu_{ri}} \times l_i$$

$$= \dfrac{0.59}{(4\pi \times 10^{-7}) \mu_{ri}} \times (\pi \times 15 \times 10^{-2} - 0.5 \times 10^{-3})$$

$$= \dfrac{221015.25}{\mu_{ri}} \text{ A}$$

∴ Total m.m.f., $F = F_g + F_i = \left(234.75 + \dfrac{221015.25}{\mu_{ri}}\right)$ A ... (I)

But, Total m.m.f. provided,

$$F = N \times I = 1500 \times 1 = 1500 \text{ A} \qquad \text{... (II)}$$

Hence, equating equations (I) and (II), we get

$$234.75 + \dfrac{221015.25}{\mu_{ri}} = 1500$$

∴ Relative permeability of iron,

$$\mu_{ri} = \mathbf{174.68} \qquad \text{... Ans.}$$

Example 2.15 : *An iron ring of relative permeability 1100 is uniformly wound with the coil having 1000 turns. The coil carries a current of 1 A. In the iron ring, air gap is of 2 mm. If the effective iron path length is 1 m, calculate the flux density in the air gap. Neglect leakage. Fringing factor is 1.05.* **(May 2008/8 Marks)**

Solution : Given : $\mu_{ri} = 1100$, $N = 1000$, $I = 1$ A, $l_g = 2$ mm, $l_i = 1$ m, Fringing factor = 1.05.

Fig. 2.25 shows the necessary magnetic circuit.

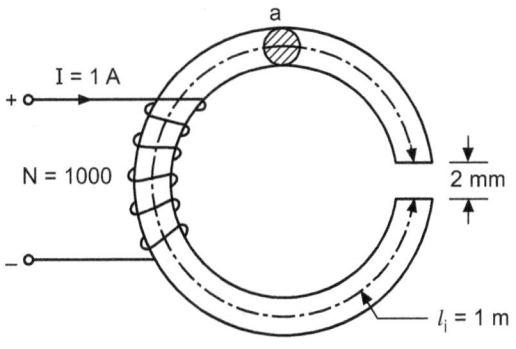

Fig. 2.25

Let 'a' be the cross-sectional area for the iron part of the magnetic circuit, in m². Then,
Reluctance of the iron part,

$$S_i = \frac{l_i}{\mu_0 \mu_{ri} a_i} = \frac{1}{4\pi \times 10^{-7} \times 1100 \times a} = \frac{723.43}{a} \text{ A/Wb}$$

Effective area of an air gap due to fringing effect, in m²

$$a_g = 1.05 \times a$$

∴ Reluctance of an air gap,

$$S_g = \frac{l_g}{\mu_0 \mu_{rg} a_g} = \frac{2 \times 10^{-3}}{4\pi \times 10^{-7} \times 1 \times 1.05 \times a} = \frac{1515.76}{a} \text{ A/Wb}$$

∴ Total reluctance, $S = S_i + S_g = \frac{723.43}{a} + \frac{1515.76}{a} = \frac{2239.19}{a}$ A/Wb

Now, M.M.F. provided, $F = N \cdot I = 1000 \times 1 = 1000$ A

∴ Flux, $\phi = \frac{M.M.F.}{S} = \frac{1000 \times a}{2239.19} = (0.4466 \times a)$ Wb

∴ Flux density in the air gap,

$$B_g = \frac{\phi}{a_g} = \frac{0.4466 \times a}{1.05 \times a} = \mathbf{0.43 \text{ T}} \qquad \text{... Ans.}$$

Example 2.16 : *A circular ring with mean diameter 600 mm has radial air gap of 2 mm width. The uniformly wound coil on it has 900 turns. The coil carries 2 A current. If the flux density in the air gap is 0.35 Wb/m², calculate the relative permeability of iron. Consider the leakage factor 1.15.* **(May 2009/6 Marks)**

Solution : Given : $D = 600$ mm $= 60$ cm, $l_g = 2$ mm, $N = 900$,

$$I = 2 \text{ A}, \ B_g = 0.35 \text{ Wb/m}^2, \ \lambda = 1.15$$

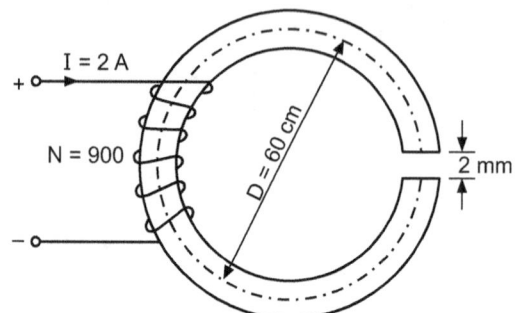

Fig. 2.26

Air Gap : $B_g = 0.35$ Wb/m^2, $l_g = 2$ mm

$\therefore$ M.M.F. required, $F_g = H_g \times l_g = \dfrac{B_g}{\mu_0 \mu_{rg}} \times l_g = \dfrac{0.35}{(4\pi \times 10^{-7} \times 1)} \times 2 \times 10^{-3}$

$\qquad = 557.04$ A

Iron Path : $B_i = 1.15 \times 0.35 = 0.403$ Wb/m^2 (neglecting fringing)

$l_i = \pi D -$ Air gap length $= \pi \times 60 - 0.2 = 188.296$ cm

$\therefore$ M.M.F. required, $F_i = H_i \times l_i = \dfrac{B_i}{\mu_0 \mu_{ri}} \times l_i = \dfrac{0.403}{(4\pi \times 10^{-7} \times \mu_{ri})} \times 188.296 \times 10^{-2}$

$\qquad = \dfrac{603860.02}{\mu_{ri}}$ A

$\therefore$ Total M.M.F. required,

$$F_T = F_g + F_i = \left(557.04 + \dfrac{603860.02}{\mu_{ri}}\right) \text{A} \qquad \ldots \text{(I)}$$

But Total M.M.F. provided,

$$F_T = N \cdot I = 900 \times 2 = 1800 \text{ A} \qquad \ldots \text{(II)}$$

Hence, equating the Equation (I) with Equation (II), we have

Relative permeability of iron,

$$\mu_{ri} = 485.82 \qquad \ldots \text{Ans.}$$

Example 2.17 : *An iron ring of 27 cm mean diameter and circular cross-section 40 cm^2 is uniformly wound with the coil. Flux produced in 3 mm air gap is 2.5 mWb. The coil carries 5 A current. Relative permeability of iron is 1200. Calculate the number of turns of the coil if leakage factor is 1.2.* **(December 2009/8 Marks)**

Solution : Given : D = 27 cm, a = 40 cm^2, ϕ_g = 2.5 mWb, l_g = 3 mm, I = 5 A, μ_{ri} = 1200, λ = 1.2.

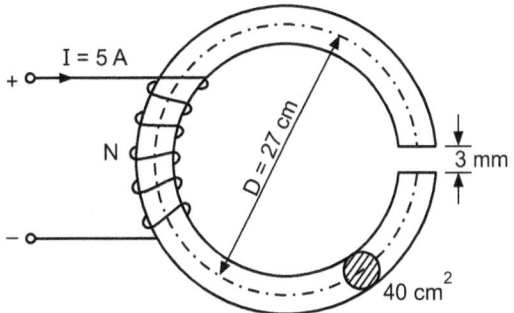

Fig. 2.27

Air Gap :

$$B_g = \frac{\phi_g}{a} = \frac{2.5 \times 10^{-3}}{40 \times 10^{-4}} = 0.625 \text{ Wb/m}^2$$

$$l_g = 3 \text{ mm}$$

$\therefore$ M.M.F. required, $F_g = H_g \times l_g = \dfrac{B_g}{\mu_0 \mu_{rg}} \times l_g$

$$= \frac{0.625}{(4\pi \times 10^{-7} \times 1)} \times 3 \times 10^{-3} = 1492.08 \text{ A}$$

Iron Path :

$$\phi_i = 1.2 \times \phi_g = 1.2 \times 2.5 \times 10^{-3} = 3 \times 10^{-3} \text{ Wb}$$

$\therefore$

$$B_i = \frac{\phi_i}{a} = \frac{3 \times 10^{-3}}{40 \times 10^{-4}} = 0.75 \text{ Wb/m}^2$$

$l_i = \pi D -$ Air gap length $= \pi \times 27 - 0.3 = 84.523$ cm

$\therefore$ M.M.F. required, $F_i = H_i \times l_i = \dfrac{B_i}{\mu_0 \mu_{ri}} \times l_i$

$$= \frac{0.75}{(4\pi \times 10^{-7} \times 1200)} \times 84.523 \times 10^{-2}$$

$$= 420.38 \text{ A}$$

$\therefore$ Total M.M.F., $F_T = F_g + F_i = 1492.08 + 420.38$

$$= 1912.46 \text{ A} \qquad \ldots \text{(I)}$$

If the coil has N turns, then with a current of 5 A flowing through it,

Total M.M.F., $F_T = N \cdot I = 5 N$ amperes $\qquad \ldots \text{(II)}$

$\therefore$ Equating the Equation (I) with the Equation (II), we get

Coil turns, N = **382.49** ... **Ans.**

Example 2.18 : *A mild steel ring is wound with two coils having the number of turns 500 and 300 respectively. Currents flowing through the coils are 3 A and 2 A respectively. Currents flowing through the coils are in opposition with each other. The length of the iron path is 50 cm and uniform cross-section of the steel ring is 4 cm². Calculate the reluctance of the magnetic path and flux density in the ring. Assume no leakage and fringing. Relative permeability of the ring material is 800.* **(May 2010/6 Marks)**

Solution : Fig. 2.28 shows the magnetic circuit for the given condition.

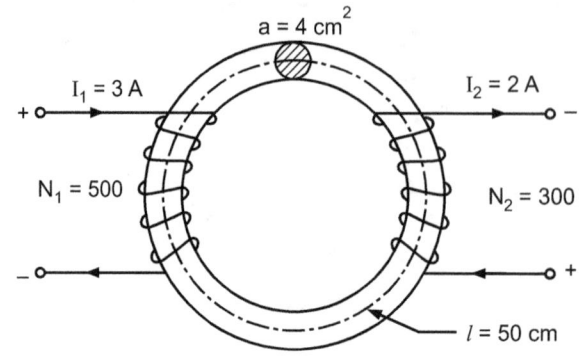

Fig. 2.28

Reluctance of the magnetic path,

$$S = \frac{l}{\mu_0 \mu_r a} = \frac{50 \times 10^{-2}}{4\pi \times 10^{-7} \times 800 \times 4 \times 10^{-4}}$$

$$= \mathbf{1243398 \text{ A/Wb}} \qquad \ldots \text{ Ans.}$$

Net m.m.f. acting in the circuit,

$$F = N_1 \cdot I_1 - N_2 I_2 \qquad \text{(being in opposition)}$$

$$= 500 \times 3 - 300 \times 2$$

$$= 900 \text{ A, forcing the flux in the clockwise direction.}$$

∴ Flux in the ring, $\phi = \dfrac{F}{S} = \dfrac{900}{1243398} = 7.24 \times 10^{-4}$ Wb or 0.724 mWb

∴ Flux density in the ring,

$$B = \frac{\phi}{a} = \frac{0.724 \times 10^{-4}}{4 \times 10^{-4}} = \mathbf{0.18 \text{ T}} \qquad \ldots \text{ Ans.}$$

Example 2.19 : *A circular iron ring with mean diameter 50 cm and uniform cross-section 6 cm² is uniformly wound 8000 turns. Air-gap of 6 mm is in it. Flux density in the air-gap is 0.5 Wb/m². Current flowing through the coil is 2.6 A and leakage factor is 1.1. Calculate the relative permeability of iron.* **(December 2010/6 Marks)**

Solution : Given : D = 50 cm, a = 6 cm², N = 8000, l_g = 6 mm, B_g = 0.5 Wb/m², I = 2.6 A, λ = 1.1.

Fig. 2.29 shows the magnetic circuit for this case.

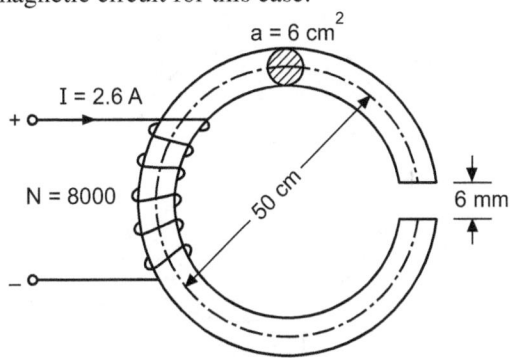

Fig. 2.29

Air Gap : $B_g = 0.5$ Wb/m^2, $l_g = 6$ mm, $\mu_{rg} = 1$

∴ M.M.F. required, $F_g = H_g \times l_g = \dfrac{B_g}{\mu_0 \mu_{rg}} \times l_g$

$= \dfrac{0.5}{(4\pi \times 10^{-7} \times 1)} \times 6 \times 10^{-3}$

$= 2387.32$ A

Iron Path : $B_i = 1.1 \times 0.5 = 0.55$ Wb/m^2 (neglecting fringing)

$l_i = \pi D -$ Air gap length $= \pi \times 50 - 0.6 = 156.48$ cm

∴ M.M.F. required, $F_i = H_i \times l_i = \dfrac{B_i}{\mu_0 \mu_{ri}} \times l_i$

$= \dfrac{0.55}{(4\pi \times 10^{-7} \times \mu_{ri})} \times 156.48 \times 10^{-2}$

$= \dfrac{684875.55}{\mu_{ri}}$ A

∴ Total m.m.f. required,

$F_T = F_g + F_i = 2387.32 + \dfrac{684875.55}{\mu_{ri}}$ ... (I)

But Total m.m.f. provided, $F_T = N \cdot I = 8000 \times 2.6 = 20800$ A ... (II)

Hence, equating the Equation (I) with Equation (II), we have

Relative permeability of iron,

$\mu_{ri} = \mathbf{37.2}$ ... **Ans.**

Example 2.20 : *An iron ring with a mean length of 50 m has an air gap of 1 mm and a winding of 200 turns. If the relative permeability of iron is 300, find the flux density when a current of 1 A flows through the coil.* **(May 2011/8 Marks)**

Solution : Given : $l = 50$ cm, $l_g = 1$ mm, $N = 200$, $\mu_{ri} = 300$, $I = 1$ A.

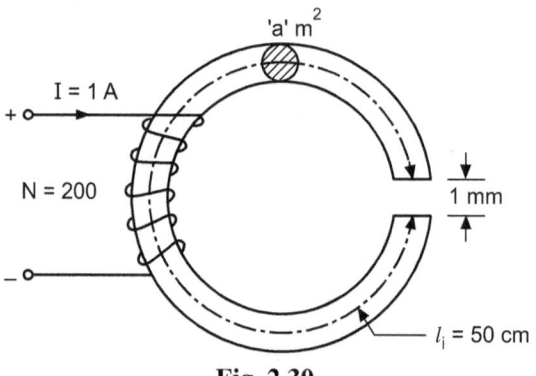

Fig. 2.30

Fig. 2.30 shows the given magnetic circuit. Let 'a' be the cross-sectional area of the magnetic circuit in m^2. We know that

$$\text{Reluctance, } S = \frac{l}{\mu_0 \mu_r a}$$

Therefore, reluctances of iron part and air gap will be as follows :

Reluctance of the iron part,

$$S_i = \frac{50 \times 10^{-2}}{4\pi \times 10^{-7} \times 300 \times a} \quad \text{(taken } l_i = l = 50 \text{ cm)}$$

$$= \frac{1326.29}{a} \text{ A/Wb}$$

Reluctance of the air gap, $\quad S_g = \dfrac{1 \times 10^{-3}}{4\pi \times 10^{-7} \times 1 \times a} = \dfrac{795.77}{a}$ A/Wb

∴ Total reluctance, $S = S_i + S_g = \dfrac{1326.29}{a} + \dfrac{795.77}{a}$

$$= \frac{2122.06}{a} \text{ A/Wb}$$

Now, M.M.F. provided $= N \cdot I = 200 \times 1 = 200$ A

∴ $\quad$ Flux, $\phi = \dfrac{\text{M.M.F.}}{S} = \dfrac{200 \times a}{2122.06} = 0.0942 \times a$ webers

∴ $\quad$ Flux density, $B = \dfrac{\phi}{a} = \dfrac{0.0942 \times a}{a} = \mathbf{0.0942 \text{ T}}$ ... **Ans.**

Example 2.21 : *An iron ring of mean circumference 1.2 m is uniformly wound with 400 turns of wire. When a current of 1.5 A is passed through the coil, a flux density of 1.25 Wb/m^2 is produced in the iron. Find the relative permeability of iron.* **(December 2011/6 Marks)**

Solution : Given : $l = 1.2$ m, $N = 400$, $I = 1.5$ A, $B = 1.25$ Wb/m^2

Magnetic field strength, $\quad H = \dfrac{NI}{l} = \dfrac{400 \times 1.5}{1.2} = 500$ A/m

But $\quad B = \mu_0 \mu_{ri} H$

∴ $\quad 1.25 = 4\pi \times 10^{-7} \times \mu_{ri} \times 500$

∴ Relative permeability of iron,

$$\mu_{ri} = \mathbf{1989.44} \quad \text{... \textbf{Ans.}}$$

Example 2.22 : *A toroidal air-cored coil with 2000 turns has a mean radius of 25 cm, diameter of each turn being 6 cm. If the current in the coil is 10 A, find : (i) M.M.F., (ii) Flux, (iii) Flux density.* **(May 2012/8 Marks)**

Solution : Given : N = 2000, R = 25 cm, d = 6 cm, I = 10 A.

(i) $\quad$ M.M.F. = N · I = 2000 × 10 = **20000 A** ... Ans.

(ii) Mean circumference of the coil,

$$l = 2\pi R = 2\pi \times 25 = 157.08 \text{ cm}$$

Cross-sectional area of the coil,

$$a = \frac{\pi}{4} \times d^2 = \frac{\pi}{4} \times 6^2 = 28.27 \text{ cm}^2$$

∴ $\quad$ Reluctance $S = \dfrac{l}{\mu_0 \mu_r a} = \dfrac{157.08 \times 10^{-2}}{4\pi \times 10^{-7} \times 1 \times 28.27 \times 10^{-4}}$ $\quad$ (∵ For air, $\mu_r = 1$)

$$= 4.42 \times 10^8 \text{ A/Wb}$$

∴ $\quad$ Flux $\phi = \dfrac{\text{M.M.F.}}{S} = \dfrac{20000}{4.42 \times 10^8}$

$$= 4.52 \times 10^{-5} \text{ Wb or } 0.0452 \text{ mWb} \quad \text{... Ans.}$$

(iii) $\quad$ Flux density $B = \dfrac{\phi}{a} = \dfrac{4.52 \times 10^{-5}}{28.27 \times 10^{-4}}$

$$= 0.016 \text{ T} \quad \text{... Ans.}$$

Alternative Method :

Magnetic field strength, $H = \dfrac{NI}{l} = \dfrac{2000 \times 10}{157.08 \times 10^{-2}} = 12732.37 \text{ A/m}$

∴ $\quad$ Flux density $B = \mu_0 \mu_r H = 4\pi \times 10^{-7} \times 1 \times 12732.37$

$$= 0.016 \text{ T} \quad \text{... Ans.}$$

Flux $\phi = B \times a = 0.016 \times 28.27 \times 10^{-4}$

$$= 4.52 \times 10^{-5} \text{ Wb or } 0.452 \text{ mWb} \quad \text{... Ans.}$$

Example 2.23 : *A mild steel ring has a mean circumference of 500 mm and a uniform cross-sectional area of 300 mm². An air gap of 1 mm is cut in the ring. Determine the current required in the coil of 500 turns wound over the ring, to produce a flux of 147 μWb in the air gap. Neglect fringing and assume the relative permeability of iron as 1200.* **(December 2012/8 Marks)**

Solution : Fig. 2.31 shows the given magnetic circuit.

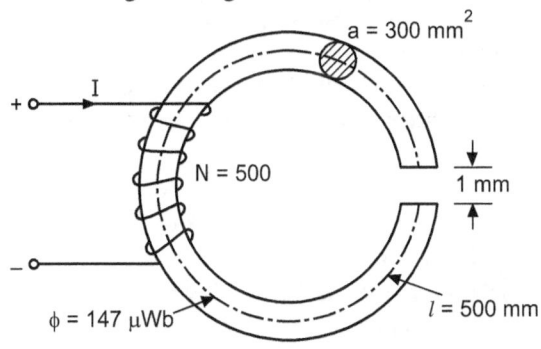

Fig. 2.31

$$a = 300 \text{ mm}^2$$
$$\phi = 147 \text{ μWb}$$

$$\therefore \quad \text{Flux density } B = \frac{\phi}{a} = \frac{147 \times 10^{-6}}{300 \times 10^{-6}} = 0.49 \text{ T}$$

For Mild Steel Path :
$$H_i = \frac{B}{\mu_0 \mu_{ri}} = \frac{0.49}{4\pi \times 10^{-7} \times 1200} = 324.94 \text{ A/m}$$
$$l_i = 500 - 1 = 499 \text{ mm}$$

$$\therefore \quad \text{M.M.F. required, } F_i = H_i \times l_i = 324.94 \times 499 \times 10^{-3}$$
$$= 162.15 \text{ A}$$

For Air Gap :
$$H_g = \frac{B}{\mu_0 \mu_{rg}} = \frac{0.49}{4\pi \times 10^{-7} \times 1} \qquad (\because \text{ For air, } \mu_r = 1)$$
$$= 389929.61 \text{ A/m}$$
$$l_g = 1 \text{ mm}$$

$$\therefore \quad \text{M.M.F. required, } F_g = H_g \times l_g = 389929.61 \times 1 \times 10^{-3} = 389.93 \text{ A}$$
$$\therefore \quad \text{Total m.m.f. required} = F_i + F_g = 162.15 + 389.93 = 552.08 \text{ A}$$
$$\therefore \quad \text{Current required I} = \frac{\text{Total m.m.f.}}{N} = \frac{552.08}{500}$$
$$= 1.1 \text{ A} \qquad \qquad \text{... Ans.}$$

2.12 EXERCISES

2.12 1 Review Questions

1. Define magnetic flux, flux density, magnetic field strength. State their units.
2. Differentiate between absolute permeability, relative permeability and permeability of free space.
3. Explain the following terms with reference to a magnetic circuit :
   (i) Magnetomotive force, (ii) Reluctance, (iii) Permeance.
4. Compare magnetic and electric circuits stating clearly similarities and dissimilarities between them.
5. State the simple law governing the relation which exists among flux, magnetomotive force and reluctance. To which law in the electric circuit does this law correspond ?
6. What is magnetization curve ? Comment on its practical importance.
7. How are the reluctances in series combined ? List the usual steps which are followed for finding the total magnetomotive force for a series magnetic circuit.
8. Explain the following terms :
   (i) Useful flux, (ii) Leakage flux, (iii) Leakage co-efficient, (iv) Fringing.

2.12.2 Classified Theory Questions from University Papers

1. Define the terms given below :
   Magnetic flux (ϕ), Magnetic flux density (B), Magnetic field strength (H), Magnetomotive force (F), Reluctance (S), Magnetic leakage factor (λ).
   (Answer : Sections 2.2, 2.8.1, 2.8.5)
   (December 2008, 2012; May 2012/Some of these for 2 Marks each)
2. Explain Fleming's left hand rule.
   (Answer : Section 2.4) *(May 2010/3 Marks)*

3. Compare the electric and magnetic circuits.
   (Answer : Section 2.8.2) (December 2011/6 Marks)
4. State the difference between the electric and magnetic circuits.
   (Answer : Section 2.8.2) (May 2012/4 Marks)
5. State six similarities and minimum two dissimilarities between the electric and magnetic circuits.
   (Answer : Section 2.8.2) (December 2008/8 Marks)
6. State four dissimilarities between the electric and magnetic circuits.
   (Answer : Section 2.8.2) (December 2010/4 Marks)
7. Explain the magnetization curve and its importance.
   (Answer : Section 2.8.3) (December 2010/4 Marks)
8. Draw and explain the B-H curve for a magnetic material.
   (Answer : Section 2.8.3) (December 2011/6 Marks)
9. With the help of a neat diagram, explain 'Magnetic leakage' and 'Fringing'.
   (Answer : Section 2.8.5) (May 2009, 2010/4 Marks)

2.12.3 Examples for Practice

1. Two long straight parallel conductors, placed 1.5 m apart in air, carry currents of I_1 and I_2 amperes in the same direction. The magnetic field strength at a point midway between the conductors is 7.5 A/m. If the force on each conductor per metre length is 2.5×10^{-4} N, calculate the values of I_1 and I_2. (I_1 = 64.44 A, I_2 = 29.1 A)
2. A toroid has a mean diameter of 20 cm and a cross-sectional area of 5 sq.cm. It is wound uniformly with 500 turns. If the relative permeability of the material is 1000, find the flux density when a current of 1 A flows through the winding. (1.0 T)
3. An iron ring of mean circumference of 0.8 m is uniformly wound with 500 turns of wire. When a current of 1 A is passed through the coil, a flux density of 1.1 T is produced in the iron. Find the permebilility of the iron under given condition.(1400.56)
4. An iron ring having a mean length of 50 cm has an air-gap of 1 mm and a winding of 200 turns. The relative permeability of iron is 300 when a current of 1 A flows through the coil. Find the flux density. (0.0943 T)
5. An iron ring of 300 cm mean circumference and a circular cross-section of 5 cm^2 has a saw cut of 2 mm wide in it. It has been wound with 500 turns of wire. Find the current required to produce 0.5 mWb across the gap. Assume the relative permeability of iron to be 500. Neglect leakage and fringing. (12.73 A)
6. An iron ring of mean circumference of 60 cm has an air-gap of 1 mm cut in it. It has a circular cross-section with area 6 cm^2. It carries a coil with 250 turns wound uniformly. The relative permeability of iron is 300. If the coil carries a current of 1.1 A, find the flux in the air-gap. (69.12×10^{-6} Wb)
7. An iron ring wound with 500 turns has a flux denity of 0.94 T while carrying a current of 2.4 A. The mean length of iron path is 80 cm and that of an air-gap is 1 mm. Determine the relative permeability of iron. (1324)
8. An electromagnet has area of cross-section of core, 12 cm^2. It has mean length of magnetic path of 50 cm and air-gap of 0.4 cm cut in it. It is excited by two separate coils each having 500 turns. When the current in the coils is 1 A, the resultant flux density (with additive coil fluxes) gives relative permeability of 1300. Calculate the flux in the air-gap. (0.3439×10^{-3} Wb)

9. An iron ring of cross-sectional area 3 cm³ and a mean circumference of 40 cm has an air-gap 2 mm wide cut in it. It is wound with 200 turns of wire. Calculate the magnetizing current necessary to provide a flux of 0.3 mWb in the air-gap. Neglect leakage and fringing. The magnetization curve of the iron is given by

B (Wb/m^2)	0.9	1.0	1.1	1.2
H (A/m)	1270	1510	1830	2300

(10.98 A)

10. Fig. 2.32 shows a magnetic circuit excited by the three coils A, B and C. Find the net m.m.f. acting in the circuit. (1400 A, forcing the flux in the clockwise direction)

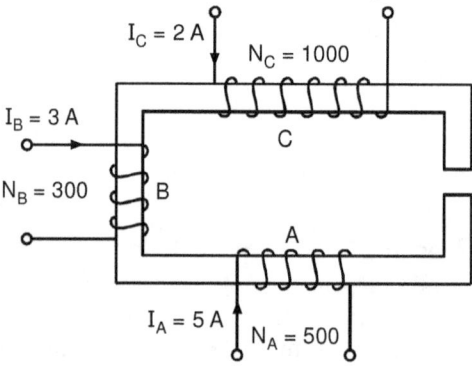

Fig. 2.32

11. A cast steel ring has a mean length of 200 cm and circular cross-section of 4 cm diameter. The ring is uniformly wound with a coil of 100 turns.
    (i) Calculate the exciting current required to produce a flux of 0.3 mWb in the ring.
    (ii) If an air-gap of 2 mm wide is cut in the ring, find the flux produced by the current calculated in (i). Take μ_r = 1500. (2.5327 A, 0.12 mWb)

12. A series magnetic circuit comprises three sections :
    (i) Length of 80 mm with cross-sectional area 60 mm².
    (ii) Length of 70 mm with cross-sectional area 80 mm² and
    (iii) An air-gap of length 0.5 mm with cross-sectional area 60 mm².
    Sections (i) and (ii) are of a material having magnetic characteristics given by the following table :

H (A/m)	100	210	340	500	800	1500
B (T)	0.2	0.4	0.6	0.8	1.0	1.2

Determine the current necessary in a coil of 4000 turns wound on section (ii) to produce a flux density of 0.7 T in the air-gap. Neglect magnetic leakage. (82.9175 mA)

13. An iron ring of 10 cm² cross-section and 50 cm mean circumference has 0.1 cm wide saw cut made in it. A flux of 1 mWb is required in the air-gap. If leakage co-efficient is 1.2 and iron is such that when B = 1.2 T, μ_r = 400, calculate the total magnetomotive force required. (1990 A)

CHAPTER 3

A.C. FUNDAMENTALS

3.1 INTRODUCTION

Basically, the electrical circuit or network serves as means of energy transfer from the source of electrical energy to the load with the help of the connecting wires or in simple words, it provides a path for the current flow from the source to the load. An electrical circuit is actually a combination of various elements consisting of sources of energy and parameters like resistors, capacitors and inductors either in lumped or distributed form. In this chapter, starting with the study of these basic elements, we shall also get acquainted with some fundamental aspects regarding alternating currents and voltages. Response of pure resistance, inductance and capacitance to alternating current supplies will also be studied at the end.

3.2 ELECTRIC CIRCUIT ELEMENTS R, L AND C

Any network consists of one or more of the following passive elements : resistors, inductors and capacitors. Under ideal circumstances only, these elements can be considered as pure elements.

3.2.1 Resistance Parameter

Resistance is the property of a material by virtue of which it opposes the flow of current through it. This opposition is due to the collisions between the electrons and between electrons and other atoms in the material, which converts electrical energy into heat. Resistance as a circuit element is denoted by the letter R and symbolically represented as shown in Fig. 3.1 (a).

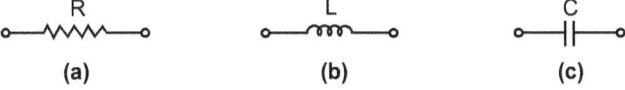

Fig. 3.1 : **Symbolic representation of circuit parameters R, L and C**

The unit of resistance is *ohm* (Ω). *The resistance offered by the material is said to be one ohm if a current of one ampere flowing through it, produces heat at the rate of one joule per second.*

The resistance of any material with a uniform cross-sectional area is determined by the following factors :

(i) Material.

(ii) Length.

(iii) Cross-sectional area.

(iv) Temperature.

The resistance of some material at a given temperature is given by

$$R = \rho \frac{l}{a} \text{ ohms} \qquad \ldots (3.1)$$

where ρ is a constant which depends on the type of material used. It is known as the *specific resistance* or *resistivity* of the material. The unit of specific resistance is *ohm-metre*.

Resistance of most of the metallic conductors increases with the increase of temperature linearly over a limited temperature range (approximately, –50 to 200°C). If the resistance of a metallic conductor at temperature $T_1°C$ is R_1, then over a normal temperature range, the resistance at temperature $T_2 °C$ is given by

$$R_2 = R_1 [1 + \alpha_1 (T_2 - T_1)] \qquad \ldots (3.2)$$

where, α_1 is the *temperature co-efficient of resistance* of the material at temperature $T_1 °C$.

According to Ohm's law, the current flow through a solid conductor is directly proportional to the difference of potential across the conductor and inversely proportional to its resistance, provided the temperature remains constant i.e.

$$i = \frac{v}{R} \text{ amperes} \qquad \ldots (3.3)$$

We can also write the above equation as follows :

$$i = \frac{v}{R} = G \cdot v \text{ amperes} \qquad \ldots (3.4)$$

where G is the *conductance* of a conductor. The unit of conductance is *siemens*.

The power absorbed by the resistance is given by,

$$p = vi = (iR) i = i^2 R \text{ watts} \qquad \ldots (3.5)$$

where i is the current flowing through the resistor in amperes and v is the voltage across the resistor in volts. The corresponding amount of energy consumed by a resistance in time t is given by

$$W = \int_0^t p \cdot dt = p \cdot t = i^2 R t = \frac{v^2}{R} \cdot t \text{ joules (Joule's law)} \qquad \ldots (3.6)$$

This energy is ultimately converted into heat.

3.2.2 Inductance Parameter

Self-inductance or *simply inductance is defined as that property of a coil by virtue of which it opposes any change in current flowing through it.* Inductance as a circuit element is denoted by the letter L and symbolically represented as shown in Fig. 3.1 (b). It is measured in *henries (H)*.

A coil has an inductance of one henry when a current changing uniformly at the rate of one ampere per second induces an opposing e.m.f. of one volt in it.

Inductors are the coils of various dimensions designed to introduce specified amounts of inductance into a circuit. The relationship between the inductance of a coil and its physical dimensions is given by the following expression :

$$L = \frac{N^2 \mu a}{l} \text{ henries} \qquad \ldots (3.7)$$

where N represents the number of turns, μ the absolute permeability of the core, a the cross-sectional area of the core in square metres, and l the mean length of the core in metres.

The current-voltage relationship for inductance parameter is given by

$$v = L \frac{di}{dt} \text{ volts} \qquad \ldots (3.8)$$

where v is the voltage across the inductor in volts, and i is the current flowing through it in amperes. However, to express the current in terms of the voltage across the inductor, we can rewrite the above equation as

$$di = \frac{1}{L} v \cdot dt \qquad \ldots (3.9)$$

Integrating both sides, we get

$$\int_0^t di = \frac{1}{L} \int_0^t v \cdot dt$$

$$i(t) - i(0) = \frac{1}{L} \int_0^t v \cdot dt$$

$$\therefore \quad i(t) = \frac{1}{L} \int_0^t v \cdot dt + i(0) \text{ amperes} \qquad \ldots (3.10)$$

Thus, the current in an inductor is dependent upon the integral of voltage across its terminals and the initial current in the coil, i(0). Equations (3.8) and (3.10) reveal an important property of inductance that *the current in an inductor cannot change abruptly in zero time*. Equation (3.8) clearly shows that a finite change in current in zero time calls for an infinite voltage to appear across the inductor, which is physically impossible. Further, Equation (3.10) shows that in zero time, the contribution to the inductor current from the integral term is zero, so that current immediately before and after the application of voltage to the inductor is the same. Thus, the inductance exhibits the property similar to that of mechanical inertia.

The power absorbed by the inductor is

$$p = vi = Li\frac{di}{dt} \text{ watts} \qquad \ldots (3.11)$$

Therefore, the energy stored by the inductor is given by

$$W = \int_0^t p \cdot dt = \int_0^t Li\frac{di}{dt} \cdot dt = \int_0^i Li\, di = \frac{1}{2} Li^2 \text{ joules} \qquad \ldots (3.12)$$

It should be remembered that a pure inductor never consumes energy like the resistor, but only stores it in its magnetic field. This energy is then returned to the source at a later time when the field of the inductor is allowed to collapse.

3.2.3 Capacitance Parameter

Two conducting surfaces or plates separated by an insulating medium called dielectric form a *capacitor. The property of such a capacitor to store an electric charge when a potential difference is applied across it is known as its capacitance.* Capacitance as a circuit element is denoted by the letter C and symbolically represented as shown in Fig. 3.1 (c).

The unit of capacitance is *farad (F). A capacitor is said to have a capacitance of one farad if it acquires a charge of one coulomb when a potential difference of one volt is applied across its terminals.*

Capacitance of a capacitor is decided by its geometrical configuration and the physical property of the dielectric material lying between its two metal surfaces. This will be clear from the following expression :

$$C = \frac{\varepsilon_0 \varepsilon_r a}{d} \text{ farads} \qquad \ldots (3.13)$$

where ε_0 is the permittivity of free space, ε_r is the relative permittivity (or dielectric constant) of the dielectric material, a is the cross-sectional area in square metres of the plates and d is the distance in metres between the plates.

The charge stored by a capacitor is always proportional to the voltage across the capacitor plates. The relation between the voltage across the capacitor and its charge can be mathematically expressed as

$$q = Cv \text{ coulombs} \qquad \ldots (3.14)$$

Or,

$$C = \frac{q}{v} \text{ farads} \qquad \ldots (3.15)$$

Different capacitors with the same potential difference across their plates acquire greater or lesser amounts of charge on their plates and accordingly have greater or lesser capacitance, respectively.

We can write the above Equation (3.14) in terms of current as

$$i = \frac{dq}{dt} = \frac{d}{dt}(Cv) = C\frac{dv}{dt} \text{ amperes} \qquad \ldots (3.16)$$

$$\therefore \quad dv = \frac{1}{C} i \, dt \qquad \ldots (3.17)$$

Integrating both sides, we have

$$\int_0^t dv = \frac{1}{C} \int_0^t i \, dt$$

$$\therefore \quad v(t) - v(0) = \frac{1}{C} \int_0^t i \, dt$$

$$\therefore \quad v(t) = \frac{1}{C} \int_0^t i \, dt + v(0) \text{ volts} \qquad \ldots (3.18)$$

From the above equation, it is clear that the voltage appearing across the capacitor plates is dependent upon the integral of current through it, and the value of the initial voltage across it.

Equations (3.16) and (3.18) reveal the important property of the capacitor that *the voltage across a capacitor cannot change instantaneously*. Equation (3.16) shows that with a finite change in v in zero time gives a value of infinity for dv/dt, and therefore, for the capacitor current which is a physical impossibility. Further, Equation (3.18) points out that for any finite change in capacitor current, the integral term contribution to the capacitor voltage in zero time must necessarily be zero. Hence, the capacitor voltage cannot change instantaneously.

The power absorbed by the capacitor is given by

$$p = vi = vC\frac{dv}{dt} \text{ watts} \qquad \ldots (3.19)$$

Therefore, the energy stored by the capacitor is

$$W = \int_0^t p \cdot dt = \int_0^t vC\frac{dv}{dt} \cdot dt = \int_0^v Cv \cdot dv = \frac{1}{2} Cv^2 \text{ joules} \qquad \ldots (3.20)$$

This energy is actually stored in the electric field of a capacitor and is returned at a later time when the capacitor is discharged.

3.3 ALTERNATING CURRENT AND VOLTAGE

In the early days, small installations supplying power mainly for lighting homes and factories were utilizing direct currents (d.c.). *The direct current is that current which flows continuously in one direction and has constant magnitude with respect to time.* Fig. 3.2 (a) illustrates the graph for such current against time.

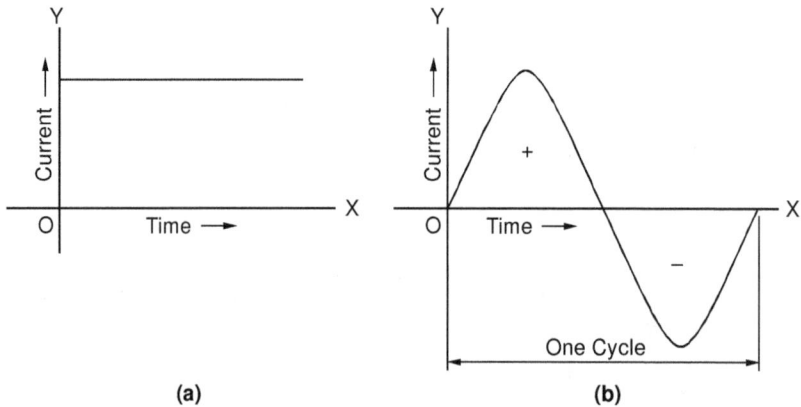

Fig. 3.2 : (a) Direct current, (b) Alternating current

The subsequent developments led to the extensive use of alternating currents. *An alternating current (a.c.) is the one which periodically passes through a definite cycle of changes in respect of magnitude as well as direction.* Each cycle consists of two half cycles. During one of these half cycles, the current flows in one direction around the circuit and during the other in the opposite direction (Fig. 3.2 b). While flowing in one particular direction, the magnitude of the current also changes in some regular manner with time.

Use of alternating current offers following principal advantages :

(i) Since it is possible to build up high-voltage, high-speed a.c. generators with very large capacities, their construction and operating costs per kilowatt are low. This is not possible in case of d.c. generators.

(ii) The a.c. voltage can be raised or lowered very easily with the help of a simple static device known as *transformer*. Raising and lowering of d.c. voltage is not so easy and economical.

(iii) Due to adoption of high voltages, a.c. transmission is always efficient and economical. This is because, higher the voltage, lesser is the current flowing through the transmission line conductors for the given power. Consequently, the volume of conductor material and power loss in the line itself are reduced.

(iv) A.C. motors are simple in construction, cheaper and more efficient than d.c. motors and require less maintenance.

(v) A.C. can be easily converted to d.c. for the applications like traction, electrolytic and other electro-chemical processes, arc lamps (used for search lights and cinema projectors), telephone and telegraph systems, charging storage batteries, modern protection systems, etc. Due to the small requirement, the generation of d.c. power for the above applications at ordinarily used voltages would be very uneconomical.

Because of the above advantages, now-a-days, electrical energy is almost exclusively generated, transmitted, distributed and ultimately utilized in the form of alternating current only. Therefore, the study of a.c. fundamentals is of prime importance.

3.4 GENERATION OF ALTERNATING CURRENT AND VOLTAGE

An electric current, whether d.c. or a.c., is now commonly produced by means of an electrical machine known as a *generator* which converts mechanical energy into electrical energy. The mechanical energy is provided by a steam turbine, an internal combustion engine, a water turbine or other prime mover which drives the generator.

Principle of Generator : The operation of all electrical generators, whether d.c. or a.c., is based on the fact that when a conductor is moved in magnetic field or a magnetic field moved with respect to the conductor, according to Faraday's law of electromagnetic induction, an electromotive force is set up in the conductor. Thus, as long as there is relative motion between a conductor and a magnetic field, a voltage will always be generated in the conductor.

A.C. generators are normally known as *alternators*.

3.4.1 Simple One Loop A.C. Generator or Elementary Alternator

Fig. 3.3 illustrates the elementary alternator.

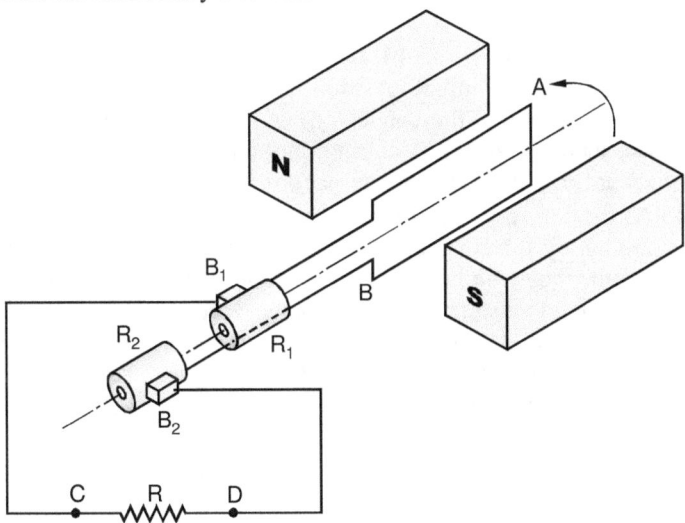

Fig. 3.3 : The elementary alternator with two poles

Construction : It consists of a single-turn rectangular coil (AB) made up of some conducting material like copper or aluminium. The coil is so placed that it can be rotated about its own axis at a constant speed in a uniform magnetic field provided by the North and South poles of the magnet. The coil is known as *armature* of the alternator. The ends of the armature coil are connected to rings (R_1 and R_2) called *slip rings* which rotate with the armature. Two carbon brushes (B_1 and B_2) pressed against the slip rings collect the current induced in the coil and carry it to the external resistor (R).

Operation : Assume that the armature coil is rotating in an anticlockwise direction. As the conductors (A and B) of the coil cut through the magnetic field, according to Faraday's law of electromagnetic induction, an e.m.f. is produced in them, which causes a current to flow through the external circuit. The magnitude of this e.m.f. is dependent on the position of the armature coil in relation to the magnetic field. Let us consider the few selected positions of the coil as shown in Fig. 3.4.

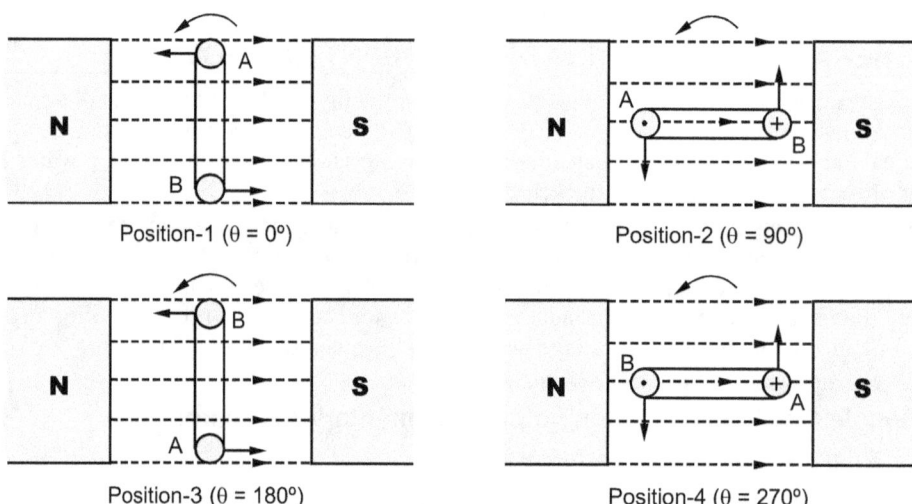

Fig. 3.4 : **The end views of the armature coil in different positions**

Position No. 1 : This is the initial position of the coil. The plane of the coil being perpendicular to the magnetic field, the conductors (A and B) of the coil move parallel to the magnetic field. Since there is no flux cutting, no e.m.f. is generated in the conductors and, therefore, no current flows through the external circuit.

Position No. 2 : As the coil rotates from Position-1 ($\theta = 0°$) to Position-2 ($\theta = 90°$), more and more lines of force are cut by the conductors. In the Position-2, both the conductors of the coil move at right angles to the magnetic field and cut through a maximum number of lines of force, so the e.m.f. induced in them is also maximum. In other words, between zero and 90°, the e.m.f. generated in the conductors builds up from zero to a maximum value. The e.m.f.s. in both the conductors being in series, the resultant coil e.m.f. is the sum of the two conductor e.m.f.s. It is, therefore, twice that of one of the conductors, since the voltages are equal.

The current through the circuit varies just as the e.m.f. varies, being zero at 0° and rising to a maximum at 90°. In Position-2 of the coil, according to Fleming's right hand rule, the direction of the induced current in conductor A is towards the observer (i.e. out of the plane of paper) and in conductor B, it is away from the observer (i.e. into the plane of paper) as indicated. Therefore, the current flows through external resistor from the terminal C to the terminal D.

Position No. 3 : As the coil continues to rotate further from Position-2 ($\theta = 90°$) to Position-3 ($\theta = 180°$), the lines of force cut by the conductors gradually reduce. This decreases the generated e.m.f. in them. In Position-3, the conductors again move parallel to the field and hence, no e.m.f. is induced in them. Therefore, the current through the external resistor is also zero. It should be noted that during the rotation of the coil from 0° to 180° (i.e. during the first half revolution), the conductors of the coil move in the same direction through the magnetic field. Therefore, throughout this period, the polarity of the generated e.m.f. remains same and current flows through the external resistor from C to D only.

Position No. 4 : As the coil rotates beyond Position-3, the direction of the cutting action of the conductors through the magnetic field reverses. Now, the conductor A cuts up through the field and the conductor B cuts down through the field. In consequence, both the polarity of the generated e.m.f. and the current flow reverse. To make it more clear, consider the coil in Position-4 ($\theta = 270°$). By applying Fleming's right hand rule, it is seen that the direction of induced current in conductor A is away from the observer and in conductor B it is towards the observer. As such, current flows through the external resistor from D to C. Thus, during the entire second half revolution, i.e. when the coil rotates from the Position-3 to Position-4 and back to Position-1, the current flows in the opposite direction to that in the first half revolution. Also, similar to Position-2, e.m.f. in the coil is maximum in Position-4. In general, the variations in the magnitude of e.m.f. of the alternator when the armature coil rotates from 180° to 360° are exactly similar to those in the first half revolution.

Graphical Representation of E.M.F. or Current : The graph of e.m.f. or current for the complete revolution of the coil under consideration is shown in Fig. 3.5.

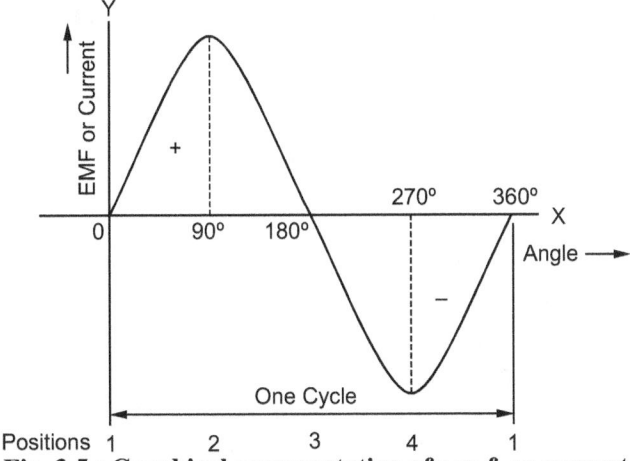

Fig. 3.5 : Graphical representation of e.m.f. or current

From the above graph, it will be readily seen that the voltage and the current supplied by such an alternator are alternating and follow a sine curve. In practice, an alternator has a number of poles and a number of coils suitably connected to obtain the necessary e.m.f.

3.5 SOME IMPORTANT TERMS

Before discussing further details, it is essential to know some basic terms which are frequently used in relation to alternating quantities.

Instantaneous Values : *Value of an alternating quantity at a particular instant is known as its instantaneous value*, e.g. i_1 and i_2 shown in Fig. 3.6 are the instantaneous values of an alternating current at different instances. The instantaneous values are always represented by small letters.

Waveform : *It is the pictorial representation of an alternating quantity in a graphical form.* In other words, *the graph obtained by plotting the instantaneous values of an alternating quantity against time gives its waveform.* The theory of alternating current is based on the assumption that the voltages and currents have sinusoidal waveforms. This greatly simplifies the theory and calculations in a.c. circuits. In actual practice, the waveforms slightly differ from sinusoidal nature.

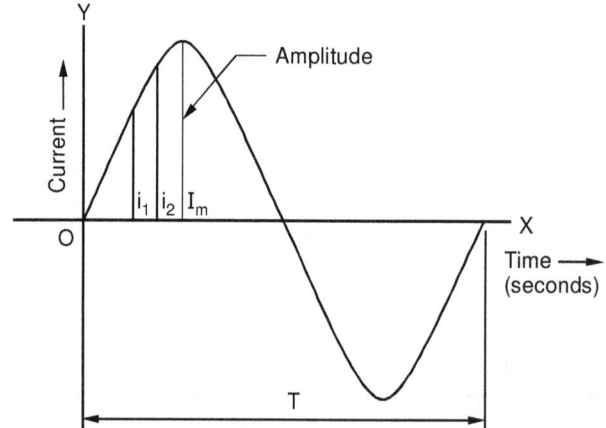

Fig. 3.6 : A cycle of an alternating current

Cycle : *Each repetition of a complete set of changes undergone by the alternating quantity is called cycle.* These repetitions recur at equal intervals. One such cycle of an alternating current is shown in Fig. 3.6.

Period or Periodic Time (T) : *It is the time (in seconds) required by an alternating quantity to complete its one cycle.*

Frequency (f) : *The number of cycles completed per second by an alternating quantity is known as its frequency.* It is measured in *hertz* (Hz). From the definitions of period and frequency, it is observed that

$$f = \frac{1}{T} \text{ hertz} \qquad \ldots(3.21)$$

Our country has adopted a frequency of 50 Hz for alternating currents and voltages. Naturally, with this frequency, the alternating current or voltage has time period of

$$T = \frac{1}{f} = \frac{1}{50} = 0.02 \text{ s}$$

Amplitude : *The maximum value attained by an alternating quantity during its positive or negative half cycle is called its amplitude or peak value.*

Electrical Angle : In the elementary two-pole alternator, we have seen that one revolution of the coil generates one cycle of e.m.f. Thus, one cycle of e.m.f. wave spans 360 mechanical degrees or 2π mechanical radians. In practical multipolar generators of alternating current, one revolution of the coil generates more than one cycle. But still, for mathematical convenience, each cycle of e.m.f. is assumed to span 360 degrees or 2π radians. But now the angles measured by these units do not necessarily correspond to the mechanical angles actually turned through by the rotating parts of the generator. These new units of angle are called *electrical degrees* and *electrical radians*. The angle measured in electrical degrees or electrical radians is called *electrical angle*.

In 2-pole machine, one revolution of the coil which generates one cycle of e.m.f., corresponds to angular rotation through

$$360° \text{ mechanical} = 360° \text{ electrical}$$

∴ $$1° \text{ mechanical} = 1° \text{ electrical}$$

But with 4-pole machine, one revolution of the coil which generates 2 cycles of e.m.f., corresponds to angular rotation through

$$360° \text{ mechanical} = 2 \times 360° \text{ electrical}$$

∴ $$1° \text{ mechanical} = 2° \text{ electrical}$$

In general, in a P-pole machine, $\frac{P}{2}$ cycles are generated in one revolution, so in that case,

$$1° \text{ mechanical} = \left(\frac{P}{2}\right)° \text{ electrical} \qquad \ldots (3.22)$$

Angular Frequency : *It is the frequency expressed in electrical radians per second.* Since one cycle of an alternating quantity spans 2π electrical radians, the angular frequency is given by

$$\omega = 2\pi f \text{ electrical radians / second} \qquad \ldots (3.23)$$

where f is the frequency in hertz.

3.6 EQUATIONS OF ALTERNATING VOLTAGES AND CURRENTS

In the Section (3.4.1), we have seen that when the single turn rectangular armature coil of an elementary alternator rotates at constant angular velocity in a uniform magnetic field, an alternating e.m.f. is induced in it which follows a sine curve. Now, let us derive the mathematical equation to represent such an e.m.f. For that purpose, let

  B = Flux density of the magnetic field, in teslas

  l = Active length of each conductor (coil side), in metres

  r = Radius of circular path traced out by the conductors, in metres

  ω = Angular velocity of the coil, in radians/second

  v = Linear velocity of the coil sides, in metres/second (= r ω)

Reckon time from the instant when the coil lies in the plane of reference YOY and has zero e.m.f. Angle turned through by the coil in t seconds will be given by $\theta = \omega t$.

Fig. 3.7 shows the coil AB after it has rotated through this angle θ. At this instant, the peripheral velocity of each coil side can be resolved into two components, one perpendicular and other parallel to the direction of the magnetic flux as shown in Fig. 3.7.

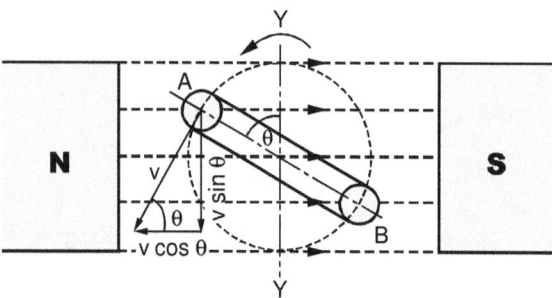

Fig. 3.7 : Instantaneous value of generated e.m.f.

The e.m.f. generated in each coil side is entirely due to the component, 'v sin θ' of the velocity perpendicular to the magnetic field. Therefore, using the standard expression for the magnitude of a dynamically induced e.m.f., it follows that at any instant,

E.M.F. generated in each coil side $= Blv \sin \theta$ volts

∴ Total e.m.f. generated in the coil, $e = 2Blv \sin \theta$ volts ...(3.24)

When $\theta = 90°$, the coil will be in the horizontal plane and both the conductors A and B will cut the magnetic flux at a maximum rate. Naturally, e.m.f. in this position of the coil will reach its maximum value, E_m. From Expression (3.24), it follows that when $\theta = 90°$,

$$E_m = 2Blv \text{ volts} \qquad (\because \sin \theta = 1)$$

The Equation (3.24) for the instantaneous value of e.m.f. generated in the coil can, therefore, be written in different forms as follows :

$$e = E_m \sin \theta = E_m \sin \omega t = E_m \sin 2\pi ft \qquad (\because \omega = 2\pi f)$$

$$= E_m \sin \frac{2\pi t}{T} \qquad ...(3.25)$$

The instantaneous value of sinusoidal alternating current set up by the above e.m.f. can also be expressed by similar equations as follows :

$$i = I_m \sin \theta = I_m \sin \omega t = I_m \sin 2\pi ft = I_m \sin \frac{2\pi t}{T} \qquad ...(3.26)$$

Example 3.1 : *If the e.m.f. is represented by the equation $e = 150 \sin 314\, t$, what is its maximum value and the frequency ? Reckoning time from the instant the e.m.f. is zero and is changing from negative to positive, calculate the instantaneous value of this e.m.f. at $\frac{1}{300}$ second from the origin.*

Solution : Comparing with the standard form of the equation

$$e = E_m \sin 2\pi ft, \text{ we get}$$

Maximum value, $E_m = $ **150 V** ... Ans.

and $\omega = 2\pi f = 314$

∴ $f = \dfrac{314}{2\pi} = $ **50 Hz** ... Ans.

The instantaneous value of the e.m.f. at $t = \dfrac{1}{300}$ second from the origin will be given by,

$$e = 150 \sin\left(314 \times \dfrac{1}{300}\right)$$

It should be remembered that in the above equation, the angle is in radians. If converted to degrees, the instantaneous value of the e.m.f. will be given by

$$e = 150 \sin\left(314 \times \dfrac{1}{300} \times \dfrac{180°}{\pi}\right)$$

$$= \mathbf{129.86 \ V} \qquad \text{... Ans.}$$

Example 3.2 : *In an a.c. circuit, supply voltage is given in usual notations by*

$$e = 100 \sin \omega t \text{ volts}$$

Calculate the magnitudes of 'e' at time t = 0.005 s for (i) f = 50 Hz, (ii) f = 150 Hz. Sketch the approximate waveforms of 'e' from time t = 0 to t = 0.01 s for both cases, with the same time axis.

Solution : (i)

$$\begin{aligned} e &= 100 \sin \omega t = 100 \sin 2\pi f t \\ &= 100 \sin 2\pi \times 50 \times t \\ &= 100 \sin 314\, t \end{aligned}$$

At $t = 0.005$ s,

$$e = 100 \sin (314 \times 0.005) \times \dfrac{180°}{\pi}$$

$$= \mathbf{100 \ V} \qquad \text{... Ans.}$$

(ii)

$$\begin{aligned} e &= 100 \sin \omega t = 100 \sin 2\pi f t \\ &= 100 \sin 2\pi \times 150 \times t \\ &= 100 \sin (942.48\, t) \end{aligned}$$

At $t = 0.005$ s,

$$e = 100 \sin (942.48 \times 0.005)\, \dfrac{180°}{\pi}$$

$$= \mathbf{-100 \ V} \qquad \text{... Ans.}$$

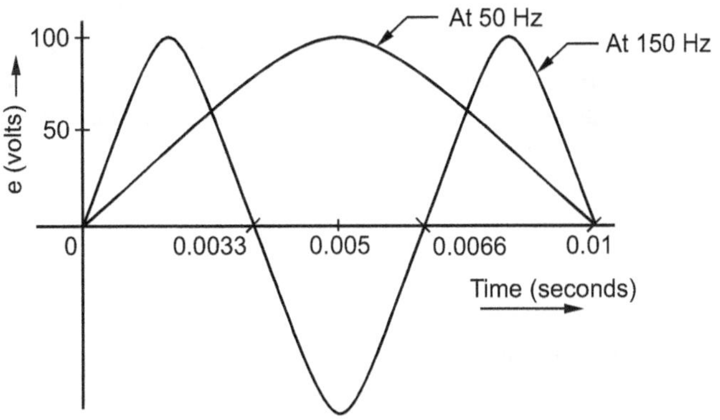

Fig. 3.8 : Supply voltage waveforms, Example 3.2

3.7 EFFECTIVE OR ROOT MEAN SQUARE (R.M.S.) VALUE OF SINUSOIDAL CURRENT OR VOLTAGE

The magnitude of an alternating current varies from instant to instant, whereas the magnitude of a direct current remains constant with respect to time. Therefore, we need a common measure to judge the relative effectiveness of the two currents in performing useful functions. Such a measure may be developed from the consideration of the effects produced by the two currents. One such effect is heating in resistance. Based on this, the effective or r.m.s. value of an alternating current is defined as follows :

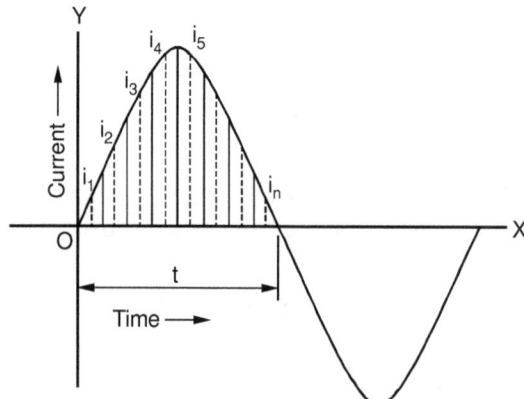

Fig. 3.9 : Mid-ordinate method to find r.m.s. value

The effective or r.m.s. value of an alternating current is given by that direct current which, when flowing through a given circuit for a given time, produces the same amount of heat as produced by the alternating current when flowing through the same circuit for the same time.

Now, let us consider the case of an alternating current having sinusoidal waveform as shown in Fig. 3.9. Its effective or r.m.s. value can be found by the following two methods :

(a) Graphical method, (b) Analytical method.

Graphical Method : As heating effect is proportional to the square of the current, it is not directional. Moreover, both the half cycles are perfectly symmetrical as far as the numerical values of current are concerned. Therefore, for finding the r.m.s. value, we need to consider only half wave. Divide the time base 't' of this half wave into n equal intervals, each of t / n seconds. Erect the mid-ordinates $i_1, i_2, i_3, \ldots, i_n$ which give the average values of instantaneous currents during these intervals. Let the resistance be R ohms through which this alternating current is passed. We know that passage of current through the resistance causes loss of electrical energy which ultimately appears in the form of heat. Then,

$$\text{Heat produced in the 1}^{st} \text{ interval} = i_1^2 R \frac{t}{n} \text{ joules}$$

$$\text{Heat produced in the 2}^{nd} \text{ interval} = i_2^2 R \frac{t}{n} \text{ joules}$$

$$\text{Heat produced in the n}^{th} \text{ interval} = i_n^2 R \frac{t}{n} \text{ joules}$$

$$\text{Total heat produced in t seconds} = Rt \frac{(i_1^2 + i_2^2 + \ldots + i_n^2)}{n} \text{ joules} \qquad \ldots (3.27)$$

Now, let the effective value of this current be I amperes. The heat developed by a direct current of I amperes when flowing in a resistance of R ohms for t seconds is

$$= I^2 R t \qquad \ldots (3.28)$$

By definition, the amount of heat given by two expressions (3.27) and (3.28) should be equal.

Therefore, we get $\qquad I^2 R t = R t \dfrac{(i_1^2 + i_2^2 + \ldots + i_n^2)}{n}$

i.e. $\qquad\qquad I = \sqrt{\dfrac{(i_1^2 + i_2^2 + \ldots + i_n^2)}{n}} \qquad \ldots (3.29)$

$\qquad\qquad\quad =$ Square root of mean of squares of the successive ordinates (i.e. instantaneous values)

The effective value is also called the *root mean square (r.m.s.) value* because of the nature of the above Expression (3.29). Sometimes, it is also called as *virtual value*.

The r.m.s. value of sinusoidal voltage can be obtained in a similar fashion and is given by the following expression :

$$V = \sqrt{\dfrac{(v_1^2 + v_2^2 + \ldots + v_n^2)}{n}} \qquad \ldots (3.30)$$

Analytical Method : Since the alternating current or voltage can be represented by a simple mathematical expression, it is possible to find its r.m.s. value by analytical method. With a sinusoidal current, we have

$$i = I_m \sin \theta$$

$\therefore \qquad\qquad\qquad i^2 = I_m^2 \sin^2 \theta$

If the square curve, i.e. the curve for $i^2 = I_m^2 \sin^2 \theta$ be plotted (Fig. 3.10), the area under this curve over half a cycle will be given by

$$\text{Area of squared curve over half a cycle} = \int_0^\pi i^2 \, d\theta$$

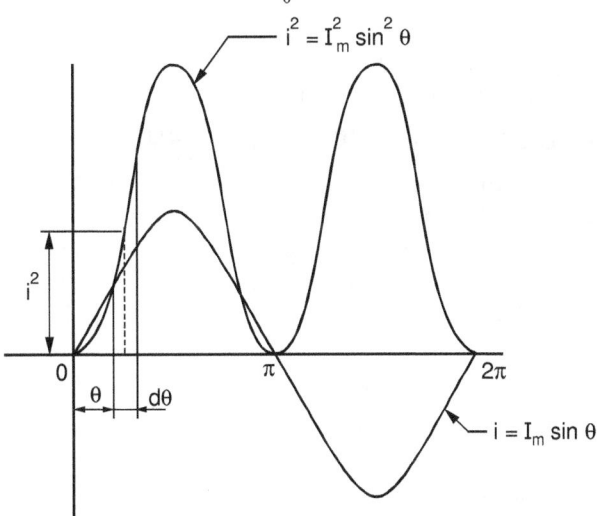

Fig. 3.10 : R.M.S. value of sinusoidal current

Since the length of the base is π, mean height or mean value of ordinates of squared curve (i^2) over half a cycle

$$= \frac{\text{Area of squared curve over half a cycle}}{\text{Length of base over half a cycle}}$$

$$= \frac{1}{\pi} \int_0^\pi i^2 \, d\theta$$

$$= \frac{1}{\pi} \int_0^\pi I_m^2 \sin^2 \theta \, d\theta \qquad (\because i = I_m \sin \theta)$$

$$= \frac{I_m^2}{\pi} \int_0^\pi \left[\frac{1 - \cos 2\theta}{2} \right] d\theta$$

$$= \frac{I_m^2}{2\pi} \left[\theta - \frac{\sin 2\theta}{2} \right]_0^\pi = \frac{I_m^2}{2\pi} \times \pi = \frac{I_m^2}{2}$$

Hence, the r.m.s. value of sinusoidal current is

$$I = \sqrt{\frac{I_m^2}{2}} = \frac{I_m}{\sqrt{2}}$$

Or, $\qquad I = 0.707 \, I_m \qquad \ldots (3.31)$

Thus, *r.m.s. value of sinusoidal current is 0.707 times its maximum or peak value*. In a similar way, it can be shown that r.m.s. value of sinusoidal voltage is given by

$$V = 0.707 \, V_m \qquad \ldots (3.32)$$

It should be noted that r.m.s. values of alternating quantities are always represented by capital letters, e.g. V, I, E, etc.

Practical Importance of R.M.S. Values : The r.m.s. values are extremely important as these are the values invariably used in actual practice for specifying the magnitudes of alternating quantities. Moreover, the most common a.c. instruments inherently indicate r.m.s. values only.

3.8 AVERAGE VALUE OF SINUSOIDAL CURRENT OR VOLTAGE

For sinusoidal current or voltage, *average value is that value which is obtained by averaging all the instantaneous values of its wave over a period of half cycle*. For such a current or voltage, the two half cycles being exactly similar, average value over a complete cycle is zero. Hence, a period of half cycle only is considered for obtaining average value. Similar to r.m.s. value, average value for sinusoidal current or voltage can also be found by either graphical or analytical method.

Graphical Method : As mentioned previously, in graphical method for finding r.m.s. value, if n equidistant mid-ordinates are erected over the half cycle of sinusoidal current wave (Fig. 3.9), then

Average value of current over half a cycle,

$$I_{av} = \frac{(i_1 + i_2 + \ldots + i_n)}{n} \qquad \ldots (3.33)$$

Similarly, for a sinusoidal voltage,

$$V_{av} = \frac{(v_1 + v_2 + \ldots + v_n)}{n} \quad \ldots (3.34)$$

Analytical Method : For sinusoidal current, its instantaneous value is represented by

$$i = I_m \sin \theta$$

Fig. 3.11 shows one cycle of such sinusoidal current wave.

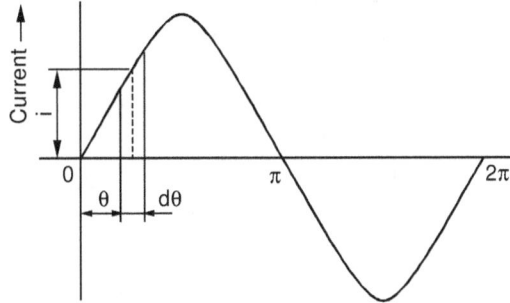

Fig. 3.11 : Average value of sinusoidal current

Total area under the current wave over half a cycle

$$= \int_0^\pi i \, d\theta$$

∴ Average value of current over half a cycle,

$$I_{av} = \frac{\text{Area under the curve over half a cycle}}{\text{Length of base over half a cycle}} = \frac{1}{\pi} \int_0^\pi i \, d\theta$$

$$= \frac{1}{\pi} \int_0^\pi I_m \sin \theta \cdot d\theta \quad (\because i = I_m \sin \theta)$$

$$= \frac{I_m}{\pi} [-\cos \theta]_0^\pi = \frac{2I_m}{\pi}$$

i.e. $\quad I_{av} = 0.637 \, I_m \quad \ldots (3.35)$

Thus, *for sinusoidal current, average value is 0.637 times its maximum value.* The same thing is true for sinusoidal voltage, i.e.

$$V_{av} = 0.637 \, V_m \quad \ldots (3.36)$$

Practical Importance of Average Values : Since alternating current flows in one direction during the first half cycle and then in the opposite direction during the next half cycle, it cannot be employed for electrochemical work (e.g. battery charging, electroplating, etc.). If, however, the a.c. wave be rectified, i.e. made to flow in one direction only, we get a fluctuating but unidirectional current. If such current is used for electrochemical work, the useful effect that is produced is directly proportional to the average value of the current. This is the only field where average value has some practical importance.

3.9 PEAK FACTOR AND FORM FACTOR

These are the factors which relate the maximum, average and r.m.s. values of an alternating quantity.

Peak Factor : It is defined as *the ratio of maximum value of an alternating quantity to its r.m.s. value.* This factor is also many times called as *crest factor* or *amplitude factor*. For sinusoidal current or voltage,

$$\text{Peak factor} = \frac{\text{Maximum value}}{\text{R.M.S. value}} = \frac{\text{Maximum value}}{0.707 \times \text{Maximum value}}$$

$$= 1.414 \qquad \ldots (3.37)$$

Since this factor gives the relationship between maximum value and r.m.s. value, its knowledge is very useful in the applications like insulation testing and measurement of iron losses.

Form Factor : *The ratio of r.m.s. value to average value is called the form factor of an alternating quantity.* For sinusoidal current or voltage,

$$\text{Form Factor} = \frac{\text{R.M.S. value}}{\text{Average value}} = \frac{0.707 \times \text{Maximum value}}{0.637 \times \text{Maximum value}}$$

$$= 1.11 \qquad \ldots (3.38)$$

The knowledge of this factor helps in determining the r.m.s. value of an alternating quantity from its average value and vice versa.

Example 3.3 : *What are the r.m.s. and average values of a sinusoidal alternating current with maximum value of 25 A ?*

Solution :

$$\text{R.M.S. value} = \frac{\text{Maximum value}}{\text{Peak factor}} = \frac{25}{1.414} = \textbf{17.68 A} \qquad \ldots \text{Ans.}$$

$$\therefore \quad \text{Average value} = \frac{\text{R.M.S. value}}{\text{Form factor}} = \frac{17.68}{1.11} = \textbf{15.93 A} \qquad \ldots \text{Ans.}$$

Example 3.4 : *Draw the waveform of an a.c. voltage given by $e = E_m \sin \omega t$ which reaches a maximum value of 5 V and has a time period of 1/100 s. Also find its average value.*

Solution : $E_m = 5$ V, $f = \dfrac{1}{T} = \dfrac{1}{0.01} = 100$ Hz

Therefore, equation for the waveform will be as follows :

$$e = E_m \sin \omega t = E_m \sin 2\pi f t = 5 \sin 2\pi \times 100 \times t = 5 \sin 628.32\, t \text{ volts}$$

Average value of the voltage, $E_{av} = 0.637 \times 5 = \textbf{3.185 V}$ ... Ans.

Fig. 3.12 shows the necessary waveform.

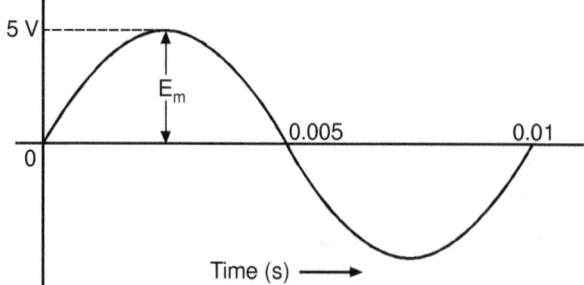

Fig. 3.12 : Waveform of an a.c. voltage, Example 3.4

Example 3.5 : *An alternating voltage is mathematically expressed as*

$$v = 141.42 \sin\left(157.08\, t + \frac{\pi}{12}\right) \text{ volts}$$

Find its effective value, frequency and periodic time.

Solution : $\quad v = 141.42 \sin\left(157.08\, t + \frac{\pi}{12}\right)$ volts

Hence, $\quad V_m = 141.42$ V

∴ Effective (r.m.s.) value,

$$V = \frac{141.42}{\sqrt{2}} = 100 \text{ V} \qquad \text{... Ans.}$$

Frequency, $f = \dfrac{157.08}{2\pi} = 25$ Hz $\qquad$ ... Ans.

Periodic time, $T = \dfrac{1}{f} = \dfrac{1}{25} = 0.04$ s $\qquad$ ... Ans.

Example 3.6 : *A 60 Hz sinusoidal alternating current has a peak value of 14.14 A. Its zero crossing entering the positive half cycle occurs at t = 0.*

  (i) *Write down the time equation of the current.*

  (ii) *Calculate its r.m.s. value.*

  (iii) *Determine the time taken for the current to reach a value of −10 A for the first time in the cycle.*

Solution :

(i) $\quad i = I_m \sin \omega t = 14.14 \sin(2\pi f t) = 14.14 \sin(2\pi \times 60\, t)$

Or, $\quad i = 14.14 \sin(120\,\pi\, t)$ **amperes** $\qquad$ ... Ans.

(ii) R.M.S. value, $I = \dfrac{I_m}{\sqrt{2}} = \dfrac{14.14}{\sqrt{2}} = 10$ A $\qquad$ ... Ans.

(iii) Time t to reach the value of −10 A is given by

$$i = -10 = 14.14 \sin 120\,\pi t$$

∴ $\quad \sin 120\,\pi t = \dfrac{-10}{14.14} = -0.707$

∴ $\quad 120\,\pi t = \dfrac{5\pi}{4}$ radians (i.e. 225°) or $\dfrac{7\pi}{4}$ radians (i.e. 315°)

Since we want the time taken for the current to reach a value of −10 A for the first time in the cycle, taking the first value, we have

$$120\,\pi t = \frac{5\pi}{4}$$

∴ $\qquad\qquad t = 0.0104$ s $\qquad$ ... Ans.

Example 3.7 : *An alternating current varying sinusoidally with a frequency of 50 Hz has a r.m.s. value of 20 A. If the waveform of this current enters into its positive half cycle at t = 0, write down the equation for the instantaneous value and find this value : (i) 0.0025 s, (ii) 0.0125 s after passing through a positive maximum value.*

Solution : (i) R.M.S. value of the current, I = 20 A

∴ Maximum value of the current,

$$I_m = 20\sqrt{2} = 28.28 \text{ A}$$

Hence, instantaneous value of the current is given by

$$i = I_m \sin \omega t = I_m \sin 2\pi ft = 28.28 \sin (2\pi \times 50 \times t)$$

Or, $i = 28.28 \sin 314 \, t$ ... **Ans.**

(ii) Time to reach positive maximum value $= \dfrac{\text{Periodic time}}{4} = \dfrac{0.02}{4} = 0.005$ s

At t = 0.005 + 0.0025 = 0.0075 s,

$$i = 28.28 \sin (314 \times 0.0075) \dfrac{180°}{\pi} = \mathbf{20.02 \text{ A}} \quad \text{... \textbf{Ans.}}$$

(iii) At t = 0.005 + 0.0125 = 0.0175 s,

$$i = 28.28 \sin (314 \times 0.0175) \dfrac{180°}{\pi} = \mathbf{-20.06 \text{ A}} \quad \text{... \textbf{Ans.}}$$

Example 3.8 : *A periodically varying voltage has following values over one half of its cycle, the other half being repeated symmetrically on negative side.*

Time (ms)	0	20	40	60	80	100	120	140	160	180	200
Voltage (V)	0	4	8	12	16	20	16	12	8	4	0

At the end of each time interval, the value of the voltage changes instantaneously from one value to the next. Determine :

(i) The average value, (ii) The r.m.s. value, (iii) The form factor.

Solution : Fig. 3.13 shows the waveform for the voltage.

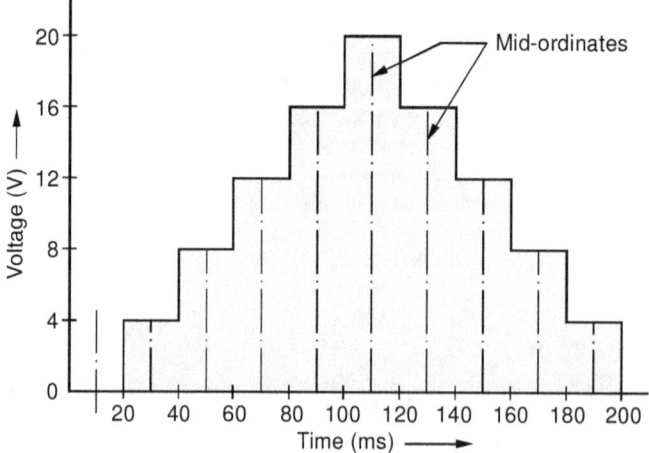

Fig. 3.13 : Waveform for voltage, Example 3.8

Even though the voltage waveform is not sinusoidal, it is symmetrical. Hence, its r.m.s. value may be found by considering either half-cycle or full one cycle. But its average value must be found by considering half-cycle only (average over a cycle being zero). Hence, using mid-ordinate method, we have

(i) Average value, $V_{av} = \dfrac{v_1 + v_2 + v_3 + \ldots + v_n}{n}$

$= \dfrac{0 + 4 + 8 + 12 + 16 + 20 + 16 + 12 + 8 + 4}{10}$

$= \dfrac{100}{10} = \mathbf{10\ V}$ ... Ans.

(ii) Mean value of v^2 over half a cycle $= \dfrac{0^2 + 4^2 + 8^2 + 12^2 + 16^2 + 20^2 + 16^2 + 12^2 + 8^2 + 4^2}{10}$

$= \dfrac{1360}{10} = 136\ V$

∴ R.M.S. value, $V = \sqrt{\text{Mean value of } v^2 \text{ over half a cycle}}$

$= \sqrt{136} = \mathbf{11.66\ V}$ ... Ans.

(iii) Form factor $= \dfrac{\text{R.M.S. value}}{\text{Average value}} = \dfrac{11.66}{10} = \mathbf{1.166}$ ... Ans.

Example 3.9 : *Find the average and r.m.s. values of a resultant current in a wire which carries simultaneously a direct current of 5 A and a sinusoidal alternating current with a peak value of 5 A.*

Solution : Fig. 3.14 shows the resultant current wave.

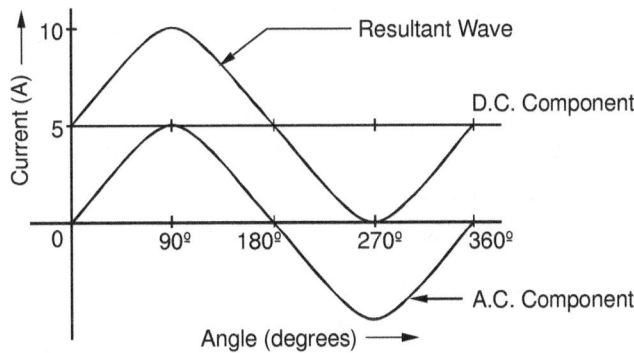

Fig. 3.14 : Current waveforms, Example 3.9

The instantaneous value of the resultant current can be represented by the following expression :

$i = i_{dc} + i_{ac} = 5 + 5 \sin \omega t = 5 + 5 \sin \theta$ amperes

(i) Average value of sinusoidal current over one complete cycle is zero. Hence, the average value of the resultant current over a cycle is equal to the value of d.c. component.

Thus, Average value of the resultant current, $I_{av} = \mathbf{5\ A}$ ... Ans.

(ii) Let I be the r.m.s. value of the resultant current and R be the resistance of the wire through which this current is passed for t seconds. Then, by definition, equating heat produced by the resultant current with the sum of heat produced by its individual components under identical condition, we have

$$I^2 R t = 5^2 \times R \times t + \left(\frac{5}{\sqrt{2}}\right)^2 \times R \times t$$

Here, it should be remembered that r.m.s. value of the a.c. component is $\frac{5}{\sqrt{2}}$.

∴ R.M.S. value of the resultant current,

$$I = 6.1237 \text{ A} \qquad \text{... Ans.}$$

Example 3.10 : *A 60 Hz sinusoidal current has an instantaneous value of 7.07 A at t = 0 and r.m.s. value of $10\sqrt{2}$. Assuming the current increasing positively at t = 0, determine :*

(i)   Expression for current.

(ii) Magnitude of current at t = 0.0125 s and t = 0.025 s after t = 0.

Solution : (i) Since the given sinusoidal current has instantaneous value of +7.07 A at t = 0 and it is increasing positively, its waveform must have started earlier with respect to the point from which time is reckoned (i.e. origin) as illustrated in Fig. 3.15.

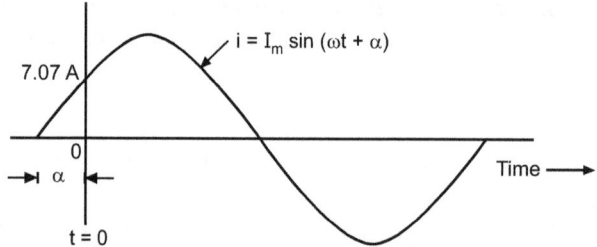

Fig. 3.15 : Sine wave with phase angle α, Example 3.10

The sine wave for such a current can be represented by the equation,

$$i = I_m \sin(\omega t + \alpha) = I_m \sin(2\pi f t + \alpha)^*$$

where α is generally known as *phase angle* of a wave.

Now with $\quad f = 60 \text{ Hz}, \quad I_m = \sqrt{2} I_{rms} = \sqrt{2} \times 10\sqrt{2} = 20 \text{ A}.$

$$i = 20 \sin(2\pi \times 60 \times t + \alpha)$$

$$= 20 \sin(376.99 \, t + \alpha)$$

---

* *Depending upon the value of the phase angle (i.e. the angle from zero point on the wave to the value at the point from which time is reckoned), the general expression for sinusoidal current is given by*

$$i = I_m \sin(\omega t \pm \alpha) \text{ amperes}$$

Similarly, for sinusoidal voltage, the expression is

$$v = V_m \sin(\omega t \pm \alpha) \text{ volts}$$

Further, it is given that when t = 0, i = 7.07 A. Hence,

$$7.07 = 20 \sin (376.99 \times 0 + \alpha)$$

∴ $\quad \sin \alpha = \dfrac{7.07}{20} = 0.3535$

∴ $\quad \alpha = 20.7°$ or 0.3613 radian.

Hence, the expression for current is

$$i = \mathbf{20 \sin (376.99\, t + 0.3613)} \textbf{ amperes} \quad \text{... Ans.}$$

(ii) At t = 0.0125 s,

$$i = 20 \sin (376.99 \times 0.0125 + 0.3613) \dfrac{180°}{\pi}$$

$$= \mathbf{-18.7 \text{ A}} \quad \text{... Ans.}$$

At t = 0.025 s,

$$i = 20 \sin (376.99 \times 0.025 + 0.3613) \dfrac{180°}{\pi}$$

$$= \mathbf{-7.07 \text{ A}} \quad \text{... Ans.}$$

3.10 PHASOR REPRESENTATION OF ALTERNATING QUANTITIES

In the study of a.c. circuits, we have to deal with many alternating quantities. It is, however, always cumbersome to handle these quantities in the form of their waves or mathematical equations (like $i = I_m \sin \omega t$, etc.). It is, therefore, appropriate to devise a shorthand method of representing these quantities. One such method is to represent them with the help of rotating phasors. A phasor is a directed arrow analogous to vector used to represent the magnitude and direction of a quantity in space, e.g. force in mechanics. Consider a phasor OA rotating in an anti-clockwise direction with uniform angular velocity (Fig. 3.16).

If the projections on Y-axis of this phasor in its different positions are plotted against the angle turned through (or time), we get a sine waveform. Therefore, the alternating quantity following a sine waveform can always be represented by such a rotating phasor.

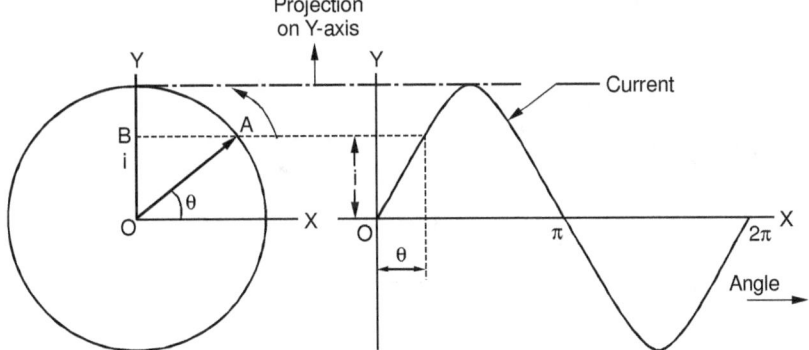

Fig. 3.16 : Phasor representation of the alternating quantity

Let the phasor OA in Fig. 3.16 represent some sinusoidal alternating quantity, say current. If the length of OA is taken equal to maximum value, I_m of the sinusoidal current, then at any instant, the projection on Y-axis will be

$$OB = OA \sin \theta = I_m \sin \theta$$

Hence, OB = i, the instantaneous value of the current. Thus, if the length of phasor is taken equal to the maximum value of the alternating quantity, then its orientation in space at any instant is such that the length of its projection on Y-axis gives the instantaneous value of alternating quantity at that particular instant.

In practice, we deal more frequently with the r.m.s. values of the alternating quantities. Moreover, r.m.s. value bears a definite relationship to the maximum value. Therefore, the phasors are normally drawn to represent r.m.s. values of alternating quantities. In this case, the projection of a phasor on Y-axis does not give directly the instantaneous value but it is to be multiplied by $\sqrt{2}$ to get such a value. It is important to note that the phasors are always assumed to rotate in a counter-clockwise direction. This is purely a conventional direction which has been universally adopted. The phasor representation greatly simplifies the calculation work involved in a.c. circuits.

3.11 PHASE AND PHASE DIFFERENCE

Considering the instant when alternating quantity passes through zero and increases in the positive direction as a reference point, the fraction of the time period (T) that elapses in achieving certain instantaneous value is known as *phase* of that alternating quantity. For example, in Fig. 3.17, phase of the alternating quantity at point P is T/4 seconds or when expressed in terms of angle, it is π/2 radians.

In other words, the orientation in space at a particular instant (i.e. the angle turned through from reference axis) of the rotating phasor representing a certain alternating quantity also gives its *phase*. Considering again the case of point P (Fig. 3.17), the corresponding rotation of phasor OA will be through $\frac{\pi}{2}$ radians from the reference axis OX. Therefore, phase at this point is $\frac{\pi}{2}$ radians.

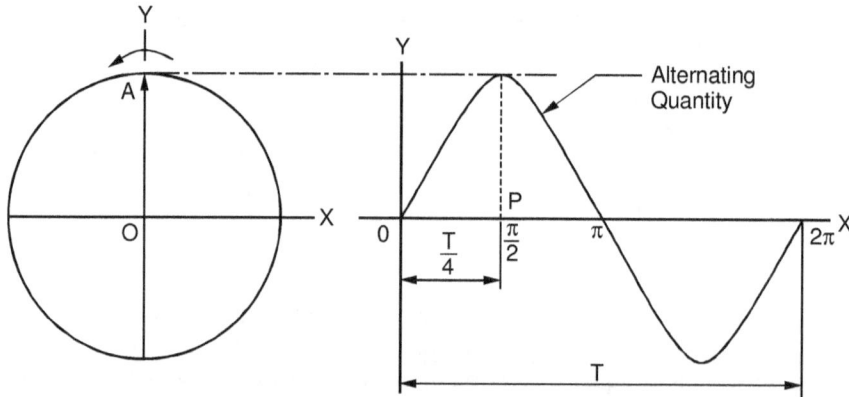

Fig. 3.17 : Phase of an alternating quantity

In practice, we are, however, more concerned with *relative phases* or *phase difference* between different alternating quantities rather than with their absolute phases.

Phase Difference : Consider two single-turn coils A and B of different dimensions arranged radially in the same plane and mounted rigidly on the common shaft as shown in Fig. 3.18 (a).

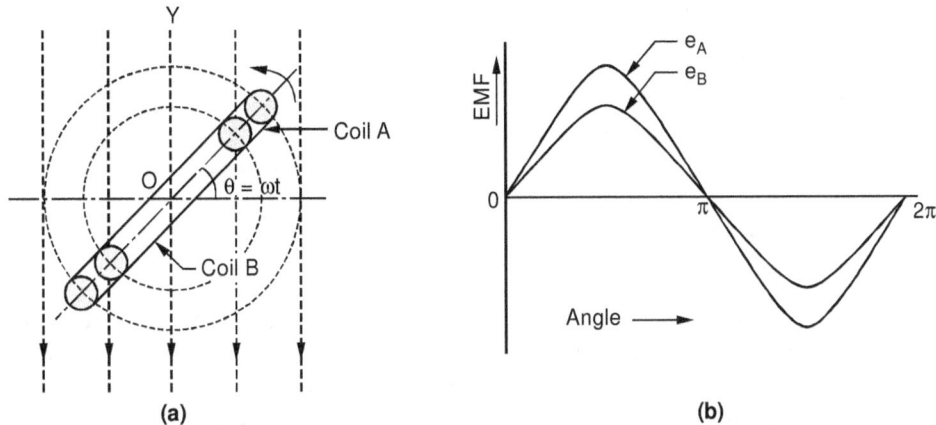

Fig. 3.18 : Two alternating quantities in phase

Let the two coils rotate together with some constant angular velocity in the uniform magnetic field. Then, as seen in the case of an elementary alternator (Fig. 3.3), sinusoidal e.m.f.s will be induced in these two coils. These e.m.f.s will have the same frequency but different values at every instant. Even though the values of these e.m.f.s will be different at every instant, they would reach their respective maximum or zero values at the same time (Fig. 3.18 b). Such e.m.f.s are said to be *in phase* (i.e. in step) with each other.

Thus, *when two alternating quantities of the same frequency attain their corresponding values (e.g. zero, positive maximum, etc.) simultaneously, they are said to be in phase with each other.*

The two alternating e.m.f.s in the coils A and B considered above can be represented by the following equations :

$$e_A = E_{mA} \sin \theta = E_{mA} \sin \omega t \qquad \ldots (3.39)$$

$$e_B = E_{mB} \sin \theta = E_{mB} \sin \omega t \qquad \ldots (3.40)$$

Now, assume that coil B is displaced from coil A by an angle α as shown in Fig. 3.19 (a). In this condition, it will be observed that the e.m.f.s induced in the two coils will not reach their maximum or zero values at the same instant. Thus, the two e.m.f.s will be out of step with one another. In technical terms, *such two alternating quantities of the same frequency which attain their corresponding values at different instants are said to be out of phase.*

Fig. 3.19 (b) shows the waveforms for the e.m.f.s induced in the two coils. It will be seen that there is an angular displacement of α between the two curves. This angular displacement between the waveforms of the two e.m.f.s is known as *phase difference* between them. When the phase difference between the two alternating quantities is $\pi/2$ radians (90º), they are said to be in *quadrature*, and when it is 180º, they are in *phase opposition*.

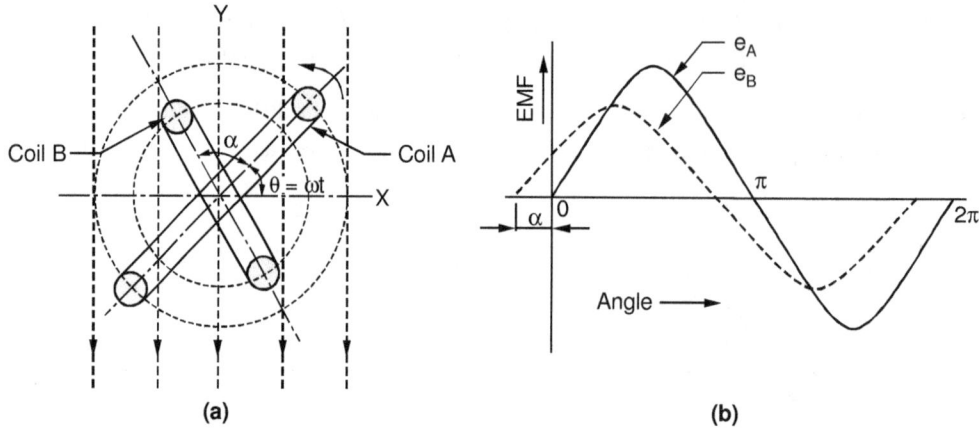

Fig. 3.19 : Two alternating quantities out of phase

The waveforms shown in Fig. 3.19 (b) also reveal that the e.m.f. induced in the coil B attains its zero or maximum value earlier than the e.m.f. in the coil A by an angle α. Therefore, the e.m.f. in the coil B is said to be *leading* by an angle α with respect to the e.m.f. in the coil A or alternatively, the e.m.f. in the coil A is said to be *lagging* by an angle α behind the e.m.f. in the coil B.

Thus, we can define a *leading alternating quantity as one which attains its zero or maximum value earlier as compared with the other quantity.* Similarly, *lagging alternating quantity is that which attains its zero or maximum value latter than the other quantity.*

In the case considered above, if the e.m.f. in the coil A is represented by the equation,

$$e_A = E_{mA} \sin \omega t \qquad \ldots (3.41)$$

then, the e.m.f. in the coil B will be represented by

$$e_B = E_{mB} \sin (\omega t + \alpha) \qquad \ldots (3.42)$$

On the other hand, if the e.m.f. in the coil B is taken as a reference and represented by the equation,

$$e_B = E_{mB} \sin \omega t \qquad \ldots (3.43)$$

then the e.m.f. in the coil A will be represented by the equation :

$$e_A = E_{mA} \sin (\omega t - \alpha) \qquad \ldots (3.44)$$

Thus, *in connection with the phase difference, a plus (+) sign indicates lead whereas a minus (−) sign indicates lag in reference to the given alternating quantity.*

3.12 PHASOR DIAGRAMS

The diagram in which different alternating quantities (sinusoidal) of the same frequency are represented by phasors with their correct phase relationships is known as a phasor diagram. The phasors representing different alternating quantities of the same frequency rotate in an anti-clockwise direction with the same angular velocity ($\omega = 2\pi f$). As such they maintain a fixed position relative to each other. Therefore, a phasor diagram can be considered as a still picture of these phasors in one particular position.

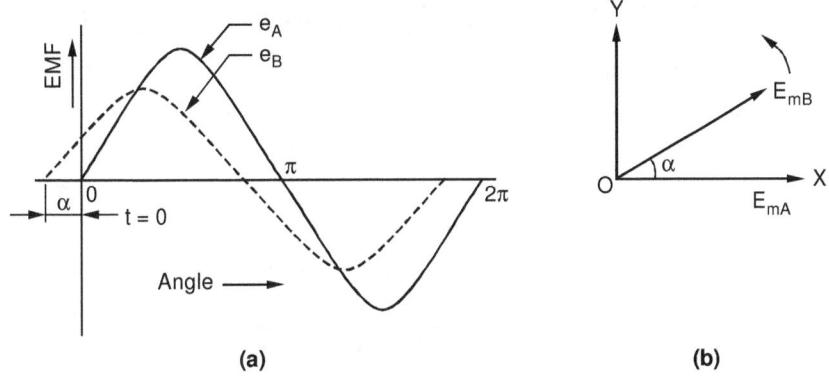

Fig. 3.20 : Phasor diagram for two alternating quantities

As an example, let us again consider the case of the e.m.f.s in two single-turn coils A and B shown in Fig. 3.19 (a). If the wave for the e.m.f. in coil A is supposed to pass upward in positive direction through zero at the instant when t = 0, then at the same instant, the wave for the e.m.f. in the coil B already attains some positive value because of its advancement through an angle α from its zero value (Fig. 3.20 a). This can be shown with the help of phasors in the phasor diagram as illustrated in Fig. 3.20 (b). The angle α between two phasors is obviously the phase difference between the two e.m.f.s.

Following few points should be noted in connection with the phasor diagrams :

(i) X and Y axes are fixed in space. Therefore, it is not necessary to include them in the diagram.

(ii) The phasors are drawn normally to represent r.m.s. values.

(iii) The phasor chosen as a *reference phasor* is drawn in the horizontal position (merely for convenience) e.g. the phasor E_{mA} in Fig. 3.20 (b) is the reference phasor.

(iv) Since the phasors representing different alternating quantities are assumed to rotate in the counter clockwise direction, the phasors ahead in this direction from a given phasor are said to lead the given phasor, while those behind are said to lag the given phasor. e.g. in Fig. 3.20 (b), the phasor E_{mB} leads the phasor E_{mA} by an angle α. The angle between two phasors represents the phase difference between two alternating quantities.

(v) In order to distinguish between different alternating quantities like current, voltage or flux, different types of arrow heads may be used. e.g. the current phasors may be drawn with closed arrow heads while the voltage phasors with open arrow heads.

In this way, when different alternating quantities of the same frequency are represented by phasors in the same phasor diagram, their addition and subtraction becomes simple. It is similar to addition and subtraction of vectors in mechanics as seen in the next section.

3.13 ADDITION AND SUBTRACTION OF SINUSOIDAL ALTERNATING QUANTITIES

While analysing the a.c. circuits, we are often required to add the sine waves of the same frequency but different magnitude and phase. These waves can be added by the use of trigonometric transformations or they are plotted and then added graphically. However, these methods are inherently cumbersome. Phasor representation of alternating quantities, as said earlier, greatly simplifies this addition. When the magnitudes and phase angles of the various voltages or currents are known, the phasor diagram can be constructed. Once such phasor diagram is constructed, the addition of phasors becomes a simple geometric problem. The phasors are added in the same manner as are force vectors in mechanics. For example, if two alternating e.m.f.s are to be added, the resultant is obtained by means of *a parallelogram of e.m.f.s* or *a triangle of e.m.f.s*. If there are several such e.m.f.s, then the resultant is given by the closing side of a *phasor polygon*. These graphical methods are rather inconvenient and often time-wasting. A more systematic method is to split each phasor into its components along the horizontal and vertical axes. The horizontal component of the resultant is then given by the *algebraic sum* of the individual horizontal components and the vertical component of the resultant is given by the *algebraic sum* of the individual vertical components. It should be remembered that the operation of subtraction of one phasor from the other is simply that of their addition with one of the phasors reversed. The following examples will illustrate all these methods.

Example 3.11 : *The instantaneous values of two alternating e.m.f.s are given by the following expressions :*

$$e_1 = 30 \sin \omega t$$

$$e_2 = 20 \sin\left(\omega t - \frac{\pi}{4}\right)$$

Derive an expression for the instantaneous value of (a) the sum and (b) the difference of these e.m.f.s.

Solution : (a) From the given equations, the maximum values of the two e.m.f.s are obviously, $E_{1\,max} = 30$ V and $E_{2\,max} = 20$ V

The equation of the e.m.f. e_2 shows that the phasor $\bar{E}_{2\,max}^{*}$ lags the phasor $\bar{E}_{1\,max}$ by $\pi/4$ radian or 45°. With this information, the phasor diagram is constructed and the parallelogram of e.m.f.s is drawn to scale in Fig. 3.21.

---

* *To distinguish the phasor quantity from a scalar quantity, a bar (–) or dot (·) is placed on the top of the letter representing the phasor quantity, e.g.*

$$\bar{E}, \bar{E}_1, \bar{E}_2, \bar{I} \quad \text{or} \quad \dot{E}, \dot{E}_1, \dot{E}_2, \dot{I}$$

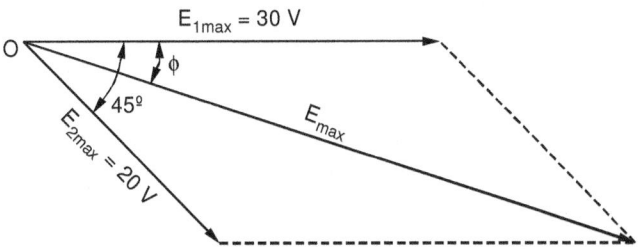

Fig. 3.21 : Addition of phasors, Example 3.11

By measurement, we find that the maximum value of the resultant e.m.f. $\bar{E}_{max}$ is

E_{max} = 46.25 V, while ϕ = 18° or 0.31 radian.

Hence, the instantaneous value of the sum of the two voltages will be given by

$$e = 46.25 \sin(\omega t - 0.31) \text{ volts} \quad \text{... Ans.}$$

The minus sign is used because phasor $\bar{E}_{max}$ of the total e.m.f. lags the reference phasor $\bar{E}_{1\,max}$. Alternatively, this expression can also be found as follows :

The phasors representing the maximum values of the two e.m.f.s are shown in Fig. 3.21.

Resolving these phasors into their X and Y components, we get

Resultant horizontal component,

$$\bar{X} = 30 + 20 \cos 45° = 44.14 \text{ V}$$

Resultant vertical component,

$$\bar{Y} = 0 - 20 \sin 45° = -14.14 \text{ V}$$

Hence, the maximum value of resultant e.m.f.

$$\begin{aligned} E_{max} &= \sqrt{(\bar{X})^2 + (\bar{Y})^2} \\ &= \sqrt{(44.14)^2 + (-14.14)^2} \\ &= 46.35 \text{ V} \end{aligned}$$

If ϕ is the phase difference between resultant e.m.f. $\bar{E}_{max}$, and the reference phasor $\bar{E}_{1\,max}$,

$$\tan \phi = -\frac{14.14}{44.14} = -0.3203$$

$\therefore \quad \phi = -17.76°$ or -0.31 radian

Hence, the instantaneous value of the resultant voltage will be given by the expression

$$e = 46.35 \sin(\omega t - 0.31) \text{ volts} \quad \text{... Ans.}$$

(b) The construction for subtracting $\bar{E}_{2\,max}$ from $\bar{E}_{1\,max}$ will be clear from Fig. 3.22. By measurement,

E_{max} = 21 V and ϕ = 42° or 0.733 radian

Since the resultant phasor $\bar{E}_{max}$ leads the reference phasor $\bar{E}_{1\,max}$, its instantaneous value will be given by the equation,

$$e = 21 \sin(\omega t + 0.733) \text{ volts} \quad \text{... Ans.}$$

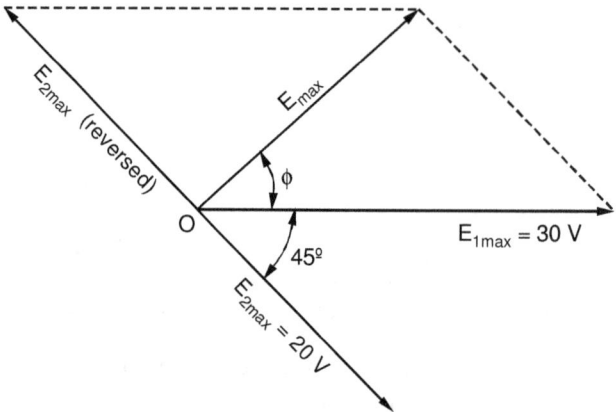

Fig. 3.22 : Subtraction of phasors, Example 3.11

Alternatively, resolving the phasors into their X and Y components, we get
Resultant horizontal component,

$$\overline{X} = 30 - 20 \cos 45° = 15.86 \text{ V}$$

Resultant vertical component,

$$\overline{Y} = 0 + 20 \sin 45° = 14.14 \text{ V}$$

∴ Maximum value of the resultant voltage,

$$E_{max} = \sqrt{(\overline{X})^2 + (\overline{Y})^2}$$
$$= \sqrt{(15.86)^2 + (14.14)^2} = 21.25 \text{ V}$$
$$\tan \phi = \frac{14.14}{15.86} = 0.8916$$

∴ $\phi = 41.72°$ or 0.728 radian

Hence, the instantaneous value of the resultant voltage will be given by

$$e = 21.25 \sin (\omega t + 0.728) \text{ volts} \qquad \ldots \text{Ans.}$$

Example 3.12 : *Three alternating currents are given by*

$$i_1 = 150 \sin \left(\omega t + \frac{\pi}{4}\right)$$

$$i_2 = 40 \sin \left(\omega t + \frac{\pi}{2}\right)$$

$$i_3 = 80 \sin \left(\omega t - \frac{\pi}{6}\right)$$

and are fed into a common conductor. Find graphically or otherwise the equation of the resultant current and its r.m.s. value.

Solution : The current phasors representing their maximum values are shown in Fig. 3.23 (a) and the phasor polygon is set out to scale in Fig. 3.23 (b). From this phasor polygon, we see that

$$I_{max} = 205 \text{ A} \quad \text{while} \quad \phi = 31° \quad \text{or} \quad 0.541 \text{ radian.}$$

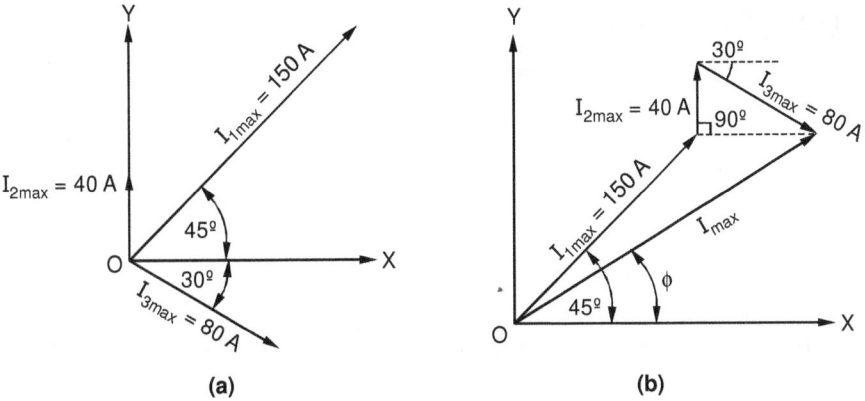

Fig. 3.23 : (a) Phasor diagram, Example 3.12, (b) Phasor polygon

We also see that the resultant current phasor, $\bar{I}_{max}$ leads the reference axis so that

$$i = 205 \sin(\omega t + 0.541) \text{ amperes} \qquad \text{... Ans.}$$

The r.m.s. value of the resultant current,

$$I = \frac{205}{\sqrt{2}} = 144.96 \text{ A} \qquad \text{... Ans.}$$

Alternatively, resolving the current phasors into their X and Y components, we get

The resultant horizontal component,

$$\bar{X} = 150 \cos 45° + 0 + 80 \cos 30°$$
$$= 106.07 + 0 + 69.28$$
$$= 175.35 \text{ A}$$

The resultant vertical component,

$$\bar{Y} = 150 \sin 45° + 40 - 80 \sin 30°$$
$$= 106.07 + 40 - 40$$
$$= 106.07 \text{ A}$$

∴ Maximum value of the resultant current,

$$I_{max} = \sqrt{(\bar{X})^2 + (\bar{Y})^2} = \sqrt{(175.35)^2 + (106.07)^2}$$
$$= 204.94 \text{ A}$$
$$\tan \phi = \frac{106.07}{175.35} = 0.6049$$

∴ $\qquad \phi = 31.17°$ or 0.544 radian.

Hence, the equation for the resultant current is

$$i = 204.94 \sin(\omega t + 0.544) \text{ amperes} \qquad \text{... Ans.}$$

The r.m.s. value of the resultant current,

$$I = \frac{204.94}{\sqrt{2}} = 144.92 \text{ A} \qquad \text{... Ans.}$$

3.14 COMPLEX NOTATION

Simple a.c. circuits can be solved with the aid of phasor diagrams. However, this method is not much useful in solving more complex circuits. Such circuits can be more easily analysed using complex algebra. In this method, the phasor quantities, such as alternating voltages and currents, and their phase relationships are expressed in simple algebraic forms. The circuits are then solved by algebraic operations alone. The simple algebraic forms which are normally used to represent the phasors mainly include :

(i) Rectangular form, (ii) Polar form

These two forms and the general principles of complex notation method are discussed in the following sections. The application of this method to a.c. circuits will be studied later on in the next chapters.

3.15 PHASORS IN RECTANGULAR FORM

Consider the phasor $\bar{V}$ at the angle θ with the reference axis as shown in Fig. 3.24 (a). The phasor $\bar{V}$ has two components, x along the reference axis and y at 90° to the reference axis. Thus, phasor $\bar{V}$ is the phasor addition of components x and y. This may be expressed symbolically as,

$$\bar{V} = x + j\,y \qquad \ldots (3.45)$$

Here, the actual magnitude of the phasor is

$$V = \sqrt{x^2 + y^2}$$

while its phase angle, i.e. its inclination to the reference axis is given by

$$\tan \theta = \frac{y}{x}$$

Thus, Equation (3.45) completely specifies the magnitude and the position of the phasor. Phasors represented in this form are said to be in *rectangular, Cartesian* or *symbolic form* (or *notation*).

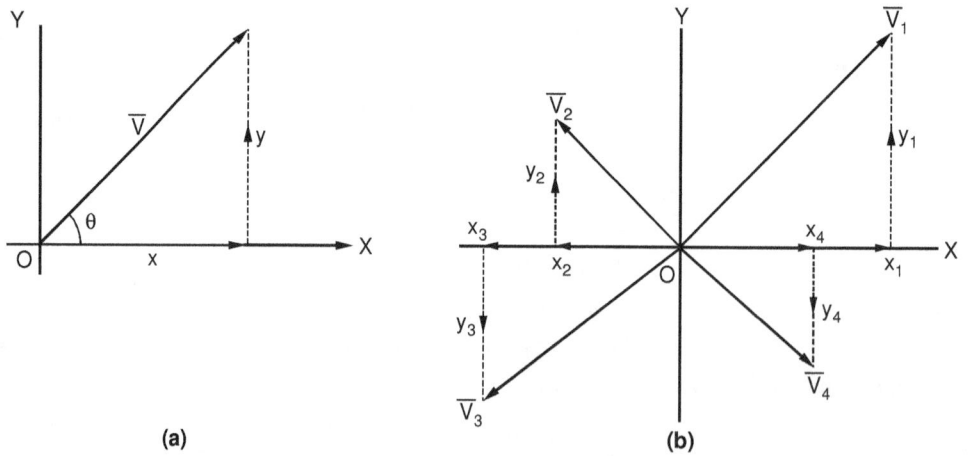

Fig. 3.24 : Phasors and their components

3.15.1 The j Operator

The symbol j used in Equation (3.45) indicates that the component y is perpendicular to the component x. In other words, the symbol j denotes rotation of the quantity to which it is attached through 90° in the counter-clockwise direction. The symbol j is thus a phasor operator indicating rotation through 90°. Hence, if applied twice, it turns the quantity through 180°, e.g.

$$j\,j\,y = j^2\,y = -y$$

This gives
$$j^2 = -1 \quad \text{or} \quad j = \sqrt{-1}$$

The quantities when expressed in the form x + j y are called *complex numbers*. Complex numbers follow all fundamental laws of algebra. In all the algebraic operations with complex numbers, the operator j may be handled as if it were $\sqrt{-1}$. In mathematics, x is called the *real* and y the *imaginary* component of the complex number. However, in connection with a.c. circuits, these components are normally referred to as *in-phase (or active)* and the *quadrature (or reactive)* component respectively. While expressing the different phasors in the rectangular form, due regard must be paid to the sign of their in-phase and quadrature components. e.g. consider the phasors $\bar{V}_1, \bar{V}_2, \bar{V}_3$ and $\bar{V}_4$ shown in Fig. 3.24 (b). These phasors can be expressed in their rectangular forms as given below :

$$\bar{V}_1 = x_1 + j\,y_1, \qquad \bar{V}_2 = -x_2 + j\,y_2,$$

$$\bar{V}_3 = -x_3 - j\,y_3, \qquad \bar{V}_4 = x_4 - j\,y_4$$

3.15.2 Addition and Subtraction of Phasors in Rectangular Form

While adding two phasors in rectangular form, their in-phase and quadrature components are added separately. Similarly, while subtracting one phasor from the another, their in-phase and quadrature components are separately subtracted. However, it should be remembered that when phasors are added or subtracted, they must all represent quantities of the same physical kind.

Example 3.13 : *Two phasors are* $\bar{V}_1 = (7 + j9)$ V, $\bar{V}_2 = (3 - j5)$ V.

Find : (a) $\bar{V}_1 + \bar{V}_2$, (b) $\bar{V}_1 - \bar{V}_2$.

Solution : $\bar{V}_1 + \bar{V}_2 = (7 + j\,9) + (3 - j\,5) = (7 + 3) + j\,(9 - 5)$

$= (10 + j\,4)$ V ... Ans.

and $\bar{V}_1 - \bar{V}_2 = (7 + j\,9) - (3 - j\,5) = (7 - 3) + j\,(9 + 5)$

$= (4 + j\,14)$ V ... Ans.

3.15.3 Multiplication and Division of Phasors in Rectangular Form

Multiplication of two phasors expressed in rectangular form is carried out as in ordinary algebraic multiplication, substituting –1 for j^2. While dividing one phasor by another, a process called *rationalisation* is adopted to remove j terms from the denominator. In this process, numerator and denominator are multiplied by the *conjugate* of the denominator. The conjugate of complex number is obtained by reversing the sign of the j term. The process of multiplication and division is best illustrated by a numerical example.

Example 3.14 : *For the phasors given in Example 3.13, find : (a)* $\bar{V}_1 \cdot \bar{V}_2$, *(b)* $\dfrac{\bar{V}_1}{\bar{V}_2}$.

Solution :
$$\bar{V}_1 \cdot \bar{V}_2 = (7 + j\,9)(3 - j\,5) = 21 - j\,35 + j\,27 - j^2\,45$$
$$= 21 - j\,8 + 45 \qquad (\because j^2 = -1)$$
$$= (66 - j\,8) \text{ V} \qquad \text{... Ans.}$$

and
$$\dfrac{\bar{V}_1}{\bar{V}_2} = \dfrac{7+j9}{3-j5} = \dfrac{7+j9}{3-j5} \times \dfrac{3+j5}{3+j5} = \dfrac{21 + j35 + j27 + j^2\,45}{3^2 - j^2\,5^2}$$
$$= \dfrac{21 + j62 - 45}{9 + 25}$$
$$= \dfrac{-24 + j62}{34}$$
$$= (-0.71 + j\,1.82) \text{ V} \qquad \text{... Ans.}$$

3.16 PHASORS IN POLAR FORM

In this form, a phasor is specified by its magnitude and its angular position with respect to the X-axis taken as a reference axis. For example, the phasor $\bar{V}$ in Fig. 3.24 (a) can be represented in polar form as shown below :

$$\bar{V} = V \angle \theta \qquad \text{... (3.46)}$$

where V is the magnitude of the phasor $\bar{V}$ and θ is the angle made by it with the X-axis. The magnitude V is called the *modulus* or *absolute value* of the phasor $\bar{V}$ and $\angle \theta$ is called the *argument* of this phasor. If the phasor is given in rectangular form, it can be easily converted into its polar form and its vice-versa. For example, we have seen that the phasor $\bar{V}$ shown in Fig. 3.24 (a) can be expressed in rectangular form as

$$\bar{V} = x + j\,y$$

This phasor can be expressed in polar form as

$$\bar{V} = V \angle \theta$$

where, from the geometry of Fig. 3.24 (a),

$$V = \sqrt{x^2 + y^2}$$

and
$$\theta = \tan^{-1} \dfrac{y}{x}$$

For reverse operation, $x = V \cos \theta$, $y = V \sin \theta$

Thus, summarizing the various ways of representing the phasors in algebraic forms, we have

$$\bar{V} = x + jy = V \angle \theta = V(\cos \theta + j \sin \theta)$$

3.16.1 Multiplication and Division of Phasors in Polar Form

Multiplication of two phasors in polar form is done by taking the product of their magnitudes and the sum of their angles. On the other hand, their division is done by taking the quotient of their magnitudes and the difference of their angles.

Example 3.15 : *Two phasors are,*

$$\bar{V}_1 = 12 \angle 60° \, V \quad and \quad \bar{V}_2 = 3 \angle -30° \, V$$

Find : (a) $\bar{V}_1 \cdot \bar{V}_2$, *(b)* $\dfrac{\bar{V}_1}{\bar{V}_2}$.

Solution : $\bar{V}_1 \cdot \bar{V}_2 = 12 \angle 60° \times 3 \angle -30° = 12 \times 3 \angle (60° - 30°) = \mathbf{36 \angle 30° \, V}$ ... **Ans.**

and $\dfrac{\bar{V}_1}{\bar{V}_2} = \dfrac{12 \angle 60°}{3 \angle -30°} = \dfrac{12}{3} \angle (60° + 30°) = \mathbf{4 \angle 90° \, V}$ ... **Ans.**

3.17 INTERCONVERSION OF RECTANGULAR AND POLAR FORMS

For addition and subtraction, phasors must be essentially in their rectangular forms. Multiplication and division, however, are less laborious in polar forms. The use of scientific calculator is very helpful in converting quantities from rectangular to polar form and vice versa.

Following example will illustrate how the use of complex notation method gives a more quick, direct, and accurate technique for finding the algebraic sum of sinusoidal alternating quantities. In the next chapter, this technique will be extended to permit the analysis of sinusoidal a.c. networks.

Example 3.16 : *Solve Example 3.12 using complex notation method.*

Solution : Referring to the phasor diagram of Fig. 3.23 (a), three current phasors can be expressed in their complex forms as given below :

$$\bar{I}_{1\,max} = 150 \angle 45° = (106.07 + j\,106.07) \, A$$

$$\bar{I}_{2\,max} = 40 \angle 90° = (0 + j\,40) \, A$$

$$\bar{I}_{3\,max} = 80 \angle -30° = (69.28 - j\,40) \, A$$

∴ Resultant current,

$$\begin{aligned}\bar{I}_{max} &= \bar{I}_{1\,max} + \bar{I}_{2\,max} + \bar{I}_{3\,max} \\ &= (106.07 + j\,106.07) + (0 + j\,40) + (69.28 - j\,40) \\ &= 175.35 + j\,106.07 = 204.94 \angle 31.17° \, A\end{aligned}$$

∴ $|I_{max}| = 204.94 \, A$

and $\phi = 31.17°$ or 0.544 radian

Hence, as already seen,

$$i = \mathbf{204.94 \sin(\omega t + 0.544) \text{ amperes}} \quad \text{... Ans.}$$

The r.m.s. value of the resultant current,

$$I = \dfrac{204.94}{\sqrt{2}} = \mathbf{144.92 \, A} \quad \text{... Ans.}$$

Example 3.17 : *Draw a neat sketch, in each case (not to scale), of the waveform and write the equation for instantaneous value, for the following :*

(i) Sinusoidal current of 10 A (r.m.s.), 50 Hz, passing through its zero value at $\omega t = \dfrac{\pi}{3}$ radians and rising positively.

(ii) Sinusoidal current of amplitude of 8 A, 50 Hz, passing through its zero value at $\omega t = -\dfrac{\pi}{6}$ radians and rising positively.

Solution :

(i) Maximum value of current = $10\sqrt{2}$ = 14.14 A

$\therefore$ $i = I_m \sin(\omega t - \alpha) = 14.14 \sin\left(2\pi \times 50 \times t - \dfrac{\pi}{3}\right)$ = **14.14 sin $\left(100\,\pi t - \dfrac{\pi}{3}\right)$ amperes**

... Ans.

The waveform is as shown in Fig. 3.25 (a).

(ii) Maximum value of current = 8 A

$\therefore$ $i = I_m \sin(\omega t + \alpha) = 8 \sin\left(2\pi \times 50 \times t + \dfrac{\pi}{6}\right)$ = **8 sin $\left(100\,\pi t + \dfrac{\pi}{6}\right)$ amperes** ... Ans.

The waveform is as shown in Fig. 3.25 (b).

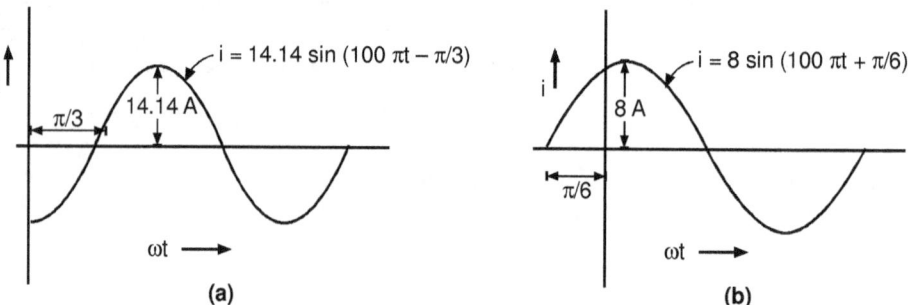

Fig. 3.25 : Current waveforms, Example 3.17

Example 3.18 : *An alternating current is represented by the expression,*

$$i = 10 \sin\left(2\pi \times 60 \times t - \dfrac{\pi}{6}\right) \text{ amperes}$$

Find its periodic time. Also find :

(i) its instantaneous value at t = 0,

(ii) time 't' at which it first reaches zero value after t = 0, and

(iii) time at which it first reaches its negative maximum value after t = 0.

Draw a neat sketch of its waveform for one cycle from time t = 0, and indicate in it the co-ordinates of the above three points.

Solution :

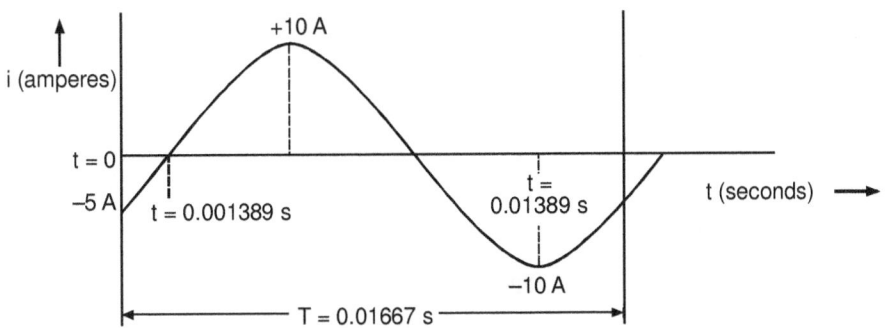

Fig. 3.26 : Current waveform, Example 3.18

Fig. 3.26 shows the waveform for the given alternating current.

$$\text{Frequency, } f = \frac{\omega}{2\pi} = \frac{2\pi \times 60}{2\pi} = 60 \text{ Hz}$$

∴ $\quad$ Periodic time, $T = \frac{1}{f} = \frac{1}{60} = \mathbf{0.01667 \text{ s}}$ ... **Ans.**

(i) Value of current at t = 0,

$$i = 10 \sin\left(2\pi \times 60 \times 0 - \frac{\pi}{6}\right) = \mathbf{-5 \text{ A}} \qquad \text{... \textbf{Ans.}}$$

(ii) Time when current first reaches zero value will be given by

$$i = 0 = 10 \sin\left(2\pi \times 60 \times t - \frac{\pi}{6}\right)$$

∴ $\quad 2\pi \times 60 \times t - \frac{\pi}{6} = 0$

∴ $\quad t = \mathbf{0.001389 \text{ s}}$ ... **Ans.**

(iii) Time at which the current first reaches its negative maximum value will be given by

$$t = 0.001389 + \frac{3T}{4} = 0.001389 + \frac{3 \times 0.01667}{4}$$

$$= \mathbf{0.01389 \text{ s}} \qquad \text{... \textbf{Ans.}}$$

Example 3.19 : *A sinusoidal wave of frequency 50 Hz has its maximum value of 9.2 A. What will be its value at (a) 0.002 s after the wave passes through zero in positive direction, (b) 0.0045 s after the wave passes through positive maximum ? Show the values of current in a neat sketch of the waveform.*

Solution :

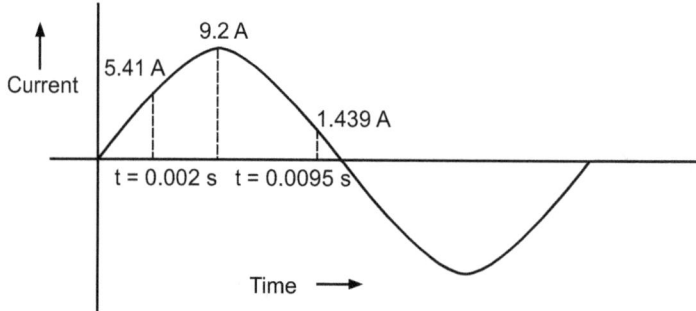

Fig. 3.27 : Current waveform, Example 3.19

Maximum value of current, $I_m = 9.2$ A

Hence, instantaneous value of current will be given by

$i = I_m \sin \omega t = I_m \sin 2\pi ft = 9.2 \sin 2\pi \times 50 \times t = 9.2 \sin 314\,t$ amperes

(a)   At $t = 0.002$ s, $i = 9.2 \sin (314 \times 0.002) \dfrac{180°}{\pi} = \mathbf{5.41\ A}$ ... **Ans.**

(b) Time to reach positive maximum value $= \dfrac{\text{Periodic time}}{4} = \dfrac{0.02}{4} = 0.005$ s

Hence,   at $t = 0.005 + 0.0045 = 0.0095$ s,

$$i = 9.2 \sin (314 \times 0.0095) \dfrac{180°}{\pi} = \mathbf{1.439\ A} \qquad \text{... \textbf{Ans.}}$$

Fig. 3.27 shows the waveform for the current.

Example 3.20 : *At $t = 0$, the instantaneous value of a 60 Hz sinusoidal current is + 5 A and it increases in magnitude further. Its r.m.s. value is 10 A.*

(i) *Write the expression for its instantaneous value.* (ii) *Find the current at $t = 0.01$ s and $t = 0.015$ s.*

(iii) *Sketch the waveform indicating these values.*

Solution :

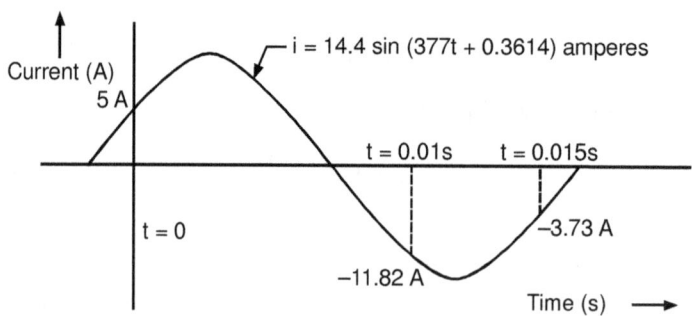

Fig. 3.28 : Current waveform, Example 3.20

(i)   R.M.S. value of current, $I = 10$ A

       Maximum value of current, $I_m = 10\sqrt{2} = 14.14$ A

Therefore, instantaneous value of the current will be given by the equation (generalized form),

$$i = I_m \sin(\omega t + \alpha) = 14.14 \sin(2\pi \times 60 \times t + \alpha) = 14.14 \sin(377 t + \alpha)$$

But, it is given that when $t = 0$, $i = +5$ A

$$\therefore \quad 5 = 14.14 \sin(377 \times 0 + \alpha)$$

$$\therefore \quad \sin \alpha = \frac{5}{14.14} = 0.3536$$

$$\therefore \quad \alpha = 20.7° \text{ or } 0.3614 \text{ radian}$$

Hence, the expression for current will be

$$i = 14.14 \sin(377 t + 0.3614) \text{ amperes} \qquad \text{... Ans.}$$

(ii) At $t = 0.01$ s, $i = 14.14 \sin(377 \times 0.01 + 0.3614) = -11.82$ A ... Ans.

At $t = 0.015$ s, $i = 14.14 \sin(377 \times 0.015 + 0.3614) = -3.73$ A ... Ans.

The waveform for the current is shown in Fig. 3.28.

Example 3.21 : *Find the effective value of a resultant current in a wire which carries simultaneously a direct current of 10 A and alternating current given by*

$$i = 12 \sin \omega t + 6 \sin\left(3\omega t - \frac{\pi}{6}\right) + 4 \sin\left(5\omega t + \frac{\pi}{3}\right)$$

Solution : Let I be the r.m.s. value of the resultant current and R be the resistance of the wire through which this current is passed for t seconds. Then by definition, equating heat produced by the resultant current with the sum of heat produced by its individual components under identical condition, we have

$$I^2 R t = 10^2 \times R \times t + \left(\frac{12}{\sqrt{2}}\right)^2 \times R \times t + \left(\frac{6}{\sqrt{2}}\right)^2 \times R \times t + \left(\frac{4}{\sqrt{2}}\right)^2 \times R \times t$$

(Here, it should be remembered that the r.m.s. value of each a.c. component is $I_m/\sqrt{2}$.)

∴ Effective or r.m.s. value of a resultant current,

$$I = \sqrt{10^2 + \left(\frac{12}{\sqrt{2}}\right)^2 + \left(\frac{6}{\sqrt{2}}\right)^2 + \left(\frac{4}{\sqrt{2}}\right)^2} = 14.07 \text{ A} \qquad \text{... Ans.}$$

Example 3.22 : *Find the resultant of three voltages given by,*

$$v_1 = 10 \sin \omega t, \quad v_2 = 20 \sin\left(\omega t - \frac{\pi}{4}\right) \text{ and } v_3 = 30 \cos\left(\omega t + \frac{\pi}{6}\right)$$

Solution : The voltages must all be of the same function, either sine or cosine, before they can be expressed as phasors for the purpose of their addition or subtraction. Remembering this, the three given voltages given by

$$v_1 = 10 \sin \omega t,$$

$$v_2 = 20 \sin\left(\omega t - \frac{\pi}{4}\right),$$

and $\quad v_3 = 30 \cos\left(\omega t + \frac{\pi}{6}\right) = 30 \sin\left(\omega t + \frac{2\pi}{3}\right)$

can be expressed in their complex forms as given below :

$$\bar{V}_1 = \frac{10}{\sqrt{2}} \angle 0° = 7.07 \angle 0° = (7.07 + j0) \text{ V}$$

$$\bar{V}_2 = \frac{20}{\sqrt{2}} \angle -45° = 14.14 \angle -45° = (10 - j10) \text{ V}$$

$$\bar{V}_3 = \frac{30}{\sqrt{2}} \angle 120° = 21.21 \angle 120° = (-10.61 + j18.37) \text{ V}$$

∴   Resultant voltage, $\bar{V} = \bar{V}_1 + \bar{V}_2 + \bar{V}_3 = (7.07 + j0) + (10 - j10) + (-10.61 + j18.37)$
$$= 6.46 + j8.37 = 10.57 \angle 52.34° \text{ V}$$

This resultant voltage can be expressed in the equation form as given below :

$$v = \sqrt{2} \times 10.57 \sin\left(\omega t + 52.34° \times \frac{\pi}{180°}\right) = 14.95 \sin(\omega t + 0.91) \quad \text{... Ans.}$$

Example 3.23 : *The instantaneous current is given by*

$$i = 7.071 \sin\left(157.08\, t - \frac{\pi}{4}\right) \text{ amperes}$$

Find its effective value, periodic time and the instant at which it reaches its positive maximum value. Sketch the waveform from t = 0 over one complete cycle.

Solution : From the expression for the current, it is obvious that

$$I_m = 7.071 \text{ A and } \omega = 157.08 \text{ radians/s}$$

∴   Effective value of the current,

$$I = \frac{I_m}{\sqrt{2}} = \frac{7.071}{\sqrt{2}} = 5 \text{ A} \quad \text{... Ans.}$$

$$\text{Frequency, } f = \frac{\omega}{2\pi} = \frac{157.08}{2\pi} = 25 \text{ Hz}$$

∴   Periodic time, $T = \frac{1}{f} = \frac{1}{25} = \textbf{0.04 s or 40 ms}$ ... Ans.

Further, $i = 7.071 \sin\left(157.08\, t - \frac{\pi}{4}\right)$

Therefore,   when i = 7.071 A, we have

$$7.071 = 7.071 \sin\left(157.08\, t - \frac{\pi}{4}\right)$$

∴ $\sin\left(157.08\, t - \frac{\pi}{4}\right) = 1$

∴ $157.08\, t - \frac{\pi}{4} = 1.571 \text{ radian}$

∴   Time to reach positive maximum value,

$$t = \textbf{0.015 s or 15 ms} \quad \text{... Ans.}$$

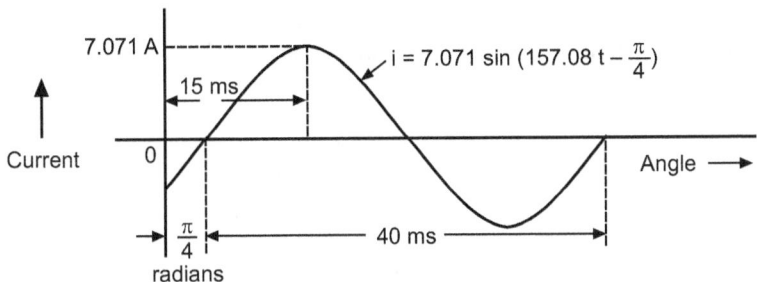

Fig. 3.29 : Current waveform, Example 3.23

Fig. 3.29 shows the necessary waveform for the current.

3.18 RESPONSE OF PURE R, L AND C TO SINUSOIDAL A.C. SUPPLIES

Using Ohm's law and the basic equations for the capacitor and inductor, we can now study the response of basic circuit elements R, L and C to a sinusoidal voltage or current. This will enable us to establish the phase-angle relationships existing between the current and voltage for each circuit parameter. It will be seen that these relationships are fixed and are always satisfied irrespective of whether a given circuit element is in a series or parallel arrangement with other circuit elements.

3.19 PURELY RESISTIVE A.C. CIRCUIT

Consider a purely resistive circuit containing a resistance of R ohms as shown in Fig. 3.30 (a).

Let an alternating voltage represented by the equation $v = V_m \sin \omega t$ be applied across its terminals. As a result, the alternating current will be set up in the circuit. By Ohm's law, the value of the current at any instant will be given by

$$i = \frac{v}{R} = \frac{V_m \sin \omega t}{R} \qquad \ldots (3.47)$$

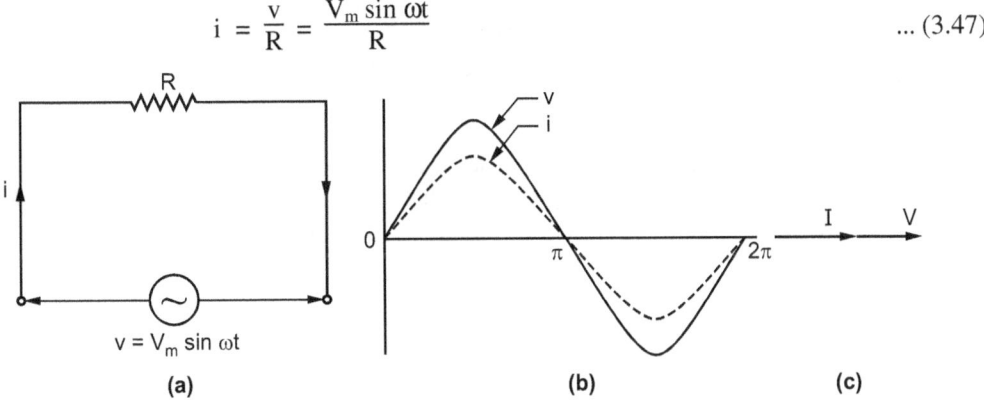

Fig. 3.30 : A.C. circuit containing resistance only

The current will be maximum (I_m) when $\sin \omega t$ is unity.

$$\therefore \quad I_m = \frac{V_m}{R} \qquad \ldots (3.48)$$

Hence, Equation (3.47) can be rewritten as

$$i = I_m \sin \omega t \qquad \ldots (3.49)$$

Comparing the Equation (3.49) for the current with that of the voltage, we find that this current will be sinusoidal similar to the applied voltage and will be in phase with it.

Hence, we can conclude that *in a purely resistive a.c. circuit, the current set up by a sinusoidal applied voltage is also sinusoidal and both are in phase with each other.*

Fig. 3.30 (b) illustrates the waveforms of the current and voltage and Fig. 3.30 (c) the phasor diagram for purely resistive circuit under consideration. The phase difference between the applied voltage and the current being zero, the two phasors representing them (V and I) are drawn in line with each other in the phasor diagram.

Now, as already seen, from Equation (3.48),

$$I_m = \frac{V_m}{R}$$

If V and I are the r.m.s. values of voltage and current, then

$$\frac{I}{0.707} = \frac{V}{0.707\,R}$$

$$\therefore \quad I = \frac{V}{R} \quad \ldots (3.50)$$

Thus, *for a purely resistive a.c. circuit, Ohm's law is applicable, even if r.m.s. values of voltage and current are used.*

Power : In the d.c. circuit, power in watts is given by the product of voltage (in volts) and current (in amperes). In a.c. circuit also, power at any instant is given by the product of instantaneous value of voltage (v) and instantaneous value of current (i). Fig. 3.31 shows the power curve obtained by plotting the instantaneous values of power at number of points during the cycle.

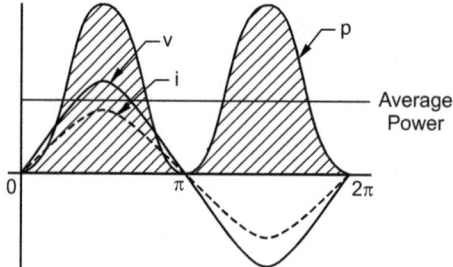

Fig. 3.31 : Power curve for a purely resistive circuit

From the power curve, it will be observed that the power even though always positive, pulsates between zero and a certain maximum value with time. Since the wattmeter indicates average value of the power over a cycle, it is of more practical importance.

Now, as $v = V_m \sin \omega t$ and $i = I_m \sin \omega t$

Instantaneous power, $p = v\,i$

$$= V_m I_m \sin^2 \omega t = \frac{V_m I_m}{2} (1 - \cos 2\omega t)$$

$$= \frac{V_m I_m}{2} - \frac{V_m I_m}{2} \cos 2\omega t \quad \ldots (3.51)$$

The above expression shows that the instantaneous power has a constant part $\frac{V_m I_m}{2}$ and a fluctuating part $\frac{V_m I_m}{2} \cos 2\omega t$. The fluctuating part is a cosine curve of frequency double that of voltage and current waves. Therefore, if such a curve is drawn for a complete cycle, its average value is zero.

∴ Average power over a cycle,

$$P = \text{Average of } \frac{V_m I_m}{2} - \text{Average of } \frac{V_m I_m}{2} \cos 2\omega t$$

$$= \frac{V_m I_m}{2} = \frac{V_m}{\sqrt{2}} \times \frac{I_m}{\sqrt{2}} = V \cdot I \text{ watts} \qquad \ldots (3.52)$$

Hence, in a *purely resistive circuit, average power is given by the product of the r.m.s. values of applied voltage and the current.* Alternatively,

$$P = V \cdot I = \frac{V^2}{R} = I^2 R \text{ watts} \qquad \ldots (3.53)$$

3.20 PURELY INDUCTIVE A.C. CIRCUIT

Consider a purely inductive coil * with inductance L henries and almost negligible ohmic resistance connected across an a.c. supply as shown in Fig. 3.32 (a).

Let an alternating voltage applied across the coil be

$$v = V_m \sin \omega t$$

The resulting alternating current flowing through the coil will set up an alternating field. The changing flux linking with the coil will induce an e.m.f. of self-induction in it. We know that this e.m.f. of self-induction will be always in opposition with the applied voltage and given by

$$e = -L \frac{di}{dt}$$

Now, since the ohmic resistance of the coil is negligibly small, the applied voltage will have to overcome the e.m.f. of self-induction only. Therefore, the applied voltage will be equal and opposite to the e.m.f. of self-induction at every instant i.e.

$$v = -e = L \frac{di}{dt} \qquad \ldots (3.54)$$

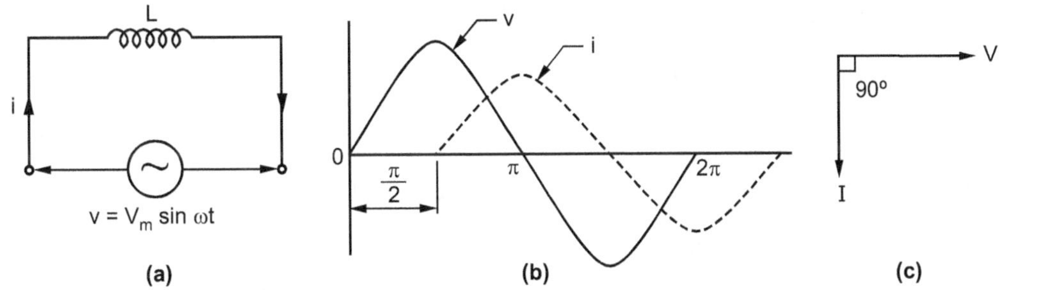

Fig. 3.32 : A circuit containing inductance only

---

* A purely inductive coil is that coil which has only inductance and no ohmic resistance. In practice, it is not possible to have such a coil. But a coil of heavy section copper wire wound on a laminated iron core can be considered as a purely inductive coil for all practical purposes due to its negligible ohmic resistance.

Substituting $v = V_m \sin \omega t$ in the above expression, we get

$$V_m \sin \omega t = L \frac{di}{dt}$$

$$\therefore \quad di = \frac{V_m}{L} \sin \omega t \cdot dt$$

Integrating both sides, we have

$$i = \int \frac{V_m}{L} \sin \omega t \cdot dt = \frac{V_m}{\omega L} (-\cos \omega t)$$

$$= \frac{-V_m}{\omega L} \sin \left(\frac{\pi}{2} - \omega t\right)$$

$$= \frac{V_m}{\omega L} \sin \left(\omega t - \frac{\pi}{2}\right) \qquad \ldots (3.55)$$

The current will be maximum (I_m) when $\sin \left(\omega t - \frac{\pi}{2}\right)$ will be unity.

$$\therefore \quad I_m = \frac{V_m}{\omega L} \qquad \ldots (3.56)$$

Substituting this in Equation (3.55), it gives

$$i = I_m \sin \left(\omega t - \frac{\pi}{2}\right) \qquad \ldots (3.57)$$

Equation (3.57) clearly shows that the current will be sinusoidal and lag behind the applied voltage by 90°.

Thus, it is important to note that *when a sinusoidal alternating voltage is applied to a purely inductive circuit, the resulting current is also sinusoidal and lags 90° behind the applied voltage (or the voltage leads the current by 90°).*

The waveforms and phasor diagram are shown in Figs. 3.32 (b) and (c) respectively.

Inductive Reactance : According to Equation (3.56),

$$I_m = \frac{V_m}{\omega L}$$

If V and I are the r.m.s. values of voltage and current, then

$$\frac{I}{0.707} = \frac{V}{0.707 \, \omega L}$$

$$\therefore \quad I = \frac{V}{\omega L} \qquad \ldots (3.58)$$

The term ωL in the above expression is called the *inductive reactance* and denoted by X_L.

$$\therefore \quad I = \frac{V}{X_L} \qquad \ldots (3.59)$$

This expression is of the same form as Expression (3.50) for a purely resistive circuit. Similar to resistance, the inductive reactance also opposes the current flow. Therefore, it can be defined as *opposition offered by the inductance of a circuit to the flow of an alternating current.*

Logically, inductive reactance is expressed in units of resistance, namely *ohms*.

Since

$$X_L = \omega L = 2 \pi f L \qquad \ldots (3.60)$$

$$X_L \propto f, \quad \text{if L is constant}$$

Fig. 3.33 shows the graph of inductive reactance against frequency under such condition. It is a straight line passing through the origin.

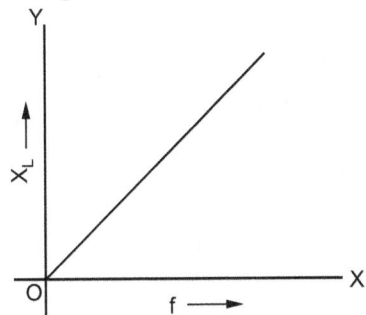

Fig. 3.33 : Variation of X_L with f

Power : Fig. 3.34 shows the power curve obtained by plotting the instantaneous values of power at number of points during the cycle as before.

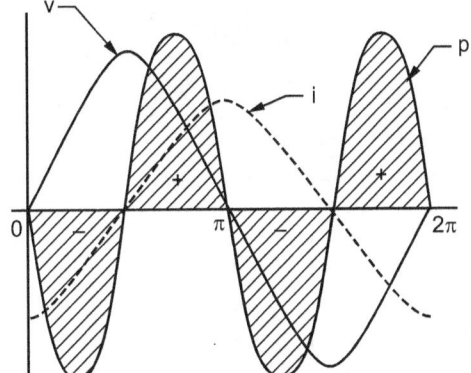

Fig. 3.34 : Power curve for a purely inductive circuit

With $v = V_m \sin \omega t$ and $i = I_m \sin\left(\omega t - \frac{\pi}{2}\right)$,

Instantaneous power, $p = v\,i$

$$= V_m I_m \sin \omega t \cdot \sin\left(\omega t - \frac{\pi}{2}\right)$$

$$= -V_m I_m \sin \omega t \cdot \cos \omega t$$

$$= -\frac{V_m I_m}{2} \sin 2\omega t \qquad \ldots (3.61)$$

Thus, the power curve is a sine curve of frequency double that of voltage and current waves. *Its mean value taken over a cycle will be zero.*

∴ Average power, P = Average of $\left(\dfrac{-V_m I_m}{2} \sin 2\omega t\right) = 0$ ... (3.62)

This will be also clear if the total energy supplied to the circuit during a cycle is considered. The shaded areas under the power curve of Fig. 3.34 represent energy. During the parts of the cycle when power is positive, the energy is stored in the magnetic field established due to increasing current. This energy is represented by area of the positive loops. When power is negative, the same energy is returned back to the supply due to collapse of the magnetic field as current decreases. The areas of the negative loops represent the energy returned back to the supply. The areas of the positive loops are exactly equal to the areas of the negative loops. Therefore, total energy supplied over a cycle is zero. Hence,

$$\text{Average power, P} = \frac{\text{Energy supplied over a cycle}}{\text{Periodic time, T}} = 0 \qquad \ldots(3.63)$$

Thus, the average demand for power in a purely inductive circuit over the whole period is always zero.

Example 3.24 : *Find the current which will flow through a coil of negligible resistance and inductance of 0.5 H, when connected to 230 V, 50 Hz supply.*

Solution : Inductive reactance,

$$X_L = \omega L = 2\pi f L = 2\pi \times 50 \times 0.5 = 157 \, \Omega$$

$$\therefore \quad I = \frac{V}{X_L} = \frac{230}{157} = 1.47 \text{ A} \qquad \ldots \text{Ans.}$$

3.21 PURELY CAPACITIVE A.C. CIRCUIT

When a capacitor is connected across an a.c. supply, its charging (when applied voltage is increasing) and discharging (when applied voltage is decreasing) during alternate quarter cycles, gives rise to an alternating current in the circuit.

Suppose a voltage $v = V_m \sin \omega t$ is applied to a purely capacitive circuit containing capacitance of C farads only (Fig. 3.35 a).

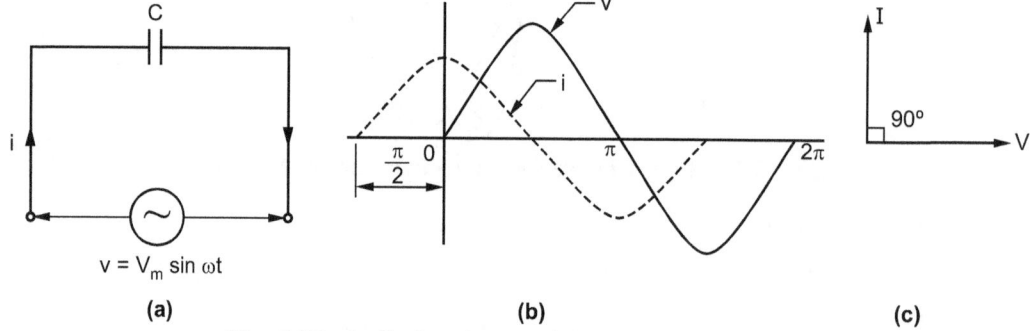

Fig. 3.35 : A.C. circuit containing capacitance only

Using the standard equation for the charge on the capacitor, the instantaneous charge (q) on the capacitor plate is given by

$$q = C \cdot v = C V_m \sin \omega t$$

If dq is the small charge which accumulates on a capacitor plate in small time interval dt, at the instant when current is i, then

$$dq = i \, dt \qquad (\because \text{Charge} = \text{Current} \times \text{Time})$$

$$\therefore \quad i = \frac{dq}{dt} = \frac{d}{dt}(C V_m \sin \omega t) = \omega C V_m \cos \omega t$$

i.e. $$i = \omega C V_m \sin\left(\omega t + \frac{\pi}{2}\right) \qquad \ldots(3.64)$$

Current reaches its maximum value (I_m) when

$$\sin\left(\omega t + \frac{\pi}{2}\right) = 1$$

$\therefore \qquad I_m = \omega C V_m \qquad \qquad \ldots (3.65)$

Substituting this in the Expression (3.64), it can be rewritten as

$$i = I_m \sin\left(\omega t + \frac{\pi}{2}\right) \qquad \ldots (3.66)$$

From the Expression (3.66), we find that the current varies sinusoidally and leads the applied voltage by 90°.

Thus, it should be remembered that *when a sinusoidal alternating voltage is applied to a purely capacitive circuit, the current that is set up varies sinusoidally with the same frequency as that of the applied voltage and leads it by 90°.*

Figs. 3.35 (b) and (c) illustrate the waveforms and the phasor diagram respectively for this case.

Capacitive Reactance : Now, referring to Equation (3.65), we know that

$$I_m = \omega C V_m$$

$\therefore \qquad \dfrac{I}{0.707} = \omega C \times \dfrac{V}{0.707}$

$\therefore \qquad I = \omega C V = \dfrac{V}{(1/\omega C)} \qquad \ldots (3.67)$

where V and I are the r.m.s. values of voltage and current. The term $\dfrac{1}{\omega C}$ is known as *capacitive reactance* and denoted by X_C.

$\therefore \qquad I = \dfrac{V}{X_C} \qquad \ldots (3.68)$

Thus, similar to resistance and inductive reactance, the capacitive reactance also limits the current and hence can be defined as *opposition offered by the capacitance of the circuit to the flow of an alternating current*. Its unit is *ohm*.

Since $\qquad X_C = \dfrac{1}{\omega C} = \dfrac{1}{2\pi f C} \qquad \ldots (3.69)$

$X_C \propto \dfrac{1}{f}$, if C is constant.

The capacitive reactance thus being inversely proportional to frequency, the curve X_C versus f is a rectangular hyperbola as shown in Fig. 3.36.

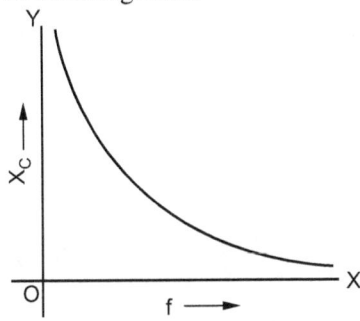

Fig. 3.36 : Variation of X_C with f

Power : As $v = V_m \sin \omega t$ and $i = I_m \sin\left(\omega t + \frac{\pi}{2}\right)$,

Instantaneous power,

$$p = vi$$

$$= V_m I_m \sin \omega t \cdot \sin\left(\omega t + \frac{\pi}{2}\right) = V_m I_m \sin \omega t \cdot \cos \omega t$$

$$= \frac{V_m I_m}{2} \sin 2\omega t \qquad \ldots (3.70)$$

Thus, similar to a purely inductive circuit, in this case also, the power curve is a sine wave of frequency double that of voltage and current waves. *Its mean value taken over a cycle is zero.*

$$\therefore \quad \text{Average power, P} = \text{Average of}\left(\frac{V_m I_m}{2} \sin 2\omega t\right) = 0 \qquad \ldots (3.71)$$

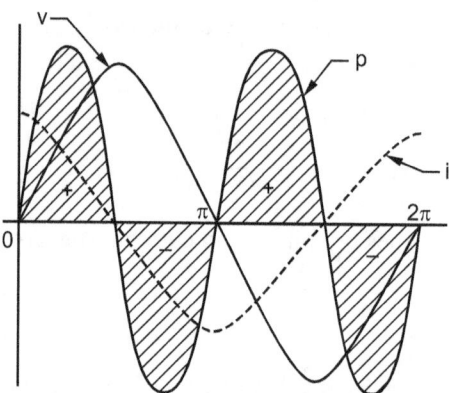

Fig. 3.37 : Power curve for a purely capacitive circuit

Fig. 3.37 shows the power curve for a purely capacitive circuit. The areas of the positive loops represent the value of the electrostatic energy stored in the capacitor during charging and the areas of the negative loops represent the energy returned back to the supply during discharging of the capacitor. The two areas being exactly equal, the total energy supplied to the capacitor over a cycle is zero. This also shows that *the average power demand of the purely capacitive circuit over a complete cycle is always zero.*

Example 3.25 : *Find the current taken by a 100 μF capacitor when it is connected across a 230 V, 50 Hz supply.*

Solution : We know that

$$I = \frac{V}{X_C}$$

where

$$X_C = \frac{1}{\omega C} = \frac{1}{2\pi f C} = \frac{1}{2\pi \times 50 \times 100 \times 10^{-6}} = 31.83 \ \Omega$$

$$\therefore \quad I = \frac{230}{31.83} = 7.23 \text{ A} \qquad \ldots \text{Ans.}$$

Example 3.26 : *A 50 Hz voltage of 230 V r.m.s. value is applied across a capacitor of capacitance 26.5 μF.*

(i) *Write the time equations for the voltage and the resulting current. Let the zero axis of the voltage be at t = 0.*

(ii) *Show the voltage and current on a time diagram.*

(iii) *Show the voltage and current on a phasor diagram.*

(iv) *Calculate the capacitive reactance.*

Solution :

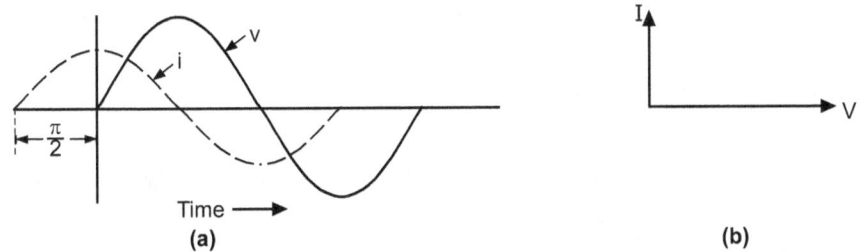

Fig. 3.38 : Waveforms and phasor diagram for voltage and current, Example 3.26

$$\text{Capacitive reactance, } X_C = \frac{1}{\omega C} = \frac{1}{2\pi f C} = \frac{1}{2\pi \times 50 \times 26.5 \times 10^{-6}}$$

$$= 120.12 \ \Omega \quad \text{... Ans.}$$

∴ R.M.S. value of the current, $I = \frac{V}{X_C} = \frac{230}{120.12} = 1.91$ A

Taking voltage as a reference quantity, its equation can be written as :

$$v = V_m \sin \omega t = V_m \sin 2\pi f t = \sqrt{2} \times 230 \sin 2\pi \times 50 \times t$$

$$= 325.27 \sin 314 \ t \text{ volts} \quad \text{... Ans.}$$

Further, since the circuit is a purely capacitive circuit, the current will lead the voltage by 90° $\left(\text{i.e. } \frac{\pi}{2} \text{ radian}\right)$. Therefore, the equation for the current can be written as :

$$i = I_m \sin\left(\omega t + \frac{\pi}{2}\right) = I_m \sin\left(2\pi f t + \frac{\pi}{2}\right)$$

$$= \sqrt{2} \times 1.91 \sin\left(2\pi \times 50 \times t + \frac{\pi}{2}\right)$$

$$= 2.7 \sin\left(314 \ t + \frac{\pi}{2}\right) \text{ amperes} \quad \text{... Ans.}$$

Fig. 3.38 (a) shows the voltage and current on a time diagram and Fig. 3.38 (b) shows the voltage and current on a phasor diagram.

3.22 POINTS TO REMEMBER

- The direct current is that current which flows continuously in one direction and has constant magnitude with respect to time.
- An alternating current (a.c.) is one which periodically passes through a definite cycle of changes in respect of magnitude as well as direction.
- Value of an alternating quantity at a particular instant is known as its instantaneous value.
- The graph obtained by plotting the instantaneous values of an alternating quantity against time gives its waveform.
- Each repetition of a complete set of changes undergone by the alternating quantity is called cycle.
- Periodic time (T) is the time (in seconds) required by an alternating quantity to complete its one cycle.
- The number of cycles completed per second by an alternating quantity is known as its frequency. It is measured in hertz (Hz).
- The maximum value attained by an alternating quantity during its positive or negative half cycle is called its amplitude or peak value.
- The angle measured in electrical degrees or electrical radians is called electrical angle.
- Angular frequency is the frequency expressed in electrical radians per second.
- The effective or r.m.s. value of an alternating current is given by that direct current which, when flowing through a given circuit for a given time, produces the same amount of heat as produced by the alternating current when flowing through the same circuit for the same time.
- For sinusoidal current or voltage, average value is that value which is obtained by averaging all the instantaneous values of its wave over a period of half cycle.
- Peak factor is defined as the ratio of maximum value of an alternating quantity to its r.m.s. value.
- The ratio of r.m.s. value to average value is called the form factor of an alternating quantity.
- When two alternating quantities of the same frequency attain their corresponding values (e.g. zero, positive maximum, etc.) simultaneously, they are said to be in phase with each other.
- A leading alternating quantity is defined as one which attains its zero or maximum value earlier as compared with the other quantity.
- A lagging alternating quantity is that which attains its zero or maximum value later than the other quantity.
- The diagram in which different alternating quantities (sinusoidal) of the same frequency are represented by phasors with their correct phase relationships is known as phasor diagram.
- In a purely resistive a.c. circuit, the current set up by a sinusoidal applied voltage is also sinusoidal and both are in phase with each other.

- In a purely resistive circuit, average power is given by the product of the r.m.s. values of applied voltage and the current.
- When a sinusoidal alternating voltage is applied to a purely inductive circuit, the resulting current is also sinusoidal and lags 90° behind the applied voltage (or the voltage leads the current by 90°).
- Inductive reactance can be defined as opposition offered by the inductance of a circuit to the flow of an alternating current. Logically, inductive reactance is expressed in units of resistance, namely ohms.
- The average demand for power in a purely inductive circuit over the whole period is always zero.
- When a sinusoidal alternating voltage is applied to a purely capacitive circuit, the current that is set up varies sinusoidally with the same frequency as that of the applied voltage and leads it by 90°.
- Capacitive reactance is defined as opposition offered by the capacitor of the circuit to the flow of an alternating current. Its unit is ohm.
- The average power demand of the purely capacitive circuit over a complete cycle is always zero.

3.23 IMPORTANT FORMULAE AT A GLANCE

- Periodic time $T = \dfrac{1}{f}$ seconds

  where f = Frequency of the supply, in hertz

- Angular frequency, $\omega = 2\pi f$ electrical radians/second

  where f = Frequency of the supply, in hertz

- R.M.S. value of a sinusoidal alternating current,

  $$I = \sqrt{\dfrac{(i_1^2 + i_2^2 + i_3^2 + \ldots + i_n^2)}{n}} \text{ amperes}$$

  where $i_1, i_2, i_3, \ldots, i_n$ = Instantaneous values of an alternating current over a period of half cycle, in amperes

- R.M.S. value of a sinusoidal alternating current,

  $$I = \dfrac{I_m}{\sqrt{2}} = 0.707\, I_m \text{ amperes}$$

  where I_m = Peak value of the sinusoidal alternating current, in amperes

- Average value of a sinusoidal alternating current,

  $$I_{av} = \dfrac{(i_1 + i_2 + i_3 + \ldots + i_n)}{n} \text{ amperes}$$

  where $i_1, i_2, i_3, \ldots, i_n$ = Instantaneous values of an alternating current over a period of half cycle, in amperes

- Average value of a sinusoidal alternating current,

$$I_{av} = \frac{2I_m}{\pi} = 0.637 \, I_m \text{ amperes}$$

  where I_m = Peak value of the sinusoidal alternating current, in amperes

- Peak factor of a sinusoidal alternating quantity $= \dfrac{\text{Maximum value}}{\text{R.M.S. value}} = 1.414$

- Form factor of a sinusoidal alternating quantity $= \dfrac{\text{R.M.S. value}}{\text{Average value}} = 1.11$

- Current (r.m.s. value) in a purely resistive a.c. circuit, $I = \dfrac{V}{R}$ amperes.

  where V = R.M.S. value of the applied alternating voltage, in volts

  R = Resistance of the resistor in a circuit, in ohms

- Average power consumed in a purely resistive a.c. circuit,

$$P = V \cdot I = \frac{V^2}{R} = I^2 R \text{ watts}$$

  where V = R.M.S. value of the applied alternating voltage, in volts

  I = R.M.S. value of the alternating current in a circuit, in amperes

  R = Resistance of the resistor in a circuit, in ohms

- Inductive reactance $X_L = \omega L = 2\pi f L$ ohms

  where ω = Angular frequency, in electrical radians/second

  f = Frequency of the supply, in hertz

  L = Inductance of an inductor in the circuit, in henrys

- Current (r.m.s. value) in a purely inductive circuit, $I = \dfrac{V}{X_L}$ amperes

  where V = R.M.S. value of the applied alternating voltage, in volts

  X_L = Inductive reactance, in ohms

- Capacitive reactance $X_C = \dfrac{1}{\omega C} = \dfrac{1}{2\pi f C}$ ohms

  where ω = Angular frequency, in electrical radians/second

  f = Frequency of the supply, in hertz

  C = Capacitance of a capacitor in the circuit, in farads

- Current (r.m.s. value) in a purely capacitive circuit,

$$I = \frac{V}{X_C} \text{ amperes}$$

  where V = R.M.S. value of the applied alternating voltage, in volts

  X_C = Capacitive reactance, in ohms

3.24 SOLUTIONS OF NUMERICAL EXAMPLES FROM UNIVERSITY PAPERS

Example 3.27: *Explain the concept of phasor representation of alternating currents. A sinusoidal voltage is given by (325.269 sin ωt) volts at 50 Hz. Determine the r.m.s. value, average value and time period of the voltage.* **(November 2004/4 Marks)**

Solution : R.M.S. value of the voltage,

$$V = \frac{V_m}{\sqrt{2}} = \frac{325.269}{\sqrt{2}}$$

$$= 230 \text{ volts} \quad \text{... Ans.}$$

Average value of the voltage,

$$V_{av} = 0.637 \, V_m = 0.637 \times 325.269$$

$$= 207.2 \text{ volts} \quad \text{... Ans.}$$

Time period, $T = \frac{1}{f} = \frac{1}{50}$

$$= 0.02 \text{ s} \quad \text{... Ans.}$$

Example 3.28 : *A 50 Hz sinusoidal alternating current has a peak value of 14.14 A. Its zero crossing entering the positive half cycle occurs at t = 0.*
  (i)   *Write down the time equation of the current.*
  (ii) *Calculate its r.m.s. value.*
  (iii) *Determine the time taken for the current to reach a value of –10 A for the first time in the cycle.* **(May 2006/6 Marks)**

Solution : (i) $\quad i = I_m \sin \omega t = 14.14 \sin (2\pi f t) = 14.14 \sin (2\pi \times 50 t)$

Or, $\quad i = \mathbf{14.14 \sin (100 \pi t) \text{ amperes}} \quad \text{... Ans.}$

(ii) R.M.S. value, $I = \dfrac{I_m}{\sqrt{2}} = \dfrac{14.14}{\sqrt{2}}$

$$= \mathbf{10 \text{ A}} \quad \text{... Ans.}$$

(iii) Time t to reach the value of –10 A is given by

$$i = -10 = 14.14 \sin 100\pi t$$

$$\therefore \quad \sin 100\pi t = \frac{-10}{14.14} = -0.707$$

$$\therefore \quad 100\pi t = \frac{5\pi}{4} \text{ radians (i.e. 225°) or } \frac{7\pi}{4} \text{ radians (i.e. 315°)}$$

Since we want the time taken for the current to reach a value of –10 A for the first time in the cycle, taking the first value, we have

$$100\pi t = \frac{5\pi}{4}$$

$$\therefore \quad t = \mathbf{0.0125 \text{ s}} \quad \text{... Ans.}$$

Example 3.29 : *A sinusoidal alternating current of frequency 25 Hz has a maximum value of 125 A. How long will it take for the current to attain values of 25 A, 50 A and 100 A ?* **(May 2007/8 Marks)**

Solution : Expression for the instantaneous value of the current can be written as :

$$i = I_m \sin \omega t = I_m \sin 2\pi f t = 125 \sin 2\pi \times 25 \times t$$

$$= 125 \sin 50\pi t$$

(i) Now, time to reach the value, $i = 25$ A will be given by

$$25 = 125 \sin 50\pi t$$

$\therefore \quad \sin 50\pi t = \dfrac{25}{125} = 0.2$

$\therefore \quad 50\pi t = 0.2014$ radian

$\therefore \quad t = \mathbf{0.001282\ s}$ ... Ans.

(ii) When $i = 50$ A,

$$50 = 125 \sin 50\pi t$$

$\therefore \quad \sin 50\pi t = \dfrac{50}{125} = 0.4$

$\therefore \quad 50\pi t = 0.4115$ radian

$\therefore \quad t = \mathbf{0.00262\ s}$ ... Ans.

(iii) When $i = 100$ A,

$$100 = 125 \sin 50\pi t$$

$\therefore \quad \sin 50\pi t = \dfrac{100}{125} = 0.8$

$\therefore \quad 50\pi t = 0.9273$ radian

$\therefore \quad t = \mathbf{0.005903\ s}$ ... Ans.

Example 3.30 : *Find the current flowing through a purely inductive circuit containing a voltage source, $v = 325 \sin(100\pi)$ and an inductance $L = 2$ H.* **(December 2012/8 Marks)**

Solution : Comparing the equation of a voltage source with the standard form of equation for an alternating voltage $v = V_m \sin \omega t$, we have

$$V_m = 325 \text{ volts}$$
$$\omega = 100\pi \text{ radians/s}$$

$\therefore \quad$ Supply frequency $f = \dfrac{\omega}{2\pi} = \dfrac{100\pi}{2\pi} = 50$ Hz

and R.M.S. value of the voltage, $V = \dfrac{V_m}{\sqrt{2}} = \dfrac{325}{\sqrt{2}} = 229.81$ volts

Further, $\quad L = 2H$ (given)

$\therefore \quad$ Inductive reactance $X_L = 2\pi f L = 2\pi \times 50 \times 2 = 628.32\ \Omega$

and R.M.S. value of the current flowing through a purely inductive circuit,

$$I = \dfrac{V}{X_L} = \dfrac{229.81}{628.32} = 0.37 \text{ A}$$

Being a purely inductive circuit, this current will lag behind the applied voltage by 90° or $\pi/2$ radian. Hence expressing it in the same form as given applied voltage, we have

Current flowing through an inductive circuit,

$$i = \sqrt{2} \times 0.37 \sin\left(100\pi t - \dfrac{\pi}{2}\right) = \mathbf{0.52 \sin\left(100\pi t - \dfrac{\pi}{2}\right) \text{ amperes}} \quad \text{... Ans.}$$

3.25 EXERCISES

3.25.1 Review Questions

1. What is an alternating current ? Compare it with a direct current.
2. With reference to alternating quantities, define the following terms : Waveform, Cycle, Frequency, Amplitude and Periodic time.
3. State the relationship between angular velocity and frequency.
4. Explain clearly the terms : Instantaneous and Maximum values of an alternating quantity.
5. Define r.m.s. value of an alternating quantity. Prove that in an alternating quantity varying sinusoidally, the maximum value is $\sqrt{2}$ times the r.m.s. value.
6. Explain the practical significance of the r.m.s. value of an alternating quantity.
7. Prove that for a sinusoidally varying current and voltage, the average value is $2/\pi$ times the maximum value.
8. Define peak factor and form factor. State their values for a sinusoidal quantity.
9. Explain the meaning of the terms phase and phase difference.
10. What do you understand by the terms lag and lead in relation to alternating quantities ?
11. How are the two alternating quantities added ?
12. With the help of waveforms and phasor diagrams, comment on the phase relationship between the voltage and the current in pure resistive, pure inductive and pure capacitive circuits.
13. Discuss in brief the effect of frequency on inductive and capacitive reactances.
14. What is the average power taken by a pure inductor and a pure capacitor when connected across an a.c. supply ?

3.25.2 Classified Theory Questions from University Papers

1. Define : (i) Inductive reactance, (ii) Capacitive reactance, (iii) Time period of an a.c. cycle, (iv) Amplitude of an a.c. quantity.
   (Answer : Sections 3.5, 3.20, 3.21) **(May 2009/4 Marks)**
2. Derive an expression for the instantaneous value of an alternating current in terms of its maximum value, angular velocity and time.
   (Answer : Section 3.6) **(December 2011/8 Marks)**
3. Explain the importance of r.m.s. value of an a.c. quantity. Derive analytically the equation to calculate the r.m.s. value of sinusoidal a.c. quantity.
   (Answer : Section 3.7) **(December 2008, 2010/6 Marks)**
4. Define the terms : (i) R.M.S. value, (ii) Average value, (iii) Form factor, (iv) Peak or Crest factor.
   (Answer : Sections 3.7, 3.8, 3.9) (May 2008, 2011, 2012/Some of these for 2 Marks each)
5. When a pure resistance is connected across an a.c. supply, prove that power consumed by the resistance is equal to the multiplication of r.m.s. voltage across it and r.m.s. current through it. Draw the voltage, current and power waveforms.
   (Answer : Section 3.19) **(May 2008, 2010/8 Marks)**
6. Show that when a sinusoidal a.c. is applied across a pure inductance, current flowing through it lags behind the voltage by 90°.
   (Answer : Section 3.20) **(May 2009/6 Marks)**

7. Show that in a pure inductance, average power consumed is zero. Draw the voltage, current and power waveforms.

   (Answer : Section 3.20) (December 2008, 2012/8 Marks)

8. Show that the average power consumed by a pure capacitance is zero when it is supplied with an a.c. supply. Draw the voltage, current and power waveforms.

   (Answer : Section 3.21) (May 2010/6 Marks)

3.25.3 Examples for Practice

1. The waveform of a voltage has a form factor of 1.15 and peak factor of 1.5 and if the maximum value of the voltage is 4500 V, calculate the average and r.m.s. values of the voltage. (2608.7 V, 3000 V)

2. An alternating voltage is represented as

   $$v = 141.42 \sin\left(628\,t + \frac{\pi}{6}\right) \text{ volts}$$

   Find its r.m.s. value, frequency and periodic time. (100 V, 100 Hz, 0.01 s)

3. A sinusoidal alternating current of frequency 25 Hz, has a maximum value of 100 A. How long will it take for the current to attain values of 20 A and 50 A starting from zero ?

   (0.00128 s, 0.0033 s)

4. An alternating current, varying sinusoidally with a frequency of 50 Hz, has an r.m.s. value of 10 A. Write down the equation for instantaneous value and find this value for

   (i) 0.0015 s after passing through the positive maximum value.

   (ii) 0.0075 s after passing through zero and increasing negatively.

   (i = 14.14 sin 314 t, 12.61 A, − 10.03 A)

5. A certain resultant current is made up of two components, a 10 A d.c. component and a 50 Hz a.c. component of sinusoidal waveform having a maximum value of 14.14 A. Draw a sketch of the waveform of the resultant current and find out its r.m.s. value. (14.14 A)

6. An alternating voltage is applied to three circuit elements connected in series. The voltages across the elements are respectively

   $$e_1 = 100 \sin 314\,t$$

   $$e_2 = 60 \sin\left(314\,t - \frac{\pi}{2}\right)$$

   $$e_3 = 150 \sin\left(314\,t + \frac{\pi}{4}\right)$$

   Find graphically or otherwise the equation for the resultant voltage.

   [e = 211.1 sin (314 t + 0.22)]

CHAPTER

4

SINGLE-PHASE A.C. SERIES CIRCUITS

4.1 INTRODUCTION

As already mentioned earlier, all practical electric circuits consist of combinations of three basic circuit elements namely *resistance (R), inductance (L)* and *capacitance (C)*. In the previous chapter, we have studied the behaviour of simple single-parameter circuits on application of sinusoidal voltages. Now in this chapter, we shall study the analysis of series a.c. circuits and, power and energy considerations in such circuits.

4.2 SERIES A.C. CIRCUITS

So far, we have studied simple single-element a.c. circuits such as circuits containing resistance only, inductance only and capacitance only. In practice, a.c. circuits consist of series and parallel combinations of these three types of circuit elements. In the following sections, we shall study few cases of simple series circuits.

4.3 CIRCUIT WITH RESISTANCE AND INDUCTANCE IN SERIES

Consider the circuit containing resistance of R ohms in series with an inductance of L henries connected across an a.c. supply as shown in Fig. 4.1 (a). If the circuit draws a current of I amperes, then we have,

Voltage drop across R, $V_R = I.R$ (in phase with I)

Voltage drop across L, $V_L = I.X_L$ (leading I by 90°)

where $X_L (= \omega L)$ is the inductive reactance of the inductance L.

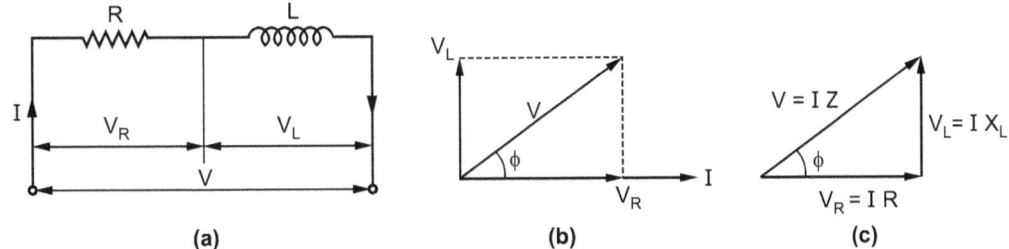

Fig. 4.1 : A.C. circuit containing resistance and inductance in series

These voltage drops across resistance and inductance are represented with the help of phasors taking current as the reference phasor in the phasor diagram of Fig. 4.1 (b). The current is chosen as a reference phasor because it is common to all circuit elements. Now, we know that in the d.c. series circuits, the total applied voltage is the sum of the voltage drops in the individual parts of the circuit. In the a.c. series circuits also, the same general rule is applicable with the exception that the addition must be the phasor addition. Therefore, in the circuit under consideration, the applied voltage can be obtained by the phasor addition of V_R and V_L i.e.

$$\bar{V} = \bar{V}_R + \bar{V}_L \quad \text{(Phasor addition)}$$

Then, from the voltage triangle shown in Fig. 4.1 (c),

$$V = \sqrt{V_R^2 + V_L^2} = \sqrt{(IR)^2 + (IX_L)^2} = I\sqrt{R^2 + X_L^2}$$

$$\therefore \qquad I = \frac{V}{\sqrt{R^2 + X_L^2}} = \frac{V}{Z} \qquad \ldots (4.1)$$

where

$$Z = \sqrt{R^2 + X_L^2} \qquad \ldots (4.2)$$

Impedance : The quantity $\sqrt{R^2 + X_L^2}$ in the above expression is called the impedance of the circuit and denoted by Z. It is defined as *the opposition of the circuit to the flow of alternating current*. The resistance (R) and inductive reactance (X_L) being in ohms, unit of impedance is also ohm.

Phase Relationship between Voltage and Current : From the phasor diagram shown in Fig. 4.1 (b), it is clear that in such circuit, the current lags behind the applied voltage by an angle ϕ such that

$$\tan \phi = \frac{V_L}{V_R} = \frac{I \cdot X_L}{I \cdot R} = \frac{X_L}{R} \qquad \ldots (4.3)$$

Or,

$$\cos \phi = \frac{V_R}{V} = \frac{I \cdot R}{I \cdot Z} = \frac{R}{Z} \qquad \ldots (4.4)$$

It means that if the applied voltage is represented by

$$v = V_m \sin \omega t$$

then,

$$i = I_m \sin (\omega t - \phi)$$

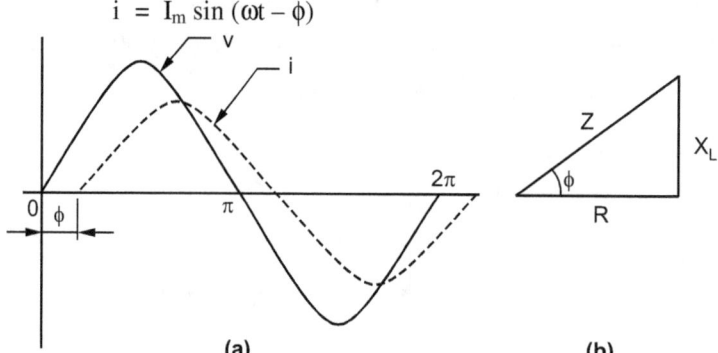

Fig. 4.2 : R-L series circuit (a) Waveforms, (b) Impedance triangle

Fig. 4.2 (a) shows the waveforms for the voltage and the current.

Impedance Triangle : By dividing each side of the voltage triangle (Fig. 4.1 c) by I, a similar triangle as shown in Fig. 4.2 (b) is obtained. As sides of this triangle represent the resistance, reactance and impedance of the circuit, it is known as *impedance triangle*. From this triangle also, we have the following relationships :

$$Z = \sqrt{R^2 + X_L^2}$$

i.e. $\quad$ Impedance $= \sqrt{(\text{Resistance})^2 + (\text{Reactance})^2}$ ... (4.5)

and $\quad \cos\phi = \dfrac{R}{Z}, \quad \tan\phi = \dfrac{X_L}{R}$

where ϕ is the phase angle between the applied voltage and circuit current.

Power : It is obvious that, average power supplied to the circuit,

P = (Average power taken by the resistance)

+ (Average power taken by the inductance)

But we have seen that the average power taken by a pure inductance over a complete cycle is always zero. Hence, the inductance L in the circuit consumes no power.

$\therefore \quad$ P = Average power taken by the resistance

$= I^2 R = (IR) I = V_R I$

$= V \cos\phi \times I \quad\quad$ ($\because$ from voltage triangle, $V_R = V \cos\phi$)

i.e. $\quad$ P = V I $\cos\phi$ ... (4.6)

Following terms are worth noting in connection with the power in a.c. circuits :

Apparent Power (S) : The product of r.m.s. values of voltage (V) and current (I) in the Expression (4.6) for power is called the *apparent power*.

It is measured in *volt-amperes (VA)* or *kilovolt-amperes (kVA)*.

True Power (P) : The average power given by the expression P = V I $\cos\phi$ is called the *true power* or *real power*. It is measured in *watts (W)* or *kilowatts (kW)*.

Power Factor (cos ϕ) : *It is the factor by which the apparent power must be multiplied in order to obtain the true power* or in other words, *it is the ratio of the true power to the apparent power* i.e.

$$\text{Power factor} = \dfrac{\text{True power}}{\text{Apparent power}} = \dfrac{VI \cos\phi}{VI} = \cos\phi \quad ...(4.7)$$

Thus, *the numerical value of the cosine of the phase angle between the voltage and current gives the power factor of the circuit*. The value of the power factor, therefore, can never be more than *unity*.

Alternatively, we can also get the power factor from the impedance triangle (Fig. 4.2 b) as

$$\text{Power factor} = \cos\phi = \dfrac{R}{Z}$$

The nature of the power factor is always decided by the lag or lead of the current with respect to the voltage. In the case of the inductive circuit where current lags behind the voltage, power factor is said to be *lagging*. On the other hand, in a capacitive circuit, it is said to be *leading* as current leads the voltage.

For a purely inductive circuit, power factor is *zero lagging* and for a purely capacitive circuit, it is *zero leading* as in both the cases, $\phi = 90°$. For a purely resistive circuit with $\phi = 0$, power factor is simply stated as *unity*. Sometimes, power factor is also expressed as percentage e.g. 0.7 lagging p.f. can be expressed as 70 % lagging.

From the Expression (4.6) for power, it is clear that more current is required for supplying a given power at a low power factor than at a high power factor. An increase in the current caused by low power factor leads to many disadvantages such as increased cost of the equipments, increased power losses and reduced efficiency. Therefore, the value of the power factor is of practical importance.

Choking Coil : Majority of a.c. series circuits which occur in practice have negligibly small capacitance. Such circuits, therefore, come under the category of R-L series circuit. The most common example is of a *choking coil*. A choking coil consists of a coil wound on a laminated iron core. Its inductance is very high in comparison with its ohmic resistance. The resistance and inductance of the coil are not physically separate. However, in effect, such a coil is always considered equivalent to R-L series circuit.

In many cases, it is necessary to use the a.c. power at a voltage lower than that of the supply. Under such conditions, a reduction of voltage may be obtained by means of a choking coil connected in series with the circuit, e.g. this is one of the purposes for which a choke is used in fluorescent tube circuit. The use of choking coil for such purpose involves very little power loss in comparison with the simple resistor if used in its place.

Since the introduction of a choking coil in the circuit reduces the circuit current ($\because$ I = V / Z), it can also be used as a *current limiting device*. In this case also, because of its small power loss, a choking coil is preferred over simple resistor, e.g. the reactors are used in the modern power stations to limit the excessive short-circuit current and thereby to protect the machinery and switchgear.

Example 4.1 : *A circuit has a resistance of 110 Ω and an inductance of 0.5 H. It is connected to a 230 V, 50 Hz supply. Calculate (a) the inductive reactance, (b) the impedance, (c) the current and (d) phase difference between the voltage and current.*

Solution : Referring to Fig. 4.1 (a), we have

(a)   Inductive reactance, $X_L = \omega L = 2\pi f L = 2\pi \times 50 \times 0.5 = \mathbf{157\ \Omega}$ ... Ans.

(b)   Impedance, $Z = \sqrt{R^2 + X_L^2}$

$\qquad\qquad\qquad\qquad = \sqrt{110^2 + 157^2} = \mathbf{191.7\ \Omega}$ ... Ans.

(c)   Current, $I = \dfrac{V}{Z} = \dfrac{230}{191.7} = \mathbf{1.2\ A}$ ... Ans.

(d)   Power factor, $\cos\phi = \dfrac{R}{Z} = \dfrac{110}{191.7} = \mathbf{0.574\ lagging}$ ... Ans.

$\therefore \qquad\qquad\qquad \phi = \mathbf{54.98° \approx 55°}$ ... Ans.

Thus, the phase difference between the current and voltage will be 55°. The current will lag the voltage by this angle.

Example 4.2 : *A 110 V, 100 W lamp is to be operated on 230 V, 50 Hz supply mains by connecting it in series with either a choking coil of negligible resistance or a non-inductive resistor. Calculate the values of inductance of a choking coil and resistance of a non-inductive resistor respectively required in the two cases. Which method is preferable and why ?*

Solution :

Case-1 : A Lamp in Series with a Choking Coil :

The circuit is given in Fig. 4.3 (a), where R* represents the lamp and L the inductance of a choking coil. In the phasor diagram of Fig. 4.3 (b), the voltage V_R across R is in phase with the current I, while the voltage V_L across a choking coil leads I by 90°. The resultant voltage V is the phasor sum of V_R and V_L.

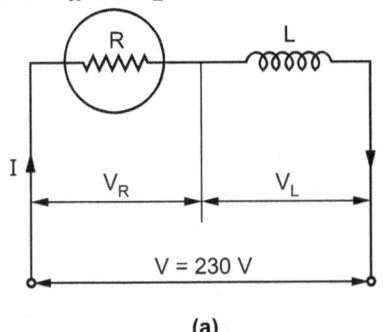
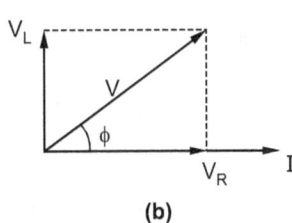

(a)   (b)

Fig. 4.3 : (a) A lamp in series with a choking coil, Example 4.2, (b) Phasor diagram

Therefore, from the phasor diagram,

$$V^2 = V_R^2 + V_L^2$$

∴ $\quad 230^2 = 110^2 + V_L^2$

∴ $\quad V_L = 201.99 \text{ V}$

Rated current of the lamp, $I = \dfrac{100}{110} = 0.91 \text{ A}$

∴ Inductive reactance of a choking coil,

$$X_L = \dfrac{V_L}{I} = \dfrac{201.99}{0.91} = 221.97 \ \Omega$$

∴ $\quad L = \dfrac{X_L}{\omega} = \dfrac{X_L}{2\pi f} = \dfrac{221.97}{2\pi \times 50} = \mathbf{0.71 \text{ H}}$ **... Ans.**

Since the resistance of a choking coil is negligible, it will consume very small amount of power.

Case-2 : A Lamp in Series with a Non-inductive Resistor :

As illustrated in Fig. 4.4 (a), let R' be the resistance of the non-inductive resistor required in series with the lamp (R). The voltages V_R and V'_R both are in phase with the current I (Fig. 4.4 b). The resultant voltage V is, therefore, mere arithmetic addition of these two voltages i.e. $V = V_R + V'_R$.

∴ $\quad V'_R = V - V_R = 230 - 110 = 120 \text{ V}$

With rated current of 0.91 A for the lamp,

$$R' = \dfrac{V'_R}{I} = \dfrac{120}{0.91} = \mathbf{131.87 \ \Omega} \quad\quad\quad \text{... Ans.}$$

---

* *The filament lamp is always considered to be purely resistive in nature with unity power factor.*

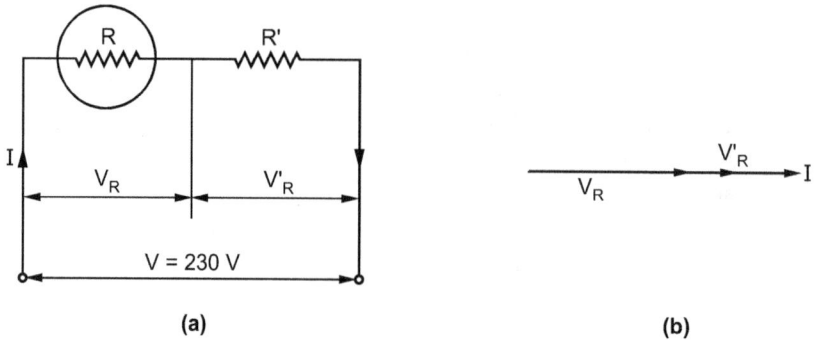

Fig. 4.4 : (a) A lamp in series with a non-inductive resistor, Example 4.2, (b) Phasor diagram

Power consumed by a non-inductive resistor = $I^2 R' = 0.91^2 \times 131.87 = 109.2$ W

Obviously, the first method which involves least power consumption is preferable.

Example 4.3 : *The inductive coils A and B are connected in series across a 100 V, single-phase supply. The current drawn by the circuit is 10 A and the total power loss is 300 W. If the power loss in coil A is twice of that in coil B and the voltage across coil A is 50 V, calculate the resistance and inductive reactance of each coil.*

Solution : Referring to the circuit diagram (Fig. 4.5), let R_A, X_{LA}, Z_A be the resistance, reactance and impedance of coil A, and R_B, X_{LB}, Z_B be the resistance, reactance and impedance of coil B. Then,

Total resistance of the circuit, $R = R_A + R_B$ and
Total reactance of the circuit, $X_L = X_{LA} + X_{LB}$

Now, impedance of the circuit, $Z = \sqrt{R^2 + X_L^2} = \dfrac{V}{I} = \dfrac{100}{10} = 10\ \Omega$

Also, Total power loss, $P = I^2 R = 300$ W (given)

∴ $R = \dfrac{300}{10^2} = 3\ \Omega$

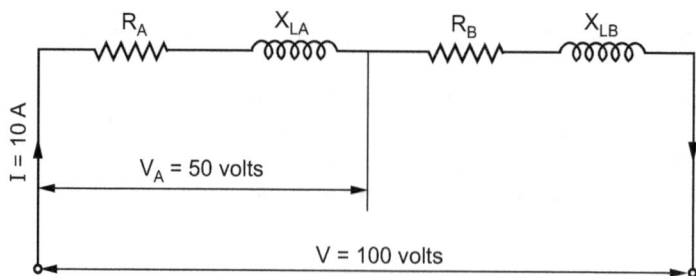

Fig. 4.5 : Circuit diagram for Example 4.3

∴ $X_L = \sqrt{Z^2 - R^2} = \sqrt{10^2 - 3^2} = 9.539\ \Omega$

As Power loss in coil A = $I^2 R_A$ and
Power loss in coil B = $I^2 R_B$

$I^2 R_A = 2 I^2 R_B$ (given)

∴ $R_A = 2 R_B$ ... (I)

Also, as already seen above, $R = R_A + R_B = 3\ \Omega$ ... (II)

Substituting the value of R_A from Equation (I) in Equation (II), we get

$$2 R_B + R_B = 3$$

∴ $\quad R_B = 1\,\Omega$ ... Ans.

∴ $\quad R_A = 2 R_B = 2\,\Omega$ ... Ans.

Impedance of coil A,

$$Z_A = \frac{V_A}{I} = \frac{50}{10} = 5\,\Omega$$ ... Ans.

∴ $\quad X_{LA} = \sqrt{Z_A^2 - R_A^2} = \sqrt{5^2 - 2^2} = 4.583\,\Omega$ ... Ans.

Since, $\quad X_L = X_{LA} + X_{LB} = 9.539\,\Omega$

$$X_{LB} = 9.539 - 4.583 = 4.956\,\Omega$$ ... Ans.

Thus, we have, $R_A = 2\,\Omega$, $X_{LA} = 4.583\,\Omega$, $R_B = 1\,\Omega$, $X_{LB} = 4.956\,\Omega$

Example 4.4 : *A choke coil is connected to 240 V, a.c. supply. When the frequency of supply is 50 Hz, an ammeter connected in series with the choke coil reads 60 A. On increasing the frequency to 100 Hz, the same ammeter reads 40 A. Calculate the resistance and inductance of the coil.*

Solution : Let R be the resistance and L be the inductance of the choke coil.

With 50 Hz Supply :

$$Z = \frac{V}{I} = \frac{240}{60} = 4\,\Omega$$

∴ $\quad \sqrt{R^2 + (2\pi \times 50 \times L)^2} = 4$

Or, $\quad R^2 + (2\pi \times 50 \times L)^2 = 16$ ... (i)

With 100 Hz Supply :

$$Z = \frac{V}{I} = \frac{240}{40} = 6\,\Omega$$

∴ $\quad \sqrt{R^2 + (2\pi \times 100 \times L)^2} = 6$

Or, $\quad R^2 + (2\pi \times 100 \times L)^2 = 36$ ... (ii)

Solving the equations (i) and (ii), we get

$$R = 3.055\,\Omega, \quad L = 8.22 \times 10^{-3}\,H$$ ... Ans.

Example 4.5 : *A bank of four lamps each rated at 100 W at 100 V, is to be operated from 250 V, 50 Hz, single-phase, a.c. supply. A choke coil is connected in series to manage this. If the angle between supply voltage and current is 65°, determine :*

(i) Resistance and inductance of the choke coil.

(ii) Power consumed by choke coil.

(iii) Total power.

Solution :

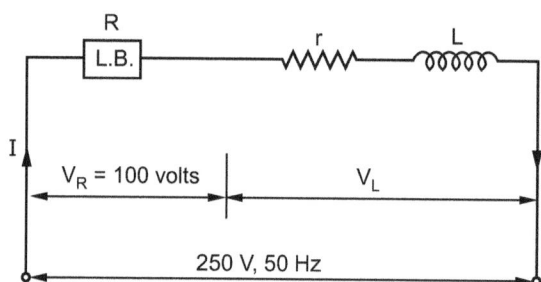

Fig. 4.6 : Circuit diagram for Example 4.5

Power consumed by lamp bank, P_R = 4 × 100 = 400 W

Current drawn by lamp bank, $I = \dfrac{P_R}{V_R} = \dfrac{400}{100}$ = 4 A

Resistance of the lamp bank, $R = \dfrac{V_R}{I} = \dfrac{100}{4}$ = 25 Ω

Total power supplied to the circuit, P_T = V I cos φ = 250 × 4 × cos 65°

   = **422.62 W** ... **Ans.**

∴ Power consumed by choke coil, $P_L = P_T - P_R$ = 422.62 − 400

   = **22.62 W** ... **Ans.**

∴ Resistance of choke coil, $r = \dfrac{P_L}{I^2} = \dfrac{22.62}{4^2}$ = **1.414 Ω** ... **Ans.**

Total impedance of the circuit, $Z = \dfrac{V}{I} = \dfrac{250}{4}$ = 62.5 Ω

∴ Inductive reactance of the choke coil,

$$X_L = \sqrt{Z^2 - (R + r)^2} = \sqrt{(62.5)^2 - (25 + 1.414)^2}$$

   = 56.64 Ω

∴ Inductance of choke coil, $L = \dfrac{X_L}{2\pi f} = \dfrac{56.64}{2\pi \times 50}$ = **0.18 H** ... **Ans.**

4.3.1 Measurement of Power in an Inductive Circuit using Three-Voltmeter Method

The power in an a.c. circuit is generally measured with the help of a wattmeter. In an inductive circuit, it may, however, be measured using *three-voltmeter method*. In this method, the inductive load in which power is to be measured is connected in series with a non-inductive resistor (say, a lamp bank) across an a.c. supply as shown in Fig. 4.7 (a). The voltages V_L, V_R and V are then measured (generally using one voltmeter only in turn) where

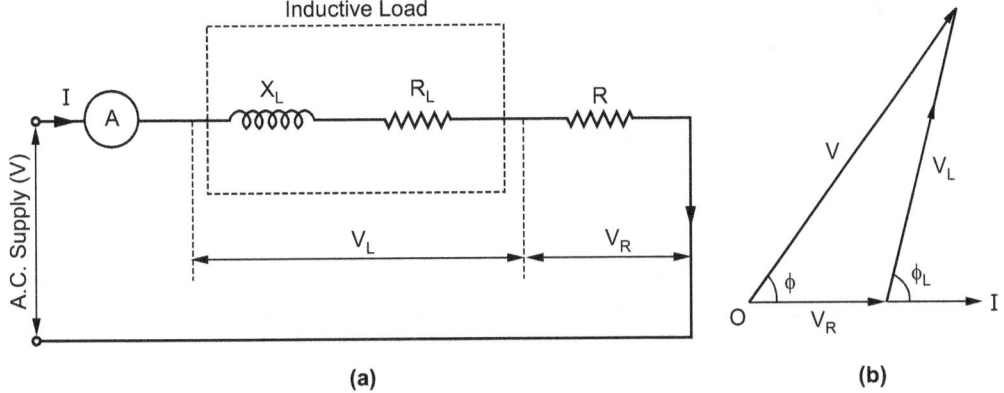

Fig. 4.7 : Three-voltmeter method of measuring power

V_L = Voltage across an inductive load (with resistance R_L and inductive reactance X_L), leading the current I by ϕ_L.

V_R = Voltage across the non-inductive resistor R, in phase with the current I.

V = Supply voltage

Fig. 4.7 (b) shows the phasor diagram of voltages. From this diagram, the power factor angle ϕ_L of the inductive load can be found by using the *cosine rule* as follows :

$$V^2 = V_L^2 + V_R^2 - 2 V_L V_R \cos(180° - \phi_L)$$
$$= V_L^2 + V_R^2 + 2 V_L V_R \cos \phi_L$$

∴ $$\cos \phi_L = \frac{V^2 - V_L^2 - V_R^2}{2 V_L \cdot V_R}$$

Hence, power consumed by the inductive load,

$$P_L = V_L \cdot I \cos \phi_L = \frac{I(V^2 - V_L^2 - V_R^2)}{2 V_R} \text{ watts} \qquad \ldots (4.8)$$

Or, since $\frac{V_R}{I} = R$ (Ohm's law),

$$P_L = \frac{1}{2R}(V^2 - V_L^2 - V_R^2) \text{ watts} \qquad \ldots (4.9)$$

Following are the limitations of this method :

(i) Small errors in the voltmeter readings produce much larger errors in the power measurement.

(ii) This method gives reliable results only if the load power factor angle ϕ_L is sufficiently large, i.e. if the voltage drop across R is nearly equal to that across the inductive load.

(iii) A supply voltage much higher than the rated voltage of the load is required for accurate results.

Example 4.6 : *The three-voltmeter method is used to measure the power input to an inductive load. The following measurements are made :*

Supply voltage = 230 V

Voltage across non-inductive resistor in series with the load = 140 V

Voltage across the inductive load = 120 V

Current = 5 A

Calculate : (i) Impedance of the inductive load; (ii) Impedance of combination; (iii) Power absorbed by the inductive load; (iv) Power absorbed by non-inductive resistor; (v) Total power taken from the supply; (vi) Power factor of the load and of whole circuit; (vii) Reactance and resistance of the inductive load.

Solution : Referring to Figs. 4.7 (a) and (b) for the circuit diagram and phasor diagram respectively and using usual notations, we have

Current, $I = 5$ A

Impedance of the inductive load,

$$Z_L = \frac{V_L}{I} = \frac{120}{5} = 24 \ \Omega \qquad \text{... Ans.}$$

Impedance of combination,

$$Z = \frac{V}{I} = \frac{230}{5} = 46 \ \Omega \qquad \text{... Ans.}$$

Power absorbed by the inductive load,

$$P_L = \frac{I(V^2 - V_L^2 - V_R^2)}{2V_R}$$

$$= \frac{5(230^2 - 120^2 - 140^2)}{2 \times 140} = 337.5 \text{ W} \qquad \text{... Ans.}$$

Or alternatively, $\quad R = \dfrac{V_R}{I} = \dfrac{140}{5} = 28 \ \Omega$

$\therefore \qquad P_L = \dfrac{1}{2R}(V^2 - V_L^2 - V_R^2)$

$$= \frac{1}{2 \times 28}(230^2 - 120^2 - 140^2) = \textbf{337.5 W} \qquad \text{... Ans.}$$

Power absorbed by non-inductive resistor,

$$P_R = I^2 \cdot R = 5^2 \times 28 = \textbf{700 W} \qquad \text{... Ans.}$$

Or alternatively, $\quad P_R = V_R \cdot I = 140 \times 5 = \textbf{700 W} \qquad \text{... Ans.}$

Total power taken from the supply,

$$P = P_L + P_R = 337.5 + 700 = \textbf{1037.5 W} \qquad \text{... Ans.}$$

Power factor of the inductive load,

$$\cos\phi_L = \frac{P_L}{V_L \cdot I} = \frac{337.5}{120 \times 5} = 0.563 \text{ lagging} \quad \text{... Ans.}$$

Power factor of combination,

$$\cos\phi = \frac{P}{V \cdot I} = \frac{1037.5}{230 \times 5}$$

$$= 0.902 \text{ lagging} \quad \text{... Ans.}$$

Now, the resistance (R_L) and inductive reactance (X_L) of the load can be calculated from its impedance triangle.

Resistance of the load, $R_L = Z_L \cos\phi_L = 24 \times 0.563 = \mathbf{13.51\ \Omega}$ ... Ans.

Reactance of the load, $X_L = Z_L \sin\phi_L = 24 \times 0.827 = \mathbf{19.84\ \Omega}$ ... Ans.

4.4 CIRCUIT WITH RESISTANCE AND CAPACITANCE IN SERIES

Fig. 4.8 (a) shows a circuit containing a resistor of R ohms in series with a capacitor of C farads capacitance connected across an a.c. supply. If circuit current is I amperes, then

Voltage drop across R, $V_R = I \cdot R$ (in phase with I)

Voltage drop across C, $V_C = I \cdot X_C$ (lagging I by 90°)

where $X_C \left(= \dfrac{1}{\omega C}\right)$ is the capacitive reactance of the capacitor.

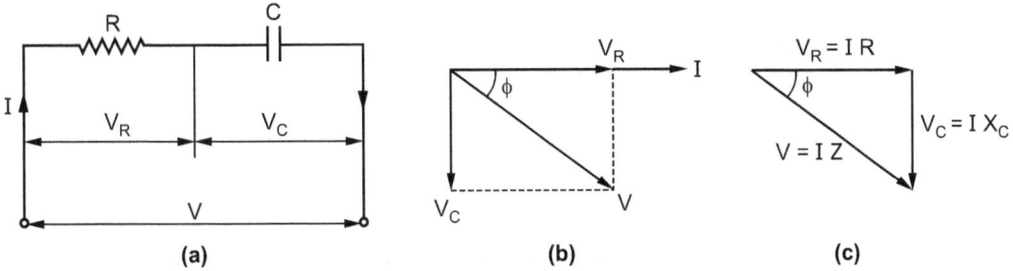

(a) (b) (c)

Fig. 4.8 : A.C. circuit containing resistance and capacitance in series

Fig. 4.8 (b) shows the phasor diagram with current as a reference phasor. The applied voltage V must be the phasor sum of its component parts V_R and V_C which are in quadrature. Therefore, from the voltage triangle shown in Fig. 4.8 (c), we have

$$V = \sqrt{V_R^2 + V_C^2} = \sqrt{(IR)^2 + (IX_C)^2}$$

$$= I\sqrt{R^2 + X_C^2}$$

$$\therefore \quad I = \frac{V}{\sqrt{R^2 + X_C^2}} = \frac{V}{Z} \quad \ldots(4.10)$$

where
$$Z = \sqrt{R^2 + X_C^2} \quad \ldots(4.11)$$

Impedance : Similar to R-L series circuit, the quantity $\sqrt{R^2 + X_C^2}$ denoted by Z is called the *impedance* of the circuit when resistance and capacitance are connected in series. *It gives the combined opposition due to all elements of the circuit to the flow of an alternating current* and is measured in *ohms*.

Phase Relationship between Voltage and Current : The phasor diagram shown in Fig. 4.8 (b) clearly shows that in this case, the current leads the applied voltage by an angle φ such that

$$\tan \phi = \frac{-V_C}{V_R} = \frac{-I \cdot X_C}{I \cdot R} = \frac{-X_C}{R} \quad \ldots(4.12)$$

Or,
$$\cos \phi = \frac{V_R}{V} = \frac{I \cdot R}{I \cdot Z} = \frac{R}{Z} \quad \ldots(4.13)$$

Therefore, voltage and current in the circuit can be represented by the following equations :

$$v = V_m \sin \omega t$$
$$i = I_m \sin (\omega t + \phi)$$

The waveforms for the current and voltage are shown in Fig. 4.9 (a).

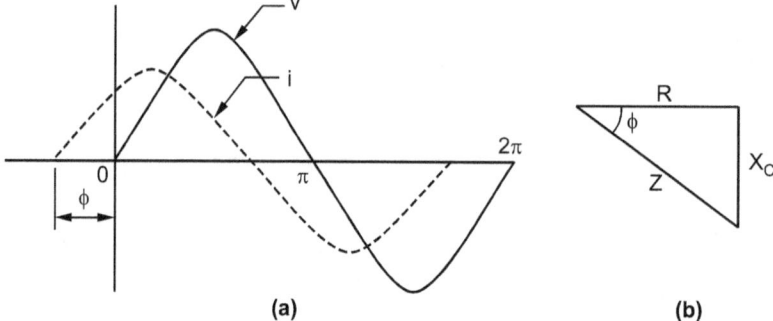

(a)   (b)

Fig. 4.9 : R-C series circuit (a) Waveforms, (b) Impedance triangle

Impedance Triangle : Fig. 4.9 (b) illustrates the impedance triangle for the circuit. As already mentioned in the previous case, this triangle is obtained by dividing each side of the voltage triangle (Fig. 4.8 c) by I. Since X_C is along negative direction of Y-axis, it is taken as negative. From impedance triangle also, we have

$$Z = \sqrt{R^2 + X_C^2}$$
$$\tan \phi = \frac{-X_C}{R} \quad \text{and} \quad \cos \phi = \frac{R}{Z}$$

where φ is the phase angle between the applied voltage and circuit current.

Power : Since the average power taken by a pure capacitance over a complete cycle is zero, the capacitor in the circuit under consideration consumes no power. Therefore, the average power P, supplied to the circuit is entirely utilized by the resistance R only.

∴ P = Average power taken by the resistance

$$= I^2 R = (IR) I = V_R I$$

$$= V \cos \phi \times I \qquad (\because \text{from voltage triangle, } V_R = V \cos \phi)$$

i.e. $\qquad P = V I \cos \phi$ watts $\qquad$ ... (4.14)

where $\cos \phi$ is the power factor of the circuit. The Expression (4.14) for power is similar to that of R-L series circuit.

Example 4.7 : *A resistance of 100 Ω and a 50 μF capacitor are connected in series across a 230 V, 50 Hz supply. Find (a) the circuit impedance, (b) the current flowing, (c) voltage across the resistance, (d) voltage across the capacitor, (e) power factor and (f) the power.*

Solution : Circuit diagram is similar to that shown in Fig. 4.8 (a).

(a) $\qquad X_C = \dfrac{1}{\omega C} = \dfrac{1}{2\pi f C} = \dfrac{1}{2\pi \times 50 \times 50 \times 10^{-6}} = 63.66 \ \Omega$

∴ $\qquad Z = \sqrt{R^2 + X_C^2} = \sqrt{100^2 + 63.66^2} = \mathbf{118.54 \ \Omega} \qquad$ ... Ans.

(b) $\qquad I = \dfrac{V}{Z} = \dfrac{230}{118.54} = \mathbf{1.94 \ A} \qquad$ ... Ans.

(c) $\qquad V_R = I \cdot R$

$\qquad = 1.94 \times 100 = \mathbf{194 \ V} \qquad$ ... Ans.

(d) $\qquad V_C = I \cdot X_C = 1.94 \times 63.66$

$\qquad = \mathbf{123.5 \ V} \qquad$ ... Ans.

(e) $\qquad$ Power factor $= \cos \phi = \dfrac{R}{Z} = \dfrac{100}{118.54} = \mathbf{0.8435 \ leading} \qquad$ ... Ans.

Alternatively, from voltage triangle of Fig. 4.8 (c),

$\qquad \cos \phi = \dfrac{V_R}{V} = \dfrac{194}{230} = \mathbf{0.8435 \ leading} \qquad$ ... Ans.

(f) $\qquad P = V I \cos \phi = 230 \times 1.94 \times 0.8435$

$\qquad = \mathbf{376.36 \ W} \qquad$ ... Ans.

Or, $\qquad P = I^2 R = 1.94^2 \times 100 = \mathbf{376.36 \ W} \qquad$ ... Ans.

Example 4.8 : *The waveforms of the voltage and current of a circuit are given by*

$$e = 150 \sin 314 t$$

and $\qquad i = 10 \sin \left(314t + \dfrac{\pi}{4}\right)$

Sketch these waveforms. Find the values of the resistance and capacitance which are connected in series to form the circuit.

Solution : From the equation for the current, it is clear that the current leads the voltage by $\pi/4$ radian or 45°. Therefore, the waveforms for the voltage and the circuit current will be similar to those shown in Fig. 4.9 (a) with $\phi = \pi/4$ radian or 45°. From the equations for the voltage and current,

Maximum value of the voltage, V_m = 150 V

∴ R.M.S. value of the voltage, V = 0.707 × 150 = 106.05 V

Similarly, Maximum value of current,

$$I_m = 10 \text{ A}$$

∴ R.M.S. value of the current, I = 0.707 × 10 = 7.07 A

∴ Impedance of the circuit, $Z = \dfrac{V}{I} = \dfrac{106.05}{7.07} = 15.00 \, \Omega$

Now, the resistance (R) and the capacitive reactance (X_C) of the circuit can be calculated from its impedance triangle (Fig. 4.9 b).

$$R = Z \cos\phi = 15 \cos 45° = 15 \times 0.707 = \mathbf{10.61 \, \Omega} \qquad \text{... Ans.}$$
$$X_C = Z \sin\phi = 15 \sin 45° = 15 \times 0.707 = \mathbf{10.61 \, \Omega} \qquad \text{... Ans.}$$

Since, $X_C = \dfrac{1}{\omega C}$ and $\omega = 314$ (from equation for the voltage),

$$C = \dfrac{1}{\omega X_C} = \dfrac{1}{314 \times 10.61} = \mathbf{300.16 \times 10^{-6} \, F} \qquad \text{... Ans.}$$

4.5 CIRCUIT WITH RESISTANCE, INDUCTANCE AND CAPACITANCE IN SERIES

Fig. 4.10 (a) represents a circuit with resistance R ohms, inductance L henrys and capacitance C farads in series, connected across an a.c. supply.

Let V and I be the r.m.s. values of the applied voltage and the circuit current. Then, we have

Voltage drop across R, $V_R = I \cdot R$ (in phase with I)

Voltage drop across L, $V_L = I \cdot X_L$ (leading I by 90°)

Voltage drop across C, $V_C = I \cdot X_C$ (lagging I by 90°)

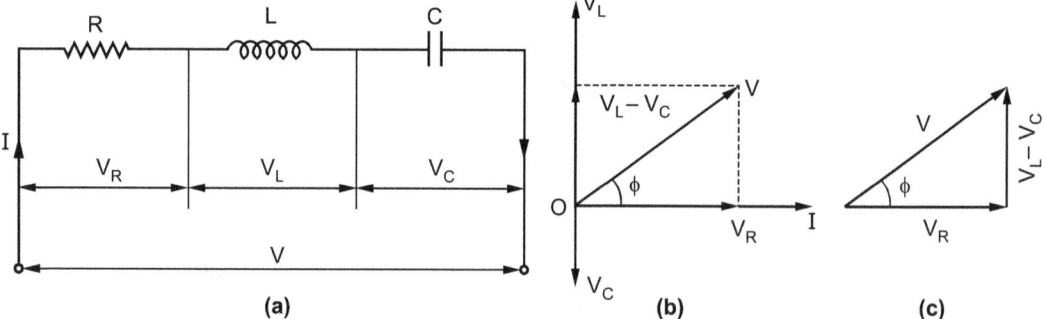

Fig. 4.10 : (a) R-L-C series circuit, (b) Phasor diagram when $X_L > X_C$, (c) Voltage triangle where X_L (=$2\pi f L$) and $X_C \left(= \dfrac{1}{2\pi f C}\right)$ are the inductive and capacitive reactances of the inductance and capacitance respectively.

The relative values of X_L and X_C play a very important role in determining the behaviour of R-L-C series circuit. In general, according to the values of X_L and X_C, there are three possible cases. We shall study these cases one by one.

Case (i) $X_L > X_C$: When X_L is greater than X_C, voltage drop across X_L is obviously greater than that across X_C (i.e. $V_L > V_C$). Fig. 4.10 (b) shows the phasor diagram for this condition with the current I as a reference phasor. The applied voltage V is the phasor sum of its component voltages V_R, V_L and V_C i.e.

$$\bar{V} = \bar{V}_R + \bar{V}_L + \bar{V}_C \qquad \text{... (Phasor sum)}$$

Now, since V_L is in direct phase opposition with V_C, their resultant ($V_L - V_C$) is given by their simple arithmetic subtraction. Moreover, V_L being greater than V_C, this resultant is along the direction of V_L. Therefore, from the voltage triangle of Fig. 4.10 (c),

$$V = \sqrt{V_R^2 + (V_L - V_C)^2} = \sqrt{(IR)^2 + (IX_L - IX_C)^2}$$
$$= I\sqrt{R^2 + (X_L - X_C)^2}$$

$$\therefore \quad I = \frac{V}{\sqrt{R^2 + (X_L - X_C)^2}} = \frac{V}{Z} \qquad \text{... (4.15)}$$

where
$$Z = \sqrt{R^2 + (X_L - X_C)^2} \qquad \text{... (4.16)}$$

Case (ii) $X_L < X_C$: In this case, V_C is greater than V_L. Therefore, their resultant ($V_C - V_L$) is along the direction of V_C. Fig. 4.11 (a) shows the phasor diagram and Fig. 4.11 (b) the corresponding voltage triangle.

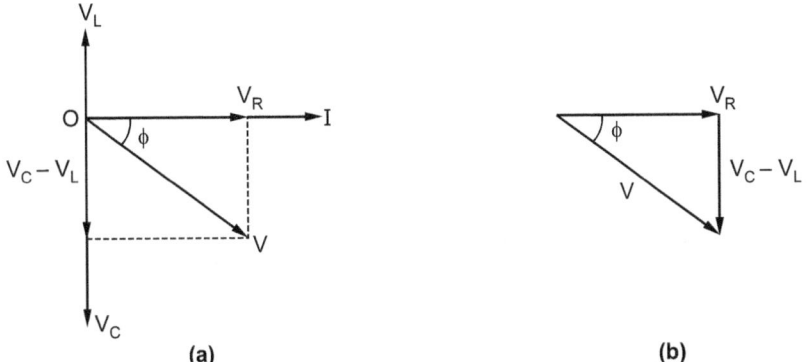

**Fig. 4.11 : (a) Phasor diagram for R-L-C series circuit with $X_L < X_C$,
(b) Voltage triangle**

From the voltage triangle, we get

$$V = \sqrt{V_R^2 + (V_C - V_L)^2} = \sqrt{(IR)^2 + (IX_C - IX_L)^2}$$
$$= I\sqrt{R^2 + (X_C - X_L)^2}$$

$$\therefore \quad I = \frac{V}{\sqrt{R^2 + (X_C - X_L)^2}} = \frac{V}{\sqrt{R^2 + (X_L - X_C)^2}} = \frac{V}{Z} \qquad \text{... (4.17)}$$

where, as mentioned in the previous case,
$$Z = \sqrt{R^2 + (X_L - X_C)^2}$$

Case (iii) $X_L = X_C$: Fig. 4.12 shows the phasor diagram for this condition.

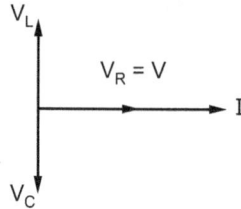

Fig. 4.12 : Phasor diagram for R-L-C series circuit with $X_L = X_C$

In this case, V_L and V_C being equal and in direct phase opposition with each other, their resultant is zero. Therefore, the applied voltage V is equal to the voltage drop across resistance R i.e.

$$V = V_R = I \cdot R$$

∴ $$I = \frac{V}{R} \qquad \ldots (4.18)$$

Impedance : The quantity $\sqrt{R^2 + (X_L - X_C)^2}$ denoted by Z in expressions (4.15) and (4.17) is the *impedance* of a circuit containing resistance, inductance and capacitance in series and measured in *ohms* as already seen in the previous cases. The quantity $(X_L - X_C)$ gives the total reactance of the circuit and is usually denoted by X. Therefore, the Expression (4.16) for impedance of the circuit can also be written as

$$Z = \sqrt{R^2 + X^2} \qquad \ldots (4.19)$$

It should be noted that the capacitive reactance (X_C) is always regarded as negative. This has already been mentioned previously in the Section (4.4). Therefore, the total reactance of the circuit (X) is negative if $X_C > X_L$.

For the particular case, when $X_L = X_C$, the total reactance of the circuit is zero. As such,

$$Z = \sqrt{R^2 + X^2} = R$$

Phase Relationship between Voltage and Current : The phase relationship between the voltage and the current in R-L-C series circuit is purely dependent upon the relative values of X_L and X_C. Let us again consider the three cases mentioned above.

Case (i) $X_L > X_C$: When X_L is greater than X_C (i.e. $V_L > V_C$), the inductive reactance predominates and the total reactance of the circuit $(X_L - X_C)$ is inductive in nature (as indicated by its positive value). Therefore, the current lags the applied voltage (or, applied voltage leads the current) as indicated by the phasor diagram of Fig. 4.10 (b). In this respect, the overall behaviour of the circuit is similar to that of R-L series circuit. Referring to the voltage triangle of Fig. 4.10 (c), the angle φ by which the current lags the applied voltage under this condition can be obtained from the following expressions :

$$\tan \phi = \frac{(V_L - V_C)}{V_R} = \frac{IX_L - IX_C}{IR}$$

$$= \frac{X_L - X_C}{R} = \frac{X}{R} \qquad \ldots (4.20)$$

Or, $$\cos \phi = \frac{V_R}{V} = \frac{I \cdot R}{I \cdot Z} = \frac{R}{Z} \qquad \ldots (4.21)$$

Case (ii) $X_L < X_C$: In this case, the capacitive reactance predominates and the total reactance of the circuit $(X_L - X_C)$ is capacitive in nature (as indicated by its negative value). Therefore, the current leads the applied voltage (or, applied voltage lags the current) as illustrated in the phasor diagram of Fig. 4.11 (a). In this respect, the overall behaviour of the circuit is similar to that of R-C series circuit.

The expressions (4.20) and (4.21) are applicable to this condition also. In this case, X_L being less than X_C, the total reactance $(X_L - X_C)$ is negative. Therefore, $\tan \phi$ and hence the angle ϕ becomes negative. This indicates that the current leads the voltage.

Case (iii) $X_L = X_C$: As already mentioned previously, in this case, total reactance of the circuit $(X_L - X_C)$ is zero. Hence, numerically, $Z = R$. The circuit under such condition behaves as a purely resistive circuit and the current is in phase with the applied voltage (Fig. 4.12).

Impedance Triangle : The impedance triangles for R-L-C series circuit when $X_L > X_C$ and $X_L < X_C$ are shown in Figs. 4.13 (a) and (b) respectively.

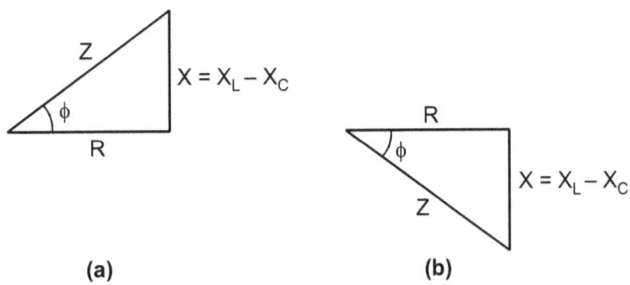

(a)   (b)

Fig. 4.13 : Impedance triangle for R-L-C series circuit (a) $X_L > X_C$, (b) $X_L < X_C$

From these impedance triangles also, we get

$$Z = \sqrt{R^2 + (X_L - X_C)^2} = \sqrt{R^2 + X^2}$$

$$\tan \phi = \frac{X_L - X_C}{R} = \frac{X}{R} \quad \text{and} \quad \cos \phi = \frac{R}{Z}$$

Power : The inductance and capacitance in the circuit consume no power. Therefore, the average power (P) supplied to the circuit is entirely consumed by the resistance R only.

∴   P = Average power taken by the resistance

                 $= I^2 R = (IR) I = V_R I$

                 $= V \cos \phi \times I$ (∵ from voltage triangle, $V_R = V \cos \phi$)

Thus,   P = V I $\cos \phi$ watts   ... (4.22)

where $\cos \phi$ is power factor of the circuit.

The Expression (4.22) for power is similar to that of R-L series circuit or R-C series circuit.

Alternative Proof : An alternative proof for the expression for power in a single-phase a.c. circuit can be given as follows :

Let instantaneous value of voltage, $v = V_m \sin \omega t = V_m \sin \theta$

and instantaneous value of current, $i = I_m \sin (\omega t - \phi) = I_m \sin (\theta - \phi)$

The angle ϕ which represents the phase difference between voltage and current in these expressions is positive for current lagging the voltage and negative for leading current.

∴ Instantaneous value of power,

$$p = vi = V_m \sin \theta \times I_m \sin(\theta - \phi) = V_m I_m \sin \theta \cdot \sin(\theta - \phi)$$

Now, we know that for any angles A and B,

$$2 \sin A \sin B = \cos(A - B) - \cos(A + B)$$

Using the above trigonometric identity, we have

$$p = \frac{V_m I_m}{2}[\cos \phi - \cos(2\theta - \phi)]$$

$$= \frac{1}{2} V_m I_m \cos \phi - \frac{1}{2} V_m I_m \cos(2\theta - \phi) \qquad \ldots (4.23)$$

∴ Average power over a cycle is given by

$$P = \frac{1}{2\pi} \int_0^{2\pi} p \cdot d\theta$$

$$= \frac{1}{2\pi} \int_0^{2\pi} \left[\frac{1}{2} V_m I_m \cos \phi - \frac{1}{2} V_m I_m \cos(2\theta - \phi) \right] d\theta$$

$$= \frac{V_m I_m}{4\pi} \left[(\cos \phi) \theta - \frac{\sin(2\theta - \phi)}{2} \right]_0^{2\pi}$$

$$= \frac{V_m I_m}{4\pi} \left[(\cos \phi) 2\pi - \frac{\sin(4\pi - \phi)}{2} + \frac{\sin(-\phi)}{2} \right]$$

$$= \frac{V_m I_m}{4\pi} \left[(\cos \phi) 2\pi + \frac{\sin \phi}{2} - \frac{\sin \phi}{2} \right]$$

$$= \frac{1}{2} V_m I_m \cos \phi$$

This result was obvious from Expression (4.23) itself. Because, the first term $\frac{1}{2} V_m I_m \cos \phi$ of this expression is a constant quantity and the mean value of the second term $\frac{1}{2} V_m I_m \cos(2\theta - \phi)$ over a cycle is zero. Thus,

$$\text{Average power, } P = \frac{1}{2} V_m I_m \cos \phi = \frac{V_m}{\sqrt{2}} \times \frac{I_m}{\sqrt{2}} \cos \phi = VI \cos \phi$$

where V and I are the r.m.s. values of the voltage and current respectively.

4.6 ACTIVE POWER AND REACTIVE POWER IN A.C. CIRCUIT

We have seen that the current in the a.c. circuit either lags or leads the applied voltage depending upon whether the circuit is predominantly inductive (with $X_L > X_C$) or capacitive (with $X_C > X_L$) in nature. Fig. 4.14 shows phasor diagrams for the two conditions taking the voltage as a reference phasor. In both the cases, the current phasor I can be resolved into two components, I cos φ in phase with the voltage and I sin φ in quadrature (at 90°) with it.

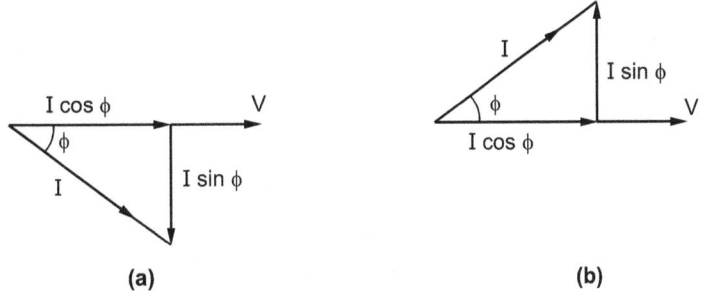

Fig. 4.14 : Active and reactive components of current (a) $X_L > X_C$, (b) $X_L < X_C$

Active Component of Current : For an a.c. circuit,

　　　Power = V I cos φ

　　　　　 = Voltage × Component of the current in phase with the voltage

The in-phase component, I cos φ is, therefore, called *active, power, wattful* or *energy component* of the current.

Reactive Component of Current : The component I sin φ which is 90° out of phase with the voltage is known as the *reactive, wattless* or *idle component* of the current.

Active Power (P) : The true or real power in the a.c. circuit which is given by the product of the applied voltage and the active component of the current (i.e. P = V I cos φ) is also called *active power*. As already seen previously, it is measured in *watts (W)* or *kilowatts (kW)*.

Reactive Power (Q) : The quantity VI sin φ which is the product of applied voltage and reactive component of the current, is called the *reactive power*. It represents the energy alternately stored in the magnetic or electric field and returned to the circuit without doing any useful work. The unit for reactive power is *reactive volt-ampere (VAr)* or *reactive kilovolt-ampere (kVAr)*.

Power Triangle : If all three sides of the impedance triangle (Fig. 4.13) are multiplied by I^2, it becomes a *power triangle* as shown in Fig. 4.15.

From the power triangle, it is obvious that

$$S = \sqrt{P^2 + Q^2}, \quad P = S \cos \phi \quad \text{and} \quad Q = S \sin \phi \qquad \ldots (4.24)$$

Conventionally, inductive reactive power is always considered as positive, whereas capacitive reactive power as negative.

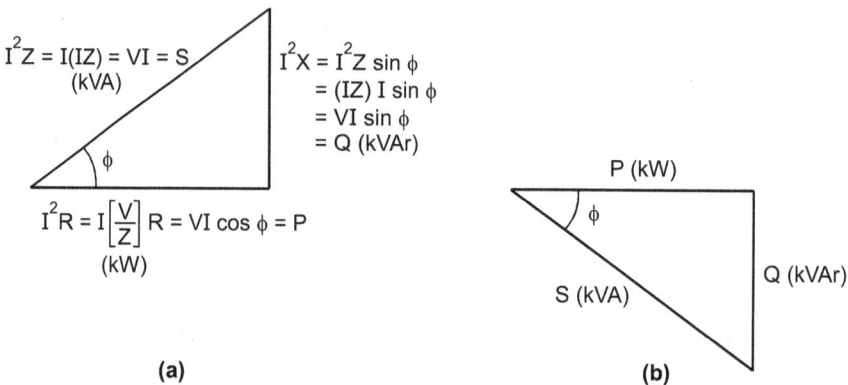

Fig. 4.15 : Power triangle (a) Inductive circuit, (b) Capacitive circuit

Example 4.9 : *A coil of resistance 15 Ω and inductance 0.05 H is connected in series with a 100 μF capacitor across a 230 V, 50 Hz supply. Find the current taken and the phase difference between the supply voltage and the current. Find also the voltage drop across the coil and the capacitor.*

Solution : Fig. 4.16 (a) shows the circuit diagram.

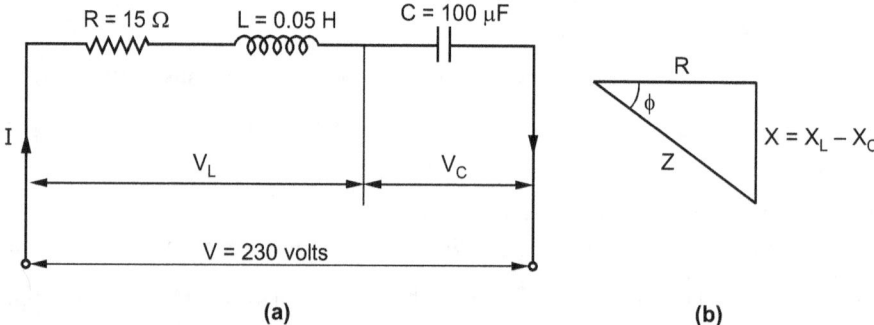

Fig. 4.16 : (a) Circuit diagram for Example 4.9, (b) Impedance triangle

$$\text{Inductive reactance, } X_L = \omega L = 2\pi f L$$
$$= 2\pi \times 50 \times 0.05$$
$$= 15.70 \, \Omega$$

$$\text{Capacitive reactance, } X_C = \frac{1}{\omega C} = \frac{1}{2\pi f C} = \frac{1}{2\pi \times 50 \times 100 \times 10^{-6}}$$
$$= 31.83 \, \Omega$$

$$\therefore \quad \text{Impedance of the circuit, } Z = \sqrt{R^2 + (X_L - X_C)^2}$$
$$= \sqrt{15^2 + (15.70 - 31.83)^2} = 22.03 \, \Omega$$

$$\therefore \quad I = \frac{V}{Z} = \frac{230}{22.03} = \mathbf{10.44 \, A} \quad \text{... Ans.}$$

Now, from the impedance triangle of Fig. 4.16 (b),

$$\tan \phi = \frac{X_L - X_C}{R} = \frac{15.70 - 31.83}{15}$$

$$= \frac{-16.13}{15} = -1.075$$

∴ $\phi = -47.08°$ ... Ans.

Since $X_C > X_L$, the current will lead the applied voltage by 47.08°. This is also indicated by the minus (–) sign for the angle.

Impedance of the coil, $Z_{coil} = \sqrt{R^2 + X_L^2} = \sqrt{15^2 + 15.70^2} = 21.71\ \Omega$

∴ Voltage drop across the coil, $V_L = I \cdot Z_{coil} = 10.44 \times 21.71$

$= 226.65$ V ... Ans.

Also, voltage drop across the capacitor,

$V_C = I \cdot X_C$

$= 10.44 \times 31.83 = 332.31$ V ... Ans.

Example 4.10 : *A circuit consisting of resistance, inductive reactance and capacitive reactance in series is connected across an a.c. single-phase, 100 V, 50 Hz supply. If the voltages across the resistance and inductive reactance are 80 V and 120 V respectively, and if the power consumed by the resistance is 800 W, find (i) Current in the circuit; (ii) Value of the capacitive reactance; (iii) Voltage across the capacitive reactance; and (iv) Additional resistance to reduce the current to 5 A. Take overall power factor of the circuit as lagging.*

Solution : Fig. 4.17 (a) shows the circuit diagram. Let R, X_L and X_C be the resistance, inductive reactance and capacitive reactance respectively and I be the r.m.s. value of the current. Now,

Power consumed by the resistance, $P = \dfrac{V^2}{R}$

∴ $800 = \dfrac{80^2}{R}$

∴ $R = \dfrac{6400}{800} = 8\ \Omega$

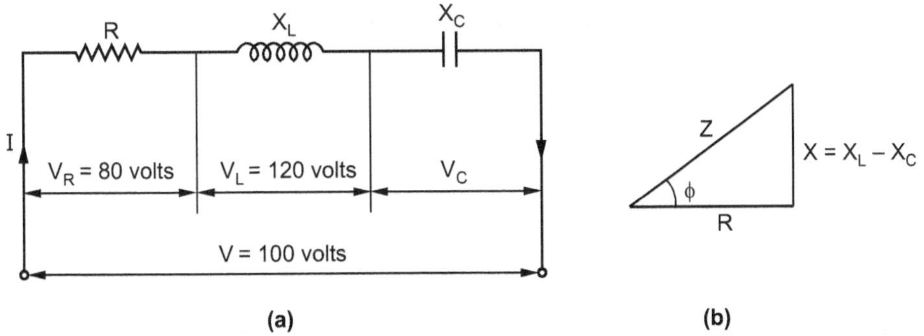

Fig. 4.17 : (a) Circuit diagram for Example 4.10, (b) Impedance triangle

Voltage drop across R, $V_R = I \cdot R$

∴ $80 = I \times 8$

∴ $I = \dfrac{80}{8} = 10 \text{ A}$ ... Ans.

Impedance of the circuit, $Z = \dfrac{V}{I} = \dfrac{100}{10} = 10 \text{ }\Omega$

Voltage drop across X_L, $V_L = I \cdot X_L$

∴ $X_L = \dfrac{V_L}{I} = \dfrac{120}{10} = 12 \text{ }\Omega$

Now, $Z = \sqrt{R^2 + (X_L - X_C)^2}$

∴ $X_L - X_C = \sqrt{Z^2 - R^2} = \sqrt{10^2 - 8^2} = 6 \text{ }\Omega$

∴ $X_C = X_L - 6 = 12 - 6 = 6 \text{ }\Omega$ ... Ans.

Hence, voltage drop across X_C, $V_C = I \cdot X_C = 10 \times 6 = \mathbf{60 \text{ V}}$ ... Ans.

Let, R' be the additional resistance which, when connected in series with the circuit, reduces the current to 5 A. Then,

Impedance of the circuit with additional resistance,

$$Z' = \dfrac{V}{I} = \dfrac{100}{5} = 20 \text{ }\Omega$$

Total resistance of the circuit, $R_T = R + R'$

$= \sqrt{(Z')^2 - (X_L - X_C)^2}$

$= \sqrt{(20)^2 - (6)^2} = 19.08 \text{ }\Omega$

∴ Additional resistance, $R' = R_T - R = 19.08 - 8 = \mathbf{11.08 \text{ }\Omega}$ ... Ans.

Example 4.11 : *A coil of power factor 0.6 is in series with a 100 μF capacitor. When connected to a 50 Hz supply, the potential difference across the coil is equal to the potential difference across the capacitor. Find the resistance and the inductance of the coil.*

Solution : Fig. 4.18 shows the circuit diagram.

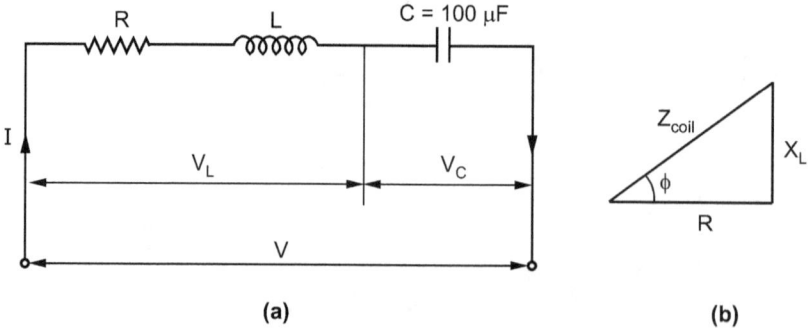

(a)   (b)

Fig. 4.18 : (a) Circuit diagram for Example 4.11, (b) Impedance triangle for the coil

Let R and L be the resistance (in ohms) and inductance (in henrys) of the coil and I be the circuit current.

Capacitive reactance of the capacitor, $X_C = \dfrac{1}{\omega C} = \dfrac{1}{2\pi f C} = \dfrac{1}{2\pi \times 50 \times 100 \times 10^{-6}}$

$= 31.85 \; \Omega$

If Z_{coil} is the impedance of the coil,

Voltage drop across the coil, $V_L = I \cdot Z_{coil}$ and

Voltage drop across the capacitor, $V_C = I \cdot X_C$

Now, since $V_L = V_C$ (given)

$I \cdot Z_{coil} = I \cdot X_C$

∴ $Z_{coil} = X_C = 31.85 \; \Omega$

Also, Power factor of the coil $= \dfrac{R}{Z_{coil}} = 0.6$ (given)

∴ Resistance of the coil, $R = 0.6 \times Z_{coil} = 0.6 \times 31.85 = \mathbf{19.11 \; \Omega}$ ... **Ans.**

∴ Inductive reactance of the coil,

$$X_L = \sqrt{Z_{coil}^2 - R^2} = \sqrt{31.85^2 - 19.11^2} = 25.48 \; \Omega$$

But, $X_L = \omega L = 2\pi f L$

∴ Inductance of the coil, $L = \dfrac{X_L}{2\pi f} = \dfrac{25.48}{2\pi \times 50} = \mathbf{0.081 \; H}$ ... **Ans.**

Example 4.12 : *The maximum values of the alternating voltage and current are 400 V and 20 A respectively, in a circuit connected to 50 Hz supply, and these quantities are sinusoidal. The instantaneous values of the voltage and current are 283 V and 10 A respectively at t = 0, both increasing positively.*

(i) Write down the expressions for voltage and current at time t.

(ii) Determine the power consumed in the circuit.

Solution : Let the equations for the voltage and current be

$v = V_m \sin(\omega t + \alpha)$ volts

$i = I_m \sin(\omega t + \beta)$ amperes

As $V_m = 400 \; V, \quad I_m = 20 \; A,$

$\omega = 2\pi f = 2\pi \times 50 = 314$ radians/s, we have

$v = 400 \sin(314 \, t + \alpha)$ volts

$i = 20 \sin(314 \, t + \beta)$ amperes

Now, it is given that at t = 0, v = 283 V and i = 10 A. Therefore, from the equation for the voltage, we have

$283 = 400 \sin(314 \times 0 + \alpha)$

Or, $\sin \alpha = \dfrac{283}{400} = 0.7075$

∴ $\alpha = 45°$ or $\pi/4$ radian

Similarly, from the equation for current, we get

$$10 = 20 \sin(314 \times 0 + \beta)$$

Or, $\quad \sin \beta = \dfrac{10}{20} = 0.5$

$\therefore \quad \beta = 30°$ or $\pi/6$ radian

Hence, equations for the voltage and current are

$$v = 400 \sin\left(314t + \dfrac{\pi}{4}\right) \text{ volts} \qquad \text{... Ans.}$$

$$i = 20 \sin\left(314t + \dfrac{\pi}{6}\right) \text{ amperes} \qquad \text{... Ans.}$$

$$P = VI \cos\phi = \dfrac{400}{\sqrt{2}} \times \dfrac{20}{\sqrt{2}} \times \cos(45° - 30°) = 3864 \text{ W} \qquad \text{... Ans.}$$

Example 4.13 : *A non-inductive resistor is connected in series with a coil and a capacitor. The circuit is connected to a single-phase, a.c. supply. If the voltages measured across the various circuit components are as indicated in Fig. 4.19 (a), when the current flowing through the circuit is 0.345 A, find the applied voltage and the power loss in the coil.*

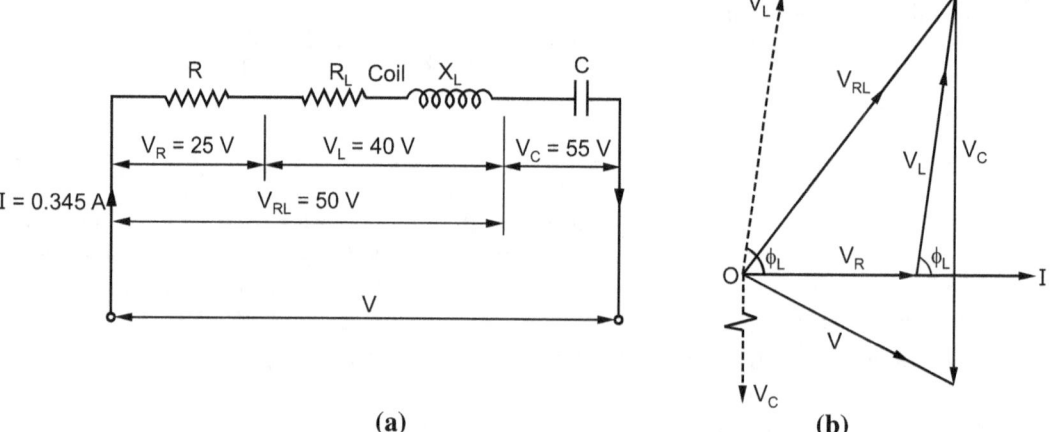

Fig. 4.19 : (a) Circuit diagram for Example 4.13, (b) Phasor diagram

Solution : Resistance of non-inductive resistor,

$$R = \dfrac{V_R}{I} = \dfrac{25}{0.345} = 72.46 \, \Omega$$

Impedance of the coil, $\quad Z_L = \dfrac{V_L}{I} = \dfrac{40}{0.345} = 115.94 \, \Omega$

Capacitive reactance of the capacitor,

$$X_C = \dfrac{V_C}{I} = \dfrac{55}{0.345} = 159.42 \, \Omega$$

From the phasor diagram of Fig. 4.19 (b), we have

$$V_{RL}^2 = V_R^2 + V_L^2 - 2 V_R V_L \cos(180° - \phi_L)$$
$$= V_R^2 + V_L^2 + 2 V_R V_L \cos\phi_L$$

∴ Power factor of the coil,

$$\cos\phi_L = \frac{V_{RL}^2 - V_R^2 - V_L^2}{2V_R \cdot V_L} = \frac{50^2 - 25^2 - 40^2}{2 \times 25 \times 40} = 0.1375 \text{ lagging}$$

∴ $\phi_L = 82.1°$

Hence, the resistance of the coil,
$$R_L = Z_L \cos\phi_L = 115.94 \times 0.1375 = 15.94 \ \Omega$$

Reactance of the coil,
$$X_L = Z_L \sin\phi_L = 115.94 \times 0.991 = 114.84 \ \Omega$$

∴ Impedance of the entire circuit,
$$Z = \sqrt{(R + R_L)^2 + (X_L - X_C)^2}$$
$$= \sqrt{(72.46 + 15.94)^2 + (114.84 - 159.42)^2}$$
$$= 99 \ \Omega$$

∴ Supply voltage, $V = I \cdot Z$
$$= 0.345 \times 99 = \mathbf{34.16 \ V} \qquad \text{... Ans.}$$

Power loss in coil, $P_L = I^2 R_L = (0.345)^2 \times 15.94 = \mathbf{1.9 \ W} \qquad \text{... Ans.}$

4.7 IMPEDANCES IN SERIES

A general series circuit may consist of a combination of resistances, inductances and capacitances distributed through the circuit in different fashions. Fig. 4.20 (a) shows one such general circuit arrangement.

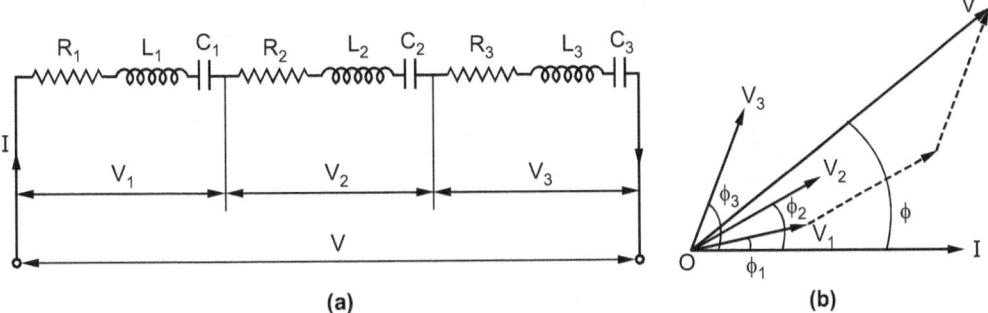

Fig. 4.20 : (a) Circuit containing impedances in series, (b) Phasor diagram

Let V be the applied voltage, I the circuit current and let V_1, V_2 and V_3 be the voltages taken in order across the different portions of the circuit. The voltages across the different parts of the circuit are not in phase with the current. Let the phase differences between the current I and the voltages V_1, V_2 and V_3 be ϕ_1, ϕ_2 and ϕ_3 respectively, the values of which are obtained from the reactance and resistance of each portion of the circuit, e.g.

$$\tan\phi_1 = \frac{\left(\omega L_1 - \dfrac{1}{\omega C_1}\right)}{R_1}$$

Fig. 4.20 (b) shows the phasor diagram for the given circuit in which the current I is considered as the reference phasor. The applied voltage V is the phasor addition of the voltages across the several portions of the circuit. Hence, from the phasor diagram, its value is given by

$$V^2 = (V_1 \cos \phi_1 + V_2 \cos \phi_2 + V_3 \cos \phi_3)^2 + (V_1 \sin \phi_1 + V_2 \sin \phi_2 + V_3 \sin \phi_3)^2$$
$$= (IR_1 + IR_2 + IR_3)^2 + (IX_1 + IX_2 + IX_3)^2$$

where $X_1 = \omega L_1 - \dfrac{1}{\omega C_1}$, $X_2 = \omega L_2 - \dfrac{1}{\omega C_2}$, $X_3 = \omega L_3 - \dfrac{1}{\omega C_3}$

Hence, the joint impedance Z of the circuit is given by

$$Z = \frac{V}{I} = \sqrt{(R_1 + R_2 + R_3)^2 + (X_1 + X_2 + X_3)^2}$$
$$= \sqrt{R^2 + X^2} \qquad \ldots (4.25)$$

and $\qquad \tan \phi = \dfrac{X_1 + X_2 + X_3}{R_1 + R_2 + R_3} = \dfrac{X}{R} \qquad \ldots (4.26)$

where, $R = R_1 + R_2 + R_3$ and $X = X_1 + X_2 + X_3$

Hence, impedance of the complex series circuit may be calculated by combining the values of the resistances and reactances. If Z_1, Z_2 and Z_3 are the impedances of the different portions of the series circuit, then Equation (4.25) clearly shows that the joint impedance is given by their phasor addition i.e.,

$$\bar{Z} = \bar{Z}_1 + \bar{Z}_2 + \bar{Z}_3 \qquad \ldots (4.27)$$

Actually, impedance itself is not a phasor in the real sense, but being a complex quantity, it is always treated as a phasor.

Example 4.14 : *The circuit shown in Fig. 4.21 (a) is connected to a 230 V, 50 Hz supply. Calculate : (i) Total impedance, (ii) The current and its phase relationship with the supply voltage, and (iii) The potential differences V_1 and V_2 with their phase angles.*

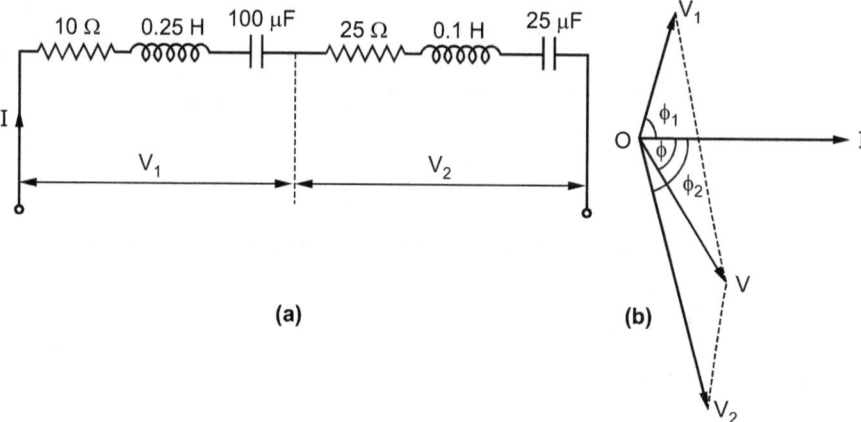

Fig. 4.21 : (a) Circuit diagram for Example 4.14, (b) Phasor diagram

Solution : Since the potential differences V_1 and V_2 are to be calculated, let us calculate the impedances of the two portions of the given circuit separately.

$$R_1 = 10 \, \Omega$$
$$X_{L1} = 2\pi \times 50 \times 0.25 = 78.54 \, \Omega$$

$$X_{C1} = \frac{1}{2\pi \times 50 \times 100 \times 10^{-6}} = 31.83 \, \Omega$$

$$X_1 = 78.54 - 31.83 = 46.71 \, \Omega$$

∴ $\quad Z_1 = \sqrt{10^2 + 46.71^2} = 47.77 \, \Omega$

and $\quad \tan \phi_1 = \dfrac{46.71}{10} = 4.671$

∴ $\quad \phi_1 = 77.92°$

Similarly, $\quad R_2 = 25 \, \Omega$

$$X_{L2} = 2\pi \times 50 \times 0.1 = 31.42 \, \Omega$$

$$X_{C2} = \frac{1}{2\pi \times 50 \times 25 \times 10^{-6}} = 127.32 \, \Omega$$

$$X_2 = 31.42 - 127.32 = -95.9 \, \Omega$$

∴ $\quad Z_2 = \sqrt{25^2 + (-95.9)^2} = 99.11 \, \Omega$

and $\quad \tan \phi_2 = \dfrac{-95.9}{25} = -3.836$

∴ $\quad \phi_2 = -75.39°$

∴ Total impedance, $Z = \sqrt{(R_1 + R_2)^2 + (X_1 + X_2)^2}$

$\qquad = \sqrt{(10 + 25)^2 + (46.71 - 95.9)^2}$

$\qquad = \mathbf{60.37 \, \Omega}$ ... Ans.

and $\quad I = \dfrac{V}{Z} = \dfrac{230}{60.37} = \mathbf{3.81 \, A}$ ... Ans.

$\quad \tan \phi = \dfrac{46.71 - 95.9}{10 + 25} = -1.41$

∴ $\quad \phi = \mathbf{54.57° \text{ leading}}$ ... Ans.

$\quad V_1 = I Z_1 = 3.81 \times 47.77 = \mathbf{182 \, V}$ ... Ans.

$\quad \phi_1 = \mathbf{77.92° \text{ lagging}}$ ... Ans.

$\quad V_2 = I Z_2 = 3.81 \times 99.11 = \mathbf{377.61 \, V}$ ... Ans.

$\quad \phi_2 = \mathbf{75.39° \text{ leading}}$ ... Ans.

Phasor diagram is shown in Fig. 4.21 (b).

4.8 RESONANCE IN THE R-L-C SERIES CIRCUIT

In the Section (4.5), we have seen that the impedance of the circuit containing resistance, inductance and capacitance in series (Fig. 4.10) is given by,

$$Z = \sqrt{R^2 + (X_L - X_C)^2}$$

Now, if the voltage applied across the circuit is maintained constant and the frequency is gradually increased from zero to a high value, the inductive reactance increases from zero value ($\because X_L \propto f$) while the capacitive reactance decreases from its infinitely large value $\left(\because X_C \propto \dfrac{1}{f}\right)$ as illustrated in Fig. 4.22 (a). Hence, at some frequency (f_r), the two become numerically equal i.e. at this frequency,

$$X_L = X_C$$

Or, $$X_L - X_C = 0$$

$$\therefore \quad Z = R$$

and $$I = \dfrac{V}{Z} = \dfrac{V}{R}$$

Thus, under these conditions, the effects of the inductive and capacitive reactances completely neutralize each other. As a result, the impedance falls to a minimum value ($Z = R$) and the current reaches a maximum value $\left(I = \dfrac{V}{R}\right)$ with unity power factor. This condition is known as *series resonance* and the frequency at which this occurs is called *resonant frequency*. Since in series resonance, the voltages across the inductance and capacitance also reach their maximum values, it is called as *voltage resonance*. Fig. 4.22 (a) shows curves of X_L, X_C, $X_L - X_C$, R, Z and I plotted against frequency and Fig. 4.22 (b) shows the phasor diagram for the resonance condition.

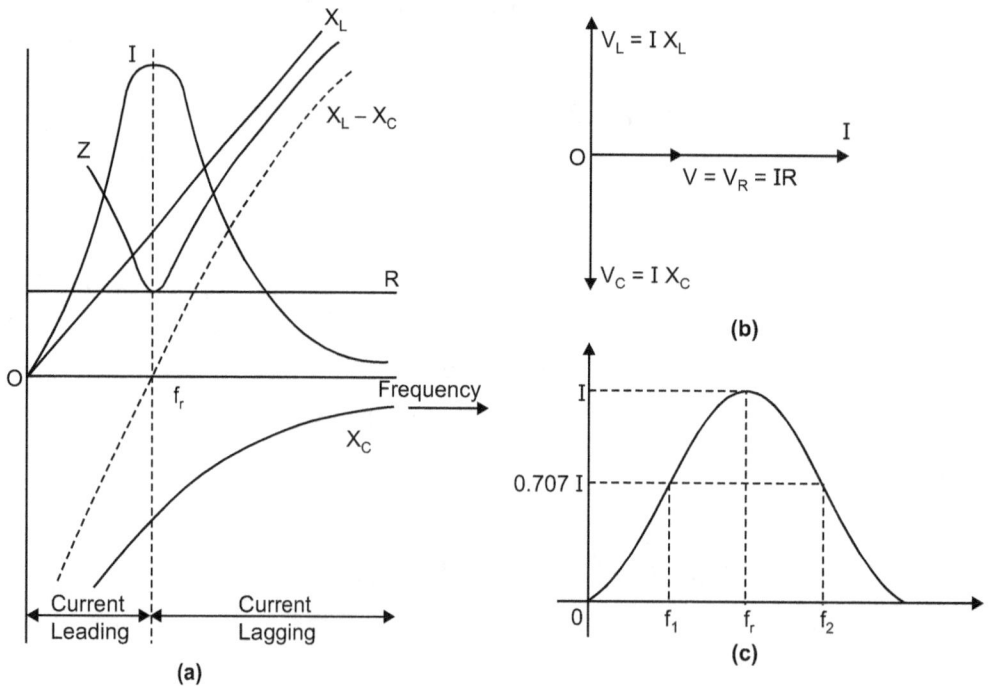

Fig. 4.22 : Series resonance

4.8.1 Resonant Frequency

Let f_r be the resonant frequency. Then, at this frequency,

$$X_L = X_C$$

i.e.
$$\omega L = \frac{1}{\omega C}$$

Or,
$$2\pi f_r L = \frac{1}{2\pi f_r C}$$

From this, it follows that the resonant frequency is given by,

$$f_r = \frac{1}{2\pi \sqrt{LC}} \text{ hertzs} \qquad \ldots (4.28)$$

4.8.2 Bandwidth of a Resonant Circuit

For a series resonant circuit, there is a definite range of frequencies at which the current is near its maximum value and the impedance is at a minimum. The term *bandwidth* is used for describing this frequency range. *For the series resonant circuit, bandwidth is defined as the range of frequency over which the magnitude of the current is equal to or greater than 0.707 of the current at resonance.* Fig. 4.22 (c) shows the resonance curve (i.e. current vs. frequency curve) for a series R–L–C circuit separately. Here, the frequencies f_1 and f_2 are the frequencies at which the current is 0.707 times the current at resonance. These frequencies are called the *cutoff frequencies*. Obviously, the bandwidth is the frequency difference between the lower cutoff frequency f_1 and the upper cutoff frequency f_2, i.e.

$$\text{Bandwidth} = f_2 - f_1 \qquad \ldots (4.29)$$

If P_1, P_2 and P are magnitudes of power delivered to a resistance R at frequencies f_1, f_2 and f_r (resonant frequency) respectively, then we can write,

$$P_1 = P_2 = (0.707\, I)^2 R = 0.5\, I^2 R$$

and
$$P = I^2 R$$

where I is the maximum circuit current under resonance condition. Hence,

$$P_1 = P_2 = 0.5 P$$

Due to the above relationship, cut-off frequencies f_1 and f_2 are also called as *half-power frequencies*.

Since the resonant circuit is adjusted to select a band of frequencies, the resonance curve shown in Fig. 4.22 (c) is also called the *selectivity curve* of the circuit. *Selectivity* indicates how well a resonant circuit responds to a certain frequency and eliminates all other frequencies. The smaller the bandwidth, the higher is the selectivity.

4.8.3 Q-Factor of a Series Circuit

Under resonance condition, potential difference across the inductance is given by,

$$V_L = I \cdot X_L = \frac{V}{R} \times \omega L = \frac{V}{R} \times 2\pi f_r L$$

$$= \frac{V}{R} \times 2\pi L \left(\frac{1}{2\pi \sqrt{LC}}\right) = \frac{V}{R} \sqrt{\frac{L}{C}}$$

Or, potential difference across the capacitor,

$$V_C = I \cdot X_C = \frac{V}{R} \times \frac{1}{\omega C} = \frac{V}{R} \times \frac{1}{2\pi f_r C}$$

$$= \frac{V}{R} \times \frac{1}{2\pi C} (2\pi \sqrt{LC})$$

$$= \frac{V}{R} \sqrt{\frac{L}{C}}$$

If R is small, V_L and V_C are many times the supply voltage. The ratio V_L / V or V_C / V at resonant frequency is called the *voltage magnification*. Therefore, from the above equations,

$$\text{Voltage magnification} = \frac{\text{Voltage across L (or C)}}{\text{Supply voltage}}$$

$$= \frac{1}{R} \sqrt{\frac{L}{C}} \qquad \ldots (4.30)$$

The quality factor or the Q-factor in the case of an R-L-C series circuit is defined as equal to the voltage magnification in the circuit at resonance.

$$\therefore \qquad \text{Q-factor} = \frac{1}{R} \sqrt{\frac{L}{C}} \qquad \ldots (4.31)$$

Alternatively, *the quality factor Q of a series circuit is also defined as the ratio of the reactive power of either the inductor or the capacitor to the average power of the resistor at resonance.* Thus,

$$\text{Q-factor} = \frac{\text{Reactive power}}{\text{Average power}} \qquad \ldots (4.32)$$

Firstly, considering the reactive power of the inductive reactance, we have

$$\text{Q-factor} = \frac{I^2 X_L}{I^2 R} = \frac{X_L}{R} = \frac{\omega L}{R} = \frac{2\pi f_r L}{R}$$

$$= \frac{2\pi L}{R} \times \frac{1}{2\pi \sqrt{LC}}$$

$$= \frac{1}{R} \sqrt{\frac{L}{C}}$$

Or, considering the reactive power of the capacitive reactance, we get

$$\text{Q-factor} = \frac{I^2 X_C}{I^2 R} = \frac{X_C}{R} = \frac{1}{\omega CR} = \frac{1}{2\pi f_r \times CR}$$

$$= \frac{1}{2\pi CR} \times (2\pi \sqrt{LC})$$

$$= \frac{1}{R} \sqrt{\frac{L}{C}}$$

The quality factor is an indication of how much energy is placed in storage (continual transfer from one reactive element to the other) as compared to that dissipated. The lower the level of dissipation for the same reactive power, the larger the Q-factor and the more concentrated and intense the region of resonance.

If the resistance R in the circuit is just the resistance of the coil, the quality factor of the circuit (Q) may be considered as *Q-factor of the coil* i.e. under this condition,

$$Q_{coil} = Q$$

The manufacturers of inductors often provide the Q-factor of the coil.

Further, it can be shown that

$$\text{Bandwidth} = f_2 - f_1 = \frac{f_r}{Q}$$

Or, $$Q = \frac{f_r}{f_2 - f_1} \qquad \qquad \ldots (4.33)$$

Hence, *Q-factor of a resonant circuit may also be defined as the ratio of resonant frequency to bandwidth.* The larger the Q-factor, the smaller is the bandwidth and higher is the selectivity.

Thus, Q-factor is a measure of the selectivity or sharpness of the tuning of a series R-L-C circuit. The potential differences across the inductance and the capacitance under resonance condition may reach values far in excess of the supply voltage and cause damage to insulation. Hence, resonance condition is to be avoided in power circuits. The series resonant circuit offers minimum impedance to the currents of one particular frequency. Hence, it is sometimes called an *acceptor circuit* for that frequency. Such circuits are employed in many radio circuits.

Example 4.15 : *An R-L-C series circuit has R = 1.5 Ω, L = 0.2 H and C = 100 µF. Calculate the frequency for resonance. If the applied voltage is 230 V of this frequency, calculate : (i) the current, (ii) the voltage drops across L and C, and (iii) the Q-factor of the circuit.*

Solution : From Equation (4.28),

$$\text{Resonant frequency, } f_r = \frac{1}{2\pi \sqrt{LC}} \text{ hertzs}$$

Here, L = 0.2 H and C = 100 µF = 100 × 10⁻⁶ F

∴ $$f_r = \frac{1}{2\pi \sqrt{0.2 \times 100 \times 10^{-6}}} = 35.59 \text{ Hz} \qquad \ldots \text{Ans.}$$

(i) At this frequency,
$$Z = R$$

∴ $$I = \frac{V}{Z} = \frac{V}{R} = \frac{230}{1.5} = 153.33 \text{ A} \qquad \ldots \text{Ans.}$$

(ii) Now, $X_L = \omega L = 2\pi f_r L = 2\pi \times 35.59 \times 0.2 = 44.72 \ \Omega$

∴ Voltage drop across inductance,
$$V_L = I \cdot X_L = 153.33 \times 44.72 = 6857 \text{ V} \qquad \ldots \text{Ans.}$$

and voltage drop across capacitance,
$$V_C = 6857 \text{ V} \qquad \ldots \text{Ans.}$$

Or, alternatively, $X_C = \dfrac{1}{\omega C} = \dfrac{1}{2\pi f_r C} = \dfrac{1}{2\pi \times 35.59 \times 100 \times 10^{-6}}$

$= 44.72 \, \Omega$

$\therefore \quad V_C = I \cdot X_C = 153.33 \times 44.72 = \mathbf{6857 \, V}$ ... Ans.

Notice that these voltages are very much higher than the applied voltage.

(iii) $\quad$ Q-factor $= \dfrac{V_L \text{ or } V_C}{V} = \dfrac{6857}{230} = \mathbf{29.81}$ ... Ans.

Or, alternatively,

$\quad$ Q-factor $= \dfrac{1}{R}\sqrt{\dfrac{L}{C}} = \dfrac{1}{1.5}\sqrt{\dfrac{0.2}{100 \times 10^{-6}}} = \mathbf{29.81}$ ... Ans.

Example 4.16 : *A series circuit consisting of resistance of 10 Ω, inductive reactance of 20 Ω and capacitive reactance of X_C Ω, is connected to 100 V, 50 Hz supply. It is observed that current in the circuit is maximum. Find :*

(i) *Value of capacitance and inductance in the circuit,*
(ii) *Impedance of the circuit,*
(iii) *Power factor of the circuit,*
(iv) *Value of maximum current,*
(v) *Power consumed by the circuit.*

Solution :

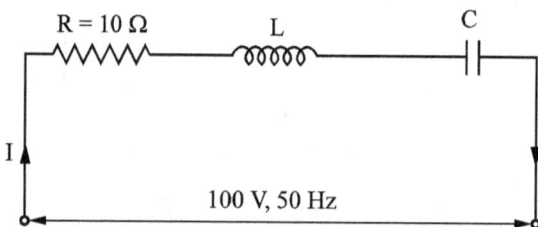

Fig. 4.23 : Circuit diagram for Example 4.16

(i) The current being maximum, the circuit is under resonance. Hence,

$$X_L = X_C = 20 \, \Omega$$

$\therefore \quad L = \dfrac{X_L}{2\pi f} = \dfrac{20}{2\pi \times 50} = \mathbf{0.06366 \, H}$ ... Ans.

and $\quad C = \dfrac{1}{(2\pi f) X_C} = \dfrac{1}{2\pi \times 50 \times 20}$

$= \mathbf{0.1592 \times 10^{-3} \, F}$ ... Ans.

(ii) $\quad Z = \sqrt{R^2 + (X_L - X_C)^2} = R = \mathbf{10 \, \Omega}$ ... Ans.

(iii) Power factor of the circuit,

$$\cos \phi = \dfrac{R}{Z} = \dfrac{10}{10} = \mathbf{1}$$ ... Ans.

(iv) Maximum current (r.m.s. value),

$$I_{max} = \frac{V}{R} = \frac{100}{10} = 10 \text{ A} \qquad \text{... Ans.}$$

(v) Power consumed,

$$P = I_{max}^2 \times R = 10^2 \times 10 = \mathbf{1000 \text{ W}} \qquad \text{... Ans.}$$

4.9 APPLICATION OF COMPLEX NOTATION METHOD TO A.C. SERIES CIRCUITS

In the previous chapter, we have already seen the general principles of complex notation method. Now, in the following few sections, let us study how this method can be employed in the analysis of a.c. series circuits.

Voltage, Current and Impedance : Let us first consider a simple circuit in which resistance R is connected in series with an inductive reactance X_L (Fig. 4.1 a). In this case, voltage-current relations as given by the phasor diagram of Fig. 4.1 (b) can be completely derived using complex notation as follows :

Since the current is considered as a reference quantity, we have

$$\overline{I} = I + j0 = I \angle 0°$$

From the impedance triangle, (Fig. 4.2 b), the impedance of the circuit can be represented as,

$$\overline{Z} = R + jX_L = Z \angle \phi$$

where

$$Z = \sqrt{R^2 + X_L^2}$$

and

$$\phi = \tan^{-1}\frac{X_L}{R}$$

Then, voltage across the circuit is given by,

$$\overline{V} = \overline{I} \cdot \overline{Z} = I \angle 0° \times Z \angle \phi°$$
$$= IZ \angle \phi$$

Thus, the phasor $\overline{V}$ leads the reference phasor $\overline{I}$ by $\phi°$. The numerical value of the supply voltage is IZ. Next, consider the circuit containing a resistance R in series with a capacitive reactance X_C (Fig. 4.8 a). Again, the current being a reference quantity,

$$\overline{I} = I + j0 = I \angle 0°$$

From impedance triangle (Fig. 4.9 b),

$$\overline{Z} = R - jX_C = Z \angle -\phi$$

where

$$Z = \sqrt{R^2 + X_C^2}$$

and

$$\phi = \tan^{-1}\frac{-X_C}{R}$$

$\therefore$

$$\overline{V} = \overline{I} \cdot \overline{Z} = I \angle 0° \times Z \angle -\phi°$$
$$= IZ \angle -\phi$$

Thus, phasor $\bar{V}$ lags behind the reference current phasor by $\phi°$ as shown in the phasor diagram of Fig. 4.8 (b) and has a numerical value I Z. In a similar manner, for the circuit containing R, X_L and X_C in series (Fig. 4.10 a),

$$\bar{I} = (I + j\,0) = I \angle 0°$$

where
$$\bar{Z} = R + j\,(X_L - X_C) = Z \angle \phi$$
$$Z = \sqrt{R^2 + (X_L - X_C)^2}$$

and
$$\phi = \tan^{-1} \frac{X_L - X_C}{R}$$

Hence,
$$\bar{V} = \bar{I} \cdot \bar{Z} = I \angle 0° \times Z \angle \phi°$$
$$= I Z \angle \phi$$

which is in agreement with the phasor diagram of Fig. 4.10 (b). The angle ϕ will be negative if $X_L < X_C$ as illustrated by the phasor diagram of Fig. 4.11 (a).

Impedances in Series : If circuits having impedances $\bar{Z}_1, \bar{Z}_2, \bar{Z}_3$ etc. are connected in series across a supply voltage $\bar{V}$, (Fig. 4.20 a) and if $\bar{I}$ is the circuit current, then using complex notation, we have

$$\bar{V} = \bar{V}_1 + \bar{V}_2 + \bar{V}_3 + ...$$

$\therefore \qquad \bar{I} \cdot \bar{Z} = \bar{I} \cdot \bar{Z}_1 + \bar{I} \cdot \bar{Z}_2 + \bar{I} \cdot \bar{Z}_3 + ...$

where $\bar{Z}$ is the equivalent impedance of $\bar{Z}_1, \bar{Z}_2, \bar{Z}_3$ etc. in series.

Hence, $\qquad \bar{Z} = \bar{Z}_1 + \bar{Z}_2 + \bar{Z}_3 ...$ ... (4.34)

Further, in general, if

$$\bar{Z}_1 = R_1 + j\,X_1, \quad \bar{Z}_2 = R_2 + j\,X_2, \quad \bar{Z}_3 = R_3 + j\,X_3 \text{, etc., then}$$

$$\bar{Z} = (R_1 + j\,X_1) + (R_2 + j\,X_2) + (R_3 + j\,X_3) + ...$$
$$= (R_1 + R_2 + R_3 + ...) + j\,(X_1 + X_2 + X_3 + ...)$$
$$= R + j\,X = Z \angle \phi$$

where $\qquad R = R_1 + R_2 + R_3 + ... \quad$ and $\quad X = X_1 + X_2 + X_3 + ...$

$$Z = \sqrt{R^2 + X^2} \quad \text{and} \quad \phi = \tan^{-1} \frac{X}{R}$$

ILLUSTRATIVE EXAMPLES INVOLVING A.C. FUNDAMENTALS

Example 4.17 : *In a circuit, the equations of instantaneous voltage and current are given by*

$$v = 35.35 \sin\left(\omega t - \frac{2\pi}{5}\right) \text{ volts.}$$

$$i = 7.07 \sin\left(\omega t - \frac{\pi}{3}\right) \text{ amperes}$$

where $\omega = 314$ radians/s.

Sketch the phasor diagram. Calculate the impedance, average power, power factor and frequency.

Solution : Fig. 4.24 shows the necessary phasor diagram.

(i) Maximum value of voltage, V_m = 35.35 V

∴ R.M.S. value of voltage, $V = \dfrac{35.35}{\sqrt{2}} = 25$ V

Maximum value of current, I_m = 7.07 A

∴ R.M.S. value of current, $I = \dfrac{7.07}{\sqrt{2}} = 5$ A

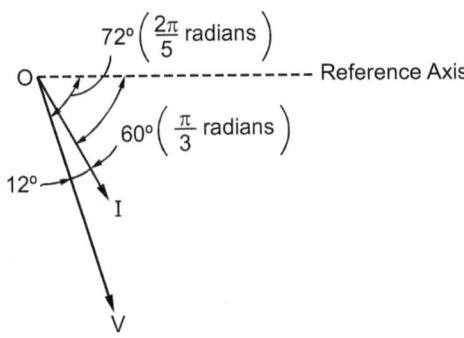

Fig. 4.24 : Phasor diagram for Example 4.17

Hence, when expressed with respect to reference axis (or phasor), we have

$$\bar{V} = 25 \angle -72° \text{ V} \quad \text{and} \quad \bar{I} = 5 \angle -60° \text{ A}$$

∴ Impedance of the circuit,

$$\bar{Z} = \dfrac{\bar{V}}{\bar{I}} = \dfrac{25 \angle -72°}{5 \angle -60°} = 5 \angle -12° \ \Omega \qquad \text{... Ans.}$$

(ii) Average power,

$$P = V I \cos \widehat{V\,I} = V I \cos \phi = 25 \times 5 \times \cos 12°$$
$$= \mathbf{122.27 \ W} \qquad \text{... Ans.}$$

(iii) Power factor,

$$\cos \phi = \cos 12° = \mathbf{0.978 \ (leading)} \qquad \text{... Ans.}$$

(iv) Frequency, $f = \dfrac{\omega}{2\pi} = \dfrac{314}{2\pi} = \mathbf{50 \ Hz}$ ... Ans.

Example 4.18 : *The sources of voltages represented by $20 \sin \omega t$ and $20 \sin \left(\omega t + \dfrac{\pi}{6}\right)$ volts are in series. Express the resultant in phasor notation with first voltage as a reference. If the resultant voltage is given to a circuit of impedance $(8 + j6) \ \Omega$, calculate the r.m.s. current and power in the circuit.*

Solution : Let,
$$v_1 = 20 \sin \omega t \text{ volts}$$
$$v_2 = 20 \sin \left(\omega t + \dfrac{\pi}{6}\right) \text{ volts}$$

Therefore, their r.m.s. values will be given by

$$V_1 = \frac{V_{m1}}{\sqrt{2}} = \frac{20}{\sqrt{2}} = 14.14 \text{ V}$$

$$V_2 = \frac{V_{m2}}{\sqrt{2}} = \frac{20}{\sqrt{2}} = 14.14 \text{ V}$$

From the equations representing two given voltages, it is obvious that V_2 leads V_1 by $\pi/6$ radian i.e. 30°. Therefore, taking V_1 as a reference, the two voltages can be represented in complex form as

$$\overline{V}_1 = 14.14 \angle 0° = (14.14 + j\,0) \text{ V}$$

$$\overline{V}_2 = 14.14 \angle 30° = (12.25 + j\,7.07) \text{ V}$$

When the two sources of voltages are in series, the resultant voltage will be given by

$$\overline{V} = \overline{V}_1 + \overline{V}_2 = (14.14 + j0) + (12.25 + j\,7.07)$$

$$= 26.39 + j\,7.07 = \mathbf{27.32 \angle 15° \text{ V}} \quad \text{... Ans.}$$

$$\overline{Z} = 8 + j\,6 = 10 \angle 36.87° \; \Omega$$

$$\therefore \quad \overline{I} = \frac{\overline{V}}{\overline{Z}} = \frac{27.32 \angle 15°}{10 \angle 36.87°} = \mathbf{2.732 \angle -21.87° \text{ A}} \quad \text{... Ans.}$$

$$P = VI \cos \widehat{VI} = VI \cos \phi$$

$$= 27.32 \times 2.732 \times \cos(15° + 21.87°) = \mathbf{59.71 \text{ W}} \quad \text{... Ans.}$$

Example 4.19 : *An alternating current, i = 1.414 sin (2π × 50 × t) amperes, is passed through a series circuit consisting of a resistance of 100 Ω and an inductance of 0.31831 H. Find the expressions for the instantaneous values of the voltages across (i) the resistance, (ii) the inductance and (iii) the combination.*

Solution :

$$i = 1.414 \sin(2\pi \times 50 \times t) \text{ amperes}$$

$\therefore$ Frequency, $f = 50$ Hz

Hence, $X_L = 2\pi fL = 2\pi \times 50 \times 0.31831 = 100 \; \Omega$

(i) R.M.S. value of current, $I = \dfrac{I_m}{\sqrt{2}} = \dfrac{1.414}{\sqrt{2}} = 1$ A

$$V_R = IR = 1 \times 100 = 100 \text{ V}$$

This voltage will be in phase with the current. Therefore, its instantaneous value can be represented by the equation,

$$v_R = V_m \sin \omega t = \sqrt{2} \times 100 \sin(2\pi \times 50 \times t)$$

$$= \mathbf{141.42 \sin 314\,t \text{ volts}} \quad \text{... Ans.}$$

(ii) $\qquad V_L = IX_L = 1 \times 100 = 100$ V

This voltage will lead the current by 90° or $\frac{\pi}{2}$ radian. Therefore, its instantaneous value will be given by,
$$v_L = \sqrt{2} \times 100 \sin\left(\omega t + \frac{\pi}{2}\right)$$
$$= 141.42 \sin\left(314\, t + \frac{\pi}{2}\right) \text{ volts} \qquad \text{... Ans.}$$

(iii) Impedance of the circuit,
$$Z = \sqrt{R^2 + X_L^2} = \sqrt{100^2 + 100^2} = 141.42\ \Omega$$

∴ Voltage across the combination,
$$V = IZ = 1 \times 141.42 = 141.42 \text{ V}$$

Power factor of the circuit, $\cos\phi = \dfrac{R}{Z} = \dfrac{100}{141.42} = 0.707$ lagging

∴ $\qquad \phi = 45°$ or $\dfrac{\pi}{4}$ radian.

Since the voltage across the combination leads the current by $\dfrac{\pi}{4}$ radian, its instantaneous value can be represented by
$$v = \sqrt{2} \times 141.42 \sin\left(314\, t + \frac{\pi}{4}\right)$$
$$= 200 \sin\left(314\, t + \frac{\pi}{4}\right) \text{ volts} \qquad \text{... Ans.}$$

Example 4.20 : *A voltage, e = 200 sin 100 πt is applied to a load having R = 200 Ω in series with L = 638 mH. Estimate :*
  (i) *Expression for current in* $i = I_m \sin(\omega t \pm \phi)$ *form,*
  (ii) *Power consumed by the load,*
  (iii) *Reactive power of the load,*
  (iv) *Voltages across R and L.*

Solution : (i) R.M.S. value of voltage, $V = \dfrac{200}{\sqrt{2}} = 141.421$ V

$$\omega = 2\pi f = 100\pi$$

∴ $\qquad f = 50$ Hz

$$X_L = \omega L = 2\pi f L = 2\pi \times 50 \times 638 \times 10^{-3} = 200.43\ \Omega$$

$$\overline{Z} = R + jX_L = 200 + j\, 200.43 = 283.149\ \angle 45.06°\ \Omega$$

$$\overline{I} = \dfrac{\overline{V}}{\overline{Z}} = \dfrac{141.421\ \angle 0°}{283.149\ \angle 45.06°} = 0.5\ \angle -45.06°\ \text{A}$$

Hence, $\qquad I_m = \sqrt{2} \times 0.5 = 0.707$ A and $\phi = -45.06°$ or $-\dfrac{\pi}{4}$ radian

∴ $\qquad i = 0.707 \sin\left(100\pi t - \dfrac{\pi}{4}\right)$ amperes $\qquad$ ... Ans.

(ii) Power consumed, $P = VI \cos\phi = 141.421 \times 0.5 \times \cos 45.06°$
$$= 50 \text{ W} \qquad \text{... Ans.}$$

(iii) Reactive power, $\quad Q = VI \sin \phi = 141.421 \times 0.5 \times \sin 45.06°$
$\quad\quad\quad\quad\quad\quad\quad\quad\quad = \mathbf{50\ VAr}$ ... Ans.

(iv) Voltage across R, $\quad V_R = IR = 0.5 \times 200 = \mathbf{100\ V}$ ... Ans.

$\quad\quad$ Voltage across L, $\quad V_L = I \cdot X_L = 0.5 \times 200.43 = \mathbf{100.21\ V}$ ... Ans.

Example 4.21 : *A voltage of v = 100 sin 314 t is applied to a circuit consisting of 25 Ω resistance and 80 µF capacitor in series. Find :*

(i) Expression for the instantaneous value of current, (ii) Power consumed.

Solution : (i) R.M.S. value of the voltage,

$$V = \frac{100}{\sqrt{2}} = 70.71 \text{ volts}$$

$$\omega = 2\pi f = 314$$

$$\therefore \quad f = \frac{314}{2\pi} = 50 \text{ Hz}$$

$$X_C = \frac{1}{\omega C} = \frac{1}{2\pi f C} = \frac{1}{2\pi \times 50 \times 80 \times 10^{-6}} = 39.8\ \Omega$$

$$\overline{Z} = R - jX_C = 25 - j\,39.8 = 47 \angle -57.87°\ \Omega$$

$$\overline{I} = \frac{\overline{V}}{\overline{Z}} = \frac{70.71 \angle 0°}{47 \angle -57.87°} = 1.504 \angle 57.87°\ A$$

$\therefore \quad I_m = \sqrt{2} \times 1.504 = 2.13\ A$ and $\phi = 57.87°$ or 1 radian

$\therefore \quad i = 2.13 \sin(\omega t + 1) = \mathbf{2.13 \sin(314\,t + 1)}$ **amperes** ... Ans.

(ii) Power consumed, $\quad P = VI \cos \phi = 70.71 \times 1.504 \times \cos 57.87° = \mathbf{56.56\ W}$ ... Ans.

Or, alternatively, $\quad P = I^2 R = (1.504)^2 \times 25 = \mathbf{56.55\ W}$ ... Ans.

Example 4.22 : *A load of 22 kW operates at 0.8 power factor (lagging) when connected to a 420 V, 1-phase, 50 Hz source. Find :*

(i) Current in the load, (ii) Power factor angle, (iii) Impedance, (iv) Resistance of load, (v) Reactance of load, (vi) Write equation of voltage and current, (vii) Draw the phasor diagram.

Solution :

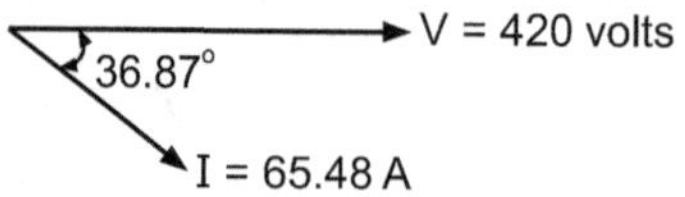

$\quad\quad\quad\quad$ 36.87° $\quad\quad\quad\quad\to V = 420$ volts

$\quad\quad\quad\quad\quad\quad\quad I = 65.48$ A

Fig. 4.25 : Phasor diagram for Example 4.22

(i) $\quad$ Current, $I = \dfrac{P}{V \cos \phi} = \dfrac{22 \times 10^3}{420 \times 0.8} = \mathbf{65.48\ A}$ ... Ans.

(ii) $\quad$ Power factor angle, $\phi = \cos^{-1} 0.8 = \mathbf{36.87°}$ ... Ans.

(iii) $\quad\quad\quad$ Impedance, $\overline{Z} = \dfrac{\overline{V}}{\overline{I}} = \dfrac{420 \angle 0°}{65.48 \angle -36.87°}$

$$= 6.414 \angle 36.87° = (5.13 + j\,3.85)\ \Omega$$

(iv) ∴ $R = 5.13\ \Omega$ ... Ans.
(v) and $X_L = 3.85\ \Omega$ ... Ans.
(vi) $V_m = \sqrt{2}\ V = \sqrt{2} \times 420 = 593.97$ volts

∴ Instantaneous voltage, $v = V_m \sin \omega t = 593.97 \sin 2\pi \times 50 \times t$

$= \mathbf{593.97 \sin 314\ t}$ **volts** ... Ans.

$I_m = \sqrt{2}\ I = \sqrt{2} \times 65.48 = 92.6$ A

Angle of lag of the current w.r.t. voltage, $\phi = 36.87°$ or 0.644 radian

∴ Instantaneous current, $i = I_m \sin(\omega t - \phi) = 92.6 \sin(2\pi \times 50 \times t - 0.644)$

$= \mathbf{92.6 \sin(314\ t - 0.644)}$ **amperes** ... Ans.

(vii) Fig. 4.25 shows the necessary phasor diagram.

Example 4.23 : *An e.m.f. given by $v = 100 \sin 100\pi t$ is impressed across a circuit consisting of resistance of 40 Ω in series with 100 μF capacitor and 0.25 H inductor. Determine : (i) r.m.s. value of the current, (ii) power consumed, (iii) power factor.*

Solution : R.M.S. value of the voltage, $V = \dfrac{100}{\sqrt{2}} = 70.71$ volts

$X_L = \omega L = 100\pi \times 0.25 = 78.54\ \Omega$

$X_C = \dfrac{1}{\omega C} = \dfrac{1}{100\pi \times 100 \times 10^{-6}} = 31.83\ \Omega$

∴ Impedance, $\bar{Z} = R + j(X_L - X_C) = 40 + j(78.54 - 31.83)$

$= 40 + j\ 46.71 = 61.5\ \angle\ 49.42°\ \Omega$

∴ R.M.S. value of the current, $\bar{I} = \dfrac{\bar{V}}{\bar{Z}} = \dfrac{70.71\ \angle\ 0°}{61.5\ \angle\ 49.42°} = \mathbf{1.15\ \angle\ -49.42°}$ **A** ... Ans.

Power factor, $\cos \phi = \cos 49.42° = \mathbf{0.65\ lagging}$ ... Ans.

Power consumed, $P = VI \cos \phi = 70.71 \times 1.15 \times 0.65$

$= \mathbf{52.9\ W}$ ... Ans.

ILLUSTRATIVE EXAMPLES ON A.C. SERIES CIRCUITS

Example 4.24 : *A resistor of 10 Ω and an inductance 0.1 H are connected in series across a 230 V, 50 Hz supply. Find (a) the circuit impedance, (b) current, (c) phase angle of the current relative to the applied voltage.*

Solution : The circuit is as shown in Fig. 4.1 (a).

Now, $X_L = \omega L = 2\pi f L = 2\pi \times 50 \times 0.1 = 31.42\ \Omega$

∴ $\bar{Z} = R + j X_L = 10 + j\ 31.42$

$= \mathbf{32.97\ \angle\ 72.35°\ \Omega}$ ... Ans.

If the applied voltage is taken as the reference quantity, then

$$\overline{V} = 230 + j\,0 = 230 \angle 0° \text{ V}$$

$$\therefore \quad \overline{I} = \frac{\overline{V}}{\overline{Z}} = \frac{230 \angle 0°}{32.97 \angle 72.35°}$$

$$= 6.98 \angle -72.35° \text{ A} \qquad \text{... Ans.}$$

Thus, current lags behind the voltage by 72.35°.

Example 4.25 : *Calculate the resistance and inductance or capacitance in series for each of the following impedances. Assume the frequency to be 50 Hz.*
(i) $25 + j\,30\ \Omega$, (ii) $-j\,80\ \Omega$, (iii) $20 \angle 60°\ \Omega$

Solution :

(i) $\quad 25 + j\,30 = (R + j\,X_L)\ \Omega$

$\therefore \quad R = 25\ \Omega$ ... Ans.

$$L = \frac{X_L}{2\pi f} = \frac{30}{2\pi \times 50} = 0.0955 \text{ H} \qquad \text{... Ans.}$$

(ii) $\quad 0 - j\,80 = (R - j\,X_C)\ \Omega$

$\therefore \quad R = 0$

$$C = \frac{1}{(2\pi f)\cdot X_C} = \frac{1}{(2\pi \times 50)\times 80}$$

$$= 3.98 \times 10^{-5} \text{ F or } 39.8\ \mu\text{F} \qquad \text{... Ans.}$$

(iii) $\quad 20 \angle 60° = 10 + j\,17.32 = (R + j\,X_L)\ \Omega$

$\therefore \quad R = 10\ \Omega$

$$L = \frac{X_L}{2\pi f} = \frac{17.32}{2\pi \times 50} = 0.055 \text{ H} \qquad \text{... Ans.}$$

Example 4.26 : *A coil A takes 3 A at 0.8 power factor lagging with applied voltage of 15 V. A second coil B takes 3 A with 0.7 power factor lagging with applied voltage of 7.5 V. What voltage will be required to produce a total current of 3 A with coils A and B connected in series ? Find the power factor in this case.*

Solution : $\quad \cos \phi_A = 0.8$ (lagging)

$\therefore \quad \phi_A = 36.87°$

$$\overline{Z}_A = \frac{\overline{V}}{\overline{I}_A} = \frac{15 \angle 0°}{3 \angle -36.87°} = 5 \angle 36.87° = (4 + j3)\ \Omega$$

$\cos \phi_B = 0.7$ (lagging)

$\therefore \quad \phi_B = 45.57°$

$$\overline{Z}_B = \frac{\overline{V}}{\overline{I}_B} = \frac{7.5 \angle 0°}{3 \angle -45.57°} = 2.5 \angle 45.57° = (1.75 + j\,1.79)\ \Omega$$

∴ Total circuit impedance after series connection of coils A and B,

$$\overline{Z} = \overline{Z}_A + \overline{Z}_B$$
$$= (4 + j3) + (1.75 + j\,1.79) = 5.75 + j\,4.79$$
$$= 7.48 \angle 39.8° \;\Omega$$

∴ Voltage required, $V = IZ = 3 \times 7.48 =$ **22.44 V** ... Ans.

Power factor, $\cos\phi = \cos 39.8° =$ **0.768 (lagging)** ... Ans.

Example 4.27 : *A series circuit consisting of 25 Ω resistor, 64 mH inductor and 80 μF capacitor, is connected to a 110 V, 50 Hz, single-phase supply as shown in Fig. 4.26 (a). Calculate the current, voltage across individual elements and the overall power factor of the circuit. Draw a neat phasor diagram showing $\overline{I}$, $\overline{V}_R$, $\overline{V}_L$, $\overline{V}_C$ and $\overline{V}$.*

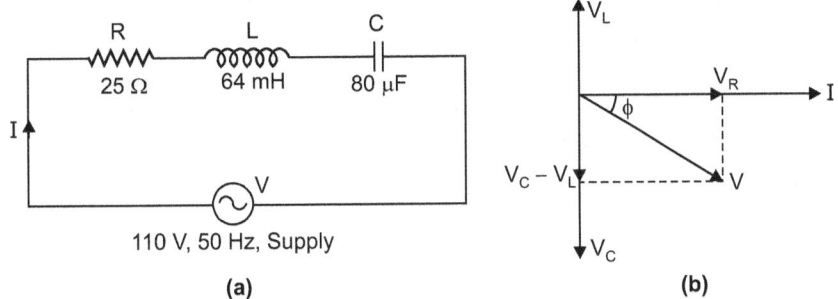

Fig. 4.26 : (a) Circuit diagram for Example 4.27, (b) Phasor diagram

Solution : $X_L = 2\pi fL = 2\pi \times 50 \times (64 \times 10^{-3}) = 20.11\;\Omega$

$$X_C = \frac{1}{2\pi fC} = \frac{1}{2\pi \times 50 \times (80 \times 10^{-6})} = 39.79\;\Omega$$

∴ $\overline{Z} = R + j(X_L - X_C) = 25 + j(20.11 - 39.79)$
$$= 25 - j\,19.68 = 31.82 \angle -38.21°\;\Omega$$

$$\overline{I} = \frac{\overline{V}}{\overline{Z}} = \frac{110 \angle 0°}{31.82 \angle -38.21°} = \mathbf{3.46 \angle 38.21°\;A} \qquad \text{... Ans.}$$

Overall p.f. $= \cos\phi = \cos(38.21°) =$ **0.7857 leading** ... Ans.

$V_R = IR = 3.46 \times 25 =$ **86.5 V** ... Ans.

$V_L = I \cdot X_L = 3.46 \times 20.11 =$ **69.58 V** ... Ans.

$V_C = I \cdot X_C = 3.46 \times 39.79 =$ **137.67 V** ... Ans.

Fig. 4.26 (b) shows the necessary phasor diagram taking current as a reference phasor.

Example 4.28 : *A resistance of 120 Ω and a capacitive reactance of 250 Ω are connected in series across an a.c. voltage source. If a current of 0.9 A is flowing in the circuit, find out : (i) power factor, (ii) supply voltage, (iii) voltages across resistance and capacitance, (iv) active power and reactive power.*

Solution :

$$\overline{Z} = 120 - j\,250 = 277.3 \angle -64.4° \; \Omega$$

∴ Power factor, $\cos \phi = \cos(64.4°) = $ **0.43 leading** ... Ans.

Supply voltage, $V = IZ = 0.9 \times 277.3 = $ **249.6 V** ... Ans.

Voltage across the resistance,

$$V_R = IR = 0.9 \times 120 = \textbf{108 V}$$ ... Ans.

Voltage across the capacitance,

$$V_C = IX_C = 0.9 \times 250 = \textbf{225 V}$$ ... Ans.

Power, $P = VI \cos \phi = 249.6 \times 0.9 \times 0.43 = $ **96.6 W** ... Ans.

Reactive power,

$$Q = VI \sin \phi = 249.6 \times 0.9 \times \sin(64.4°) = \textbf{202.6 VAr}$$ ...Ans.

Example 4.29 : *A coil of resistance 10 Ω and inductance 0.1 H is connected in series with a 150 μF capacitor, across a 200 V, 50 Hz supply. Calculate :*
(i) Impedance, (ii) Current, (iii) Power factor, (iv) Total power consumed,
(v) Voltage across the coil and capacitor, (vi) Draw the phasor diagram.

Solution : Fig. 4.27 (a) shows the necessary connection diagram.

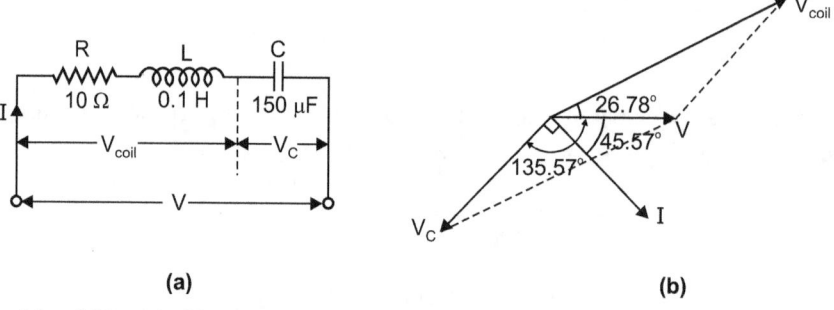

Fig. 4.27 : (a) Circuit diagram for Example 4.29, (b) Phasor diagram

$$R = 10 \; \Omega$$
$$X_L = 2\pi fL = 2\pi \times 50 \times 0.1 = 31.42 \; \Omega$$
$$X_C = \frac{1}{2\pi fC} = \frac{1}{2\pi \times 50 \times (150 \times 10^{-6})} = 21.22 \; \Omega$$

∴ Impedance of the circuit, $\overline{Z} = R + j(X_L - X_C)$
$$= 10 + j(31.42 - 21.22)$$
$$= 10 + j\,10.2 = \textbf{14.28} \angle \textbf{45.57°} \; \Omega$$ ... Ans.

Circuit current, $\overline{I} = \dfrac{\overline{V}}{\overline{Z}} = \dfrac{200 \angle 0°}{14.28 \angle 45.57°} = \textbf{14} \angle \textbf{-45.57° A}$ ... Ans.

Circuit power factor, $\cos \phi = \cos(45.57°) = $ **0.7 lagging** ... Ans.

Total power consumed, $P = VI \cos \phi = 200 \times 14 \times 0.7 =$ **1960 W** ... **Ans.**
Impedance of the coil, $Z_{coil} = R + j X_L = 10 + j\, 31.42$
$$= 32.97 \angle 72.35° \, \Omega$$

∴ Voltage across the coil, $\overline{V}_{coil} = \overline{I}\, \overline{Z}_{coil} = 14 \angle -45.57° \times 32.97 \angle 72.35°$
$$= \mathbf{461.58 \angle 26.78° \ V} \qquad \text{... \textbf{Ans.}}$$

Voltage across the capacitor,
$$\overline{V}_C = \overline{I} \cdot \overline{Z}_C = \overline{I}\, (0 - j\, X_C)$$
$$= 14 \angle -45.57° \times (0 - j\, 21.22)$$
$$= 14 \angle -45.57° \times 21.22 \angle -90°$$
$$= \mathbf{297.08 \angle -135.57° \ V} \qquad \text{... \textbf{Ans.}}$$

Fig. 4.27 (b) shows the necessary phasor diagram taking supply voltage as a reference phasor.

Example 4.30 : *A coil connected across a 250 V, 50 Hz supply takes a current of 10 A at 0.8 power factor lag. What will be the power taken by the choke coil, when connected across a 200 V, 25 Hz supply ? Also calculate the resistance and inductance of the coil.*

Solution : 250 V, 50 Hz Supply :

Current drawn, $\overline{I} = 10 \angle -\cos^{-1} 0.8 = 10 \angle -36.87°$
$$= (8 - j\, 6) \ A$$

∴ Impedance of the coil, $\overline{Z} = \dfrac{\overline{V}}{\overline{I}} = \dfrac{250 \angle 0°}{10 \angle -36.87°} = 25 \angle 36.87°$
$$= (20 + j\, 15) \ \Omega$$

∴ Resistance of the coil, $R = \mathbf{20 \ \Omega}$ ... **Ans.**

and Inductance of the coil, $L = \dfrac{X_L}{2\pi f} = \dfrac{15}{2\pi \times 50} = \mathbf{0.0477 \ H}$ ... **Ans.**

200 V, 25 Hz Supply :
Inductive reactance of the coil,
$$X_L = 2\pi f L = 2\pi \times 25 \times 0.0477 = 7.49 \ \Omega$$

∴ Impedance of the coil,
$$\overline{Z} = R + j\, X_L = 20 + j\, 7.49 = 21.36 \angle 20.53° \ \Omega$$

∴ Current drawn, $\overline{I} = \dfrac{\overline{V}}{\overline{Z}} = \dfrac{200 \angle 0°}{21.36 \angle 20.53°} = 9.36 \angle -20.53° \ A$

∴ Power taken by the coil, $P = I^2 R = (9.36)^2 \times 20 = \mathbf{1752.2 \ WS}$ ... **Ans.**
Or alternatively, $P = VI \cos \phi = 200 \times 9.36 \times \cos 20.53° = \mathbf{1753.1 \ W}$ ... **Ans.**

Example 4.31 : *Two impedances, one inductive and the other capacitive are connected in series across the voltage of $120 \angle 30°$ V and frequency of 50 Hz. The current flowing in the circuit is $3 \angle -15°$A. If one of the impedances is $(10 + j48.3) \ \Omega$, find the other. Also calculate the values of L and C in the impedances.*

Solution : Inductive impedance,
$$\overline{Z}_1 = 10 + j48.3 = 49.32 \angle 78.3° \ \Omega$$

Total circuit impedance, $\bar{Z} = \dfrac{\bar{V}}{\bar{I}} = \dfrac{120 \angle 30°}{3 \angle -15°} = 40 \angle 45° = (28.28 + j28.28)\ \Omega$

∴ Capacitive impedance,

$$\bar{Z}_2 = \bar{Z} - \bar{Z}_1 = (28.28 + j28.28) - (10 + j48.3)$$
$$= 18.28 - j20.02 = \mathbf{27.11 \angle -47.6°\ \Omega} \qquad \text{... Ans.}$$

From the expression for $\bar{Z}_1$, we have

$$X_L = 48.3\ \Omega$$

But $\qquad X_L = 2\pi f L$

∴ $\qquad 48.3 = 2\pi \times 50 \times L$

∴ Inductance, $L = \mathbf{0.1537\ H}$ ... Ans.

Also, from the expression for $\bar{Z}_2$, we have

$$X_C = 20.02\ \Omega$$

But $\qquad X_C = \dfrac{1}{2\pi f C}$

∴ $\qquad 20.02 = \dfrac{1}{2\pi \times 50 \times C}$

∴ Capacitance, $C = \mathbf{1.59 \times 10^{-4}\ F\ or\ 159\ \mu F}$ ... Ans.

Example 4.32 : *Two impedances $Z_1 = 40 \angle 30°\ \Omega$ and $Z_2 = 30 \angle 60°\ \Omega$ are connected in series across single-phase, 230 V, 50 Hz supply. Calculate :*

(i) Current drawn, (ii) Power factor and (iii) Power consumed by the circuit.

Solution : $\qquad \bar{Z}_1 = 40 \angle 30° = (34.64 + j20)\ \Omega$

$\qquad \bar{Z}_2 = 30 \angle 60° = (15 + j25.98)\ \Omega$

∴ Total impedance of the circuit,

$$\bar{Z} = \bar{Z}_1 + \bar{Z}_2 = (34.64 + j20) + (15 + j25.98)$$
$$= 49.64 + j45.98 = 67.66 \angle 42.81°\ \Omega$$

(i) Current drawn, $\bar{I} = \dfrac{\bar{V}}{\bar{Z}} = \dfrac{230 \angle 0°}{67.66 \angle 42.81°}$

$\qquad = \mathbf{3.4 \angle -42.81°\ A}$ ... Ans.

(ii) Power factor, $\cos \phi = \cos 42.81° = \mathbf{0.73\ lagging}$ ... Ans.

(iii) Power consumed by the circuit,

$\qquad P = VI \cos \phi = 230 \times 3.4 \times 0.73 = \mathbf{570.86\ W}$ ... Ans.

4.10 POINTS TO REMEMBER

- Impedance is defined as the opposition of the circuit to the flow of alternating current. The resistance (R), inductive reactance (X_L) and capacitive reactance (X_C) being in ohms, unit of impedance is also ohm.
- It should be noted that the capacitive reactance (X_C) is always regarded as negative. Therefore, the total reactance of the circuit (X) is negative if $X_C > X_L$.
- The product of r.m.s. values of voltage (V) and current (I) is called the apparent power (S). It is measured in volt-amperes (VA) or kilovolt-amperes (kVA).
- The average power given by the expression $P = V I \cos \phi$ is called the true power or real power (P). It is measured in watts (W) or kilowatts (kW).
- Power factor ($\cos \phi$) is the factor by which the apparent power must be multiplied in order to obtain the true power or in other words, it is the ratio of the true power to the apparent power.
- The numerical value of the cosine of the phase angle between the voltage and the current gives the power factor of the circuit. The value of the power factor, therefore, can never be more than unity.
- The in-phase component (w.r.t. voltage), $I \cos \phi$ is called active power, wattful or energy component of the current.
- The component $I \sin \phi$ which is 90° out of phase with the voltage is known as the reactive, wattless or idle component of the current.
- The true or real power in the a.c. circuit which is given by the product of the applied voltage and the active component of the current (i.e. $P = VI \cos \phi$) is also called active power. It is measured in watts (W) or kilowatts (kW).
- The quantity $VI \sin \phi$ which is the product of applied voltage and reactive component of the current, is called the reactive power. The unit for reactive power is reactive volt-ampere (VAr) or reactive kilovolt-ampere (kVAr).
- If all three sides of the impedance triangle (with resistance, reactance and impedance as its sides) are multiplied by I^2, it becomes a power triangle (with active, reactive and apparent powers as its sides).
- A series circuit is said to be under resonance when its net reactance $X (= X_L - X_C)$ is zero, and the frequency at which this happens, is known as resonant frequency.
- For the series resonant circuit, bandwidth is defined as the range of frequency over which the magnitude of the current is equal to or greater than 0.707 of the current at resonance.
- Selectivity indicates how well a resonant circuit responds to a certain frequency and eliminates all other frequencies. The smaller the bandwidth, the higher is the selectivity.
- The ratio V_L / V or V_C / V at resonant frequency is called the voltage magnification.

- The quality factor or the Q-factor in the case of an R-L-C series circuit is defined as equal to the voltage magnification in the circuit at resonance.
- Q-factor of a resonant R-L-C series circuit may also be defined as the ratio of resonant frequency to bandwidth. The larger the Q-factor, the smaller is the bandwidth and higher is the selectivity.

4.11 IMPORTANT FORMULAE AT A GLANCE

R-L Series Circuit :

- Impedance $Z = \sqrt{R^2 + X_L^2}$ ohms

  where R = Resistance, in ohms
  X_L = Inductive reactance of the inductance L, in ohms

- Circuit current $I = \dfrac{V}{Z}$ amperes

  where V = Supply voltage, in volts
  Z = Circuit impedance, in ohms

- Power factor $\cos \phi = \dfrac{R}{Z}$ lagging

  where R = Resistance, in ohms
  Z = Circuit impedance, in ohms

- Average power $P = V \cdot I \cdot \cos \phi$ watts

  where V = Supply voltage, in volts
  I = Circuit current, in amperes
  $\cos \phi$ = Power factor of the circuit

Three-Voltmeter Method :

- Power consumed by the inductive load,

$$P_L = \frac{I(V^2 - V_L^2 - V_R^2)}{2V_R} = \frac{1}{2R}(V^2 - V_L^2 - V_R^2) \text{ watts}$$

  where V = Supply voltage, in volts
  V_L = Voltage across the inductive load, in volts
  V_R = Voltage across the non-inductive resistor R, in volts
  I = Circuit current, in amperes
  R = Resistance of the non-inductive resistor, in ohms.

- Power factor of the inductive load,

$$\cos \phi_L = \frac{V^2 - V_L^2 - V_R^2}{2V_L \cdot V_R} \text{ lagging}$$

  where V = Supply voltage, in volts
  V_L = Voltage across the inductive load, in volts
  V_R = Voltage across the non-inductive resistor R, in volts

R-C Series Circuit :

$$\text{Impedance } Z = \sqrt{R^2 + X_C^2} \text{ ohms}$$

where R = Resistance, in ohms
 X_C = Capacitive reactance of the capacitance C, in ohms

- $$\text{Circuit current } I = \frac{V}{Z} \text{ amperes}$$

where V = Supply voltage, in volts
 Z = Circuit impedance, in ohms

- $$\text{Power factor, } \cos\phi = \frac{R}{Z} \text{ leading}$$

where R = Resistance, in ohms
 Z = Circuit impedance, in ohms

- $$\text{Average power } P = V \cdot I \cdot \cos\phi \text{ watts}$$

where V = Supply voltage, in volts
 I = Circuit current, in amperes
 $\cos\phi$ = Power factor of the circuit

R-L-C Series Circuit :

- $$\text{Impedance } Z = \sqrt{R^2 + (X_L - X_C)^2} \text{ ohms}$$

where R = Resistance, in ohms
 X_L = Inductive reactance of the inductance L, in ohms
 X_C = Capacitive reactance of the capacitance C, in ohms

- $$\text{Circuit current } I = \frac{V}{Z} \text{ amperes}$$

where V = Supply voltage, in volts
 Z = Circuit impedance, in ohms

- $$\text{Power factor, } \cos\phi = \frac{R}{Z}$$

where R = Resistance, in ohms
 Z = Circuit impedance, in ohms

- $$\text{Average power } P = V \cdot I \cdot \cos\phi \text{ watts}$$

where V = Supply voltage, in volts
 I = Circuit current, in amperes
 $\cos\phi$ = Power factor of the circuit

Apparent Power, Active Power and Reactive Power :

- $$\text{Apparent power } S = V \cdot I \text{ volt-amperes}$$

where V = Supply voltage, in volts
 I = Circuit current, in amperes

- Active power $P = V \cdot I \cos \phi$ watts

  where
  - V = Supply voltage, in volts
  - I = Circuit current, in amperes
  - $\cos \phi$ = Power factor of the circuit

- Reactive power $Q = V \cdot I \cdot \sin \phi$ reactive volt-amperes

  where
  - V = Supply voltage, in volts
  - I = Circuit current, in amperes
  - $\sin \phi$ = Sine of the phase angle between the supply voltage and circuit current

Resonance in R-L-C Series Circuit :

- Resonant frequency $f_r = \dfrac{1}{2\pi \sqrt{LC}}$ hertzs

  where
  - L = Inductance, in henrys
  - C = Capacitance, in farads

- Q-factor $= \dfrac{1}{R} \sqrt{\dfrac{L}{C}}$

  where
  - R = Resistance, in ohms
  - L = Inductance, in henrys
  - C = Capacitance, in farads

Impedances in Series :

- Equivalent impedance $\bar{Z} = \bar{Z}_1 + \bar{Z}_2 + \bar{Z}_3 + \ldots + \bar{Z}_n$ ohms

  where $\bar{Z}_1, \bar{Z}_2, \bar{Z}_3, \ldots, \bar{Z}_n$ = Impedances connected in series, in ohms.

4.12 SOLUTIONS OF NUMERICAL EXAMPLES FROM UNIVERSITY PAPERS

Example 4.33 : *A sinusoidal voltage is given by (325.269 sin ωt) volts at 50 Hz. If this voltage is applied to an R-L series circuit, a current with r.m.s. value of 35.919 A, lagging behind the voltage by 38.659°, flows. Calculate the values of R and L. Draw the phasor diagram for the circuit.* **(November 2003/6 Marks)**

Solution :

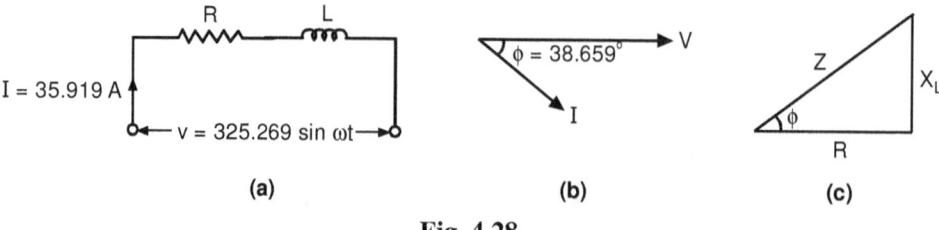

Fig. 4.28

Fig. 4.28(a) shows the circuit diagram and Fig. 4.28(b) shows the necessary phasor diagram.

R.M.S. value of the voltage,

$$V = \frac{V_m}{\sqrt{2}} = \frac{325.269}{\sqrt{2}} = 230 \text{ volts}$$

R.M.S. value of the current, $I = 35.919$ A

∴ Impedance of the circuit,

$$Z = \frac{V}{I} = \frac{230}{35.919} = 6.4 \, \Omega$$

Hence, from the impedance triangle of Fig. 4.28 (c),

$$R = Z \cos \phi = 6.4 \times \cos(38.659)° = 5 \, \Omega \quad \text{... Ans.}$$
$$X_L = Z \sin \phi = 6.4 \times \sin(38.659)° = 4 \, \Omega$$

∴ $$L = \frac{X_L}{2\pi f} = \frac{4}{2\pi \times 50} = 0.0127 \text{ H} \quad \text{... Ans.}$$

Alternatively,

$$\bar{Z} = \frac{\bar{V}}{\bar{I}} = \frac{230 \angle 0°}{35.919 \angle -(38.859)°} = 6.4 \angle (38.859)°$$

$$= (5 + j4) \, \Omega$$

∴ $R = 5 \, \Omega$, $X_L = 4 \, \Omega$ and $L = 0.0127$ H ... **Ans.**

Example 4.34: *When an inductive coil is connected across a 250 V, 50 Hz, a.c. supply, the current is found to be 10 A and the power absorbed is 1.25 kW. Calculate the impedance, resistance and inductance of the coil.* **(November 2003/6 Marks)**

Solution :

$$P = VI \cos \phi$$

∴ $$1.25 \times 10^3 = 250 \times 10 \times \cos \phi$$

∴ Power factor of the coil, $\cos \phi = 0.5$ lagging

∴ Power factor angle, $\phi = 60°$

Now, Impedance of the coil, $$\bar{Z} = \frac{\bar{V}}{\bar{I}} = \frac{250 \angle 0°}{10 \angle -60°} = 25 \angle 60° \, \Omega \quad \text{... Ans.}$$

$$= (12.5 + j\,21.65) \, \Omega$$

∴ Resistance of the coil, R = **12.5 Ω** ... **Ans.**

and Inductive reactance of the coil, $X_L = 21.65 \, \Omega$

∴ Inductance of the coil, $$L = \frac{X_L}{2\pi f} = \frac{21.65}{2\pi \times 50}$$

$$= \mathbf{0.0689 \text{ H}} \quad \text{... Ans.}$$

Example 4.35: *A circuit has a resistance of 115 Ω and an inductance of 0.7 H. It is connected to a 250 V, 50 Hz supply. Calculate:*

(a) inductive reactance, (b) the impedance, (c) current. **(May 2004/6 Marks)**

Solution : Inductive reactance, $X_L = \omega L = 2\pi f L = 2\pi \times 50 \times 0.7$

$$= 219.91 \, \Omega \quad \ldots \text{Ans.}$$

Impedance, $Z = \sqrt{R^2 + X_L^2} = \sqrt{115^2 + (219.91)^2}$

$$= 248.164 \, \Omega \quad \ldots \text{Ans.}$$

Current, $I = \dfrac{V}{Z} = \dfrac{250}{248.164} = \mathbf{1.0074 \, A} \quad \ldots \text{Ans.}$

Example 4.36: *Calculate the impedance of R-L-C series circuit having resistance = 90 Ω, inductance = 0.8 H and capacitance = 78 μF. Take f = 60 Hz and supply voltage = 250 V. Calculate the current flowing.* **(May 2006/4 Marks)**

Solution : Given : $R = 90 \, \Omega$, $L = 0.8$ H, $C = 78$ μF, $f = 60$ Hz and $V = 250$ volts.

$$X_L = \omega L = 2\pi f L = 2\pi \times 60 \times 0.8 = 301.59 \, \Omega$$

$$X_C = \dfrac{1}{\omega C} = \dfrac{1}{2\pi f C} = \dfrac{1}{2\pi \times 60 \times 78 \times 10^{-6}} = 34.01 \, \Omega$$

∴ Impedance, $Z = \sqrt{R^2 + (X_L - X_C)^2} = \sqrt{90^2 + (301.59 - 34.01)^2}$

$$= 282.31 \, \Omega \quad \ldots \text{Ans.}$$

∴ Current, $I = \dfrac{V}{Z} = \dfrac{250}{282.31} = \mathbf{0.89 \, A} \quad \ldots \text{Ans.}$

Example 4.37 : *A resistance, inductance and capacitance are connected in series across a 230 V, 50 Hz supply. The current flowing through the circuit is in phase with the voltage. If the current flowing through the circuit is 10 A and capacitance is 300 μF, calculate the resistance and inductance in the circuit.* **(May 2008/6 Marks)**

Solution : Given : $V = 230$ volts, $f = 50$ Hz, $I = 10$ A, $C = 300$ μF, $\cos\phi = 1$.

We know that for the a.c. circuit with R, L and C in series,

$$\text{Impedance, } Z = \sqrt{R^2 + (X_L - X_C)^2}$$

In a particular case when $X_L = X_C$,

$$\text{Impedance, } Z = R$$

The circuit under such condition (called as series resonance) behaves as a purely resistive circuit. As such, the current is in phase with the applied voltage and the power factor of the circuit is unity. The given circuit is under this condition. Hence,

Impedance, $Z = R = \dfrac{V}{I} = \dfrac{230}{10} = \mathbf{23 \, \Omega} \quad \ldots \text{Ans.}$

Further, $X_C = \dfrac{1}{2\pi f C} = \dfrac{1}{2\pi \times 50 \times 300 \times 10^{-6}} = 10.61\ \Omega$

$\therefore \quad X_L = X_C = 10.61\ \Omega$

$\therefore \quad$ Inductance, $L = \dfrac{X_L}{2\pi f} = \dfrac{10.61}{2\pi \times 50}$

$\qquad\qquad\qquad = \mathbf{0.034\ H}$ ... **Ans.**

Example 4.38 : *An R-C series circuit takes 4 A from 230 V, 50 Hz, a.c. supply. If power consumed by the circuit is 640 W, calculate the values of the resistance and capacitance.*
(December 2008/6 Marks)

Solution : Given : $I = 4$ A, $V = 230$ volts, $f = 50$ Hz, $P = 640$ W.
Fig. 4.29 shows the necessary circuit diagram.

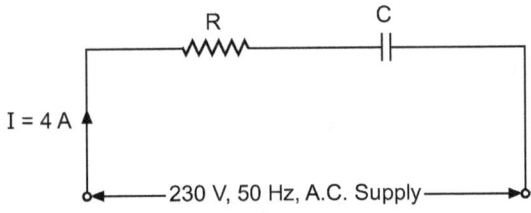

Fig. 4.29

Impedance of the circuit, $\quad Z = \dfrac{V}{I} = \dfrac{230}{4} = 57.5\ \Omega$

$\qquad\qquad$ Power, $P = I^2 R$

$\therefore \qquad\qquad 640 = 4^2 \times R$

$\therefore \qquad$ Resistance, $R = \dfrac{640}{16} = \mathbf{40\ \Omega}$ ... **Ans.**

Capacitive reactance, $X_C = \sqrt{Z^2 - R^2} = \sqrt{(57.5)^2 - 40^2} = 41.31\ \Omega$

$\therefore \qquad$ Capacitance, $C = \dfrac{1}{2\pi f \cdot X_C} = \dfrac{1}{2\pi \times 50 \times 41.31}$

$\qquad\qquad\qquad = \mathbf{7.71 \times 10^{-5}\ F}$ or $\mathbf{77.1\ \mu F}$ ... **Ans.**

Example 4.39 : *A resistance of 50 Ω, inductance of 200 mH and capacitance of 100 μF are connected in series across 230 V, 60 Hz supply. Calculate the current taken by the circuit and power consumed by the circuit.*
(May 2009/6 Marks)

Solution : Given : $R = 50\ \Omega$, $L = 200$ mH, $C = 100\ \mu F$, $V = 230$ volts, $f = 60$ Hz.

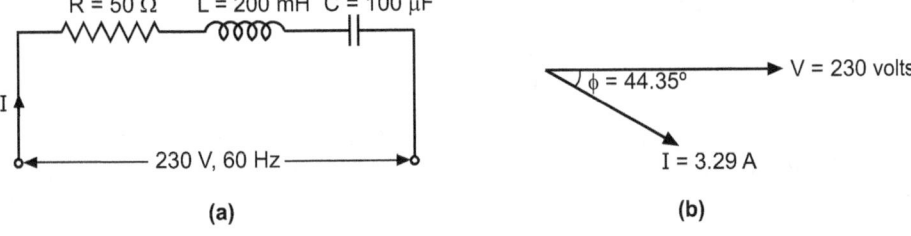

Fig. 4.30

$$R = 50 \, \Omega$$
$$X_L = 2\pi f L = 2\pi \times 60 \times (200 \times 10^{-3}) = 75.4 \, \Omega$$
$$X_C = \frac{1}{2\pi f C} = \frac{1}{2\pi \times 60 \times (100 \times 10^{-6})} = 26.53 \, \Omega$$

∴ Impedance, $\bar{Z} = R + j(X_L - X_C) = 50 + j(75.4 - 26.53)$
$$= 50 + j48.87 = 69.92 \angle 44.35° \, \Omega$$

∴ Current taken by the circuit,
$$\bar{I} = \frac{\bar{V}}{\bar{Z}} = \frac{230 \angle 0°}{69.92 \angle 44.35°} = 3.29 \angle -44.35° \, A \quad \ldots \text{Ans.}$$

Power factor of the circuit,
$$\cos \phi = \cos 44.35° = 0.72 \text{ lagging}$$

∴ Power consumed by the circuit,
$$P = VI \cos \phi = 230 \times 3.29 \times 0.72$$
$$= 544.82 \, W \quad \ldots \text{Ans.}$$

Example 4.40 : *A resistance of 50 Ω is connected in series with the inductance of 100 mH and capacitance. When this R-L-C series circuit is connected across 230 V, 50 Hz supply, it is found that the power factor is unity. Calculate the value of the capacitance and current taken by the circuit.* **(December 2009/6 Marks)**

Solution : Given : $R = 50 \, \Omega$, $L = 100$ mH, $V = 230$ volts, $f = 50$ Hz,
$$X_L = 2\pi f L = 2\pi \times 50 \times 100 \times 10^{-3} = 31.42 \, \Omega$$

Since the power factor of the R-L-C series circuit is unity,

Total reactance of the circuit,
$$X = X_L - X_C = 0$$
∴ $$X_C = X_L = 31.42 \, \Omega$$

∴ Capacitance, $C = \dfrac{1}{2\pi f \cdot X_C} = \dfrac{1}{2\pi \times 50 \times 31.42}$ F
$$= 101.31 \, \mu F \quad \ldots \text{Ans.}$$

Further, Impedance, $Z = \sqrt{R^2 + (X_L - X_C)^2} = R \quad (\because X_L = X_C)$

∴ Current taken by the circuit,
$$I = \frac{V}{Z} = \frac{V}{R} = \frac{230}{50} = 4.6 \, A \quad \ldots \text{Ans.}$$

Example 4.41 : *A resistance, an inductance of 50 mH and a capacitance of 100 μF are connected in series across 220 V, 50 Hz, a.c. supply. The circuit takes 10 A from the supply. Calculate the resistance in the circuit.* **(May 2010/6 Marks)**

Solution : Given : $L = 50$ mH, $C = 100 \, \mu F$, $V = 220$ volts, $I = 10$ A.

Fig. 4.31 shows the circuit diagram.

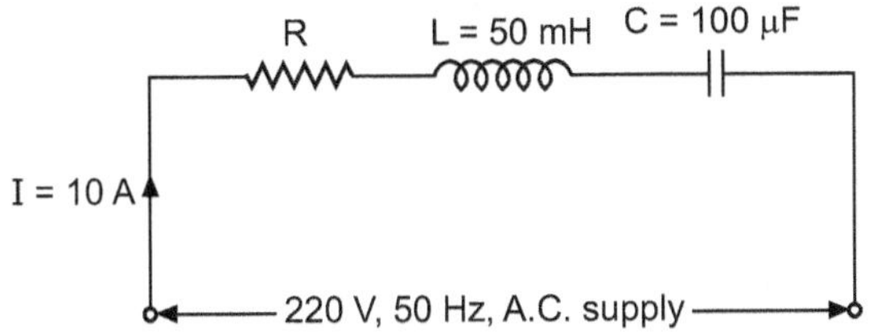

Fig. 4.31

$$X_L = 2\pi fL = 2\pi \times 50 \times 50 \times 10^{-3} = 15.71 \ \Omega$$

$$X_C = \frac{1}{2\pi fC} = \frac{1}{2\pi \times 50 \times 100 \times 10^{-6}} = 31.83 \ \Omega$$

$$Z = \frac{V}{I} = \frac{220}{10} = 22 \ \Omega$$

Now,
$$Z = \sqrt{R^2 + (X_L - X_C)^2}$$

∴ $\quad 22 = \sqrt{R^2 + (15.71 - 31.83)^2}$

∴ Resistance in the circuit, **R = 14.97 Ω** ... Ans.

Example 4.42 : *A resistance and inductance are connected in series. The series circuit consumes 500 W power from 230 V, 50 Hz supply. If the current taken from the supply is 5 A, calculate the resistance and inductance.* **(December 2010/6 Marks)**

Solution : Given : P = 500 W, V = 230 volts, f = 50 Hz, I = 5 A

$$P = VI \cos \phi$$

∴ $\quad 500 = 230 \times 5 \times \cos \phi$

∴ Power factor of the circuit,
$$\cos \phi = 0.435 \text{ lagging}$$

∴ Power factor angle, $\phi = 64.23°$

Now, Impedance of the coil, $\bar{Z} = \dfrac{\bar{V}}{\bar{I}} = \dfrac{230 \angle 0°}{5 \angle -64.23°}$

$$= 46 \angle 64.23° = (20 + j\, 41.43) \ \Omega$$

∴ Resistance, **R = 20 Ω** ... Ans.

and Inductive reactance, $X_L = 41.43 \ \Omega$

∴ Inductance, $L = \dfrac{X_L}{2\pi f} = \dfrac{41.43}{2\pi \times 50}$

$$= \mathbf{0.13 \ H} \qquad \text{... Ans.}$$

Example 4.43 : *An inductive coil takes 10 A and dissipates 1000 W when connected to a supply at 250 V, 25 Hz. Calculate impedance, reactance, inductance and power factor.*

(May 2012/8 Marks)

Solution : Given : P = 1000 W, I = 10 A, V = 250 volts, f = 25 Hz.

Now, $\quad\quad\quad\quad P = VI \cos\phi$

$\therefore \quad\quad\quad\quad 1000 = 250 \times 10 \times \cos\phi$

$\therefore$ Power factor of the coil,

$$\cos\phi = \mathbf{0.4 \text{ lagging}} \quad\quad\quad\quad \text{... Ans.}$$

and $\quad$ Power factor angle $\phi = 66.42°$

Further, Impedance of the coil, $\bar{Z} = \dfrac{\bar{V}}{\bar{I}} = \dfrac{250 \angle 0°}{10 \angle -66.42°} = \mathbf{25 \angle 66.42° \, \Omega} \quad\quad \text{... Ans.}$

But $\quad\quad\quad\quad \bar{Z} = R + jX_L = 25 \angle 66.42° = (10 + j\, 22.91) \, \Omega$

$\therefore$ Inductive reactance of the coil,

$$X_L = \mathbf{22.91 \, \Omega} \quad\quad\quad\quad \text{... Ans.}$$

$\therefore$ Inductance of the coil, $L = \dfrac{X_L}{2\pi f} = \dfrac{22.91}{2\pi \times 25} = \mathbf{0.15 \, H} \quad\quad \text{... Ans.}$

4.13 EXERCISES

4.13.1 Review Questions

1. What is the impedance of an a.c. circuit ? What is its unit ? State the factors on which it depends.
2. What is an impedance triangle ? What information does it convey ?
3. Define power factor of an a.c. circuit. State its value for purely resistive, purely inductive and purely capacitive circuits.
4. State any two practical applications of a choking coil.
5. What is meant by the active and reactive components of an alternating current ?
6. As applied to a.c. circuits, explain the terms :
   (i) Apparent power, $\quad\quad\quad$ (ii) True power, and
   (iii) Reactive power.
   State their units.
7. A circuit is connected to an a.c. voltage of $V_m \sin \omega t$ volts and carries a current of $I_m \sin(\omega t - \phi)$ amperes. Prove that the average power consumed by the circuit under this condition is given by $P = VI \cos\phi$ watts.
8. Explain three-voltmeter method of measuring power in an inductive circuit. State the limitations of this method.
9. What is meant by resonance in a series R-L-C circuit connected across a sinusoidal a.c. supply ? Deduce the necessary condition for this to occur.
10. Derive the expression for resonant frequency in series resonance.
11. Define the bandwidth of a series resonant circuit and explain its Q-factor.
12. Define the Q-factor for the series resonant circuit and express it in terms of the circuit parameters.

4.13.2 Classified Theory Questions from University Papers

1. Explain the term 'Power Factor' in an a.c. circuit.
   (Answer : Section 4.3) **(May 2012/4 Marks)**
2. Sketch the waveforms of voltage, current and power if $v = V_m \sin \omega t$ is applied across an R-C series circuit and state the expressions for current and power.
   (Answer : Section 4.4) **(December 2011/8 Marks)**
3. Draw and explain the phasor diagram of an R-L-C series circuit when
   (i) $X_L > X_C$, (ii) $X_L < X_C$, (iii) $X_L = X_C$.
   (Answer : Section 4.5) **(December 2011/8 Marks)**
4. With a neat circuit diagram and phasor diagram, discuss R-L-C series circuit.
   (Answer : Section 4.5) **(May 2011/8 Marks)**

4.13.3 Examples for Practice

1. The expressions of the voltage and the current of a circuit are given by :
$$e = 125 \sin (377 t) \text{ volts}$$
$$i = 12 \sin \left(377 t - \frac{\pi}{6}\right) \text{ amperes.}$$

   Find the resistance, inductance or capacitance of the series circuit. Calculate also the power consumed by the circuit. $(9.02 \ \Omega, 0.0138 \ H, 649.89 \ W)$

2. In a circuit, the equations for instantaneous voltage and current are given by
$$v = 141.4 \sin \left(\omega t - \frac{2\pi}{3}\right) \text{ volts}$$
$$i = 7.07 \sin \left(\omega t - \frac{\pi}{2}\right) \text{ amperes}$$

   where $\omega = 314$ radians/s.
   (i) Sketch a neat phasor diagram for the circuit.
   (ii) Use polar notation to calculate impedance with phase angle.
   (iii) Calculate average power.
   (iv) Calculate the instantaneous power at the instant t = 0.
   $(20 \angle -30° \ \Omega, 433 \ W, 866 \ W)$

3. (a) A 100 V (r.m.s.), 80 Hz supply when applied to a certain impedance delivers 2 A (r.m.s.) current at 0.5 lagging power factor. Write the equation of a current waveform with voltage as a reference. State any assumption made.
   (b) Find the values of resistance and reactance parts of the impedance in the above case. State the nature of reactance and find the value of that element. How much power is delivered by the source ?

   $(i = 2.828 \sin \left(502.66 t - \frac{\pi}{3}\right)$ amperes, 25 Ω, 43.3 Ω, 0.086 H, 100 W$)$

4. A 60 Hz sinusoidal voltage, v = 141 sin ωt is applied to a series R-L circuit. The values of the resistance and the inductance are 3 Ω and 0.0106 H respectively.
   (i) Compute the r.m.s. value of the current in the circuit and its phase angle with respect to the voltage.
   (ii) Write the expression for the instantaneous current in the circuit.
   (iii) Compute the r.m.s. value and phase of the voltages appearing across the resistance and the inductance.
   (iv) Find the average power dissipated by the circuit.
   (v) Calculate the power factor of the circuit.

   (20 ∠ – 53.13° A, i = 28.28 sin (ωt – 0.927) amperes,
   60 ∠ – 53.13° V, 80 ∠ 36.87° V, 1200 W, 0.6 lagging)

5. A non-inductive load takes a current of 15 A at 125 V. An inductor is then connected in series in order that the same current shall be supplied from 240 V, 50 Hz mains. Ignore the resistance of the inductor and calculate :
   (i) Inductance of the inductor,
   (ii) Impedance of the circuit, and
   (iii) Phase difference between current and applied voltage.   (0.0435 H, 16 Ω, 58.63°)

6. An air-cored coil draws a current of 10 A when connected across 200 V, 50 Hz supply. If the coil resistance is 5 Ω, calculate its inductance, assuming that the coil is equivalent to a series impedance.

   What is the real power, apparent power and reactive power ? What are their magnitudes in the above example ?   (0.062 H, 500 W, 2000 VA, 1936.5 VAr)

7. A coil takes a current of 1.5 A when connected to 6 V, d.c. supply. To obtain the same current with a 50 Hz, a.c. supply, the voltage required was 7.5 V. Calculate :
   (i) Resistance of the coil,
   (ii) Inductance of the coil,
   (iii) Power factor of the coil, and
   (iv) Current drawn by the coil when connected to 10 V, 60 Hz, a.c. supply.

   (4 Ω, 9.549 × 10⁻³ H, 0.8 lagging, 1.859 A)

8. A resistor R of 100 Ω is connected in series with a choke coil of impedance (50 + j 80) Ω. The circuit is connected to a single-phase, 230 V, 50 Hz supply. Calculate :
   (i) Current drawn by the circuit,
   (ii) Voltage across the choke coil and across the resistor, and
   (iii) Circuit power factor.

   (1.3529 ∠ – 28.07° A, 127.63 ∠ 29.92° V, 135.29 ∠ – 28.07° V, 0.8824 lagging)

9. A 100 Ω resistance is connected in series with a choke coil. When a 400 V, 50 Hz, single-phase alternating voltage is applied to this combination, the voltages across the resistance and the choke coil are 200 V and 300 V respectively. Find the power consumed by the choke coil. Sketch a neat phasor diagram indicating the current and all the voltages. (150 W)

10. A series combination of a resistance of 100 Ω and a capacitance of 50 μF is connected to a 230 V, 50 Hz supply. Determine :
    (i) Current in the circuit,
    (ii) Voltage across the resistance,
    (iii) Voltage across the capacitance,
    (iv) Power factor of the circuit, and
    (v) Power consumed.
    Draw a neat phasor diagram.   (1.94 A, 194 V, 123.5 V, 0.8436 leading, 376.41 W)

11. The potential difference measured across a coil is 4.5 V, when it carries a direct current of 9 A. The same coil when carries an alternating current of 9 A at 25 Hz, the potential difference is 24 V. Find the current, the power and the power factor when it is supplied by 50 V, 50 Hz supply.
    (9.49 A, 45 W, 0.095 lagging)

12. A coil of resistance 10 Ω and inductance 0.1 H is connected in series with a condenser of capacitance 150 μF across a 200 V, 50 Hz supply. Calculate :
    (i) Inductive reactance,   (ii) Capacitive reactance,
    (iii) Impedance,   (iv) Current, and
    (v) Power factor of the circuit.
    Find also the voltage across the coil and the condenser respectively.
    (31.4 Ω, 21.2 Ω, 14.28 Ω, 14 A, 0.7 lagging, 461.3 V, 296.8 V)

13. A circuit has a resistor of 10 Ω connected in series with a capacitor of 100 μF. If a variable frequency supply of 100 V is connected across the circuit, calculate the voltage drop across the resistor and capacitor for supply frequency of (i) 50 Hz and (ii) 100 Hz. Calculate the circuit power factors for both the conditions. What will be the new values of the power factors if a pure inductance of 50 mH is connected in series with the circuit to form R-L-C circuit ?
    (R-C circuit at 50 Hz : V_R = 29.98 V, V_C = 95.43 V, cos φ = 0.3 leading
    R-C circuit at 100 Hz : V_R = 53.2 V, V_C = 84.67 V, cos φ = 0.53 leading
    R-L-C circuit at 50 Hz : cos φ = 0.53 leading
    R-L-C circuit at 100 Hz : cos φ = 0.54 lagging)

14. A pure resistance R, choke coil and a pure capacitor of 15.91 μF are connected in series across a supply of V volts and carry a current of 0.25 A. Voltage across the choke is 40 V and voltage across the capacitor is of 50 V. Voltage across the resistance is 20 V. Voltage across the combination of R and choke coil is 45 V. Calculate :
    (i) Supply voltage,
    (ii) Frequency, and
    (iii) Power loss in the choke coil.   (22.92 V, 50.02 Hz, 0.156 W)

15. When a resistor and an inductor in series are connected to a 240 V supply, a current of 3 A flows lagging 37° behind the supply voltage, while the voltage across the inductor is 171 V. Find the resistance of the resistor and the resistance and reactance of the inductor.
    (33.37 Ω, 30.52 Ω and 48.144 Ω)

16. A resistor and a capacitor are connected in series across a 150 V, a.c. supply. When the frequency is 40 Hz, the current is 5 A and when the frequency is 50 Hz, the current is 6 A. Find the resistance and capacitance of the resistor and capacitor respectively.

(11.67 Ω, 143.96 μF)

17. A coil consumes power of 250 W when connected to a 100 V, 50 Hz, single-phase supply. The current taken by the coil is 5 A. A capacitive reactance is then connected in series which results into a change in power factor to 0.866 lagging. Find the value of the capacitive reactance added in the circuit. Also find the current in the circuit.

(11.54 Ω, 8.66 A)

18. Two coils are connected in series. With 2 A d.c. through the circuit, the potential differences across the coils are 20 V and 30 V respectively. With 2 A a.c. at 40 Hz, the potential differences across the coils are 140 V and 100 V respectively. If the two coils in series are connected to a 230 V, 50 Hz supply, calculate :
    (i) Current,
    (ii) Power, and
    (iii) Power factor. (1.551 A, 60.1 W, 0.169 lagging)

19. A non-inductive resistor takes 10 A at 100 V. Calculate the inductance of a choking coil to be connected in series in order that the same current be applied from 220 V, 50 Hz mains. What is the phase angle between 220 V supply and the current ? Neglect the resistance of the choking coil. (0.0624 H, 63°)

20. A series circuit consists of two pure elements, resistance of 10 Ω and inductance of 20 mH. Current flowing in the circuit is $i = 2 \sin 500\, t$. Calculate the voltage applied to the circuit.

(20 V)

21. A current of 12 A flows through a non-inductive resistance in series with a choking coil when supplied at 100 V, 50 Hz. If the voltage across the resistance is 48 V and across the coil 55 V, calculate :
    (i) Impedance, reactance and resistance of the coil,
    (ii) Power absorbed by the coil, and
    (iii) Total power supplied.
    Draw the phasor diagram. (4.583 Ω, 2.137 Ω, 4.055 Ω, 583.88 W, 1159.88 W)

22. A coil having a resistance of 5 Ω and an inductance of 0.1 H is connected in series with a 50 μF capacitor. A variable frequency alternating voltage of 200 V is applied to the circuit. At what value of the frequency will the current be maximum ? Calculate this current and the voltages across the coil and capacitor for this frequency.

(71.2 Hz, 40 A, 1799.2 V, 1788 V)

23. A resistor and a capacitor are in series with a variable inductor. When the circuit is connected to a 230 V, 50 Hz supply, the maximum current obtainable by varying the inductance is 0.314 A. The voltage across the capacitor is then 300 V. Find the circuit constants. (3.043 H, 3.33 μF, 732.48 Ω)

❑❑❑

CHAPTER 5

SINGLE-PHASE A.C. PARALLEL CIRCUITS

5.1 PARALLEL A.C. CIRCUITS

A parallel circuit consists of two or more series circuits connected in parallel across the same supply as illustrated in Fig. 5.1. All these series circuits are called the branches of the parallel circuits. Depending upon the way in which R, L and C are connected, we have a variety of a.c. parallel circuits.

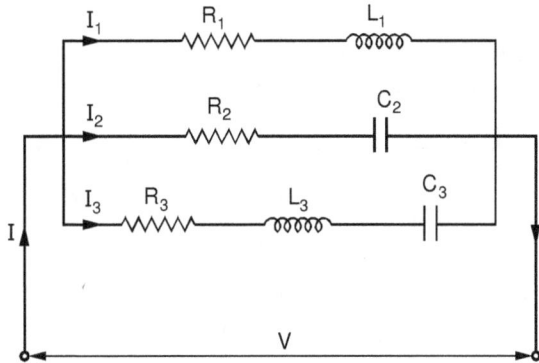

Fig. 5.1 : A parallel circuit

In this chapter, we are going to study the analysis of such circuits.

5.2 SOLUTION OF PARALLEL CIRCUITS

Parallel a.c. circuits can be solved by the following two basic methods :

(i) Phasor method, (ii) Admittance method.

Let us study these methods in the following sections.

5.3 PHASOR METHOD AND ITS APPLICATION TO PARALLEL CIRCUITS

In this case, each branch of the circuit is analysed separately as a series circuit using phasor diagram in the same manner in which we have analysed series circuits in the previous articles and then the effects of separate branches are combined, e.g. if the total current drawn by a particular parallel circuit is to be calculated, following procedure is adopted :

(i) The currents in the individual branches and their phase angles are determined using the following expressions separately for each branch :

$$I = \frac{V}{Z} \quad \text{and} \quad \tan \phi = \frac{X}{R}$$

(5.1)

(ii) Then, the phasor diagram is drawn, taking the voltage as a reference phasor. In this case, voltage is chosen as a reference quantity because it is common to all the branches of the circuit.

(iii) Finally, using this phasor diagram, the total current is calculated by a phasor addition of all branch currents.

The procedure is best illustrated by a numerical example.

Example 5.1 : *A circuit consists of three branches. Branch A has a resistance of 10 Ω. Branch B has a resistance of 6 Ω in series with an inductive reactance of 8 Ω and branch C has a resistance of 4 Ω in series with a capacitive reactance of 9 Ω. The whole circuit is connected across a 230 V, 50 Hz supply. Find :*

(i) *Current in each branch,*
(ii) *Power factor of each branch,*
(iii) *Total current taken and power factor of the whole circuit,*
(iv) *Total power consumed by the circuit, and*
(v) *Equivalent impedance of the circuit.*

Solution : Fig. 5.2 (a) shows the necessary circuit diagram.

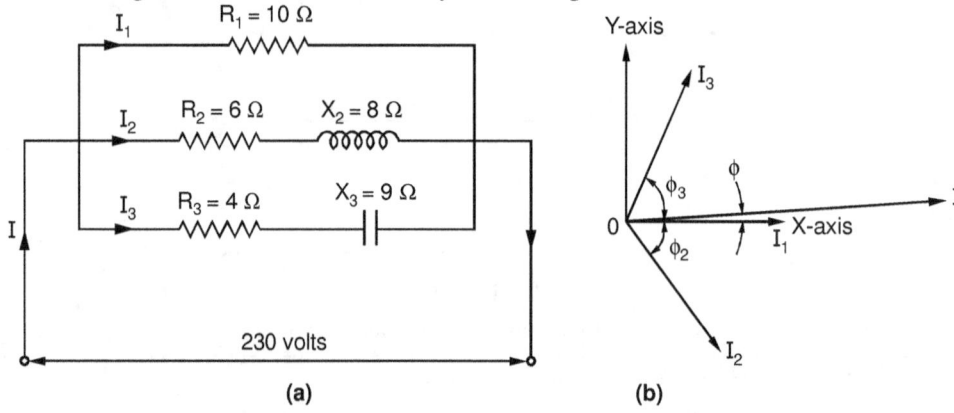

Fig. 5.2 : (a) Circuit diagram for Example 5.1, (b) Phasor diagram

Branch A :

$$\text{Impedance, } Z_1 = R_1 = 10 \ \Omega$$

∴ $$\text{Current, } I_1 = \frac{V}{Z_1} = \frac{230}{10} = 23 \text{ A} \quad \text{... Ans.}$$

$$\cos \phi_1 = \frac{R_1}{Z_1} = \frac{10}{10} = 1 \quad \text{... Ans.}$$

∴ $$\phi_1 = 0°$$

Branch B :

$$\text{Impedance, } Z = \sqrt{R_2^2 + X_2^2} = \sqrt{6^2 + 8^2} = 10 \ \Omega$$

∴ $$\text{Current, } I_2 = \frac{V}{Z_2} = \frac{230}{10} = 23 \text{ A} \quad \text{... Ans.}$$

$$\cos \phi = \frac{R_2}{Z_2} = \frac{6}{10} = 0.6 \text{ (lagging)} \quad \text{... Ans.}$$

∴ $$\phi_2 = 53.13°$$

Branch C : Impedance, $Z_3 = \sqrt{R_3^2 + X_3^2} = \sqrt{4^2 + 9^2} = 9.849 \, \Omega$

∴ Current, $I_3 = \dfrac{V}{Z_3} = \dfrac{230}{9.849} = $ **23.35 A** ... Ans.

$\cos \phi = \dfrac{R_3}{Z_3} = \dfrac{4}{9.849} = $ **0.406 (leading)** ... Ans.

∴ $\phi_3 = 66.04°$

Fig. 5.2 (b) shows the phasor diagram for different branch currents. The total current may now be found either graphically or by calculations. Resolving each current horizontally and vertically, we have

Sum of the active components $= I_1 + I_2 \cos \phi_2 + I_3 \cos \phi_3$
$= 23 + 23 \times 0.6 + 23.35 \times 0.406 = 46.28$

Sum of the reactive components $= 0 - I_2 \sin \phi_2 + I_3 \sin \phi_3$
$= 0 - 23 \times 0.8 + 23.35 \times 0.914 = 2.942$

∴ Total current, $I = \sqrt{(46.28)^2 + (2.942)^2} = $ **46.37 A** ... Ans.

Circuit power factor, $\cos \phi = \dfrac{46.28}{46.37} = $ **0.998 (leading)** ... Ans.

∴ $\phi = 3.66°$

Total power consumed, $P = V I \cos \phi = 230 \times 46.37 \times 0.998 \text{ W} = $ **10.64 kW** ... Ans.

Equivalent impedance of the circuit,

$Z = \dfrac{V}{I} = \dfrac{230}{46.37} = $ **4.96 Ω** ... Ans.

Example 5.2 : *An inductive circuit is connected in parallel with a pure resistance of 21 Ω. The parallel combination is connected across 50 Hz, a.c. supply. If the current in inductive circuit is 7 A and current in resistive branch is 12 A and total current drawn from the supply is 16 A, calculate :*
(i) Supply voltage,
(ii) Resistance of the inductive circuit,
(iii) Reactance of the inductive circuit,
(iv) Total power consumed by the circuit.

Solution : Fig. 5.3 (a) shows the circuit diagram for this case.

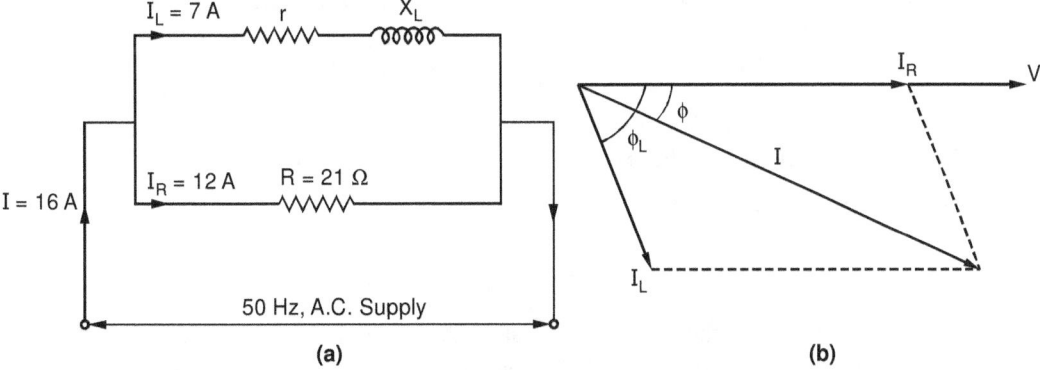

Fig. 5.3 : (a) Circuit diagram for Example 5.2, (b) Phasor diagram

Supply voltage, $V = I_R \cdot R = 12 \times 21 = \mathbf{252\ V}$ ... **Ans.**

Impedance of the inductive circuit,

$$Z_L = \frac{V}{I_L} = \frac{252}{7} = \mathbf{36\ \Omega} \quad \text{... \textbf{Ans.}}$$

From phasor diagram of Fig. 5.3 (b), using the law of parallelogram of phasors, we have

$$I^2 = I_L^2 + I_R^2 + 2\,I_L\,I_R \cos \phi_L$$

$$\therefore \quad \cos \phi_L = \frac{I^2 - I_L^2 - I_R^2}{2 I_L\, I_R} = \frac{16^2 - 7^2 - 12^2}{2 \times 7 \times 12} = 0.375 \text{ (lagging)}$$

Resistance of the inductive circuit,

$$r = Z_L \cos \phi_L = 36 \times 0.375 = \mathbf{13.5\ \Omega} \quad \text{... \textbf{Ans.}}$$

Reactance of the inductive circuit,

$$X_L = Z_L \sin \phi_L = 36 \times 0.927 = \mathbf{33.37\ \Omega} \quad \text{... \textbf{Ans.}}$$

Total power, $P = I_R^2 \cdot R + I_L^2 \cdot r = 12^2 \times 21 + 7^2 \times 13.5$

$= \mathbf{3685.5\ W}$ ... **Ans.**

5.4 ADMITTANCE AND ALLIED CONCEPTS

The concept of admittance simplifies the analysis of parallel a.c. circuits to a large extent. The *reciprocal of impedance* $\left(\frac{1}{Z}\right)$ *is known as admittance* and its symbol is Y. The unit in which it is measured is *siemens* (abbreviation, S) *which is the admittance of the circuit whose impedance is one ohm.*

Now, consider the case of a simple circuit containing a resistance R and an inductive reactance X (Fig. 5.4 a). Let the current drawn by a circuit be I amperes at the phase angle of ϕ when connected across the supply of V volts. Then,

$$I = \frac{V}{Z} = V \cdot Y$$

Further, the active component of the current in the circuit is given by,

$$I \cos \phi = \frac{V}{Z} \times \frac{R}{Z} = V \cdot \frac{R}{Z^2} = V \cdot G \quad \text{... (5.1)}$$

where, the quantity G which is the ratio of resistance to the square of the impedance is known as the *conductance* of the circuit (in the special case when $X = 0$, then $G = 1 / R$).

Also, the reactive component of the current in the circuit is given by,

$$I \sin \phi = \frac{V}{Z} \times \frac{X}{Z} = V \cdot \frac{X}{Z^2} = V \cdot B \quad \text{... (5.2)}$$

The quantity B which is the ratio of reactance to the square of impedance is known as *susceptance* of the circuit. The unit of the conductance as well as susceptance is again the siemens. Fig. 5.4 (b) shows the phasor diagram taking the voltage as a reference quantity.

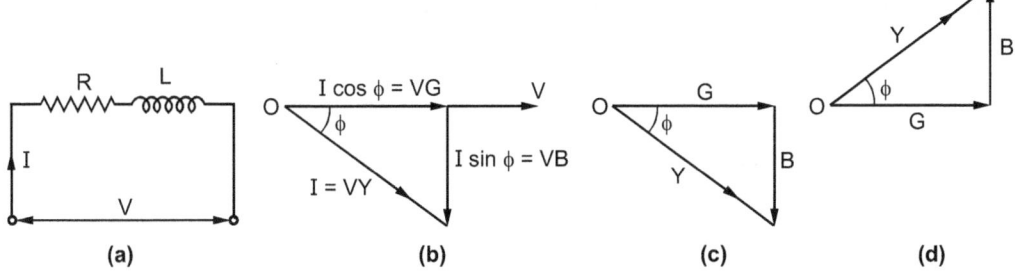

Fig. 5.4 : Admittance, conductance, susceptance

By dividing each side of the current triangle by V, a similar triangle as shown in Fig. 5.4 (c) can be obtained. As sides of this triangle represent the conductance, susceptance and admittance of the circuit, it is known as *admittance triangle*. If the circuit has resistance and capacitive reactance in series, then the current leads the voltage and in that case, the admittance triangle is as shown in Fig. 5.4 (d). From the admittance triangle, we have the following relationships :

$$G = Y \cos \phi, \quad B = Y \sin \phi, \quad Y = \sqrt{G^2 + B^2} \quad \ldots (5.3)$$

and
$$\tan \phi = \frac{B}{G} \quad \ldots (5.4)$$

It should be remembered that the capacitive susceptance is always considered as positive and inductive susceptance as negative. This will obviously be clear from the corresponding admittance triangles.

5.5 APPLICATION OF ADMITTANCE METHOD TO PARALLEL CIRCUITS

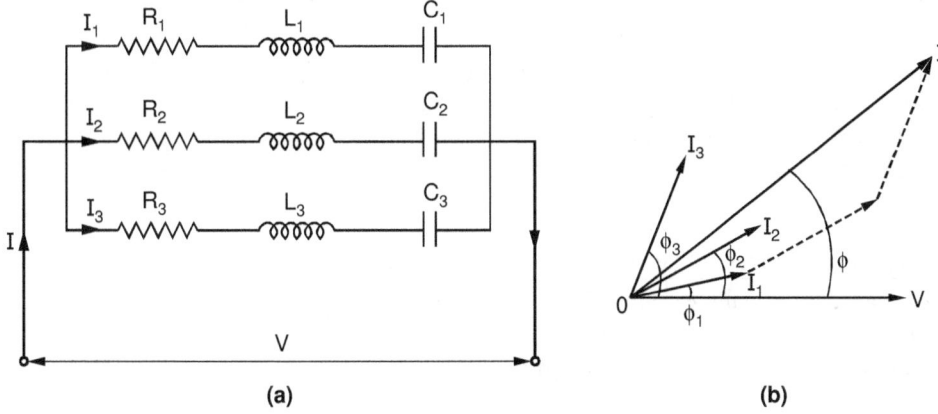

Fig. 5.5 : (a) Circuit containing impedances in parallel, (b) Phasor diagram

Consider the general parallel circuit consisting of three branches shown in Fig. 5.5 (a).

Let V be the applied voltage, I the total circuit current and let I_1, I_2 and I_3 be the branch currents. These branch currents will differ in phase with respect to the applied voltage. Let the phase difference between V and the branch currents I_1, I_2 and I_3 be ϕ_1, ϕ_2 and ϕ_3 respectively, the values of which are obtained from reactance and resistance of each branch. e.g.

$$\tan \phi_1 = \frac{\left(\omega L_1 - \dfrac{1}{\omega C_1}\right)}{R_1}$$

Fig. 5.5 (b) shows the phasor diagram for the given circuit in which V is considered as a reference quantity. The total current is the phasor addition of all the branch currents. Hence, from the phasor diagram,

$$I^2 = (I_1 \cos \phi_1 + I_2 \cos \phi_2 + I_3 \cos \phi_3)^2 + (I_1 \sin \phi_1 + I_2 \sin \phi_2 + I_3 \sin \phi_3)^2$$

$$= (VG_1 + VG_2 + VG_3)^2 + (VB_1 + VB_2 + VB_3)^2$$

where $\quad G_1 = \dfrac{R_1}{Z_1^2}, \quad G_2 = \dfrac{R_2}{Z_2^2}, \quad G_3 = \dfrac{R_3}{Z_3^2}$

$\quad B_1 = \dfrac{X_1}{Z_1^2}, \quad B_2 = \dfrac{X_2}{Z_2^2}, \quad B_3 = \dfrac{X_3}{Z_3^2}$

Here, the branch reactances X_1, X_2 and X_3 are obviously,

$$X_1 = \omega L_1 - \dfrac{1}{\omega C_1}, \quad X_2 = \omega L_2 - \dfrac{1}{\omega C_2} \quad \text{and} \quad X_3 = \omega L_3 - \dfrac{1}{\omega C_3}$$

Hence, the total admittance, of the whole circuit is given by

$$Y = \dfrac{I}{V} = \sqrt{(G_1 + G_2 + G_3)^2 + (B_1 + B_2 + B_3)^2}$$

$$= \sqrt{G^2 + B^2} \quad \ldots (5.5)$$

and $\quad \tan \phi = \dfrac{(B_1 + B_2 + B_3)}{(G_1 + G_2 + G_3)} = \dfrac{B}{G} \quad \ldots (5.6)$

where $\quad G = G_1 + G_2 + G_3 \quad$ and $\quad B = B_1 + B_2 + B_3$

Thus, total conductance of a parallel circuit can be found by merely adding the branch conductances. Similarly, its total susceptance can be found by algebraically adding the individual susceptances of different branches. If Y_1, Y_2 and Y_3 are admittances of the different branches, then, Equation (5.5) clearly shows that the total admittance of the parallel circuit is given by their phasor addition i.e.

$$\bar{Y} = \bar{Y}_1 + \bar{Y}_2 + \bar{Y}_3 \quad \ldots (5.7)$$

It should be remembered that similar to impedance, admittance is always treated as a phasor.

Example 5.3 : *Solve the Example 5.1 by admittance method.*
Solution : Refer to Fig. 5.2 (a) for circuit diagram.
Branch A : $\quad R_1 = 10 \, \Omega, \quad X_1 = 0 \, \Omega, \quad Z_1 = 10 \, \Omega$

$\therefore \quad$ Conductance, $G_1 = \dfrac{R_1}{Z_1^2} = \dfrac{10}{10^2} = 0.1 \text{ S}$

and $\quad$ Susceptance, $B_1 = \dfrac{X_1}{Z_1^2} = 0$

Hence, $\quad Y_1 = \sqrt{G_1^2 + B_1^2} = \sqrt{(0.1)^2 + (0)^2} = 0.1 \text{ S}$

$\quad I_1 = V \cdot Y_1 = 230 \times 0.1 = \textbf{23 A} \quad \ldots$ **Ans.**

and $\quad \cos \phi_1 = \dfrac{G_1}{Y_1} = \dfrac{0.1}{0.1} = \textbf{1} \quad \ldots$ **Ans.**

Branch B : $\quad R_2 = 6\ \Omega,\quad X_2 = 8\ \Omega,\quad Z_2 = 10\ \Omega$

∴ Conductance, $G_2 = \dfrac{R_2}{Z_2^2} = \dfrac{6}{10^2} = 0.06\ S$

and Susceptance, $B_2 = \dfrac{-X_2}{Z_2^2} = \dfrac{-8}{10^2} = -0.08\ S$

Hence, $Y_2 = \sqrt{G_2^2 + B_2^2} = \sqrt{(0.06)^2 + (0.08)^2} = 0.1\ S$

$I_2 = V \cdot Y_2 = 230 \times 0.1 = \mathbf{23\ A}$ ... Ans.

and $\cos\phi_2 = \dfrac{G_2}{Y_2} = \dfrac{0.06}{0.1} = \mathbf{0.6\ (lagging)}$ ... Ans.

Branch C : $\quad R_3 = 4\ \Omega,\quad X_3 = 9\ \Omega,\quad Z_3 = 9.849\ \Omega$

∴ Conductance, $G_3 = \dfrac{R_3}{Z_3^2} = \dfrac{4}{9.849^2} = 0.041\ S$

and Susceptance, $B_3 = \dfrac{X_3}{Z_3^2} = \dfrac{9}{9.849^2} = 0.093\ S$

Hence, $Y_3 = \sqrt{G_3^2 + B_3^2} = \sqrt{(0.041)^2 + (0.093)^2} = 0.1016\ S$

$I_3 = V \cdot Y_3 = 230 \times 0.1016 = \mathbf{23.37\ A}$ ... Ans.

and $\cos\phi_3 = \dfrac{G_3}{Y_3} = \dfrac{0.041}{0.1016} = \mathbf{0.404\ (leading)}$ ... Ans.

Total Circuit :

Total conductance, $G = G_1 + G_2 + G_3 = 0.1 + 0.06 + 0.041 = 0.201\ S$

Total susceptance, $B = B_1 + B_2 + B_3 = 0 - 0.08 + 0.093 = 0.013\ S$

∴ Total admittance, $Y = \sqrt{G^2 + B^2} = \sqrt{(0.201)^2 + (0.013)^2} = 0.2014\ S$

$I = V \cdot Y = 230 \times 0.2014 = \mathbf{46.32\ A}$ ... Ans.

$\cos\phi = \dfrac{G}{Y} = \dfrac{0.201}{0.2014} = \mathbf{0.998\ (leading)}$ ... Ans.

The power factor is leading because total susceptance of the circuit is positive i.e. capacitive in nature. For phasor diagram, refer to Fig. 5.2 (b).

Total power consumed, $P = VI\cos\phi = 230 \times 46.32 \times 0.998\ W$

$= \mathbf{10.63\ kW}$ ... Ans.

Equivalent impedance of the circuit,

$$Z = \frac{V}{I} = \frac{230}{46.32} = 4.966 \, \Omega \qquad \text{... Ans.}$$

Or, alternately, $\quad Z = \dfrac{1}{Y} = \dfrac{1}{0.2014} = 4.965 \, \Omega \qquad \text{... Ans.}$

5.6 MEASUREMENT OF POWER IN AN INDUCTIVE CIRCUIT USING THREE-AMMETER METHOD

In Section 4.3.1, we have seen that the power in an inductive circuit can be measured by using a simple three-voltmeter method. It can also be measured by one more method called *three-ammeter method*. In this method, a non-inductive resistor is placed in parallel with the inductive load in which power is to be measured and the combination is connected across the a.c. voltage source as shown in Fig. 5.6 (a). Following current measurements are then carried out with the help of three ammeters connected in the circuit.

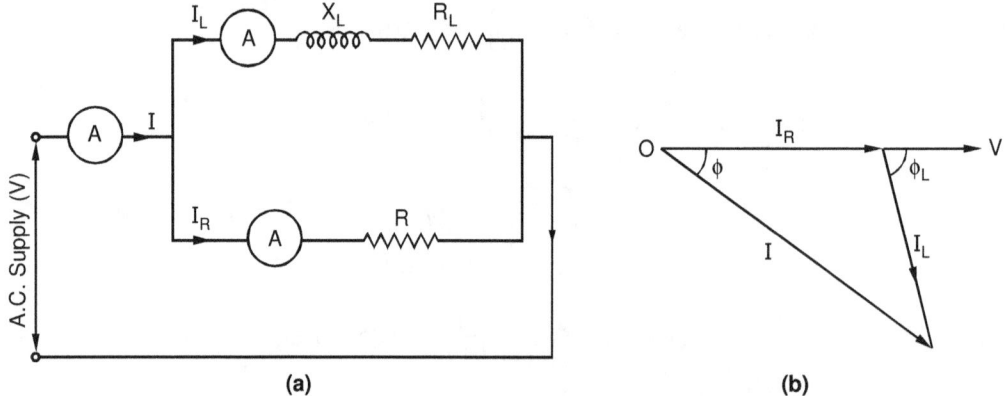

Fig. 5.6 : Three-ammeter method of measuring power

I_L = Current taken by the inductive load (with resistance R_L and inductive reactance X_L), lagging behind the supply voltage V by an angle ϕ_L.

I_R = Current taken by the non-inductive resistor R in phase with the voltage V.

I = Total current taken from the supply

Fig. 5.6 (b) shows the corresponding phasor diagram with voltage V as a reference phasor. From this diagram, we have

$$I^2 = I_L^2 + I_R^2 - 2 \, I_L \cdot I_R \, \cos(180° - \phi_L) \qquad \text{(Cosine rule)}$$

$$= I_L^2 + I_R^2 + 2 \, I_L \cdot I_R \, \cos \phi_L$$

$$\therefore \qquad \cos \phi_L = \frac{I^2 - I_L^2 - I_R^2}{2 I_L \, I_R}$$

Hence, power absorbed by the inductive load,

$$P_L = V \cdot I_L \cos \phi_L = \frac{V \, (I^2 - I_L^2 - I_R^2)}{2 I_R} \text{ watts} \qquad \text{... (5.8)}$$

Or, since $\dfrac{V}{I_R} = R$ (Ohm's law),

$$P_L = \dfrac{R}{2}(I^2 - I_L^2 - I_R^2) \text{ watts} \quad \ldots (5.9)$$

The advantage of this method over three-voltmeter method is that the supply voltage only equal to the rated voltage of the load is required as the load is directly connected across the supply. However, this method also has the following limitations :

(i) The accuracy of the method depends on the choice of a suitable value of R. The choice of R should be such as to give I_L nearly equal to I_R.

(ii) The method is suitable only for low power measurement. This is because the power wasted in R may be as high as or even higher than that to be measured.

Example 5.4 : *The three-ammeter method is used to measure the power consumed by a choking coil. The following measurements are made :*

Current through non-inductive resistor in parallel with the choking coil = 3 A.

Current through the choking coil = 4.5 A

Total current = 7 A

If the supply voltage is 230 V at 50 Hz, find :

(i) *power consumed by the choking coil,*

(ii) *power factor of the coil,*

(iii) *inductance of the choking coil.*

Solution : Figs. 5.6 (a) and (b) show the circuit diagram and the phasor diagram respectively.

Power consumed by the choking coil,

$$P_L = \dfrac{V(I^2 - I_L^2 - I_R^2)}{2I_R} \text{ watts}$$

Here V = 230 V, I = 7 A, I_L = 4.5 A and I_R = 3 A

$\therefore \quad P_L = \dfrac{230\,(7^2 - 4.5^2 - 3^2)}{2 \times 3} = \mathbf{757.1\ W}$ ... Ans.

Or, alternatively, $R = \dfrac{V}{I_R} = \dfrac{230}{3} = 76.67\ \Omega$

$\therefore \quad P_L = \dfrac{R}{2}(I^2 - I_L^2 - I_R^2) = \dfrac{76.67}{2}(7^2 - 4.5^2 - 3^2)$

$= \mathbf{757.1\ W}$ ... Ans.

Power factor of the coil,

$\cos \phi_L = \dfrac{P_L}{V \cdot I_L} = \dfrac{757.1}{230 \times 4.5} = \mathbf{0.732\ lagging}$ ... Ans.

Impedance of the coil,

$Z_L = \dfrac{V}{I_L} = \dfrac{230}{4.5} = 51.11\ \Omega$

Inductive reactance of the coil can be calculated from the impedance triangle for the coil.

Inductive reactance of the coil,

$X_L = Z_L \sin \phi_L = 51.11 \times 0.682 = 34.857\ \Omega$

∴ Inductance of the choking coil,

$$L = \frac{X_L}{2\pi f} = \frac{34.857}{2\pi \times 50} = 0.111 \text{ H} \qquad \text{... Ans.}$$

5.7 THE PRACTICAL IMPORTANCE OF POWER FACTOR

We know that, in an a.c. circuit, $P = VI \cos \phi$.

∴ $$I = \frac{P}{V \cos \phi}$$

From the above expression, it is clear that more current is required for supplying a given power at a low power factor than at a high power factor. An increase in the system current caused by low power factor leads to the following disadvantages :

(i) Larger alternators, transformers and transmission line conductors are required. This increases the cost of these equipments.
(ii) Increased power losses reduce the efficiency of the supply system as a whole.
(iii) A large voltage drop in the transmission line necessitates the installation of expensive equipments in order to keep up the voltage at the far end.

In general, it can be concluded that for a given power, the lower the power factor, the greater is the cost of generation and transmission. The supply undertakings, therefore, always encourage the consumers to increase their power factor by way of charging less for their consumption of electricity. Thus, it is always advantageous for both, the consumers as well as supplier, to work at higher improved power factor.

5.8 CAPACITOR AS A POWER FACTOR IMPROVING DEVICE

The usual industrial loads on a power system operate at a lagging power factor. In many cases, this power factor is very low and needs improvement. The simplest method to accomplish this is to connect a bank of capacitors in parallel with the load. To understand this, consider the circuit consisting of a resistance R in series with an inductance L connected across an a.c. supply (Fig. 5.7 a).

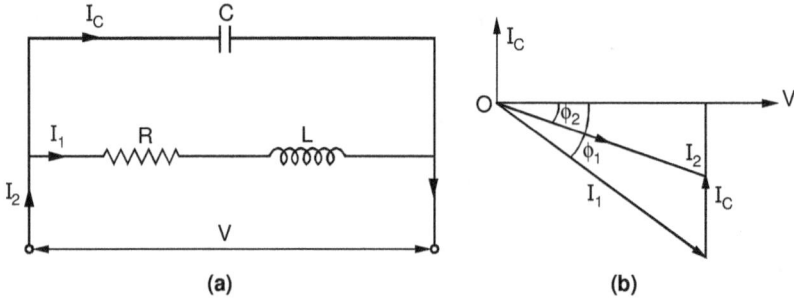

Fig. 5.7 : Capacitor as a power factor improving device

Let, I_1 be the current drawn by the circuit lagging the applied voltage V by an angle ϕ_1. If now, a capacitor C is connected across the circuit, it will draw current I_C leading the voltage by 90°. The new current I_2 drawn from the supply will then be given by the phasor addition of I_1 and I_C and will lag the voltage by an angle ϕ_2 as shown in the phasor diagram of Fig. 5.7 (b). This is how the use of a capacitor brings the line current more nearly into phase with the applied voltage and improves the power factor of the circuit. However, considering the added expenditure on the capacitor, improving the power factor all the way to unity is not always economically feasible.

5.9 RESONANCE IN PARALLEL CIRCUITS

A parallel circuit like the one that is illustrated in Fig. 5.8 (a) is said to be under *resonance* when the resultant current drawn by it and the line voltage across its terminals are in phase. The frequency at which this happens is known as *resonant frequency*. To make this more clear, consider the commonly used circuit (generally called as a tank circuit) shown in Fig. 5.8 (a). It consists of an inductive coil of L henrys and having a resistance of R ohms connected in parallel with a capacitor of capacitance C farads across a variable frequency supply of V volts. Then at any frequency f, we have

Inductive reactance of the coil, $X_L = \omega L = 2\pi f L$ ohms

Capacitive reactance of the capacitor,

$$X_C = \frac{1}{\omega C} = \frac{1}{2\pi f C} \text{ ohms}$$

Impedance of the coil, $Z_L = \sqrt{R^2 + X_L^2}$ ohms

Current in the inductive branch, $I_L = \dfrac{V}{Z_L}$ amperes

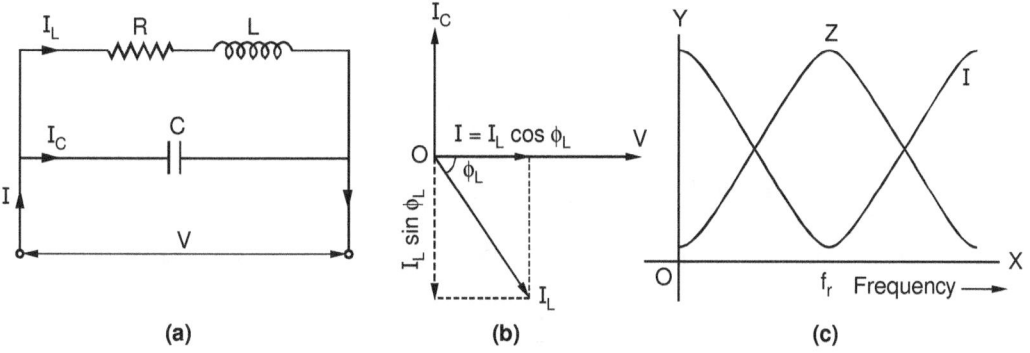

Fig. 5.8 : Parallel resonance

Phase angle between I_L and $V = \phi_L = \tan^{-1}\left(\dfrac{X_L}{R}\right)$

Current in the capacitive branch, $I_C = \dfrac{V}{X_C}$ amperes, leading V by 90°.

The resultant is obtained from the phasor addition of I_L and I_C. If f is of such a value that $I_C = I_L \sin \phi_L$, then, the resultant current I is minimum (= $I_L \cos \phi_L$) and is in phase with the supply voltage as shown in Fig. 5.8 (b). As said earlier, the circuit under this condition is said to be in *resonance* and the frequency at which this happens is known as *resonant frequency*.

5.9.1 Resonant Frequency

The expression for the resonant frequency for the circuit under consideration can be derived from the conditions prevailing at the time of resonance. We know that at resonance,

$$I_L \sin \phi_L = I_C$$

$$\therefore \quad \frac{V}{Z_L} \times \frac{X_L}{Z_L} = \frac{V}{X_C}$$

$$\therefore \quad X_L \cdot X_C = Z_L^2 \qquad \ldots (5.10)$$

$$\therefore \quad \omega L \cdot \frac{1}{\omega C} = R^2 + X_L^2 = R^2 + \omega^2 L^2$$

$$\therefore \quad \frac{L}{C} = R^2 + \omega^2 L^2 \qquad \ldots (5.11)$$

$$\therefore \quad \omega^2 L^2 = \frac{L}{C} - R^2$$

Or,

$$\omega^2 = \frac{1}{LC} - \frac{R^2}{L^2}$$

If f_r is the resonant frequency, then,

$$(2\pi f_r)^2 = \frac{1}{LC} - \frac{R^2}{L^2}$$

$$\therefore \quad f_r = \frac{1}{2\pi} \sqrt{\frac{1}{LC} - \frac{R^2}{L^2}} \qquad \ldots (5.12)$$

If R is small, then, $f_r = \dfrac{1}{2\pi \sqrt{LC}}$ ... (5.13)

Thus, we get the same expression as for series resonance. Now, from Expression (5.10), we have

$$\frac{X_L}{Z_L^2} = \frac{1}{X_C}$$

Hence, it should be noted that at resonance, the susceptances of both the parallel branches are numerically equal and net susceptance of the whole circuit is always zero.

5.9.2 Dynamic Impedance

As mentioned earlier, at resonance, the resultant current is given by,

$$I = I_L \cos \phi_L$$

$$= \frac{V}{Z_L} \times \frac{R}{Z_L} = \frac{V \cdot R}{Z_L^2}$$

$$= \frac{V \cdot R}{R^2 + X_L^2} = \frac{V \cdot R}{R^2 + \omega^2 L^2}$$

But, from Equation (5.11),

$$R^2 + \omega^2 L^2 = \frac{L}{C}$$

Putting this value in the above equation, we get

$$I = \frac{V \cdot R}{L/C} = \frac{V}{L/CR} \qquad \ldots (5.14)$$

The term (L / CR) at the denominator in the above equation is known as *the equivalent* or *dynamic impedance* of the parallel circuit under resonance. Obviously, it represents the maximum impedance of the circuit as corresponding resultant current is minimum (Fig. 5.8 c). Since the power factor of the circuit is unity under this condition, the nature of the dynamic impedance is purely resistive. As the parallel circuit under resonance offers maximum impedance to currents of one particular frequency, it is sometimes called a *rejector circuit*. Such circuits may be used in radio or electric circuits to filter out or reject the currents of the desired frequency.

5.9.3 Q-Factor of a Parallel Circuit

Parallel resonance is often referred to as *current resonance* because even though very little current is drawn from the supply by the parallel circuit under resonance, yet large circulating currents may flow in its branches. This can be readily seen from Fig. 5.8 (b). Thus, parallel resonant circuit can be used to greatly magnify the current taken from the supply.

Now, from Equation (5.14), the line current drawn from the supply at resonance is given by

$$I = \frac{V}{L/CR}$$

The current in the inductive branch is given by

$$I_L = \frac{V}{Z_L} = \frac{V}{\sqrt{R^2 + \omega^2 L^2}}$$

$$= \frac{V}{\sqrt{L/C}} \quad \text{(Refer to Equation 5.11)} \qquad \ldots (5.15)$$

The ratio of current circulating between the two parallel branches to the line current drawn from the supply is called the *current magnification*. Therefore, from the above equations, we have

$$\text{Current magnification} = \frac{I_L}{I} = \frac{V}{\sqrt{L/C}} \times \frac{L/CR}{V}$$

$$= \frac{1}{R}\sqrt{\frac{L}{C}} \qquad \ldots (5.16)$$

Or alternatively,

$$\text{Current magnification} = \frac{I_C}{I} = \tan \phi_L = \frac{X_L}{R} = \frac{2\pi f_r L}{R}$$

$$= \frac{2\pi L}{R}\left(\frac{1}{2\pi\sqrt{LC}}\right) \qquad \text{(Assuming R to be small)}$$

$$= \frac{1}{R}\sqrt{\frac{L}{C}} \qquad \ldots (5.17)$$

The quality factor or Q-factor of the parallel circuit is defined as equal to the current magnification in the circuit at resonance.

$$\therefore \quad \text{Q-factor} = \frac{1}{R}\sqrt{\frac{L}{C}} \quad \ldots (5.18)$$

It is the same as that for a series resonant circuit. This relationship is important in the design of radio circuits.

5.10 COMPARISON OF SERIES AND PARALLEL RESONANT CIRCUITS

The comparison between the series and parallel circuits at resonance is given below in the tabular form.

Table 5.1

Details	Series Circuit	Parallel Circuit
Impedance	Minimum, equal to R	Maximum, equal to L/CR
Current	Maximum, equal to V/R	Minimum, equal to $\frac{V}{L/CR}$
Power factor	Unity	Unity
Frequency	$\frac{1}{2\pi\sqrt{LC}}$	$\frac{1}{2\pi}\sqrt{\frac{1}{LC}-\frac{R^2}{L^2}}$
Magnification	Voltage	Current
Value of magnification	$\frac{1}{R}\sqrt{\frac{L}{C}}$	$\frac{1}{R}\sqrt{\frac{L}{C}}$

Example 5.5 : *A coil of inductance 31.8 mH and resistance 10 Ω is connected in parallel with a capacitor across a 250 V, 50 Hz supply. Determine the value of the capacitance if no reactive current is taken from the supply.*

Solution : Referring to Fig. 5.8 (a), we have for the coil,

$$\text{Inductive reactance, } X_L = \omega L = 2\pi f L$$
$$= 2\pi \times 50 \times 31.8 \times 10^{-3} = 9.99 \ \Omega$$
$$\text{Impedance, } Z_L = \sqrt{R^2 + X_L^2} = \sqrt{10^2 + 9.99^2}$$
$$= 14.14 \ \Omega$$
$$\text{Current, } I_L = \frac{V}{Z_L} = \frac{250}{14.14} = 17.68 \text{ A}$$
$$\tan \phi_L = \frac{9.99}{10} = 0.999$$
$$\therefore \quad \phi_L = 44.97° \text{ (lagging)}$$

Since no reactive current is taken from the supply, from the phasor diagram of Fig. 5.8 (b), we have

$$I_C = I_L \sin \phi_L$$
$$= 17.68 \times 0.707$$
$$= 12.5 \text{ A}$$

∴ Capacitive reactance of a capacitor,

$$X_C = \frac{V}{I_C}$$
$$= \frac{250}{12.5}$$
$$= 20 \, \Omega$$

∴ Capacitance, $C = \dfrac{1}{X_C \omega} = \dfrac{1}{20 \times 2\pi \times 50}$

$$= 1.59 \times 10^{-4} \text{ F} \quad \text{or} \quad 159 \, \mu\text{F} \qquad \text{... Ans.}$$

Alternative method : Since no reactive current is taken from the supply, it means that the given circuit is under resonance at 50 Hz. Now, resonant frequency is given by,

$$f_r = \frac{1}{2\pi} \sqrt{\frac{1}{LC} - \frac{R^2}{L^2}}$$

∴ $$50 = \frac{1}{2\pi} \sqrt{\frac{1}{31.8 \times 10^{-3} \times C} - \frac{10^2}{(31.8 \times 10^{-3})^2}}$$

∴ $$C = 1.59 \times 10^{-4} \text{ F} \quad \text{or} \quad 159 \, \mu\text{F} \qquad \text{... Ans.}$$

Example 5.6 : *A series circuit consisting of a 12 Ω resistance, 0.3 H inductance and a variable capacitor is connected across 100 V, 50 Hz, a.c. supply. The capacitance value is adjusted to obtain maximum current. Find this capacitance value and the power drawn by the circuit under this condition. Now, the supply frequency is raised to 60 Hz, the voltage remaining same at 100 V. Find the value of capacitor C_1 to be connected across the above series circuit, so that current drawn from the supply is the minimum.*

Solution :

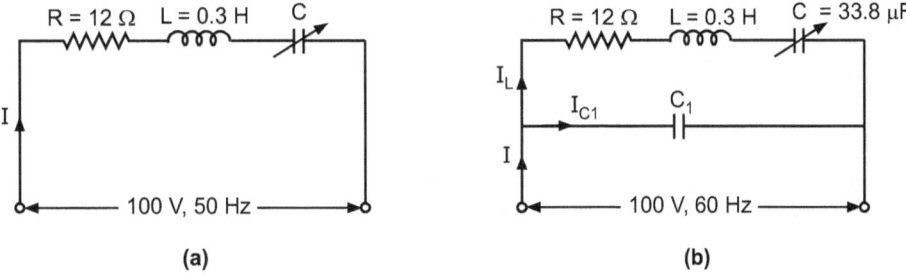

Fig. 5.9 : Circuit diagrams for Example 5.6 under two given conditions

Case I : Since the current in the circuit is maximum, the given series circuit (Fig. 5.9 a) is under resonance.

∴ $\quad X_C = X_L = 2\pi f L = 2\pi \times 50 \times 0.3 = 94.25 \ \Omega$

∴ $\quad C = \dfrac{1}{2\pi f \cdot X_C} = \dfrac{1}{2\pi \times 50 \times 94.25} \ F = \mathbf{33.8 \ \mu F}$ ... **Ans.**

$\quad I = \dfrac{V}{R} = \dfrac{100}{12} = 8.33 \ A$

∴ Power drawn by the circuit, $P = I^2 R = (8.33)^2 \times 12 = \mathbf{833 \ W}$ ... **Ans.**

Case II : With $f = 60$ Hz, for the given series circuit, we have

$\quad X_L = 2\pi f L = 2\pi \times 60 \times 0.3 = 113.1 \ \Omega$

$\quad X_C = \dfrac{1}{2\pi f C} = \dfrac{1}{2\pi \times 60 \times 33.8 \times 10^{-6}} = 78.48 \ \Omega$

$\quad X = X_L - X_C = 113.1 - 78.48 = 34.62 \ \Omega$

$\quad Z = \sqrt{R^2 + X^2} = \sqrt{12^2 + (34.62)^2} = 36.64 \ \Omega$

$\quad I_L = \dfrac{V}{Z} = \dfrac{100}{36.64} = 2.73 \ A$

$\quad \tan \phi_L = \dfrac{X}{R} = \dfrac{34.62}{12} = 2.885$

∴ $\quad \phi_L = 70.88°$

Since the current drawn by the parallel circuit (Fig. 5.9 b), formed after connecting the capacitor C_1 across the above series circuit, is to be minimum, it must be under resonance. Hence,

$\quad I_{C1} = I_L \sin \phi_L = 2.73 \times 0.945 = 2.58 \ A$ (Refer to Section 5.9)

∴ $\quad X_{C1} = \dfrac{V}{I_{C1}} = \dfrac{100}{2.58} = 38.76 \ \Omega$

∴ $\quad C_1 = \dfrac{1}{2\pi f X_{C1}} = \dfrac{1}{2\pi \times 60 \times 38.76} \ F = \mathbf{68.44 \ \mu F}$ ... **Ans.**

5.11 APPLICATION OF COMPLEX NOTATION METHOD TO A.C. PARALLEL CIRCUITS

In the previous chapter, we have studied the application of complex notation method to a.c. series circuits. Now, let us study how this method can be employed in the analysis of a.c. parallel circuits.

Current, Voltage and Impedance : If circuits having impedances $\bar{Z}_1, \bar{Z}_2, \bar{Z}_3$, etc. are connected in parallel across an applied alternating voltage $\bar{V}$ (Fig. 5.5 a), then using complex notation, currents in the various branches are respectively

$$\bar{I}_1 = \dfrac{\bar{V}}{\bar{Z}_1}, \quad \bar{I}_2 = \dfrac{\bar{V}}{\bar{Z}_2}, \quad \bar{I}_3 = \dfrac{\bar{V}}{\bar{Z}_3}, \text{ etc.}$$

Hence, total current is given by

$$\bar{I} = \bar{I}_1 + \bar{I}_2 + \bar{I}_3 + \ldots$$

$$= \frac{\bar{V}}{\bar{Z}_1} + \frac{\bar{V}}{\bar{Z}_2} + \frac{\bar{V}}{\bar{Z}_3} + \ldots$$

If $\bar{Z}$ is the equivalent impedance of $\bar{Z}_1, \bar{Z}_2, \bar{Z}_3$, etc. in parallel, then, from the above equation,

$$\frac{\bar{V}}{\bar{Z}} = \frac{\bar{V}}{\bar{Z}_1} + \frac{\bar{V}}{\bar{Z}_2} + \frac{\bar{V}}{\bar{Z}_3} + \ldots$$

$$\therefore \quad \frac{1}{\bar{Z}} = \frac{1}{\bar{Z}_1} + \frac{1}{\bar{Z}_2} + \frac{1}{\bar{Z}_3} + \ldots \qquad \ldots (5.19)$$

With two impedances in parallel, we have
Equivalent impedance,

$$\bar{Z} = \frac{\bar{Z}_1 \cdot \bar{Z}_2}{\bar{Z}_1 + \bar{Z}_2} \qquad \ldots (5.20)$$

Further using division of current rule, we have

$$\bar{I}_1 = \frac{\bar{Z}_2}{\bar{Z}_1 + \bar{Z}_2} \cdot \bar{I}$$

and

$$\bar{I}_2 = \frac{\bar{Z}_1}{\bar{Z}_1 + \bar{Z}_2} \cdot \bar{I} \qquad \ldots (5.21)$$

where $\bar{I}$ = Total circuit current, in amperes

$\bar{I}_1, \bar{I}_2$ = Current shared by two impedances $\bar{Z}_1$ and $\bar{Z}_2$ respectively, in amperes.

Admittance : The admittance of a circuit having resistance R and an inductive reactance X_L in series can be expressed using complex notation in the following manner :

$$\bar{Y} = \frac{1}{\bar{Z}} = \frac{1}{R + jX_L} = \frac{1}{R + jX_L} \times \frac{R - jX_L}{R - jX_L} = \frac{R}{R^2 + X_L^2} - j\frac{X_L}{R^2 + X_L^2}$$

Or, $\quad \bar{Y} = G - jB = Y \angle -\phi° \qquad \ldots (5.22)$

where $\quad G = $ Conductance $= \dfrac{R}{R^2 + X_L^2} = \dfrac{R}{Z^2}$

$B = $ Susceptance $= \dfrac{X_L}{R^2 + X_L^2} = \dfrac{X_L}{Z^2}$

$Y = \sqrt{G^2 + B^2}$

and $\quad \phi = \tan^{-1}\dfrac{-B}{G}$

Similarly, for a circuit having a resistance R and capacitive reactance X_C in series,

$$\bar{Y} = \frac{1}{\bar{Z}} = \frac{1}{R - jX_C} = \frac{1}{R - jX_C} \times \frac{R + jX_C}{R + jX_C}$$

$$= \frac{R}{R^2 + X_C^2} + j\frac{X_C}{R^2 + X_C^2}$$

Or, $\qquad \bar{Y} = G + jB = Y \angle \phi°$ ... (5.23)

where $\qquad G = \dfrac{R}{R^2 + X_C^2} = \dfrac{R}{Z^2}$

$\qquad B = \dfrac{X_C}{R^2 + X_C^2} = \dfrac{X_C}{Z^2}$

$\qquad Y = \sqrt{G^2 + B^2}$ and $\phi = \tan^{-1}\dfrac{B}{G}$

It should be remembered that, *with an inductive circuit, the susceptance is negative, whereas reactance is positive.* On the other hand, *with a capacitive circuit, the susceptance is positive, and the reactance is negative.*

Total Admittance of a Parallel Circuit : From the Equation (5.19), total admittance is given by

$$\bar{Y} = \bar{Y}_1 + \bar{Y}_2 + \bar{Y}_3 + ...$$ ... (5.24)

where $\bar{Y}_1, \bar{Y}_2, \bar{Y}_3$, etc. are the branch admittances.

Further, in general, if $\bar{Y}_1 = G_1 + jB_1$, $\bar{Y}_2 = G_2 + jB_2$, $\bar{Y}_3 = G_3 + jB_3$, etc.

then, $\quad \bar{Y} = (G_1 + jB_1) + (G_2 + jB_2) + (G_3 + jB_3) + ...$
$\qquad = (G_1 + G_2 + G_3 + ...) + j(B_1 + B_2 + B_3 + ...)$
$\qquad = G + jB = Y \angle \phi°$

where $G = G_1 + G_2 + G_3 + ...$ and $B = B_1 + B_2 + B_3 + ...$

$\qquad Y = \sqrt{G^2 + B^2}$

and $\qquad \phi = \tan^{-1}\dfrac{B}{G}$

The analysis of parallel a.c. circuits using complex notation method is best illustrated by few worked examples given below.

Example 5.7 : *An inductor of 0.5 H inductance and 90 Ω resistance is connected in parallel with 20 μF capacitor. Find :*
  (i) *Total r.m.s. current.*
  (ii) *Power factor of the circuit.*
  (iii) *Total power drawn from the source.*

A voltage of 230 V, 50 Hz is maintained across the circuit. Draw the phasor diagram of the circuit.

Solution : Given : R = 90 Ω, L = 0.5 H, C = 20 μF, V = 230 volts.

Fig. 5.10 (a) shows the circuit diagram.

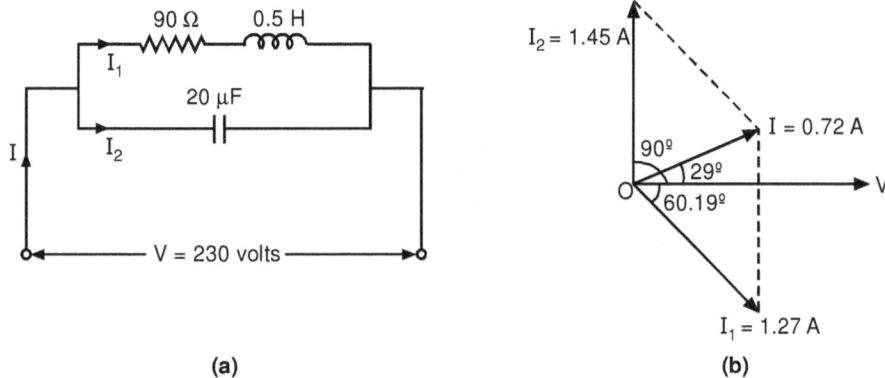

Fig. 5.10 : (a) Circuit diagram for Example 5.7, (b) Phasor diagram

(i) $X_L = 2\pi fL = 2\pi \times 50 \times 0.5 = 157.08\ \Omega$

$\overline{Z}_1 = R + jX_L = 90 + j\,157.08 = 181.04\ \angle 60.19°\ \Omega$

∴ $\overline{I}_1 = \dfrac{\overline{V}}{\overline{Z}_1} = \dfrac{230\ \angle 0°}{181.04\ \angle 60.19°} = 1.27\ \angle -60.19° = (0.63 - j\,1.1)\ A$

$X_C = \dfrac{1}{2\pi fC} = \dfrac{1}{2\pi \times 50 \times 20 \times 10^{-6}} = 159.15\ \Omega$

$\overline{Z}_2 = 0 - j\,X_C = 0 - j\,159.15 = 159.15\ \angle -90°\ \Omega$

∴ $\overline{I}_2 = \dfrac{\overline{V}}{\overline{Z}_2} = \dfrac{230\ \angle 0°}{159.15\ \angle -90°} = 1.45\ \angle 90° = (0 + j\,1.45)\ A$

∴ Total current, $\overline{I} = \overline{I}_1 + \overline{I}_2 = (0.63 - j\,1.1) + (0 + j\,1.45)$

$= 0.63 + j\,0.35 =$ **0.72 ∠ 29° A** ... Ans.

(ii) Power factor of the circuit,

$\cos \phi = \cos 29° =$ **0.87 leading** ... Ans.

(iii) Total power drawn from the source,

$P = V \cdot I \cdot \cos \phi = 230 \times 0.72 \times 0.87 =$ **144.07 W** ... Ans.

Fig. 5.10 (b) shows the necessary phasor diagram.

Example 5.8 : *A single-phase, a.c. circuit contains a resistor of 30 Ω and an inductor of 0.15 H connected in parallel across 230 V, 50 Hz supply. Determine :*
(i) Admittance, (ii) Circuit current, (iii) Power factor, (iv) Power.

Solution : Given : R = 30 Ω, L = 0.15 H, V = 230 volts, f = 50 Hz.

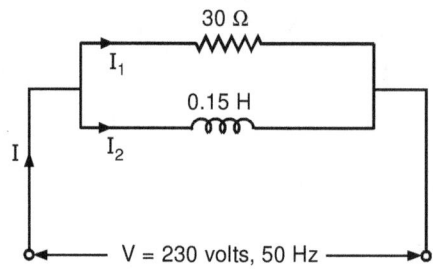

Fig. 5.11 : Circuit diagram for Example 5.8

Fig. 5.11 shows the necessary circuit diagram.

(i) $$\bar{Z}_1 = R + j0 = 30 + j0 = 30 \angle 0° \, \Omega$$

∴ $$\bar{Y}_1 = \frac{1}{\bar{Z}_1} = \frac{1}{30 \angle 0°} = 0.0333 \angle 0° = (0.0333 + j0) \, S$$

$$X_L = 2\pi f L = 2\pi \times 50 \times 0.15 = 47.12 \, \Omega$$

$$\bar{Z}_2 = 0 + jX_L = 0 + j\,47.12 = 47.12 \angle 90° \, \Omega$$

∴ $$\bar{Y}_2 = \frac{1}{47.12 \angle 90°} = 0.0212 \angle -90° = (0 - j\,0.0212) \, S$$

∴ Total admittance of the circuit,

$$\bar{Y} = \bar{Y}_1 + \bar{Y}_2 = (0.0333 + j0) + (0 - j\,0.0212)$$
$$= 0.0333 - j\,0.0212 = 0.0395 \angle -32.48° \, S$$

(ii) Circuit current, $\bar{I} = \bar{V} \cdot \bar{Y} = 230 \angle 0° \times 0.0395 \angle -32.48°$
$$= \mathbf{9.09 \angle -32.48° \, A} \qquad \text{... Ans.}$$

(iii) Power factor of the circuit,
$$\cos \phi = \cos 32.48° = \mathbf{0.84 \, lagging} \qquad \text{... Ans.}$$

(iv) Power, $P = V \cdot I \cdot \cos \phi = 230 \times 9.09 \times 0.84$
$$= \mathbf{1756.19 \, W} \qquad \text{... Ans.}$$

Example 5.9 : *Calculate the branch currents I_1 and I_2 for the given circuit.*

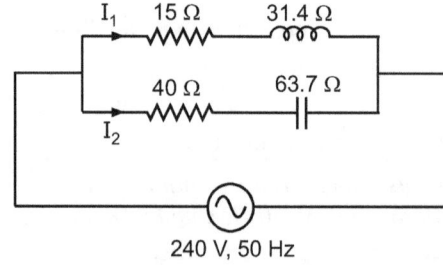

Fig. 5.12 : Circuit diagram for Example 5.9

Solution :

$$\bar{Z}_1 = R_1 + jX_{L1} = 15 + j31.4 = 34.8 \angle 64.47° \, \Omega$$

$$\bar{Z}_2 = R_2 - jX_{C2} = 40 - j63.7 = 75.22 \angle -57.87° \, \Omega$$

$$\bar{V} = 240 \angle 0° \, V \text{ (taken as a reference)}$$

∴ Branch current, $\bar{I}_1 = \dfrac{\bar{V}}{\bar{Z}_1} = \dfrac{240 \angle 0°}{34.8 \angle 64.47°} = \mathbf{6.9 \angle -64.47° A}$ ... Ans.

Branch current, $\bar{I}_2 = \dfrac{\bar{V}}{\bar{Z}_2} = \dfrac{240 \angle 0°}{75.22 \angle -57.87°} = \mathbf{3.19 \angle 57.87° A}$ ... Ans.

Fig. 5.13 shows the necessary phasor diagram.

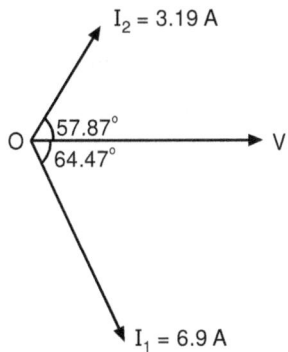

Fig. 5.13 : Phasor diagram for Example 5.9

Example 5.10 : *Solve Example 5.1 using complex notation.*

Solution : Referring to Fig. 5.2 (a), we have for

Branch A : $\bar{Z}_1 = 10 + j0 = 10 \angle 0° \, \Omega$

Taking applied voltage as a reference quantity,

$$\bar{V} = 230 + j0 = 230 \angle 0° \, V$$

∴ $\bar{I}_1 = \dfrac{\bar{V}}{\bar{Z}_1} = \dfrac{230 \angle 0°}{10 \angle 0°} = 23 \angle 0° = \mathbf{(23 + j0) \, A}$ ... Ans.

$\phi_1 = 0°$

∴ $\cos \phi_1 = \mathbf{1}$ ... Ans.

Branch B : $\quad \bar{Z}_2 = 6 + j\,8 = 10 \angle 53.13° \; \Omega$

$\therefore \quad \bar{I}_2 = \dfrac{\bar{V}}{\bar{Z}_2} = \dfrac{230 \angle 0°}{10 \angle 53.13°} = 23 \angle -53.13°$

$\qquad\qquad = (13.8 - j\,18.4)\text{ A} \qquad\qquad\qquad\qquad\qquad$ ... Ans.

$\qquad \phi_2 = 53.13°$

$\therefore \quad \cos \phi_2 = \mathbf{0.6 \text{ (lagging)}} \qquad\qquad\qquad\qquad\qquad$ ... Ans.

Branch C : $\quad \bar{Z}_3 = 4 - j\,9 = 9.849 \angle -66.04° \; \Omega$

$\therefore \quad \bar{I}_3 = \dfrac{\bar{V}}{\bar{Z}_3}$

$\qquad\qquad = \dfrac{230 \angle 0°}{9.849 \angle -66.04°} = 23.35 \angle 66.04°$

$\qquad\qquad = (9.48 + j\,21.34)\text{ A} \qquad\qquad\qquad\qquad\qquad$ ... Ans.

$\qquad \phi_3 = 66.04°$

$\therefore \quad \cos \phi_3 = \mathbf{0.406 \text{ (leading)}} \qquad\qquad\qquad\qquad\qquad$ ... Ans.

Total Circuit : Total current drawn by the circuit is given by,

$\qquad \bar{I}_1 = \bar{I}_1 + \bar{I}_2 + \bar{I}_3$

$\qquad\quad = (23 + j\,0) + (13.8 - j\,18.4) + (9.48 + j\,21.34)$

$\qquad\quad = 46.28 + j\,2.94$

$\qquad\quad = \mathbf{46.37 \angle 3.64°}$ **A** $\qquad\qquad\qquad\qquad\qquad$ ... Ans.

Hence, Circuit power factor,

$\qquad \cos \phi = \cos 3.64° = \mathbf{0.998 \text{ (leading)}} \qquad\qquad\qquad$ ... Ans.

For phasor diagram, refer to Fig. 5.2 (b).

$\qquad \text{Power} = V\,I\,\cos \phi$

$\qquad\qquad\quad = 230 \times 46.37 \times 0.998 \text{ W}$

$\qquad\qquad\quad = \mathbf{10.64 \text{ kW}} \qquad\qquad\qquad\qquad\qquad$ ... Ans.

$\qquad \text{Equivalent impedance} = \dfrac{\bar{V}}{\bar{I}} = \dfrac{230 \angle 0°}{46.37 \angle 3.64°} = \mathbf{4.96 \angle -3.64° \; \Omega} \qquad$ ... Ans.

For parallel circuit, equivalent impedance may also be found by,

$$\dfrac{1}{\bar{Z}} = \dfrac{1}{\bar{Z}_1} + \dfrac{1}{\bar{Z}_2} + \dfrac{1}{\bar{Z}_3}$$

Substituting the values of $\bar{Z}_1, \bar{Z}_2$ and $\bar{Z}_3$ in the above equation, we have

$$\frac{1}{\bar{Z}} = \frac{1}{10+j0} + \frac{1}{6+j8} + \frac{1}{4-j9}$$

$$= \frac{1}{10 \angle 0°} + \frac{1}{10 \angle 53.13°} + \frac{1}{9.849 \angle -66.04°}$$

$$= 0.1 \angle 0° + 0.1 \angle -53.13° + 0.1015 \angle 66.04°$$

$$= 0.2012 + j\,0.0128 = 0.2016 \angle 3.64°$$

$\therefore \qquad \bar{Z} = \dfrac{1}{0.2016 \angle 3.64°} = $ **4.96 $\angle$ –3.64° Ω** ... Ans.

Admittance Method : Alternatively, this problem can also be solved by admittance method as follows :

Branch A : $\qquad \bar{Z}_1 = 10 + j\,0 = 10 \angle 0°\ \Omega$

$\therefore \qquad \bar{Y}_1 = \dfrac{1}{\bar{Z}_1} = \dfrac{1}{10 \angle 0°} = 0.1 \angle 0° = (0.1 + j\,0)$ S

Taking voltage as a reference quantity,

$$\bar{V} = 230 + j\,0 = 230 \angle 0°\ V$$

$\therefore \qquad \bar{I}_1 = \bar{V} \cdot \bar{Y}_1 = 230 \angle 0° \times 0.1 \angle 0°$

$\qquad\qquad = 23 \angle 0°$

$\qquad\qquad =$ **(23 + j 0) A** ... Ans.

$\qquad \phi_1 = 0°$

$\therefore \qquad \cos \phi_1 =$ **1** ... Ans.

Branch B : $\qquad \bar{Z}_2 = 6 + j\,8 = 10 \angle 53.13°\ \Omega$

$\qquad \bar{Y}_2 = \dfrac{1}{\bar{Z}_2} = \dfrac{1}{10 \angle 53.13°}$

$\qquad\qquad = 0.1 \angle -53.13° = (0.06 - j0.08)$ S

$\therefore \qquad \bar{I}_2 = \bar{V} \cdot \bar{Y}_2$

$\qquad\qquad = 230 \angle 0° \times 0.1 \angle -53.13°$

$\qquad\qquad = 23 \angle -53.13° =$ **(13.8 – j 18.4) A** ... Ans.

$\qquad \phi_2 = -53.13°$

$\therefore \qquad \cos \phi_2 =$ **0.6 (lagging)** ... Ans.

Branch C : $\qquad \bar{Z}_3 = 4 - j\,9 = 9.85 \angle -66.04°\ \Omega$

$\qquad \bar{Y}_3 = \dfrac{1}{\bar{Z}_3} = \dfrac{1}{9.85 \angle -66.04°}$

$\qquad\qquad = 0.1015 \angle 66.04° = (0.0412 + j\,0.0928)$ S

∴ $\bar{I}_3 = \bar{V} \cdot \bar{Y}_3 = 230 \angle 0° \times 0.1015 \angle 66.04°$

$= 23.35 \angle 66.04° = \mathbf{(9.475 + j\, 21.34)\ A}$ ... Ans.

$\phi_3 = 66.04°$

∴ $\cos \phi_3 = \mathbf{0.406\ (leading)}$ ... Ans.

Total Circuit : $\bar{Y} = \bar{Y}_1 + \bar{Y}_2 + \bar{Y}_3$

$= (0.1 + j\, 0) + (0.06 - j\, 0.08) + (0.0412 + j\, 0.0928)$

$= 0.2012 + j\, 0.0128$

$= 0.2016 \angle 3.64°\ S$

∴ $\bar{I} = \bar{V} \cdot \bar{Y} = 230 \angle 0° \times 0.2016 \angle 3.64°$

$= \mathbf{46.37 \angle 3.64°\ A}$ ... Ans.

Alternatively, $\bar{I} = \bar{I}_1 + \bar{I}_2 + \bar{I}_3$

$= (23 + j\, 0) + (13.8 - j\, 18.4) + (9.475 + j\, 21.34)$

$= 46.275 + j\, 2.94$

$= \mathbf{46.37 \angle 3.64°\ A}$ ... Ans.

Thus, as before, $\cos \phi = \mathbf{0.998\ (leading)}$ ... Ans.

Power = **10.64 kW** ... Ans.

Equivalent impedance of the circuit is given by,

$$\bar{Z} = \frac{1}{\bar{Y}} = \frac{1}{0.2016 \angle 3.64°}$$

$= \mathbf{4.96 \angle -3.64°\ \Omega}$ **(as before)** ... Ans.

Or alternatively, as already seen,

$$\bar{Z} = \frac{\bar{V}}{\bar{I}} = \frac{230 \angle 0°}{46.37 \angle 3.64°} = \mathbf{4.96 \angle -3.64°\ \Omega}$$ ... Ans.

Example 5.11 : *In the circuit shown in Fig. 5.14, a voltage, v = 100 sin 3t volts is applied. Determine :*

(i) Branch currents I_1 and I_2 with their phase angles.

(ii) Total current supplied by the source and its phase angle.

(iii) Total power supplied.

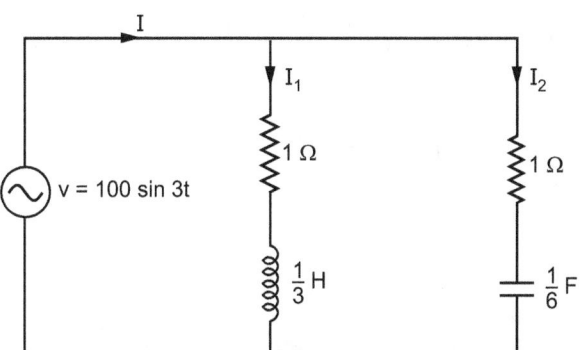

Fig. 5.14 : Circuit diagram for Example 5.11

Solution : From the equation for voltage, we have R.M.S. value of the voltage,

$$V = \frac{V_m}{\sqrt{2}} = \frac{100}{\sqrt{2}} = 70.71 \text{ V}$$

$$\omega = 3 \text{ radians/s}$$

∴ $\quad X_L = \omega L = 3 \times \frac{1}{3} = 1 \, \Omega$

and $\quad X_C = \dfrac{1}{\omega C} = \dfrac{1}{3 \times \left(\frac{1}{6}\right)} = 2 \, \Omega$

$$\bar{Z}_1 = R_1 + jX_L = 1 + j1 = 1.414 \angle 45° \, \Omega$$

$$\bar{Z}_2 = R_2 - jX_C = 1 - j2 = 2.236 \angle -63.43° \, \Omega$$

∴ $\quad \bar{I}_1 = \dfrac{\bar{V}}{\bar{Z}_1} = \dfrac{70.71 \angle 0°}{1.414 \angle 45°}$

$$= 50 \angle -45° = (35.36 - j\,35.36) \text{ A} \qquad \text{... Ans.}$$

∴ $\quad \bar{I}_2 = \dfrac{\bar{V}}{\bar{Z}_2} = \dfrac{70.71 \angle 0°}{2.236 \angle -63.43°}$

$$= 31.62 \angle 63.43° = (14.14 + j\,28.28) \text{ A} \qquad \text{... Ans.}$$

Total current, $\bar{I} = \bar{I}_1 + \bar{I}_2 = (35.36 - j\,35.36) + (14.14 + j\,28.28)$

$$= 49.5 - j\,7.08 = 50 \angle -8.14° \text{ A} \qquad \text{... Ans.}$$

Total power supplied, $P = V \cdot I \cos \phi$

$$= 70.71 \times 50 \times \cos 8.14° = \textbf{3499.88 W} \qquad \text{... Ans.}$$

Example 5.12 : *Two circuits having same numerical value of ohmic impedance are connected in parallel. The power factor of one circuit having impedance Z_1 is 0.8 and the other having impedance Z_2 is 0.6. What is the power factor of the combination when :*

(i) Both the impedances are inductive ?

(ii) Z_1 is inductive and Z_2 is capacitive ?

Solution : $\cos \phi_1 = 0.8$ ∴ $\phi_1 = 36.87°$

$\cos \phi_2 = 0.6$ ∴ $\phi_2 = 53.13°$

Let the ohmic value of the impedance of each circuit be Z Ω.

(i) When both the impedances Z_1 and Z_2 are inductive in nature, they can be expressed in the complex form as follows :

$$\overline{Z}_1 = Z \angle 36.87° = Z(0.8 + j\, 0.6)\, \Omega$$

$$\overline{Z}_2 = Z \angle 53.13° = Z(0.6 + j\, 0.8)\, \Omega$$

∴ Impedance of the parallel combination,

$$\overline{Z}_p = \frac{\overline{Z}_1 \cdot \overline{Z}_2}{\overline{Z}_1 + \overline{Z}_2} = \frac{Z\angle 36.87° \times Z\angle 53.13°}{Z(0.8 + j0.6) + Z(0.6 + j0.8)}$$

$$= \frac{Z^2 \angle (36.87° + 53.13°)}{Z(1.4 + j1.4)} = \frac{Z \angle 90°}{1.98 \angle 45°}$$

$$= 0.51\, Z \angle 45°\, \Omega$$

∴ Power factor of the combination,

$\cos \phi = \cos 45° = \mathbf{0.707\ (lagging)}$ ... **Ans.**

(ii) When Z_1 is inductive and Z_2 is capacitive, they can be expressed in the complex form as follows :

$$\overline{Z}_1 = Z \angle 36.87° = Z(0.8 + j\, 0.6)\, \Omega$$

$$\overline{Z}_2 = Z \angle -53.13° = Z(0.6 - j\, 0.8)\, \Omega$$

∴ Impedance of the parallel combination,

$$\overline{Z}_p = \frac{\overline{Z}_1 \cdot \overline{Z}_2}{\overline{Z}_1 + \overline{Z}_2}$$

$$= \frac{Z\angle 36.87° \times Z\angle -53.13°}{Z(0.8 + j0.6) + Z(0.6 - j0.8)}$$

$$= \frac{Z^2 \angle (36.87° - 53.13°)}{Z(1.4 - j0.2)} = \frac{Z \angle -16.26°}{1.41 \angle -8.13°}$$

$$= 0.71\, Z \angle -8.13°\, \Omega$$

∴ Power factor of the combination,

$\cos \phi = \cos 8.13° = \mathbf{0.99\ (leading)}$ ... **Ans.**

Example 5.13 : *An a.c. circuit connected across 200 V, 50 Hz supply has two parallel branches A and B. The current in branch A is 4 A at 0.8 lagging power factor. The total supply current is 5 A at unity power factor. Find for the branch B, the power consumed and the impedance.*

Solution : $\overline{V} = 200 \angle 0°\ V$

$\cos \phi_A = 0.8\ \text{(lagging)}$

∴ $\phi_A = 36.87°$

Hence, $\bar{I}_A = 4\angle -36.87° = (3.2 - j\,2.4)$ A
$\cos\phi = 1$
∴ $\phi = 0°$
Hence, Total current, $\bar{I} = 5\angle 0° = (5 + j\,0)$ A
∴ $\bar{I}_B = \bar{I} - \bar{I}_A$
$= (5 + j\,0) - (3.2 - j\,2.4)$
$= 1.8 + j\,2.4 = 3\angle 53.13°$ A
$P_B = V\,I_B \cos\phi_B$
$= 200 \times 3 \times \cos 53.13° = $ **360 W** ... Ans.

$\bar{Z}_B = \dfrac{\bar{V}}{\bar{I}_B} = \dfrac{200\angle 0°}{3\angle 53.13°}$

$= 66.67\angle -53.13° = $ **(40 − j 53.34) Ω** ... Ans.

Example 5.14 : *A mercury vapour lamp unit consists of a 25 μF condenser in parallel with a series circuit containing the resistive lamp and a reactor of negligible resistance. The whole unit takes 400 W at 240 V, 50 Hz and unity power factor. What is the voltage across the lamp ?*

Solution : Let R be the resistance of the lamp and L the inductance of the reactor.

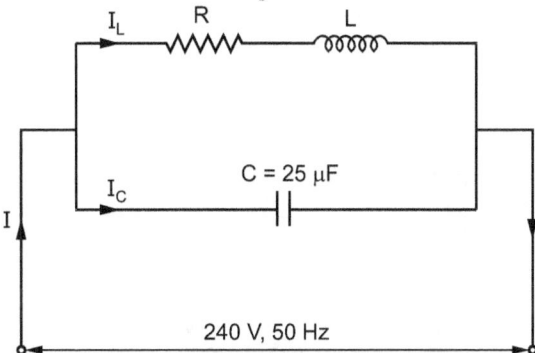

Fig. 5.15 : Circuit diagram for Example 5.14

Total current, $I = \dfrac{P}{V\cos\phi} = \dfrac{400}{240 \times 1} = 1.67$ A

Hence, total power factor being unity, we have

$\bar{I} = 1.67\angle 0° = (1.67 + j\,0)$ A

$X_C = \dfrac{1}{2\pi fC} = \dfrac{1}{2\pi \times 50 \times 25 \times 10^{-6}} = 127.32$ Ω

∴ $\bar{I}_C = \dfrac{V\angle 0°}{X_C \angle -90°} = \dfrac{240\angle 0°}{127.32\angle -90°} = 1.885\angle 90°$

$= (0 + j\,1.885)$ A

∴ Current through a series circuit containing the lamp and reactor,

$$\bar{I}_L = \bar{I} - \bar{I}_C = (1.67 + j\,0) - (0 + j\,1.885)$$

$$= 1.67 - j\,1.885 = 2.52 \angle -48.46° \text{ A}$$

∴ Impedance of a series circuit containing the lamp and reactor,

$$\bar{Z}_L = \frac{\bar{V}}{\bar{I}_L} = \frac{240 \angle 0°}{2.52 \angle -48.46°} = 95.24 \angle 48.46°$$

$$= (63.16 + j\,71.3)\ \Omega$$

Resistance of the lamp, $R = 63.16\ \Omega$

∴ Voltage across the lamp $= I_L \cdot R = 2.52 \times 63.16$

$$= 159.16 \text{ V} \qquad \text{... Ans.}$$

Example 5.15 : *Two coils of resistances 5 Ω and 3 Ω and inductances 0.03 H and 0.04 H respectively are connected in parallel across 200 V, 50 Hz supply. Calculate :*

(i) *The conductance, susceptance and admittance of each coil.*

(ii) *Total current drawn by the circuit and power factor.*

(iii) *Power absorbed by the circuit.*

Solution :

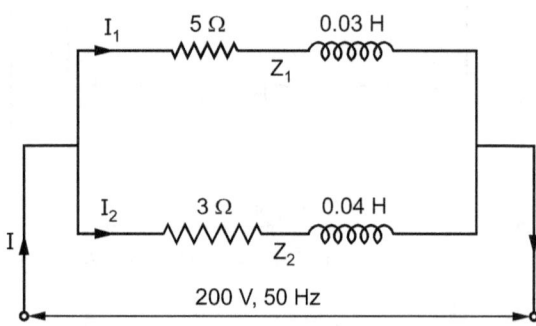

Fig. 5.16 : Circuit diagram for Example 5.15

$$\bar{Z}_1 = R_1 + j2\pi f L_1 = 5 + j2\pi \times 50 \times 0.03$$

$$= 5 + j\,9.425 = 10.669 \angle 62.05°\ \Omega$$

∴ $$\bar{Y}_1 = \frac{1}{\bar{Z}_1} = 0.0937 \angle -62.05°$$

$$= (0.0439 - j\,0.0828)\ \text{S} \qquad \text{... Ans.}$$

Hence, $G_1 = 0.0439$ S and $B_1 = -0.0828$ S ... Ans.

$$\bar{Z}_2 = R_2 + j2\pi f L_2 = 3 + j2\pi \times 50 \times 0.04$$

$$= 3 + j\,12.566 = 12.919 \angle 76.57° \;\Omega$$

∴ $$\bar{Y}_2 = \frac{1}{\bar{Z}_2} = 0.0774 \angle -76.57°$$

$$= (0.018 - j\,0.0753)\; S \qquad \text{... Ans.}$$

Hence, $\quad G_2 = \mathbf{0.018\;S}\quad$ and $\quad B_2 = \mathbf{-0.0753\;S} \qquad$ ... Ans.

$$\bar{Y} = \bar{Y}_1 + \bar{Y}_2 = (0.0439 - j\,0.0828) + (0.018 - j\,0.0753)$$

$$= 0.0619 - j\,0.1581 = 0.1698 \angle -68.62° \; S$$

∴ $$\bar{I} = \bar{V} \cdot \bar{Y} = 200 \angle 0° \times 0.1698 \angle -68.62°$$

$$= \mathbf{33.96 \angle -68.62°\; A} \qquad \text{... Ans.}$$

Power factor, $\cos\phi = \cos 68.62° = \mathbf{0.365\;(lagging)} \qquad$ ... Ans.

$$P = VI\cos\phi = 200 \times 33.96 \times 0.365$$

$$= \mathbf{2479.08\;W} \qquad \text{... Ans.}$$

Example 5.16 : *Two impedances $(8 + j6)\;\Omega$ and $(3 - j4)\;\Omega$ are connected in parallel. If the total current taken by this combination is 25 A, find the current and power taken by each impedance.*

Solution :

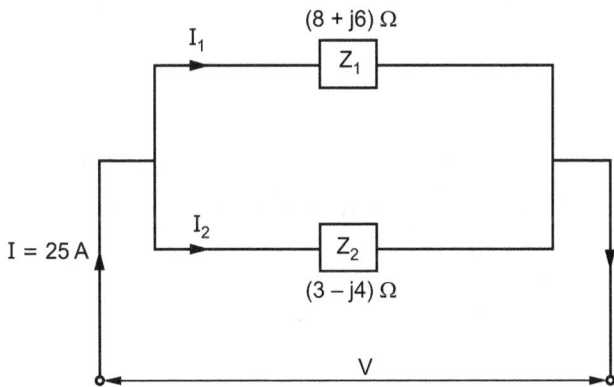

Fig. 5.17 : Circuit diagram for Example 5.16

$$\bar{Z}_1 = 8 + j6 = 10 \angle 36.87° \;\Omega$$

$$\bar{Z}_2 = 3 - j4 = 5 \angle -53.13° \;\Omega$$

∴ Impedance of the parallel combination,

$$\bar{Z} = \frac{\bar{Z}_1 \cdot \bar{Z}_2}{\bar{Z}_1 + \bar{Z}_2} = \frac{10 \angle 36.87° \times 5 \angle -53.13°}{(8 + j6) + (3 - j4)} = \frac{50 \angle -16.26°}{11.18 \angle 10.3°}$$

$$= 4.47 \angle -26.56° \; \Omega$$

$$V = IZ = 25 \times 4.47 = 111.75 \text{ V}$$

∴ $$\bar{I}_1 = \frac{\bar{V}}{\bar{Z}_1} = \frac{111.75 \angle 0°}{10 \angle 36.87°}$$

$$= \mathbf{11.175 \angle -36.87° \text{ A}} \qquad \qquad \text{... Ans.}$$

∴ $$\bar{I}_2 = \frac{\bar{V}}{\bar{Z}_2} = \frac{111.75 \angle 0°}{5 \angle -53.13°}$$

$$= \mathbf{22.35 \angle 53.13° \text{ A}} \qquad \qquad \text{... Ans.}$$

$$P_1 = I_1^2 R_1 = (11.175)^2 \times 8$$
$$= \mathbf{999.05 \text{ W}} \qquad \qquad \text{... Ans.}$$

$$P_2 = I_2^2 R_2 = (22.35)^2 \times 3$$
$$= \mathbf{1498.57 \text{ W}} \qquad \qquad \text{... Ans.}$$

Example 5.17 : *Two circuits A and B are connected in parallel to a 115 V, 50 Hz supply. The total current taken by the combination is 10 A at unity power factor. Circuit A consists of 10 Ω resistor and 200 × 10⁻⁶ F capacitor connected in series. Circuit B consists of a resistor and an inductive reactor in series. Determine the following data for circuit B :*

(i)   Current.
(ii)   Power factor.
(iii) Impedance.
(iv) Resistance.
(v)   Reactance.

Solution :

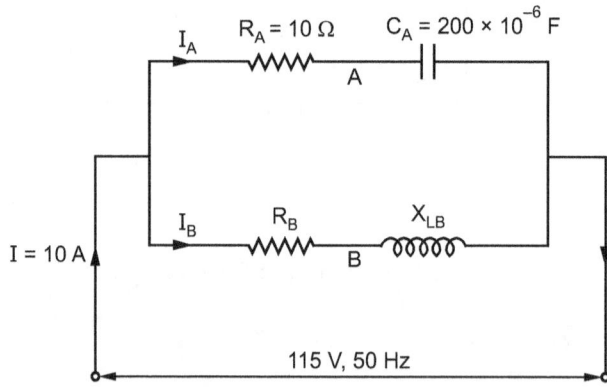

Fig. 5.18 : Circuit diagram for Example 5.17

$$\bar{V} = 115 \angle 0° \text{ V}$$

$$\bar{I} = 10 \angle 0° = (10 + j\,0) \text{ A}$$

$$\therefore \quad \bar{Z} = \frac{\bar{V}}{\bar{I}} = \frac{115 \angle 0°}{10 \angle 0°} = 11.5 \angle 0° = (11.5 + j\,0) \text{ }\Omega$$

$$X_{CA} = \frac{1}{2\pi f C} = \frac{1}{2\pi \times 50 \times 200 \times 10^{-6}} = 15.92 \text{ }\Omega$$

$$\bar{Z}_A = R_A - j\,X_{CA} = 10 - j\,15.92 = 18.8 \angle -57.87° \text{ }\Omega$$

$$\bar{I}_A = \frac{\bar{V}}{\bar{Z}_A} = \frac{115 \angle 0°}{18.8 \angle -57.87°} = 6.117 \angle 57.87°$$

$$= (3.253 + j\,5.18) \text{ A}$$

$$\therefore \quad \bar{I}_B = \bar{I} - \bar{I}_A = (10 + j\,0) - (3.253 + j\,5.18) = 6.747 - j\,5.18$$

$$= \mathbf{8.51 \angle -37.52°\text{ A}} \quad \quad \text{... Ans.}$$

$$\cos \phi_B = \cos 37.52° = \mathbf{0.793 \text{ (lagging)}} \quad \quad \text{... Ans.}$$

$$\therefore \quad \bar{Z}_B = \frac{\bar{V}}{\bar{I}_B} = \frac{115 \angle 0}{8.51 \angle -37.52°}$$

$$= 13.51 \angle 37.52° \text{ }\Omega = \mathbf{(10.72 + j\,8.23) \text{ }\Omega} \quad \quad \text{... Ans.}$$

$$\therefore \quad R_B = \mathbf{10.72 \text{ }\Omega}, \quad X_{LB} = \mathbf{8.23 \text{ }\Omega} \quad \quad \text{... Ans.}$$

Example 5.18 : *Find I, I_1, I_2 and power factor of the circuit in Fig. 5.19 and also draw the complete phasor diagram.*

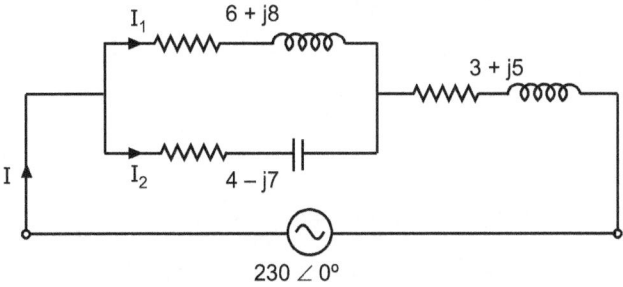

Fig. 5.19 : Circuit diagram for Example 5.18

Solution : Fig. 5.20 (a) shows the given network with the substitution of subscripted impedances. Here,

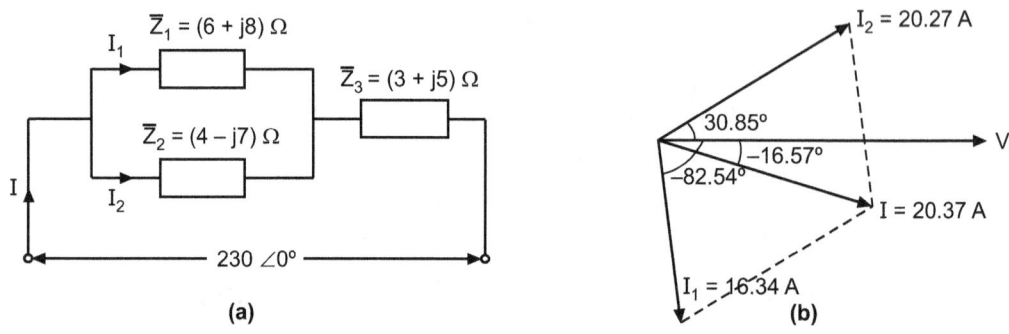

Fig. 5.20 : (a) Circuit of Fig. 5.19 with the substitution of subscripted impedances, (b) Phasor diagram

$$\bar{Z}_1 = 6 + j8 = 10 \angle 53.13° \, \Omega$$

$$\bar{Z}_2 = 4 - j7 = 8.06 \angle -60.26° \, \Omega$$

$$\bar{Z}_3 = 3 + j5 = 5.83 \angle 59.04° \, \Omega$$

As $\bar{Z}_1$ and $\bar{Z}_2$ are in parallel, their equivalent impedance will be given by

$$\bar{Z}_p = \frac{\bar{Z}_1 \bar{Z}_2}{\bar{Z}_1 + \bar{Z}_2} = \frac{10 \angle 53.13° \times 8.06 \angle -60.26°}{(6 + j8) + (4 - j7)}$$

$$= \frac{80.6 \angle -7.13°}{(10 + j1)} = \frac{80.6 \angle -7.13°}{10.05 \angle 5.71°}$$

$$= 8.02 \angle -12.84° = (7.82 - j1.78) \, \Omega$$

Hence, it is obvious that

Total impedance of the entire circuit,

$$\bar{Z}_T = \bar{Z}_p + \bar{Z}_3 = (7.82 - j1.78) + (3 + j5)$$

$$= 10.82 + j3.22 = 11.29 \angle 16.57° \, \Omega$$

∴ Circuit current, $\bar{I} = \dfrac{\bar{V}}{\bar{Z}_T} = \dfrac{230 \angle 0°}{11.29 \angle 16.57°} = \mathbf{20.37 \angle -16.57°\ A}$ ... **Ans.**

Now, the voltage across the parallel combination of $\bar{Z}_1$ and $\bar{Z}_2$,

$$\bar{V}_p = \bar{I} \cdot \bar{Z}_p = 20.37 \angle -16.57° \times 8.02 \angle -12.84°$$

$$= 163.37 \angle -29.41° \, V$$

$$\therefore \quad \bar{I}_1 = \frac{\bar{V}_p}{\bar{Z}_1} = \frac{163.37 \angle -29.41°}{10 \angle 53.13°} = \mathbf{16.34 \angle -82.54° \; A} \quad \ldots \text{Ans.}$$

and
$$\bar{I}_2 = \frac{\bar{V}_p}{\bar{Z}_2} = \frac{163.37 \angle -29.41°}{8.06 \angle -60.26°} = \mathbf{20.27 \angle 30.85° \; A} \quad \ldots \text{Ans.}$$

Power factor of the circuit,

$$\cos \phi = \cos 16.57° = \mathbf{0.96 \; lagging} \quad \ldots \text{Ans.}$$

Fig. 5.20 (b) shows the necessary phasor diagram.

5.12 POINTS TO REMEMBER

- The reciprocal of impedance $\left(\frac{1}{Z}\right)$ is known as admittance and its symbol is Y. The unit in which it is measured is siemens (abbreviation, S) which is the admittance of the circuit whose impedance is one ohm.

- The quantity G which is the ratio of resistance to the square of the impedance is known as the conductance of the circuit. The unit of the conductance is siemens.

- The quantity B which is the ratio of reactance to the square of impedance is known as susceptance of the circuit. The unit of the susceptance is siemens.

- It should be remembered that, with an inductive circuit, the susceptance is negative, whereas reactance is positive. On the other hand, with a capacitive circuit, the susceptance is positive, and the reactance is negative.

- The sides of the admittance triangle represent the conductance, susceptance and admittance of the circuit.

- A practical a.c. circuit like the one consisting of an inductive coil of L henrys and having a resistance of R ohms connected in parallel with a capacitor of capacitance C farads is said to be under resonance when the reactive component of the line current is zero, and the corresponding frequency at which this happens, is called resonant frequency.

- The ratio of current circulating between the two parallel branches to the line current drawn from the supply is called the current magnification.

- The quality factor or Q-factor of the parallel circuit is defined as equal to the current magnification in the circuit at resonance.

5.13 IMPORTANT FORMULAE AT A GLANCE

Three-Ammeter Method :

- Power consumed by the inductive load,

$$P_L = \frac{V(I^2 - I_L^2 - I_R^2)}{2I_R} = \frac{R}{2}(I^2 - I_L^2 - I_R^2) \text{ watts}$$

  where V = Supply voltage, in volts

  I = Total circuit current, in amperes

  I_L = Current taken by the inductive load, in amperes

  I_R = Current taken by the non-inductive resistor R, in amperes

- Power factor of the inductive load,

$$\cos \phi_L = \frac{I^2 - I_L^2 - I_R^2}{2 I_L I_R} \text{ lagging}$$

  where I = Total circuit current, in amperes

  I_L = Current taken by the inductive load, in amperes

  I_R = Current taken by the non-inductive resistance R, in amperes

Impedances in Parallel :

- $$\frac{1}{\bar{Z}} = \frac{1}{\bar{Z}_1} + \frac{1}{\bar{Z}_2} + \frac{1}{\bar{Z}_3} + \ldots + \frac{1}{\bar{Z}_n} \text{ siemens}$$

  where $\bar{Z}$ = Equivalent impedance, in ohms

  $\bar{Z}_1, \bar{Z}_2, \bar{Z}_3, \ldots, \bar{Z}_n$ = Impedances connected in parallel, in ohms.

- Total admittance of a parallel circuit,

$$\bar{Y} = \bar{Y}_1 + \bar{Y}_2 + \bar{Y}_3 + \ldots + \bar{Y}_n \text{ siemens}$$

  where $\bar{Y}_1, \bar{Y}_2, \bar{Y}_3, \ldots, \bar{Y}_n$ = Branch admittances of a parallel circuit, in siemens.

- $$\bar{I}_1 = \frac{\bar{Z}_2}{\bar{Z}_1 + \bar{Z}_2} \cdot I \text{ amperes}$$

$$\bar{I}_2 = \frac{\bar{Z}_1}{\bar{Z}_1 + \bar{Z}_2} \cdot I \text{ amperes}$$

  where I = Total circuit current with impedances $\bar{Z}_1$ and $\bar{Z}_2$ in parallel, in amperes.

  I_1 and I_2 = Currents shared by $\bar{Z}_1$ and $\bar{Z}_2$ respectively, in amperes.

Resonance in Parallel Circuit :

In a most practical a.c. circuit like the one consisting of an inductive coil of L henrys and having a resistance of R ohms connected in parallel with a capacitor of capacitance C farads, we have the following :

- $$\text{Resonant frequency } f_r = \frac{1}{2\pi}\sqrt{\frac{1}{LC} - \frac{R^2}{L^2}} \text{ hertzs}$$

  where   L = Inductance of a coil, in henrys
  R = Resistance of a coil, in ohms
  C = Capacitance in parallel with a coil, in farads

- $$\text{Dynamic impedance} = \frac{L}{CR} \text{ ohms}$$

  where   L = Inductance of a coil, in henrys
  R = Resistance of a coil, in ohms
  C = Capacitance in parallel with a coil, in farads

- $$\text{Q-factor} = \frac{1}{R}\sqrt{\frac{L}{C}}$$

  where   L = Inductance of a coil, in henrys
  R = Resistance of a coil, in ohms
  C = Capacitance in parallel with a coil, in farads

5.14 SOLUTIONS OF NUMERICAL EXAMPLES FROM UNIVERSITY PAPERS

Example 5.19 : *A coil of inductance 31.8 mH and resistance 10 Ω is connected in parallel with a capacitor across a 250 V, 50 Hz supply. Determine the value of capacitor if no reactive current is taken from the supply.* **(May 2007/10 Marks)**

Solution : Given : L = 31.8 mH, R = 10 Ω, f = 50 Hz, V = 250 volts, f = 50 Hz.

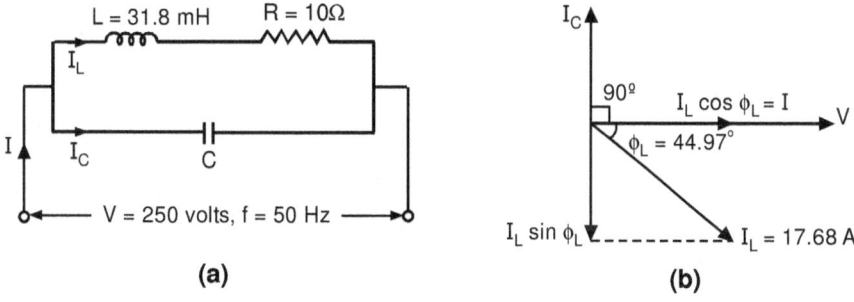

Fig. 5.21

Fig. 5.21 (a) shows the circuit diagram. Here,

$$X_L = \omega L = 2\pi f L = 2\pi \times 50 \times 31.8 \times 10^{-3} = 9.99 \text{ } \Omega$$

$$\overline{Z}_L = R + jX_L = 10 + j\,9.99 = 14.14 \angle 44.97° \text{ } \Omega$$

$$\therefore \quad \overline{I}_L = \frac{\overline{V}}{\overline{Z}_L} = \frac{250 \angle 0°}{14.14 \angle 44.97°} = 17.68 \angle -44.97° \text{ A}$$

Thus, the current I_L drawn by inductive branch will lag the voltage by 44.97° whereas current I_C drawn by the capacitive branch will lead the voltage by 90°. Fig. 5.21 (b) shows the necessary phasor diagram. If no reactive current is drawn by the circuit from the supply, then obviously,

$$I_C = I_L \sin \phi_L = 17.68 \times \sin 44.97° = 12.495 \text{ A}$$

∴ $$X_C = \frac{V}{I_C} = \frac{250}{12.495} = 20 \, \Omega$$

But $$X_C = \frac{1}{\omega C} = \frac{1}{2\pi f C}$$

∴ $$20 = \frac{1}{2\pi \times 50 \times C}$$

∴ Capacitance, $C = \dfrac{1}{2\pi \times 50 \times 20}$ F $= \mathbf{159.15 \, \mu F}$ ... Ans.

It should be noted that in this case,

Current drawn from the supply,

$$I = I_L \cos \phi_L = 17.68 \times \cos 44.97° = 12.5 \text{ A}$$

This current will be in phase with the voltage. As such, circuit power factor will be unity.

5.15 EXERCISES

5.15.1 Review Questions

1. Explain the terms :
   (i) Admittance.
   (ii) Conductance.
   (iii) Susceptance.
   State their units.

2. Explain three-ammeter method of measuring power in an inductive circuit. State the limitations of this method.

3. Why is it advantageous for both consumers as well as suppliers to work at higher improved power factor ?

4. Explain the phenomenon of current resonance (i.e. parallel resonance) in an a.c. circuit and explain its Q-factor.

5. Derive an expression for the resonant frequency of a parallel circuit consisting of inductance of L henries and resistance of R ohms in one branch and a capacitance of C farads in the other.

6. A coil of resistance R ohms and inductance L henries is shunted by a capacitor. Show that when this circuit is under resonance, the effective resistance of the circuit is L/CR.

7. The series resonant circuit is often regarded as the acceptor circuit and the parallel resonant circuit as the rejector circuit. Explain.

8. Compare the properties of series resonance and parallel resonance.

5.15.2 Classified Theory Questions from University Papers

1. Explain the concept of admittance and impedance.

   (Answer : Sections 5.4, 5.5) **(May 2011/8 Marks)**

5.15.3 Examples for Practice

1. A coil having a resistance of 4 Ω and inductive reactance of 3 Ω is connected in parallel with another impedance consisting of a resistance of 8 Ω in series with a capacitive reactance of 6 Ω. This combined circuit is then connected across a single-phase, a.c. supply. If the power loss in the coil is 1600 W, calculate :

   (i) Total current drawn and p.f. of the circuit and

   (ii) Total power loss.

   (24.74 A, 0.9701 lagging, 2400 W)

2. The current taken by an inductive circuit is 2.5 A. The current taken by a resistor of 105 Ω placed in parallel is 2.38 A, while the total current taken from the supply is 4.5 A.

   Calculate :

   (i) Power absorbed by the inductive circuit,

   (ii) Supply voltage, and

   (iii) Power factor of inductive circuit.

   (437.62 W, 249.9 V, 0.7 lagging)

3. Two impedances are having equal magnitudes and power factors of these impedances are 0.7 lagging and 0.9 leading respectively. Calculate the power factor of their :

   (i) Series combination, and

   (ii) Parallel combination.

   (0.985 lagging, 0.985 lagging)

4. Two impedances $(6 + j\,8)$ Ω and $(8 - j\,6)$ Ω are connected in parallel across a 200 V, 50 Hz mains. Calculate :

   (i) Conductance, susceptance and admittance of the combined circuit,

   (ii) Total current taken from the mains and its power factor.

   (0.14 S, – 0.02 S, 0.1414 ∠ – 8.13° S, 28.28 A, 0.99 lagging)

5. A circuit consists of a 12.5 Ω non-inductive resistor in series with a coil having an inductive reactance of 6 Ω and a resistance of 8 Ω. A capacitor with a reactance of 16.67 Ω is connected in parallel with the above circuit. The circuit so formed is then connected across a 250 V, 50 Hz, single-phase supply. Calculate the current in each branch and its phase relative to the supply voltage. Also find out the total power dissipated.

$(11.7 \angle -16.3° \text{ A}, 15 \angle 90° \text{ A}, 2807 \text{ W})$

6. A coil of resistance 10 Ω and inductance 0.5 H is connected in series with a capacitor. On applying a sinusoidal voltage, the current is maximum when the frequency is 50 Hz. A second capacitor is in parallel with the circuit. What capacitance must it have so that the combination acts like a non-inductive resistor at 100 Hz ? Calculate the total current supplied in each case if the applied voltage is 220 V. $(6.7 \text{ μF}, 22 \text{ A}, 0.039 \text{ A})$

❏❏❏

CHAPTER 6

EARTHING AND LAMPS

6.1 NECESSITY OF EARTHING

In order to ensure safety in electrical installations, it is essential that all metal casings containing conductors (e.g. conduits, the frames of the motors and other appliances) must be connected to the general mass of earth, supposed to be at zero potential, by a wire of negligible resistance. This is generally known as *earthing* or *grounding*.

To understand the utility of such earthing, consider a non-earthed piece of metal-cased appliance such as a heater connected to the supply (Fig. 6.1).

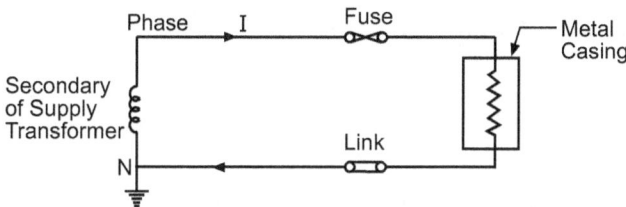

Fig. 6.1 : Non-earthed appliance connected to the supply

If a fault develops causing contact between the conductor and the casing, the casing becomes live with respect to earth by acquiring a potential equal to that of the phase wire (Fig. 6.2).

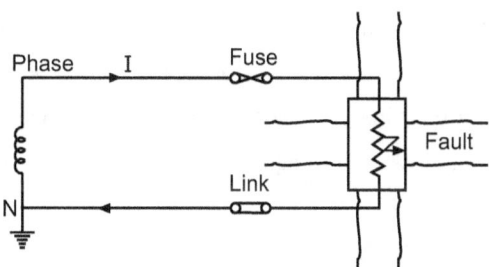

Fig. 6.2 : Fault with non-earthed appliance

If the casing is standing on an insulating or partially insulating surface, there will be no leakage current and the appliance continues to operate. But this state of affairs is highly dangerous. When a person touches the metal casing of the appliance, a circuit to earth is completed as shown in Fig. 6.3.

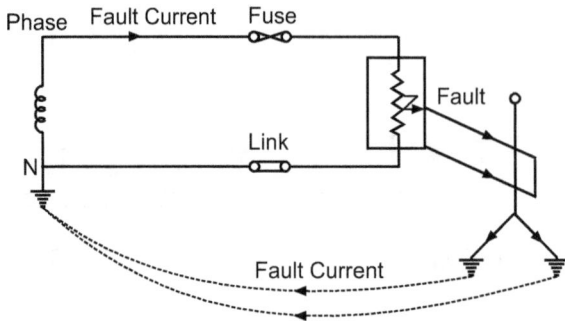

Fig. 6.3 : Faulty non-earthed appliance giving an electric shock

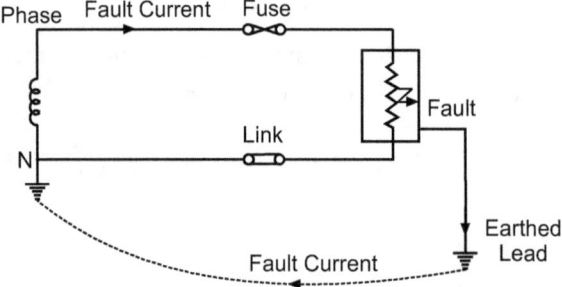

Fig. 6.4 : Fault with earthed appliance

The fault current flows through the phase conductor, the fault and the person to earth. In this condition, the person completing the circuit to earth receives an electric shock. If, however, the casing is well earthed (Fig. 6.4), its potential cannot rise appreciably and immediately upon occurrence of a severe type of fault, a large current flows through the earth lead, back to the earthed neutral point, blowing the fuse and disconnecting the appliance from the supply. This isolation of the appliance not only makes it safe from the point of view of electric shock but also saves it from further damage. However, to achieve this, a fuse must be provided in the live wire only and not in the neutral wire.

6.2 METHODS OF EARTHING

Any metal plate, pipe, rod, other conductor embedded in earth and which makes an effective electrical connection with the general mass of earth is known as *earth electrode*. For small installations such as residential buildings, one electrode is sufficient, in addition to the earth connection through the overhead or underground service connection. For larger installations including substations, several electrodes connected together in parallel are to be provided.

Depending upon the type of electrode used, following are the commonly used methods of earthing : (i) Earthing through a water main, (ii) Plate earthing, (iii) Pipe earthing.

6.2.1 Earthing through a Water Main

In city areas, an underground water main system having metal to metal joints is sometimes used for earthing purposes. While making the earthing connection to the main water pipe, a specially designed earthing clamp is normally used to limit the contact resistance to the minimum. This method is, however, not useful if water mains are of concrete or cement.

6.2.2 Plate Earthing

In this method as illustrated in Fig. 6.5, the earth wire is securely bolted to the earth plate either of copper (minimum size : 60 cm × 60 cm × 3.18 mm) or of galvanized iron (minimum size : 60 cm × 60 cm × 6.35 mm) burried in the ground to the depth of 3 m.

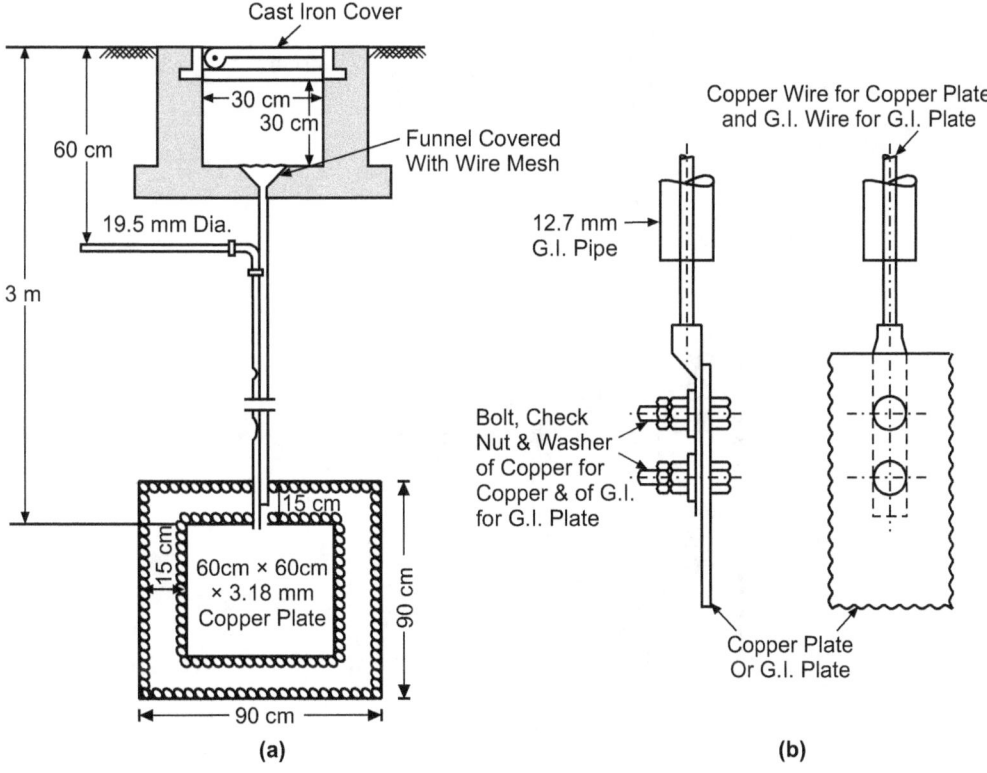

Fig. 6.5 : Plate earthing

The plate is kept in vertical position and is embedded in an alternate layer of coke and salt, each with a minimum thickness of about 15 cm. The layers of coke and salt help to reduce the earth resistance. A galvanized iron pipe fitted with funnel at the top is provided to pour salty water in the pit of earth plate from time to time in the summer season when the moisture content in the soil reduces to a large extent.

6.2.3 Pipe Earthing

In this method (Fig. 6.6), the galvanized iron pipe of not less than 38.1 mm diameter and 2 m in length for ordinary soil and 2.75 m for dry and rocky soil is embedded vertically in the ground to work as earth electrode. The depth at which the pipe should be burried in the ground depends upon the soil condition. The earth wire is fastened to the top section of the pipe with nut bolts. The pit area around the galvanized iron pipe is filled with alternate layers of salt and broken pieces of coke or charcoal. A funnel is fitted to the galvanized iron pipe at the top to pour salty water in the pit of earth electrode from time to time in the summer season as mentioned in the case of plate earthing.

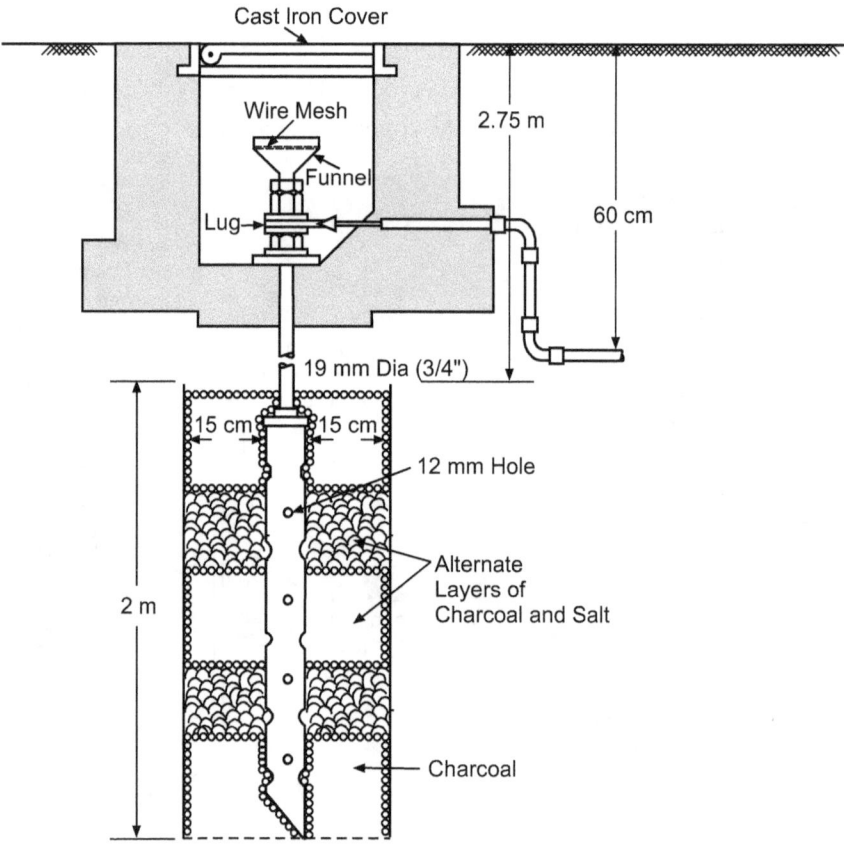

Fig. 6.6 : Pipe earthing

In this method, the earth wire connection with galvanized iron pipe being above the ground level, it can be easily checked for carrying out continuity tests as and when desired. It is an advantage of this method over the plate earthing.

6.3 MAXIMUM PERMISSIBLE RESISTANCE OF EARTH SYSTEMS

The overall resistance of the earth system should be low enough to allow the passage of sufficient current to operate the overload relays or blow fuses, in the event of an earth fault. It follows that the larger the installation, the lower should be the total earth resistance. Even though there is no hard and fast rule about the maximum permissible resistance for the earth systems, their representative values for different installations are listed in the following table :

Table 6.1 : Maximum Permissible Resistance of Earth Systems

Type of Installation	Maximum Permissible Value of the Combined Overall Resistance of the Earth System
Large power stations	0.5 Ω
Major substations	1.0 Ω
Small substations	2.0 Ω
All other cases	8.0 Ω

6.4 WIRING ACCESSORIES

Apart from wires, wooden battens, wooden blocks, clips, nails, screws, screw plugs (commonly known as rawl plugs), etc., the various electrical wiring systems also need accessories such as switches, lamp holders, ceiling roses, socket outlets, plugs and various circuit protection devices such as fuses, moulded case circuit breakers (MCCBs), miniature circuit breakers (MCBs) and earth leakage circuit breakers (ELCBs). Discussion here is restricted to only these circuit protection devices.

6.5 FUSES

An electrical circuit must be safeguarded against the harmful effects of excessive currents. These excessive currents may be because of overloading or short-circuit faults. When an electrical motor is overloaded, it draws an excessive current. If proper precautions are not taken, this excessive current results in the overheating of the motor which ultimately leads to its damage. In case of domestic installation, short circuiting takes place when there is direct connection between the live and neutral conductor. Under these circumstances, the resistance to the supply being very low, enormous current will flow through the conductors. Such a high current leads to an excessive heat rise which, if adjacent to inflammable materials will almost certainly cause an outbreak of fire. In all such cases, therefore, it is necessary to interrupt these excessive currents before they cause any damage. Fuse is the simplest current interrupting device for the protection against excessive currents.

General Construction of the Fuse : In general, the fuse consists of a small piece of metal connected in between two terminals mounted on the insulated base.

Function of the Fuse : When the fuse is inserted in a circuit to be protected, it carries the normal working current safely without heating. But when the current exceeds the predetermined value, it melts due to its rapid overheating. The circuit is then interrupted thereby preventing any damage due to excessive current. Thus, the fuse is in effect a *safety valve* for the electrical circuit.

Fuse Element Material : Metals like tin, lead, zinc, silver, antimony, copper and aluminium can be used for fuse elements. However, metals with low melting points like tin, lead, zinc or lead-tin alloys are found more suitable for this purpose. The main objection for the lead-tin alloys is that these alloys being soft are apt to spread under pressure. The most preferred lead-tin alloys for a fuse element contain 37 % lead and 63 % tin. Normally, lead-tin alloy wire is not used beyond 10 amperes because with higher currents, a wire with a large diameter will be required and after fusing, the metal released will be excessive. Copper wire is most suitable for higher currents. The present trend, however, is to use silver for higher currents despite its higher cost as it is comparatively free from oxidation.

6.6 TYPES OF FUSES

Following two types of fuses are commonly used in practice :

(i) Semi-enclosed or rewirable type, (ii) High rupturing capacity (H.R.C.) cartridge type.

6.6.1 Semi-enclosed or Rewirable Type Fuses

Construction : In this type of fuses, the fuse element is semi-enclosed i.e. neither open nor totally closed. They are available in various forms. Fig. 6.7 illustrates a typical rewirable fuse bridge and base (also known as a *kit-kat* type fuse unit).

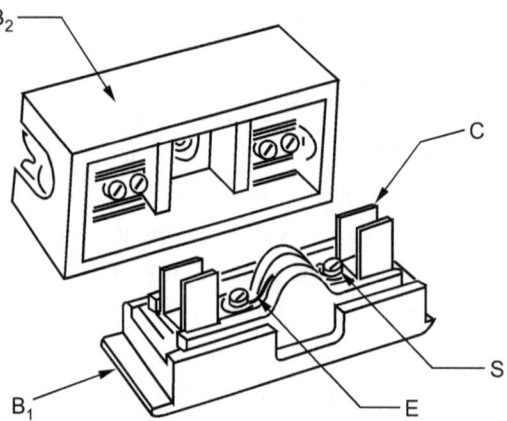

Fig. 6.7 : Rewirable fuse bridge and base

The fuse element (E) consists of a short length of fuse wire of diameter depending upon the current rating of the circuit the fuse is protecting. The wire is threaded through a small hole in the porcelain fuse bridge (B_1) and secured to the contacts (C) by means of screws (S). The incoming and outgoing live or phase wires are connected permanently with the help of connecting terminals to the base (B_2). These terminals of the base are bridged by the contacts of the bridge through the fuse element when the bridge fits into the base.

Operation : The fuse is wired in series with the circuit to be protected. At the fuse, because of the highest resistance, more heat is developed than at any other point in the circuit. During the fault, the circuit current rises in value. Therefore, the heat produced at the fuse causes temperature of the fuse wire to rise to a value high enough to melt the wire and thus break the circuit.

Application : Commonly used in domestic installations and the other circuits where very low values of fault currents are to be handled.

Advantages :

(i) They are cheaper.

(ii) After blowing off the fuse element, the bridge can be pulled out and again rewired with a new fuse wire. Thus, service can be restored very quickly with negligible additional expenditure.

Disadvantages :

(i) Cannot be used for higher values of fault current.

(ii) Protection is not reliable due to inaccurate characteristics.

(iii) Since the wire is exposed to air, it is subjected to deterioration due to oxidation caused by heating. This decreases the effective diameter of the wire. Heating due to increased resistance causes premature failure under normal load.

(iv) Slow speed i.e. current interruption is not quick in comparison with other interrupting devices.

(v) Risk of fire hazards due to external flash on blowing.

6.6.2 High Rupturing Capacity (H.R.C.) Cartridge Fuses

With the increase in fault current level, the fuse clearing the fault would be called upon to withstand extremely heavy stresses in the process. A rewirable fuse would not be able to withstand these stresses and would probably disintegrate violently. The totally enclosed type high rupturing capacity cartridge fuses, specially designed for extremely rapid operation are, therefore, used for such duties.

Construction : H.R.C. cartridge fuse in its simplest form is shown in Fig. 6.8.

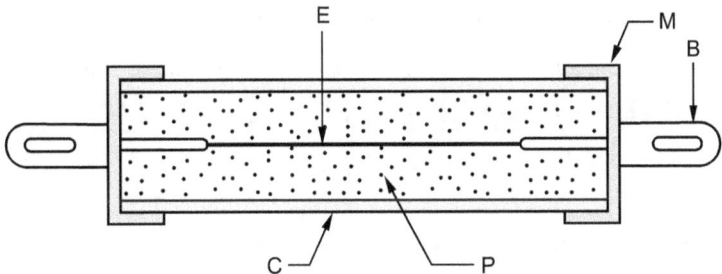

Fig. 6.8 : H.R.C. Cartridge fuse

Fuse element (E), either of silver or copper is totally enclosed and hermetically sealed inside the container known as cartridge (C). The body of the cartridge is of a ceramic material or epoxy-resins having good mechanical strength. The ends of the enclosed fuse element are connected to the metal end caps (M) normally of brass. The contact blades (B) of some conducting material are welded to the metal end caps. The fuse body is filled with powdered pure quartz (P) and some form of indicator is provided on it to provide an indication of the blowing up to the fuse element. The cartridge is bolted on the stationary terminals of the fuse base.

Operation : When the fuse is inserted in a circuit to be protected, it carries the normal working current safely without heating. When a fault occurs, the large current passing through the fuse element produces heat to such an extent that it causes melting of the fuse element. The metal released in the vapour form diffuses with the quartz powder. The chemical reaction between the two produces a substance of high electrical resistance like an insulator. This substance, which is in the form of glass beads, helps in quenching the arc quickly.

An indicator may consist of a resistance wire of fine gauge connected in parallel with the fuse element and led through a small quantity of a mild explosive held in a pocket in the side of the fuse and covered by a label. The fine wire is automatically fused when the fuse operates and the resulting combustion of the explosive material chars the label. Thus, the charred label will indicate the blowing up of the fuse.

Application : With the increasing loads and sizes of the networks, H.R.C. cartridge fuses are now gradually replacing the rewirable types, particularly in industrial installations. They are also frequently used in low-voltage distribution systems.

Advantages :

(i) Being totally closed, there is no deterioration of the fuse element.

(ii) Due to accurate characteristics and consistent performance, protection is reliable.

(iii) High speed operation.

(iv) Ability to clear high values of fault current.

(v) Its operation is silent and without flame, gas or smoke. Hence safe from the point of view of fire hazards.

Disadvantages :

(i) Costly in comparison with rewirable type fuses.

(ii) The cartridge is to be replaced by a new one after each operation.

(iii) Overheating of the adjacent contacts is possible during the operation of the fuse.

6.7 CURRENT RATING AND MINIMUM FUSING CURRENT

These are the terms which are very commonly used in respect of fuses. They are defined as follows :

Current Rating of Fusing Element : It is that value of continuous current which the fusing element can carry safely without undue heating, melting and deterioration.

Minimum Fusing Current : It is that minimum value of current which causes melting of the fuse.

Fusing Factor : It is defined as the ratio of minimum fusing current to the current rating of the fusing element i.e.

$$\text{Fusing factor} = \frac{\text{Minimum fusing current}}{\text{Current rating of the fusing element}}$$

Its value is always more than 1.

6.8 INTRODUCTION TO LOW-VOLTAGE CIRCUIT BREAKERS

A circuit breaker is an automatic type mechanical switching device capable of making, carrying and breaking current, under normal and under specified abnormal conditions.

Basic Principle of Operation of a Circuit Breaker :

Fig. 6.9 illustrates the basic principle of operation of a circuit breaker. When a fault occurs in the protected circuit, the fault impedance being low, the current increases. This actuates the relay connected to the line through the current transformer (C.T.) and closes its contacts. Closing of the relay contacts results in closing of the trip circuit of the circuit breaker and the trip coil is energized due to current flow from the battery. As the trip coil of the circuit breaker is energized, the circuit breaker operating mechanism is actuated and it opens the circuit breaker contacts. On the separation of the circuit breaker contacts, the flow of current is interrupted, resulting in the formation of arc between the contacts. These contacts are placed in a closed chamber containing some insulating medium (like air, oil or gas) which extinguishes the arc.

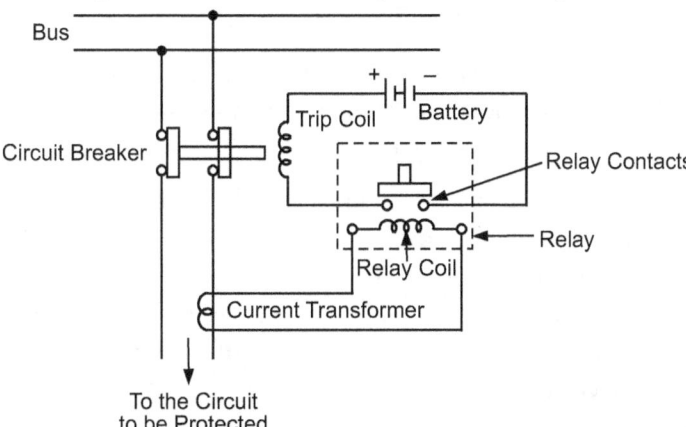

Fig. 6.9 : Basic principle of operation of a circuit breaker

The difference between the fuse and circuit breaker is that under fault conditions, the fuse melts and a new one is to be replaced while the circuit breaker can close the circuit as well as break the circuit without any replacement.

There are various types of circuit breakers. These types are based on the medium used in their operation for arc quenching. Here, we shall restrict our discussion mainly to the following types of circuit breakers which are extensively used in low-voltage domestic, commercial and industrial applications to replace fuse-switch units.

6.8.1 Moulded Case Circuit Breaker (MCCB)

Moulded case circuit breaker is a compact type of air circuit breaker enclosed in a moulded (insulating body) case. It uses air (at atmospheric pressure) as an arc quenching medium. The resistance of the arc is increased by cooling, lengthening and splitting the arc with the help of arc chute. The arc resistance is increased to such an extent that the system voltage cannot maintain the arc and it gets extinguished. When used on a.c., the arc extinction process is further assisted by the current zeros in the a.c. wave.

Protections Provided : Moulded case circuit breaker mainly provides protection against the overload and short-circuits. Overload protection is given by bimetal strips and short-circuit protection is achieved by magnetic attraction.

Advantages : Inspite of its high initial cost, MCCB is preferred over traditionally used switch-fuse unit becasue of the following advantages :

  (i)   Practically, no maintenance is required.
  (ii) No recurring cost.
  (iii) It avoids single-phasing.
  (iv) Gives indication in case it trips on fault.

Ratings : Ratings available are 16 A to 1600 A with breaking capacities as high as 85 kA, for both 3-pole as well as 4-pole versions.

Applications : MCCBs are suitable for both a.c. as well as d.c. applications. Some of these applications are as mentioned below :

Distribution feeders, distribution transformers, diesel generating sets, L.T. capacitors, rectifier panels, U.P.S. and other electronic equipment, motors, furnaces, etc.

6.8.2 Miniature Circuit Breaker (MCB)

In this case also, tripping mechanism and the terminal contacts are assembled in a moulded case, moulded out of thermosetting powders. This ensures high mechanical strength, high dielectric strength and virtually no ageing. The current carrying parts are made of electrolytic copper or silver alloy depending upon the rating of the breaker. All other metal parts are of non-ferrous, non-rusting type. The arc chute has a special construction which increases the length of arc by the magnetic field created by the arc itself.

The breaker has unit construction whereby multiple-pole breakers can be made by assembly of single-pole breakers. For single-phase, either 1-pole or 2-pole versions of MCB are used. On the other hand, for 3-phase circuits, either 3-pole or 4-pole versions are used.

Protections Provided : MCB is used for overload and short-circuit protections. Overload protection is given by bimetal strips and short-circuit protection is achieved by magnetic attraction.

Advantages :
  (i)   It can be used by skilled/unskilled workmen.
  (ii) It can be used as a functional switch or as an isolator.
  (iii) Its a fully enclosed unit and hence no ageing problem.
  (iv) MCB is a cost effective device.

Ratings : Available from 0.5 A to 100 A at voltage ratings of 240 V/415 V and breaking capacity upto 3 kA.

Applications : Commonly used for lighting circuits, distribution feeders, switching of motors, capacitors, control transformers, etc.

6.8.3 Earth Leakage Circuit Breaker (ELCB)

When the fault current flows through the earth return path, the fault is called *earth fault*. An earth leakage circuit breaker gives protection against direct or indirect contact with the live circuit under such fault condition. Fig. 6.10 diagrammatically represents 2-pole earth leakage circuit breaker suitable for single-phase load.

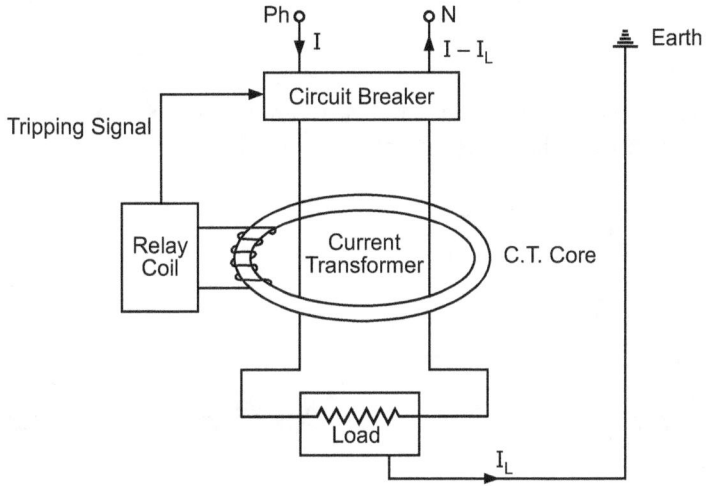

Fig. 6.10 : Earth leakage circuit breaker

Principle of Operation : During normal condition, the currents through the phase and neutral wires are equal and opposite. So the fluxes produced by these currents in the current transformer core are equal and opposite. So they neutralize each other. But during the earth fault condition, small leakage current (I_L) starts returning back to earth through the earthing conductor or human body as illustrated in Fig. 6.10. This disturbs the balance between the currents in the phase and neutral wire. So, certain resultant flux is set up in the current transformer core which induces an e.m.f. in the secondary winding of the C.T. The output current of the current transformer under this condition energizes the relay coil. The relay produces a tripping signal and applies it to the circuit breaker. The circuit breaker then operates and breaks the supply to the circuit to be protected.

The 4-pole earth leakage circuit breaker suitable for three-phase loads also works on the same principle.

Ratings : ELCB is available in following sensitivities :

30 mA   :   For personal protection (e.g. domestic applications)
100 mA :   Installation protection in industries.
300 mA :   Installation protection in industries having inherently high leakage currents.

Applications : A combination of ELCB and MCB modules can be used to give overload, short-circuit and earth leakage protection in low-voltage domestic, commercial and industrial applications.

6.9 ELECTRIC LAMPS

The *lamp*, whether oil, gas, electric or any other type, may be regarded as a piece of equipment for converting a certain form of energy into light waves. Electric lamps produce light using electrical energy and have almost replaced other types of lamps due to their cleanliness, ease of control and low cost. Their application has particularly helped industries in reducing the accidents and increasing the outputs. The following types of electric lamps are in common use in our day to day life.

6.10 INCANDESCENT LAMPS

Incandescent lamps work on the principle that when a filament of fine wire is maintained at incandescence (white-hot condition) by the passage of current, it emits sufficient energy in the form of light.

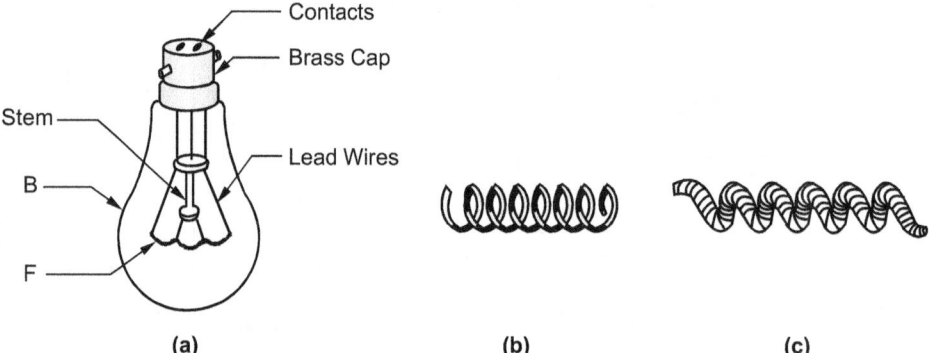

Fig. 6.11 : (a) Modern gas filled incandescent lamp, (b) Coiled or helical filament, (c) Coiled-coil filament

Construction : Fig. 6.11 (a) shows the construction of the modern type of gas-filled incandescent lamp.

It consists of a tungsten filament (F) placed in a glass bulb (B). Tungsten is used as filament material because it has a high melting point (3500° C), high specific resistance and a low rate of evaporation in addition to ductility and good mechanical strength. The glass bulb is filled with a chemically inert gas such as argon or nitrogen at about atmospheric pressure to further reduce the rate of evaporation and avoid oxidation. This increases the life and efficiency of the lamp. The filament is supported on wire hooks fixed on a glass stem and is normally in the coiled (helical) or coiled-coil (Figs. 6.11 b and c) form to reduce the surface area exposed to gas, thereby reducing heat loss due to convection. It also requires less space. The coiled-coil lamp has higher efficiency than a single-coil lamp and requires less number of supports for the filament. In small sizes upto 25 watts, the filament may be worked in vacuum.

Operation : When the current is passed through the tungsten filament, it is heated to incandescence (white-hot condition) which then starts emitting energy in the form of light.

Applications : These lamps are very commonly used for indoor lighting, flood lights for buildings, head lights for the vehicles, photographic and projection work. For applications requiring glare-free lamps, silica lamps with a milk-white diffusing layer of silicon oxide spread over the internal surface of the glass bulbs are used. Carbon filament lamps are used as loading resistances. The commonly used ratings for the incandescent lamps vary from 10 to 1500 watts.

Advantages :
  (i) Cheapest among all types of lamps.
  (ii) Available in various shapes and shades.
  (iii) Operates at unity power factor.

Disadvantages :
  (i) Shorter life (about 1000 working hours).
  (ii) Much lower efficiency in comparison with discharge lamps i.e. lesser light output for given wattage.
  (iii) High heat radiation.
  (iv) They are very sensitive to changes in supply voltage. Efficiency and operating life of the lamp is dependent upon voltage fluctuations. Violent voltage fluctuations shorten the life of the lamp.

6.11 ELECTRIC DISCHARGE LAMPS

If a high voltage is applied between two electrodes situated at the ends of a tube containing certain gas, then, the discharge (passage of current) in a gas is always accompanied by a glow. This phenomenon is utilized in the modern electric discharge lamps described below.

6.11.1 Fluorescent Lamps or Fluorescent Tubes

Construction : The fluorescent lamp (Fig. 6.12 a and Fig. 16.13) is a low-pressure mercury discharge lamp. It generally consists of a long glass tube (G) with an electrode at each end (E_1 and E_2). These electrodes are made of coiled tungsten filament coated with an electron emitting material. The tube is internally coated with a fluorescent powder and contains a small amount of argon together with a little mercury at a very-low pressure. The control circuit of the tube consists of a starting switch (S) known as a *starter*, an iron-cored inductive coil called a *choke* (L) and two capacitors (C_1 and C_2).

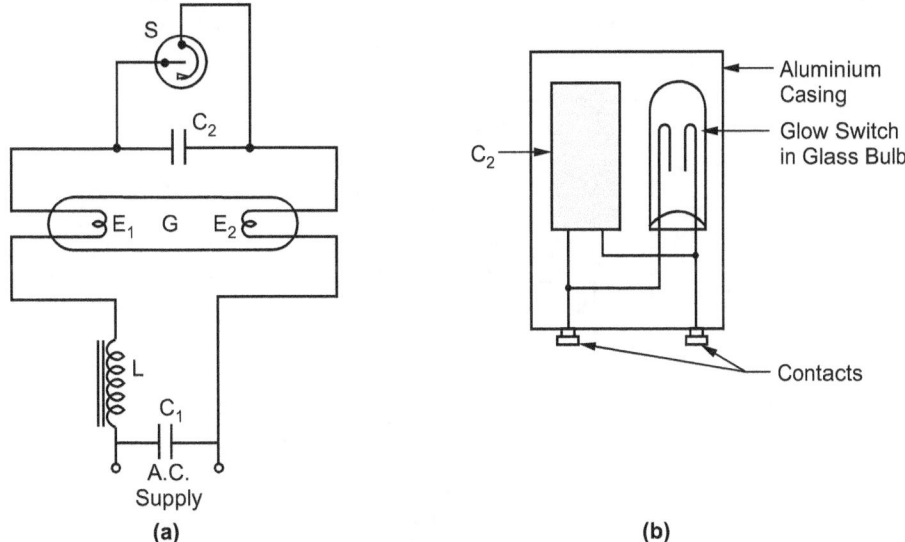

**Fig. 6.12 : (a) Fluorescent lamp circuit with a glow type starting switch,
(b) Cutaway view of a starter**

Operation : Two types of starting switches, namely the glow type (a voltage operated device) and the thermal type (a current operated device) are in general use. A tube fitted with a glow type starter (S) is shown in Fig. 6.12 (a). This starter (Fig. 6.12 b) consists of two electrodes hermetically sealed in a glass bulb filled with a mixture of helium and hydrogen. One electrode is fixed and the other is a U-shaped bimetallic strip made of two metals having different temperature co-efficients of expansion. The contacts are normally open. When the supply is switched on, heat produced due to a glow discharge between electrodes of the starter is sufficient to bend the bimetallic strip (due to uneven expansions of two metals) until it makes contact with the fixed electrode. Thus, the circuit between two tube electrodes (E_1 and E_2) is completed and a relatively large current is circulated through them. The electrodes are then heated to incandescence by this circulating current and the gas in their immediate vicinity is ionized. After a second or two, due to the absence of a glow discharge which ceases after the closing of the contacts of the starting switch, the bimetallic strip cools sufficiently. This causes it to break contact and the sudden reduction of current induces an e.m.f. of the order of 800-1000 V in the choke coil. This voltage is sufficient to strike an arc between the two electrodes E_1 and E_2 due to the ionization of argon. The heat generated in the tube vaporizes the mercury and the potential difference across the tube falls to about 100-110 V. This potential difference is not sufficient to restart the glow in the starter.

If a thermal type starting switch is used, the circuit arrangement will be as shown in Fig. 6.13. This switch (S), either open type or enclosed in a hydrogen filled glass bulb, has a bimetallic strip close to a heater element (R). The two electrodes of the switch are normally closed. Consequently, when the lamp is switched on, the circuit being complete through the thermal switch, a relatively large current flows through the two filaments (E_1 and E_2) of the tube. This circulating current heats the filaments to incandescence and the gas in their immediate vicinity is ionized. Since the same current is also passing through the heater element (R), it causes the bimetallic strip to break contact and the inductive voltage surge due to the choke starts the discharge in the tube. The starter contacts, then remain open till the lamp is in operation due to the heat generated in the heater element.

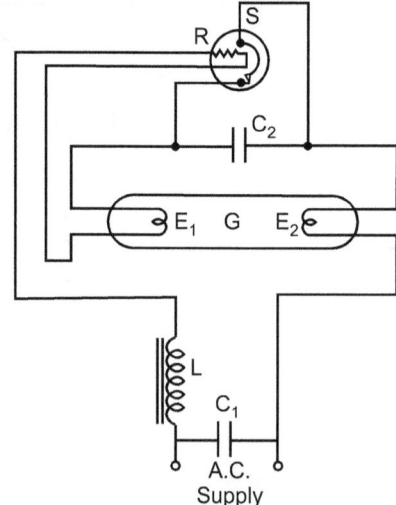

Fig. 6.13 : Fluorescent lamp circuit with thermal type starting switch

Most of the energy radiated by this low-pressure mercury vapour lamp is not in visible form. The fluorescent coating absorbs this energy and converts it into visible radiation i.e. light. Different fluorescent powders re-radiate the absorbed energy at different colours.

Functions of the Auxiliary Circuit Components :

Choke :

(i) It provides a necessary high voltage to start the discharge in the tube (i.e. the voltage required to strike an arc between the two electrodes of the tube).

(ii) Since the voltage required across the tube during normal operation is small (about 100-110 V), the excess voltage is dropped across the choke.

(iii) The choke acts as a stabilizer. The discharge has a negative characteristic i.e. the resistance falls with an increase in current. Under such conditions, the choke helps in maintaining a constant current in the tube. For example, if the current increases, the voltage drop across the choke will increase and the voltage across the tube will decrease which will tend to decrease the current and vice-versa.

Capacitor C_1 : The choke lowers the power factor of the circuit. C_1 connected across the supply improves this power factor.

Capacitor C_2 : It is connected across the starting switch to suppress radio interference due to high frequency voltage oscillations which may occur across its contacts.

Applications : They are very popularly used for interior lighting in residential buildings, shops and hotels. They are also extensively used with reflectors for street lighting. Due to their glare-free shadowless light, they are ideal for workshops, factories, laboratories and drawing rooms. The fluorescent tubes are normally manufactured with 20, 40 and 80 W ratings.

Advantages :

(i) Lower power consumption.

(ii) Longer life which is about 3 to 4 times that of filament lamps.

(iii) Compared to filament lamps, the efficiency is also about 3 to 4 times, thus gives much more light for the same wattage.

(iv) Superior quality of light. Gives diffused, glare-free, shadowless and cool white light (approaching a day light).

(v) No warming up period is required as in the case of other discharge lamps.

(vi) Different colour lights can be obtained using different types of fluorescent powders.

(vii) Low heat radiation.

Disadvantages :

(i) Initial cost of the lamp alongwith the auxiliary equipment needed is very high. However, considering its long life, its use is still economical.

(ii) With frequent switching operations, life reduces.

(iii) Voltage fluctuations affect it, but not to the extent that filament lamps are affected.

(iv) Produce radio interference.

(v) Fluctuating light output (flicker) produces undesirable stroboscopic effect with rotating machinery. Due to this effect, rotating machinery may appear to be stationary or even seem to rotate in the opposite direction. This can be eliminated by using groups of three lamps distributed between three phases of a three-phase supply or twin lamps on a single-phase supply with certain circuit modifications.

6.11.2 Mercury Vapour Lamps

Construction : Mercury vapour lamps are available in various forms. Fig. 6.14 shows one form of this lamp. It consists of the discharge tube (G_1) enclosed within an evacuated outer glass tube (G_2). This arrangement reduces heat loss thereby improving the operating efficiency of the lamp. The inner tube contains a small quantity of mercury and argon (or neon). The two cathodes made from electron emitting material and held in tungsten wire helices form the main electrodes (E_1 and E_2). The pressure inside the discharge tube is of the order of 1 to 2 atmospheres. The control circuit of the lamp consists of a stabilizing choke (L) and a capacitor (C).

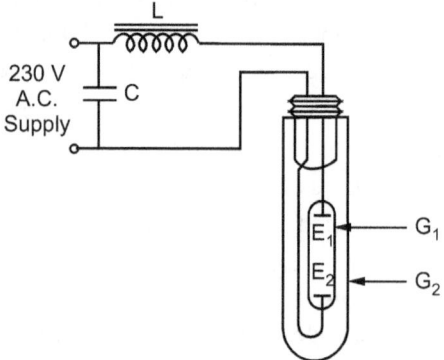

Fig. 6.14 : Mercury vapour lamp

Operation : When the lamp is switched on, the initial discharge takes place through neon or argon gas. The heat produced during the next few minutes due to the discharge through this gas vaporises the mercury. The lamp then commences normal operation and emits its characteristic light with a bluish tinge. During normal operation, the cathode is maintained incandescent (at very high temperature) by the ionic bombardment and therefore no heating of the cathode is necessary.

The choke stabilizes the discharge i.e. limits the current to a safe value as already explained in the case of a fluorescent lamp. The power factor lowered by the presence of the choke is improved with the help of a capacitor connected across the supply.

Applications : These lamps are widely used for out-door yard lighting and street lighting where a high level of illumination is essential and the colour of the light is not important. Such lamps are made in sizes of 125, 250 W and upwards.

Advantages :

(i) Efficiency well in excess of that of filament lamps (nearly 3 times). Therefore, gives more light output for a given wattage.

(ii) Longer life (about 3000 working hours).

Disadvantages :

(i) Requires warming up time of about 3 to 5 minutes.

(ii) If the lamp goes out while in service, for its restarting, cooling is necessary. Cooling reduces the vapour pressure to sufficiently low value, which then allows restriking of the discharge in the neon or argon to take place.

6.11.3 Sodium Vapour Lamps

Construction : Fig. 6.15 illustrates one form of the modern low-pressure sodium vapour lamp. The sodium vapour lamp is similar in construction to the mercury vapour lamp. The two electrodes (E_1 and E_2) are mounted in a glass tube or bulb (G_1) containing sodium along with a small quantity of neon or argon. Sodium vapour being chemically very active, the glass of the tube is of special composition in order to resist the action of hot sodium vapour. As already mentioned previously, to obtain best operating conditions and efficiency, it is essential to maintain the correct temperature in the discharge tube (about 300ºC) and to reduce loss of heat from it.

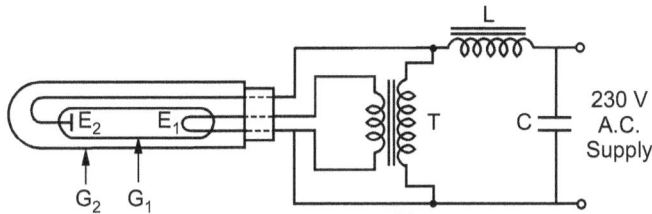

Fig. 6.15 : Sodium vapour lamp

Therefore, the discharge tube itself is placed in an evacuated outer tube (G_2). In addition to the stabilizing choke (L) and the capacitor (C), a small step-down transformer (T) is also included in the circuit for heating the cathode (E_1).

Operation : Similar to mercury vapour lamp, an initial discharge on switching on takes place in the neon (or argon) gas and the heat generated during the next few minutes is then sufficient to vaporize the sodium. This enables the main discharge to take place through the sodium vapour. Thus, the lamp starts emitting its characteristic bright yellow light. The choke stabilizes the discharge and the capacitor improves the power factor.

Applications : These lamps are extensively used for the illumination of roads, goods yards, air-ports, etc. They are also sometimes used for advertisement purposes. The lamps with 250 watts and upward ratings are more commonly employed.

Advantages :

(i) Highest efficiency, about 3 to 4 times that of the filament lamps.

(ii) Longer life.

Disadvantages :

(i) Bright yellow colour is not suitable for indoor lighting.

(ii) Long tubes are required for sufficient light output.

(iii) Requires 5 to 10 minutes for giving full output. This factor is however of little importance in its practical use.

(iv) Since the sodium solidifies when the tube cools, it is necessary to ensure that the sodium is deposited reasonably uniformly along the whole length of the tube and not concentrated at one end. Consequently, the lamp is to be used preferably in a horizontal position.

6.11.4 Neon Lamps

Construction : It uses glass bulb of the size similar to that of an ordinary incandescent lamp.

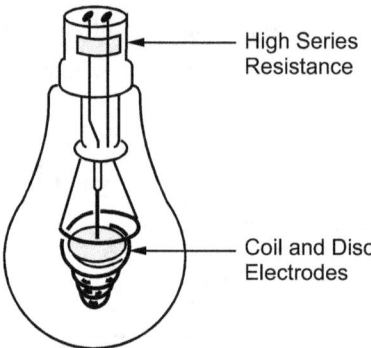

Fig. 6.16 : Neon lamp

The bulb is filled with the rare gas neon at a pressure of about 10 mm of mercury. Pure iron electrodes in the form of two thick parallel wire spirals or a tapering spiral and a disk or two flat plates are placed close together (but not touching each other) in the glass bulb (Fig. 6.16). A series resistance of about 2000 ohms is mounted inside the cap.

Operation : On switching on, the lamp lights with a luminous orange red glow. With d.c., glow is around the cathode (negative electrode) but on a.c., both the electrodes glow with equal intensity. Ballast resistance in the cap reduces the fluctuations in current drawn by the lamp.

Applications : Such type of neon lamps are used only when a small amount of light is required e.g. a night lamp or a pilot lamp. They are available for the voltages as low as 110 V, a.c. or 150 V d.c.

Advantages :

(i) Long life (about 5000 working hours).

(ii) Low power consumption of the order of 3 to 5 W.

Disadvantages :

(i) Low efficiency.

(ii) Cannot be used for ordinary lighting purposes.

Special Applications of Neon Lamps :

Neon Signs :

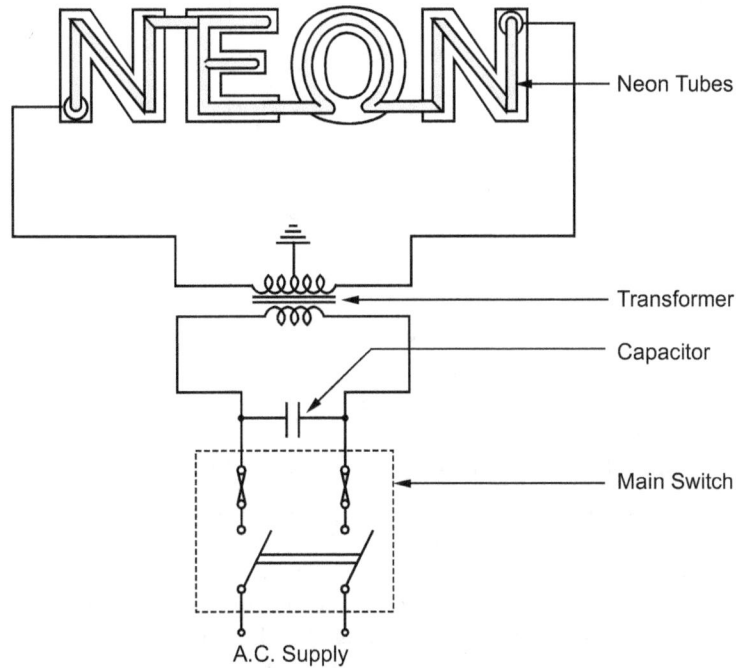

Fig. 6.17 : Neon sign tubes

Construction : These are the neon lamps in the form of long tubes (Fig. 6.17) of desired shape filled with neon gas at a low pressure. Metal electrodes with the coating of electron emissive material are provided at each end of the tube. A transformer having a high internal reactance is used to provide a high voltage ranging between 1500 to 6000 V depending upon the length and internal diameter of the tubing, gas pressure and the type of gas filling. The center of the high-tension winding of the transformer is connected to earth so as to keep the maximum potential to earth of any part of the high-tension circuit within permissible limits. Capacitors may be connected across the primary terminals of the transformer for improvement of power factor and elimination of radio interference.

Operation : On switching on, a high voltage (about 50 % higher than the normal working voltage across the tube) is applied across the electrodes which starts the discharge. Once the discharge starts, this voltage is reduced due to high internal reactance of the transformer, thus stabilizing the discharge.

Applications : Neon signs are mainly used for advertising and decoration purposes. By varying the composition of the glass and adding substances to the neon gas, a wide range of colours can be obtained. Other inert gases like argon (for blue colour) and helium (for yellow colour) are also used frequently depending upon the colour requirements.

6.11.5 Compact Fluorescent Lamps (C.F.Ls.)

Construction : Basically compact fluorescent lamp (Fig. 6.18) is a type of fluorescent lamp. There are two types of these lamps :

(i) Integrated type, (ii) Non-integrated type.

Fig. 6.18 : A typical compact fluorescent lamp (C.F.L.)

Integrated type lamps have a compact arc tube, an electronic ballast (choke) and either a screw or bayonet type fitting combined in a single unit. With such a construction, these lamps work well in standard incandescent fixtures and therefore can easily replace incandescent lamps. In non-integrated type, compact fluorescent lamp does not include a ballast in itself. Therefore, such lamps allow low cost replacement of consumable tubes and the extended use of electrical ballasts in a light fixture. Non-integrated compact fluorescent lamp housings are both more expensive and sophisticated, providing options such as dimming, less flicker, faster starts, etc.

Operation : Compact arc tube of a lamp contains a high-pressure mixture of argon and mercury. Like ordinary fluorescent tubes, in this case also, the light is produced by passing an electric arc through a mixture of these gases.

The ballast used provides proper starting and operating voltages and regulate the current flow in the lamp. Increasing use of electronic ballasts has removed most of the flickering and slow starting traditionally associated with fluorescent lighting. Compact fluorescent lamps generally radiate a different light spectrum from that of incandescent lamps. However, now-a-days with the improved phosphor formulations, the lamps emitting soft white light similar in colour to standard incandescent lamps are also available.

Applications :
(i) Compact fluorescent lamps are produced for both alternating current and direct current. Integrated type compact fluorescent lamps are finding increasing use in domestic applications. D.C. compact fluorescent lamps are popular for use in recreational vehicles and off-the-grid housing. D.C. fluorescent lamps operating on car batteries, solar panels and small wind generators are increasingly used in rural parts to replace kerosene lanterns.
(ii) Non-integrated compact fluorescent lamps with external ballasts having dimming capabilities are more popular for professional users, such as hotels and office buildings.

Advantages :
(i) Modern compact fluorescent lamps generally have a lifespan of between 6000 to 15000 hours as against 750 to 1000 hours for incandescent lamps.
(ii) For a given light output, compact fluorescent lamps use between 20 to 25% of the power of an equivalent incandescent lamp.

Disadvantages :
(i) Purchase cost of a compact fluorescent lamp is nearly 3 to 10 times greater than that of an equivalent incandescent lamp. However, extended lifespan and lower energy use compensate for the higher initial cost in many applications.
(ii) Compact fluorescent lamps can fail prematurely if overheated.

6.11.6 Metal Halide Lamps

Construction : Metal halide lamps (Fig. 6.19) are basically compact high-intensity discharge lamps producing high light output and operating under the conditions of high pressure and temperature. Metal halide lamp has a metal base and a glass shield to protect the inner components. Inside the glass shield, a series of support and lead wires hold the inner fused quartz or alumina arc tube with its embedded tungsten electrodes. The compact arc tube contains a high-pressure mixture of argon, mercury and a variety of metal halides (iodides or sometimes bromides of different metals).

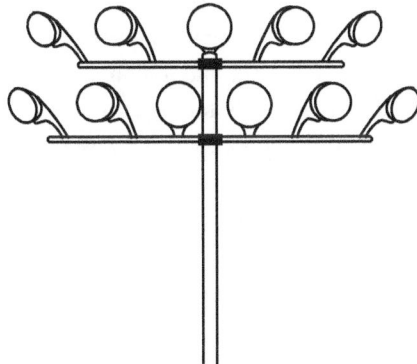

Fig. 6.19 : Metal halide lighting pole at a sport field

Operation : The argon gas in the lamp is easily ionized and facilitates striking of the arc across the two electrodes when voltage is first applied to the lamp. The heat generated by the arc then vaporizes the mercury and metal halides which produce light as the temperature and pressure increase. The mixture of halides affects the nature of light produced. Sometimes, a phosphor coating is provided on the inner side of the outer glass bulb (shield) to improve the spectrum and diffuse the light.

Like other gas discharge lamps, metal halide lamps require electrical or electronic ballasts to regulate the arc current flow and deliver the proper voltage to the arc.

Applications : Because of their availability in numerous sizes (150, 250, 575 and 1200 W ratings) and configurations, these lamps are now increasingly used for industrial, commercial and domestic applications. They are most often used in athletic facilities. They are preferred to mercury vapour lamps in instances where natural light is desired.

Advantages :

(i) Metal halide lamps are more efficient than fluorescent lamps and substantially more efficient than incandescent lamps.

(ii) Longer lifespan.

Disadvantages : In general, a cold metal halide lamp requires some starting or warm up time. It cannot immediately begin producing its full light because the temperature and pressure in the inner arc tube require time to reach full operating levels. However, now the lamps having 'instant restriking' capabilities, have also been developed. In this case, the lamp, ballast and socket are built to withstand 30 kV re-ignition pulse supplied via a separate anode wire.

6.11.7 LED Lamps

Construction : LED lamp is a solid-state lamp that uses light-emitting diodes (LEDs) as the source of light. LED lamps are available with a variety of colour properties depending upon the semiconductor materials used in their construction and on the techniques incorporated in their operation, such as use of phosphor, colour mixing, etc. For general lighting purposes, LED lamps are now available as a directly compatible drop-in-replacement for incandescent or fluorescent lamps and multiple LEDs are used in their construction. This makes them brighter.

LEDs need controlled direct current (d.c.) electrical power for their operation. Hence, LED lamps include circuitry to rectify the a.c. power and to convert the voltage to a level usable by the LEDs. LEDs are adversely affected by high temperature. Therefore, LED lamps need heat dissipation elements such as heat sinks and cooling fins as part of their construction.

Operation : Light-emitting diode used as the source of light in LED lamps is basically a semiconductor device that converts electrical energy into light. When an electron falls from higher energy level to lower energy level, energy is always released in the form of either heat or light. In the LED, this happens when electrons move around in its semiconductor structure, and energy is released in the form of light.

Applications : LED lamps are commonly used as indicator lamps in many electrical and electronic devices. With the development of high efficiency, high-power LEDs, now it has become possible to use LED lamps for general and special-purpose lighting. Now-a-days, these lamps are used in the applications as diverse as aviation lighting, automotive lighting, advertising, general-purpose lighting, street lights, traffic signals, flash lights, solar powered garden or walkway lights, aquarium lights, stage lights, flood lights, etc.

Advantages :
- (i) High light emitting efficiency.
- (ii) Lower energy consumption.
- (iii) Improved mechanical robustness.
- (iv) Long lifespans.
- (v) Smaller sizes.
- (vi) Faster response.
- (vii) More environmental friendly (being free from toxic materials).

Disadvantages :
- (i) Relatively more expensive.
- (ii) Require more precise current and heat management.

6.12 ELECTRICAL POWER SYSTEM

In general, the modern power system consists of the following three principal elements :

(i) Generating stations,

(ii) Transmission lines,

(iii) Distribution systems.

Electrical energy is produced in bulk at the generating stations. Transmission lines transmit this energy to distribution systems and thus serve as connecting links between the generating stations and distribution systems. Distribution systems then distribute the energy received by them to all the individual loads.

6.13 TRANSMISSION AND DISTRIBUTION OF ELECTRICAL POWER

While discussing the three-phase supply systems later on in Article 7.3, we have assumed there that the electrical power is directly supplied by an alternator to the load. However, this is the case with only small alternators supplying power over relatively short distances. The present-day electric systems involve the extensive use of transformers to step up the generation voltage before the power is transmitted to the distant load centres. The reasons for adoption of high voltage for transmission of electrical power are discussed briefly in the Section 3.3. The power stations (particularly the hydro-power stations) are normally located at favourable places, quite away from the load centres. Under such conditions, it is the high voltage which makes the long distance transmission economical. However, since the cost of the transmission equipments is rising with the increase in transmission voltage, compromise is to be made in the selection of transmission voltage. The high voltage at the transmitting end is again reduced at the load centres.

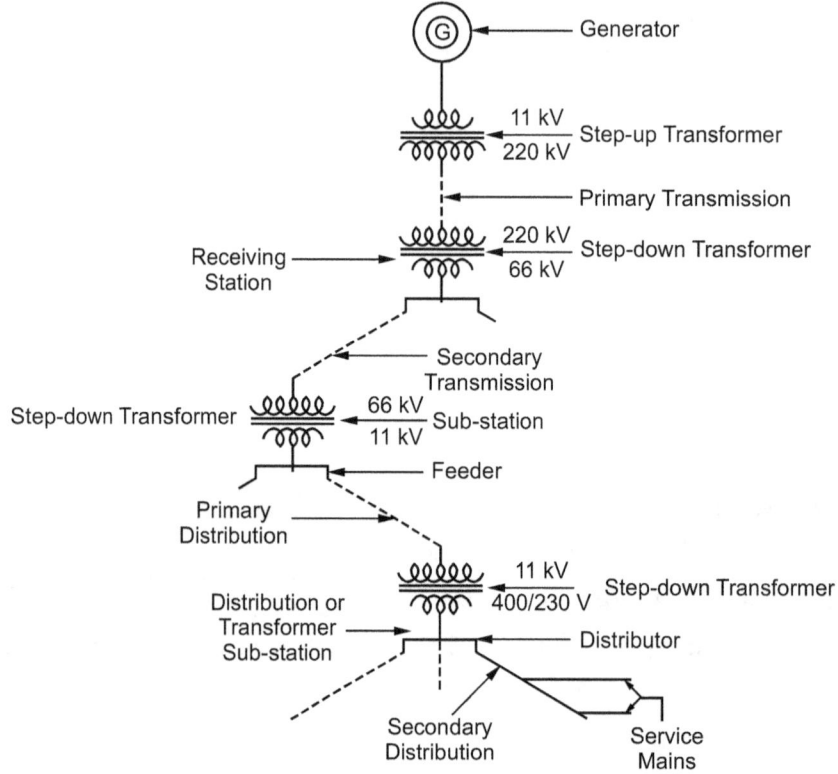

Fig. 6.20 : Layout (single-line diagram) of a typical power system

Fig. 6.20 shows a typical alternating current transmission and distribution system with the help of a single line diagram.

Stages Involved in Transmission and Distribution of Electrical Power : The various stages involved in the transmission and distribution of electrical power are as follows :

(i) Generating Station : The generating station, as already seen, is equipped with number of three-phase alternators. These alternators run in parallel to generate large power and are driven by various types of prime movers depending upon the type of power station.

Usual generation voltages are 6.6, 11 or 33 kV. The generation voltage is then stepped up with the help of transformers to some suitable value such as 132, 220, 275 or 400 kV for transmission purposes.

(ii) Primary or High-Voltage Transmission : The transmission lines carry the power at the high voltage from generating station to the receiving station which is usually located at the outskirts of a city. This forms the primary transmission system. It should be noted that the distance between the generating station and the receiving station is normally very large.

(iii) Secondary or Low-Voltage Transmission : At the receiving station which is also equipped with the transformers, the primary transmission voltage is stepped down to 33 or 66 kV. The power is further transmitted at this voltage to the sub-stations located in different areas in the city. This stage is known as secondary or low-voltage transmission.

(iv) Primary or High-Voltage Distribution : During this stage, the transformers at the substations step down the voltage to a value as low as 3.3, 6.6 or 11 kV and feed the transformer sub-stations (also known as distribution sub-stations) serving the various localities. Big factories may be supplied directly at this voltage.

(v) Secondary or Low-Voltage Distribution : The voltage is further reduced to 400/230 volts at the transformer sub-stations to suit the secondary distribution system which feeds the consumers.

In the context of the a.c. transmission and distribution systems, the following points are worth noting :

(i) All the existing systems do not include all the stages discussed above. e.g. Some may have no primary transmission and others may be so small that there is, in effect, distribution only and so on.

(ii) Generation, transmission and distribution are almost exclusively three-phase.

(iii) For transmission and primary distribution, the three-phase, three wire system with high voltage has been universally adopted. For secondary distribution, the three-phase, four wire system has been standardized as it gives 400 volts between phases for large industrial loads such as motors and 230 volts between any phase and the neutral for small domestic consumers.

(iv) For ensuring continuity of service and to meet the future demand, transmission is generally by the duplicate lines. Such lines are known as *double circuit lines*. These two 3-phase transmission lines work in parallel and are run on the same towers.

(v) In general, the conductors in the distribution system may be grouped under three headings, *feeders*, *distributors* and *service mains*. Feeders are the conductors, between the sub-station and distribution substation and distributors normally radiate off from the distribution substation and are tapped at various points for supply to the consumers. The tappings in the consumer's premises from the distributors are known as service mains.

6.14 ENERGY METERS

We know that electricity bills are charged on the basis of electrical energy utilized by the consumers. The measurement of electrical energy is, therefore, of vital importance from the point of view of both, the consumers as well as supply undertakings. Energy meters are the integrating type of instruments used to measure the quantity of energy supplied (in kWhs) to the consumers, over a period of time. These metes fall into two basic categories :

(i) Electromechanical type energy meters,

(ii) Electronic type energy meters.

For many years, traditional electromechanical type energy meters are in use for measuring energy consumptions in the residential, commercial and industrial fields. However, within the last few years, due to the developments in the semiconductor technology, manufacture of cost-effective electronic energy meters with high accuracy has become possible. Hence, these energy meters are fastly replacing the traditional electromechanical type meters. Energy meters of both these types are, therefore, briefly discussed in the following sections.

6.15 ELECTROMECHANICAL TYPE ENERGY METERS

Among the various types of electromechanical energy meters, induction type meters are almost universally used for a.c. energy measurements and are in every day use in domestic, commercial and industrial installations. The discussion here is, therefore, limited to induction type energy meters only.

6.15.1 Induction Type Single-Phase Energy Meters

Principle of Operation : Induction instruments operate only in alternating current circuits. Their action depends basically on the principle of electromagnetic induction i.e. on the production of induced alternating currents (known as eddy currents) in the element of the moving system of the instrument by alternating fluxes. The driving torque produced by the interaction of the eddy currents and the inducing fluxes is utilized in the operation of the instrument.

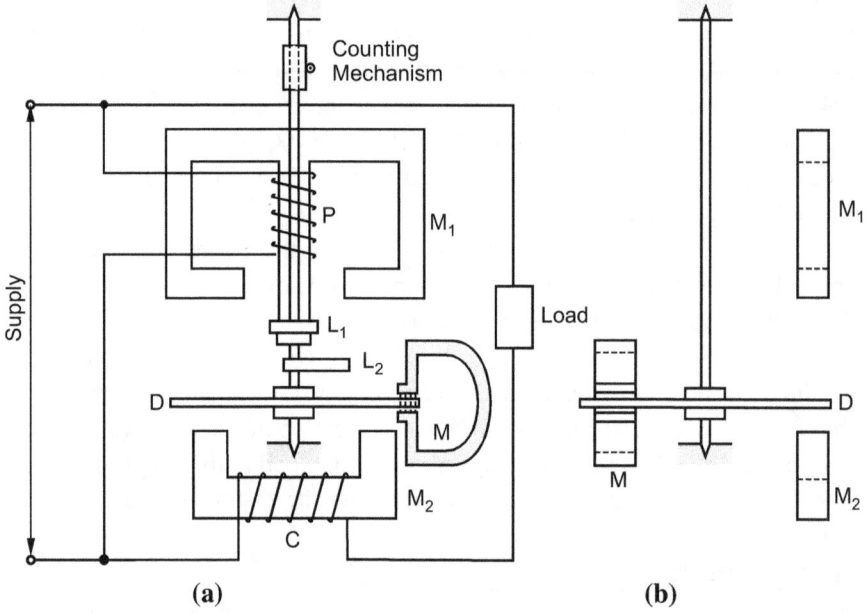

Fig. 6.21 : Induction type single-phase energy meter

Construction : Fig. 6.21 (a) shows the construction of the induction type single-phase energy meter in its simplified form.

Following are the main parts of its operating mechanism :

Driving System : The driving system of the meter mainly consists of the two a.c. electromagnets. M_1 is the voltage magnet or shunt magnet of laminated construction built up of silicon steel stampings. It carries the highly inductive pressure (or voltage) coil P having a large number of turns and which is connected across the supply. The current magnet or series magnet M_2, also of laminated construction, carries the current coil C with a small number of turns. This coil is connected in series with the load and, therefore, load current flows through it. Adjustable shading ring L_1 placed over the central limb of the electromagnet M_1 is used as power factor compensator whereas metallic stamping (or vane) L_2 moving laterally between the central limb of the electromagnet M_1 and the disc by means of some lever provides necessary compensation for friction.

Moving System : This consists of an aluminium disc D mounted on a light alloy shaft which is supported between the jewel bearings. This disc is positioned in the air gap between shunt and series magnets. A pinion cut on the shaft at the top, meshes with a gear wheel of the counting or registering mechanism.

Breaking System : The arrangement is similar to the eddy current damping as in an indicating instrument. A permanent magnet M (or a pair of magnets) produces the necessary braking torque under the condition of continuous rotation of the disc between its poles. This magnet is mounted diametrically opposite to the a.c. magnets (Fig. 6.21 b). The strength (with the help of the magnetic shunt) or the position of the permanent magnet is adjustable so that the value of the braking torque can be changed.

Registering or Counting Mechanism : The dial and pointer arrangement in case of an indicating instrument is replaced here by a registering or counting mechanism which is a form of revolution counter. Its function is to record continuously the energy consumed by the circuit over a given period of time in terms of units i.e. kWhs and is driven by the pinion on the rotor shaft through the train of reduction gears.

Operation : Since the pressure coil P carried by the electromagnet M_1 is connected across the supply, current flowing through it is proportional to voltage. The current coil C carried by the electromagnet M_2 being in series with the load carries a load current. Both these coils produce alternating fluxes which are proportional to the currents flowing through them. Part of each of these fluxes links with the disc and induces an e.m.f. in it. These e.m.f.s produce eddy currents proportional to them. The currents induced in the disc by the electromagnet M_2 react with the magnetic field produced by the electromagnet M_1. Also the currents induced in the disc by the electromagnet M_1 react with the magnetic field produced by the electromagnet M_2. Consequently, each portion of the disc carrying the currents experiences a mechanical force. Thus, the motor action results and the disc rotates. Basically, since the current coil carries load current and the pressure coil carries current proportional to the supply voltage, the resulting driving torque (T_d) is proportional to the average power supplied to the load. This torque causes the continuous rotation of the disc in the absence of control springs. However, the control or braking action is effected by eddy currents induced in the disc due to its rotation in the field between the poles of a single permanent magnet or a pair of magnets. The braking torque (T_B) provided is proportional to the speed of rotation (N) of the disc. Thus,

$$T_D \propto \text{Power} \quad \text{and} \quad T_B \propto N$$

For any particular value of driving torque, the disc speeds up until the braking torque is equal to the driving torque. Therefore, for a steady speed, equating the two torques, we have

$$N \propto \text{Power} \qquad \ldots (6.1)$$

Hence, in given time (t), the total number of revolutions (N × t) is proportional to the electrical energy (power × t) supplied to the load. The energy supplied to the load is continuously recorded by the registering or counting mechanism.

Meter Adjustments : Some adjustments are provided in the energy meter so as to correct its reading by minimising the different errors. They are as follows :

Power-factor Adjustment : It is necessary that the energy meter should read substantially correctly at all power factors. This is achieved by adjusting the position of the shading ring L_1 over the central limb of the voltage magnet M_1. This shading ring is therefore known as power-factor compensator. Alternatively, a small auxiliary coil of few turns is placed on the central limb of the electromagnet M_1 and its ends are connected to the variable resistance. By properly adjusting this resistance, the necessary power-factor compensation can be achieved.

Main Speed Adjustment : This may be effected by adjusting the radial position of the brake magnet M with respect to the centre of the disc. The braking torque varies as the effective radius at which the braking force acts changes. Movement of the poles of the braking magnet towards the centre of the disc reduces the braking torque and consequently increases the speed of rotation of the disc and vice-versa.

Variation of braking torque can also be achieved by by-passing some part of the flux of the braking magnet using a magnetic shunt or flux diverter.

Friction Adjustment : Friction at the bearings and counting mechanism tends to reduce the speed of the disc thereby introducing the error in the reading of the energy meter. To compensate this, a metallic stamping (or vane) L_2 which can be moved laterally with the help of some lever is placed between the central limb of the electromagnet M_1 and the disc. The interaction of the fluxes between shaded and unshaded portions of the central limb of the magnet M_1 and the currents induced by them in the disc causes a small driving torque. This additional driving torque is used for compensating reduction in speed due to friction.

Creep Adjustment : The slow but continuous rotation of the disc of the meter when only its pressure coil is excited and no current flows through its current coil is known as *creeping*. It may be caused due to various factors like incorrect friction compensation, vibrations, stray magnetic fields, excess supply voltage, etc.

In order to prevent the creeping on no load, two holes are drilled in the disc on diametrically opposite sides of the spindle. This causes sufficient distortion of the field to prevent rotation of the disc when one of the holes comes under the pole of a shunt magnet.

In some cases, small piece of iron wire is attached to the edge of the disc. The force of attraction exerted by the brake magnet on this iron wire is sufficient to prevent continuous rotation of the disc under no-load condition.

Application : Universally used in domestic and industrial installations for measurement of a.c. energy.

Standard Specifications : As an illustration, the standard specifications of a typical induction type single-phase energy meter are given below :

Voltage	:	240 V
Current	:	5 to 20 A
Frequency	:	50 Hz
Meter constant	:	750 R/kWh
Accuracy class	:	2.0

6.15.2 Induction Type Three-Phase Energy Meters

Induction type three-phase energy meters are commonly employed to measure the energy supplied to three-phase circuits.

Construction : These meters consist of two or three meter elements depending upon whether the circuit is three-phase three wire or three-phase four wire. The construction of the individual elements is in most respects similar to that of the single-phase energy meters. These meter elements are mounted in a vertical line in a common case and have a common spindle, gearing and registering mechanism.

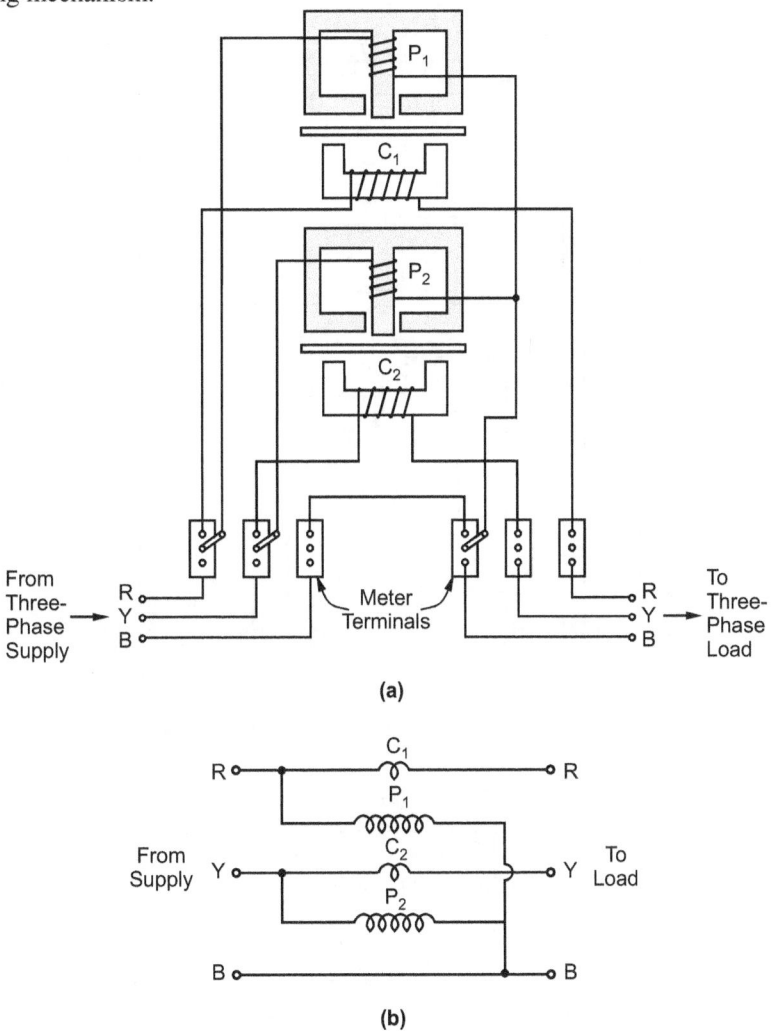

Fig. 6.22 : (a) Two-element energy meter, (b) Simplified connection diagram

Fig. 6.22 (a) shows a two-element energy meter and Fig. 6.22 (b) its simplified connection diagram. The current coils C_1 and C_2 of two elements are connected in series with lines R and Y respectively. Pressure coil P_1 is connected across lines R and B while the pressure coil P_2 of other element is connected across lines Y and B.

Fig. 6.23 (a) illustrates a three-element energy meter and Fig. 6.23 (b) its simplified connection diagram. In this case, current coils C_1, C_2 and C_3 of three elements are connected in series with lines R, Y and B respectively. Three pressure coils P_1, P_2 and P_3 are connected across these respective lines and the neutral as shown in the connection diagram.

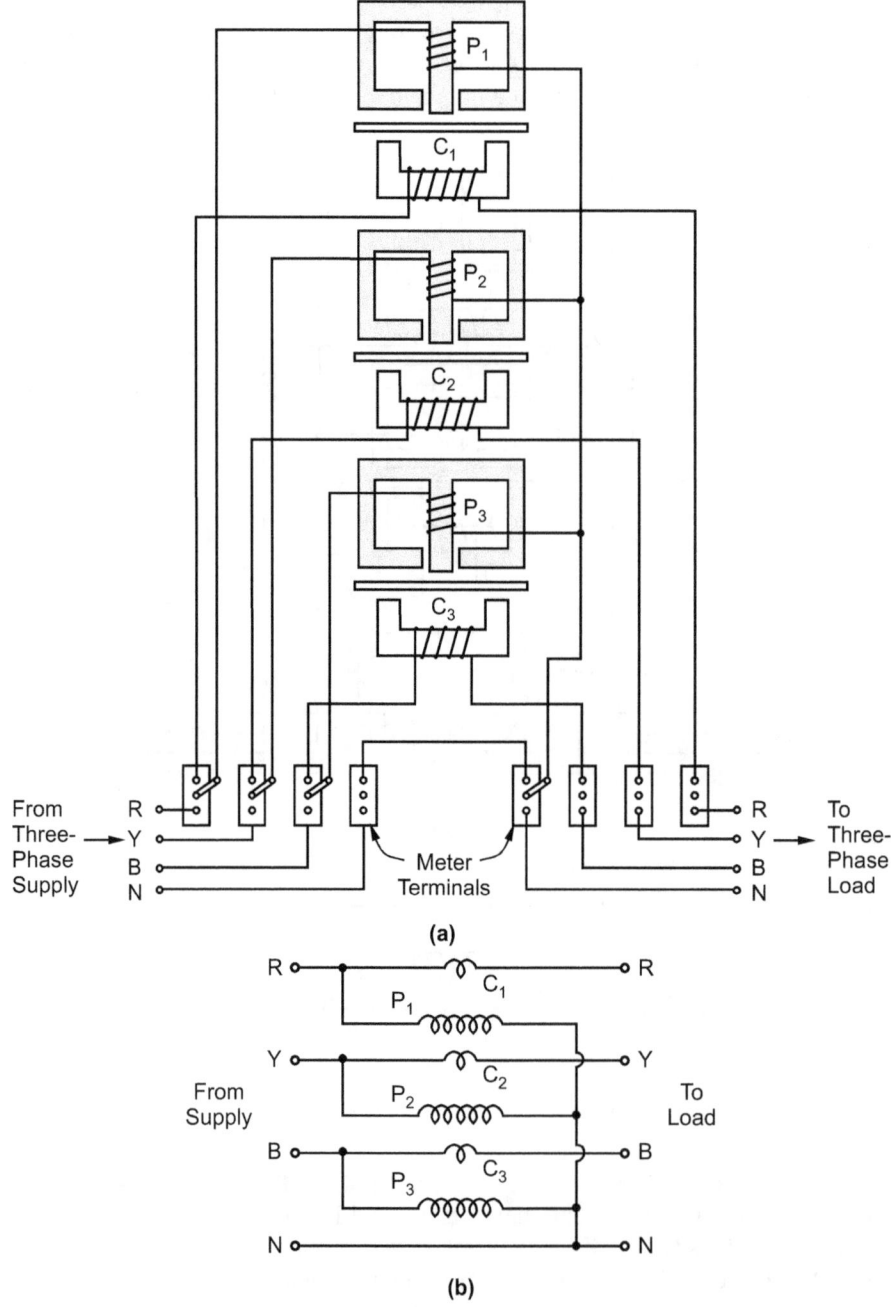

Fig. 6.23 : (a) Three-element energy meter, (b) Simplified connection diagram

Operation : Each meter element produces torque in a manner similar to that of single-phase energy meter. The total torque on the moving system is, therefore, the sum of the torques of the individual elements. The meter thus registers the total energy in the three-phase circuit.

Application : Induction type three-phase energy meters are commonly employed to measure the energy supplied to three-phase circuits. Two-element energy meters are suitable for measuring the energy in three-phase, three-wire circuits in both balanced and unbalanced load conditions. Three-element energy meters are necessary for three-phase, four-wire circuits to enable the total energy to be measured under all conditions of loading.

Standard Specifications : As an illustration, the standard specifications of a typical induction type two or three-element, three-phase energy meter are given below :

Voltage	:	$3 \times 240/415$ V
Current	:	10 to 40 A
Frequency	:	50 Hz
Meter constant	:	550 R/kWh
Accuracy class	:	2.0

6.16 ELECTRONIC TYPE ENERGY METERS

As already mentioned previously, electronic type energy meters, also called *solid-state energy meters*, are a more recent introduction. These meters commonly utilize a potential transformer* (PT) connected to the power lines as a voltage sensor for producing an electrical voltage signal proportional to a load voltage and a current transformer** (CT) connected to the power lines as a current sensor for producing an electrical voltage signal proportional to a load current. These small signals are then passed to the general electronic circuits or dedicated energy measurement chips which calculate the energy consumption (in kWhs) and display it on the screen of the display unit.

The detailed study of electronic type energy meters is beyond the scope of this book. However, these meters are just introduced here with the help of simple schematic block diagrams in the following sections.

6.16.1 Electronic Type Single-Phase Energy Meters

Fig. 6.24 shows the simple schematic block diagram of a typical electronic type single-phase energy meter. The potential transformer (PT) used as a voltage sensor steps down the line voltage to a suitable level. The current transformer (CT) used as a current sensor senses the current in the line and converts it to corresponding voltage signal. Both these voltage and current (i.e. corresponding voltage signal) signals are further downscaled to the suitable level using

---

* *High alternating voltages are reduced in some fixed proportion for measurement purposes with the help of this special-purpose transformer.*

** *Large alternating currents are reduced in some fixed proportion for measurement purposes with the help of this special-purpose transformer.*

voltage and current scaling networks and then applied as input to an analog multiplier. The analog multiplier produces output signal in the form of a d.c. voltage (V_{dc}) proportional to the product of its two input signals. Hence, the output signal produced by the analog multiplier is proportional to the product of the instantaneous values of the line voltage (v) and line current (i) i.e. it is proportional to the instantaneous electrical power (p) flowing through the lines. Thus, we have

$$V_{dc} \propto v \cdot i \propto p$$

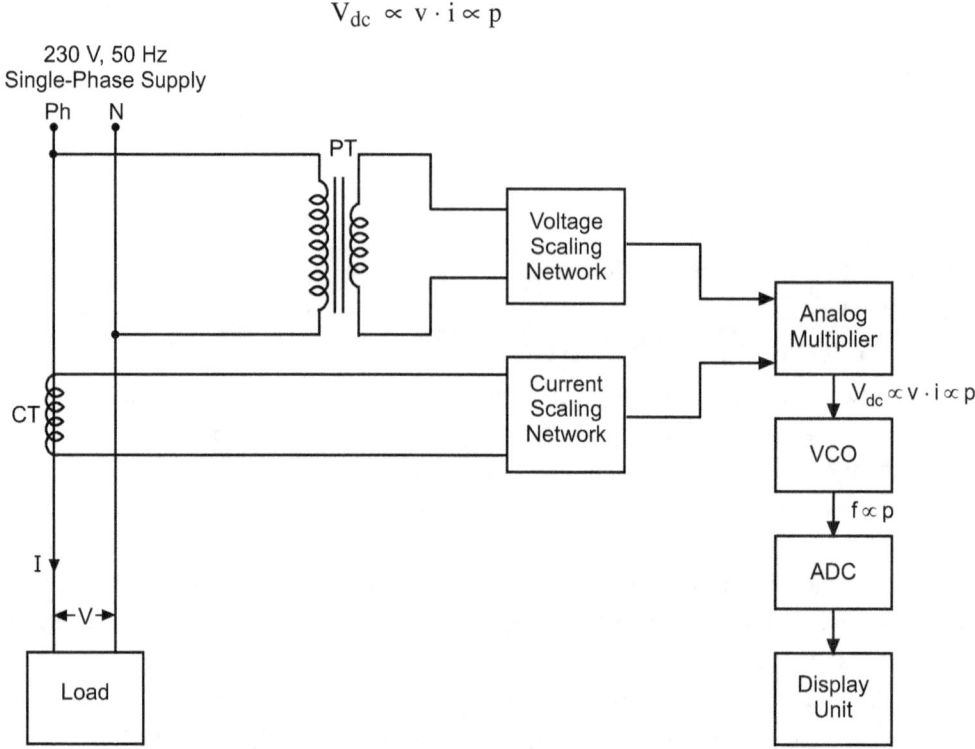

Fig. 6.24 : Block diagram of a typical electronic type single-phase energy meter

To calculate the energy, it is now necessary to complete the process of integrating this power over the observation time. For that the power signal in the form of a d.c. voltage (V_{dc}) at the output terminals of the analog multiplier is applied as input to the voltage controlled oscillator (VCO) which is basically a voltage to frequency converter with a square-wave output. The frequency of this square wave from the voltage controlled oscillator is proportional to the d.c. input voltage from the analog multiplier and therefore proportional to the instantaneous electric power flowing through the lines. Further, the analog signal at the output terminals of the voltage controlled oscillator is converted into a digital signal by means of an analog to digital converter (ADC). The digital output of the analog to digital converter is applied to the display unit which actually measures the input pulses whose frequency is proportional to the instantaneous electrical power flowing through the line. The pulse counting process here performs the integration of the power over the observation interval and thereby carries out the measurement of energy supplied. Finally, the display unit displays on its screen the number of units (kWhs) supplied to the load over the period under consideration.

Standard Specifications : As an illustration, the standard specifications of a typical electronic type single-phase energy meter are given below :

Voltage	:	240 V
Current	:	10 to 60 A
Frequency	:	50 Hz
Pulse rate	:	3200 imp/kWh
Accuracy class	:	1.0
Reference temperature	:	27°C

6.16.2 Electronic Type Three-Phase Energy Meters

Fig. 6.25 shows the simple schematic block diagram of a typical electronic type three-phase energy meter using microcontrollers[*].

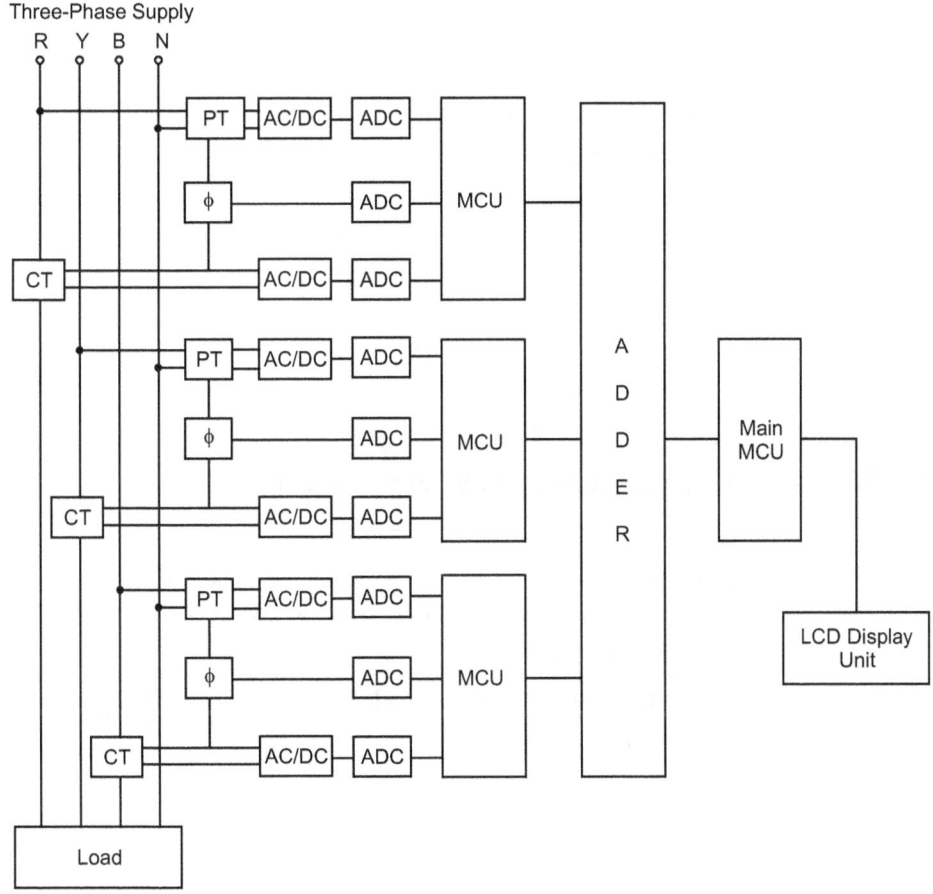

Fig. 6.25 : Block diagram of a typical electronic type three-phase energy meter

---

[*] *A microcontroller is a single integrated chip designed for small or dedicated applications. It functions as a tiny computer.*

The values of phase voltages and line currents are stepped down to a suitable level through potential transformers (PTs) and current transformers (CTs) respectively. The blocks with symbol 'ϕ' in the diagram represent the circuits for finding the phase difference between the current and the voltage for different phases. The outputs from the current and potential transformers are given as inputs to the blocks 'AC/DC' representing circuits which convert a.c. signals to d.c. signals. These analog d.c. signals are then converted into digital form using analog to digital converters (ADCs). There are three microcontroller units (MCUs), each of which receives the digital values of voltage, current and phase angle between them from their respective analog to digital converters and calculates the power of one individual phase. The powers of all the phases are then added with the help of 'adder' which is a type of integrated circuit. Next to adder, is a main microcontroller unit which performs various important tasks like calculation of energy (in kWhs), saving the data and also displaying the units with the help of a liquid-crystal-display (LCD) unit.

Standard Specifications : As an illustration, the standard specifications of a typical electronic type three-phase energy meter are given below :

Voltage	:	3×240 (P-N)
Current	:	10 – 40 A
Frequency	:	50 Hz
Pulse rate	:	416.66667 imp/unit
Accuracy class	:	1.0
Reference temperature	:	27°C

6.16.3 Advantages of Electronic Type Energy Meters

(i) Electronic type energy meters are less prone to tampering.

(ii) Since these meters do not involve moving parts, they do not suffer from frictional losses and mechanical wear and tear. Hence, these meters remain consistent and accurate throughout their life period.

(iii) Due to electronic circuitry, these meters have a lot of flexibility for change.

(iv) As electronic components are getting cheaper and cheaper day by day, these meters are now available at reasonable costs.

(v) These meters inherently have high accuracy, high sensitivity, high resolution, high frequency range and less loading effect.

(vi) These meters can be designed to measure and record energy parameters like active energy (in kWh), reactive energy (in kVArh), apparent energy (in kVAh), maximum demand (in kW and kVA), power factor and frequency (in Hz). Such meters are called *electronic trivector meters*. They have almost replaced the traditional electromagnetic trivector meters.

6.17 EXERCISES

6.17.1 Review Questions

1. Why earthing is necessary in a wiring installation ? How it is achieved ?
2. Discuss, in brief, the commonly used methods of earthing.
3. State the various wiring accessories generally needed.
4. What is a fuse ? Explain the principle of operation of a fuse.
5. State the various types of metals used for making fuse elements.
6. Describe the construction and operating principle of a low-voltage H.R.C. cartridge fuse. Explain why cartridge fuses are preferred over the rewirable type, particularly for high values of current.
7. Why fuses should always be provided in the live (phase) wire ?
8. Define the following terms :
   (i) Current rating
   (ii) Minimum fusing current
   (iii) Fusing factor
9. Write briefly on : MCCB, MCB and ELCB.
10. Enumerate the different types of electric light sources. State the principles on which they work and give their relative advantages.
11. Describe the constructional details of gas-filled incandescent lamp, explaining what advantage is derived from coiling the filament.
12. Explain with a connection diagram, the operation of the fluorescent lamp. State the purpose of each component used in its control circuit. Discuss its advantages and disadvantages.
13. Explain the construction and working of the following types of electric discharge lamps :

    (i) Mercury vapour lamp.

    (ii) Sodium vapour lamp.

    (iii) Neon lamp.

    (iv) Compact fluorescent lamp (C.F.L.).

    (v) Metal halide lamp.

14. Write briefly on LED lamps stating their general constructional features, operating principle, applications, advantages and disadvantages.

15. Draw a layout of a typical power system and explain in brief the stages involved in the transmission of electrical power from the generating station to consumer's premises.

16. Describe the construction and principle of operation of a single-phase, induction-type watthour meter.

17. Draw neat sketches of induction type, three-phase energy meters with two and three elements. Label the parts.

18. Explain the working of electronic type, single-phase energy meter with the help of a simple schematic block diagram.

19. Explain the working of electronic type, three-phase energy meter with the help of a simple schematic block diagram.

6.17.2 Classified Theory Questions from University Papers

1. Why earthing is necessary ? Explain briefly.
   (Answer : Section 6.1)   **(May 2008/6 Marks)**

2. With a neat diagram, explain the construction and working of a fluorescent tube/lamp.
   (Answer : Section 6.11.1)   **(December 2008, 2009; May 2009/6 Marks)**

3. Draw a neat diagram and explain the working of a mercury vapour lamp. State the advantages and limitations of the mercury vapour lamp.
   (Answer : Section 6.11.2)   **(May 2009, 2010/6 Marks)**

4. Explain with a neat diagram, construction and working principle of a sodium vapour lamp.
   (Answer : Section 6.11.3)   **(May 2008/6 Marks)**

5. Compare CFL with an ordinary fluorescent lamp.
   (Answer : Sections 6.11.1, 6.11.5)   **(December 2010/4 Marks)**

6. Write short notes on :
   (i) Fluorescent tubes, (ii) Mercury vapour lamps, (iii) CFLs, (iv) Metal halide lamps.
   (Answer : Sections 6.11.1, 6.11.2, 6.11.5, 6.11.6)
   (May 2011, 2012; December 2008, 2011, 2012/Some of these for 6 Marks each)

CHAPTER 7
THREE-PHASE A.C. CIRCUITS

7.1 POLYPHASE SYSTEMS

The alternator with the number of armature coils suitably connected to form one winding is known as *single-phase (winding) alternator*. The elementary alternator with one armature coil shown in Fig. 3.3 schematically represents such a single-phase alternator. The single alternating voltage generated by such an alternator is known as *single-phase voltage (or e.m.f.)* and the current that results from the action of this single-phase alternating voltage is called *single-phase alternating current*.

Polyphase[*] (*or multiphase*) *alternators* have two or more windings symmetrically spaced around the armature. Such alternators produce as many independent alternating voltages as the number of windings (phases). These voltages in the individual windings have the same magnitude and frequency but they have definite phase difference. The amount of phase difference depends on the number of windings. Thus, by using appropriate polyphase alternator, it is possible to generate two-phase and three-phase a.c. and from these to obtain four, six, nine and twelve-phase a.c. depending upon the requirements. These systems are collectively known as *polyphase systems*.

Inspite of increased complications, the polyphase systems have enormous advantages. Principal among these are listed below :

(i) The output of a polyphase machine is greater than that of a single-phase machine of the same size or in other words, a polyphase machine is always smaller, lighter and therefore, cheaper than a single-phase machine of the same rating.

(ii) The total power output of a polyphase machine is not fluctuating as in the case of a single-phase machine. It has a higher efficiency. In general, the operating characteristics and overall performance of a polyphase machine are better.

(iii) A polyphase transmission line requires less copper than a single-phase line to transmit a given amount of power at a given voltage over a given distance. Hence, transmission becomes economical.

(iv) Most of the single-phase motors are not self-starting. Polyphase motors are self-starting.

---

[*] *In the word 'polyphase', poly means many and phase means winding or circuit.*

(v) Power factor of a single-phase motor is lower than that of a three-phase motor of the same output and speed.

(vi) Parallel operation of polyphase alternators is more easy.

Since, it is observed that there is little advantage in any further increase in the number of phases beyond *three*, the three-phase system has become the standard system throughout the world for generation, transmission and distribution of electrical energy. Therefore, in this chapter, we shall confine our discussion to three-phase system only.

7.2 GENERATION OF THREE-PHASE VOLTAGES

The generation of three-phase voltages can be very well understood by considering an elementary three-phase alternator shown in Fig. 7.1 (a).

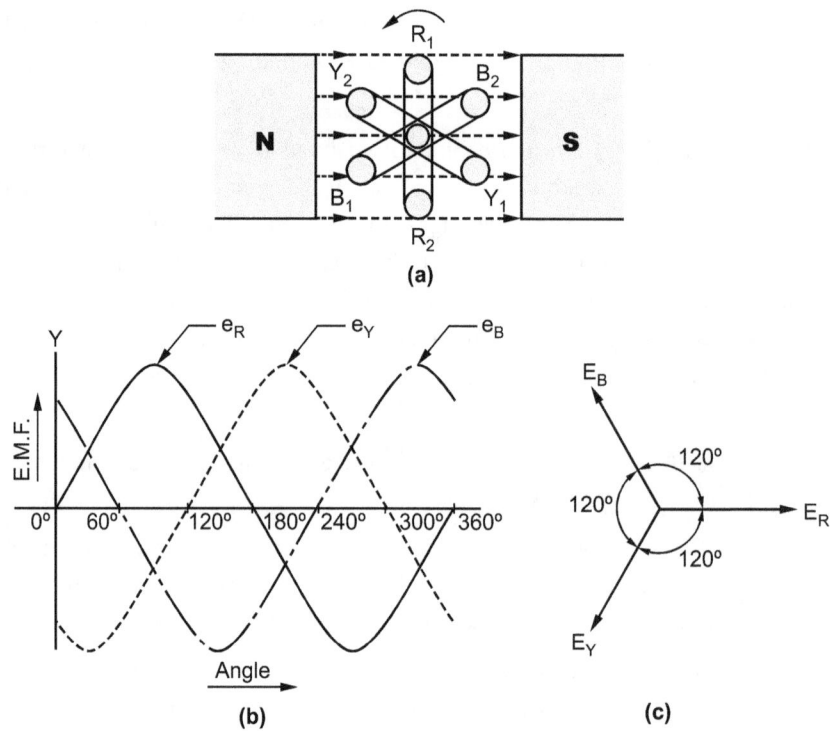

Fig. 7.1 : (a) Elementary three-phase alternator with two poles,
(b) Waveforms of three phase e.m.fs., (c) Phasor diagram

Construction : The armature of the alternator consists of three single-turn rectangular coils $R_1 R_2$, $Y_1 Y_2$ and $B_1 B_2$ fixed to one another at angles of 120°. This means that the corresponding terminals (i.e. starting terminals R_1, Y_1 and B_1 or finishing terminals R_2, Y_2 and B_2) of the three coils are 120° apart. The ends of each coil are connected to a pair of slip-rings carried on the shaft. The coils are placed in the uniform magnetic field provided by the North and South poles of the magnet. The carbon brushes are pressed against the slip-rings to collect the induced currents in the coils (Some of these details are omitted in the figure for simplicity).

Operation : Suppose the three coils are rotating in an anti-clockwise direction at uniform speed. Then as seen previously in the case of an elementary single-phase alternator (with only one armature coil), each coil will have its own generated e.m.f. and current which will be alternating in nature. In the position shown in Fig. 7.1 (a), the plane of the coil $R_1 R_2$ is perpendicular to the magnetic field and its conductors move parallel to the field. Since there is no flux cutting, e.m.f. generated in the coil is zero. After exactly 120°, the coil $Y_1 Y_2$ will occupy this position and e.m.f. induced in it will be zero. Same thing will be true regarding the maximum values achieved by the e.m.f.s in the respective coils when in their horizontal positions. Thus, it will be observed that e.m.f. generated in the coil $Y_1 Y_2$ will be attaining its zero or maximum value of 120° later than e.m.f. generated in the coil $R_1 R_2$. In other words, the e.m.f. generated in the coil $Y_1 Y$ will be lagging that in the coil $R_1 R_2$ by 120°. Similarly, the e.m.f. generated in the coil $B_1 B_2$ will lag that in the coil $Y_1 Y_2$ by 120°. The waveforms of the respective electromotive forces even though identical will, therefore, be displaced through 120° as shown in Fig. 7.1 (b). It means that these three e.m.f.s with the same amplitude will have a phase difference of 120°. The phasor diagram shown in Fig. 7.1 (c) also shows their phase relationships (E_R, E_Y and E_B being the r.m.s. values of e.m.f.s in the coils R_1R_2, Y_1Y_2 and $B_1 B_2$ respectively).

If the instantaneous value of the e.m.f. generated in the coil $R_1 R_2$ is represented by

$$e_R = E_m \sin \omega t$$

then, the instantaneous values of the e.m.f.s generated in the coils $Y_1 Y_2$ and $B_1 B_2$ will be given by

$$e_Y = E_m \sin (\omega t - 120°)$$
$$e_B = E_m \sin (\omega t - 240°)$$

Thus, we get three independent alternating voltages from the three-phase alternator having three windings (phases) spaced 120° apart around the armature. These voltages have the same magnitude and frequency but they have a phase difference of 120°. Such voltages are, therefore, called *three-phase voltages* and corresponding currents *three-phase alternating currents.*

Symmetrical System : *A polyphase system is said to be symmetrical when the e.m.f.s of the same frequency in different phases are equal in magnitude and displaced from one another by equal phase angles.* Three-phase is the most important symmetrical system. Four, six, nine and twelve-phase systems mentioned earlier are other symmetrical systems.

Phase Sequence : *The order in which the voltages in three phases reach their maximum positive values is called the phase sequence.* In the above case which we have discussed, the phase sequence is R-Y-B[*]. The knowledge of phase sequence is essential in many applications, e.g. for finding the direction of rotation of a.c. motors, in parallel operation of alternators and transformers, etc.

---

[*] *In practice, red, yellow and blue coloured wires are used for three phases to distinguish one phase from the other. These phases are, therefore, designated as R, Y and B from their respective colours.*

7.3 THREE-PHASE SUPPLY SYSTEMS

Similar to d.c. systems (two wire), for the single-phase supply systems, two wires are sufficient for transmitting electrical energy from generator to the load. Now, as already seen, the three-phase alternator has three independent armature windings (or phases). Therefore, if power generated in each phase is to be transmitted independently, total six wires will be required as shown in Fig. 7.2.

This arrangement, however, will make the whole system complicated as well as expensive. Therefore, in actual practice, the three armature windings of the alternator are interconnected to give the following systems with reduced number of wires.

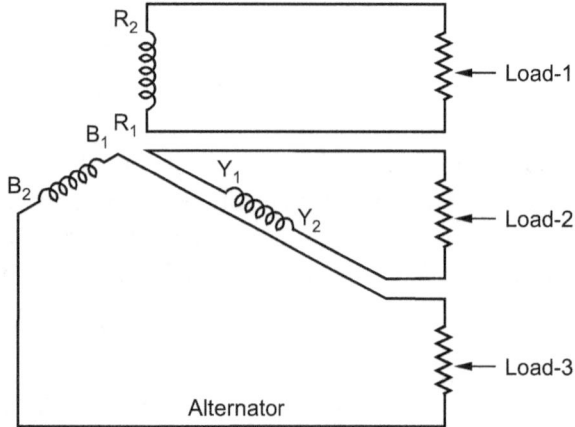

Fig. 7.2 : Three-phase supply system with six line conductors

7.3.1 Three-Phase, Three-Wire System

Depending upon the method used for the interconnection of the three armature windings of the alternator, we have two types of three-phase, three-wire systems.

(a) Three-Phase, Three-Wire, Star-Connected System : In this method, the similar ends (either starting or finishing) of the three armature windings of the alternator are connected together and the three line conductors are run from the remaining free ends as shown in Fig. 7.3 (a).

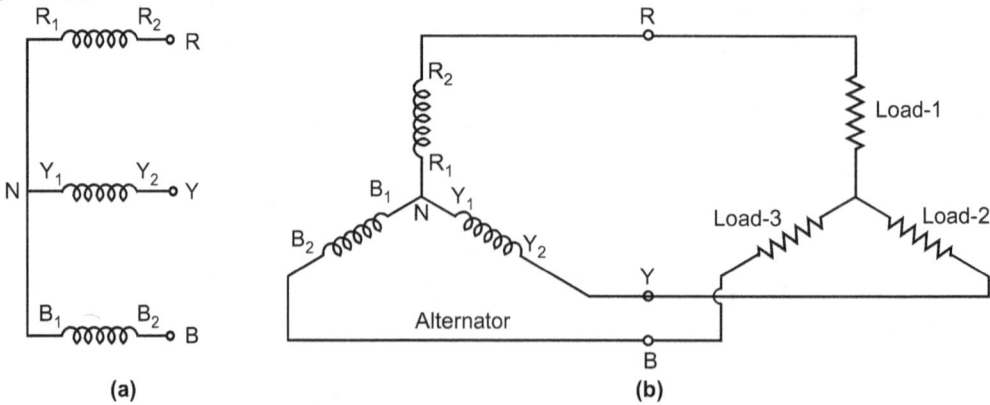

Fig. 7.3 : Three-phase, three-wire, star-connected system

The common point is called *star* or *neutral point* (N). Such an arrangement is called *star* or *wye* (Y) *connection*. A star connection is usually represented as shown in Fig. 7.3 (b). The three loads may also be connected in star (or delta as seen later) and supplied by three conductors only (Fig. 7.3 b).

(b) Three-Phase, Three-Wire, Delta or Mesh-Connected System : In this method of interconnection, starting end of one armature winding of an alternator is connected to the finishing end of the other winding and so on to obtain a closed circuit as shown in Fig. 7.4 (a).

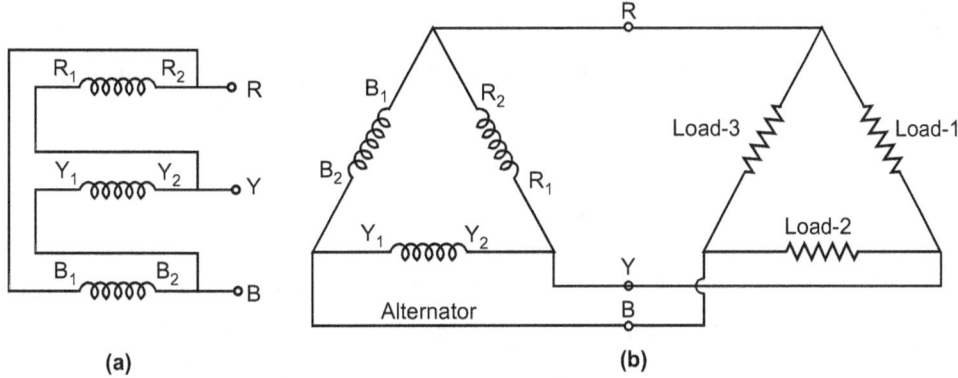

Fig. 7.4 : Three-phase, three-wire, delta-connected system

The line conductors are taken out from the three junction points. This type of interconnection is more conveniently represented as shown in Fig. 7.4 (b) and known as *delta* (from Greek capital letter Δ) or *mesh* (meaning a closed circuit) *connection*. The loads may also be star or delta connected (Fig. 7.4 b).

7.3.2 Three-Phase, Four-Wire System

In order to obtain a four-wire distribution system, the fourth conductor is connected to the star or neutral point as shown in Fig. 7.5.

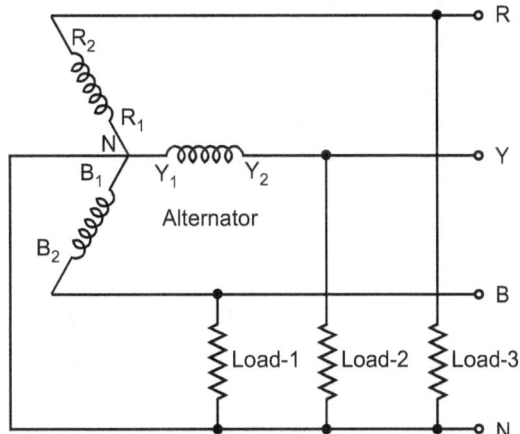

Fig. 7.5 : Three-phase, four-wire system

This system is normally employed for low voltage distribution of electrical power. The advantage of such an arrangement is that it provides :

(i) A three-phase medium voltage supply for heavy industrial loads such as motors when using all the three line conductors, and

(ii) A low voltage supply for lighting, heating and domestic loads when using one of the three line conductors and the neutral conductor (Fig. 7.5).

7.4 BALANCED LOAD

As already mentioned previously, the load on a three-phase system may be either star or delta connected irrespective of type of connection for armature windings of the alternator. *If all phase impedances of the three-phase load are exactly identical in respect of magnitude and their nature, it is said to be a balanced, three-phase load.*

For example, if each phase of the three-phase load has a resistance of 10 Ω and inductive reactance 25 Ω, it will form a balanced, three-phase load. However, if one of the phases has a capacitive reactance of 25 Ω in place of inductive reactance, then inspite of equal impedances in all the phases, the load will not be the balanced one. In practice, a three-phase motor connected across the supply forms a balanced load (Fig. 7.6).

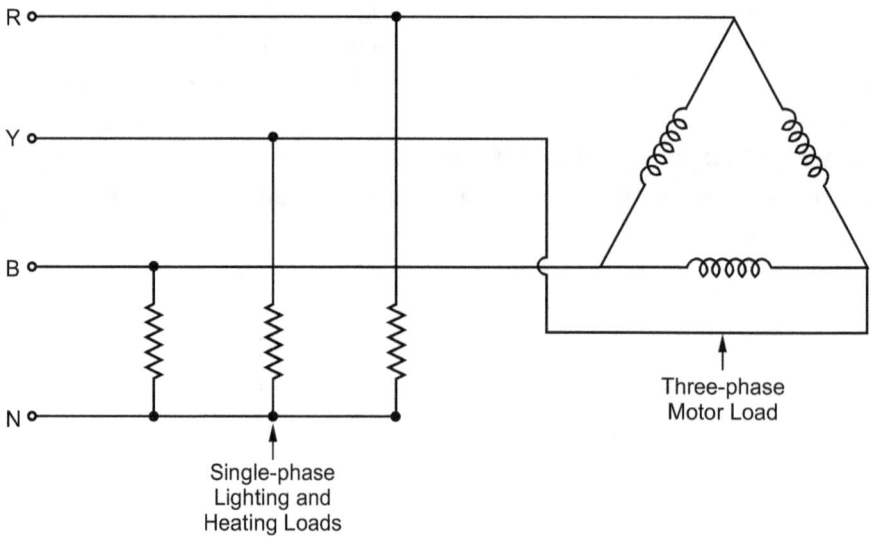

Fig. 7.6 : Loading of a three-phase system

The lighting and heating loads which are resistive in nature are normally connected between one line and neutral. The electricity authorities always try to distribute such single-phase loads on all the three phases as equally as possible. Thus, in such condition, all these single-phase loads also form a balanced, star-connected load.

7.5 BALANCED SYSTEM

A three-phase system is said to be balanced when it possesses following characteristics :
(i) The e.m.f.s (voltages) for three phases are equal and phase displaced by 120 electrical degrees.
(ii) The impedance in any one phase is identical to that in either of the other two phases.
(iii) The resulting currents in different phases are equal and have same phase angles. Or, in other words, they are also phase displaced from each other by 120 electrical degrees.
(iv) Equal power and equal reactive power flow in each phase.

As already mentioned previously, definite efforts are made to keep the three-phase system in balanced condition by using balanced loading. It is important to note that all the relations which are developed or conclusions which are reached in the following articles in respect of three-phase systems are entirely based on the assumption that these systems are balanced.

7.6 VOLTAGE, CURRENT AND POWER RELATIONS IN A STAR CONNECTION

(a) **Star-Connected, Three-Phase Supply System :** The e.m.f. generated in each winding (phase) on the armature of the alternator is known as *phase e.m.f.* and corresponding current as *phase current*. However, the voltage between any two line conductors coming out from the terminals of the alternator is called *line voltage* and the current flowing in each line conductor is called *line current*. Now, let us derive the relationships between these line and phase quantities for a star-connected, three-phase system.

Referring to Fig. 7.7 (a), let E_r, E_y, E_b be the phase e.m.f.s and I_r, I_y, I_b the corresponding phase currents. Similarly, let E_{RY}, E_{YB}, E_{BR} be the line e.m.f.s and I_R, I_Y, I_B the line currents.

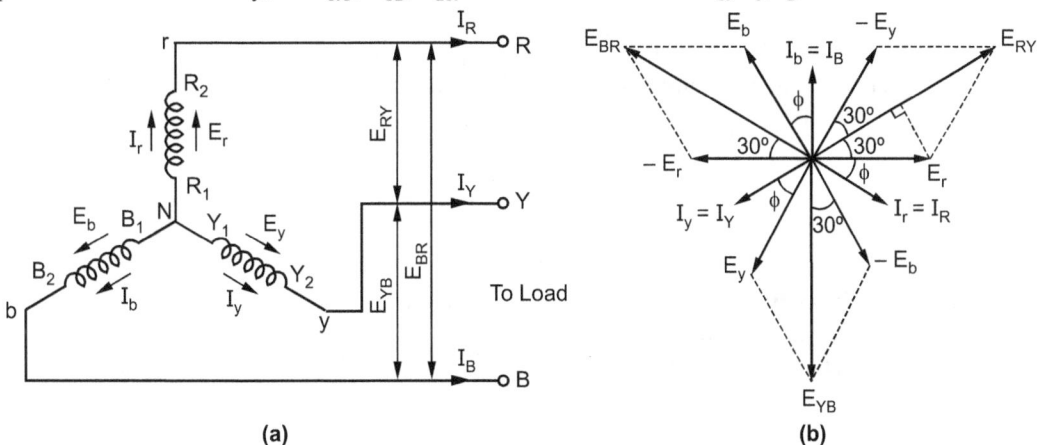

Fig. 7.7 : Star-connected, three-phase system

If the balanced three-phase inductive load is assumed, phase currents will be equal and lag behind their respective phase e.m.f.s by a constant angle ϕ as shown in the phasor diagram of Fig. 7.7 (b). This phasor diagram is drawn taking E_r as a reference phasor and phase sequence as R-Y-B. Let us adopt the convention that an e.m.f. and a current are positive when they act from start to finish of the winding. Therefore, positive direction of the phase currents and phase e.m.f.s are as indicated by the arrows in Fig. 7.7 (a).

Voltage Relation : Consider first the terminals R and Y of the alternator. There are two phase windings connected in series opposition (similar ends being together) across these terminals. Hence, the instantaneous value of e.m.f. between the terminals (or lines) R and Y is the arithmetic difference of the phase e.m.f.s (instantaneous values) in these two windings i.e.

$$e_{RY} = e_r - e_y$$

However, the r.m.s. value of this e.m.f. is given by the phasor difference of the r.m.s. values of the two phase e.m.f.s.

$$\therefore \quad \bar{E}_{RY} = \bar{E}_r - \bar{E}_y$$

Alternatively, this can be also achieved by applying Kirchhoff's voltage law to the loop between the lines R and Y i.e. loop RYNR.

$$-\bar{E}_{RY} - \bar{E}_y + \bar{E}_r = 0^*$$

$$\therefore \quad \bar{E}_{RY} = \bar{E}_r - \bar{E}_y$$

Thus, $\bar{E}_{RY}$ can be obtained by finding the resultant of $\bar{E}_r$ and $-\bar{E}_y$ (obtained by reversing the phasor $\bar{E}_y$) by completing the parallelogram of phasors as shown in Fig. 7.7 (b). Similarly, by considering the other two pairs of terminals (or lines) namely Y-B and B-R, we have

$$\bar{E}_{YB} = \bar{E}_y - \bar{E}_b$$

and

$$\bar{E}_{BR} = \bar{E}_b - \bar{E}_r$$

Now, let

$$E_r = E_y = E_b = E_{ph} \quad \ldots \text{(Numerically)}$$

and

$$E_{RY} = E_{YB} = E_{BR} = E_L \quad \ldots \text{(Numerically)}$$

Then, from one of the parallelograms, say for E_{RY}, we have

$$E_{RY} = E_L = 2E_{ph} \cos 30°$$

$$= 2E_{ph} \times \frac{\sqrt{3}}{2}$$

$$= \sqrt{3}\, E_{ph}$$

Alternatively, E_{RY} being the diagonal of the parallelogram, can also be obtained as

$$E_{RY} = E_L = \sqrt{E_r^2 + E_y^2 + 2\, E_r\, E_y \cos 60°} = \sqrt{E_{ph}^2 + E_{ph}^2 + 2E_{ph} \cdot E_{ph} \times \frac{1}{2}} = \sqrt{3}\, E_{ph}$$

Thus,

$$E_L = \sqrt{3}\, E_{ph} \quad \ldots (7.1)$$

i.e.

$$\text{Line E.M.F.} = \sqrt{3}\, \text{(Phase E.M.F.)}$$

It should also be noted that there is always a phase displacement of 30° between them.

---

* While applying the Kirchhoff's voltage law to the loop under consideration, it should be remembered that E_r and E_y are the source e.m.f.s similar to that of a battery and the line e.m.f. E_{RY} symbolizes that the potential of R is positive with respect to that of Y.

Current Relation : Further, since each line conductor is connected to one-phase winding only, the current in a particular line conductor is the same as in the phase winding to which that line conductor is connected. Therefore, if

$$I_r = I_y = I_b = I_{ph} \quad \text{... (Numerically)}$$

and
$$I_R = I_Y = I_B = I_L \quad \text{... (Numerically)}$$

then,
$$I_L = I_{ph} \quad \text{... (7.2)}$$

i.e. *Line Current = Phase Current*

Power : With balanced system, total power supplied,

$$P = 3 \times \text{(Power supplied by each phase)}$$

$$= 3 \, E_{ph} \, I_{ph} \cos \phi$$

$$= 3 \, \frac{E_L}{\sqrt{3}} \, I_L \cos \phi \quad \text{(Refer to the equations 7.1 and 7.2)}$$

$$= \sqrt{3} \, E_L \, I_L \cos \phi$$

Thus,
$$P = \sqrt{3} \, E_L \, I_L \cos \phi \quad \text{... (7.3)}$$

i.e. *Total Power = $\sqrt{3}$ (Line E.M.F. × Line Current × Phase Power Factor)*

While using this important relationship, it should be remembered that ϕ is the phase difference between a phase current and phase e.m.f. and not between a line current and line e.m.f.

(b) Star-Connected, Three-Phase Load : The above voltage, current and power relations are also applicable to balanced, three-phase, star-connected loads. Fig. 7.8 (a) shows a balanced, three-phase, star-connected load. Let V_r, V_y, V_b be the phase voltages and I_r, I_y, I_b be the corresponding phase currents. Similarly, let V_{RY}, V_{YB}, V_{BR} be the line voltages and I_R, I_Y, I_B the line currents. Positive directions of the phase currents and phase voltages are assumed as indicated by the arrows in Fig. 7.8 (a). If the load is assumed to be inductive in nature, then the phasor diagram will be similar to that in the case of three-phase, star-connected alternator seen above (Fig. 7.8 b).

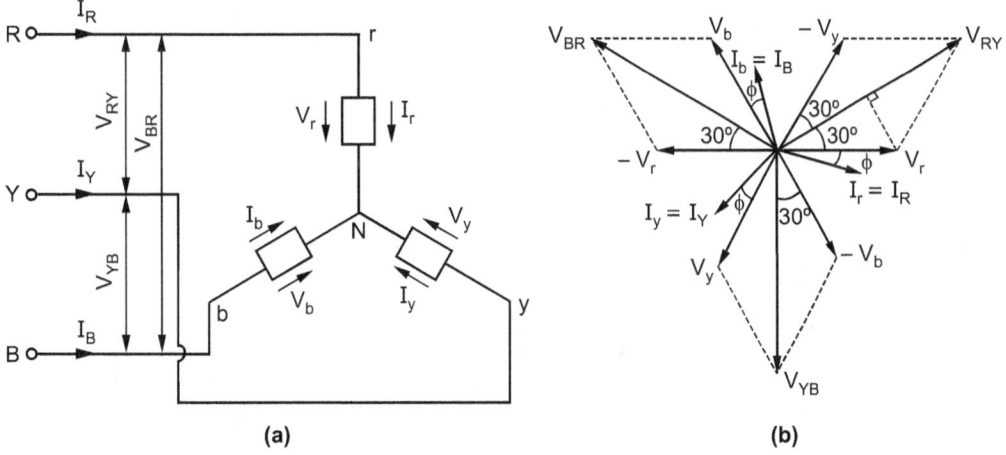

Fig. 7.8 : A balanced, three-phase, star-connected load

Voltage Relation : Consider first the two terminals (or lines) R and Y. As voltage between the lines is equal to the phasor difference between the two corresponding phase voltages,

$$\overline{V}_{RY} = \overline{V}_r - \overline{V}_y$$

Or alternatively, by applying Kirchhoff's voltage law to the loop between the lines R and Y i.e. loop RNYR, we have

$$-\overline{V}_r + \overline{V}_y + \overline{V}_{RY}^* = 0$$

$$\therefore \quad \overline{V}_{RY} = \overline{V}_r - \overline{V}_y$$

Similarly, considering other pairs of terminals (or lines),

$$\overline{V}_{YB} = \overline{V}_y - \overline{V}_b$$

and

$$\overline{V}_{BR} = \overline{V}_b - \overline{V}_r$$

Now, let

$$V_r = V_y = V_b = V_{ph} \quad \ldots \text{(Numerically)}$$

and

$$V_{RY} = V_{YB} = V_{BR} = V_L \quad \ldots \text{(Numerically)}$$

Then, from the phasor diagram of Fig. 7.8 (b), considering the parallelogram for V_{RY}, we have

$$V_{RY} = V_L = 2 V_{ph} \cos 30^\circ = 2 V_{ph} \times \frac{\sqrt{3}}{2} = \sqrt{3} V_{ph}$$

Alternatively, V_{RY} being the diagonal of the parallelogram, can also be obtained as

$$V_{RY} = V_L = \sqrt{V_r^2 + V_y^2 + 2V_r \cdot V_y \cos 60^\circ} = \sqrt{V_{ph}^2 + V_{ph}^2 + 2V_{ph} \cdot V_{ph} \times \frac{1}{2}} = \sqrt{3} V_{ph}$$

Thus

$$V_L = \sqrt{3} V_{ph} \quad \ldots (7.4)$$

i.e. $\quad$ Line Voltage $= \sqrt{3}$ (Phase Voltage)

It should be noted that there is a phase displacement of 30° between them.

Current Relation : Since each line is connected to one phase of the load, obviously

$$I_L = I_{ph} \quad \ldots (7.5)$$

i.e. $\quad$ Line Current $=$ Phase Current

Power : The load being balanced,

Total power consumed, $\quad P = 3 \times$ (Power consumed by each phase of the load)

$$= 3 V_{ph} \cdot I_{ph} \cdot \cos \phi$$

$$= 3 \frac{V_L}{\sqrt{3}} \cdot I_L \cdot \cos \phi \quad \text{(Refer to the equations 7.4 and 7.5)}$$

$$= \sqrt{3} V_L \cdot I_L \cos \phi$$

Thus,

$$P = \sqrt{3} V_L I_L \cos \phi \quad \ldots (7.6)$$

i.e. $\quad$ Total Power $= \sqrt{3}$ (Line Voltage $\times$ Line Current $\times$ Phase Power Factor)

7.7 VOLTAGE, CURRENT AND POWER RELATIONS IN A DELTA CONNECTION

(a) **Delta-Connected, Three-Phase Supply System :** Fig. 7.9 (a) shows a delta-connected, three-phase system. The same notations as in the previous case of a star-connected, supply system are used to represent different line and phase quantities. The positive directions of phase

---

* $\quad$ *The voltage V_{RY} symbolizes that the potential of R is positive with respect to that of Y.*

e.m.f.s and phase currents are indicated by arrows, also as before. Since the balanced, three-phase, inductive load is assumed, the phase currents are shown lagging behind their respective phase e.m.f.s by a constant angle φ in the phasor diagram of Fig. 7.9 (b). The phase sequence that is assumed is R-Y-B.

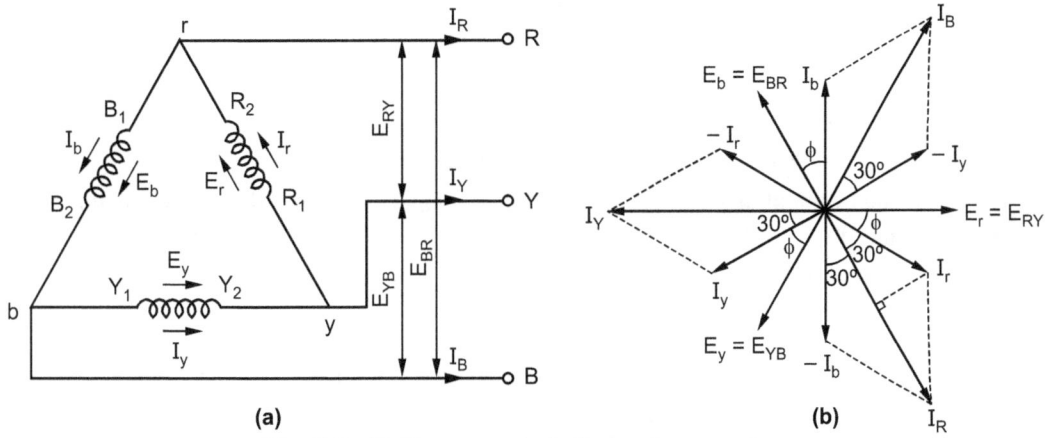

Fig. 7.9 : Delta-connected, three-phase system

Voltage Relation : In this case, each pair of line conductors is taken out from the two ends of a phase winding. Therefore, it is obvious that a line e.m.f. is the same as a phase e.m.f.. Therefore, if

$$E_r = E_y = E_b = E_{ph} \quad \text{(Numerically)}$$

and
$$E_{RY} = E_{YB} = E_{BR} = E_L \quad \text{(Numerically)}$$

Then,
$$E_L = E_{ph} \quad \ldots (7.7)$$

i.e. *Line E.M.F. = Phase E.M.F.*

Current Relation : The current in any line is obviously the phasor difference between the currents in the two phases to which the line is connected. Consider first, the line connected to the junction of R_2 and B_1. In this case, we have

$$\overline{I}_R = \overline{I}_r - \overline{I}_b$$

Alternatively, applying Kirchhoff's current law to the junction under consideration, we have

$$-\overline{I}_R - \overline{I}_b + \overline{I}_r = 0$$

$$\therefore \quad \overline{I}_R = \overline{I}_r - \overline{I}_b \quad \ldots \text{(Phasor difference)}$$

Thus, $\overline{I}_R$ is clearly the resultant of the phasors, $\overline{I}_r$ and $-\overline{I}_b$ (obtained by reversing the phasor $\overline{I}_b$) as shown in the phasor diagram (Fig. 7.9 b). Now, let

$$I_r = I_y = I_b = I_{ph} \quad \text{(Numerically)}$$

Then, from the phasor diagram of Fig. 7.9 (b), considering the parallelogram for I_R, we have

$$I_R = 2 I_{ph} \cos 30° = 2 I_{ph} \times \frac{\sqrt{3}}{2} = \sqrt{3} I_{ph}$$

Alternatively, I_R being the diagonal of the parallelogram, can also be obtained as

$$I_R = \sqrt{I_r^2 + I_b^2 + 2 I_r \cdot I_b \cos 60°} = \sqrt{I_{ph}^2 + I_{ph}^2 + 2 I_{ph} \cdot I_{ph} \times \frac{1}{2}} = \sqrt{3} I_{ph}$$

Similarly, $\bar{I}_Y = \bar{I}_y - \bar{I}_r$

∴ $I_Y = \sqrt{3} I_{ph}$

and $\bar{I}_B = \bar{I}_b - \bar{I}_y$

∴ $I_B = \sqrt{3} I_{ph}$

If $I_R = I_Y = I_B = I_L$ ... (Numerically)

then, it follows that $I_L = \sqrt{3} I_{ph}$ ... (7.8)

i.e. Line Current = $\sqrt{3}$ (Phase Current)

It should also be noted that there is always a phase displacement of 30° between them.

Power : Since the system is balanced,

Total power supplied, $P = 3 \times$ (Power supplied by each phase)

$= 3 E_{ph} I_{ph} \cos \phi$

$= 3 E_L \dfrac{I_L}{\sqrt{3}} \cos \phi$ (Refer to the equations 7.7 and 7.8)

$= \sqrt{3} E_L I_L \cos \phi$

Thus, $P = \sqrt{3} E_L I_L \cos \phi$ ... (7.9)

i.e. Total Power = $\sqrt{3}$ (Line E.M.F. × Line Current × Phase Power Factor)

Here, it should be remembered that the power factor (cos φ) refers to the phase and not to line. The expression for the power is thus identical to that for a star-connected supply system.

(b) Delta-Connected, Three-Phase Loads : The expressions (7.7), (7.8) and (7.9) are also applicable to a delta-connected, three-phase, balanced load. To verify this, consider a balanced, three-phase, delta-connected load shown in Fig. 7.10 (a). Notations used to represent the different line and phase quantities are similar to those used in the case of a three-phase, star-connected load. Assumed positive directions of phase currents and phase voltages are indicated as before by arrows. Fig. 7.10 (b) shows the phasor diagram assuming the load to be inductive in nature.

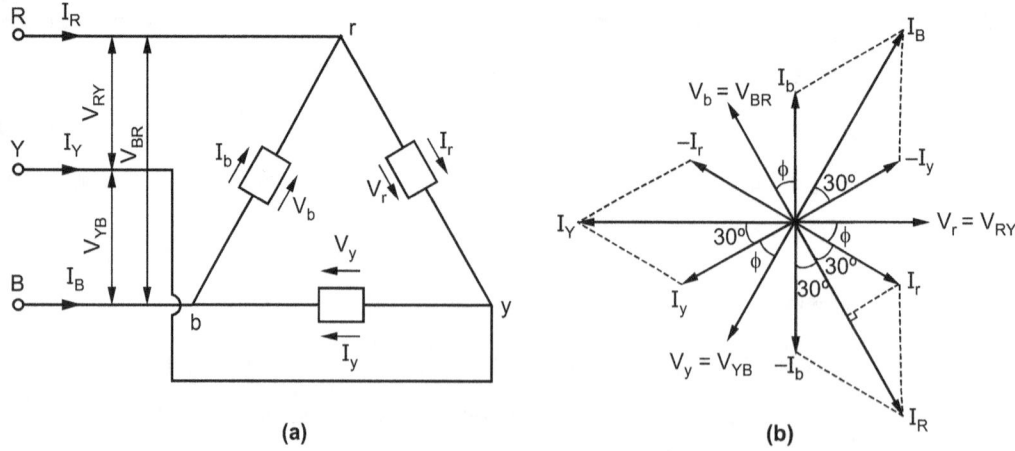

Fig. 7.10 : A balanced, three-phase, delta-connected load

Voltage Relation : There being one phase winding between each pair of lines,
$$V_L = V_{ph} \qquad \ldots (7.10)$$
i.e. $\qquad$ Line Voltage = Phase Voltage

Current Relation : Since in this type of connection, the line current is equal to phasor difference between two phase currents, for line current I_R, we have
$$\overline{I}_R = \overline{I}_r - \overline{I}_b$$
Or alternatively, applying Kirchhoff's current law to the junction r, we have
$$\overline{I}_R - \overline{I}_r + \overline{I}_b = 0$$
$\therefore \qquad \overline{I}_R = \overline{I}_r - \overline{I}_b$

Now, let $\qquad I_r = I_y = I_b = I_{ph} \qquad \ldots$ (Numerically)

Then, from the phasor diagram of Fig. 7.10 (b), considering the parallelogram for I_R, we have
$$I_R = 2 I_{ph} \cos 30° = 2 I_{ph} \times \frac{\sqrt{3}}{2} = \sqrt{3}\, I_{ph}$$

Alternatively, I_R being the diagonal of the parallelogram, can also be obtained as
$$I_R = \sqrt{I_r^2 + I_b^2 + 2 I_r \cdot I_b \cos 60°} = \sqrt{I_{ph}^2 + I_{ph}^2 + 2 I_{ph} \cdot I_{ph} \times \frac{1}{2}} = \sqrt{3}\, I_{ph}$$

Similarly, $\qquad \overline{I}_Y = \overline{I}_y - \overline{I}_r$
$\therefore \qquad I_Y = \sqrt{3}\, I_{ph}$
and $\qquad \overline{I}_B = \overline{I}_b - \overline{I}_y$
$\therefore \qquad I_B = \sqrt{3}\, I_{ph}$

If $\qquad I_R = I_Y = I_B = I_L \qquad \ldots$ (Numerically)

then, $\qquad I_L = \sqrt{3}\, I_{ph} \qquad \ldots (7.11)$

i.e. $\qquad$ Line Current = $\sqrt{3}$ (Phase Current)

From the phasor diagram of Fig. 7.10 (b), it will be clear that the phase displacement between the line currents and the respective phase currents is 30°.

Power : With a balanced load,

Total power consumed, $\quad P = 3 \times$ (Power consumed by each phase of the load)
$$= 3\, V_{ph} \cdot I_{ph} \cdot \cos \phi$$
$$= 3\, V_L \cdot \frac{I_L}{\sqrt{3}} \cos \phi \quad \text{(Refer to the equations 7.10 and 7.11)}$$
$$= \sqrt{3}\, V_L \cdot I_L \cos \phi$$

i.e. $\qquad P = \sqrt{3}\, V_L \cdot I_L \cos \phi \qquad \ldots (7.12)$

Hence it follows that for any balanced star or delta-connected load,

$\qquad$ Total Power = $\sqrt{3}$ *(Line Voltage × Line Current × Phase Power Factor)*

7.8 APPARENT POWER AND REACTIVE POWER

For a balanced, three-phase system,

$$\text{Total apparent power, } S = 3 \times (\text{Apparent power per phase})$$
$$= 3\, V_{ph} \cdot I_{ph}$$

Therefore, with star connection,

$$\text{Total apparent power, } S = 3 \frac{V_L}{\sqrt{3}} \times I_L = \sqrt{3}\, V_L \cdot I_L$$

Similarly, with delta connection,

$$\text{Total apparent power, } S = 3\, V_L \times \frac{I_L}{\sqrt{3}} = \sqrt{3}\, V_L \cdot I_L$$

Hence in general, for a balanced, three-phase system, we have

$$\text{Total Apparent Power, } S = \sqrt{3}\, V_L \cdot I_L \text{ volt-amperes} \qquad \ldots (7.13)$$

Also, when the system is balanced,

$$\text{Total reactive power, } Q = 3\, V_{ph} \cdot I_{ph} \sin \phi$$

Therefore, obviously for both star or delta connection,

$$\text{Total Reactive Power, } Q = \sqrt{3}\, V_L \cdot I_L \cdot \sin \phi \text{ reactive volt-amperes} \qquad \ldots (7.14)$$

7.9 APPLICATIONS OF STAR AND DELTA CONNECTIONS

As seen above, for a star connection, the phase voltage is $1/\sqrt{3}$ times the line voltage. Therefore, for producing a particular line voltage, a star-connected alternator needs less number of turns per phase than a delta-connected alternator and as such, they can be easily insulated. Three-phase, four-wire system, obtained with star-connected alternators is useful for both lighting and power purposes. The neutral provided by a star connection, if grounded enables the use of different protective devices for the protection of the alternator. Further, with star connection, the problem of circulating currents is also totally eliminated. Because of all these advantages, it is customary to use star connection for the alternators, more particularly for the large capacity alternators. With motors (such as induction motors) and transformers, both star and delta connections are satisfactory.

Example 7.1 : *A balanced, three-phase load of 3 kW at a power factor of 0.8 lagging is connected across a three-phase supply. If the line current is 12.5 A, calculate the resistance and reactance in each branch of the star-connected load. What will be the line current and the power loss if the same load is connected in delta ?*

Solution :

Case-1 : Three-Phase Load with Star Connection :

Fig. 7.11 (a) shows the star-connected load connected across a three-phase supply.

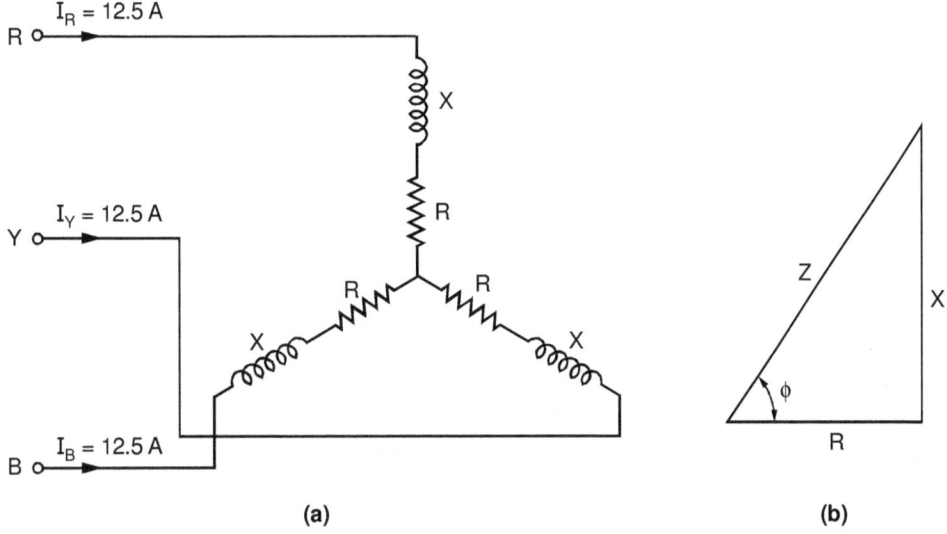

Fig. 7.11 : Three-phase system with a star-connected load, Example 7.1

Since,
$$P = \sqrt{3}\, V_L \cdot I_L \cos \phi$$

$$V_L = \frac{P}{\sqrt{3}\, I_L \cos \phi}$$

$$= \frac{3 \times 1000}{\sqrt{3} \times 12.5 \times 0.8} = 173.2 \text{ V}$$

∴ $\quad V_{ph} = \dfrac{V_L}{\sqrt{3}} = \dfrac{173.2}{\sqrt{3}} = 100$ volts   ... (Refer to Equation 7.4)

Also, $\quad I_{ph} = I_L = 12.5$ A   ... (Refer to Equation 7.5)

∴ Impedance of each branch, $Z = \dfrac{V_{ph}}{I_{ph}} = \dfrac{100}{12.5} = 8\, \Omega$.

Now, since $\cos \phi = 0.8$ lagging (given), from the impedance triangle of Fig. 7.11 (b), we get

$$R = Z \cos \phi = 8 \times 0.8 = \mathbf{6.4\, \Omega} \quad \text{... Ans.}$$
$$X = Z \sin \phi = 8 \times 0.6 = \mathbf{4.8\, \Omega} \quad \text{... Ans.}$$

Case-2 : Three-Phase Load with Delta Connection :

With delta connection (Fig. 7.12),

$$V_{ph} = V_L = 173.2 \text{ volts} \quad \text{... (Refer to Equation 7.10)}$$

∴ $\quad I_{ph} = \dfrac{V_{ph}}{Z} = \dfrac{173.2}{8} = 21.65$ A

Therefore, from Equation (7.11),

$$I_L = \sqrt{3}\, I_{ph} = \sqrt{3} \times 21.65 = \mathbf{37.50\, A} \quad \text{... Ans.}$$

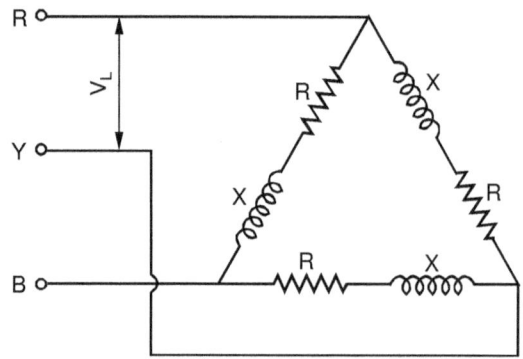

Fig. 7.12 : Three-phase system with a delta-connected load, Example 7.1

Hence, power consumed, $P = \sqrt{3} \, V_L \, I_L \cos \phi$
$= \sqrt{3} \times 173.2 \times 37.50 \times 0.8$
$= 8999.74 \text{ W}$
$\approx 9 \text{ kW}$ ... Ans.

Thus, with delta connection, the load consumes power which is three times that with star connection.

Example 7.2 : *A balanced, star-connected load is supplied from a symmetrical three-phase 415 V system. The current in each phase is $20 \angle -30°$ A.*

(a) *Determine : (i) Phase voltage, (ii) Line current, (iii) Total power and power factor of the load.*

(b) *If one of the branch impedances of the star-connected load becomes open-circuited, calculate : (i) Current, (ii) Power taken from the lines.*

Solution : Line voltage, $V_L = 415$ V

(a) The load is star connected. Hence,

Phase voltage, $V_{ph} = \dfrac{V_L}{\sqrt{3}} = \dfrac{415}{\sqrt{3}} = $ **239.6 V** ... Ans.

Line current, $I_L = I_{ph} = $ **20 A** ... Ans.

Power factor of load, $\cos \phi = \cos 30° = $ **0.866 (lagging)** ... Ans.

Total power, $P = \sqrt{3} \, V_L \, I_L \cos \phi = \sqrt{3} \times 415 \times 20 \times 0.866$
$= $ **12450 W** ... Ans.

(b) Impedance per phase of given star-connected load,

$$\bar{Z}_{ph} = \dfrac{\bar{V}_{ph}}{\bar{I}_{ph}} = \dfrac{239.6 \angle 0°}{20 \angle -30°}$$

$= 11.98 \angle 30° = (10.37 + j\, 5.99) \, \Omega$

When one of the branches becomes open-circuited, the circuit merely reduces to a single-phase circuit in which two similar impedances are joined in series across a supply of 415 V. Therefore, under this condition,

Total impedance, $\bar{Z} = 2 \times 11.98 \angle 30° = 23.96 \angle 30° \, \Omega$

Current drawn from the supply,

$$\bar{I} = \frac{415 \angle 0°}{23.96 \angle 30°} = 17.32 \angle -30° \text{ A} \qquad \text{... Ans.}$$

Power taken from the supply, $P = VI \cos \phi = 415 \times 17.32 \times \cos 30° = \textbf{6225 W}$ ... Ans.

Example 7.3 : *A three-phase, 440 V, star-connected alternator supplies a three-phase, 50 kW, delta-connected induction motor. If the motor works at 0.8 lagging power factor and has efficiency of 0.85, find current per phase for motor and alternator.*

Solution : Induction Motor :

Line voltage for the motor, V_L = 440 V

Power factor of the motor, $\cos \phi$ = 0.8 (lagging)

Output of the motor = 50 kW

$\therefore$ Input to the motor $= \dfrac{\text{Output}}{\text{Efficiency}} = \dfrac{50}{0.85} = 58.82$ kW

Hence, line current drawn by the motor,

$$I_L = \frac{\text{Input}}{\sqrt{3}\ V_L \cos \phi} = \frac{58.82 \times 10^3}{\sqrt{3} \times 440 \times 0.8} = 96.48 \text{ A}$$

Since the motor is delta connected, its phase current,

$$I_{ph} = \frac{I_L}{\sqrt{3}} = \frac{96.48}{\sqrt{3}} = \textbf{55.7 A} \qquad \text{... Ans.}$$

Alternator : Alternator being star connected, its phase current will be equal to line current.

$\therefore$ Phase current for alternator, I_{ph} = **96.48 A** ... Ans.

Example 7.4 : *A series combination of 3 Ω resistance and a 796.18 μF capacitor in each branch forms a three-phase, star-connected, balanced load which is connected to a 415 V, three-phase, 50 Hz, a.c. supply. Calculate : (i) the power consumed and (ii) current drawn by the load. If the same load is now connected as a 'delta', determine : (i) the power consumed and (ii) current drawn from the supply.*

Solution : Star Connection :

Capacitive reactance, $X_C = \dfrac{1}{2\pi fC} = \dfrac{1}{2\pi \times 50 \times 796.18 \times 10^{-6}} = 4 \ \Omega$

Impedance per phase, $\bar{Z}_{ph} = R - jX_C = 3 - j4 = 5 \angle -53.13° \ \Omega$

Phase voltage, $V_{ph} = \dfrac{415}{\sqrt{3}} = 239.6$ V

$\therefore$ Phase current, $\bar{I}_{ph} = \dfrac{\bar{V}_{ph}}{\bar{Z}_{ph}} = \dfrac{239.6 \angle 0°}{5 \angle -53.13°} = 47.92 \angle 53.13°$ A

$\therefore$ Line current, $I_L = I_{ph} = \textbf{47.92 A}$ ... Ans.

Power factor, $\cos \phi = \cos 53.13° = 0.6$ leading

$\therefore$ Power consumed, $P = \sqrt{3}\ V_L I_L \cos \phi = \sqrt{3} \times 415 \times 47.92 \times 0.6$ W

$= \textbf{20.67 kW}$ ... Ans.

Delta Connection : $\quad V_{ph} = V_L = 415\ V$

$$\therefore\quad \bar{I}_{ph} = \frac{\bar{V}_{ph}}{\bar{Z}_{ph}} = \frac{415\angle 0°}{5\angle -53.13°} = 83\angle 53.13°\ A$$

$\therefore\quad$ Line current, $I_L = \sqrt{3}\ I_{ph} = \sqrt{3}\times 83 =$ **143.76 A** ... Ans.

$\cos\phi = 0.6$ leading (as before)

$\therefore\quad$ Power consumed, $P = \sqrt{3}\ V_L\ I_L\cos\phi = \sqrt{3}\times 415\times 143.76\times 0.6\ W$

$= $ **62 kW** ... Ans.

Example 7.5 : *A delta-connected, balanced load across a 400 V, 3-phase supply consists of three identical impedances, each equal to $(15 + j\ 12)\ \Omega$. Find the line current. Also find the power and reactive voltamperes of the load.*

Solution : $\quad \bar{Z}_{ph} = 15 + j\ 12 = 19.21\angle 38.66°\ \Omega$

$V_L = 400\ V = V_{ph}$

$$\therefore\quad \bar{I}_{ph} = \frac{\bar{V}_{ph}}{\bar{Z}_{ph}} = \frac{400\angle 0°}{19.21\angle 38.66°} = 20.82\angle -38.66°\ A$$

$\therefore\quad I_L = \sqrt{3}\ I_{ph} = \sqrt{3}\times 20.82 =$ **36.06 A** ... Ans.

$\therefore\quad$ Power, $P = \sqrt{3}\ V_L\ I_L\cos\phi = \sqrt{3}\times 400\times 36.06\times \cos(38.66°)\ W$

$= $ **19.51 kW** ... Ans.

Reactive power, $Q = \sqrt{3}\ V_L I_L\sin\phi = \sqrt{3}\times 400\times 36.06\times \sin(38.66°)\ VAr$

$= $ **15.61 kVAr** ... Ans.

Example 7.6 : *It is observed that 3 kW is the total power consumed in a balanced, star-connected, three-phase load when connected to a 3-phase, 400 V, 50 Hz supply. If the power factor of the load is 0.866 leading, calculate values of the resistance and capacitance in each branch of the load.*

Solution : Total power consumed,

$P = \sqrt{3}\ V_L\ I_L\cos\phi$

$\therefore\quad 3000 = \sqrt{3}\times 400\times I_L\times 0.866$

$\therefore\quad I_L = 5\ A$

Hence, $I_{ph} = I_L = 5\ A$

$V_{ph} = \dfrac{V_L}{\sqrt{3}} = \dfrac{400}{\sqrt{3}} = 230.94\ V$

$$Z_{ph} = \frac{V_{ph}}{I_{ph}} = \frac{230.94}{5} = 46.19 \, \Omega$$

$$\cos \phi = 0.866, \; \phi = 30°, \; \sin \phi = 0.5$$

∴ Resistance, $R = Z \cos \phi = 46.19 \times 0.866 = \mathbf{40 \, \Omega}$ ... **Ans.**

Capacitive reactance, $X_C = Z \sin \phi = 46.19 \times 0.5 = 23.095 \, \Omega$

Now, $X_C = \dfrac{1}{2\pi f C}$

∴ $23.095 = \dfrac{1}{2\pi \times 50 \times C}$

∴ Capacitance, $C = \mathbf{137.83 \, \mu F}$ ... **Ans.**

Example 7.7 : *Prove that a three-phase, balanced load with delta connection, consumes power which is three times that with star connection.*

Solution : Let Z_{ph} be the impedance per phase of a given three-phase, balanced load and $\cos \phi$ be its power factor. The value of this power factor is decided by the parameters of each phase of the load. Further, let V_L be the line voltage of the supply system. Hence,

With Star Connection :

$$V_{ph} = \frac{V_L}{\sqrt{3}}$$

$$I_{ph} = \frac{V_{ph}}{Z_{ph}} = \frac{V_L}{\sqrt{3} \, Z_{ph}}$$

∴ $$I_L = I_{ph} = \frac{V_L}{\sqrt{3} \, Z_{ph}}$$

∴ Total power consumed,

$$P_{star} = \sqrt{3} \, V_L I_L \cos \phi = \sqrt{3} \, V_L \times \frac{V_L}{\sqrt{3} \, Z_{ph}} \times \cos \phi$$

$$= \frac{V_L^2 \cos \phi}{Z_{ph}} \quad \ldots \text{(I)}$$

With Delta Connection :

$$V_{ph} = V_L$$

$$I_{ph} = \frac{V_{ph}}{Z_{ph}} = \frac{V_L}{Z_{ph}}$$

∴ $$I_L = \sqrt{3} \, I_{ph} = \sqrt{3} \times \frac{V_L}{Z_{ph}}$$

∴ Total power consumed,

$$P_{delta} = \sqrt{3} \, V_L I_L \cos \phi = \sqrt{3} \, V_L \times \frac{\sqrt{3} \, V_L}{Z_{ph}} \times \cos \phi$$

$$= \frac{3 \, V_L^2 \cos \phi}{Z_{ph}} \quad \ldots \text{(II)}$$

From the equations (I) and (II), we have

$$P_{delta} = 3 \, P_{star} \quad \ldots \textbf{Ans.}$$

Example 7.8 : *A 220 V, 3-phase voltage is applied to a balanced, delta-connected load of phase impedance (15 + j 20) Ω. Find the line current and power consumed by each phase. What is the phasor sum of three line currents ? Why does it have to be this value ?*

Solution : Since the load is delta connected,

Voltage per phase for the load,
$$V_{ph} = V_L = 220 \text{ V}$$

Impedance per phase of the load,
$$\overline{Z}_{ph} = (15 + j\,20) = 25 \angle 53.13° \text{ Ω}$$

∴ Current per phase, $\overline{I}_{ph} = \dfrac{\overline{V}_{ph}}{\overline{Z}_{ph}} = \dfrac{220 \angle 0°}{25 \angle 53.13°} = 8.8 \angle -53.13° \text{ A}$

∴ Line current drawn by the load,
$$I_L = \sqrt{3}\,I_{ph} = \sqrt{3} \times 8.8 = \mathbf{15.24 \text{ A}} \qquad \text{... Ans.}$$

Power factor, $\cos \phi = \cos(53.13°) = 0.6$ lagging

Power consumed per phase,
$$P = V_{ph}\,I_{ph}\cos\phi = 220 \times 8.8 \times 0.6 = \mathbf{1161.6 \text{ W}} \qquad \text{... Ans.}$$

Phasor sum of three line currents = 0

This is because due to balanced loading, these currents are equal in magnitude and have a phase difference of 120°.

Example 7.9 : *A delta-connected, balanced load is connected to a 3-phase, 400 V supply. The load p.f. is 0.8 lagging. The line current is 34.64 A. Find :*

(i) Resistance, reactance and impedance of the load per phase,

(ii) Total power, and

(iii) Total reactive volt-amperes.

Draw the phasor diagram showing all the quantities.

Solution : The load being delta connected,

Voltage per phase for the load, $V_{ph} = V_L = 400$ V

Line current, $I_L = 34.64$ A (given)

∴ Phase current, $I_{ph} = \dfrac{I_L}{\sqrt{3}} = \dfrac{34.64}{\sqrt{3}} = 20$ A

Load power factor, $\cos\phi = 0.8$ lagging (given)

∴ $\phi = 36.87°$

(i) Impedance per phase of the load,

$$\overline{Z}_{ph} = \dfrac{\overline{V}_{ph}}{\overline{I}_{ph}} = \dfrac{400 \angle 0°}{20 \angle -36.87°}$$

$$= 20 \angle 36.87° = (16 + j\,12) \text{ Ω} \qquad \text{... Ans.}$$

∴ Resistance per phase, $R = \mathbf{16 \text{ Ω}}$ ... Ans.

and Reactance per phase, $X_L = \mathbf{12 \text{ Ω}}$ ... Ans.

(ii) Total power,
$$P = \sqrt{3}\, V_L \cdot I_L \cdot \cos\phi = \sqrt{3} \times 400 \times 34.64 \times 0.8 = \mathbf{19199.44\ W} \quad \ldots \text{Ans.}$$

(iii) Total reactive power, $Q = \sqrt{3}\, V_L \cdot I_L \cdot \sin\phi = \sqrt{3} \times 400 \times 34.64 \times 0.6$
$$= \mathbf{14399.58\ VAr} \quad \ldots \text{Ans.}$$

For phasor diagram, refer to Fig. 7.10 (b).

Example 7.10 : *A symmetrical, 3-phase, 400 V system supplies a balanced load of 0.8 lagging power factor and connected in star. If the line current is 34.64 A, find : (i) Impedance, (ii) Resistance and reactance per phase, (iii) Total power, and (iv) Total reactive volt-amperes.*

Solution : Line voltage, $V_L = 400$ V

$\therefore$ Phase voltage, $V_{ph} = \dfrac{400}{\sqrt{3}} = 230.94$ V ($\because$ star connection)

Current per phase, I_{ph} = Line current, I_L ($\because$ star connection)
$= 34.64$ A

Power factor, $\cos\phi = 0.8$ lagging (given)

$\therefore \phi = 36.87°$

(i) Impedance per phase, $\overline{Z}_{ph} = \dfrac{\overline{V}_{ph}}{\overline{I}_{ph}} = \dfrac{230.94\angle 0°}{34.64\angle -36.87°} = 6.67\angle 36.87°$
$$= \mathbf{(5.34 + j\,4)\ \Omega} \quad \ldots \text{Ans.}$$

(ii) From the above expression for the impedance per phase, it is obvious that
Resistance per phase, $R = \mathbf{5.34\ \Omega}$ ... Ans.
Reactance per phase, $X_L = \mathbf{4\ \Omega}$ ... Ans.

(iii) Total power, $P = \sqrt{3}\, V_L I_L \cos\phi = \sqrt{3} \times 400 \times 34.64 \times 0.8$ W
$= \mathbf{19.2\ kW}$ ... Ans.

(iv) Total reactive volt-amperes,
$Q = \sqrt{3}\, V_L I_L \sin\phi = \sqrt{3} \times 400 \times 34.64 \times 0.6$ VAr
$= \mathbf{14.4\ kVAr}$ ... Ans.

Example 7.11 : *A balanced, three-phase, star-connected load of 100 kW takes a leading current of 80 A when connected across 3-ϕ, 1100 V, 50 Hz supply. Find the value of the resistance per phase and capacitance per phase of the load and power factor of the load. If the same load is connected in delta, calculate power consumed.*

Solution : Star Connection :

Total power with star connection,
$$P_Y = \sqrt{3}\, V_L I_L \cos\phi \text{ watts}$$
$\therefore \quad 100 \times 10^3 = \sqrt{3} \times 1100 \times 80 \times \cos\phi$

∴ Power factor of the load,

$$\cos\phi = 0.6561 \text{ leading} \quad \text{... Ans.}$$

Voltage per phase, $V_{ph} = \dfrac{V_L}{\sqrt{3}} = \dfrac{1100}{\sqrt{3}} = 635.1$ V

Current per phase, $I_{ph} = I_L = 80$ A

Power factor angle, $\phi = \cos^{-1}(0.6561) = 48.997°$

∴ Impedance per phase of the load,

$$\bar{Z}_{ph} = \dfrac{\bar{V}_{ph}}{\bar{I}_{ph}} = \dfrac{635.1 \angle 0°}{80 \angle 48.997°}$$

$$= 7.9388 \angle -48.997° = (5.21 - j\,5.99)\ \Omega$$

∴ Resistance per phase of the load,

$$R = 5.21\ \Omega \quad \text{... Ans.}$$

and Capacitive reactance per phase, $X_C = 5.99\ \Omega$

∴ Capacitance per phase of the load,

$$C = \dfrac{1}{2\pi f \cdot X_C} = \dfrac{1}{2\pi \times 50 \times 5.99}$$

$$= 5.31 \times 10^{-4}\ \text{F} \quad \text{or}\quad 531\ \mu\text{F} \quad \text{... Ans.}$$

Delta Connection : With delta connection, the load consumes power which is three times that with star connection. Hence,

Total power consumed with delta connection,

$$P_\Delta = 3P_Y = 3 \times 100 = \mathbf{300\ kW} \quad \text{... Ans.}$$

Example 7.12 : *Three inductive coils, each having resistance of 15 Ω and an inductance of 0.03 H connected in series, are connected (i) in star, and (ii) in delta to a 3-phase, 400 V, 50 Hz supply. Calculate in each case the current and total power absorbed.*

Solution : $X_L = \omega L = 2\pi f L = 2\pi \times 50 \times 0.03 = 9.42\ \Omega$

∴ $\bar{Z}_{ph} = R + jX_L = (15 + j\,9.42) = 17.71 \angle 32.13°\ \Omega$

(i) With Star Connection : $V_L = 400$ V

$$V_{ph} = \dfrac{V_L}{\sqrt{3}} = \dfrac{400}{\sqrt{3}} = 230.94\ \text{V}$$

∴ $\bar{V}_{ph} = 230.94 \angle 0°$ V

$$\bar{I}_{ph} = \dfrac{\bar{V}_{ph}}{\bar{Z}_{ph}} = \dfrac{230.94 \angle 0°}{17.71 \angle 32.13°} = 13.04 \angle -32.13°\ \text{A}$$

∴ Line current, $I_L = I_{ph} = \mathbf{13.04\ A} \quad \text{... Ans.}$

and $\cos\phi = \cos 32.13° = 0.847$ lagging

∴ Total power absorbed, $P_Y = \sqrt{3}\ V_L I_L \cos\phi = \sqrt{3} \times 400 \times 13.04 \times 0.847$
= **7652 W or 7.652 kW** ... Ans.

(ii) With Delta Connection :

$$V_{ph} = V_L = 400\ V$$

∴ $$\overline{I}_{ph} = \frac{\overline{V}_{ph}}{\overline{Z}_{ph}} = \frac{400 \angle 0°}{17.71 \angle 32.13°} = 22.59 \angle -32.13°\ A$$

∴ Line current, $I_L = \sqrt{3}\ I_{ph} = \sqrt{3} \times 22.59 = $ **39.13 A** ... Ans.

and $\cos\phi = \cos 32.13° = 0.847$ lagging

∴ Total power absorbed,

$$P_\Delta = \sqrt{3}\ V_L I_L \cos\phi = \sqrt{3} \times 400 \times 39.13 \times 0.847$$
= **22962 W or 22.962 kW** ... Ans.

Example 7.13 : *A 3ϕ load having phase impedance of $(3 + j4)\ \Omega$ is supplied from a 3ϕ, 440 V, 50 Hz a.c. supply. Calculate the power absorbed by the load when*
(i) Load is star connected.
(ii) One of the phase blows out and load is star connected.

Solution : Given : $\overline{Z}_{ph} = (3 + j4)\ \Omega,\ V_L = 440\ V,\ f = 50\ Hz$

(i) $\overline{Z}_{ph} = 3 + j4 = 5 \angle 53.13°\ \Omega$

$$V_{ph} = \frac{V_L}{\sqrt{3}} = \frac{440}{\sqrt{3}} = 254.03\ V$$

$$\overline{I}_{ph} = \frac{\overline{V}_{ph}}{\overline{Z}_{ph}} = \frac{254.03 \angle 0°}{5 \angle 53.13°} = 50.81 \angle -53.13°\ A$$

$$I_L = I_{ph} = 50.81\ A$$

Power absorbed by the load,

$$P = \sqrt{3}\ V_L I_L \cos\phi = \sqrt{3} \times 440 \times 50.81 \times \cos 53.13°$$
= **23233.51 W** ... Ans.

(ii) When one of the phase of the 3ϕ, star-connected load blows out, the remaining two phases of the load get connected in series across 440 V, a.c. supply. Hence, under this condition, we have

Total impedance of the load,

$$\overline{Z} = (3 + j4) + (3 + j4) = 6 + j8 = 10 \angle 53.13°\ \Omega$$

∴ $$\overline{I} = \frac{\overline{V}}{\overline{Z}} = \frac{440 \angle 0°}{10 \angle 53.13°} = 44 \angle -53.13°\ A$$

∴ Power absorbed by the load,

$$P = V \cdot I \cdot \cos\phi = 440 \times 44 \times \cos 53.13° = \textbf{11616.03 W} \ \text{... Ans.}$$

Example 7.14 : *A 3ϕ, 400 V a.c. generator supplies power to both delta and star-connected loads simultaneously. Both loads have identical impedances of (12 + j6) Ω per phase. Find the current supplied by the generator.*

Solution: Given: $\bar{Z}_{ph} = (12 + j6)\ \Omega,\ V_L = 400\ V$

Delta-connected Load:

$$\bar{Z}_{ph} = 12 + j6 = 13.42\ \angle 26.57°\ \Omega$$

$$V_{ph} = V_L = 400\ V$$

$$\therefore \bar{I}_{ph} = \frac{\bar{V}_{ph}}{\bar{Z}_{ph}} = \frac{400\ \angle 0°}{13.42\ \angle 26.57°} = 29.81\ \angle -26.57°\ A$$

$$\therefore I_L = \sqrt{3} \times I_{ph} = \sqrt{3} \times 29.81 = 51.63\ A$$

$$\cos \phi = \cos(26.57°) = 0.894\ \text{lagging}$$

$$\sin \phi = \sin(26.57°) = 0.447$$

$$\therefore \text{Active power } P_\Delta = \sqrt{3}\ V_L I_L \cos \phi = \sqrt{3} \times 400 \times 51.63 \times 0.894 = 31978.66\ W$$

$$\text{Reactive power } Q_\Delta = \sqrt{3}\ V_L I_L \sin \phi = \sqrt{3} \times 400 \times 51.63 \times 0.447$$

$$= 15989.33\ VAr\ \text{(lagging)}$$

Star-connected Load:

$$\bar{Z}_{ph} = 12 + j6 = 13.42\ \angle 26.57°\ \Omega$$

$$V_{ph} = \frac{V_L}{\sqrt{3}} = \frac{400}{\sqrt{3}} = 230.94\ V$$

$$\therefore \bar{I}_{ph} = \frac{\bar{V}_{ph}}{\bar{Z}_{ph}} = \frac{230.94\ \angle 0°}{13.42\ \angle 26.57°} = 17.21\ \angle -26.57°\ A$$

$$\therefore I_L = I_{ph} = 17.21\ A$$

$$\cos \phi = \cos(26.57°) = 0.894\ \text{lagging}$$

$$\sin \phi = \sin(26.57°) = 0.447$$

$$\therefore \text{Active power } P_Y = \sqrt{3}\ V_L I_L \cos \phi = \sqrt{3} \times 400 \times 17.21 \times 0.894$$

$$= 10659.55\ W$$

$$\text{Reactive power } Q_Y = \sqrt{3}\ V_L I_L \sin \phi = \sqrt{3} \times 400 \times 17.21 \times 0.447$$

$$= 5329.78\ VAr\ \text{(lagging)}$$

Combined Load: Total active power consumed,

$$P = P_\Delta + P_Y = 31978.66 + 10659.55 = 42638.21 \text{ W}$$

Total reactive power consumed,

$$Q = Q_\Delta + Q_Y = 15989.33 + 5329.78 = 21319.11 \text{ VAr (lagging)}$$

$$\tan \phi = \frac{Q}{P} = \frac{21319.11}{42638.21} = 0.5$$

∴ Power factor of the combined load,

$$\cos \phi = 0.894 \text{ lagging}$$

∴ Total line current supplied by the generator,

$$I_L = \frac{P}{\sqrt{3}\, V_L \cos \phi} = \frac{42638.21}{\sqrt{3} \times 400 \times 0.894}$$

$$= \mathbf{68.84 \text{ A}} \qquad \text{... Ans.}$$

7.10 POINTS TO REMEMBER

- The alternator with the number of armature coils suitably connected to form one winding is known as single phase (winding) alternator.
- The single alternating voltage generated by such an alternator is known as single-phase voltage (or e.m.f.) and the current that results from the action of this single-phase alternating voltage is called single-phase alternating current.
- Polyphase (or multiphase) alternators have two or more windings symmetrically spaced around the armature.
- A polyphase system is said to be symmetrical when the e.m.f.s of the same frequency in different phases are equal in magnitude and displaced from one another by equal phase angles.
- The order in which the voltages in three phases reach their maximum positive values is called the phase sequence.
- If all phase impedances of the three phase load are exactly identical in respect of magnitude and their nature, it is said to be a balanced three-phase load.
- The e.m.f. generated in each winding (phase) on the armature of the alternator is known as phase e.m.f. and corresponding current as phase current.
- The voltage between any two line conductors coming out from the terminals of the alternator is called the line e.m.f. or line voltage and the current flowing in each line conductor is called line current.

7.11 IMPORTANT FORMULAE AT A GLANCE

Star-connected, Three-phase Supply System :

- $$E_L = \sqrt{3}\, E_{ph}$$

  where, E_L = Line e.m.f., in volts

  E_{ph} = Phase e.m.f., in volts

- $$I_L = I_{ph}$$

  where, I_L = Line current, in amperes

  I_{ph} = Phase current, in amperes

- Total power $P = \sqrt{3}\, E_L I_L \cos\phi$ watts

  where E_L = Line e.m.f., in volts

  I_L = Line current, in amperes

  $\cos\phi$ = Phase power factor

Star-connected, Three-phase Loads :

- $$V_L = \sqrt{3}\, V_{ph}$$

  where V_L = Line voltage, in volts

  V_{ph} = Phase voltage, in volts

- $$I_L = I_{ph}$$

  where I_L = Line current, in amperes

  I_{ph} = Phase current, in amperes

- Total power $P = \sqrt{3}\, V_L I_L \cos\phi$ watts

  where V_L = Line voltage, in volts

  I_L = Line current, in amperes

  $\cos\phi$ = Phase power factor.

Delta-connected, Three-phase Supply System :

- $$E_L = E_{ph}$$

  where E_L = Line e.m.f., in volts

  E_{ph} = Phase e.m.f., in volts

- $$I_L = \sqrt{3}\, I_{ph}$$

  where I_L = Line current, in amperes

  I_{ph} = Phase current, in amperes

- $$\text{Total power } P = \sqrt{3}\, E_L\, I_L \cos\phi \text{ watts}$$
  where, E_L = Line e.m.f., in volts
  I_L = Line current, in amperes
  $\cos\phi$ = Phase power factor

Delta-connected, Three-phase Loads :

- $$V_L = V_{ph}$$
  where V_L = Line voltage, in volts
  V_{ph} = Phase voltage, in volts

- $$I_L = \sqrt{3}\, I_{ph}$$
  where I_L = Line current, in amperes
  I_{ph} = Phase current, in amperes

- $$\text{Total power } P = \sqrt{3}\, V_L\, I_L \cos\phi \text{ watts}$$
  where V_L = Line voltage, in volts
  I_L = Line current, in amperes
  $\cos\phi$ = Phase power factor

Apparent Power and Reactive Power for a Balanced Three-phase System :

- Total apparent power $S = \sqrt{3}\, V_L\, I_L$ volt-amperes
  where V_L = Line voltage, in volts
  I_L = Line current, in amperes

- Total reactive power $Q = \sqrt{3}\, V_L\, I_L \sin\phi$ reactive volt-amperes
  where V_L = Line voltage, in volts
  I_L = Line current, in amperes
  $\sin\phi$ = Sine of the phase angle between the phase voltage and phase current.

7.12 EXERCISES

7.12.1 Review Questions

1. Explain the difference between a single-phase and a polyphase system.
2. Briefly describe an elementary three-phase alternator and explain how it generates a three-phase supply.
3. Define : Symmetrical system, Phase sequence.
4. Why are the three phases of the armature of an alternator interconnected ? What are the different methods of interconnecting them ?
5. State the advantages of three-phase, four-wire supply system for distribution purposes.
6. Explain with reference to a three-phase system, the terms *'balanced load'* and *'balanced supply system'*.
7. Explain the difference between a line voltage and a phase voltage, a line current and a phase current.
8. For star and delta-connected loads, state and prove the numerical relationship between
   (i) Line current and phase current
   (ii) Line voltage and phase voltage
   Also state the expression for power in terms of line voltage, line current and power factor.

9. Compare the star and delta connections on the basis of way of connection, voltage relationship, current relationship and neutral wire.

10. State the reasons for using a star connection, particularly for the large-capacity alternators.

7.12.2 Examples for Practice

1. A balanced, three-phase, star-connected load is supplied from a three-phase, 400 V, 50 Hz supply. The resistance of each coil is 6 Ω and reactance is 8 Ω. Find the value of phase current, line current and the total power consumed.

   (23.09 A, 23.09 A, 9.6 kW)

2. A balanced, delta-connected load is connected across a 230 V, three-phase supply. If the resistance and inductive reactance per phase are 6 Ω and 8 Ω respectively, calculate the line current, power factor and the total power consumed.

   (39.84 A, 0.6 lagging, 9.522 kW)

3. A balanced, three-phase, star-connected load is supplied with three-phase, 400 V, 50 Hz supply. The current in each phase is 10 A and lags 60° behind the phase voltage. Calculate the power supplied to the load. What will be the power supplied if the phase current is 10 A at a leading power factor of 0.5 ?

   (3.464 kW, 3.464 kW)

4. Three identical coils, each having resistance of 15 Ω and inductance of 0.03 H, are connected in delta across a three-phase, 400 V, 50 Hz supply. Calculate :

   (i) Phase current,

   (ii) Line current, and

   (iii) Power consumed.

   Draw a neat phasor diagram.

   (22.57 A, 39.1 A, 22931.07 W)

5. A three-phase, delta-connected load having an impedance of (30 + j 40) Ω per phase is fed from the secondary of a three-phase, star-connected transformer, which has a phase voltage of 231 V. Draw the circuit diagram of the system and calculate :

   (i) Potential difference across each phase of the load.

   (ii) Magnitude of current in each phase of the load.

   (iii) Magnitude of current in the transformer secondary windings,

   (iv) Total power consumed by the load and its power factor.

   (400.1 V, 8.002 A, 13.86 A, 5762.93 W, 0.6 lagging)

6. Three similar resistances are connected in star across 440 V, three-phase supply. The line current is 15 A. Find the value of each resistor. To which value the line voltage be changed to obtain the same line current with the resistors connected in delta ?

   (16.93 Ω, 146.61 V)

CHAPTER 8
SINGLE-PHASE TRANSFORMERS

8.1 INTRODUCTION

We know that one of the most important advantages of alternating currents over direct currents is the extreme ease with which the transformation from a low to a high voltage or vice versa may be accomplished with the help of transformers. *The transformer is a static device (with no rotating parts) which transfers electrical energy from one alternating current circuit to another with the desired change in voltage or current and without any change in frequency.* Through its use, electrical energy can be generated at the economical voltage, transmitted efficiently at the increased voltage and utilized after reducing the voltage again to the value suitable for the particular application. The high-voltage, long-distance transmission with the help of transformers has made possible the utilization of electrical energy in one geographical locality from energy sources in others.

The transformers are designed to operate either on single-phase or on three-phase supply and accordingly are known as *single-phase* or *three-phase transformers*. The discussion in this chapter is confined to the single-phase transformers only. The three-phase transformers, however, work on the same principle as single-phase transformers.

8.2 PRINCIPLE OF WORKING

The operation of the transformer is based on the principle of *mutual induction between two circuits linked by a common magnetic field*. To understand the working of the transformer more clearly, consider the transformer in its elementary form shown in Fig. 8.1.

It essentially consists of two windings (P and S), electrically separate but wound on a common laminated steel core (C). The vertical portions of the core on which these windings are placed are referred to as the *limbs* and the top and bottom portions are *the yokes*. The winding (P) which is connected to the existing supply system and which receives energy from it is known as the *primary winding*. The other winding (S) delivering energy to the load at the desired voltage is called *the secondary winding*.

When the primary winding is connected to a.c. supply, applied alternating voltage circulates an alternating current through it. This current flowing through the primary winding produces an alternating flux (ϕ). Most of this varying flux links with the secondary winding through the iron core and induces an e.m.f. in it in accordance with Faraday's law of electromagnetic induction. This phenomenon, due to which an alternating current in the primary winding produces an e.m.f. in the secondary winding, is known as *mutual induction* and the e.m.f. induced in the secondary winding is known as *mutually induced e.m.f.* or an *e.m.f. of mutual induction*. The frequency of this e.m.f. is the same as that of the supply voltage.

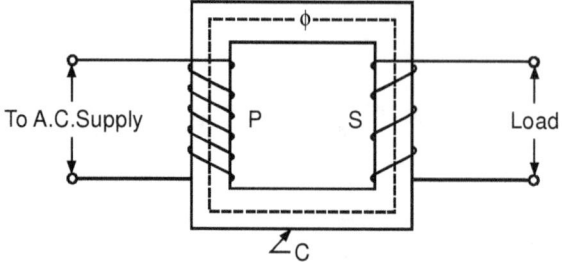

Fig. 8.1 : Elementary transformer

If now, the secondary circuit is closed through the load, the mutually induced e.m.f. in the secondary winding circulates current through the load. Thus, the energy is transferred entirely magnetically through the core from the primary circuit to the secondary circuit.

It should be noted that the transformer action is not possible with direct current of constant magnitude, as the flux produced by it will not be alternating, but will be of a constant value. Therefore, mutual induction between the primary and secondary windings will not be possible.[*]

8.3 CONSTRUCTIONAL FEATURES

As seen above, a transformer mainly consists of core and coils (windings). With the increase in the size (capacity) and the operating voltage, it also needs other parts such as suitable tank, bushings, conservator, breather, explosion vent, Buchholz relay, etc. (Fig. 8.2). Various parts of the transformer are briefly described below.

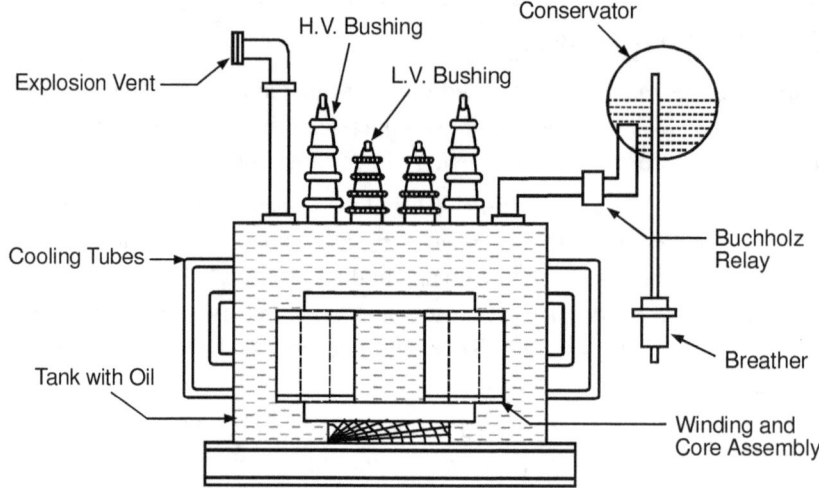

Fig. 8.2 : Schematic representation of a large capacity single-phase transformer

---

[*] *In fact, if the single-phase transformer is connected to d.c. supply of rated voltage, the resistance of the primary winding being small, it will draw a very large amount of current from the supply. This excessive current may damage the transformer. With a.c., it is the e.m.f. of self-induction (refer to Article 8.5) in the primary winding which mainly limits the current by opposing the applied voltage.*

(i) Laminated Steel Core : Basically, the core made up of magnetic material is used to provide the path of low reluctance (opposition) for the flux. Lesser the reluctance of the magnetic circuit, stronger is the field. The material actually used for the core is high grade silicon steel in the form of laminations about 0.35 to 0.5 mm thick. These laminations are varnished or coated with enamel to insulate them from each other. The core is assembled in such a fashion that it provides continuous magnetic circuit with a minimum air gap. For this, the joints in the adjacent layers are staggered. Fig. 8.3 (a) illustrates the arrangement of joints in two adjacent layers of L-shaped laminations and Fig. 8.3 (b) of I-shaped laminations.

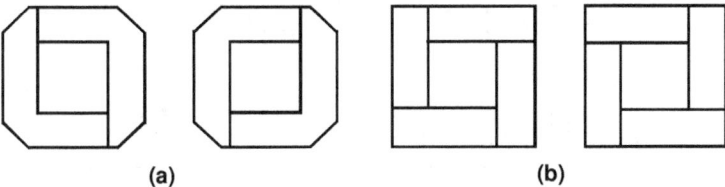

(a) (b)

Fig. 8.3 : Arrangement of joints in adjacent layers of laminations

For small transformers, the cross-section of the limb of the core can be rectangular (Fig. 8.4 a), as the coils wound on it can also be rectangular. But, as the size of the transformer increases, it becomes wasteful to employ rectangular coils and circular coils are usually preferred. Therefore, under such condition, square or stepped (Figs. 8.4 b, c, d) cross-sections are used for the limbs. More the number of steps, more the circular is the section and lesser is the copper required for the coils wound over it. This is because the circular section has the smallest perimeter for a given area. However, the saving thus effected due to core-stepping must be balanced against the increased labour charges to construct such cores.

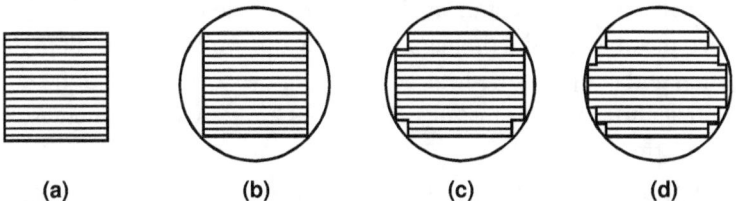

(a) (b) (c) (d)

Fig. 8.4 : Different cross-sections for the transformer limbs

(a) Rectangular, (b) Square, (c) 2-stepped or cruciform, (d) 3-stepped

The laminated construction and the choice of silicon steel as magnetic material for the core help in reducing the iron loss of the transformer (refer to Section 8.11).

(ii) Windings : The coils forming the primary and the secondary winding are former wound using well insulated copper conductor in the form of round wire or strip. These coils are then placed around the limbs of the core. These windings are insulated from each other and the core using cylinders of insulating material such as press board or bakelite.

In the elementary transformer, illustrated in Fig. 8.1, the primary and secondary windings are shown on separate limbs of the core for simplicity. However, if such an arrangement is used in actual practice, all the flux produced by the primary winding will not link with the secondary winding as some of the flux will leak out through air. Such flux is known as *leakage flux* (for more details, refer to Section 8.9.2). More the value of the leakage flux, poorer is the performance of the transformer. Therefore, to reduce this leakage flux, the primary winding and the secondary winding are placed together on the same limb in actual transformer. These windings are either cylindrical in form and concentric or sandwich type as illustrated in Fig. 8.5.

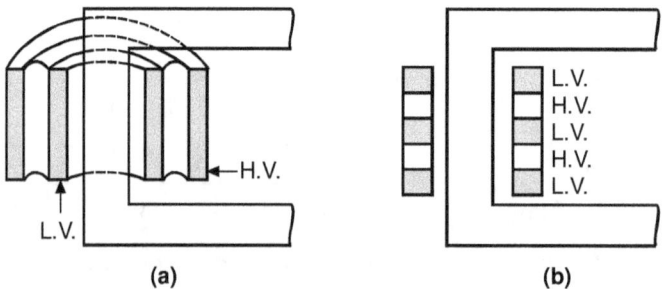

Fig. 8.5 : Transformer windings
(a) Cylindrical in form and concentric, (b) Sandwich type

While placing the cylindrical coils concentrically around the particular limb, the one which is designed for low voltage is placed near the core and the other which is designed for high voltage is placed after that. This is because, it is always easy to insulate the low voltage winding with respect to the core. In sandwich type, the windings are divided into number of small coils and these coils of high voltage (H.V.) and low voltage (L.V.) windings are interleaved. The top and bottom coils which are near the core are of low voltage winding only.

(iii) Transformer Tank : Except in small sizes, the whole transformer assembly is placed in a fabricated sheet metal tank and immersed in the oil which serves both the purposes of providing insulation and cooling. The heat generated in the windings and the core is carried by the oil to the external surface of the tank. Cooling tubes are provided to increase the surface area of the tank for more effective cooling.

(iv) Terminal Bushings : The leads of the transformer brought out from the tank are insulated from it with the help of porcelain bushings. These bushings are fitted to the tank.

(v) Conservator : In a transformer, provision of some space above the oil level is always essential to take up the expansion and contraction of the oil with changes of temperature in service. When transformer becomes warm, the oil expands and the air at the top of the oil is expelled. When the transformer cools, oil contracts and outside air is drawn into the transformer. This process is known as *breathing of the transformer*. Unless proper precautions are taken, the outside air, which enters the transformer during this process can have considerable moisture. When the oil in the transformer is exposed to such moist air, it readily absorbs the moisture from the air and loses its insulating value to some extent. This deterioration of oil can be prevented by using a *conservator*.

The conservator is an airtight cylindrical metal drum supported on the transformer tank. This drum is connected by pipe to the transformer tank and is always partly filled with oil. The expansion and contraction of the oil in the main tank with the changes of temperature is now taken up by the conservator. With this arrangement, since the main tank remains always full with oil, the surface of the oil is not directly exposed to air.

(vi) Breather : The displacement of air above the oil level in the conservator during the breathing process of the transformer takes place through the apparatus known as a *breather*. It contains a drying agent, such as *calcium chloride or silica gel*, which extracts the moisture from the air. The breather also cleans the air by removing the dust particles present in it. Thus, only dry and clean air is allowed to come in contact with the oil in the transformer.

(vii) Buchholz Relay : It is a type of protective device mounted in the pipeline connecting the main tank to the conservator. Due to excessive heat developed during the fault condition, the oil in the tank in the vicinity of the fault point gets decomposed and different types of the gases are liberated. These gases operate the Buchholz relay which in the initial condition gives alarm to the operator. If the fault developed is converted into a serious type of fault, then this relay trips off the main circuit breaker.

(viii) Explosion Vent : The bent up pipe fitted on the upper surface of the tank is known as *explosion vent or relief valve*. It is provided with a diaphragm made out of glass sheet, aluminium foil or a bakelite sheet. In the event of the fault condition, if the excessive pressure is developed inside the tank due to liberated gases, the diaphragm in the explosion vent bursts and releases the pressure, thus avoiding damage to the transformer.

8.4 TYPES OF TRANSFORMERS

Depending upon the arrangement of the core and the windings, there are three main types of the transformer :

(a) Core type, (b) Shell type and (c) Berry type.

(a) Core Type Transformers : Fig. 8.6 (a) diagrammatically illustrates a core type transformer and the actual arrangement is shown in Fig. 8.6 (b).

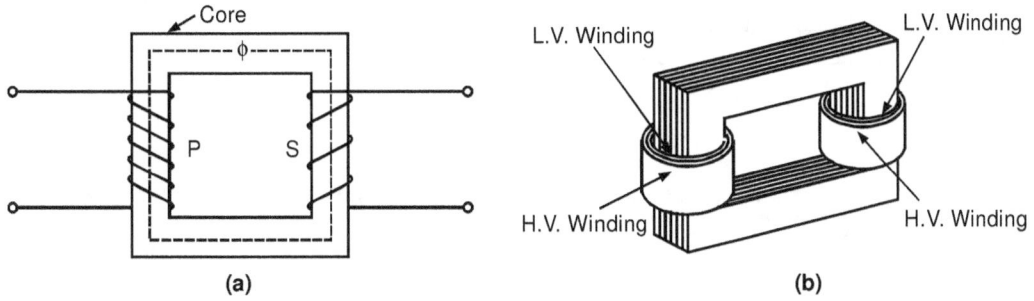

Fig. 8.6 : Core type transformer

Distinguishing Features : Some of the distinguishing features of this type of transformer are as follows :

(i) The core of this type of transformer is built of laminations to form a rectangular frame and provides a single magnetic circuit.

(ii) The windings are normally cylindrical in form and concentric, low voltage winding being placed near the core.

(iii) Both the windings are uniformly distributed over two limbs of the core.

(iv) These windings surround considerable portion of the core.

(v) Since the windings are distributed on two limbs, natural cooling is more effective.

(vi) The coils can be withdrawn for repairs just by dismantling laminations of the top yoke.

(b) Shell Type Transformers : Fig. 8.7 (a) shows the elementary scheme of a shell type transformer and Fig. 8.7 (b) shows the shell type transformer as used in actual practice.

Distinguishing Features : Some of the specialities of the shell type transformer are listed below :

(i) The core of this type of transformer provides double magnetic circuit.

(ii) The windings are normally sandwich type, always placed on the central limb of the core. H.V. and L.V. coils which are wound in the form of pancakes are interleaved. The top and bottom coils which are near the yoke of the core are of L.V. winding only.

(iii) The core nearly surrounds the windings placed on the central limb of the core. This feature is useful from the point of view of providing mechanical protection to the windings.

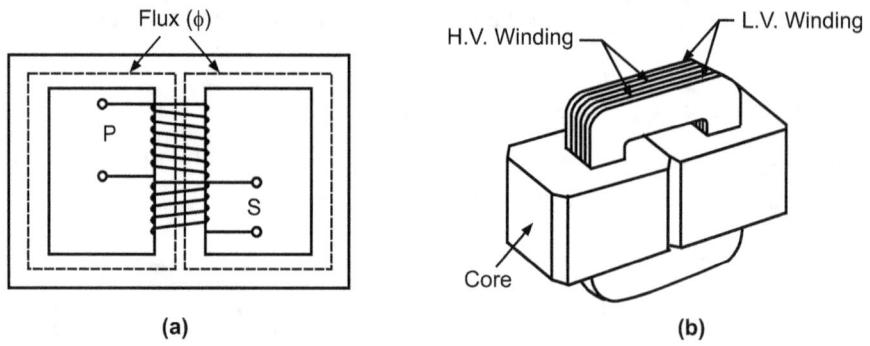

Fig. 8.7 : Shell type transformer

(iv) Since the coils are placed on one limb (central) only and are surrounded by the core, natural cooling is poor.

(v) When the coils are to be withdrawn for repairs, large number of laminations are to be dismantled.

(c) Berry Type Transformers : Fig. 8.8 diagrammatically illustrates this type of transformer.

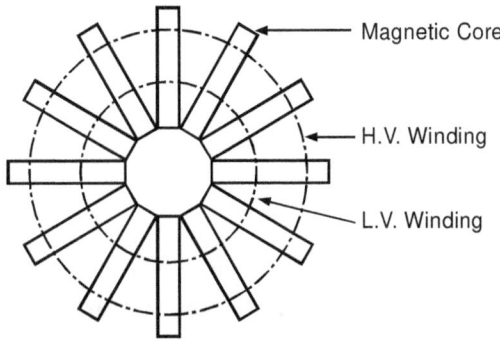

Fig. 8.8 : Berry type transformer (plan view)

Distinguishing Features : This type of transformer has distributed magnetic circuit, i.e. the number of independent magnetic circuits is more than two. The core is constructed in such a fashion that its yokes radiate out from the centre just like the spokes of a wheel. Rest of the features are similar to the shell type transformer.

8.5 E.M.F. EQUATION OF A TRANSFORMER

In the Section (8.2), we have seen that when the primary winding (P) is connected to the a.c. supply, an alternating current flowing through it produces an alternating flux (ϕ). This varying flux links with the secondary winding (S) through the core and produces an e.m.f. in it by mutual induction. But this flux produced by the primary winding while passing through the magnetic core, links not only the turns of the secondary winding but also the turns of the primary winding itself. Therefore, an e.m.f. is also induced in the primary winding due to self-induction. Now, let us derive the mathematical expressions for these e.m.f.s induced in the primary and secondary windings. For that, let

N_1 = Number of turns on the primary winding

N_2 = Number of turns on the secondary winding

ϕ_m = Maximum value of the alternating flux linking both the windings, in webers

f = Frequency of supply, in hertz.

Fig. 8.9 shows one cycle of sinusoidal flux established in the core by the sinusoidally varying alternating current in the primary winding.

From this figure, it will be readily seen that the flux grows from zero to its maximum value ϕ_m in one quarter of the cycle i.e. in a time $t = 1/(4f)$ seconds.

$\therefore$ Average rate of change of flux $= \dfrac{\phi_m}{t} = \dfrac{\phi_m}{1/(4f)} = 4\phi_m f$ webers / second

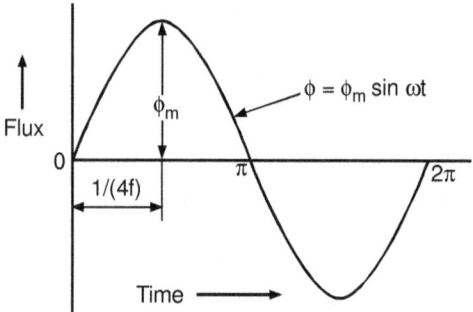

Fig. 8.9 : A cycle of flux in the transformer core

Then, from Faraday's law of electromagnetic induction, it follows that

Average e.m.f. induced in each turn = Average rate of change of flux

$$= 4 \phi_m f \text{ volts} \quad (\because \text{Numerically, } e = -N\frac{d\phi}{dt})$$

Since the flux is assumed to vary sinusoidally with time, the e.m.f. induced by it in each turn of both the windings will also be sinusoidal. Now, we know that for a sine wave,

$$\text{Form factor} = \frac{\text{R.M.S. value}}{\text{Average value}} = 1.11$$

∴ R.M.S. value of e.m.f. induced in each turn

$$= 1.11 \text{ (Average value)}$$
$$= 1.11 \times 4 \phi_m f$$
$$= 4.44 \phi_m f \text{ volts}$$

∴ R.M.S. value of induced e.m.f. in primary winding,

$$E_1 = (\text{Induced e.m.f. / turn}) \times \text{No. of primary turns}$$
$$= 4.44 \phi_m f \times N_1 \text{ volts}$$

Thus, $\quad E_1 = 4.44 \phi_m f N_1 \text{ volts} \quad \ldots (8.1)$

Similarly, R.M.S. value of induced e.m.f. in the secondary winding is given by

$$E_2 = 4.44 \phi_m f N_2 \text{ volts} \quad \ldots (8.2)$$

Alternative Method : The equations (8.1) and (8.2) for the e.m.f.s induced in the primary and secondary windings of the transformer can also be derived by the following alternative method.

Since the flux varies sinusoidally with time, the value of the flux at any instant,

$$\phi = \phi_m \sin \omega t$$

Now, we know that according to Faraday's law of electromagnetic induction, induced e.m.f. in a particular circuit is given by the expression,

$$e = -N \frac{d\phi}{dt} \text{ volts}$$

∴ Instantaneous value of the induced e.m.f. per turn of the transformer winding

$$= -\frac{d\phi}{dt} \qquad (\because N = 1)$$

$$= -\frac{d}{dt}(\phi_m \sin \omega t) \qquad (\because \phi = \phi_m \sin \omega t)$$

$$= -\omega \phi_m \cos \omega t$$

$$= \omega \phi_m \sin\left(\omega t - \frac{\pi}{2}\right) \text{ volts} \qquad \ldots (8.3)$$

Obviously, maximum value of the induced e.m.f. per turn

$$= \omega \phi_m$$

$$= 2\pi f \phi_m \text{ volts} \qquad (\because \omega = 2\pi f)$$

Further, since for a sine wave,

$$\text{R.M.S. value} = 0.707 \text{ (Maximum value)}$$

R.M.S. value of the induced e.m.f. per turn

$$= 0.707 \times 2\pi f \phi_m$$

$$= 4.44 \phi_m f \text{ volts}$$

Hence, R.M.S. value of the induced e.m.f. in the primary winding of N_1 turns is

$$E_1 = 4.44 \phi_m f N_1 \text{ volts}$$

and R.M.S. value of the induced e.m.f. in the secondary winding of N_2 turns is

$$E_2 = 4.44 \phi_m f N_2 \text{ volts}$$

Example 8.1 : *A single-phase transformer of 50 Hz, has maximum flux in the core of 0.021 Wb, the number of turns of primary being 460 and that on secondary 52. Calculate the e.m.f. induced in the primary and secondary windings of a transformer.*

Solution : E.M.F. induced in the primary winding,

$$E_1 = 4.44 \phi_m f N_1 = 4.44 \times 0.021 \times 50 \times 460$$

$$= 2144.52 \text{ V} \qquad \ldots \text{ Ans.}$$

Similarly,

E.M.F. induced in the secondary winding,

$$E_2 = 4.44 \phi_m f N_2 = 4.44 \times 0.021 \times 50 \times 52$$

$$= 242.42 \text{ V} \qquad \ldots \text{ Ans.}$$

Example 8.2 : *A single-phase, 50 Hz transformer has 300 primary turns and 750 secondary turns. The net cross-sectional area of the core is 64 sq. cm. If the primary induced e.m.f. is 440 V, find :*

(a) Maximum flux density in the core.

(b) E.M.F. induced in the secondary.

Solution : We know from Equation (8.1),

$$E_1 = 4.44\, \phi_m\, f\, N_1 \text{ volts}$$

$$\therefore \quad \phi_m = \frac{E_1}{4.44\, f\, N_1} \text{ webers}$$

Substituting the given values in the above expression, we get

$$\phi_m = \frac{440}{4.44 \times 50 \times 300} = 0.0066 \text{ Wb}$$

∴ Maximum flux density in the core,

$$B_m = \frac{\text{Maximum value of flux in webers}}{\text{Net cross-sectional area of the core in m}^2}$$

$$= \frac{0.0066}{64 \times 10^{-4}}$$

$$= \mathbf{1.032\ T} \qquad \text{... Ans.}$$

Hence, secondary induced e.m.f.,

$$E_2 = 4.44\, \phi_m\, f\, N_2 \text{ volts}$$

$$= 4.44 \times 0.0066 \times 50 \times 750$$

$$= \mathbf{1100\ V} \qquad \text{... Ans.}$$

8.6 VOLTAGE AND CURRENT RATIOS OF A TRANSFORMER

Fig. 8.10 shows a transformer with its secondary winding connected to the load.

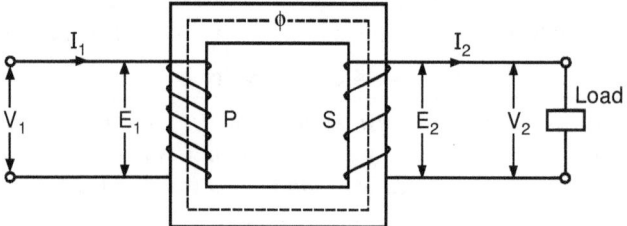

Fig. 8.10 : Voltage and current ratios

Voltage Ratio : Let N_1 and N_2 be the number of turns of the primary and secondary windings respectively and E_1 and E_2 the R.M.S. values of induced e.m.f. in the corresponding windings. Then from equations (8.1) and (8.2), we have

$$E_1 = 4.44\, \phi_m\, f\, N_1 \text{ volts}$$

and

$$E_2 = 4.44\, \phi_m\, f\, N_2 \text{ volts}$$

$$\therefore \quad \frac{E_1}{E_2} = \frac{N_1}{N_2} \qquad \text{... (8.4)}$$

Now, if the voltage applied across the primary winding is V_1 and terminal voltage of the secondary winding is V_2 as illustrated in Fig. 8.10, then at no load (i.e. when the secondary is on open circuit),

$$V_2 = E_2$$

Also, the primary current being very small under this condition, V_1 is numerically almost equal to E_1 i.e. $V_1 \approx E_1$. Hence, Equation (8.4) gives,

$$\frac{E_1}{E_2} = \frac{V_1}{V_2} = \frac{N_1}{N_2} \qquad \ldots (8.5)$$

Thus, *the primary and the secondary terminal voltages of a transformer are proportional to the respective number of turns.* The ratio of primary to secondary terminal voltage is known as *voltage ratio* and the ratio of primary to secondary turns is known as *turns ratio* of the transformer. At no load, these two ratios are equal. The impedance of the transformer windings being small, even at full load, they are nearly equal.

More often, the ratio of the secondary voltage to the primary voltage is termed as *transformation ratio* and denoted by the letter K. Therefore, from Equation (8.5),

$$\text{Transformation ratio, } K = \frac{V_2}{V_1} = \frac{E_2}{E_1} = \frac{N_2}{N_1} \qquad \ldots (8.6)$$

If $K > 1$ i.e. $V_2 > V_1$, transformer is called a *step-up transformer*. It is that transformer which receives electrical energy at one voltage and delivers it at a higher voltage.

If $K < 1$ i.e. $V_2 < V_1$, transformer is called a *step-down transformer*. It is the transformer which receives electrical energy at one voltage and delivers it at a lower voltage.

If $K = 1$, i.e. $V_2 = V_1$, transformer is called a *one to one transformer*. Obviously, such a transformer transfers electrical energy from one circuit to another circuit without any change in the voltage.

Current Ratio : Further, since the transformer transfers electrical power from one circuit to another circuit very efficiently with negligible power loss,

$$\text{Power input} = \text{Power output}$$

i.e. $\qquad V_1 I_1 \cos \phi_1 = V_2 I_2 \cos \phi_2 \qquad (\because P = V I \cos \phi)$

where I_1 and I_2 are the currents in the primary and the secondary circuits respectively and $\cos \phi_1$ and $\cos \phi_2$ are the corresponding power factors. But for a transformer, the primary and the secondary power factors are also nearly equal, particularly at full load.

$\therefore \qquad V_1 I_1 = V_2 I_2$

Or, $\qquad \dfrac{I_1}{I_2} = \dfrac{V_2}{V_1} \qquad \ldots (8.7)$

Combining the results obtained in the equations (8.6) and (8.7), we have

$$\frac{V_2}{V_1} = \frac{I_1}{I_2} = \frac{N_2}{N_1} = K \qquad \ldots (8.8)$$

Thus, from the above expression, it is clear that the *primary and the secondary currents of a transformer are inversely proportional to the respective turns or voltages.*

8.7 KILOVOLT-AMPERE RATING OF A TRANSFORMER

When the transformer transfers electrical energy from one circuit to another circuit, even though small, some energy is always lost in the transformer itself. This energy appears in the form of heat raising the temperature of the transformer. The temperature rise beyond a specified value is always harmful for the insulating materials used in the construction of the transformer. Therefore, it is the temperature rise which determines the rating (capacity) of the particular transformer. Since heating caused by the current flowing through the windings mainly limits the output of the transformer, its rating is always specified in terms of the *kilovolt-ampere (kVA)** output corresponding to the output current giving limiting temperature rise. The kVA rating of the transformer can, therefore, be defined as the *kVA output which it can deliver at rated voltage and frequency under usual service conditions without exceeding the standard limits of temperature rise*. The transformer is so designed that under full-load conditions, the temperature rise will not be excessive. Thus, a 50 Hz, 250 kVA, 1100/230 V transformer, when operated at rated full load would be delivering safely 250 kVA at 230 V, 50 Hz. The kVA rating of the transformer is given by the following expression :

$$\text{kVA rating} = \frac{V_2 I_2}{1000} = \frac{V_1 I_1}{1000} \qquad (\because V_2 I_2 = V_1 I_1) \quad \ldots (8.9)$$

where V_1 and V_2 are the terminal voltages on the primary and the secondary side respectively and I_1 and I_2 are the corresponding full-load currents.

It is worth noting that the output of the transformer in watts or kilowatts at the rated voltage is dependent upon not only the output current deciding the temperature rise, but also on the power factor of the load. Therefore, it is not used in specifying the rating of the transformer. For example, a transformer supplying a load having very low power factor may get fully loaded with full-load currents flowing in the primary and the secondary windings and have its full-load losses causing normal temperature rise, even though its power output is negligibly small.

Example 8.3 : *A 50 kVA single-phase transformer has a turns ratio of 300 / 20. The primary winding is connected to a 2200 V, 50 Hz supply. Calculate : (a) the secondary voltage on no load, (b) the approximate values of the primary and secondary currents on full load.*

Solution :

(a) Since,
$$\frac{V_2}{V_1} = \frac{N_2}{N_1}$$

$\therefore$
$$V_2 = V_1 \times \frac{N_2}{N_1}$$

With $V_1 = 2200$ V, $N_1 = 300$ and $N_2 = 20$

$$V_2 = 2200 \times \frac{20}{300}$$

$$= 146.67 \text{ V} \qquad \ldots \text{Ans.}$$

---

* *We know that the product, voltage × current is called apparent power in a.c. circuits and it is measured in VA and kVA.*

$$1 \text{ kVA} = 1000 \text{ VA}$$

(b) $$\text{kVA} = \frac{V_1 I_1}{1000} = \frac{V_2 I_2}{1000}$$

∴ Full-load primary current, $I_1 = \dfrac{\text{kVA} \times 1000}{V_1}$

With kVA = 50 and V_1 = 2200 V, we get

$$I_1 = \frac{50 \times 1000}{2200} = \mathbf{22.73 \text{ A}} \qquad \text{... Ans.}$$

Similarly, full-load secondary current,

$$I_2 = \frac{\text{kVA} \times 1000}{V_2}$$

As V_2 = 146.67 V

$$I_2 = \frac{50 \times 1000}{146.67}$$
$$= \mathbf{340.9 \text{ A}} \qquad \text{... Ans.}$$

Alternatively, $I_2 = I_1 \times \dfrac{V_1}{V_2} = 22.73 \times \dfrac{2200}{146.67}$

$$= \mathbf{340.9 \text{ A}} \qquad \text{... Ans.}$$

Or, $I_2 = I_1 \times \dfrac{N_1}{N_2} = 22.73 \times \dfrac{300}{20}$

$$= \mathbf{340.9 \text{ A}} \qquad \text{... Ans.}$$

Example 8.4 : *A 2000/200 V, single-phase, 50 Hz transformer has the maximum core flux of 20 mWb. Find out the number of turns on the primary and secondary windings.*

Solution : $E_1 = 4.44 \, \phi_m \, f N_1$

∴ $2000 = 4.44 \times 20 \times 10^{-3} \times 50 \times N_1$

∴ Number of turns on the primary winding,

$$N_1 = \mathbf{450} \qquad \text{... Ans.}$$

Further, $\dfrac{E_1}{E_2} = \dfrac{N_1}{N_2}$

∴ Number of turns on the secondary winding,

$$N_2 = \frac{E_2}{E_1} \times N_1 = \frac{200}{2000} \times 450 = \mathbf{45} \qquad \text{... Ans.}$$

Alternatively, $E_2 = 4.44 \, \phi_m \, f N_2$

∴ $200 = 4.44 \times 20 \times 10^{-3} \times 50 \times N_2$

∴ $N_2 = \mathbf{45} \qquad \text{... Ans.}$

8.8 IDEAL TRANSFORMER

An ideal transformer possesses following properties :

(i) The permeability of the core is so high that only a negligible current is required to establish the flux in it.

(ii) There is no magnetic leakage (refer to Section 8.9.2). In other words, all the flux is confined to the iron core only and links both the windings.

(iii) Its windings have no ohmic resistance.

(iv) It has no losses.

In practice, it is not possible to have such an ideal transformer. However, the concept of an ideal transformer is very useful in developing step by step, the theory of the practical transformer. Therefore, to start with, let us consider such an ideal transformer and study its behaviour on no load and on load.

8.8.1 Ideal Transformer On No Load

Let the transformer shown in Fig. 8.11 (a) be an ideal transformer. When its primary winding is connected to an alternating voltage V_1, with the secondary winding open circuited, it draws a negligibly small amount of magnetizing current I_{mag} (if the transformer is truly ideal, this magnetizing current would be zero). This current which is a purely reactive current (the primary windings being purely inductive) lags the voltage V_1 by 90° and is responsible for establishing a flux ϕ in the core in time phase with it. The flux produced is in time phase with the magnetizing current because it is obvious that if there were no magnetizing current, there would be no flux. This flux induces an e.m.f. E_1 of self-induction in the primary winding to counterbalance the applied voltage V_1 and an e.m.f. E_2 in the secondary winding by mutual induction. The magnitudes of E_1 and E_2 are proportional to the number of turns on the primary and secondary windings. As seen from the Equation (8.3), these e.m.f.s lag the flux ϕ by 90°.

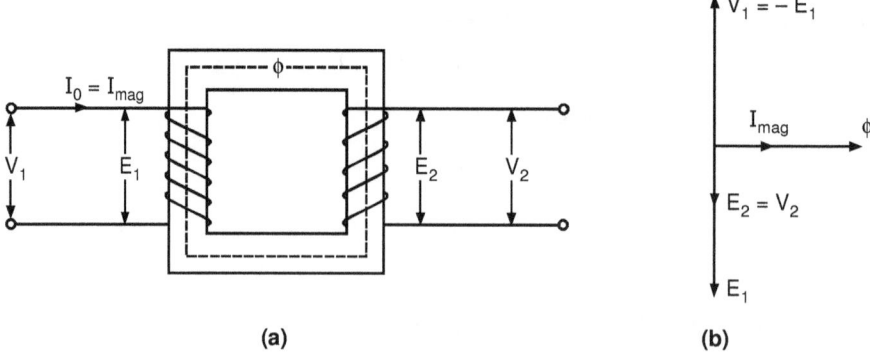

Fig. 8.11 : Ideal transformer on no load

Since the secondary circuit is open,

The secondary terminal voltage, $V_2 = E_2$

Also, there being a negligible voltage drop in the primary winding, the primary applied voltage V_1 is equal and opposite in phase to the e.m.f. E_1 induced in the primary winding. Thus, the primary applied voltage, $V_1 = -E_1$

Fig. 8.11 (b) shows the necessary phasor diagram for the ideal transformer under consideration when on no load. The flux ϕ being common to the two windings, it is considered as a reference phasor while drawing this phasor diagram.

8.8.2 Ideal Transformer On Load

Now, if a load having a finite impedance is connected across the secondary terminals of an ideal transformer (Fig. 8.12 a), the current I_2 flows in the secondary winding. If we consider a general case of an inductive load having a lagging power factor $\cos \phi_2$, then obviously the current I_2 lags V_2 by an angle ϕ_2 (Fig. 8.12 b). By Lenz's law, this secondary current I_2 produces a demagnetizing effect. Consequently, the flux and the e.m.f. induced in the primary are reduced slightly. The increased difference between the applied voltage and the e.m.f. induced in the primary causes additional current I_2' called *load component* to flow in the primary winding.

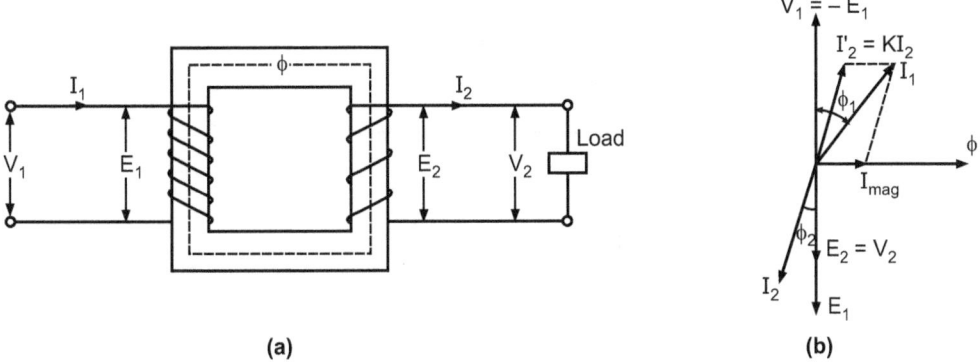

(a)   (b)

Fig. 8.12 : Ideal transformer on load

The magnitude of this current is such that the demagnetizing m.m.f. $N_2 I_2$ of the secondary is nearly neutralized by the increased primary m.m.f. $N_1 I_2'$ and thereby the core flux ϕ is maintained at a constant value. Obviously under such condition,

$$I_2' = I_2 \times \frac{N_2}{N_1} = K I_2 \qquad \ldots (8.10)$$

and is in anti-phase with I_2. This sequence of reactions, that follow the application of load enables the primary to draw more power from the line to meet the increased demand of the secondary. When the transformer is on load, the total current, I_1 in the primary is the phasor sum of I_2' and I_{mag}. Here ϕ_1 is the phase difference between V_1 and I_1. Hence the power factor on the primary side is $\cos \phi_1$.

8.9 PRACTICAL TRANSFORMERS

The above discussion is entirely based on the ideal transformer having no core losses, winding resistances and magnetic leakage. We have to take into account the effects of these factors while analysing the behaviour or the performance of the transformers used in actual practice.

8.9.1 Effect of Core Losses

Since the iron core of the practical transformer is subjected to an alternating flux, core losses (i.e. hysteresis and eddy current losses) are always present to some extent even though the core is laminated to reduce eddy currents and hysteresis is minimized by the use of high grade silicon steel (refer to Section 8.11). It follows, therefore, that even under no-load condition (i.e. with the secondary winding open circuited), the source must supply enough power to the primary winding to overcome the core losses. Therefore, in the case of transformers which are used in actual practice, on no load i.e. with no current in the secondary winding, the primary winding carries a small current I_0 which has two components :

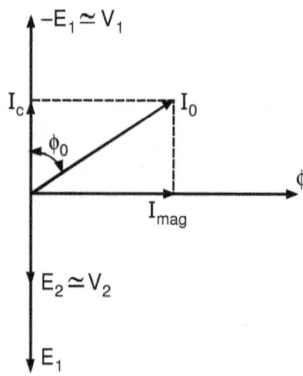

Fig. 8.13 : Phasor diagram for the practical transformer on no load

(i) A reactive or wattless magnetizing component, I_{mag}. It produces the magnetic flux and therefore is in phase with it.

(ii) An active or power or core loss component, I_c. It supplies mainly the core losses and the negligible copper loss in the primary winding. This component is in phase with component $-E_1$ of the impressed voltage.

Fig. 8.13 shows the phasor diagram for the transformer on no load. From the diagram, it is obvious that,

$$\text{No-load current,} \quad I_0 = \sqrt{(I_c^2 + I_{mag}^2)} \qquad \ldots (8.11)$$

and power factor on no load,

$$\cos \phi_0 = \frac{I_c}{I_0} \qquad \ldots (8.12)$$

The core-loss component I_c being usually very small compared with magnetizing component I_{mag}, the no-load power factor is very low.

Example 8.5 : *Power input to a 2200/220 V, single-phase transformer on no load is 330 W at a power factor of 0.3 lagging. Find :*

(i) No-load current,

(ii) Magnetizing and core-loss components of no-load current.

Solution :

No-load power input, $W_o = V_1 I_o \cos \phi_o$

∴ No-load current, $I_o = \dfrac{W_o}{V_1 \cos \phi_o}$

$= \dfrac{330}{2200 \times 0.3} = \mathbf{0.5\ A}$ ... Ans.

Referring to phasor diagram for the transformer on no load shown in Fig. 8.13, we have

Magnetizing component of no-load current,

$$I_{mag} = I_o \sin \phi_o = 0.5 \times 0.9539 = \mathbf{0.477\ A} \qquad \text{... Ans.}$$

Core-loss component of no-load current,

$$I_c = I_o \cos \phi_o = 0.5 \times 0.3 = \mathbf{0.15\ A} \qquad \text{... Ans.}$$

8.9.2 Effect of Resistance and Leakage Reactance of Windings

In practical transformer, each winding of the transformer possesses certain finite resistance which apart from causing a power loss, produces a voltage drop in it on current flow. Further, as an electric current, magnetic flux cannot be completely confined into a desired path. Therefore, all the magnetizing flux produced by the primary winding of a transformer does not link the secondary, but a part of it completes its magnetic circuit by passing through the air rather than around through the core as shown in Fig. 8.14. Such a flux is called *the primary leakage flux*.

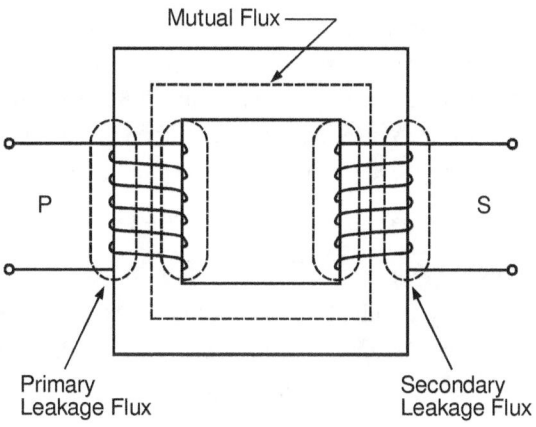

Fig. 8.14 : Primary and secondary leakage fluxes

This leakage flux does not contribute to the transfer of energy from primary to secondary and thus serves no useful purpose, since it fails to link the secondary winding to the primary winding. Secondary winding also produces opposing (in accordance with Lenz's law) flux due to the induced current flowing through it on load. Major portion of this flux links with the primary winding through the core. However, certain amount of this flux links only with the secondary winding through air as shown in Fig. 8.14. This is termed as the *secondary leakage flux*. These primary and secondary leakage fluxes produce in their respective windings e.m.f.s of self-induction which are proportional to the current and the frequency. They are, therefore, equivalent to an inductance placed in series with each winding, the reactance of which is called the *leakage reactance* of the winding. Similar to resistance, both primary and secondary leakage reactances cause a voltage drop in the respective windings. The combined effect of voltage drop due to resistance and leakage reactance of the windings of a transformer is ultimately to change its secondary terminal voltage on load from its no-load value for a given applied voltage across the primary as discussed in the next few articles. In practice, the leakage reactance is minimized by placing the windings on both the limbs of the core (half on each) and also by subdividing and interleaving the different sections of the windings.

8.9.3 Practical Transformer on Load

When the primary winding of a practical transformer is connected across the a.c. supply of voltage V_1 and a load having a finite impedance is connected across its secondary, the sequence of reactions that follow the application of load, is exactly similar to that which occurs in the case of an ideal transformer (refer to Section 8.8.2). Only exception is that increased currents in the primary and secondary windings cause increased impedance drops in the respective windings. This ultimately affects the secondary terminal voltage of the transformer.

8.10 REGULATION OF A TRANSFORMER

We are familiar with the fact that in the case of a cell, the terminal voltage is always less than its e.m.f. when it delivers current to the load due to the voltage drop caused by its internal resistance. Similar is the case of a transformer. When the transformer is not delivering any current to the load, voltage available across its secondary terminals ($_0V_2$) is equal to the induced e.m.f. (E_2) in the secondary winding. But as soon as the transformer starts delivering current to the load, due to internal voltage drop caused by the combined effect of impedances of both the windings, the secondary terminal voltage falls (assuming the normal inductive or resistive load conditions) from its no-load value. With the increase in the current delivered (I_2), the increased resistance and leakage reactance drops of the primary winding cause a decrease in the value of primary induced e.m.f. (from E_1 to say E_1'). This produces a proportional decrease in the flux and hence in the secondary induced e.m.f. (from E_2 to say E_2'). Subsequently, the secondary terminal voltage decreases. The secondary terminal voltage is then further reduced by the resistance and reactance drops of the secondary winding. The effect of load on the secondary terminal voltage can be more easily understood from the simple equivalent circuit representing a transformer shown in Fig. 8.15.

In this circuit diagram, R_1, X_1, R_2 and X_2 respectively represent the resistance and leakage reactance in lumped form of primary and secondary windings. These parameters are considered as being external to the windings. On no load (Fig. 8.15 a), with $I_1 = I_0$ and $I_2 = 0$, there will be negligibly small internal voltage drop in the impedance of the primary winding and no internal voltage drop in the impedance of the secondary winding. Hence, the voltage available at the secondary terminals under this condition will be

$$_0V_2 = E_2$$

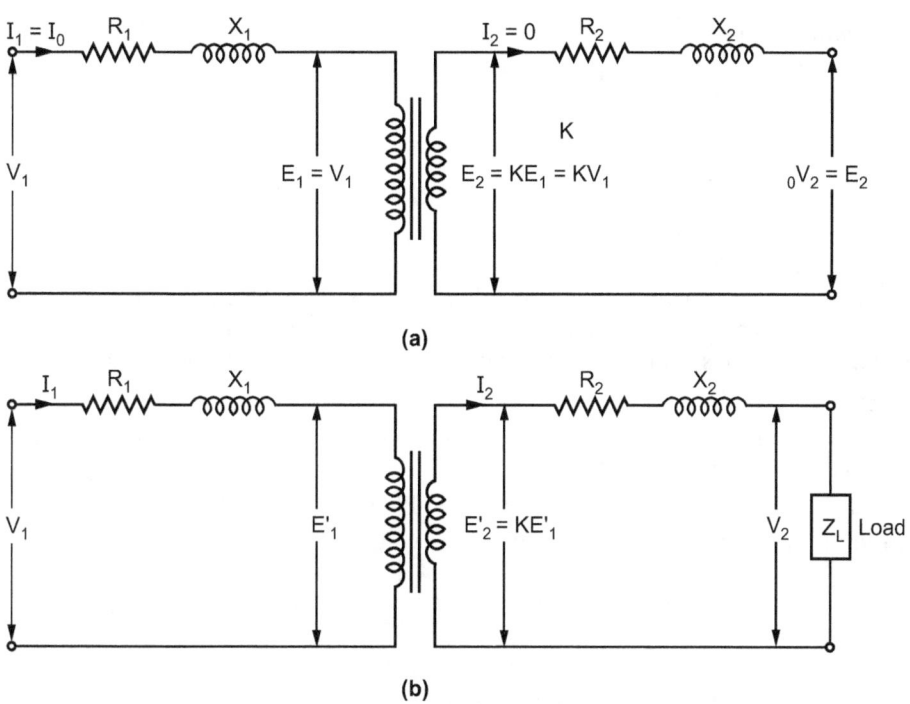

Fig. 8.15 : Simple equivalent circuit representing a transformer
(a) On no load, (b) On load

But on load (Fig. 8.15 b), due to increased internal voltage drops in the impedances of the windings, the secondary voltage will change from its no-load value $_0V_2$ (= E_2) to V_2.

The secondary terminal voltage depends not only on the magnitude of the load current but it also depends on the power factor of the load (Fig. 8.16). With inductive loads such as motors and resistive loads, the secondary terminal voltage decreases with the increase in the load on the transformer, while with capacitive loads having low leading power factors, it may even increase due to opposite effect of inductive reactance.

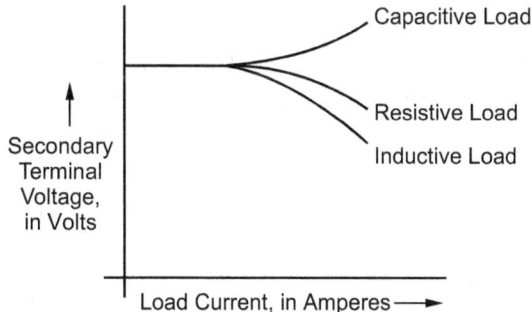

Fig. 8.16 : Effect of the nature of the load on regulation

The numerical difference between the values of the secondary terminal voltage on no load ($_0V_2$ = E_2) and with full load (V_2) is of the importance to the user and is known as the *inherent voltage regulation* of the transformer. The regulation of the transformer is, therefore, defined as *the change in the secondary terminal voltage from no-load to full load with primary impressed voltage (V_1) and temperature of the transformer maintained constant.* The regulation is usually expressed as percentage of the no-load secondary terminal voltage. Thus,

$$\text{Voltage regulation} = \frac{_0V_2 - V_2}{_0V_2} \times 100 = \frac{E_2 - V_2}{E_2} \times 100 \text{ per cent} \quad \ldots (8.13)$$

It should be remembered that *regulation is always positive for the inductive load with lagging power factor and resistive load with unity power factor and may be negative for the capacitive load with leading power factor.* Voltage regulation being dependent on the power factor of the load, it is always specified with the load power factor. The transformer having less regulation and therefore more or less constant secondary terminal voltage is always considered as a good transformer.

Example 8.6 : *Find the percentage voltage regulation of a transformer whose no-load secondary terminal voltage of 250 V drops down to 230 V while delivering full load at 0.8 lagging power factor. Assume that the primary applied voltage remains constant.*

Solution : From the definition of the percentage voltage regulation, we have

$$\text{Voltage regulation} = \frac{(_0V_2 - V_2)}{_0V_2} \times 100 \text{ per cent}$$

With $\quad _0V_2 = 250 \text{ V} \quad$ and $\quad V_2 = 230 \text{ V}$

Full-load regulation at 0.8 lagging power factor

$$= \frac{(250 - 230)}{250} \times 100$$

$$= 8 \text{ per cent} \quad \ldots \text{Ans.}$$

8.11 TRANSFORMER LOSSES

When the practical transformer transfers electrical energy from one circuit to another circuit, some energy (even though small) is always lost in this process. There are two types of power losses in the transformer.

(i) Copper losses.

(ii) Core or iron losses.

(i) Copper Losses : These losses represent the loss of power caused by the resistance of the windings (both, the primary and the secondary) due to the current flow through them. These are called *copper losses* since copper conductor is generally used for the windings. The power loss on this account is proportional to the square of the current flowing through the windings and is ultimately utilized in heating the windings. If R_1 and R_2 are the primary and the secondary resistances respectively and I_1 and I_2 are the corresponding currents, then

$$\text{Total copper loss} = I_1^2 R_1 + I_2^2 R_2 \quad \ldots (8.14)$$

The copper losses are thus proportional to the square of the current and therefore proportional to the square of the kVA output. These losses are reduced by using the material with good conductivity, like copper, for the windings of the transformer.

(ii) Core or Iron Losses : These losses consist of hysteresis and eddy current losses caused by the alternating flux in the transformer core.

(a) Hysteresis Loss : This loss takes place in the transformer core because it is continuously subjected to rapid reversals of magnetization by the alternating flux. Since this loss basically occurs due to characteristic property of hysteresis (lagging of flux density behind magnetic field strength when a magnetic material is taken through a cycle of magnetization) exhibited by the magnetic material, it is called hysteresis loss and is given by the expression :

$$\text{Hysteresis loss, } P_h = K_h B_m^{1.6} f v \text{ watts} \quad \ldots (8.15)$$

where f is the frequency in hertz, B_m is the maximum flux density in tesla, v is the volume of the magnetic material in cubic metres and K_h is a constant.

(b) Eddy Current Loss : This loss occurs due to the flow of eddy currents in the core. These are the currents induced in the core which itself is composed of conducting material like iron and is subjected to an alternating magnetic flux. Quantitatively, eddy current loss is given by the following expression :

$$\text{Eddy current loss, } P_e = K_e B_m^2 f^2 t^2 v \text{ watts} \quad \ldots (8.16)$$

where t is the thickness of laminations and K_e is a constant.

These core losses together are nearly constant and independent of the magnitude of the current delivered by the transformer. They are reduced by choosing silicon steel having small values of K_h and K_e as a core material and by using laminated construction for the core.

All the losses in the transformer are ultimately converted into heat and thereby cause heating of the core, windings and other parts. The transformer is, therefore, provided with suitable cooling system to protect the insulation of the windings against excessive temperature rise.

8.12 EFFICIENCY OF A TRANSFORMER

Due to the various losses discussed above, the power output of the transformer is always less than the corresponding power input to the transformer and is given by,

$$\text{Power output} = \text{Power input} - \text{Losses} \quad \ldots (8.17)$$

Higher the value of this power output (i.e. lesser the losses) for the given input, more efficient is the transformer. Therefore, *ordinary or commercial efficiency (symbol, η) of the transformer is defined as the ratio of the output power to the input power* (both being in W or kW). It is normally expressed as a percentage. Hence,

$$\text{Efficiency, } \eta = \frac{\text{Output power}}{\text{Input power}} \times 100 = \frac{\text{Output power}}{\text{Output power} + \text{Losses}} \times 100$$

$$= \frac{V_2 I_2 \cos \phi}{(V_2 I_2 \cos \phi + P_i + P_{cu})} \times 100 \text{ per cent} \quad \ldots (8.18)$$

where, P_i is the iron loss and P_{cu} is the total copper loss of the transformer. If this copper loss is full-load copper loss, I_2 is the full-load secondary current and $\cos \phi$ is the full-load power factor, then the efficiency under full-load condition can be expressed as

$$\text{Efficiency on full load} = \frac{\text{Full-load output (in watts)}}{\text{Full-load output (in watts)} + P_i + P_{cu}}$$

$$= \frac{\text{Full-load rating (in VA)} \times \text{p.f.}}{\text{Full-load rating (in VA)} \times \text{p.f.} + P_i + P_{cu}} \quad \ldots (8.19)$$

If the efficiency at any other load, say (x × Full load) is desired, then the copper loss at (x × Full load) being = x^2 × Copper loss at full load = $x^2 P_{cu}$, the corresponding efficiency will be given by the following expression,

$$\text{Efficiency at (x} \times \text{Full load)} = \frac{x \times \text{Full-load rating (in VA)} \times \text{p.f.}}{x \times \text{Full-load rating (in VA)} \times \text{p.f.} + P_i + x^2 P_{cu}} \quad \ldots (8.20)$$

It should be remembered that at 25% load, the value of x will be 0.25, at 50 % load, it will be 0.5 and so on. The factor x is sometimes called the *degree of loading*.

8.12.1 Condition for Maximum Efficiency of a Transformer

The efficiency of a transformer depends on the load condition. On no load, the efficiency is zero. At light loads, for the given input, the constant losses (i.e. core losses) being relatively large compared with the output, transformer efficiency is low. But as the load is increased, the efficiency rises until it reaches a maximum value. It then commences to fall more and more as the load is further increased. This is because variable losses (i.e. copper losses) become relatively large under this condition. The general shape of the efficiency curve is shown in Fig. 8.17.

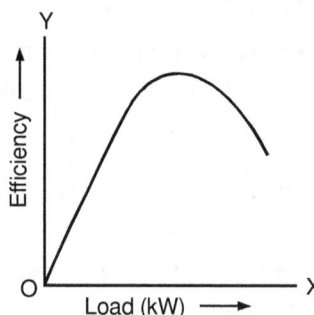

Fig. 8.17 : Efficiency curve of a transformer

It can be mathematically shown that, *efficiency of a transformer is a maximum for that load which makes the variable copper losses equal to the constant iron losses* i.e. under maximum efficiency condition,

$$\text{Variable losses} = \text{Constant losses} \quad \ldots (8.21)$$

Load at Maximum Efficiency : If we are given full load kVA of the transformer, iron loss and full-load copper loss, we can always find the load corresponding to maximum efficiency. For that, let

S = Full-load kVA of the transformer.
S' = kVA load corresponding to the maximum efficiency.
P_i = Iron loss.
P_{cu} = Full-load copper loss.

Then, Copper loss at S' kVA load = $\left(\dfrac{S'}{S}\right)^2 \times P_{cu}$ ($\because$ Copper loss $\propto$ kVA^2)

Under maximum efficiency conditions,

$$\text{Copper loss} = \text{Iron loss}$$

$\therefore \quad \left(\dfrac{S'}{S}\right)^2 \times P_{cu} = P_i$

$\therefore \quad S' = S \cdot \sqrt{\dfrac{P_i}{P_{cu}}}$

Thus, for a transformer, kVA load corresponding to maximum efficiency

$$= \text{Full-load kVA} \times \sqrt{\dfrac{\text{Iron loss}}{\text{Full-load copper loss}}} \qquad \ldots (8.22)$$

In practice, if a transformer is intended to work on full load for most of the period, it is always designed to have maximum efficiency in the neighbourhood of full load. But, if the load is variable, it is usually designed to have maximum efficiency at about 75 % of its full load. It is important to note that the transformer, being a static device (with no rotating parts), is free from friction and windage losses. Therefore, it is the most efficient equipment with the efficiency of about 96 to 99 % at its rated output.

Example 8.7 : *A 50 kVA, 2200 / 220 V, 50 Hz single-phase transformer has an iron loss of 300 W. The resistances of its low and high potential windings are 0.005 and 0.5 Ω respectively. If the power factor of the load is 0.8 lagging, calculate the efficiency when the transformer is on (a) full load and (b) half-full load. Find also the load at which the efficiency of the transformer is a maximum and calculate its value.*

Solution : Part-1 :

(a)   Full-load secondary current = $\dfrac{50 \times 1000}{220}$ = 227.27 A

$\therefore$ Full-load primary current = $227.27 \times \dfrac{220}{2200}$ = 22.727 A

$\therefore$ Total copper loss on full load = $I_1^2 R_1 + I_2^2 R_2$ = $(22.727)^2 \times 0.5 + (227.27)^2 \times 0.005$

= 516.53 W

Total loss on full load = 300 + 516.53 = 816.53 W

= 0.817 kW

Output power on full load = kVA × p.f. = 50 × 0.8 = 40 kW
Input power on full load = Output power + Total loss
= 40 + 0.817 = 40.817 kW

$\therefore$ Efficiency on full load = $\dfrac{\text{Output power}}{\text{Input power}} \times 100$

$= \dfrac{40}{40.817} \times 100$

= **98 per cent** ... Ans.

(b) Since the copper loss is proportional to the square of the current,

Copper loss on half load = $516.53 \times (0.5)^2$ = 129.13 W

$\therefore$ Total loss on half load = 129.13 + 300 = 429.13 W
= 0.429 kW

Now, output power on half load = 20 kW
Input power on half load = 20 + 0.429 = 20.429 kW

$\therefore$ Efficiency on half load = $\dfrac{20}{20.429} \times 100$

= **97.9 per cent** ... Ans.

Alternatively, with x = 0.5,

Efficiency on half load = $\dfrac{x \times \text{Full-load rating (in VA)} \times \text{p.f.}}{x \times \text{Full-load rating (in VA)} \times \text{p.f.} + P_i + x^2 P_{cu}} \times 100$

$= \dfrac{0.5 \times (50 \times 10^3) \times 0.8}{0.5 \times (50 \times 10^3) \times 0.8 + 300 + (0.5)^2 \times 516.53} \times 100$

= **97.9 per cent** ... Ans.

Part-2 : We have seen that for the full load output of 50 kVA, the total copper loss is 516.53 W. Therefore, if x is the fraction of full load kVA at which the efficiency is at maximum, then the corresponding total copper loss

$= x^2 \times 516.53$ W

Hence, from Equation (8.21), for maximum efficiency,

Total copper loss = Iron loss

$\therefore$ $x^2 \times 516.53 = 300$

$\therefore$ x = 0.762

$\therefore$ Load at maximum efficiency = 0.762 × 50
= **38.1 kVA** ... Ans.

Alternatively,

Load at maximum efficiency, $S' = S \cdot \sqrt{\dfrac{P_i}{P_{cu}}} = 50 \times \sqrt{\dfrac{300}{516.53}}$

= **38.1 kVA** ... Ans.

Now, let us calculate the value of the maximum efficiency at this load. Since the copper and iron losses are equal under this condition,

$$\text{Total loss} = 2 \times 300 = 600 \text{ W} = 0.6 \text{ kW}$$
$$\text{Output power} = \text{kVA} \times \text{Power factor}$$
$$= 38.1 \times 0.8 = 30.48 \text{ kW}$$
$$\text{Input power} = 30.48 + 0.6 = 31.08 \text{ kW}$$
$$\therefore \text{Maximum efficiency} = \frac{30.48}{31.08} \times 100$$
$$= \textbf{98.07 per cent} \quad \text{... Ans.}$$

Example 8.8 : *The iron loss of a 80 kVA, 1000/250 V, single-phase, 50 Hz transformer is 800 W. The copper loss when primary carries 50 A is 400 W. Estimate :*

(i) *Area of cross-section of limb if working flux density is 1 T and there are 1000 turns on primary,*

(ii) *Current ratio (primary to secondary),*

(iii) *Efficiency at full load and 0.8 power factor,*

(iv) *Efficiency for a load when copper loss will be equal to iron loss and power factor remains 0.8 lagging.*

Solution :

(i)
$$E_1 = 4.44 \, \phi_m \, f \, N_1 \text{ volts}$$
$$\therefore \quad 1000 = 4.44 \times \phi_m \times 50 \times 1000$$
$$\therefore \quad \phi_m = 4.5 \times 10^{-3} \text{ Wb}$$

But
$$B_m = \frac{\phi_m}{A_i}$$

$$\therefore \quad A_i = \frac{\phi_m}{B_m} = \frac{4.5 \times 10^{-3}}{1} \text{ m}^2 = \textbf{45 cm}^2 \quad \text{... Ans.}$$

(ii)
$$\text{Current ratio} = \frac{250}{1000} = \textbf{0.25} \quad \text{... Ans.}$$

(iii)
$$\text{Full-load primary current} = \frac{80 \times 1000}{1000} = 80 \text{ A}$$

$$\therefore \quad \text{Copper loss at full load} = \left(\frac{80}{50}\right)^2 \times 400 = 1024 \text{ W}$$

$$\therefore \quad \text{Efficiency at full load} = \frac{\text{kVA} \cos\phi \times 10^3}{\text{kVA} \cos\phi \times 10^3 + P_i + P_{cu}}$$

$$= \frac{80 \times 0.8 \times 10^3}{80 \times 0.8 \times 10^3 + 800 + 1024}$$

$$= \textbf{0.9723 or 97.23 \%} \quad \text{... Ans.}$$

(iv) For maximum efficiency,

$$P_i = P_{cu} = 800 \text{ W}$$

Hence, corresponding current $= 50 \times \sqrt{\dfrac{800}{400}} = 70.71 \text{ A}$

$\therefore$ Maximum efficiency $= \dfrac{VI \cos \phi}{VI \cos \phi + P_i + P_{cu}}$

$= \dfrac{1000 \times 70.71 \times 0.8}{1000 \times 70.71 \times 0.8 + 800 + 800}$

$= \mathbf{0.9725 \text{ or } 97.25 \%}$ ... **Ans.**

Please note that the load corresponding to maximum efficiency

$= \dfrac{VI}{1000} = \dfrac{1000 \times 70.71}{1000}$

$= 70.71 \text{ kVA}$

This load can also be determined directly as follows :

Load corresponding to maximum efficiency

$= \text{Full-load kVA} \times \sqrt{\dfrac{\text{Iron loss}}{\text{Full-load copper loss}}}$

$= 80 \times \sqrt{\dfrac{800}{1024}} = 70.71 \text{ kVA}$

Example 8.9 : *A 40 kVA, single-phase transformer with a ratio of 2000 / 250 V has a primary resistance of 1.15 Ω and a secondary resistance of 0.0155 Ω. If the transformer is designed for maximum efficiency at 75 % of full load, find its efficiency when delivering full load at 0.8 power factor.*

Solution :

Full-load secondary current, $I_2 = \dfrac{40 \times 10^3}{250} = 160 \text{ A}$

$\therefore$ Transformation ratio, $K = \dfrac{250}{2000} = 0.125$

$\therefore$ Full-load primary current, $I_1 = KI_2 = 160 \times 0.125 = 20 \text{ A}$

Full-load copper loss $= I_1^2 R_1 + I_2^2 R_2 = 20^2 \times 1.15 + 160^2 \times 0.0155$

$= 857.6 \text{ W}$

As efficiency is maximum at 75 % of full load, it means iron loss equals copper loss at this load.

Copper loss at 75 % of full load $= (0.75)^2 \times 857.6 \text{ W} = 482.4 \text{ W}$

Hence, Iron loss $= 482.4 \text{ W}$

Alternatively, kVA load corresponding to maximum efficiency

$$= \text{Full-load kVA} \times \sqrt{\frac{\text{Iron loss}}{\text{Full-load copper loss}}}$$

$$0.75 \times 40 = 40 \times \sqrt{\frac{\text{Iron loss}}{857.6}}$$

∴ Iron loss $= \left(\frac{0.75 \times 40}{40}\right)^2 \times 857.6 = 482.4$ W

∴ Total full-load loss $= 857.6 + 482.4 = 1340$ W

Full-load output $= 40 \times 0.8 = 32$ kW $= 32000$ W

∴ Full-load efficiency $= \dfrac{32000}{32000 + 1340} = $ **0.96 or 96 % ... Ans.**

Example 8.10 : *A single-phase, 100 kVA, 3.3 kV/230 V, 50 Hz transformer has an efficiency of 89.5 % at 0.85 lagging power factor, both at full load and at half full load. Determine the efficiency of the transformer at 75 % of full load and 0.9 leading power factor.*

Solution : Full-load Condition :

Power output $=$ kVA $\times$ Power factor $= 100 \times 0.85 = 85$ kW

Power input $= \dfrac{\text{Power output}}{\text{Efficiency}} = \dfrac{85}{0.895} = 94.97$ kW

∴ Total losses $=$ Power input $-$ Power output $= 94.97 - 85 = 9.97$ kW

Let P_i be the iron loss and P_{cu} be the full-load copper loss of the transformer. Hence,

$$P_i + P_{cu} = 9.97 \qquad \qquad \text{... (I)}$$

Half Full-load Condition :

Power output $=$ kVA $\times$ Power factor $= 50 \times 0.85 = 42.5$ kW

∴ Power input $= \dfrac{\text{Power output}}{\text{Efficiency}} = \dfrac{42.5}{0.895} = 47.49$ kW

∴ Total losses $=$ Power input $-$ Power output $= 47.49 - 42.5 = 4.99$ kW

∴ $P_i + \dfrac{P_{cu}}{4} = 4.99$ \qquad (as Copper loss $\propto$ kVA^2) \qquad ... (II)

Solving the equations (I) and (II), we get

$P_i = 3.33$ kW   and $P_{cu} = 6.64$ kW

75% of Full-load Condition :

Power output $=$ kVA $\times$ Power factor $= 75 \times 0.9 = 67.5$ kW

Copper loss $= (0.75)^2 P_{cu} = (0.75)^2 \times 6.64 = 3.735$ kW

∴ Total losses $= 3.33 + 3.735 = 7.065$ kW

∴ Power input = Power output + Total losses

= 67.5 + 7.065 = 74.565 kW

∴ Efficiency = $\frac{\text{Power output}}{\text{Power input}} \times 100 = \frac{67.5}{74.565} \times 100$

= **90.53 per cent** ... Ans.

8.13 METHODS OF FINDING EFFICIENCY AND REGULATION OF A TRANSFORMER

Efficiency and regulation of a transformer at any desired load condition and power factor can be found by either directly loading the transformer or by conducting open-circuit and short-circuit tests. The method of finding the efficiency and regulation by direct loading is rarely used for large transformers because of the difficulty of obtaining a suitable load and the large loss of power involved during testing. On the other hand, open-circuit and short-circuit tests can give the desired results without actually loading the transformer. It is for this reason, this method is known as *indirect method* of testing the performance of the transformer. The power required to carry out the open-circuit and short-circuit tests on the transformers is also very small compared with the method of direct loading and results obtained are also more accurate. However, here we are going to restrict our discussion to the method of finding efficiency and regulation of a transformer by direct loading only.

8.13.1 Efficiency and Regulation by Direct Loading

Efficiency and regulation at any desired load condition and power factor can be found by directly loading the transformer as follows :

Experimental Set-up : Fig. 8.18 shows the necessary connection diagram for the test.

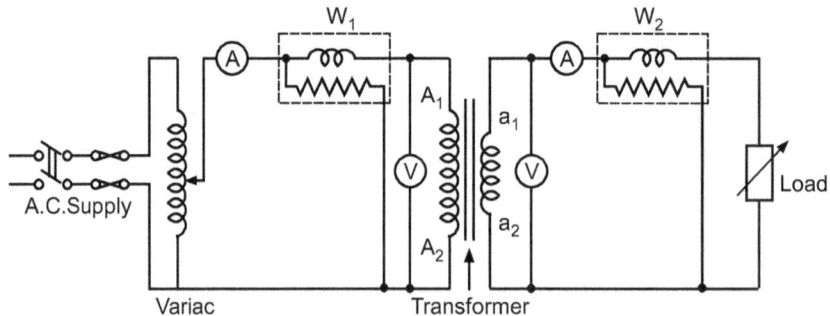

Fig. 8.18 : Direct loading of a single-phase transformer

The primary of the transformer is connected to an a.c. supply of rated voltage through the instruments like an ammeter, a voltmeter and wattmeter. A variable load is connected across the secondary. One ammeter, one voltmeter and one wattmeter are also inserted on the secondary side as shown.

Procedure : By varying the load in suitable steps, readings are taken on all meters from no load to about 25 % above full load. Suitable arrangement must be made using a variac or rheostat so as to maintain the rated voltage across the primary throughout the test. Various observations are recorded in a tabular form given below.

Table for Observations

Sr. No.	Primary Side			Secondary Side		
	V_1	I_1	W_1	V_2	I_2	W_2

Calculations for Efficiency : The wattmeters on the primary and secondary sides respectively read the input (W_1) and output (W_2) powers.

$$\therefore \quad \text{Efficiency} = \frac{\text{Output power}}{\text{Input power}} \times 100$$

$$= \frac{W_2}{W_1} \times 100 \text{ per cent} \quad \ldots (8.23)$$

If the load is purely resistive (with unity power factor) like lamp-bank, then the wattmeter on the secondary side can be eliminated. This is because with unity power factor loads, output power is also given by the product $V_2 I_2$.

$$\therefore \quad \text{Efficiency} = \frac{V_2 I_2}{W_1} \times 100 \text{ per cent} \quad \ldots (8.24)$$

Calculation for Regulation : Under no load condition (i.e. when secondary circuit is open and $I_2 = 0$), the voltmeter reading on secondary side gives no load secondary terminal voltage. Let us call it $_0V_2$. Then, for each reading, regulation is given by

$$\text{Voltage regulation} = \frac{_0V_2 - V_2}{_0V_2} \times 100 \text{ per cent} \quad \ldots (8.25)$$

where V_2 = Secondary terminal voltage on load.

Graphs : From the results obtained, curves are plotted for efficiency and regulation against load current or output power as illustrated in Fig. 8.19.

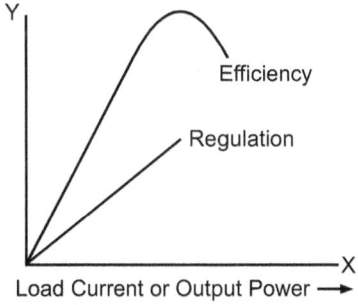

Fig. 8.19 : Efficiency and regulation curves

Then, the efficiency and regulation at any desired load can be found from these curves.

Example 8.11 : *A load test is conducted on 1 kVA, 230 / 115 V, 50 Hz, single-phase transformer using lamp load. Following are the results obtained at a particular load condition.*

Primary side			Secondary side	
V_1	I_1	W_1	V_2	I_2
230	4.2	846	111.5	7.5

If the no load secondary terminal voltage is observed to be 114 V, find the efficiency and regulation of the transformer at the given load condition.

Solution : With lamp load having unity power factor,

$$\text{Output power} = V_2 I_2 = 111.5 \times 7.5 = 836.25 \text{ W}$$

$$\text{Input power} = \text{Wattmeter reading on the primary side, } W_1$$

$$= 846 \text{ W}$$

$$\text{Efficiency} = \frac{\text{Output power}}{\text{Input power}} \times 100$$

$$= \frac{836.25}{846.0} \times 100$$

$$= \textbf{98.85 per cent} \quad \text{... Ans.}$$

Also, since no load secondary terminal voltage,

$$_0V_2 = 114 \text{ V}$$

$$\text{Voltage regulation} = \frac{_0V_2 - V_2}{_0V_2} \times 100$$

$$= \frac{114 - 111.5}{114} \times 100$$

$$= \textbf{2.19 per cent} \quad \text{... Ans.}$$

8.14 ALL-DAY EFFICIENCY OF A TRANSFORMER

Distribution transformers (i.e. the transformers supplying lighting and domestic loads and general electrical networks) have their primaries permanently connected to the power lines to give service to the consumers for 24 hours a day. Hence, in the case of these transformers, iron loss which is of constant magnitude occurs throughout 24 hours of the day irrespective of whether there is load on the transformer or not. On the other hand, since these transformers operate at different loads during different hours of the day, they have changing copper loss depending upon the load. The performance of a transformer under these conditions is best judged by its efficiency computed on energy basis. This efficiency is known as *all-day efficiency or operational efficiency*. It is defined as the *ratio of energy output (in kWh) over a period of 24 hours to the energy input (in kWh) over the same period.* Thus,

$$\text{All-day efficiency} = \frac{\text{Energy output (in kWh) over 24 hours}}{\text{Energy input (in kWh) over 24 hours}} \times 100 \text{ per cent} \quad \text{... (8.26)}$$

When a transformer is to be selected for the distribution purposes, one having a higher all-day efficiency should be always preferred.

Example 8.12 : *Find the all-day efficiency of a 500 kVA distribution transformer whose copper and iron losses at full load are 4.5 kW and 3 kW respectively. During a day of 24 hours, it is loaded as under :*

No. of hours	6	6	8	4
Load in kW	450	300	150	0
Power factor	0.9	0.75	1	–

Solution : Since the transformer is energised throughout the day, iron loss of 3 kW will occur for 24 hours irrespective of load condition. The copper loss at full load is given as 4.5 kW. Copper loss at any other load will be proportional to the square of the load current or kVA. For calculating the all-day efficiency of a transformer under consideration, all the calculations involved are made in the tabular form given below (Table 8.1).

Table 8.1

Load in kW	P. F.	Hours	kVA $\left(\dfrac{\text{Load in kW}}{\text{P. F.}}\right)$	Copper loss in kW	Copper loss in kWh (kW × Hrs.)	Iron Loss in kWh (kW × Hrs.)	Output in kWh (kW × Hrs.)
450	0.9	6	$\dfrac{450}{0.9} = 500$	4.5	27	18	2700
300	0.75	6	$\dfrac{300}{0.75} = 400$	$4.5\left(\dfrac{400}{500}\right)^2$ $= 2.88$	17.28	18	1800
150	1	8	$\dfrac{150}{1} = 150$	$4.5\left(\dfrac{150}{500}\right)^2$ $= 0.405$	3.24	24	1200
0	–	4	0	0	0	12	0
			Total		47.52	72	5700

Now, from Equation (8.26),

$$\text{All-day efficiency} = \dfrac{\text{Energy output (in kWh) over 24 hours}}{\text{Energy input (in kWh) over 24 hours}} \times 100$$

$$= \dfrac{\text{Energy output (in kWh) over 24 overs}}{[\text{Energy output (in kWh) over 24 hours} + \text{Total losses (in kWh) over 24 hours}]} \times 100$$

$$= \dfrac{5700}{(5700 + 47.52 + 72)} \times 100$$

$$= \textbf{98 per cent} \qquad \qquad \text{... Ans.}$$

Example 8.13 : *A 1000/200 V, 20 kVA, single-phase transformer absorbs 200 W at no load. The resistances of its primary and secondary windings are 0.25 Ω and 0.012 Ω respectively. It runs for 10 hours on no load, for 8 hours with a load of 100 A and for 6 hours with a load of 60 A, power factor being unity throughout. What is the all-day efficiency of the transformer ?*

Solution :

$$\text{Transformation ratio, } K = \frac{200}{1000} = 0.2$$

Total effective resistance of the transformer referred to secondary side

$$= R_1' + R_2 = K^2 R_1 + R_2$$
$$= (0.2)^2 \times 0.25 + 0.012 = 0.022 \, \Omega$$

$$\text{Secondary full-load current} = \frac{20 \times 10^3}{200} = 100 \, A$$

No-load loss = 200 W

Following table shows the losses and outputs in kWh under different load conditions :

Load condition	No. of Hours	No-load losses in kWh	Copper losses in kWh	Output in kWh
No load	10	$\frac{200 \times 10}{1000} = 2$	0	0
100 A (Full-load condition)	8	$\frac{200 \times 8}{1000} = 1.6$	$\frac{100^2 \times 0.022 \times 8}{1000} = 1.76$	$20 \times 1 \times 8 = 160$
60 A	6	$\frac{200 \times 6}{1000} = 1.2$	$\frac{60^2 \times 0.022 \times 6}{1000} = 0.48$	$\frac{20 \times 60 \times 1 \times 6}{100} = 72$
Total	24	4.8	2.24	232

$$\therefore \quad \text{All-day efficiency} = \frac{232}{(232 + 4.8 + 2.24)} \times 100$$

$$= 97.05 \% \qquad \text{... Ans.}$$

8.15 APPLICATIONS OF TRANSFORMERS

In general, the important tasks performed by the transformers are as follows :

(i) Increasing or decreasing voltage and current levels from one circuit to another circuit.

(ii) Matching the impedance of a source and its load for maximum power transfer in electronic and control circuits.

(iii) Isolating d.c. while permitting the flow of a.c. between two circuits or isolating one circuit from another.

Accordingly, the transformers are used in almost all the areas of electrical engineering. The prominent among them are listed below :

(i) Transformers are used extensively in a.c. power systems because they make possible power generation at the most desirable and economical voltage level (10 kV to 20 kV), power transmission at an economical transmission voltage level (400 kV to 1000 kV), and power utilization at the most convenient and safe distribution voltage level (400/230 V to 11 kV).

(ii) In the form of instrument transformers, they are commonly used for the electrical instruments and control circuits.

(iii) In the communication and electronic systems where frequency ranges from audio to radio and video, transformers are used for a wide variety of purposes e.g. Filament transformers are used to heat vacuum tube filaments. Input transformers (used to connect a microphone output to the first stage of an electronic amplifier), interstage transformers, and output transformers (used to connect the last amplifying stage to the loudspeaker) find their applications in radio and television circuits. Pulse transformers are used in radar, television and digital computers. Transformers are also widely used in the telephone circuits.

8.16 AUTO-TRANSFORMERS

An *auto-transformer* is a transformer having only one winding wound on a laminated magnetic core, the part of this winding being common to both the primary and secondary circuits. As an ordinary two-winding transformer, it can be used as a step-down or a step-up transformer as illustrated in Figs. 8.20 (a) and (b) respectively.

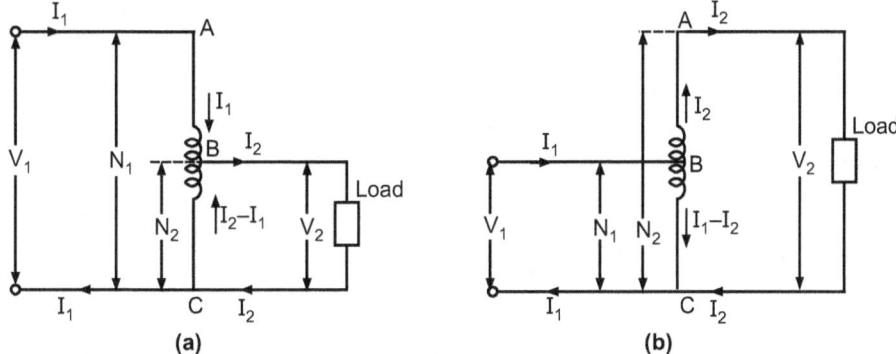

Fig. 8.20 : (a) Step-down auto-transformer, (b) Step-up auto-transformer

In Fig. 8.20 (a), the winding AC forms the primary and the portion BC forms the secondary. On the other hand, in Fig. 8.20 (b), the winding AC forms the secondary and its portion BC forms the primary. The performance of the auto-transformer is governed by the same fundamental considerations which we have already discussed for the two-winding transformers. Hence, in the case of an auto-transformer also, neglecting the losses, the leakage reactance and the magnetizing current, we have

$$\frac{V_2}{V_1} = \frac{I_1}{I_2} = \frac{N_2}{N_1} = K \quad \text{... (with usual notations) ... (8.27)}$$

Advantages :

(i) Weight of copper required in an auto-transformer is always less than that of the conventional two-winding transformer and hence, it is comparatively cheaper. The saving of copper is increased as transformation ratio approaches unity.

(ii) The resistance and leakage reactance of an auto-transformer being less than the corresponding two-winding transformer, its regulation is better.

(iii) $I^2 R$ losses being less, the efficiency of an auto-transformer is higher than that of the two-winding transformer.

Disadvantages : In the case of an auto-transformer, there is always a risk of serious electric shock particularly when it is used in high voltage circuit. This is because the low voltage and high voltage sides are not electrically separate.

Applications :
  (i)   For starting squirrel-cage induction motors and synchronous motors.
  (ii) For interconnecting a.c. systems having roughly the same operating voltage.
  (iii) As *boosters* to raise the voltage in a.c. feeders.
  (iv) As furnace transformers for getting suitable supply voltage.
  (v)   As *variacs* for getting continuously variable a.c. supply voltage. This is the most common application of auto-transformers. We know that ordinary rheostat can be used as potential divider for getting continuously variable a.c. voltage. But it is useful only for stepping down the voltage. On the other hand, the auto-transformer even though costlier has the distinct advantage that it can step-up as well as step-down the voltage and has negligible losses. Fig. 8.21 (a) shows the constructional details of a single-phase variac and Fig. 8.21 (b) the necessary connection diagram. It has its winding wound on a toroidal core. Input voltage (V_1) is applied between the terminals A and B. A continuously variable output voltage (V_2) from zero to about 120 % of the input voltage can be obtained across the output terminals D and E by moving the sliding contact S along the surface of the winding. Such variacs are many times used for dimming the lights in the theatres. Hence, they are also called as *dimmerstats*.

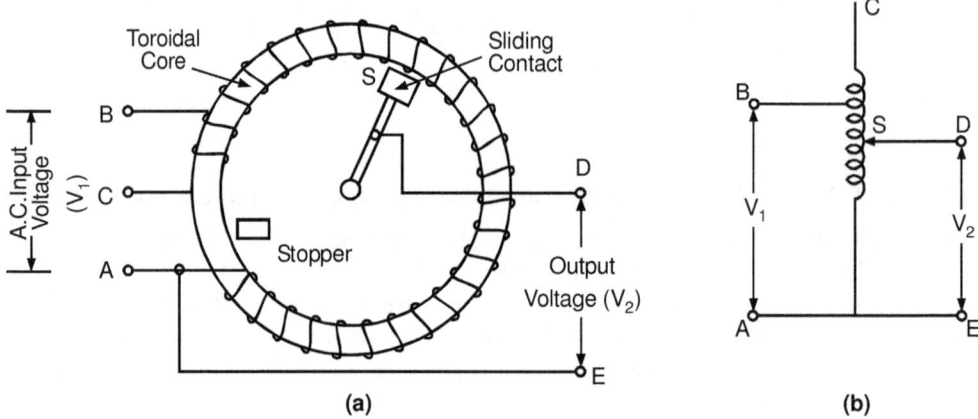

Fig. 8.21 : Single-phase variac

8.17 POINTS TO REMEMBER

- The transformer is a static device (with no rotating parts) which transfers electrical energy from one alternating current circuit to another with the desired change in voltage or current and without any change in frequency.
- The operation of the transformer is based on the principle of mutual induction between two circuits linked by a common magnetic field.
- The phenomenon, due to which an alternating current in the primary winding produces an e.m.f. in the secondary winding, is known as mutual induction and the e.m.f. induced in the secondary winding is known as mutually induced e.m.f. or an e.m.f. of mutual induction.

- The primary and the secondary terminal voltages of a transformer are proportional to the respective number of turns.
- The ratio of primary to secondary terminal voltage is known as voltage ratio and the ratio of primary to secondary turns is known as turns ratio of the transformer.
- More often, the ratio of the secondary voltage to the primary voltage is termed as transformation ratio and denoted by the letter K.
- If K > 1 i.e. $V_2 > V_1$, transformer is called a step-up transformer. It is that transformer which receives electrical energy at one voltage and delivers it at a higher voltage.
- If K < 1 i.e. $V_2 < V_1$, transformer is called a step-down transformer. It is the transformer which receives electrical energy at one voltage and delivers it at a lower voltage.
- If K = 1, i.e. $V_2 = V_1$, transformer is called a one to one transformer. Obviously, such a transformer transfers electrical energy from one circuit to another circuit without any change in the voltage.
- The primary and the secondary currents of a transformer are inversely proportional to the respective turns or voltages.
- The kVA rating of the transformer can be defined as the kVA output which it can deliver at rated voltage and frequency under usual service conditions without exceeding the standard limits of temperature rise.
- The regulation of the transformer is defined as the change in the secondary terminal voltage from no-load to full load with primary impressed voltage (V_1) and temperature of the transformer maintained constant.
- Regulation is always positive for the inductive load with lagging power factor and resistive load with unity power factor and may be negative for the capacitive load with leading power factor.
- Ordinary or commercial efficiency (symbol η) of the transformer is defined as the ratio of the output power to the input power (both being in W or kW). It is normally expressed as a percentage.
- Efficiency of a transformer is maximum for that load which makes the variable copper losses equal to the constant iron losses i.e. under maximum efficiency condition, variable losses = constant losses.
- All-day efficiency or operational efficiency of a transformer is defined as the ratio of energy output (in kWh) over a period of 24 hours to the energy input (in kWh) over the same period.
- An auto-transformer is a transformer having only one winding wound on a laminated magnetic core, the part of this winding being common to both the primary and secondary circuits.

8.18 IMPORTANT FORMULAE AT A GLANCE

- E.M.F. induced per turn of the primary or secondary winding of a transformer

$$= 4.44 \, \phi_m \cdot f \text{ volts}$$

where ϕ_m = Maximum value of the alternating flux linking both the windings of a transformer, in webers.

f = Frequency of the supply, in hertz

- E.M.F. induced in the primary winding of a transformer,

$$E_1 = 4.44 \phi_m f N_1 \text{ volts}$$

  where ϕ_m = Maximum value of the alternating flux linking both the windings of a transformer, in webers.

  f = Frequency of the supply, in hertz

  N_1 = Number of turns on the primary winding

- E.M.F. induced in the secondary winding of a transformer,

$$E_2 = 4.44 \phi_m f N_2 \text{ volts}$$

  where ϕ_m = Maximum value of the alternating flux linking both the windings of a transformer, in webers

  f = Frequency of the supply, in hertz

  N_2 = Number of turns on the secondary winding.

- Voltage ratio of a transformer = $\dfrac{\text{Primary applied voltage}}{\text{Secondary terminal voltage}} = \dfrac{V_1}{V_2}$

- Turns ratio of a transformer = $\dfrac{\text{Number of turns on the primary winding}}{\text{Number of turns on the secondary winding}} = \dfrac{N_1}{N_2}$

- Transformation ratio of a transformer,

$$K = \dfrac{\text{Secondary terminal voltage}}{\text{Primary applied voltage}} = \dfrac{V_2}{V_1}$$

- Transformation ratio of a transformer,

$$K = \dfrac{V_2}{V_1} = \dfrac{E_2}{E_1} = \dfrac{N_2}{N_1} = \dfrac{I_1}{I_2}$$

  where I_1 and I_2 = Currents in the primary and secondary windings respectively, in amperes

  E_1 and E_2 = E.M.Fs. induced in the primary and secondary windings respectively, in volts

  V_1 and V_2 = Primary applied voltage and secondary terminal voltage respectively, in volts

  N_1 and N_2 = Number of turns on the primary and secondary windings respectively.

- kVA rating of a transformer = $\dfrac{V_2 I_2}{1000} = \dfrac{V_1 I_1}{1000}$

  where V_1 and V_2 = Primary applied voltage and secondary terminal voltage respectively, in volts

  I_1 and I_2 = Full-load currents in the primary and secondary windings respectively, in amperes

- Voltage regulation $= \dfrac{_0V_2 - V_2}{_0V_2} \times 100 = \dfrac{E_2 - V_2}{E_2} \times 100$ per cent.

  where $_0V_2$ = Secondary terminal voltage on no load, in volts

  V_2 = Secondary terminal voltage on full load, in volts

  E_2 = Induced e.m.f. in the secondary winding, in volts

- Total copper loss of a transformer $= I_1^2 R_1 + I_2^2 R_2$ watts

  where I_1 and I_2 = Currents in the primary and secondary windings respectively, in amperes

  R_1 and R_2 = Primary and secondary resistances respectively, in ohms

- Hysteresis loss, $P_h = K_h B_m^{1.6} f v$ watts

  where f = Frequency of the supply, in hertz.

  B_m = Maximum value of the flux density in the core of a transformer, in teslas

  v = Volume of the magnetic material, in cubic metres

  K_h = Constant

- Eddy current loss,

  $$P_e = K_e B_m^2 f^2 t^2 v \text{ watts}$$

  where t = Thickness of laminations, in metres

  K_e = Constant

  B_m, f, v = As above

- Efficiency of a transformer, $\eta = \dfrac{\text{Output power}}{\text{Input power}} \times 100 = \dfrac{\text{Output power}}{\text{Output power} + \text{Losses}} \times 100$

  $$= \dfrac{V_2 I_2 \cos \phi}{V_2 I_2 \cos \phi + P_i + P_{cu}} \times 100 \text{ per cent}$$

  where P_i = Iron loss, in watts

  P_{cu} = Total copper loss, in watts

  V_2 = Secondary terminal voltage, in volts

  I_2 = Secondary current, in amperes

  $\cos \phi$ = Power factor of the load

- Efficiency of a transformer on full-load

  $$= \dfrac{\text{Full-load output (in watts)}}{\text{Full-load output (in watts)} + P_i + P_{cu}} \times 100$$

  $$= \dfrac{\text{Full-load rating (in VA)} \times \text{Power factor}}{\text{Full-load rating (in VA)} \times \text{Power factor} + P_i + P_{cu}} \times 100$$

  where, P_i = Iron loss, in watts

  P_{cu} = Total full-load copper loss, in watts

- Efficiency at $(x \times \text{Full load}) = \dfrac{x \times \text{Full-load rating (in VA)} \times \text{Power factor}}{x \times \text{Full-load rating (in VA)} \times \text{Power factor} + P_i + x^2 P_{cu}} \times 100$

  where, x = Degree of loading (e.g. at 25% load, $x = 0.25$)

  P_i = Iron loss, in watts

  P_{cu} = Total full-load copper loss, in watts

- Condition for maximum efficiency of a transformer : Copper losses = Iron losses.
- For a transformer, kVA load corresponding to maximum efficiency

  $$= \text{Full-load kVA} \times \sqrt{\dfrac{\text{Iron loss}}{\text{Full-load copper loss}}}$$

- All-day efficiency of a transformer

  $$= \dfrac{\text{Energy output (in kWh) over 24 hours}}{\text{Energy input (in kWh) over 24 hours}} \times 100 \text{ per cent}$$

  $$= \dfrac{\text{Energy output (in kWh) over 24 hours}}{[\text{Energy output (in kWh) over 24 hours} + \text{Total losses (in kWh) over 24 hours}]} \times 100 \text{ per cent}$$

8.19 SOLUTIONS OF NUMERICAL EXAMPLES FROM UNIVERSITY PAPERS

Example 8.14 : *A single-phase, 50 Hz transformer has 300 primary turns and 750 secondary turns. The net cross-sectional area of the core is 64 sq. cm. If the primary induced e.m.f. is 440 V, find the maximum flux density in the core and e.m.f. induced in the secondary.*

(May 2007/8 Marks)

Solution : Refer to the solution of Example 8.2 on Page 8.9.

Example 8.15 : *A 200 kVA, 3300/240 V, 50 Hz, single-phase transformer has 80 turns on the secondary winding. Assuming an ideal transformer, calculate :*

(i) *Number of primary turns,*

(ii) *Maximum value of the flux in the core,*

(iii) *Primary and secondary currents on full load.* **(May 2008/8 Marks)**

Solution : Given : Rating = 200 kVA, Voltage ratio = 3300/240 V, f = 50 Hz, $N_2 = 80$.

(i) Number of primary turns,

$$N_1 = N_2 \times \dfrac{V_1}{V_2} = 80 \times \dfrac{3300}{240} = 1100 \qquad \text{... Ans.}$$

(ii) $V_1 \approx E_1 = 4.44 \, \phi_m f N_1$ volts

∴ Maximum value of the flux in the core,

$$\phi_m = \dfrac{E_1}{4.44 \, fN_1} = \dfrac{3300}{4.44 \times 50 \times 1100} = \mathbf{0.0135 \text{ Wb}} \qquad \text{... Ans.}$$

(iii) Full-load primary current,

$$I_1 = \frac{kVA \times 10^3}{V_1} = \frac{200 \times 10^3}{3300}$$

$$= 60.606 \text{ A} \qquad \text{... Ans.}$$

Full-load secondary current,

$$I_2 = \frac{kVA \times 10^3}{V_2} = \frac{200 \times 10^3}{240}$$

$$= 833.33 \text{ A ... Ans.}$$

Alternatively, $\quad I_2 = I_1 \times \dfrac{V_1}{V_2} = 60.606 \times \dfrac{3300}{240} = \textbf{833.33 A}$ ... Ans.

Example 8.16 : *A single-phase transformer working at unity power factor has an efficiency of 92% at both half and at full load of 500 kW. Determine the amount of copper loss and core loss at full load.* **(May 2008/8 Marks)**

Solution : Full-load Condition :

Full-load output at unity power factor = 500 kW (given)

Let $\quad P_i$ = Core loss of the transformer

and $\quad P_{cu}$ = Full-load copper loss

∴ Total loss at full load = $P_i + P_{cu}$

Now, Efficiency at full load = $\dfrac{\text{Output}}{\text{Output + Total loss}}$

∴ $\quad 0.92 = \dfrac{500}{500 + (P_i + P_{cu})}$

∴ $\quad P_i + P_{cu} = 43.48 \text{ kW}$ ... (I)

Half-load Condition :

Half-load output at unity power factor = $0.5 \times 500 = 250$ kW

Half-load copper loss = $(0.5)^2 \times P_{cu}$ $\qquad$ (∵ Copper loss $\propto (kVA)^2$)

$= 0.25 \, P_{cu}$

∴ Total loss at half load = $P_i + 0.25 \, P_{cu}$

Now, Efficiency at half load = $\dfrac{\text{Output}}{\text{Output + Total loss}}$

∴ $\quad 0.92 = \dfrac{250}{250 + (P_i + 0.25 \, P_{cu})}$

∴ $\quad P_i + 0.25 \, P_{cu} = 21.74 \text{ kW}$ ... (II)

Solving the equations (I) and (II) simultaneously, we get

Copper loss at full load, P_{cu} = **28.99 kW** ... Ans.

Core loss of the transformer, P_i = **14.49 kW** ... Ans.

Example 8.17 : *The no-load current of a transformer is 5 A at 0.3 power factor when supplied at 230 V, 50 Hz. The number of turns on the primary winding is 200. Calculate :*

(i) Maximum value of the flux in the core,

(ii) Core loss,

(iii) Magnetizing current.　　　　　　　　　　　　　　　　**(December 2008/8 Marks)**

Solution : Given : $I_0 = 5$ A, $\cos \phi_0 = 0.3$ lagging, $V = V_1 = 230$ volts, $f = 50$ Hz, $N_1 = 200$.

(i) $\quad E_1 \approx V_1 = 4.44\, \phi_m\, f\, N_1$

∴ $\quad 230 = 4.44 \times \phi_m \times 50 \times 200$

∴ Maximum value of the flux in the core,

$$\phi_m = 5.18 \times 10^{-3} \text{ Wb or } 5.18 \text{ mWb} \quad \ldots \text{Ans.}$$

(ii) $\quad$ Core loss = No-load power input　　(∵ Copper loss is negligible)

$\qquad\qquad = V_1 I_0 \cos \phi_0 = 230 \times 5 \times 0.3$

$\qquad\qquad = \mathbf{345\ W}$　　　　　　　　　　　　　　　　　　　　… Ans.

(iii) $\quad \cos \phi_0 = 0.3$ lagging (given)

∴ $\quad \sin \phi_0 = 0.954$

∴ Magnetizing component,

$$I_{mag} = I_0 \sin \phi_0 = 5 \times 0.954 = \mathbf{4.77\ A} \quad \ldots \text{Ans.}$$

Example 8.18 : *A 200/400 V, 10 kVA, 50 Hz, single-phase transformer has at full load, a copper loss of 120 W. It has an efficiency of 98% at full load, unity power factor. Determine the iron losses at full load. What would be the efficiency of the transformer at half load, 0.8 power factor lagging ?*　　　　　　　　　　　　　　　　　　　**(December 2008/8 Marks)**

Solution : (i) Full-load Condition : Full-load copper loss, $P_{cu} = 120$ W.

$\qquad$ Power output = kVA × Power factor = 10 × 1 = 10 kW = 10000 W

$\qquad$ Power input = $\dfrac{\text{Power output}}{\text{Efficiency}} = \dfrac{10000}{0.98} = 10204.08$ W

∴ $\quad$ Total loss = Power input − Power output = 10204.08 − 10000

$\qquad\qquad\qquad = 204.08$ W

∴ Iron losses of the transformer,

$\qquad\qquad P_i$ = Total loss − Copper loss = 204.08 − 120

$\qquad\qquad\quad = \mathbf{84.08\ W}$　　　　　　　　　　　　　　　　　　　… Ans.

(ii) Half-load Condition :

$\qquad$ Degree of loading, $x = 0.5$

∴ Efficiency at half load, 0.8 power factor lagging

$$= \dfrac{x \times \text{Full-load rating (in VA)} \times \text{p.f.}}{x \times \text{Full-load rating (in VA)} \times \text{p.f.} + P_i + x^2 P_{cu}} \times 100$$

$$= \dfrac{0.5 \times 10000 \times 0.8}{0.5 \times 10000 \times 0.8 + 84.08 + (0.5)^2 \times 120} \times 100$$

$$= \mathbf{97.23\%} \qquad \ldots \text{Ans.}$$

Example 8.19 : *A 100 kVA, 33 kV/6.6 kV, 50 Hz, single-phase transformer has 1200 turns on primary. Determine secondary winding turns and maximum value of the flux in the core.*

(May 2009/6 Marks)

Solution :
$$\frac{V_1}{V_2} = \frac{N_1}{N_2}$$

∴ Secondary winding turns,
$$N_2 = \frac{N_1 V_2}{V_1} = \frac{1200 \times 6.6 \times 10^3}{33 \times 10^3} = \mathbf{240} \quad \ldots \text{Ans.}$$

Also, $V_1 \approx E_1 = 4.44 \, \phi_m \, f \, N_1$ volts

∴ Maximum value of the flux in the core,
$$\phi_m = \frac{E_1}{4.44 \times f \times N_1} = \frac{33 \times 10^3}{4.44 \times 50 \times 1200} = \mathbf{0.1239 \, Wb} \quad \ldots \text{Ans.}$$

Example 8.20 : *A 20 kVA, single-phase, 50 Hz transformer has full-load copper loss of 360 W and iron loss of 120 W. Calculate the efficiency of the transformer at half of the full load at 0.9 power factor lagging.* **(May 2009/6 Marks)**

Solution : Given : kVA rating = 20, f = 50 Hz,

Full-load copper loss, P_{cu} = 360 W, P_i = 120 W

We know that

$$\text{Efficiency at } (x \times \text{full load}) = \frac{x \times \text{Full-load rating (in VA)} \times \text{p.f.}}{x \times \text{Full-load rating (in VA)} \times \text{p.f.} + P_i + x^2 P_{cu}} \times 100$$

For half-load condition, degree of loading i.e. x = 0.5.

∴ Efficiency at half of the full load at 0.9 p.f. lagging,
$$\eta_{HL} = \frac{0.5 \times 20 \times 10^3 \times 0.9}{(0.5 \times 20 \times 10^3 \times 0.9) + 120 + (0.5)^2 \times 360} \times 100$$
$$= \mathbf{97.72\%} \quad \ldots \text{Ans.}$$

Example 8.21 : *The primary winding of a single-phase transformer is connected to 230 V, 50 Hz supply. The secondary winding has 1500 turns. If the maximum value of the core flux is 2.07 mWb, determine :*

(i) Number of turns on the primary winding.

(ii) Secondary induced voltage.

(iii) Net cross-sectional area if the flux density has maximum value of 0.465 T.

(December 2009/8 Marks)

Solution : Given : V = 230 volts, f = 50 Hz, N_2 = 1500, ϕ_m = 2.07 mWb, B_m = 0.465 T

(i) $V \approx E_1 = 4.44 \, \phi_m \, f \, N_1$

∴ Number of turns on the primary winding,
$$N_1 = \frac{E_1}{4.44 \, \phi_m \cdot f} = \frac{230}{4.44 \times 2.07 \times 10^{-3} \times 50}$$
$$= \mathbf{500.5} \quad \ldots \text{Ans.}$$

(ii) Secondary induced voltage,

$$V_2 = \frac{N_2}{N_1} \times V_1 = \frac{1500}{500.5} \times 230 = \mathbf{689.31\ V} \qquad \ldots \text{Ans.}$$

(iii) $\quad B_m = \dfrac{\phi_m}{A_i}$

∴ Net cross-sectional area of the core,

$$A_i = \frac{\phi_m}{B_m} = \frac{2.07 \times 10^{-3}}{0.465}\ m^2$$

$$= \mathbf{44.52\ cm^2} \qquad \ldots \text{Ans.}$$

Example 8.22 : *In a 25 kVA, 3300/230 volts, single-phase transformer, the iron and full-load copper losses are respectively 350 W and 400 W. Determine the efficiency at half load, 0.8 power factor.* **(December 2009/8 Marks)**

Solution : Given : Full-load rating = 25 kVA,

Full-load copper loss, $P_{cu} = 400\ W$, $P_i = 350\ W$

We know that

Efficiency at (x × Full load)

$$= \frac{x \times \text{Full-load rating (in VA)} \times \text{p.f.}}{x \times \text{Full-load rating (in VA)} \times \text{p.f.} + P_i + x^2\, P_{cu}} \times 100$$

For half-load condition, degree of loading i.e. x = 0.5.

∴ Efficiency at half load, 0.8 power factor,

$$\eta_{HL} = \frac{0.5 \times 25 \times 10^3 \times 0.8}{(0.5 \times 25 \times 10^3 \times 0.8) + 350 + (0.5)^2 \times 400} \times 100$$

$$= \mathbf{95.69\%} \qquad \ldots \text{Ans.}$$

Example 8.23 : *The no-load current of a transformer is 5 A at 0.25 power factor when supplied at 235 V, 50 Hz. The number of turns on the primary winding is 200. Determine :*

(i) Maximum value of the flux in the core,

(ii) Core loss,

(iii) Magnetizing component. **(May 2010/8 Marks)**

Solution : Given : $I_0 = 5\ A$, $\cos \phi_0 = 0.25$ lagging, V = 235 volts, f = 50 Hz, $N_1 = 200$.

(i) $\quad E_1 \approx V_1 = 4.44\ \phi_m\ f\ N_1$

∴ $\quad 235 = 4.44 \times \phi_m \times 50 \times 200$

∴ Maximum value of the flux in the core,

$$\phi_m = \mathbf{5.29 \times 10^{-3}\ Wb}\ \text{or}\ \mathbf{5.29\ mWb} \qquad \ldots \text{Ans.}$$

(ii) Core loss = No-load power input   (Copper loss being negligible)

$$= V_1\ I_0 \cos \phi_0 = 235 \times 5 \times 0.25$$

$$= \mathbf{293.75\ W} \qquad \ldots \text{Ans.}$$

(iii) $\quad \cos \phi_0 = 0.25$ lagging $\quad$ ∴ $\sin \phi_0 = 0.968$

∴ Magnetizing component,

$$I_{mag} = I_0 \sin \phi_0 = 5 \times 0.968 = \mathbf{4.84\ A} \qquad \ldots \text{Ans.}$$

Example 8.24 : *A single-phase, 20 kVA, 22 kV/1.1 kV, 50 Hz transformer has maximum flux density 1.2 Wb/m². If the voltage per turn is 20 V, calculate the primary and secondary number of turns and core area.* **(December 2010/6 Marks)**

Solution : Voltage per turn, E_t = 20 V

∴ Number of turns of the primary winding,

$$N_1 = \frac{V_1}{E_t} = \frac{22 \times 10^3}{20} = \mathbf{1100} \quad \text{... Ans.}$$

Number of turns of the secondary winding,

$$N_2 = \frac{V_2}{E_t} = \frac{1.1 \times 10^3}{20} = \mathbf{55} \quad \text{... Ans.}$$

Now, $E_1 \approx V_1 = 4.44 \, \phi_m \, f \, N_1$

∴ $22 \times 10^3 = 4.44 \, \phi_m \times 50 \times 1100$

∴ Maximum flux, ϕ_m = 0.09 Wb

But Maximum flux density, $B_m = \dfrac{\phi_m}{A_i}$

∴ $1.2 = \dfrac{0.09}{A_i}$

∴ Core area, A_i = **0.075 m² or 750 cm²** ... Ans.

Example 8.25 : *A 55 kVA, single-phase transformer has primary winding of 460 turns and secondary winding of 160 turns. The input side of the transformer is supplied with the voltage of 2500 V from 50 Hz a.c. supply. Calculate : Secondary voltage, Primary and secondary full-load currents, Maximum value of the flux.* **(May 2011/8 Marks)**

Solution : Given : Rating of the transformer = 55 kVA, N_1 = 460, N_2 = 160,

$V = V_1 = 2500$ volts, $f = 50$ Hz

(i) Since $\dfrac{V_2}{V_1} = \dfrac{N_2}{N_1}$

Secondary voltage, $V_2 = \dfrac{N_2}{N_1} \times V_1 = \dfrac{160}{460} \times 2500$

= **869.57 V** ... Ans.

(ii) Primary full-load current,

$$I_1 = \frac{kVA \times 1000}{V_1} = \frac{55 \times 1000}{2500} = \mathbf{22 \, A} \quad \text{... Ans.}$$

Secondary full-load current,

$$I_2 = \frac{kVA \times 1000}{V_2} = \frac{55 \times 1000}{869.57} = \mathbf{63.25 \, A} \quad \text{... Ans.}$$

Alternatively, $I_2 = \dfrac{N_1}{N_2} \times I_1 = \dfrac{460}{160} \times 22 = \mathbf{63.25 \, A}$ ... Ans.

(iii) Maximum value of the flux,

$$\phi_m = \frac{E_1}{4.44 \, f \, N_1} = \frac{2500}{4.44 \times 50 \times 460} \quad (\because E_1 \approx V_1)$$

= **0.0245 Wb** ... Ans.

Example 8.26 : *A 3000/230 V, 50 Hz, single-phase transformer is built with a core having an effective cross-sectional area of 120 cm² and 60 turns in the low-voltage winding. Calculate :*

(i) Value of the maximum flux density.

(ii) Number of turns on the high-voltage winding. **(December 2011/8 Marks)**

Solution : Given : Voltage ratio = 3000/230 V, Frequency = 50 Hz, a = 120 cm², $N_2 = 60$.

(i)
$$E_2 = 4.44 \, \phi_m \, f \, N_2$$

$$\therefore \quad 230 = 4.44 \times \phi_m \times 50 \times 60$$

∴ Value of the maximum flux,

$$\phi_m = 0.0173 \text{ Wb}$$

∴ Value of the maximum flux density,

$$B_m = \frac{\phi_m}{a} = \frac{0.0173}{120 \times 10^{-4}} = 1.44 \text{ Wb/m}^2 \quad \text{... Ans.}$$

(ii) Number of turns on the high-voltage winding,

$$N_1 = N_2 \times \frac{V_1}{V_2} = 60 \times \frac{3000}{230}$$

$$= 782.61 \approx 783 \quad \text{... Ans.}$$

Example 8.27 : *A 200 kVA, 6600/400 V, 50 Hz, single-phase transformer has 80 turns on the secondary side. Calculate :*

(i) Primary and secondary currents,

(ii) Primary turns,

(iii) Maximum value of the flux at full load.

Neglect losses. **(May 2012/8 Marks)**

Solution : Given : Rating = 200 kVA, Voltage ratio = 6600/400 V, f = 50 Hz, $N_2 = 80$.

(i) Full-load primary current,

$$I_1 = \frac{kVA \times 10^3}{V_1} = \frac{200 \times 10^3}{6600} = 30.3 \text{ A} \quad \text{... Ans.}$$

Full-load secondary current,

$$I_2 = \frac{kVA \times 10^3}{V_2} = \frac{200 \times 10^3}{400} = 500 \text{ A} \quad \text{... Ans.}$$

Alternatively, $I_2 = I_1 \times \frac{V_1}{V_2} = 30.3 \times \frac{6600}{400} = 500 \text{ A} \quad \text{... Ans.}$

(ii) Number of primary turns,

$$N_1 = N_2 \times \frac{V_1}{V_2} = 80 \times \frac{6600}{400} = 1320 \quad \text{... Ans.}$$

(iii) $\quad V_1 \approx E_1 = 4.44\, \phi_m\, f\, N_1$ volts

∴ Maximum value of the flux in the core,

$$\phi_m = \frac{E_1}{4.44\, f\, N_1} = \frac{6600}{4.44 \times 50 \times 1320} = 0.0225 \text{ Wb} \qquad \text{... Ans.}$$

Example 8.28 : *A single-phase transformer has 500 turns on the primary and 250 turns on the secondary winding. The maximum value of flux is 9 mWb. Calculate the primary voltage, secondary voltage, kVA rating of the transformer, secondary current if the full-load primary current is 10 A and supply frequency is 50 Hz.* **(December 2012/8 Marks)**

Solution : Given : $N_1 = 500$, $N_2 = 250$, $\phi_m = 9$ mWb, $I_1 = 10$ A on full load, $f = 50$ Hz.

(i) Primary voltage, $V_1 \approx E_1 = 4.44\, \phi_m\, f\, N_1$

$$= 4.44 \times 9 \times 10^{-3} \times 50 \times 500$$

$$= \mathbf{999\ V} \qquad \text{... Ans.}$$

(ii) Secondary voltage, $V_2 = V_1 \times \dfrac{N_2}{N_1}$

$$= 999 \times \frac{250}{500} = \mathbf{499.5\ V} \qquad \text{... Ans.}$$

(iii) kVA rating of the transformer $= \dfrac{V_1 I_1}{1000} = \dfrac{999 \times 10}{1000} = \mathbf{9.99\ kVA} \qquad \text{... Ans.}$

(iv) Full-load secondary current, $I_2 = I_1 \times \dfrac{V_1}{V_2} = 10 \times \dfrac{999}{499.5} = \mathbf{20\ A} \qquad \text{... Ans.}$

8.20 EXERCISES

8.20.1 Review Questions

1. What is the function of a transformer in a.c. circuit ?
2. State the principle on which transformer works.
3. Describe with a neat sketch the salient constructional features of a transformer.
4. In what way does the core type transformer differ in construction from the shell type ?
5. From first principles derive the e.m.f. equation for a transformer.
6. State the relationship between the voltages, currents and turns on the primary and the secondary side of a transformer. Explain the meaning of kVA rating of a transformer.
7. What is the transformation ratio of a transformer ?
8. What is meant by step-up and step-down transformer ?
9. Define an ideal transformer.
10. Discuss the magnetic leakage in a transformer and indicate how its value may be kept down.

11. Define regulation of a transformer.

12. Enumerate the various losses in a transformer and state the steps taken to minimize these losses.

13. What do you understand by efficiency of a transformer ?

14. State the condition for maximum efficiency of a transformer.

15. Describe the test for finding the efficiency and regulation of a transformer by direct loading. Why this test is normally conducted in case of small transformers only ?

16. What is all-day efficiency of a transformer ? How does it differ from its ordinary efficiency ?

17. List the different applications of transformers.

18. Define an auto-transformer.

19. State the different advantages and applications of an auto-transformer.

8.20.2 Classified Theory Questions from University Papers

1. State and explain the working principle of a transformer. State how the transformers are classified.

    (Answer : Sections 8.2, 8.4)   **(December 2010/6 Marks)**

2. Explain the working principle of a single-phase transformer. Also compare core-type and shelf-type transformers.

    (Answer : Sections 8.2, 8.4)   **(December 2009/8 Marks)**

3. Derive an e.m.f. equation of a single-phase transformer.

    (Answer : Section 8.5)   **(December 2008, 2012; May 2009/8 Marks)**

4. For an ideal transformer, prove that $\frac{N_2}{N_1} = \frac{E_2}{E_1} = \frac{I_1}{I_2} = K$.

    (Answer : Section 8.6)   **(May 2008/8 Marks)**

5. Explain the concept of transformer at no load.

    (Answer : Sections 8.8.1, 8.9.1)   **(December 2009; May 2012/6 Marks)**

6. State various losses in a transformer. How to minimize them ?

    (Answer : Section 8.11)   **(December 2010; May 2012/6 Marks)**

7. How the eddy current losses are minimized ? Explain.

    (Answer : Section 8.11)   **(December 2009/4 Marks)**

8. For a single-phase transformer, define : (i) Efficiency, (ii) Regulation.

    (Answer : Sections 8.10, 8.12)   **(May 2009/6 Marks)**

9. Explain the efficiency of a transformer. What is the condition for maximum efficiency ?

    (Answer : Sections 8.12, 8.12.1)   **(May 2010/6 Marks)**

10. Explain with a neat diagram, how you determine the efficiency any regulation of a single-phase transformer by direct loading.

   (Answer : Section 8.13.1)   **(May 2008, 2011; December 2010/8 Marks)**

8.20.3 Examples for Practice

1. A single-phase, 50 Hz transformer has 80 turns on the primary winding and 400 turns on the secondary winding. The net cross-sectional area of the core is 200 cm². If the primary winding is connected to a 240 V, 50 Hz supply, determine (a) The e.m.f. induced in the secondary winding and (b) The maximum value of the flux density in the core.

   (1199 V, 0.675 T)

2. A 3 kVA transformer of 230 / 115 voltage ratio is fully loaded. Find : (i) Primary full-load current, (ii) Secondary full-load current, (iii) Secondary turns, if primary turns are 60 and (iv) Half-load kVA output.

   (13.04 A, 26.08 A, 30, 1.5 kVA)

3. A 2200 / 230 V, single-phase transformer in a small distribution sub-station supplies four feeders with the following loads : (i) 7.5 kW at 0.8 power factor lagging, (ii) 30 A at 0.7 power factor lagging and (iii) 5 kVA at 0.85 power factor leading.

   Determine the primary current which the transformer draws from 2200 V mains and its power factor. Neglect losses in the transformer.

   (8.35 A, 0.9 lagging)

4. A single-phase transformer is loaded to 8 A by lamp loads. The output voltage is 215 V. The total losses at the above load are equal to 51.6 W. Find : (i) Output of the transformer; (ii) Efficiency of the transformer; (iii) Input to the transformer.

   (1720 W, 97.09 %, 1771.6 W)

5. A single-phase transformer delivers 10 A at 220 V to a resistive load while the primary draws 6 A at 0.9 lagging power factor from 450 V, 50 Hz supply. The turns ratio of the transformer is 2. Calculate the percentage efficiency and percentage regulation in this condition.

   (90.53 %, 2.22 %)

6. A 100 kVA, 2200 / 220 V, 50 Hz, single-phase transformer has an iron loss of 400 W. The full-load copper loss is 500 W. Find out the efficiency of the transformer at (i) Full-load, 0.7 power factor lagging, (ii) Half-load, 0.8 power factor lagging.

   (98.73 %, 98.7 %)

7. A 20 kVA, 3300 / 220 V, 50 Hz, single-phase transformer has iron loss of 200 W, and copper loss at full load of 400 W. Find the efficiency of the transformer at half load at 0.8 lagging power factor. Also, find the maximum efficiency and load at which it occurs.

   (96.39 %, 96.58 %, 14.14 kVA)

8. A 500 / 250 V, single-phase transformer has constant losses of 150 W. When delivering an output of 8 kW to a load, the transformer takes 21 A at a power factor of 0.8 lagging from the 500 V supply mains. (a) Calculate the variable losses of the transformer at this load and the corresponding efficiency, (b) If this load on the transformer is reduced to half, calculate its new efficiency, (c) At what load will the efficiency be maximum ? Find the maximum efficiency.

(250 W, 95.2 %, 94.96 %, 7.75 kVA, 95.4 %)

9. A 40 kVA, 2000 / 250 V, 50 Hz, single-phase transformer has (i) efficiency of 97 % at full load and 0.8 power factor, (ii) efficiency of 98 % at half load and unity power factor. Determine :

(a) Iron and copper losses at full load.

(b) Load at which copper loss is 400 W.

(c) Efficiency at the load in (ii) and 0.8 lagging power factor.

(P_i = 214.3 W, P_{cu} = 775.4 W, 28.73 kVA, 97.4 %)

10. A 500 kVA, 11000 /500 V distribution transformer is loaded as follows :

No load for 5 hours; 300 A for 5 hours; 500 A for 5 hours; 800 A for 5 hours and 1000 A for 4 hours.

If the iron losses are 10 kW and full-load copper losses are 30 kW, calculate the all-day efficiency, assuming unity power factor throughout. (92 %)

11. A transformer has its maximum efficiency of a 0.98 at 500 kVA unity power factor. During a day it is loaded as under :

Duration	Load	Power Factor
6 hours	450 kW	0.9
6 hours	250 kW	0.75
4 hours	100 kW	0.9
8 hours	No load	—

Determine its all-day efficiency. (96.48 %)

12. Two transformers A and B each rated for 50 kVA have core losses of 600 W and 300 W respectively and full-load copper losses of 600 W and 900 W respectively. Compare the all-day efficiencies of the two transformers if they are to be used to supply a lighting load with outputs varying as follows : Full load for 4 hours, Half-full load for 9 hours and No load for 11 hours. (Transformer A – 96 %, Transformer B – 97 %)

CHAPTER

9

SINGLE-PHASE ALTERNATORS

9.1 INTRODUCTION

As said earlier, a.c. generators are normally known as *alternators* or *synchronous generators* (being always run at a constant speed called *synchronous speed*). Presently, they are the most commonly used machines for generating electrical power on large scale for commercial purposes. All modern day power stations are equipped with alternators for the generation of electrical power. The general principle on which the operation of all electrical generators whether a.c. or d.c. is based, and the working of single-phase and three-phase elementary alternators have already been discussed in Sections 3.4, 3.4.1, 7.2.

Since the three-phase system has become the standard system throughout the world for generation, transmission and distribution of electrical energy, three-phase alternators are universally used by the electrical power industry for supplying three-phase as well as single-phase power to its customers. The single-phase power that is supplied originate from one phase of the three-phase system. However, single-phase alternators are also in use in many applications. They are most often used when the loads being supplied are relatively light. These alternators produce a.c. power at utilization voltage and are generally driven by petrol or diesel engines. For simplicity of understanding, in this chapter, we shall confine our discussion on alternators to single-phase alternators only.

9.2 TYPES OF ALTERNATORS

An alternator consists essentially of the field magnet system and the armature (part of the machine in which e.m.f. is induced). As already seen in Section 3.4, the generation of an e.m.f. in the armature conductors depends on the relative motion between the conductors and the field flux. Hence, in an alternator, either the armature or the field may be the rotating member. Accordingly, there are two types of alternators :

(i) Revolving armature type.

(ii) Revolving field type.

The elementary 2-pole alternators which we have studied in Section 3.4.1 (Fig. 3.3) schematically represent the revolving armature type single-phase alternator. In this type of alternator, the armature rotates through a stationary magnetic field.

The revolving field type alternator has a stationary armature winding and a rotating field winding. Fig. 9.1 illustrates the elementary single-phase alternator of this type.

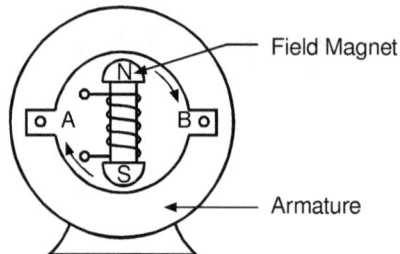

Fig. 9.1 : Rotating field type elementary 2-pole, single-phase alternator

The advantages of the rotating field construction for alternators are as follows :

(i) The high voltage generated in the armature winding need not be brought to the external circuit through slip-rings and brushes, but the load can be directly connected to the terminals of the alternator.

(ii) It permits better insulation for the armature coils than would be possible on a rotating armature. This is because with steady armature, more space can be easily provided for insulation. The increased space may be made available by either increasing the size of the stator or by deepening the slots without mechanically weakening the armature. Moreover, the centrifugal force and vibrations are also absent. Hence, it is possible to achieve high generation voltage.

(iii) Since the voltage applied to the rotating field winding is low d.c. voltage (110 or 250 V), the problem of sparking at the slip-rings is not encountered. Moreover, only two slip-rings are required and they can be easily insulated because of low voltage.

(iv) Overall construction is considerably simplified. With the simpler and more robust mechanical construction of the rotor, a higher speed is possible, so that a greater output can be obtained from a machine of given size.

(v) In the case of large machines, it is easy to make the necessary arrangements for forced air cooling or hydrogen cooling on a stationary armature by increasing the size of the stator core and providing radial air ducts and ventilation holes.

9.3 ALTERNATOR CONSTRUCTION

Because of the various advantages mentioned in the previous section, almost all single-phase alternators are constructed with a stationary armature and rotating poles, except some of the smaller low-power rating alternators in which the armature rotates within the stationary field structure. Therefore, let us see the general constructional features of only revolving field type alternators in brief. The revolving field type practical single-phase alternator has the following main parts :

Stator : The stationary armature is normally called as *stator* (stationary member). It consists of the iron core and the armature winding. (Fig. 9.2).

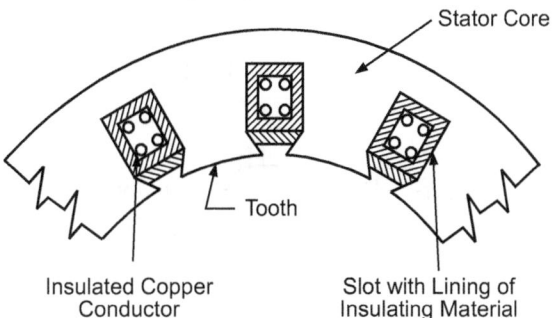

Fig. 9.2 : **Portion of an alternator stator**

The magnetic core of the stator is built-up of special steel stampings insulated from each other with paper, varnish or oxide coating. These laminations are in the form of complete rings for smaller machines and in segments for larger machines. The laminated construction of the core minimizes the iron loss occurring in it (as the stator core is continuously cut by the rotor field). The built-up core is housed in a frame which is usually fabricated from steel plates. The frame carries no flux and serves merely as a mechanical support. Both radial and axial air ducts are provided in the core for ventilation purposes. For axial ducts, the series of holes are provided through the stampings. On the other hand, radial air ducts are provided by placing spacers between the stacks of the laminations. The slots (open, semi-closed or fully-closed type) cut around the inner surface of the core hold the conductors of the armature winding. These conductors are well insulated from each other and from the core.

Rotor : The rotating field system of the alternator is normally known as *rotor* (rotating member).

In general, type of rotor construction used in an alternator, depends upon the type of primemover used to drive the alternator. In the single-phase alternators using medium-speed primemovers, like petrol or diesel engines, the number of poles is always more than two and the rotor construction that is used is invariably salient or projected pole type.

In this type of rotor, all the poles project out from the surface of the rotor. The alternators with salient pole type rotors have large diameters (to accommodate the large number of poles on the rotor) and short axial lengths. The poles built up of thick steel stampings rivetted together are either bolted or dovetailed to the rotor spider as shown in Fig. 9.3. The pole face is suitably shaped so as to obtain increasing radial air-gap length from the pole centre to pole tips. This makes the flux distribution over the armature approximately a sine wave and thereby helps to generate sinusoidal waveform of e.m.f. The overhang of the pole shoes provides mechanical support for the field coils which are often wound using rectangular copper strip.

As projected poles produce fan action, cooling is more effective in the alternators with salient-pole type rotors.

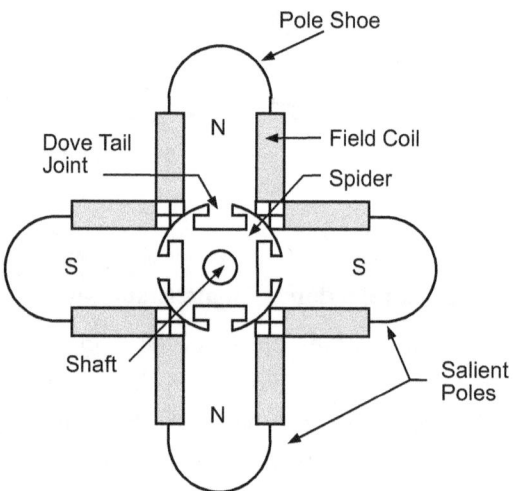

Fig. 9.3 : Salient-pole rotor

9.3.1 Excitation for Revolving Field System of an Alternator

D.C. excitation required by the field winding of the alternator is provided by using any of the following methods :

(i) The field winding of the alternator may be excited by a small d.c. generator called *an exciter*. This exciter is mounted on the same shaft with the alternator. The d.c. current is fed to the rotor (i.e. rotating field) of the alternator through slip-rings.

(ii) This method depends on the residual magnetism for initial a.c. voltage build up, after which the field is supplied with rectified voltage from the alternator itself.

(iii) With large-capacity alternators, use of slip-rings and brush arrangement presents a significant problem and involves the substantial amount of power loss. Hence, for such alternators, brushless systems that have shaft-mounted a.c. exciter and the rectifier which rotates with the rotor are in use. This avoids the need for brushes and slip-rings. The stationary field winding of the a.c. exciter requiring small d.c. current is fed from the alternator terminals after rectification.

If the d.c. excitation required for the field winding of the alternator is provided by using a separate source like shaft-mounted exciter (a self-excited d.c. generator) as mentioned in (i), then such an alternator is said to be *separately excited*. On the other hand, when a.c. current from the alternator itself is rectified and used for excitation purpose as mentioned in (ii) and (iii), it is said to be *self-excited*. Alternators using such solid-state excitation systems use silicon diodes or thyristors for rectification.

9.4 FREQUENCY OF INDUCED E.M.F.

In the case of an elementary two-pole, single-phase alternator shown in Fig. 3.3, we have seen that the e.m.f. generated in each conductor of the armature completes one cycle as it moves past both the poles (North and South). In actual practice, the alternator has more number of poles. Therefore, in general, it can be said that the e.m.f. generated in each conductor completes one cycle as it moves past one pair of poles.

If N = Speed, in revolutions per minute (r.p.m.)

P = Total number of poles, then

Number of cycles produced per revolution = $\frac{P}{2}$

∴ Frequency of generated e.m.f. (i.e. number of cycles per second),

f = (No. of cycles per revolution) × (No. of revolutions per second)

$$= \frac{P}{2} \times \frac{N}{60}$$

$$= \frac{PN}{120} \text{ hertz} \qquad \ldots (9.1)$$

Thus, there exists a definite relationship between the speed of rotation of the rotor (N), the frequency of the induced e.m.f. (f) and the number of poles (P).

9.5 SYNCHRONOUS SPEED

N in the Expression (9.1) is called the *synchronous speed* and can be defined as *the speed at which the machine must be run in order to generate the required frequency*. It is normally denoted by N_S. Thus,

$$N_S = \frac{120 \text{ f}}{P} \qquad \ldots (9.2)$$

Since the alternators operate at only one speed namely the synchronous speed, determined by the number of poles and the required line frequency, they are also called as *synchronous generators*.

50 hertz is the standard frequency which we have adopted. For this frequency, speed of the alternators with different number of poles should be as given in the following table :

No. of poles	2	4	6	8	10	12	14
Speed (r.p.m.)	3000	1500	1000	750	600	500	250

Example 9.1 : *A single-phase, 50 Hz alternator runs at 1500 r.p.m. What is the number of poles ?*

Solution : Given : $f = 50$ Hz, $N_S = 1500$ r.p.m.

Synchronous speed, $N_S = \dfrac{120\,f}{P}$

$\therefore \quad 1500 = \dfrac{120 \times 50}{P}$

$\therefore \quad$ Number of poles, $P = 4$ ... Ans.

9.6 WINDING TERMINOLOGY

Before we study the armature winding in detail, it is necessary to get acquainted with some of the commonly used terms in connection with the windings.

(i) Conductor : It is the *active length* (part actually lying in the magnetic field and in which an e.m.f. is induced) of wire or strip embedded in the slot on the armature periphery.

(ii) Turn : Every two conductors laid in a pair of slots and connected to each other form one *turn*.

(iii) Coil : A coil may consist of a single turn or may consist of many turns connected in series. A coil with one turn is called a *single-turn coil* while a coil with more than one turn is known as *multi-turn coil*.

(iv) Pole-Pitch : The pole-pitch is the centre to centre distance (over the armature periphery) between two adjacent poles. It is usually expressed in terms of *slots per pole or coil sides per pole*. e.g. if there are 24 slots, 24 coils, and 4 poles, then pole-pitch is,

$$\dfrac{24}{4} = 6 \text{ slots} \quad \text{or} \quad \dfrac{24 \times 2}{4} = 12 \text{ coil sides}$$

(v) Coil Span : It is the distance on the periphery of the armature spanned by the two sides of the coil. It is usually expressed in terms of corresponding *armature slots* (or *coil sides*).

If the coil span is exactly equal to the pole-pitch, then such a coil is called a *full-pitch coil*. On the other hand, if its span is less than a pole-pitch, it is said to be a *fractional-pitch coil*. Alternatively, this type of coil is also called a *short-pitch or chorded coil*. For example, in a 6-pole armature having 96 slots, a coil spanning 15 teeth would obviously be a fractional-pitch or chorded coil (since pole-pitch is 16). Such a coil is said to be short-pitched or chorded by one *slot-pitch*. Here, slot-pitch means the centre to centre distance between two consecutive slots.

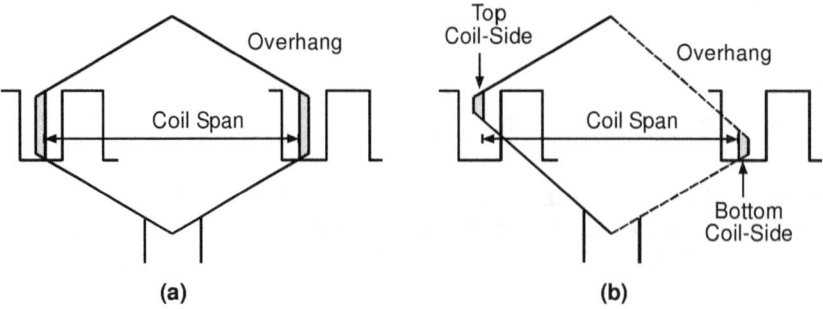

Fig. 9.4 : Single and double layer windings

The e.m.f. induced in the coil is maximum if the span of the coil is equal to the pole-pitch. This is because under this condition, the coil embraces almost whole of the useful flux per pole. However, sometimes the span is deliberately reduced as it effects a substantial saving in the copper used for end connections and gives improved performance.

(vi) Single Layer Winding : In this type of winding, the two sides of each coil are placed in the two slots separated by a distance of approximately one pole-pitch as shown in Fig. 9.4 (a). In this type of winding arrangement, since each side of a coil fully occupies the slot in which it is placed, there is only one coil side per slot. Single layer windings are rarely used for armatures of a.c. machines.

(vii) Double Layer Winding : In this type of winding arrangement, one side of every coil lies in the top half of one slot and its other side lies in the bottom half of some other slot, normally at a distance of about one pole-pitch (Fig. 9.4 b). Thus, there are at least two coil sides per slot.

9.7 SINGLE-PHASE ARMATURE WINDINGS

Fig. 9.5 (a) illustrates the cross-section of a four-pole, single-phase alternator with one slot per pole on the armature periphery and one conductor per slot. Fig. 9.5 (b) shows the developed diagram for its armature winding. The two coils connected in the wave fashion represent the wave winding in its most simplified form. Most of the alternator windings used in actual practice are the modifications of this type of simple wave winding. Fig. 9.6 shows several types of single-phase windings in their elementary forms for 4-pole alternator. Fig. 9.6 (a) shows the wave winding with multi-turn coils giving higher e.m.f. In this and the previous type of winding with single-turn coils shown in Fig. 9.5 (b), only one slot per pole is assumed. Such windings are known as *concentrated windings*.

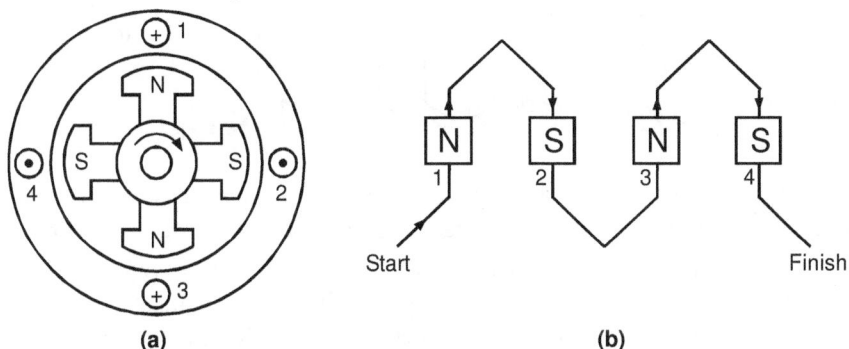

**Fig. 9.5 : (a) Cross-section of single-phase, four-pole alternator,
(b) Developed single-phase, single layer, wave type armature winding**

Even though concentrated windings give the maximum e.m.f. for a given number of conductors, they are never used in actual practice. This is because with one slot per pole, armature surface is not economically used. Also the number of conductors per slot being large, heat dissipation is poor. Moreover, with such windings, the resulting e.m.f. waveform departs considerably from the desired sinusoidal form. Hence, the winding is always distributed in several slots per pole. Such distributed windings may be *spiral* (or *concentric*), *lap* or *wave* type. Figs. 9.6 (b), (c) and (d) respectively show these types.

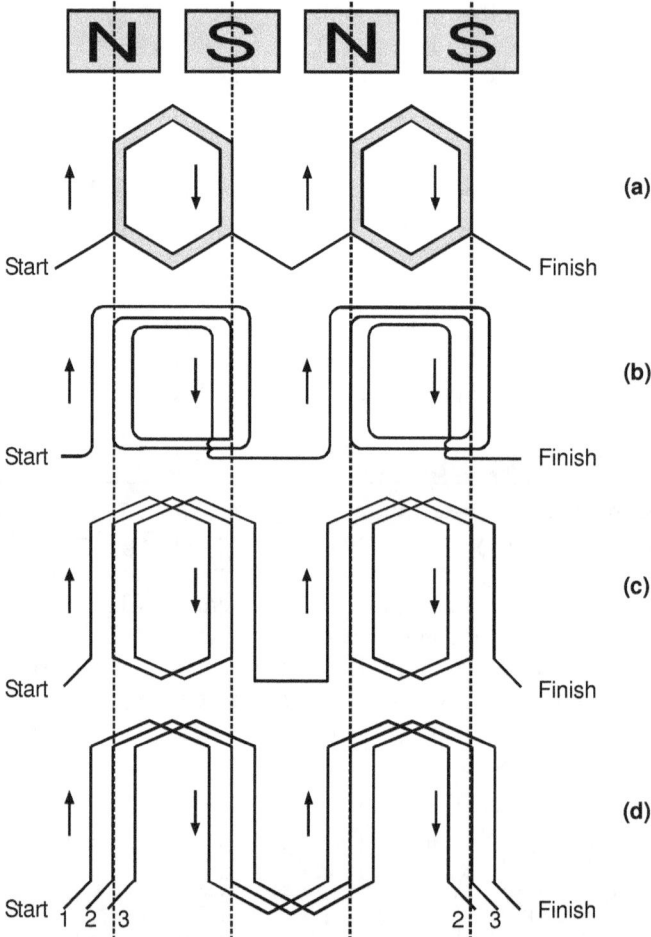

**Fig. 9.6 : Different types of single-phase, single-layer armature windings
(a) Wave winding with multi-turn coils, (b) Distributed winding with spiral coils,
(c) Distributed winding with lap coils, (d) Distributed wave winding**

In spiral windings, all the coils comprising a coil group in adjacent pole pitches are concentric. The individual coils may have a span greater or less than a pole pitch. But the average coil-span is equal to one pole-pitch. Unlike the concentric winding, in lap and wave type windings, all the coils used are identical with the same shape and pitch. These windings (i.e. lap and wave) give the same e.m.f. if the number of armature conductors, poles and other conditions are identical. This is because under such conditions, each winding has the same number of series connected armature conductors. As the end connections in the case of wave windings become somewhat problematic, they are rarely used for the armatures of the alternators.

All the above windings are *single-layer* type with only one coil side per slot. However, it is possible to arrange them as *two-layer* windings with two coil sides per slot. In fact, two layer windings are more common in a.c. machines because both, materials and space can be preserved by the use of such windings. Fig. 9.7 illustrates one such simple two-layer winding, for 4-pole alternator with one slot per pole using diamond shaped lap type coils. From the figure, it will be observed that alternate coils are reverse connected so that their e.m.f.s are additive.

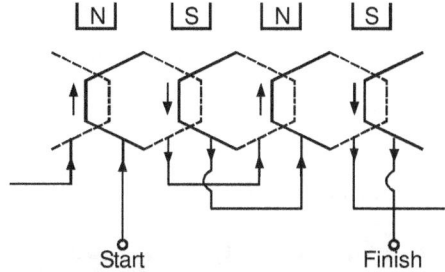

Fig. 9.7 : Single-phase, two-layer winding with 1 slot per pole using diamond-shaped lap type coils

9.8 E.M.F. EQUATION OF AN ALTERNATOR

Let, Z = Total number of armature conductors in series

ϕ = Flux per pole, in webers

P = Number of poles

N = Speed in r.p.m.

f = Frequency of induced e.m.f., in hertzs

We shall assume the alternator to be of rotating field type as is the general case.

Flux cut by each armature conductor per revolution of the rotor

$$= \phi \cdot P \text{ webers}$$

Time taken by the rotor to make one revolution

$$= \frac{60}{N} \text{ seconds}$$

Hence, in accordance with Faraday's law of electromagnetic induction,

Average e.m.f. induced in each conductor due to flux cutting

$$= \frac{\text{Flux cut}}{\text{Time taken}} = \frac{\phi \cdot P}{60/N} = \frac{\phi PN}{60}$$

$$= 2\phi \cdot f \text{ volts} \qquad \left(\because f = \frac{P \cdot N}{120}\right)$$

Now, we know that

R.M.S. value = (Average value) × (Form factor)

If the waveform of the induced e.m.f. is assumed to be sinusoidal, its form factor will be obviously 1.11. Hence,

R.M.S. value of e.m.f. per conductor

$$= 1.11 \times 2 \phi \cdot f$$
$$= 2.22 \phi \cdot f \text{ volts} \qquad \ldots (9.3)$$

To begin with, for simplicity, let us assume that the armature winding is full-pitch concentrated type (arranged in 1 slots per pole) similar to that shown in Fig. 9.5 (b) except that coils used may be multi-turn. With such winding, as far as resultant e.m.f. is concerned, the e.m.f.s induced in all the series connected conductors will be in phase with one another and therefore get added arithmetically to give the total e.m.f. Hence,

R.M.S. value of e.m.f. in a full-pitch concentrated winding

$$= 2.22 \, \phi \cdot f \cdot Z \text{ volts} \qquad \ldots (9.4)$$
$$= 4.44 \, \phi \cdot f \cdot T \text{ volts} \qquad \ldots (9.5)^*$$

where T = Total number of turns in series $\left(= \dfrac{Z}{2}\right)$

9.8.1 Effect of Distributing the Winding on Induced E.M.F.

As already mentioned previously in Section 9.7, in order to achieve economical utilization of armature surface, better heat dissipation and improvement in the e.m.f. waveform, the windings used in actual practice for the armatures of the alternators are always distributed type. We know that in such a winding, all the coils are distributed in two or more slots per pole in the manner similar to that shown in Figs. 9.6 (b), (c) and (d). This causes phase difference in the e.m.fs induced in the various coils constituting a group. Hence obviously, the resultant coil group e.m.f. which is given by the phasor sum of the individual coil e.m.fs is less than the arithmetic sum of these coil e.m.fs. To illustrate this, consider a single-phase, full pitch, single-layer, lap type winding distributed in 3 slots per pole. There being 3 slots per pole,

$$\text{Slot pitch, } \alpha = \dfrac{180°}{3} = 60 \text{ electrical degrees}$$

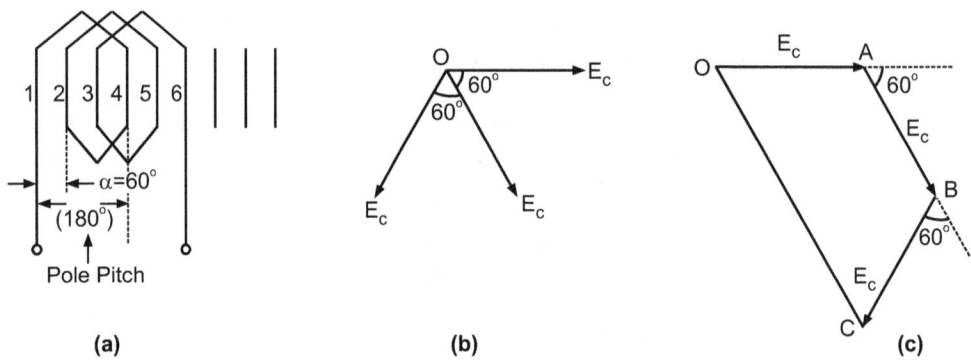

(a)   (b)   (c)

Fig. 9.8 : Representation of one coil group belonging to a given single-phase, lap type, single-layer, distributed winding using full-pitch coils and its resultant e.m.f.

Fig. 9.8 (a) shows one coil group of a given single-phase winding with 3 full pitch coils connected in series and displaced from each other through 60 electrical degrees on the armature periphery. The e.m.f.s in the two consecutive coils will, therefore, have a phase difference of 60° electrical degrees. Fig. 9.8 (b) shows the phasor diagram for the three coil e.m.f.s wherein E_c

---

*   *This expression is similar to that for the e.m.f. in the case of a transformer except for the fact that ϕ here is the flux per pole.*

denotes the e.m.f. per coil. The closing side (OC) of the phasor polygon shown in Fig. 9.8 (c) will then be resultant coil group e.m.f. It will be obviously less than the arithmetic sum of the three coil e.m.fs. As a result of this, the total e.m.f. that can be obtained with a distributed winding is always less than that due to concentrated winding having an equal number of turns. *The ratio of the e.m.f with a distributed winding to the e.m.f. with a concentrated winding having an equal number of turns is called the distribution factor or breadth factor* of the winding and is usually represented by K_d.

Let us now derive the expression for the distribution factor by considering the most general case of the single-phase winding distributed in m slots per pole. Obviously, there will be m coils connected in series per coil group and these coils will have mutual displacement of one slot pitch of α electrical degrees given by

$$\alpha = \frac{180°}{\text{Number of slots per pole}} = \frac{180°}{m}$$

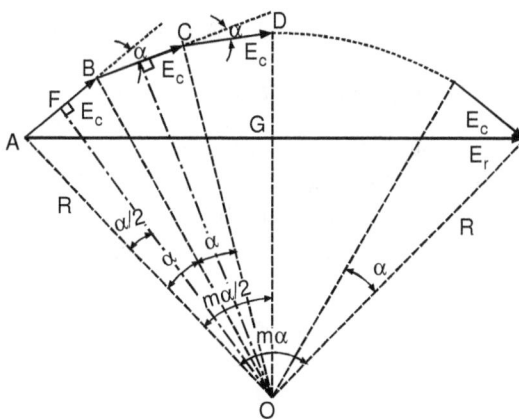

Fig. 9.9 : Coil group e.m.f. with large number of coils per group

Hence, the phase difference between the e.m.fs induced in the two consecutive coils will also be α electrical degrees. Fig. 9.9 shows the phasor polygon formed by the e.m.fs of the individual coils, each being of value E_c. The closing side of the polygon gives the resultant coil group e.m.f. E_r. Let the perpendicular bisectors of AB, BC, CD, ... etc. representing the individual coil e.m.fs meet at O which gives the centre of the circumscribing circle of radius R and passing through the points A, B, C, D, ... etc. (shown with the help of dotted line). All the phasors representing individual coil e.m.fs are thus the chords of this circle. Now, $\triangle$ OBA and $\triangle$ OBC being similar,

$$\angle OBA = \angle OBC$$

Further, $\angle OBA + \angle OBC + \alpha = 180°$

∴ $\quad 2 \angle OBA = 180° - \alpha \qquad (\because \angle OBA = \angle OBC)$

Or, $\quad \angle OBA = \left(90° - \frac{\alpha}{2}\right)$

Hence from right angled $\triangle$ OBF,

$$\angle BOF = 90° - \angle OBF = 90° - \angle OBA$$

$$= 90° - \left(90° - \frac{\alpha}{2}\right)$$

$$= \frac{\alpha}{2}$$

$\therefore \qquad \angle AOB = \angle BOC = \angle COD = \alpha$

Thus, each phasor representing the coil e.m.f. subtends an angle at the centre of the circumscribing circle equal to the phasor difference between the two phasors representing the induced e.m.fs in the two consecutive coils. Hence,

Angle subtended at the centre of the circumscribing circle by the phasor representing the resultant coil group e.m.f. E_r is

$$= m\alpha$$

Now, from Fig. 9.9, it is evident that resultant coil group e.m.f.,

$$E_r = 2\,AG = 2R\sin\frac{m\alpha}{2} \quad \left(\because \angle AOG = \frac{m\alpha}{2}\right) \qquad \ldots (9.6)$$

If all the coils of the coil group under consideration were concentrated in the same pair of slots (as is the case in concentrated winding with 1 slot per pole), all the coil e.m.fs would have been in phase and resulting coil group e.m.f. would have been

$$= \text{Arithmetic sum of the coil e.m.fs}$$

$$= m \times E_c$$

$$= m \times 2R\sin\frac{\alpha}{2} \qquad \ldots (9.7)$$

Therefore by definition,

$$\text{Distribution factor, } K_d = \frac{\text{E.M.F. with distributed winding}}{\text{E.M.F. with concentrated winding}}$$

$$= \frac{[\text{Phasor sum of coil e.m.fs in one coil group of a distributed winding}]}{[\text{Arithmetic sum of coil e.m.fs in the same coil group}]}$$

$$= \frac{2R\sin(m\alpha/2)}{m \times 2R\sin(\alpha/2)} \qquad \text{(from the equations 9.6 and 9.7)}$$

$$= \frac{\sin(m\alpha/2)}{m\sin(\alpha/2)} \qquad \ldots (9.8)$$

It should be remembered that the value of the distribution factor is always less than unity.

9.8.2 Effect of using Fractional-Pitch Coils on Induced E.M.F.

Instead of using a winding with full-pitch coils, the coil span is often intentionally reduced for improving the e.m.f. waveform, and to achieve the saving in copper and the greater stiffness of the coils due to the shorter end connections. The stiffness of the coils is more important particularly in the case of two-pole, high-speed alternators. Use of this type of windings also makes it possible to use a number of slots which is not an exact multiple of the number of poles.

Such windings using coils with spans less than a pole pitch are often called *fractional pitch windings*. The only disadvantage of using such a winding with *fractional-pitch* coils (also called *short-pitch* or *chorded coils*) is that the induced e.m.f. per coil and hence the total e.m.f. is reduced. *The ratio of the e.m.f. with a fractional-pitch winding to the e.m.f. with full-pitch winding having an equal number of turns is known as pitch, coil-span or chording factor* and is normally denoted by K_p. It can be computed as follows :

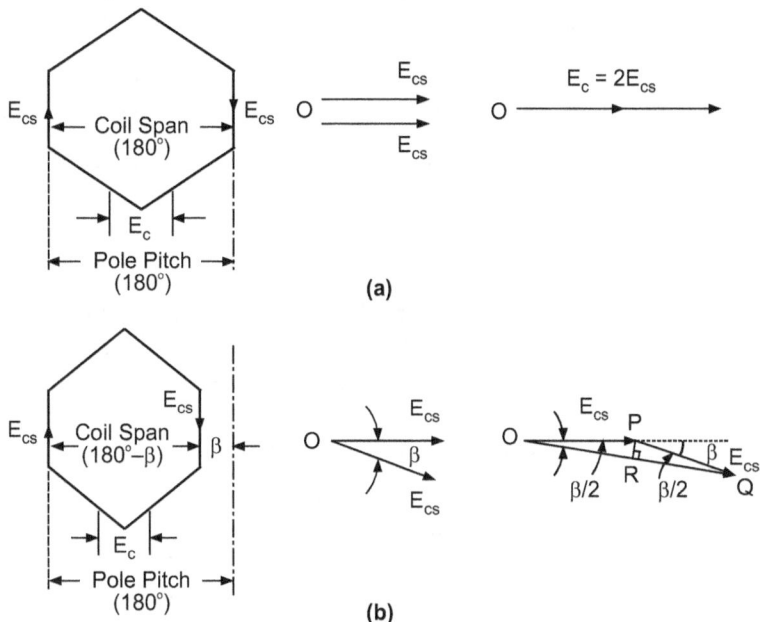

Fig. 9.10 : (a) E.M.F. with full-pitch coil, (b) E.M.F. with short-pitch coil

Fig. 9.10 (a) shows the full-pitch coil (having its two coil sides a pole-pitch apart). Let E_{cs} be the e.m.f. induced in its each coil side. With such a full-pitch coil, the e.m.fs induced in its two sides differ in time phase by 180 electrical degrees. But the coil connections are such that they act in the same general direction round the coil. Hence obviously they are in phase as far as the resultant e.m.f. is concerned. Therefore, as illustrated by the phasor diagram of Fig. 9.10 (a),

The resultant coil e.m.f., E_c

= Arithmetic sum of the e.m.fs induced in the two coil sides of a coil

= $2 E_{cs}$ ... (9.9)

Now, consider the same coil when short-pitched by β electrical degrees [i.e. with coil-span of (180° – β)] shown in Fig. 9.10 (b). In such a coil, the e.m.fs induced in the two coil sides will not be in phase as in the case of full-pitch coil but will differ by an angle β (called *chording angle*) as illustrated by the phasor diagram of Fig. 9.10 (b). From the geometry of the phasor triangle shown in Fig. 9.10 (b), it follows that in this case,

The resultant coil e.m.f., E_c

= Phasor sum of the e.m.fs induced in the two coil sides of a coil

= OQ = OR + RQ

But $\quad$ OR $= $ RQ $ = E_{cs} \cos \dfrac{\beta}{2}$

$\therefore \quad E_c = 2 E_{cs} \cos \dfrac{\beta}{2}$ ... (9.10)

$\therefore$ Pitch or coil-span factor,

$$K_p = \dfrac{\text{E.M.F. with a fractional-pitch winding}}{\text{E.M.F. with a full-pitch winding}}$$

$$= \dfrac{\text{E.M.F. induced in a fractional-pitch coil}}{\text{E.M.F. induced in a full-pitch coil}}$$

$$= \dfrac{2 E_{cs} \cos (\beta/2)}{2 E_{cs}} \quad \text{(from the equations 9.9 and 9.10)}$$

$$= \cos (\beta/2) \quad \text{... (9.11)}$$

9.8.3 General Expression for the E.M.F. of an Alternator

Assuming the general case of fractional-pitch distributed winding, Equation (9.5) derived earlier for the r.m.s. value of e.m.f. in full-pitch concentrated winding can now be modified as follows :

R.M.S. value of e.m.f. generated

$$= 4.44 \, K_d \cdot K_p \cdot \phi \cdot f \cdot T \quad \text{... (9.12)}$$

where, $\quad K_d =$ Distribution factor of the winding

$\qquad K_p = $ Pitch factor of the winding

Example 9.2 : *A 12-pole, single-phase alternator has 144 slots, $\dfrac{2}{3}$ of which are wound with 8 conductors per slot. The flux per pole is 42 mWb sinusoidally distributed. The distribution factor is 0.829 and the coil span factor is unity. If the speed is 500 r.p.m., find the frequency and e.m.f. generated.*

Solution : Given : P = 12, ϕ = 42 mWb, K_d = 0.829, K_p = 1, Number of slots = 144, Conductors per slot = 8, N_S = 500 r.p.m.

$$\text{Frequency } f = \dfrac{PN_S}{120} = \dfrac{12 \times 500}{120} = \textbf{50 Hz} \quad \text{... Ans.}$$

$$\text{Actual slots used } = \dfrac{2}{3} \times 144 = 96$$

Total number of armature conductors, Z = 96 × 8 = 768

Number of turns connected in series,

$$T = \dfrac{Z}{2} = \dfrac{768}{2} = 384$$

$\therefore \quad$ E.M.F. generated, E_o = 4.44 K_d K_p ϕ f T

$$= 4.44 \times 0.829 \times 1 \times 42 \times 10^{-3} \times 50 \times 384$$

$$= \textbf{2968.16 volts} \quad \text{... Ans.}$$

Example 9.3 : *A single-phase, 4-pole, 50 Hz, 24 slot alternator has its armature coils short-pitched by one slot. Find the distribution factor and pitch factor.*

Solution : Number of slots = 24, Number of poles = 4

$$\text{Number of slots per pole} = \frac{24}{4} = 6$$

∴ Number of coils connected in series per coil group, m = 6.

$$\text{Slot pitch, } \alpha = \frac{180°}{\text{Slots per pole}} = \frac{180°}{6} = 30°$$

∴ $$\text{Distribution factor, } K_d = \frac{\sin(m\alpha/2)}{m \sin(\alpha/2)} = \frac{\sin(6 \times 30°/2)}{6 \sin(30°/2)}$$

$$= 0.644 \quad \quad \text{... Ans.}$$

The coils are short-pitched by 1 slot.

∴ Angle of chording, β = 1 slot-pitch = 30°

∴ Pitch factor, K_p = cos (β/2) = cos (30°/2) = cos 15°

$$= 0.9659 \quad \quad \text{... Ans.}$$

Example 9.4 : *A single-phase, 4-pole, 50 Hz alternator has 48 slots having 12 conductors per slot. The coil span is 165° electrical. Calculate the generated e.m.f. on open circuit, if the flux per pole is 40 mWb.*

Solution : Number of slots per pole = $\frac{48}{4}$ = 12.

∴ Number of coils connected in series per coil group, m = 12

$$\text{Slot pitch, } \alpha = \frac{180°}{\text{Slots per pole}} = \frac{180°}{12} = 15°$$

∴ $$\text{Distribution factor, } K_d = \frac{\sin(m\alpha/2)}{m \sin(\alpha/2)}$$

$$= \frac{\sin(12 \times 15°/2)}{12 \sin(15°/2)}$$

$$= 0.6384$$

Angle of chording, β = 180° − 165° = 15°

∴ Pitch factor, K_p = cos (β/2) = cos (15°/2)

$$= 0.9914$$

Total number of armature conductors,

$$Z = 48 \times 12 = 576$$

∴ Total number of turns in series,

$$T = \frac{Z}{2} = \frac{576}{2} = 288$$

∴ Generated e.m.f., $E_0 = 4.44 \, K_d \, K_p \, \phi \, f \, T$

$= 4.44 \times 0.6384 \times 0.9914 \times 40 \times 10^{-3} \times 50 \times 288$

$= \mathbf{1618.63 \ V}$ ... Ans.

9.9 PARAMETERS OF ARMATURE WINDING

Armature Resistance : The effective resistance of the armature winding (R_a) under a.c. conditions is always greater than its d.c. resistance (as measured with direct current). This is because with alternating currents, there is additional energy loss (over normal I^2R loss under d.c. conditions) on account of various reasons, the principal among these being

(i) Eddy currents and magnetic hysteresis in the surrounding material.

(ii) Eddy currents and unequal current distribution (due to skin effect*) in the conductors themselves.

The exact value of the effective resistance varies widely from 1.25 to 1.75 times the d.c. resistance, depending upon design.

Armature Leakage Reactance : All the flux lines produced by the currents flowing in the armature conductors of an alternator when on load, do not cross the air gap and thereby modify the value and distribution of the main field produced by the poles, but some of them merely link with the conductors themselves (Fig. 9.11). This flux is called *leakage flux*. Leakage flux makes the armature winding inductive. As a result, in addition to resistance, it also possesses leakage reactance which is numerically given by the following expression.

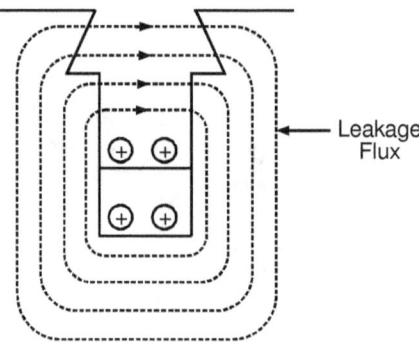

Fig. 9.11 : Slot leakage flux

Leakage reactance, $X_L = 2\pi f \, L$ ohms, where L is the leakage inductance of the armature winding in henrys.

In practice, the leakage reactance of the armature winding is much larger than its resistance. Hence, the resistance of the armature winding is often neglected in alternator regulation calculations.

---

* *Uniform distribution of current throughout the cross-section of a conductor exists only for direct current. With a.c., this current distribution becomes nonuniform, the current density increasing from the interior towards the surface (inductance of the filaments near the surface of the conductor being lower than that of the interior filaments). This phenomenon is called **skin effect**.*

9.10 CONCEPT OF SYNCHRONOUS REACTANCE AND IMPEDANCE

The terminal voltage of an alternator changes with the increase of load (field excitation and speed being kept constant). The factors which influence the terminal voltage of the alternator with increase of load include

(i) Armature resistance (R_a), causing a voltage drop $I_a R_a$.

(ii) Armature leakage reactance (X_L), causing a voltage drop $I_a X_L$.

(iii) Armature reaction, causing a change in the effective air-gap flux which in turn affects the terminal voltage. Here it should be noted that the effect of magnetic field produced by the currents flowing in the armature conductors on the value and distribution of the main magnetic field (produced by the field winding) of the machine is known as armature reaction.

First two factors have already been discussed in the previous section. The effect of armature reaction on terminal voltage under different power factor conditions is exactly similar to that of armature leakage reactance. For unity power-factor loads, these two factors produce little change in the terminal voltage. For lagging power-factor loads, both of them cause their greatest reduction in the terminal voltage and for leading power-factor loads, they cause their greatest rise in terminal voltage. In both cases, the changes caused in terminal voltage are proportional to the armature current. Because of this similarity in the effects, the effect of armature reaction may be accounted for by attributing a fictitious reactance of X_a to the armature winding. The value of X_a is such that $I_a X_a$ represents the voltage drop due to armature reaction.

The nature of the effects produced by the armature reaction and armature leakage reactance on the terminal voltage of the alternator under different power factor conditions being exactly similar, they are sometimes combined together. The sum of the fictitious reactance X_a attributed to the armature winding to account for armature reaction effect and its leakage reactance X_L is called *synchronous reactance* (X_s). Thus,

Synchronous reactance, $X_s = X_a + X_L$ ohms

Further, combining this synchronous reactance with the resistance R_a of the armature winding, we get the quantity known as *synchronous impedance* (Z_s). Obviously,

Synchronous impedance, $Z_s = \sqrt{R_a^2 + X_s^2}$ ohms.

The concept of synchronous reactance is very helpful in simplifying the analysis of performance characteristics of the alternators.

9.11 PHASOR DIAGRAMS OF AN ALTERNATOR ON LOAD

The single-phase alternator may be represented by the equivalent circuit shown in Fig. 9.12 (a) wherein the armature resistance R_a, the leakage reactance X_L and the fictitious reactance X_a for armature reaction are separated from the *ideal* alternator. E_o is the e.m.f. induced by the field flux alone. This e.m.f. obviously corresponds to the e.m.f. which would be induced under no-load condition i.e. with no armature current or armature reaction. E is the air gap e.m.f. (i.e. the e.m.f. after allowing for armature reaction) and V is the terminal voltage.

Fig. 9.12 (b) shows the simplified form of the equivalent circuit after X_a and X_L are combined to form synchronous reactance X_s. The relationship between the induced e.m.f. E_o and the terminal voltage V can now be easily derived from the equivalent circuit of an alternator.

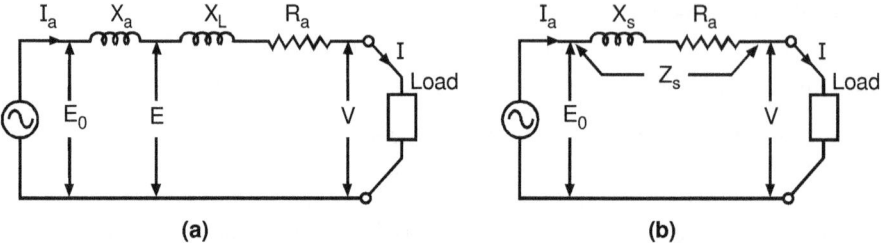

Fig. 9.12 : Equivalent circuits of an alternator

In X_a, a drop $I_a X_a$ (leading I_a by 90°) occurs to take account of armature reaction. The net e.m.f. is the air-gap e.m.f. E. The terminal voltage V is less than E by further phasor drops $I_a R_a$ (in phase with I_a) and $I_a X_L$ (leading I_a by 90°) in resistance and leakage reactance of the armature. Thus, the phasor sum of V, $I_a R_a$, $I_a X_L$ and $I_a X_a$ is the induced e.m.f. (open circuit e.m.f.) E_o. This relationship between E_o and V can be mathematically written as

$$\bar{E}_o = \bar{V} + \bar{I}_a [R_a + j(X_L + X_a)]$$

$$= \bar{V} + \bar{I}_a (R_a + j X_s)$$

$$= \bar{V} + \bar{I}_a \bar{Z}_s$$

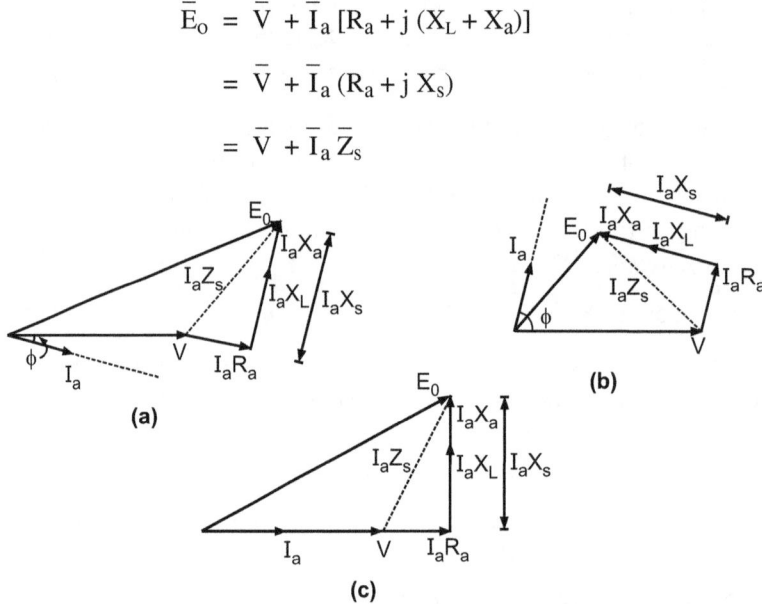

Fig. 9.13 : Phasor diagrams of an alternator with $\bar{V}$ as a reference phasor at (a) lagging power factor load, (b) leading power factor load, (c) unity power factor load

Based on above relationship, Fig. 9.13 shows the phasor diagrams for the alternator supplying different power factor loads. While drawing these phasor diagrams, we have taken the terminal voltage $\bar{V}$ as a reference phasor. These diagrams can also be drawn taking the armature current $\bar{I}_a$ as a reference phasor as shown in Fig. 9.14.

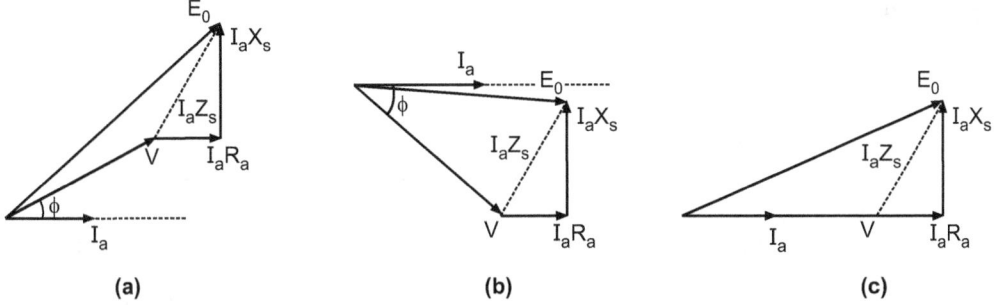

Fig. 9.14 : Phasor diagrams of an alternator with $\bar{I}_a$ as a reference phasor at (a) lagging power factor load, (b) leading power factor load, (c) unity power factor load

If other things are known, the magnitude of E_o can be obtained with the help of some simple expressions which can be derived with the help of these phasor diagrams as shown below :

(i) Lagging Power Factor Load : Fig. 9.14 (a) shows the phasor diagram (with $\bar{I}_a$ as a reference phasor) for the alternator supplying lagging power factor load. From this diagram, taking projections of phasors representing V, $I_a R_a$ and $I_a X_s$ along I_a and perpendicular to I_a, we have

Sum of the individual components along I_a,

$$\bar{X} = V \cos\phi + I_a R_a$$

Sum of the individual components perpendicular to I_a,

$$\bar{Y} = V \sin\phi + I_a X_s$$

$$\therefore \quad E_o = \sqrt{(\bar{X})^2 + (\bar{Y})^2}$$
$$= \sqrt{(V \cos\phi + I_a R_a)^2 + (V \sin\phi + I_a X_s)^2} \quad \ldots (9.13)$$

The above expression can also be derived by using complex algebra as follows :

$$\bar{E}_o = \bar{V} + \bar{I}_a \bar{Z}_s = (V \cos\phi + j V \sin\phi) + (I_a + j0)(R_a + jX_s)$$
$$= (V \cos\phi + I_a R_a) + j(V \sin\phi + I_a X_s)$$
$$\therefore \quad E_o = \sqrt{(V \cos\phi + I_a R_a)^2 + (V \sin\phi + I_a X_s)^2}$$

Alternatively, referring to the phasor diagram (with $\bar{V}$ as a reference phasor) for the alternator supplying lagging power factor load shown in Fig. 9.13 (a), the magnitude of E_o can also be determined from the expression obtained by resolving all the phasors along V and perpendicular to V as shown below :

Sum of the individual components along V,

$$\bar{X} = V + I_a R_a \cos\phi + I_a X_s \sin\phi$$

Sum of the individual components perpendicular to V,

$$\overline{Y} = I_a X_s \cos\phi - I_a R_a \sin\phi$$

$$\therefore \quad E_o = \sqrt{(\overline{X})^2 + (\overline{Y})^2}$$

$$= \sqrt{(V + I_a R_a \cos\phi + I_a X_s \sin\phi)^2 + (I_a X_s \cos\phi - I_a R_a \sin\phi)^2} \quad \ldots (9.14)$$

The above Expression (9.14) can also be derived using complex algebra as follows :

$$\overline{E}_o = \overline{V} + \overline{I}_a \overline{Z}_s = (V + j\,0) + (I_a \cos\phi - j\,I_a \sin\phi)(R_a + j X_s)$$

$$= (V + I_a R_a \cos\phi + I_a X_s \sin\phi) + j(I_a X_s \cos\phi - I_a R_a \sin\phi)$$

$$\therefore \quad E_o = \sqrt{(V + I_a R_a \cos\phi + I_a X_s \sin\phi)^2 + (I_a X_s \cos\phi - I_a R_a \sin\phi)^2}$$

(ii) Leading Power Factor Load : Referring to corresponding phasor diagram shown in Fig. 9.14 (b) and resolving the phasors V, $I_a R_a$ and $I_a X_s$ along I_a and perpendicular to I_a, we have

Sum of the individual components along I_a,

$$\overline{X} = V \cos\phi + I_a R_a$$

Sum of the individual components perpendicular to I_a,

$$\overline{Y} = -V \sin\phi + I_a X_s$$

$$\therefore \quad E_o = \sqrt{(\overline{X})^2 + (\overline{Y})^2}$$

$$= \sqrt{(V \cos\phi + I_a R_a)^2 + (-V \sin\phi + I_a X_s)^2}$$

$$= \sqrt{(V \cos\phi + I_a R_a)^2 + (V \sin\phi - I_a X_s)^2} \quad \ldots (9.15)$$

The above expression can also be derived by using complex algebra as follows :

$$\overline{E}_o = \overline{V} + \overline{I}_a \overline{Z}_s = (V \cos\phi - j V \sin\phi) + (I_a + j0)(R_a + jX_s)$$

$$= (V \cos\phi + I_a R_a) + j(-V \sin\phi + I_a X_s)$$

$$\therefore \quad E_o = \sqrt{(V \cos\phi + I_a R_a)^2 + (-V \sin\phi + I_a X_s)^2}$$

$$= \sqrt{(V \cos\phi + I_a R_a)^2 + (V \sin\phi - I_a X_s)^2}$$

Alternatively resolving all the phasors along V and perpendicular to V (refer to the phasor diagram of Fig. 9.13 b), we have

Sum of the individual components along V,

$$\overline{X} = V + I_a R_a \cos\phi - I_a X_s \sin\phi$$

Sum of the individual components perpendicular to V,

$$\overline{Y} = I_a R_a \sin\phi + I_a X_s \cos\phi$$

$$\therefore \quad E_o = \sqrt{(\overline{X})^2 + (\overline{Y})^2}$$
$$= \sqrt{(V + I_aR_a \cos\phi - I_aX_s \sin\phi)^2 + (I_aR_a \sin\phi + I_aX_s \cos\phi)^2}$$
... (9.16)*

The above Expression (9.16) can also be derived by the use of complex algebra. That is

$$\overline{E}_o = \overline{V} + \overline{I}_a \overline{Z}_s = (V + j\,0) + (I_a \cos\phi + j\,I_a \sin\phi)(R_a + j\,X_s)$$
$$= (V + I_aR_a \cos\phi - I_aX_s \sin\phi) + j(I_aR_a \sin\phi + I_aX_s \cos\phi)$$
$$\therefore \quad E_o = \sqrt{(V + I_aR_a \cos\phi - I_aX_s \sin\phi)^2 + (I_aR_a \sin\phi + I_aX_s \cos\phi)^2}$$

It will be observed that the expressions (9.15) and (9.16) for E_o under leading power factor conditions can be obtained from the corresponding expressions (9.13) and (9.14) for E_o under lagging power factor conditions simply by taking power factor angle to be negative i.e. by substituting ϕ by $-\phi$ in these expressions.

(iii) Unity Power Factor Load : From the phasor diagram of Fig. 9.13 (c) or 9.14 (c), it is obvious that

$$E_o = \sqrt{(V + I_a R_a)^2 + (I_a X_s)^2} \qquad \qquad ... (9.17)$$

Since under unity power factor conditions, power factor angle ϕ is zero, the above expression can also be obtained from the Expression (9.13) or the Expression (9.14) for E_o under lagging power factor conditions by putting $\phi = 0$ in them.

Example 9.5 : *A 50 kVA, 500 V, single-phase alternator has an effective armature resistance of 0.2 Ω and synchronous impedance of 1.71 Ω. Find the generated e.m.f. when this alternator is supplying full-load current at (i) 0.8 lagging power factor, (ii) 0.8 leading power factor, (iii) unity power factor.*

Solution : Given : Alternator rating = 50 kVA, V = 500 volts, R_a = 0.2 Ω, Z_s = 1.71 Ω.

Synchronous reactance, $X_S = \sqrt{Z_s^2 - R_a^2} = \sqrt{(1.71)^2 - (0.2)^2}$
$$= 1.698 \, \Omega$$

Full-load current, I = Full-load armature current, I_a
$$= \frac{kVA \times 10^3}{V} = \frac{50 \times 10^3}{500} = 100 \, A$$

(i) 0.8 Lagging Power Factor :

Generated e.m.f., $E_0 = \sqrt{(V \cos\phi + I_aR_a)^2 + (V \sin\phi + I_aX_S)^2}$
$$= \sqrt{(500 \times 0.8 + 100 \times 0.2)^2 + (500 \times 0.6 + 100 \times 1.698)^2}$$
$$= \textbf{630.17 volts} \qquad \qquad \text{... Ans.}$$

---

* *The approximate expression, $E_o \approx V + I_aR_a \cos\phi \pm I_aX_s \sin\phi$ (with + sign for lagging power factor and – sign for leading power factor) is not used in the case of alternators as it leads to a considerable error, particularly when power factor is near unity.*

(ii) 0.8 Leading Power Factor :

$$\text{Generated e.m.f., } E_0 = \sqrt{(V \cos \phi + I_a R_a)^2 + (V \sin \phi - I_a X_S)^2}$$

$$= \sqrt{(500 \times 0.8 + 100 \times 0.2)^2 + (500 \times 0.6 - 100 \times 1.698)^2}$$

$$= \mathbf{439.72 \text{ volts}} \qquad \text{... Ans.}$$

(iii) Unity Power Factor :

$$\text{Generated e.m.f., } E_0 = \sqrt{(V + I_a R_a)^2 + (I_a X_S)^2} \qquad (\because \cos \phi = 1)$$

$$= \sqrt{(500 + 100 \times 0.2)^2 + (100 \times 1.698)^2}$$

$$= \mathbf{547.02 \text{ volts}} \qquad \text{... Ans.}$$

9.12 VOLTAGE REGULATION OF AN ALTERNATOR

If under the conditions represented by Fig. 9.12, the load is disconnected, the speed and the field excitation remaining the same, the terminal voltage will change from V to E_0 (the effects of armature resistance, leakage reactance and armature reaction being absent). This change in the terminal voltage (i.e. the numerical difference between E_o and V) is known as *voltage regulation* of the alternator for the given conditions of load and power factor. Thus, voltage regulation of an alternator may be defined *as the change in its terminal voltage when a given load is thrown off, the excitation and speed remaining constant.* It is usually expressed as a fraction or percentage of terminal voltage on load*. Hence in general, if V is the terminal voltage for a given load and E_o is the open-circuit voltage (i.e. no-load terminal voltage), then

$$\text{Voltage regulation} = \frac{E_o - V}{V} \text{ per unit} \qquad \text{... (9.18)}$$

$$= \frac{E_o - V}{V} \times 100 \text{ per cent} \qquad \text{... (9.19)}$$

Its value depends not only on the load current but also on the power factor of the load. Fig. 9.15 shows the load characteristics (relationships between terminal voltage and load current) of an alternator under different power factor conditions. For unity and lagging power factor conditions, there is always a voltage drop with the increase in load current. As such, the voltage regulation is always positive. However, if the load is capacitive with low leading power factor, the terminal voltage may rise with the increase of load current (see phasor diagram of Fig. 9.13 b) and the regulation will then be negative. Since the voltage regulation of an alternator depends on the load power factor, it is always specified with the load power factor.

---

* *The voltage regulation of an alternator is usually expressed as a fraction or percentage of its terminal voltage on load because the alternator usually works at constant terminal voltage. To achieve this, the excitation is constantly adjusted to suit different load conditions using automatic voltage regulators.*

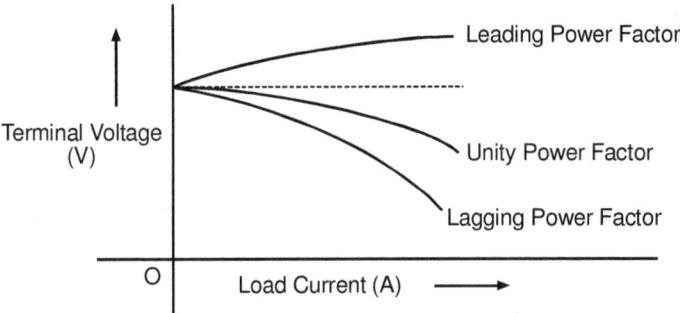

Fig. 9.15 : Load characteristics of an alternator under different power factor conditions

Alternators are designed to operate at a desired regulation limit while supplying full load usually at 0.8 lagging power factor. The amount of regulation of commercial alternators may vary from 15% in older types to 100% in the newer units (higher value being helpful in limiting the short-circuit current) at 0.8 lagging power factor. A knowledge of voltage regulation at different power factors is usually essential because it shows how closely a machine will maintain its voltage under the various conditions of load. This knowledge is also important from the point of voltage control, parallel operation and protection of alternators.

Example 9.6 : *A 55 kVA, 1100 V, single-phase alternator has an effective armature resistance of 0.3 Ω and synchronous impedance of 7 Ω. Find the full-load voltage regulation of the alternator at 0.87 leading power factor.*

Solution : Alternator rating = 55 kVA, V = 1100 volts, R_a = 0.3 Ω, Z_S = 7 Ω.

Synchronous reactance, $X_S = \sqrt{Z_S^2 - R_a^2} = \sqrt{7^2 - (0.3)^2} = 6.994\ \Omega$

Full-load current, I = Full-load armature current, I_a

$$= \frac{kVA \times 1000}{V} = \frac{55 \times 1000}{1100} = 50\ A$$

$\cos \phi$ = 0.87 leading, $\sin \phi$ = 0.493

$\therefore$ Generated e.m.f., $E_0 = \sqrt{(V \cos \phi + I_a R_a)^2 + (V \sin \phi - I_a X_S)^2}$

$$= \sqrt{(1100 \times 0.8 + 50 \times 0.3)^2 + (1100 \times 0.493 - 50 \times 6.994)^2}$$

$$= 990.9\ \text{volts}$$

$\therefore$ Full-load voltage regulation

$$= \frac{E_0 - V}{V} \times 100 = \frac{990.9 - 1100}{1100} \times 100$$

$$= -\ 9.92\ \% \qquad \qquad \qquad \text{... Ans.}$$

9.13 DETERMINATION OF VOLTAGE REGULATION

Many methods have been devised for determining the voltage regulation of an alternator. In the case of a small machine, regulation may be determined by actually loading it. But this method of direct loading is out of the question for large machines because of the prohibitive cost of providing motive power and auxiliary apparatus for absorbing the power output. In fact, in the case of very large machines, it may be impossible to obtain sufficient power required for testing purposes and to find an artificial load of sufficient magnitude. With polyphase alternators, there is the added difficulty of obtaining a balanced load. The large machines are, therefore, generally tested indirectly by simulating the load conditions. A number of such indirect methods have been developed. All these methods are based on simple no-load test and require comparatively little power. In the following section, we shall study only the method of direct loading.

9.13.1 Voltage Regulation by Direct Loading

As already mentioned earlier, in the case of a small machine, regulation at any desired load condition and power factor can be found by directly loading the machine as follows :

Circuit Diagram : Fig. 9.16 shows the schematic circuit diagram for conducting the load test on an alternator for finding its regulation. The loading arrangement may consist of lamp banks, choking coils.

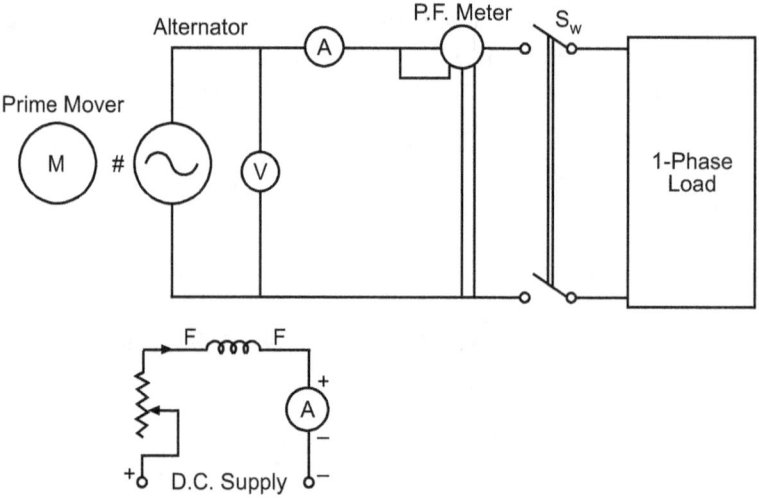

Fig. 9.16 : Schematic diagram for load test on an alternator

Test Procedure : The alternator is driven at synchronous speed using a suitable prime mover. By adjusting the excitation, its terminal voltage is raised to the rated (or slightly higher) value. Next, the alternator is loaded upto full load at desired power factor with the excitation adjusted to give the rated voltage per phase (V) under this condition. Finally, keeping the speed and excitation constant, the entire load is then thrown off by disconnecting the switch S_w and the open-circuit voltage or no-load terminal voltage E_o is observed. All these observations are recorded in a tabular form shown below.

Table for Observations

Sr. No.	V	I	Power Factor	E_o

Regulation Calculations : From the above observations, regulation of the alternator at any desired power factor can be calculated as follows :

$$\text{Regulation} = \frac{\text{(No-load terminal voltage} - \text{Full-load terminal voltage)}}{\text{Full-load terminal voltage}} \times 100$$

$$= \frac{(E_o - V)}{V} \times 100 \text{ per cent}$$

Example 9.7 : *When a single-phase alternator is fully loaded at 0.8 lagging power factor, the terminal voltage is 230 V. On throwing of this load, with speed and field excitation being maintained constant, the voltage rises to 300 V. Calculate its voltage regulation.*

Solution : Full-load terminal voltage,

$$V = 230 \text{ volts}$$

No-load terminal voltage,

$$E_o = 300 \text{ volts}$$

$\therefore$
$$\text{Regulation} = \frac{(E_o - V)}{V} \times 100 = \frac{(300 - 230)}{230} \times 100$$

$$= \textbf{30.43 per cent} \qquad \text{... Ans.}$$

9.14 APPLICATIONS OF SINGLE-PHASE ALTERNATORS

As said earlier, three-phase alternators are the most commonly used machines for generating electrical power on large scale for commercial purposes. All modern day power stations are equipped with three-phase alternators for generation of electrical power. For emergency power supply, however, small single-phase alternators driven by petrol or diesel engines are in common use in homes, shops and small commercial establishments. For the field work, where regular supply is not available, engine driven single-phase alternator is an obvious choice. Ships, aircrafts, automobiles are also equipped with these alternators.

9.15 EXERCISES

9.15.1 Review Questions

1. Discuss the advantages of rotating field type single-phase alternators.
2. With neat sketches, briefly comment on the main constructional features of single-phase alternators.
3. Differentiate between self and separate excitation in reference to alternators.
4. Derive an expression for the frequency of the e.m.f. generated by an alternator in terms of its speed and number of poles.
5. With neat sketches, comment on the different types of single-phase windings used in a.c. armatures.

6. Distinguish between a concentrated winding and a distributed winding. Explain why distributed windings are preferred over concentrated windings for the armatures of alternators.

7. What is meant by fractional-pitch winding ? State the principal advantages of such a winding.

8. Derive the e.m.f. equation for an alternator with sinusoidal flux distribution. Also derive the expressions for distribution factor and pitch factor.

9. Explain clearly what is meant by synchronous impedance of a single-phase alternator.

10. Draw the phasor diagrams of an alternator on load at unity, lagging and leading power factors.

11. What is voltage regulation of an alternator ? On what factors does the regulation of an alternator depend ?

12. Describe with the aid of connection diagram, the method of finding voltage regulation of an alternator by direct loading. State the limitations of this method.

9.15.2 Examples for Practice

1. Determine the synchronous speed of the single-phase alternator having the following data : (i) 50 Hz, 6 poles, (ii) 50 Hz, 4 poles. (1000 r.p.m., 1500 r.p.m.)

2. A part of an alternator winding consists of 6 coils in series, each coil having an e.m.f. of 10 V (r.m.s. value) induced in it. The coils are placed in successive slots. If the slot pitch in terms of electrical phase angle between the adjacent slots is 30°, calculate the e.m.f. of the six coils in series. (38.64 V)

3. A 4-pole, single-phase alternator has an armature with 24 slots and 8 conductors per slot. It rotates at 1500 r.p.m. and the flux per pole is 0.05 Wb. Calculate the e.m.f. generated if the distribution factor is 0.96 and the coils used are full-pitched. (1022.98 V)

4. A 600 V, 60 kVA, single-phase alternator has an effective armature resistance of 0.2 Ω and synchronous reactance of 2.27 Ω. Calculate its full-load voltage regulation at 0.8 power factor lagging. (28.51%)

CHAPTER 10
SINGLE-PHASE A.C. MOTORS

10.1 INTRODUCTION

As the name itself indicates, single-phase motors are designed to operate on a single-phase supply. In general, single-phase motors have less satisfactory operating characteristics (particularly with regards to efficiency, starting torque and power factor) as compared to polyphase motors. However, advances in the design have made single-phase motors quite satisfactory in their smaller sizes (fractional horse power range). As a result, now-a-days, millions of them are in use in the commercial, agricultural and domestic fields.

Wide variation in starting and maximum torque requirements of the various applications has led to the development of many different types of single-phase motors. Hence, selection of a motor meeting the requirements of a particular application and at the same time, having reasonably low cost has become possible. Of all the types of single-phase motors, the single-phase induction motors and universal motors are the commonly used types. Hence in this chapter, we shall restrict our study to these two types of single-phase motors only.

10.2 SINGLE-PHASE INDUCTION MOTORS

Fig. 10.1 schematically represents 2-pole, single-phase induction motor.

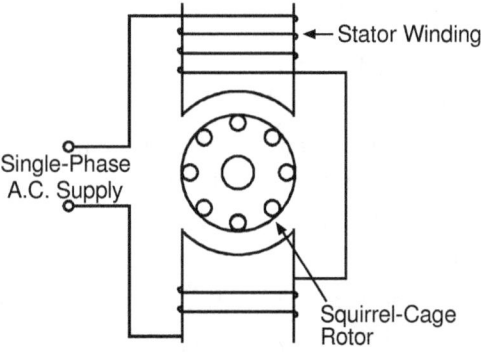

Fig. 10.1 : Schematic representation of a 2-pole, single-phase induction motor

Operating Principle : When a single-phase stator winding is connected to a source of alternating voltage, the current flowing through this winding produces a resultant field which alternates along the axis of the winding. Such a field, varying or pulsating sinusoidally with the time along a fixed space axis while acting on a stationary cage rotor* cannot produce rotation.

---

* *The rotor winding of the actual motor consists of a series of uninsulated aluminium or copper bars, accommodated in the slots of the rotor core and permanently short-circuited at each end by a conducting ring. Thus, the rotor construction resembles a squirrel cage.*

To understand this, consider a single-phase induction motor shown in Fig. 10.2 with the rotor at rest. When single-phase supply is given to the stator winding, current flowing through this winding produces an alternating flux ϕ_s acting along the axis of the winding. This alternating field induces an e.m.f. in the rotor conductors by transformer action. The rotor circuit being closed, this e.m.f. called *transformer e.m.f.* sets up current through the rotor conductors.

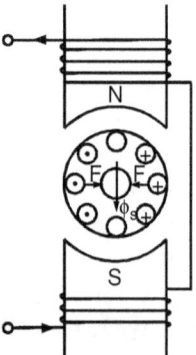

Fig. 10.2 : Transformer e.m.f.s in the rotor of a single-phase induction motor

If it is assumed that the stator flux ϕ_s is acting in the downward direction and increasing positively at a particular instant as shown in Fig. 10.2, then the current in the rotor conductors must flow in such a direction as to oppose this flux ϕ_s (Lenz's law). The direction of the current in the rotor conductors, therefore, will be as shown in Fig. 10.2. The application of Fleming's left hand rule shows that under this condition, the force experienced by the conductors on the left side of the rotor is just opposite to that experienced by the conductors on the right side of the rotor. The rotor will, therefore, experience no torque and the motor thus develops no inherent starting torque. As a result, it is not self-starting.

However, it has been observed that if the rotor is given an initial rotation in any direction, the single-phase induction motor develops torque and the rotor continues to pick up speed in that particular direction. This typical behaviour of single-phase induction motor can be explained with the help of the following theory :

Double Revolving Field Theory : As already mentioned previously, when a single-phase stator winding is connected to a source of alternating voltage, the current flowing through this winding produces a field which varies sinusoidally with time along a fixed space axis. According to double revolving field theory, such a flux can be resolved into two equal sinusoidal fields rotating in opposite directions at synchronous speed*, each having a maximum value equal to one half that of the given field as illustrated in Fig. 10.3 (a).

---

*   Synchronous speed, $N_S = \dfrac{120 f}{P}$ rpm

     where f = Supply frequency, in hertz

                               P = Number of poles

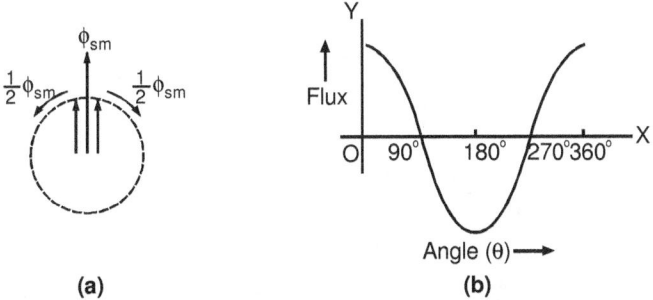

Fig. 10.3 : (a) Single-phase alternating stator field represented by two oppositely rotating fields, (b) Resultant of two oppositely rotating fields

Here, ϕ_{sm} is assumed to be the maximum value of the stator field, ϕ_s. From Fig. 10.3 (b), it can be easily verified that the resultant of these two component fields gives the original alternating stator field. Each of the component rotating fields of the stator field produces a torque in a manner similar to that produced by a rotating magnetic field in polyphase (e.g. two-phase or three-phase) induction motor.

Actually, the action of the polyphase induction motor is based on the fact that when a set of windings on its stator is connected to a polyphase a.c. supply, the rotating field of constant magnitude is produced. This rotating field, in effect, is similar to the rotation of field poles in space by some mechanical means. When this rotating field is cut by the stationary rotor conductors, according to Faraday's laws of electromagnetic induction, an e.m.f. is induced in the rotor conductors. Since, all the rotor conductors together form a closed circuit, the induced e.m.f. in the rotor conductors sets up rotor currents. According to Lenz's law, the direction of the induced current in the rotor conductors is always such as to oppose the very cause producing it. In this case, the cause producing the current in the rotor conductors being the relative speed between the rotating flux of the stator and the stationary rotor conductors, the rotor starts rotating in the same direction as that of the flux to reduce the relative speed between them.

But in the case of single-phase induction motor, the torques produced by the two component rotating fields are in opposite directions. The total torque developed by the motor is given by the resultant of these two torques. The complete torque-speed curves (extended into the other quadrant) for the two oppositely rotating component fields considered independently are shown with the help of dotted lines in Fig. 10.4. The resultant torque-speed curve (solid line) given by the sum of the two component curves is also shown in the figure. From this resultant torque-speed curve, it can be observed that at starting when the rotor is at standstill, the torques developed by two component rotating fields are exactly equal and opposite. Therefore, the torque developed by the motor is zero. Consequently, the single-phase induction motor is not self starting. However, if the rotor is given an initial rotation in any direction, the net torque developed causes the rotor to continue to rotate in the direction in which it is initially rotated and the motor gives the same type of performance as polyphase induction motor.

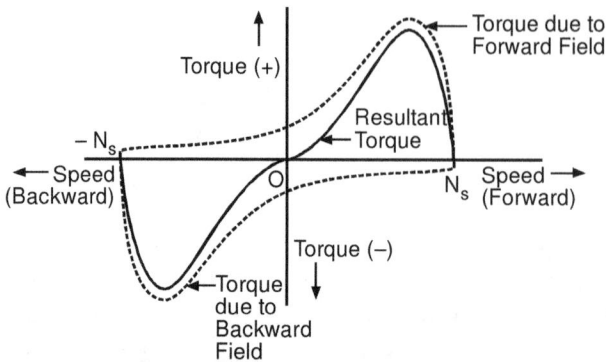

Fig. 10.4 : Torque-speed curves for the two oppositely rotating component fields and resultant torque-speed curve in a single-phase induction motor

10.3 TYPES OF SINGLE-PHASE INDUCTION MOTORS

We have seen that a single-phase induction motor has an alternating field and not a rotating field and, therefore, has no starting torque at all. However, they are made self starting by providing the various special arrangements which enable them to have a rotating magnetic field at least at starting. Accordingly, the motors are of the following commonly used types.

10.3.1 Resistance Split-Phase Motors

These motors are commonly known as *split-phase motors*. The stator of this type of motor carries two windings, one called the *main winding* (M) and the other known as *auxiliary winding* (A) or *starting winding*. The axes of these windings are displaced from each other usually by an angle of 90 electrical degrees in space. The rotor (G) of the motor is of normal cage type. Fig. 10.5 (a) shows the motor schematically and Fig. 10.5 (b) shows its connection diagram.

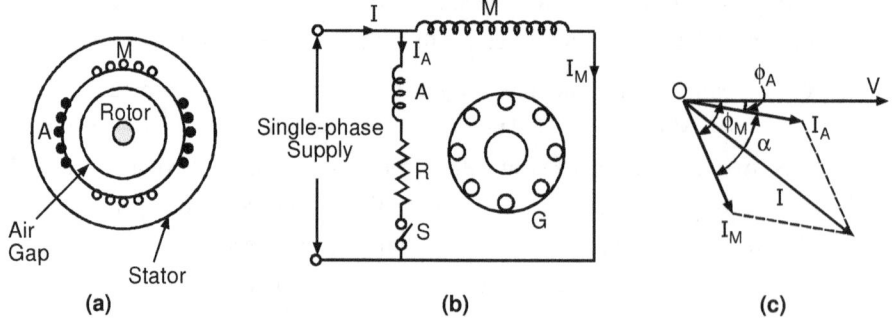

Fig. 10.5 : (a) Schematic representation of a split-phase type, single-phase induction motor, (b) Connection diagram, (c) Phasor diagram

The auxiliary winding along with the series resistor (R) is connected across the main winding. Instead of connecting externally such a high resistance in series with an auxiliary winding, its resistance may be increased by choosing a high resistance fine copper wire for winding purposes. The resistance to reactance ratio of the auxiliary winding circuit being higher than the main winding, currents through them are nearly in quadrature (Fig. 10.5 c). The resulting fluxes due to these currents are, therefore, displaced in space through 90° and have considerable time phase difference. A rotating magnetic field is, therefore, produced (as in a two-phase motor). The motor thus develops a starting torque. Once the motor is started, the auxiliary winding is disconnected with the help of a centrifugal switch (S) at about 75 to 80% of the synchronous speed.

Torque-Speed Characteristic : Fig. 10.6 shows the torque-speed characteristic of a resistance split-phase motor. The starting torque of this type of motor is generally 125 to 150 % of full-load torque.

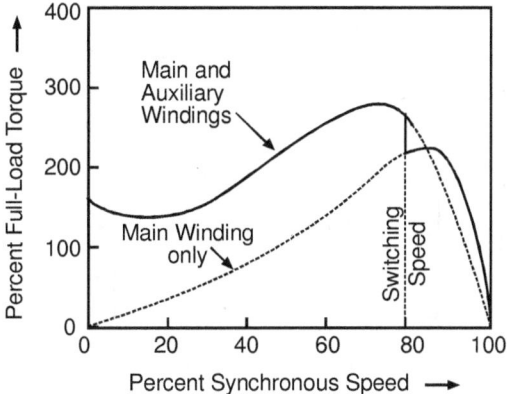

Fig. 10.6 : Typical torque-speed characteristic of a resistance split-phase motor

Reversal of Rotation : The direction of rotation of this type of motor can be reversed by reversing the terminal connections of either the main or the auxiliary winding.

Applications : These motors are commonly used in small electric tools, fans, blowers, centrifugal pumps, domestic refrigerator units, oil burners, washing machines, etc.

10.3.2 Capacitor Split-Phase Motors

These motors are commonly called as *capacitor motors*. This type of motor is similar in construction to resistance split-phase type, single-phase induction motor considered above, except that the resistance in series with the auxiliary winding is replaced by a capacitor. The high starting torque is the outstanding feature of a capacitor motor because the fluxes produced by two windings on the stator can be made to have a time phase difference of practically 90°. Thus, this type of motor becomes essentially a two-phase motor. Due to use of a capacitor, the motor also has better power factor. Following are the three main types of the capacitor motors :

(i) Capacitor-Start Motors : In this case, the auxiliary winding (A) in series with a capacitor (C) is in the circuit only during the starting period and then disconnected with the help of a centrifugally operated starting switch (S) after the motor reaches 75 to 80 % of synchronous speed. This type of motor is shown schematically in Fig. 10.7 (a) and Fig. 10.7 (b) shows the phasor diagram.

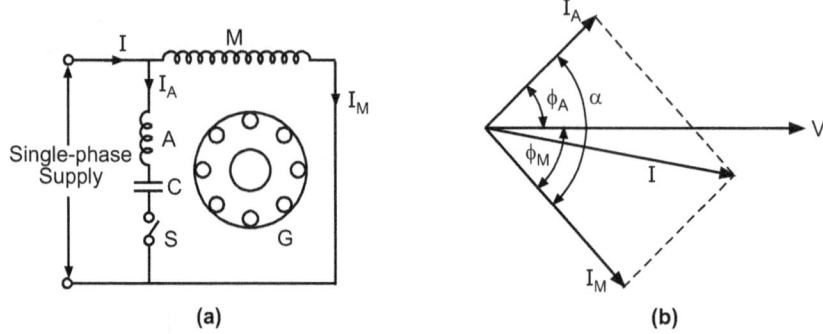

Fig. 10.7 : (a) Schematic representation of a capacitor-start, single-phase induction motor, (b) Phasor diagram

Torque-Speed Characteristic : Torque-speed characteristic of this type of motor is shown in Fig. 10.8. The starting torque of this type of motor is generally of the order of 350 to 400 % of full-load torque. Thus, high starting torque is the outstanding feature of this motor.

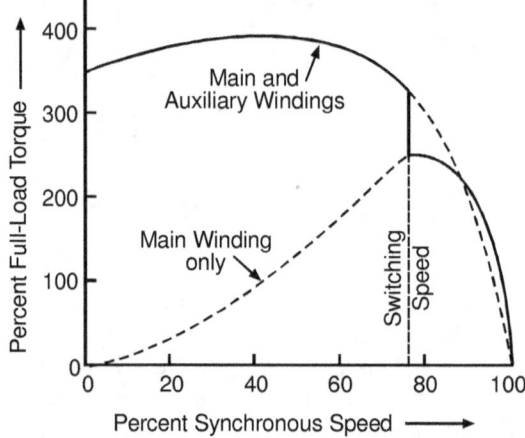

Fig. 10.8 : Typical torque-speed characteristic of a capacitor-start motor

(ii) **Permanent-Split or Single Value Capacitor Motors :** In this type of motor, the auxiliary winding (A) along with the capacitor (C) is in the circuit for both, starting and running (Fig. 10.9 a).

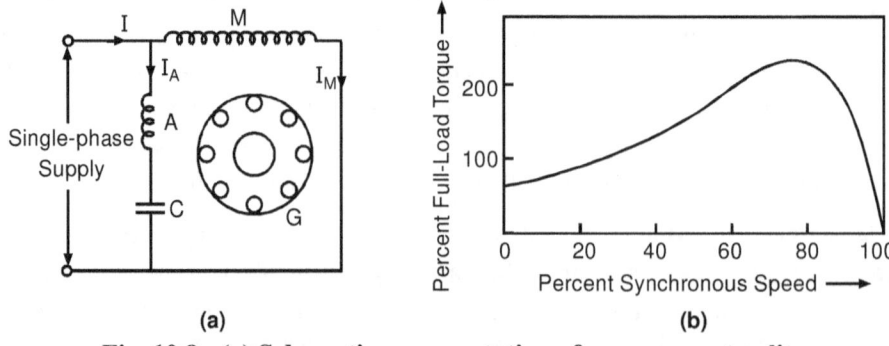

Fig. 10.9 : (a) Schematic representation of a permanent-split, capacitor type single-phase induction motor, (b) Typical torque-speed characteristic

Torque-Speed Characteristic : Since the capacitor and auxiliary winding remains permanently in the circuit, this improves the power factor and running performance of the motor. However, the starting torque of this type of motor is not good (it is only 50 to 100 % of full-load torque) as the value of the capacitor has to be chosen as a compromise between best starting and best running conditions. The resulting torque-speed characteristic of this type of motor is shown in Fig. 10.9 (b).

(iii) Capacitor Start and Run Or Two Value Capacitor Motors : This type of motor uses two capacitors (C_1 and C_2) for starting, one of them (C_2) being cut out for running by means of a centrifugal switch (S) when the motor reaches about 75 to 80 % of synchronous speed. Fig. 10.10 (a) schematically illustrates this type of motor.

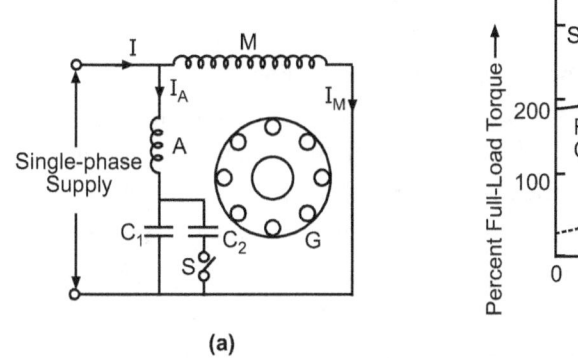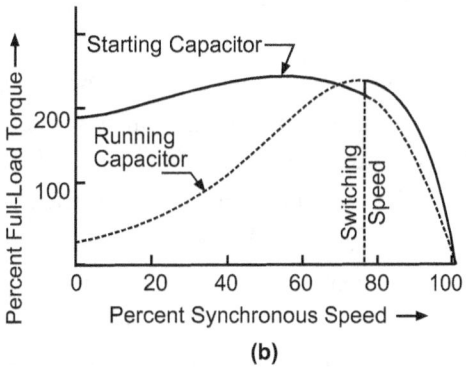

Fig. 10.10 : (a) Schematic representation of a capacitor start and run, single-phase induction motor, (b) Typical torque-speed characteristic

Torque-Speed Characteristic : This type of motor has better starting and running performance with improved power factor. Fig. 10.10 (b) shows the typical torque-speed characteristic for such a motor.

Reversal of Rotation in Capacitor Split-Phase Motors : Reversal of direction of rotation can be obtained in all types of capacitor split-phase motors by changing the terminal connections of one of the windings.

Applications of Capacitor Split-Phase Motors : These motors are in very common use for fans, blowers, drilling machines, grinders, compressors, conveyors, refrigerators, air conditioners, washing machines, domestic water pumps, etc.

10.3.3 Shaded-Pole Motors

The most usual form of a motor of this type has a rotor (G) of squirrel cage type and the stator (M) with salient poles (P_1, P_2). In addition to its own exciting coil (C_1, C_2), each pole carries a copper shading coil, band or ring (B_1, B_2) on one of its unequally divided parts (Fig. 10.11). Production of torque in this type of motor can be explained as below :

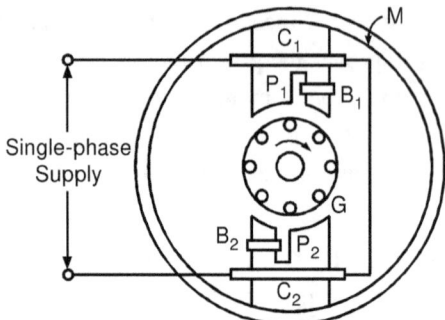

Fig. 10.11 : Shaded-pole type, single-phase induction motor

Operating Principle : When the single-phase supply is given to the stator winding, an alternating flux is produced. Fig. 10.12 (a) shows the waveform for the sinusoidally varying alternating stator current and the flux produced by it. The distribution of this flux in the pole area is greatly influenced by the magnitude of the induced e.m.f. in the shading ring by transformer action. To examine this, let us consider three instants of time, namely t_1, t_2 and t_3 on the waveform for the stator current. At the instant when $t = t_1$, the rate of rise of stator current and hence that of stator flux being high, large e.m.f. is induced in the shading ring. The direction of this induced e.m.f. and hence the current set up by it in the short-circuited shading ring will be such as to oppose the rise of the stator current (Lenz's law). The opposing flux produced by the induced current in the shading ring makes stator flux distribution in the pole area non-uniform. There is crowding of flux in the non-shaded portion of the pole and magnetic axis (MA) lies along the middle of this part. (Fig. 10.12 b).

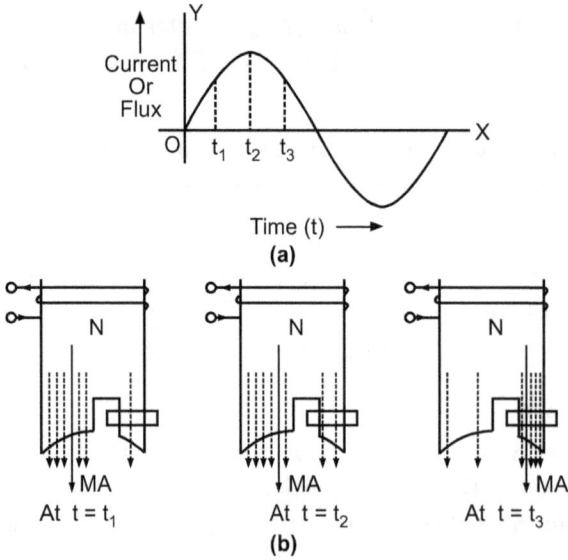

Fig. 10.12 : Production of torque in a shaded-pole type, single-phase induction motor

At the instant when t = t_2, even though the stator current is at its maximum, the rate of change of current and hence that of stator flux is minimum. Under this condition, the induced e.m.f. in the shading ring is negligible and there being practically no opposing flux, stator flux distribution in the pole area will be uniform. As a result of this, the position of magnetic axis (MA) is shifted towards the centre line of the pole.

At the instant when t = t_3, the stator current which is rapidly decreasing, again induces large e.m.f. in the shading ring. The direction of this e.m.f. and resulting induced current in the shading ring is now such as to oppose the decrease in the stator current. The flux produced by a current in the shading ring, therefore, strengthens the flux in the shaded portion of the pole. Consequently, the magnetic axis gets shifted to the middle of the shaded part of the pole. This sequence is repeated even in the negative half cycle of the stator current. This periodic shift in the stator flux from the unshaded to the shaded part of the pole gives to some extent rotating field effect and produces a low starting torque.

Torque-Speed Characteristic : Fig. 10.13 shows the typical torque-speed characteristic of this type of motor. The starting torque of this type of motor is only about 40 to 50 % of full-load torque.

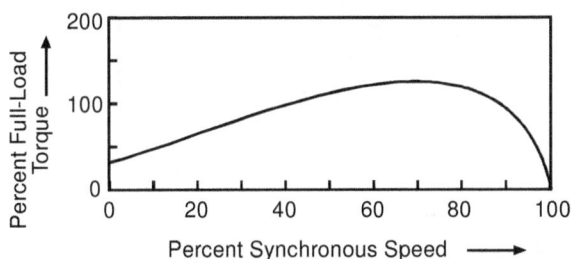

Fig. 10.13 : Typical torque-speed characteristic of a shaded-pole motor

Reversal of Rotation : The shaded-pole motor generally has a definite direction of rotation which cannot be reversed. However, if such reversal is essential, it can be achieved by providing two shading coils, one on each end of every pole. Then by open-circuiting one set of shading coils and short-circuiting the other set, desired direction of rotation can be achieved.

Applications : Due to absence of centrifugal switch, construction of the motor of this type is simple and robust. However, the motor has low efficiency and low power factor, and its starting torque is very poor. Therefore, such motors are suitable for only small powers and where the starting conditions are easy e.g. they are commonly employed for driving small fans, motorised valves, recording instruments, record players, gramophones, toy motors, photocopying machines, hair dryers, advertising displays, etc.

10.4 UNIVERSAL MOTORS

An a.c. series motor because of the simultaneous reversal of field and armature current, develops a unidirectional torque and has general characteristics similar to those of the d.c. series motor. The principal constructional difference between d.c. and a.c. series motors is that the entire field structure of the a.c. series motor is laminated to reduce the eddy currents created in the cores by the alternating flux.

Universal motors are small capacity series motors designed to operate on either direct current or single-phase alternating current supply of approximately the same voltage, with nearly similar operating characteristics. Normally the frequency of the a.c. supply used is upto 50 Hz.

Constructional Features : Two types of universal motors are in use, namely, *non-compensated* and *compensated*. The non-compensated motor is usually built with concentrated or salient poles (Fig. 10.14). On the other hand, compensated motor has distributed field windings (main field and compensating winding). Hence, the stator of such a motor resembles to that of a split-phase induction motor. The compensating winding in this type of motor is fitted to improve its performance under fluctuating load conditions. Both these types of motors have a wound armature similar to that of a small d.c. motor. Fig. 10.15 shows the connection diagrams for these motors.

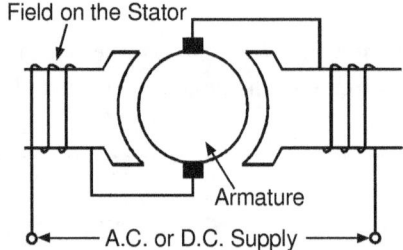

Fig. 10.14 : Cross-sectional view of a non-compensated type universal motor

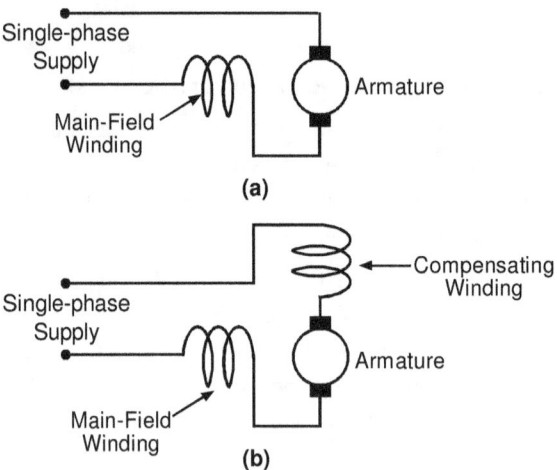

Fig. 10.15 : Connection diagrams of an universal motor
(a) Non-compensated type, (b) Compensated type

Speed-Torque Characteristics : Speed-torque characteristics of a non-compensated universal motor, for both a.c. and d.c. operations are shown in Fig. 10.16 (a). Similarly, Fig. 10.16 (b) shows the speed-torque characteristics of a compensated universal motor.

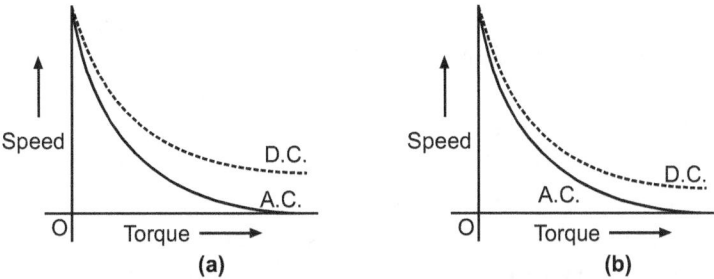

Fig. 10.16 : (a) Speed-torque characteristics of a non-compensated universal motor, (b) Speed-torque characteristics of a compensated universal motor

From these figures, it will be observed that the compensated motor has better *universal characteristics* i.e. it has nearly the same operating characteristics on d.c. as well as on a.c. supply. Depending upon their ratings, universal motors are usually designed for full-load operating speeds ranging between 3000 to 20000 r.p.m. and if necessary, are provided with in-built speed reduction gears for low speed applications. Normally, the friction and windage losses in small universal motors are sufficient to limit their no-load speeds to a safe value.

Reversal of Rotation : For universal motors, reversal can be achieved by reversing the connections to either the field or the armature winding.

Applications : Even though compensated type universal motors have more superior characteristics, non-compensated motors are in more general use, particularly for small power applications. This is because they are less expensive and simpler in construction. Being high-speed motors, universal motors are smaller in size than other types for a given output. Hence, these motors are used where light weight is important. High starting torque is also their outstanding feature. The usual applications of the universal motors are for domestic appliances like vacuum cleaners, food mixers, coffee grinders, sewing machines, hair driers, electric shavers, etc. Their other applications include blowers, mechanical computing machines, portable tools like drilling machines and other small power drives.

10.5 EXERCISES

10.5.1 Review Questions

1. Explain the principle of working of a single-phase induction motor with the help of double revolving field theory.
2. Discuss why single-phase induction motors do not have a starting torque. Describe with the aid of diagram of connections and phasor diagrams, various methods used to obtain a starting torque in the case of single-phase induction motors.
3. Compare different types of single-phase induction motors and state their applications.
4. Explain the principle of split-phasing used in single-phase induction motors. Name the different methods employed. Explain each of them.
5. Explain why the starting torque of a capacitor split-phase type, single-phase induction motor is better than resistance split-phase type, single-phase induction motor.
6. How is the direction of rotation of resistance split-phase type and capacitor split-phase type single-phase induction motors reversed ?

7. Explain the principle of working of a shaded-pole, single-phase induction motor. Draw its torque-speed characteristic and state its applications.
8. Is it possible to change the direction of rotation of a shaded-pole type, single-phase induction motor ? Explain your statement.
9. What is an universal motor ? Comment briefly on its constructional features and speed-torque characteristics. Mention its applications.
10. How is the direction of rotation of the universal motor reversed ?

10.5.2 Classified Theory Questions from University Papers

1. Why is single-phase induction motor not self-starting ?
   (Answer : Section 10.2) **(May 2012/4 Marks)**
2. Explain the construction and working principle of a single-phase induction motor.
   (Answer : Section 10.2) **(May 2011/8 Marks)**
3. Why is single-phase induction motor not self-starting ? How it is made self-starting ?
   (Answer : Sections 10.2, 10.3) **(December 2009/8 Marks)**
4. Explain how the single-phase induction motor is made self-starting. State the different methods.
   (Answer : Sections 10.3, 10.3.1, 10.3.2, 10.3.3) **(May 2009/6 Marks)**
5. Write a short note on split-phase single-phase induction motor.
   (Answer : Section 10.3.1) **(May 2012/6 Marks)**
6. Explain the construction and working principle of a split-phase induction motor. State any four applications of it.
   (Answer : Section 10.3.1) **(December 2008, 2011/8 Marks)**
7. With the help of a neat diagram, explain the working of :
   (i) Capacitor-start capacitor-run motor,
   (ii) Shaded-pole motor.
   (Answer : Sections 10.3.2, 10.3.3) **(December 2010/12 Marks)**
8. Explain the working principle of a shaded-pole induction motor.
   (Answer : Section 10.3.3) **(May 2008; December 2012/6 Marks)**
9. Draw a neat diagram and explain the working of a shaded-pole motor.
   (Answer : Section 10.3.3) **(May 2009/6 Marks)**
10. State various types of a single-phase induction motor. Explain any one of them.
    (Answer : Sections 10.3.1, 10.3.2, 10.3.3) **(May 2010/8 Marks)**
11. State the applications of single-phase induction motors and explain the working of an universal motor.
    (Answer : Sections 10.3.1, 10.3.2, 10.3.3, 10.4) **(May 1012/6 Marks)**
12. Explain the construction and working principle of an universal motor. State its applications.
    (Answer : Section 10.4) **(May 2011; December 2011/8 Marks)**

SHIVAJI UNIVERSITY
UNIVERSITY QUESTION PAPERS
Basic Electrical Engineering
Dec. 2014

Time : 3 HoursTotal Marks : 100

Section - I

1. **Answer any Two**

   (a) State and explain Kirchhoff's laws as applied to electrical circuits. [08]

   (b) An electric kettle heats 5 litres of water from 30 degree. Centigrade to 90 degree centigrade in 10 minutes. Calculate current drawn from 250 V supply and electrical energy input by kettle if kettle efficiency is 80% and heat capacity of water to be 4190 J/Kg. K and assuming mass of 1 litre of water to be 1 kg. [08]

   (c) Describe similarities between electric and magnetic circuits. Also magnetic leakage and fringing as applied to magnetic circuit. [08]

2. **Answer any Two**

   (a) Derive an expression for impedance of R-L-C series circuit. [08]

   (b) Resistance of 20 ohm, inductance of 0.2 H and capacitance of 68 microfarad are connected in series across 200 V, 50 Hz, single phase ac supply. Calculate current drawn by circuit and power consumed. [08]

   (c) What is power factor? How power factor can be improved by use of capacitor? [08]

3. **Answer any Two**

   (a) Explain construction and working of fluorescent tube light. Also state its advantages and disadvantages. [09]

   (b) Explain working of fuse. What advantages MCB is having over fuse? [09]

   (c) Describe construction and working of induction type single phase energy meter. [09]

Section - II

4. **Answer any Two**

   (a) Explain the difference between a single phase and a poly phase system. What are the advantages of three phase system over single phase system. Define - Symmetrical system, Balanced load. [08]

   (b) Explain the difference between a line voltage and a phase voltage, a line current and a phase current.

   For delta connected load obtain numerical relationship between,

(i) Line current and Phase current

   (ii) Line voltage and Phase voltage [08]

(c) Explain how the three phase voltage is induced in three phase generator. What is a phase sequence? Deduce the relation between number of poles, frequency and speed of an alternator. [08]

5. **Answer any Two**

   (a) With the help of neat circuit diagrams describe the method of testing a single phase transformer by open circuit and short circuit. Explain how efficiency can be calculated. [08]

   (b) A 50 KVA single phase transformer has 20 turns on the primary winding and 300 turns on the secondary winding. The primary winding is connected to a 2200 V, 50 Hz supply. Calculate

   (i) Secondary voltage on no load.

   (ii) Approximate value of primary and secondary current on full load and

   (iii) The maximum value of flux. [08]

   (c) What is a synchronous generator? Why should it operate at synchronous speed? Derive Emf equation of a synchronous generator. [08]

6. **Answer any Two**

   (a) Describe construction and working of an Auto-transformer. What are its advantages and disadvantages? State its applications. [09]

   (b) What are the different single phase induction motors? Explain construction and working principle of Shaded pole induction motor. State the applications. [09]

   (c) Explain the construction and working of capacitor start capacitor run induction motor. Draw the torque-speed characteristic and give its applications. [09]

Basic Electrical Engineering (S.U., F.E., Sem. I and II)   University Question Papers

May 2015

Time : 3 Hours   Total Marks : 100

Section - I

1. **Answer any Two**

   (a) Explain the following terms and state their practical importance : Magnetic saturation, Magnetic leakage, Magnetic fringing. **[09]**

   (b) Find the current in 2 ohm resistance in the following circuit. Comment on the battery currents. **[09]**

   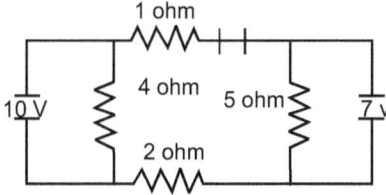

   Fig. 1

   (c) Find the efficiency of a motor centrifugal pump set that completely fills a 1000, litre tank by lifting water through 80 m in exactly 45 minutes while d.c. motor in the draws 3A from 200 V d.c. supply. The electric bill for this work is Rs. 4. Find the rate of electric energy supply in Rs/KWh. **[09]**

2. **Answer any Two**

   (a) If a current Im sin Wt' flow in a series R-L circuit, derive the expression for voltage across the combination, impedance and phase difference between voltage and current. Draw the phasors for all voltages and current. **[09]**

   (b) State the advantages of high power factor, Explain the pf improvement using a static capacitor. Draw the appropriate phasor diagram. **[09]**

   (c) A coil is connected in series with a 100 micro F condenser and 200 V, 50 Hz sinusoidal ac is applied to the circuit. The circuit draws 5A at unity pf. Find the impendance and pf of the coil. **[09]**

3. **Answer any Two**

   (a) With a neat diagram, list the elements necessary in equipment earthing. Explain the electric shock prevention to the user in case of insulation failure fault. **[07]**

(b) Explain the operating principle of LED. Hence list the advantages of LED lamp over CFL. **[07]**

(c) Explain the role of conventional choke and glow type starter in a fluorescent tube. **[07]**

Section - II

4. Answer any Two

(a) Define and explain: Symmetrical 3 phase ac supply, phase sequence, 3 phase balanced load. **[09]**

(b) Compare the star connected 3 phase load with delta connected 3 phase load in terms of phase voltage, phase current power drawn, other advantages related to the configuration. (Assume same line voltage.) **[09]**

(c) List the advantages of 3 phase power generation, transmission, distribution and 3 phase machines. **[09]**

5. Answer any Two

(a) Explain the construction of the core and the windings in a core type transformer and a shell type transformer. State the measures taken to reduce the flux leakage. **[09]**

(b) Explain the operating principle of single phase alternator. State the advantages of rotating field structure over rotating armature structure. **[09]**

(c) A 220V/110V, 1.1 KVA single phase transformer draws 80W at no load. Then a 0.8 lagging pf load is connected and gradually increased upto full load. The full load copper loss is 100W. **[09]**

    (i) Find the transformer efficiency at one fourth of the full load.

    (ii) Find the amount of load for operating this transformer at maximum efficiency (Assume zero voltage regulation throughout.)

6. Answer any Two

(a) Draw the circuit, explain the working of a capacitor run type single phase Induction motor and state its advantages. **[07]**

(b) State the dissimilarities between a split phase induction motor and a Shaded pole induction motor with respect to the stator structure, torgue, reversiblilty, appliations. **[07]**

(c) State the important features of an universal motor. Explain why the torgue does not reverse when the AC supply current reverses **[07]**

www.ingramcontent.com/pod-product-compliance
Lightning Source LLC
Chambersburg PA
CBHW081413230426
43668CB00016B/2227